Bolivia

Deanna Swaney

LONELY PLANET PUBLICATIONS
Melbourne • Oakland • London • Paris

BOLIVIA

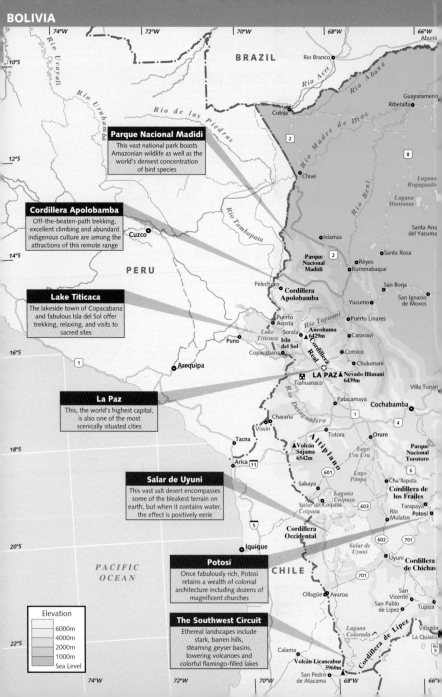

Parque Nacional Madidi
This vast national park boasts Amazonian wildlife as well as the world's densest concentration of bird species

Cordillera Apolobamba
Off-the-beaten-path trekking, excellent climbing and abundant indigenous culture are among the attractions of this remote range

Lake Titicaca
The lakeside town of Copacabana and fabulous Isla del Sol offer trekking, relaxing, and visits to sacred sites

La Paz
This, the world's highest capital, is also one of the most scenically situated cities

Salar de Uyuni
This vast salt desert encompasses some of the bleakest terrain on earth, but when it contains water, the effect is positively eerie

Potosí
Once fabulously rich, Potosí retains a wealth of colonial architecture including dozens of magnificent churches

The Southwest Circuit
Ethereal landscapes include stark, barren hills, steaming geyser basins, towering volcanoes and colorful flamingo-filled lakes

BRAZIL

PERU

PACIFIC OCEAN

CHILE

Elevation
6000m
4000m
2000m
1000m
Sea Level

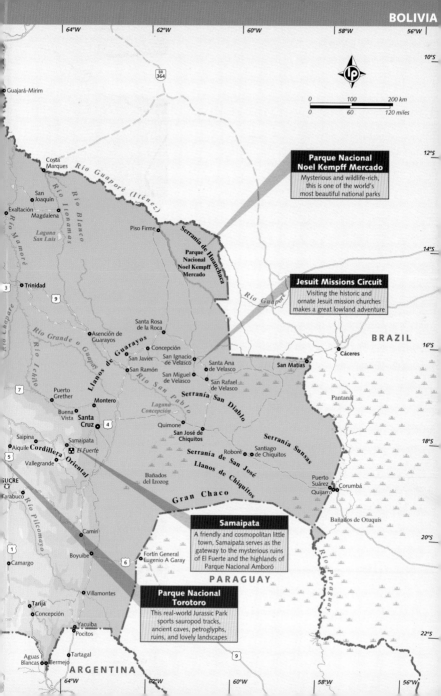

**Parque Nacional
Noel Kempff Mercado**
Mysterious and wildlife-rich,
this is one of the world's
most beautiful national parks

Jesuit Missions Circuit
Visiting the historic and
ornate Jesuit mission churches
makes a great lowland adventure

Samaipata
A friendly and cosmopolitan little
town, Samaipata serves as the
gateway to the mysterious ruins of
El Fuerte and the highlands of
Parque Nacional Amboró

**Parque Nacional
Torotoro**
This real-world Jurassic Park
sports sauropod tracks,
ancient caves, petroglyphs,
ruins, and lovely landscapes

BRAZIL

PARAGUAY

ARGENTINA

Bolivia
4th edition – March 2001
First published – December 1988

Published by
Lonely Planet Publications Pty Ltd ABN 36 005 607 983
90 Maribyrnong St, Footscray, Victoria 3011, Australia

Lonely Planet Offices
Australia Locked Bag 1, Footscray, Victoria 3011
USA 150 Linden St, Oakland, CA 94607
UK 10a Spring Place, London NW5 3BH
France 1 rue du Dahomey, 75011 Paris

Photographs
Many of the images in this guide are available for licensing from
Lonely Planet Images.
email: lpi@lonelyplanet.com.au
Web site: www.lonelyplanetimages.com

Front cover photograph
Licancabur volcano, flamingos and the moon from Laguna Blanca
(Woods Wheatcroft)

ISBN 0 86442 668 2

text & maps © Lonely Planet Publications Pty Ltd 2001
photos © photographers as indicated 2001

Printed by The Bookmaker International Ltd
Printed in China

Contents

1

THE CORDILLERAS & YUNGAS   192

LAKE TITICACA   244

SOUTHERN ALTIPLANO   269

CENTRAL HIGHLANDS   317

SOUTH CENTRAL BOLIVIA & THE CHACO   384

SANTA CRUZ & AROUND 406

EASTERN LOWLANDS 438

AMAZON BASIN 455

LANGUAGE 505

GLOSSARY 511

ACKNOWLEDGMENTS 516

INDEX 519

MAP INDEX

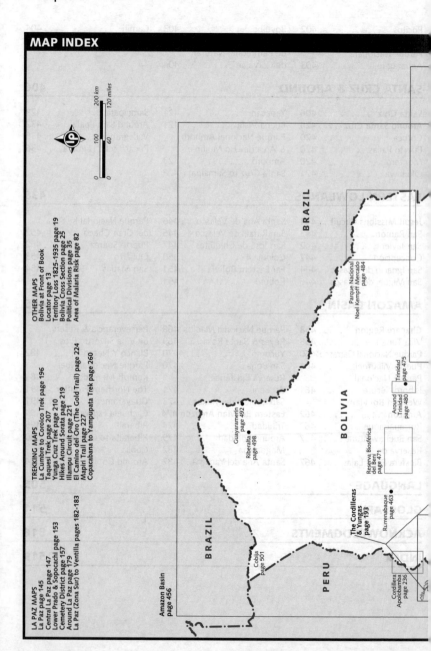

LA PAZ MAPS
La Paz page 145
Central La Paz page 147
Lower Prado & Sopocachi page 153
Cemetery District page 157
Around La Paz page 179
La Paz (Zona Sur) to Ventilla pages 182–183

TREKKING MAPS
La Cumbre to Coroico Trek page 196
Taquesi Trek page 207
Yunga Cruz Trek page 210
Hikes Around Sorata page 219
Illampu Circuit page 221
El Camino del Oro (The Gold Trail) page 224
Mapiri Trail page 227
Copacabana to Yampupata Trek page 260

OTHER MAPS
Bolivia at Front of Book
Locator page 13
Territory Loss 1825–1935 page 19
Bolivia Cross Section page 25
Political Divisions page 35
Area of Malaria Risk page 82

0   100   200 km
0   60   120 miles

BRAZIL

BRAZIL

PERU

BOLIVIA

Amazon Basin page 456

Cobija page 501

Guayaramerín page 492

Riberalta page 498

Parque Nacional Noel Kempff Mercado page 484

Trinidad page 475

Around Trinidad page 480

Reserva Biosférica del Beni page 471

The Cordilleras & Yungas page 193

Rurrenabaque page 463

Cordillera Apolobamba page 236

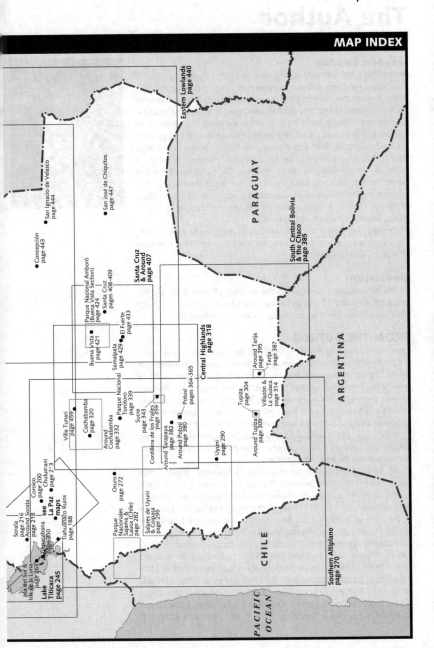

Sorata
page 216
Around Sorata
page 218
Coroico
page 200

Chulumani
page 2-3
La Paz maps

Tiahuanaco Ruins
page 188

Copacabana
page 250

Isla del Sol &
Isla de la Luna
page 263

Lake Titicaca
page 245

PACIFIC OCEAN

CHILE

Southern Altiplano
page 270

Parque Nacionales
Sajama &
Lauca (Chile)
page 282

Oruro
page 272

Salares de Uyuni
& Coipasa
page 295

Around Tupiza
page 309

Uyuni
page 290

Villa Tunari
page 459

Around Cochabamba
page 332

Cochabamba
page 320

Parque Nacional
Torotoro
page 339

Sucre
page 343

Cordillera de los Frailes
page 359

Around Tarapaya
page 382

Around Potosí
page 380

Potosí
pages 364-365

Tupiza
page 304

Villazón &
La Quiaca
page 314

Tarija
page 387

Around Tarija
page 395

ARGENTINA

Central Highlands
page 318

South Central Bolivia
& the Chaco
page 385

Buena Vista
page 421

Samaipata
page 429

El Fuerte
page 433

Parque Nacional Amboró
(Buena Vista Section)
page 424

Santa Cruz
pages 408-409

Santa Cruz
& Around
page 407

Concepción
page 443

San Ignacio de Velasco
page 444

San José de Chiquitos
page 447

Eastern Lowlands
page 440

PARAGUAY

The Author

Deanna Swaney

After completing university studies, Deanna made a shoestring circuit of Europe and has been addicted to travel ever since. Despite an erstwhile career in computer programming, she managed intermittent forays away from the corporate bustle of midtown Anchorage, and at first opportunity, made a break for South America where she wrote the 1st edition of this book. Subsequent travels steered her through a course of paradise destinations and resulted in six more Lonely Planet travel guides: *Tonga, Samoa, Iceland, Greenland & the Faroe Islands, Zimbabwe, Botswana & Namibia, Norway* and *The Arctic*. She has also co-authored the 2nd editions of the *Brazil* and *Mauritius, Réunion & Seychelles* travel guides, updated the 2nd edition of *Madagascar & Comoros* and the 3rd edition of *Russia, Ukraine & Belarus,* and contributed to shoestring guides to Africa, South America and Scandinavia.

Deanna now divides her time between traveling, writing and looking for time to work on various construction projects around her home base in Alaska's Susitna Valley.

Dedication

I'd like to dedicate this edition to the memory of Yossi Brain, climber extraordinaire, who still intends to forever remain above 3000m. *¡Que te vaya bien, dondequiera te encuentres en las alturas celestiales!*

FROM THE AUTHOR

Latin America seems to change so fast that it can make your head spin, and the Bolivia of today bears little resemblance to the country that appeared in the first edition of this book, well over a decade ago. Because I can't be there all the time to stay apprised of everything that happens, I'm especially grateful to everyone who has so graciously helped me stay on top of things.

First and foremost, I must thank Alistair Matthew of Gravity Assisted Mountain Biking and América Tours, who went far beyond the call of duty to keep this project humming down a good long downhill run! Similarly helpful was Geoffrey Groesbeck, who kindly provided lots of details on Santa Cruz and the Jesuit Missions Circuit.

I'd also like to express my appreciation to the following people for their substantial contributions: Jasminee Persaud (Chulumani & Santa Cruz); Jazmin at América Tours; Marianne at Conservación Internacional in Rurrenabaque; Roberto de Urioste, for help with Madidi, Rurrenabaque & the Reserva Biosférical del Beni; Sandro, for his expert guiding in Parque Nacional Madidi; Preston Motes in Yanacachi; Dan Hagaman in Charazani & Apolobamba; Al Liu, for his expert contributions on tinku, Aiquile, Mizque, Santa Cruz and Buena Vista; Dakin Cook, for welcome help with the Quimsa Cruz and tracking down topo sheets; Fabiola Mitru & Beatriz of Tupiza Tours, for their assistance and good times in the wild southwest; Tito Ponce López in Uyuni; Juliet at Juliet Tours in Uyuni; Juan Carlos Vargas in Oruro; Marcelo Olivera in Cochabamba; Louis Demers at Residencial Sorata in Sorata; Johny & Roxana Resnikowski of Café

Altai in Sorata; Dan Buck & Anne Meadows, for help with the Butch & Sundance connection; John Pilkington, for continuing inspiration; Elva Alfaro in Sucre for friendship and a happy day with the dinosaurs; Rosario Herrera Alé at VIVA Tours in Tarija; Denise C at PROMETA in Tarija; Margarita & Pieter at La Víspera in Samaipata; Erik & Krisztina Velde at La Chakana in Samaipata; Jaap & Celestina Kröschell in Sucre for a fortuitous flood-time return to Santa Cruz; Michel & Sophie Ridder in Santa Cruz; Lucho & Dely Loredo in Sucre; Lizzie and Janine in Sucre; Jonathan Bradbury & Alison Christian, for various tidbits of information from around Bolivia; Jeff Welpott in the Cordillera Apolobamba; Hans Rocha Torrez, for help on Torotoro; Iván Dávalos L, for information on the Parque Nacional Carrasco; Sergio Ballivián, for the section on whitewater rafting; Dr Hugo Berrios, for maps and Cordillera information; Rob Rachowiecki, for help on Peru border crossings; Wayne Bernhardson, for additional information on Lauca National Park and the aside on Andean camelids; John Meyers & Tim Miller at Neblina Forest, for insights about Noel Kempff Mercado National Park; and Tim Killeen, for continuing help with the latest on Noel Kempff Mercado National Park.

In the Lonely Planet office, this project was expertly brought together by Robert Reid, Kimra McAfee, Ben Greensfelder, Vivek Wagle and Christine Lee – among many others, I suspect; it was fun working with all of you!

Also, thanks to Peter & Christine (Australia & Austria, respectively), Jennifer Peterson (North Carolina), and Resi Botteram & Jean Keizer (Netherlands), for their sweat-stained and mosquito-plagued contributions to my burned-out home-site in Alaska

Finally, love, thanks and lots of other positive sentiments to Earl, Dean, Kim, Jennifer & Lauren Swaney and Cyndee Snyder in Fresno; Rodney, Heather & Bradley Leacock in Colorado Springs; Keith & Holly Hawkings in Anchorage; and especially to Dave Dault, back home, who provides stability, direction and ingenuity.

This Book

This is the 4th edition of *Bolivia*. It was updated by Deanna Swaney.

FROM THE PUBLISHER

This edition of Bolivia was created in Lonely Planet's Oaktown office. Ben 'Blue Shirt' Greensfelder hacked a path through the Bolivian jungle, leading the intrepid editorial team of Christine Lee, 'Speedy' Vivek Wagle and Paul 'Flares' Sheridan through the editing and proofing phases, then handed off to Christine for layout. Senior editor Robert 'Okie' Reid played coach throughout the project, and Rachel Bernstein, Gabrielle Knight and seniors Maria Donohoe and Tom Downs staged a daring rescue during layout.

A big coca leaf to all the cartographers who trekked along. Led by Andrew 'Superstar' Rebold and guided by senior Kimra McAfee, these include Molly Green, Chris Howard, Patrick Phelan, Dion Good, Matt DeMartini, Eric Thomsen, Tessa Rottiers, Kat Smith, John Spelman, Chris 'Hall & Oates' Gillis, Sean Brandt and Ed Turley. Manager Alex Guilbert and senior Monica Lepe also provided guidance on the project.

Senior designer Ruth Askevold blazed a trail for a design team that included Lora Santiago on production and Beca Lafore on illustrations. Mark Butler, Hugh D'Andrade, John Fadeff, Hayden Foell, Jun Jalbuena, Justin Marler, Hannah Reineck, Lisa Summers and Jim Swanson also contributed illustrations. Susan Rimerman oversaw design, Jenn 'Led Zeppelin II' Steffey created the cover, and Ken DellaPenta indexed the book.

Foreword

ABOUT LONELY PLANET GUIDEBOOKS

The story begins with a classic travel adventure: Tony and Maureen Wheeler's 1972 journey across Europe and Asia to Australia. Useful information about the overland trail did not exist at that time, so Tony and Maureen published the first Lonely Planet guidebook to meet a growing need.

From a kitchen table, then from a tiny office in Melbourne (Australia), Lonely Planet has become the largest independent travel publisher in the world, an international company with offices in Melbourne, Oakland (USA), London (UK) and Paris (France).

Today Lonely Planet guidebooks cover the globe. There is an ever-growing list of books, and there's information in a variety of forms and media. Some things haven't changed. The main aim is still to help make it possible for adventurous travelers to get out there – to explore and better understand the world.

At Lonely Planet we believe travelers can make a positive contribution to the countries they visit – if they respect their host communities and spend their money wisely. Since 1986 a percentage of the income from each book has been donated to aid projects and human-rights campaigns.

Lonely Planet gathers information for everyone who's curious about the planet – and especially for those who explore it firsthand. Through guidebooks, phrasebooks, activity guides, maps, literature, newsletters, image library, TV series and website, we act as an information exchange for a worldwide community of travelers.

Updates Lonely Planet thoroughly updates each guidebook as often as possible. This usually means there are around two years between editions, although for more unusual or more stable destinations the gap can be longer. Check the imprint page (following the color map at the beginning of the book) for publication dates.

Between editions, up-to-date information is available in two free newsletters – the paper *Planet Talk* and email *Comet* (to subscribe, contact any Lonely Planet office) – and on our website at www.lonelyplanet.com. The *Upgrades* section of the website covers a number of important and volatile destinations and is regularly updated by Lonely Planet authors. *Scoop* covers news and current affairs relevant to travelers. And, lastly, the *Thorn Tree* bulletin board and *Postcards* section of the site carry unverified, but fascinating, reports from travelers.

Correspondence The process of creating new editions begins with the letters, postcards and emails received from travelers. This correspondence often includes suggestions, criticisms and comments about the current editions. Interesting excerpts are immediately passed on via newsletters and the website, and everything goes to our authors to be verified when they're researching on the road. We're keen to get more feedback from organizations or individuals who represent communities visited by travelers.

Research Authors aim to gather sufficient practical information to enable travelers to make informed choices and to make the mechanics of a journey run smoothly. They also research historical and cultural background to help enrich the travel experience and allow travelers to understand and respond appropriately to cultural and environmental issues.

Authors don't stay in every hotel because that would mean spending a couple of months in each medium-size city and, no, they don't eat at every restaurant because that would mean stretching belts beyond capacity. They do visit hotels and restaurants to check standards and prices, but feedback based on readers' direct experiences can be very helpful.

Many of our authors work undercover; others aren't so secretive. None of them accept freebies in exchange for positive write-ups. And none of our guidebooks contain any advertising.

Production Authors submit their raw manuscripts and maps to offices in Australia, the USA, the UK or France. Editors and cartographers – all experienced travelers themselves – then begin the process of assembling the pieces. When the book finally hits the shops, some things are already out of date, we start getting feedback from readers and the process begins again....

WARNING & REQUEST

Things change – prices go up, schedules change, good places go bad and bad places go bankrupt – nothing stays the same. So, if you find things better or worse, recently opened or long since closed, please tell us and help make the next edition even more accurate and useful. We genuinely value all the feedback we receive. A well-traveled team reads and acknowledges every letter, postcard and email and ensures that every morsel of information finds its way to the appropriate authors, editors and cartographers for verification.

Everyone who writes to us will find their name in the next edition of the appropriate guidebook. They will also receive the latest issue of *Planet Talk*, our quarterly printed newsletter, or *Comet*, our monthly email newsletter. Subscriptions to both newsletters are free. The very best contributions will be rewarded with a free guidebook.

Excerpts from your correspondence may appear in new editions of Lonely Planet guidebooks, the Lonely Planet website, *Planet Talk* or *Comet*, so please let us know if you *don't* want your letter published or your name acknowledged.

Send all correspondence to the Lonely Planet office closest to you:

Australia: Locked Bag 1, Footscray, Victoria 3011
USA: 150 Linden St, Oakland, CA 94607
UK: 10a Spring Place, London NW5 3BH
France: 1 rue du Dahomey, 75011 Paris

Or email us at: talk2us@lonelyplanet.com.au

For news, views and updates, see our website: www.lonelyplanet.com

HOW TO USE A LONELY PLANET GUIDEBOOK

The best way to use a Lonely Planet guidebook is any way you choose. At Lonely Planet, we believe the most memorable travel experiences are often those that are unexpected, and the finest discoveries are those you make yourself. Guidebooks are not intended to be used as if they provided a detailed set of infallible instructions!

Contents All Lonely Planet guidebooks follow the same format. The Facts about the Country chapters or sections give background information ranging from history to weather. Facts for the Visitor gives practical information on issues like visas and health. Getting There & Away gives a brief starting point for researching travel to and from the destination. Getting Around gives an overview of the transport options available when you arrive.

The peculiar demands of each destination determine how subsequent chapters are broken up, but some things remain constant. We always start with background, then proceed to sights, places to stay, places to eat, entertainment, getting there and away, and getting around information – in that order.

Heading Hierarchy Lonely Planet headings are used in a strict hierarchical structure that can be visualized as a set of Russian dolls. Each heading (and its following text) is encompassed by any preceding heading that is higher on the hierarchical ladder.

Entry Points We do not assume guidebooks will be read from beginning to end, but that people will dip into them. The traditional entry points are the list of contents and the index. In addition, however, some books have a complete list of maps and an index map illustrating map coverage.

There may also be a color map that shows highlights. These highlights are dealt with in greater detail later in the book, along with planning questions. Each chapter covering a geographical region usually begins with a locator map and another list of highlights. Once you find something of interest in a list of highlights, turn to the index.

Maps Maps play a crucial role in Lonely Planet guidebooks and include a huge amount of information. A legend is printed on the back page. We seek to have complete consistency between maps and text, and to have every important place in the text captured on a map. Map key numbers usually start in the top left corner.

Although inclusion in a guidebook usually implies a recommendation, we cannot list every good place. Exclusion does not necessarily imply criticism. In fact, there are a number of reasons why we might exclude a place – sometimes it is simply inappropriate to encourage an influx of travelers.

Introduction

Bolivia is the Tibet of the Americas – the highest and most isolated of the Latin American republics. A landlocked country lying astride the widest stretch of the Andean Cordillera, Bolivia spills through a maze of tortured hills and valleys into the vast forests and savannas of the Amazon and Paraná basins, its geographical and climatic zones ranging from snowcapped Andean peaks to vast, low-lying savannas and jungles. With two major indigenous groups and several smaller ones, Bolivia is also the most traditional country on the South American continent. Over 50% of the population are of pure Indian blood, and many people maintain traditional cultural values and belief systems.

Bolivia has certainly had a turbulent and explosive history, but nowadays its image as a haunt of revolutionaries and drug barons

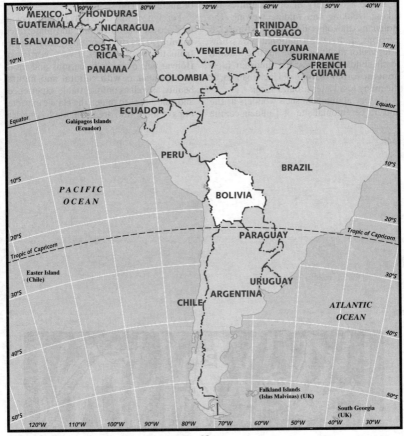

is greatly overstated. Although it still faces some difficult problems, it remains one of South America's most peaceful, secure and inviting countries. In fact, the word most often used by locals is *tranquilo*.

The country combines awe-inspiring landscapes, colonial treasures, colorful indigenous cultures and remnants of mysterious ancient civilizations. Its natural attractions range from the peaks of the Andean Cordillera to the stark beauty and startling colors of the lakes and windswept deserts of the Altiplano, from the jungle-choked waterways of the Amazon and Paraná basins to the thorny scrublands of the Chaco.

There are plenty of opportunities for hiking, trekking and wildlife viewing. The Bolivian Amazon is ideal for rain forest excursions, and several national parks now offer visitor facilities. Dinosaur trackers and fossil fiends will enjoy the dinosaur footprints at Torotoro, south of Cochabamba, or the many fossil sites around Tarija.

History abounds in such wonders as the ancient ceremonial site of Tiahuanaco; the legendary mines of Potosí, which date from the 16th century and are still worked under tortuous conditions; the ornate Jesuit churches of the eastern lowlands; and the vestiges of Inca culture set against the dramatic backdrop of the Andean mountain ranges and Lake Titicaca. Bolivia's world-renowned music is in itself a compelling reason to visit, especially when it's played on native instruments in the context of a *peña* (folk music program) or one of the country's many festivals. There are plenty of examples of colonial architecture to explore, the best of which are preserved in the churches, narrow streets and museums of Sucre and Potosí.

Foreign visitors have only recently begun to discover this intriguing and underrated country, so it's still surprisingly easy to stray from the worn routes. Every corner of Bolivia will overwhelm curious and motivated travelers with cultural and natural beauty, as well as unforgettable experiences and characters to match the classic expectations of those who dream of South America.

Facts about Bolivia

HISTORY
The Central Andes

The great Altiplano (High Plateau), the largest expanse of arable land in the Andes, extends from present-day Bolivia into southern Peru, northwestern Argentina and northern Chile. It has been inhabited for thousands of years, but the early cultures of the Altiplano were shaped by the imperial designs of two major forces: the Tiahuanaco culture of Bolivia and the Inca of Peru.

Most archaeologists define the prehistory of the Central Andes in terms of 'horizons' – Early, Middle and Late – each of which was characterized by distinct architectural and artistic trends. Cultural interchanges between early Andean peoples occurred mainly through peaceful trade and exchange, often between nomadic tribes or as a result of the diplomatic expansionist activities of powerful and well-organized societies. These interchanges resulted in the Andes' emergence as the cradle of South America's highest cultural achievements.

Early Horizon – The Chavíns

The original Andean arrivals are presumed to have descended from nomadic hunters who wandered across the Bering Strait from Siberia and eventually settled down to a sedentary agricultural existence in permanent communities. During the initial settlement of the Andes, which lasted until about 1400 BC, villages and ceremonial centers were established, and trade then emerged between coastal fishing communities and the farming villages of the highlands.

The so-called Early Horizon, which lasted from about 1400 to 400 BC, was an era of architectural innovation and activity. Its culmination is most evident in the ruins of Chavín de Huantar, on the eastern slopes of the Andes in Peru. It's postulated that during this period, a wave of Aymará-speaking Indians, possibly from the mountains of central Peru, swept across the Andes into Alto Perú (Bolivia) and

occupied the Altiplano, driving out most of the region's original settlers.

Chavín influences resounded far and wide, even after the decline of Chavín society, and spilled over into the Early Middle Horizon (400 BC to AD 500) that followed.

Middle Horizon – Tiahuanaco

The core centuries of the Middle Horizon, from about AD 500 to 900, were marked by the imperial expansion of the new Tiahuanaco-Huari culture.

The ceremonial center of Tiahuanaco, on the shores of Lake Titicaca, grew and prospered through the Middle Horizon and developed into the religious and political capital of the Alto Peruvian Altiplano. The Tiahuanaco people produced technically impressive work, the most notable example of which was the city itself. They created impressive ceramics and gilded ornamentation, and engraved pillars and slabs with calendar markings and designs representing their bearded white leader and deity, Viracocha, as well as other designs and hieroglyphs that remain undeciphered. It's believed that Tiahuanaco culture introduced and encouraged the extensive planting of maize for ceremonial purposes.

By the 7th century BC, Tiahuanaco had developed into a thriving civilization and in many respects was as advanced as that of ancient Egypt. It had an extensive system of roads, irrigation canals and agricultural terraces. Over the following centuries, wooden boats were constructed to ferry 55,000kg slabs 48km across the lake to the building site, and sandstone blocks weighing 145,000kg were moved from a quarry 10km away.

Tiahuanaco and its counterpart, Huari, in the Ayacucho valley (which is now in Peru), developed into well-organized, prosperous and ambitious societies. The relationship between these two widely separated communities isn't clear, but the architecture, iconography and changing art forms of the

Middle Horizon suggest close cultural ties. Though they may have been dual capitals of the same state, many theorists favor the idea that Tiahuanaco was the real power center. Its art and architecture were more refined than that of Huari, which might have functioned as a strategic military outpost. Whatever the relationship, through trade and political expansion, the Tiahuanaco-Huari influence – particularly artistic values and construction methods – eventually extended as far north as Ecuador.

The Tiahuanaco site had been inhabited since about 1500 BC and remained occupied until AD 1200, but its period of power lasted only from the 6th century BC to the 9th century AD (Huari had been abandoned before AD 800). During the Late Middle Horizon, Tiahuanaco's power waned and its civilization declined. One theory speculates that Tiahuanaco was uprooted by a drop in the Lake Titicaca water level, which left the lakeside settlement far from shore. Another postulates that it was attacked and its population massacred by the warlike Kollas (sometimes spelt Collas; also known as Aymará) from the west. When the Spanish arrived, they learned of an Inca legend about a battle between the Kollas and 'bearded white men' on an island in Lake Titicaca. These men were presumably Tiahuanacans, only a few of whom were able to escape. Some researchers believe that the displaced survivors migrated southward and developed into the Chipaya people of western Oruro department.

Today, the remains of the city lie on the plain between La Paz and the southern shore of Lake Titicaca, and collections of Tiahuanaco relics can be seen in several Bolivian museums. For further information, see Tiahuanaco in the La Paz chapter.

Late Horizon – The Inca

The Inca, the last of South America's indigenous conquerors, arrived shortly after the fall of Tiahuanaco. The Late Horizon, from AD 1476 to 1534, marked the zenith of Inca civilization. They pushed their empire from its seat of power in Cuzco (Peru) eastward into present-day Bolivia, southward to the northern reaches of modern Argentina and Chile, and northward through present-day Ecuador and southern Colombia. For all its widespread power and influence, however, the Inca political state thrived for less than a century before falling to the might of the invading Spanish.

Although the Inca had inhabited the Cuzco region from the 12th century, they were little more than a minor chiefdom. Inca legend recounts tales of bearded white men coming to them from the shores of Lake Titicaca and bringing civilization before pushing off to sea. It wasn't until about 1440 that the Inca became serious about extending their political boundaries beyond the immediate neighborhood. In the space of just over 50 years, they managed to establish a highly unified state that took in most of the central Andes.

The origins of the Inca are the stuff of myths and legends (see History in the Lake Titicaca chapter), but their achievements certainly are not. Renowned for their great stone cities and their skill in working with gold and silver, the Inca also set up a hierarchy of governmental and agricultural overseers, a viable social welfare scheme, and a complex road network and communication system that defied the difficult terrain of their far-flung empire.

The Inca Manco Capac, first in the line of Inca emperors, and his sister/wife Mama Ocllo (also known as Mama Huaca) convinced their people they were children of the Sun God. Their progeny were the first of the Inca nobles, and to keep the lineage pure and to extend it, they adopted a structured system of marriage. Consequently, each subsequent Inca ruler, the Sapa Inca, was considered a direct descendant of the Sun God. Nobles were permitted an unlimited number of wives and their children were considered legitimate Inca nobles.

The traditional history of the Inca told above is intriguing, but naturally there are other more down-to-earth theories regarding their origins. These include that of the 17th-century Spanish chronicler Fernando Montesinos, who believed that the Inca had descended from a lineage of Tiahuanaco wise men. There were indeed many similarities between Tiahuanaco and Inca architecture, and when the Inca arrived to conquer the shores of Lake Titicaca, the Kollas who inhabited the Tiahuanaco area regarded the site as taboo.

In a sense, the Inca government could be described as an imperialist socialist dictatorship, with the Sapa Inca as reigning monarch, head of the noble family and the extended Inca clan, and unquestionable ruler of the entire state. The state technically owned all property within its vast and expanding realm, and taxes were collected in the form of labor. The government organized a system of mutual aid in which relief supplies were collected from prosperous areas and distributed in areas suffering from natural disasters or local misfortune.

This system of benevolent rule was largely attributable to the influence of the eighth Inca, Viracocha (not to be confused with the Tiahuanaco leader/deity of the same name), who believed that the mandate from the Sun God was not just to conquer, plunder and enslave, but to organize defeated tribes and absorb them into the realm of the benevolent Sun God. When the Inca arrived in Kollasuyo (present-day Bolivia), they assimilated local tribes as they had done elsewhere: by imposing taxation, religion and their own Quechua language (the *lingua franca* of the empire) upon the region's inhabitants.

The Kollas living around the Tiahuanaco site were among the most recalcitrant additions to the empire. Although they were absorbed by the Inca and their religion was supplanted, they were permitted to keep their language and social traditions.

By the late 1520s, internal rivalries had begun to take their toll on the empire; in a brief civil war over the division of lands, Atahuallpa, the true Inca emperor's half-brother, imprisoned the emperor and assumed the throne himself.

The Spanish Conquest

The arrival of the Spanish in Ecuador in 1531 would be the ultimate blow. Within a year, Francisco Pizarro, Diego de Almagro and their bands of merry conquistadores had pushed inland toward Cuzco in search of land, wealth and adventure. When they arrived in the capital, Atahuallpa was still the incumbent emperor, but he was not considered the true heir of the Sun God. The Spanish were aided by the Inca belief that the bearded white men had been sent by the great Viracocha Inca as revenge for Atahuallpa's breach of established protocol. In fear, Atahuallpa ordered the murder of the real king, which not only ended the bloodline of the Inca dynasty, but brought shame on the family and dissolved the psychological power grip of the Inca hierarchy.

The Spanish were unconcerned about the death of the true emperor, but they did turn the resulting guilt to their own advantage. Atahuallpa's shame at having killed the divine descendant of the Sun God, combined with the Inca nobility's initial trust in the Spanish 'gods,' made the conquistadores' task easy. Within two years, the government had been conquered, the empire had been dissolved, and the invaders had divided Inca lands and booty between the two leaders of the Spanish forces.

Alto Perú, which would later become Bolivia, fell for a brief time period into the possession of Diego de Almagro, who was assassinated in 1538 and didn't have the chance to make the most of his prize. Three years later, Pizarro himself suffered the same fate at the hands of mutinous subordinates. It was during this period that the Spanish got down to exploring and settling their newly conquered land. In 1538, La Plata was founded as the Spanish capital of the Charcas region.

The Legacy of Potosí

By the time the wandering Indian Diego Huallpa revealed his earth-shattering discovery of silver at Potosí in 1544, Spanish conquerors had already firmly implanted their language, religion and customs upon the remnants of Atahuallpa's empire. Spanish Potosí, or the 'Villa Imperial de Carlos V,' was founded in 1545, when the riches of Cerro Rico (Rich Hill) were already on their way to the Spanish treasuries. Potosí, with

160,000 residents, became the largest city in the Western Hemisphere.

The Potosí mine became the world's most prolific. The silver extracted from it underwrote the Spanish economy, particularly the extravagance of its monarchy, for at least two centuries, and spawned a legendary maritime crime wave on the Caribbean Sea.

Atrocious conditions in the gold and silver mines of Potosí guaranteed a short life span for the local Indian conscripts who were herded into work gangs, as well as for the millions of African slaves brought to the mines. Those not actually worked to death or killed in accidents succumbed to pulmonary silicosis within just a few years. Africans who survived migrated to the more amenable climes of the Yungas northeast of La Paz, and developed into an Aymará-speaking minority.

The Spanish soldiers, administrators, settlers, adventurers and miners who poured into the region developed into a powerful landowning aristocracy. The indigenous peoples became tenant farmers, subservient to the Spanish lords, and were required to supply their conquerors with food and labor, in exchange for subsistence-sized plots of land. Coca, once the exclusive privilege of Inca nobles, was introduced among the general populace to keep people working without complaint.

Independence

In May of 1809, the first independence movement in Spanish America had gained momentum and was well underway in Chuquisaca (Sucre). Other cities soon followed suit, and the powder keg exploded. During the first quarter of the 19th century, General Simón Bolívar succeeded in liberating both Venezuela and Colombia from Spanish domination. In 1822 he dispatched Mariscal (Major General) Antonio José de Sucre to Ecuador to defeat the Royalists at the battle of Pichincha. In 1824, after years of guerrilla action against the Spanish and the victories of Bolívar and Sucre in the battles of Junín (6 August) and Ayacucho (9 December), Peru won its independence.

At this point, Sucre incited a declaration of independence for Alto Perú, and exactly one year later, the new Republic of Bolivia was born (see History in the Sucre chapter for further information). Bolívar and Sucre became Bolivia's first and second presidents. After a brief attempt by Andrés Santa Cruz, the third president, to form a confederation with Peru, things began to go awry. One military junta after another usurped power from its predecessor, setting a pattern of political strife that would haunt the nation for the next 162 years.

Few of Bolivia's 191 governments to date have remained in power long enough to have much intentional effect, and some were more than a little eccentric. The bizarre, cruel General Mariano Melgarejo, who ruled from 1865 to 1871, once drunkenly set off with his army on an overland march to aid France at the outset of the Franco-Prussian War. History has it that he was sobered up by a sudden downpour and the project was abandoned (to the immense relief of the Prussians, of course).

Melgarejo is also credited with a host of other gaffes, including murdering a penitent conspirator, appropriating Indian lands, squandering the nation's reserves on his mistresses and alcohol habit (among other personal projects), ceding territory to Brazil in exchange for a horse, and tying the British ambassador naked to the back of a mule and banishing him for failing to drink enough beer. This last infringement, which was the final straw for Queen Victoria, led her to declare that Bolivia did not exist and that it would thenceforth not appear on British maps.

Shrinking Territory

Bolivia's misfortunes during its earlier years were not limited to internal strife. At the time of independence, its boundaries encompassed well over 2 million square kilometers, but by the time its neighbors had finished paring away at its territory, only half the original land area remained.

The first and most significant loss occurred in the War of the Pacific, which was fought against Chile between 1879 and

1884. In the end, Chile wound up with 850km of coastline from Peru and Bolivia. The loss was most severe for Bolivia, which had been robbed of its port of Antofagasta, the copper- and nitrate-rich sands of the Atacama Desert and, most significantly, the country's only outlet to the sea. Although Chile did attempt to recompense the loss by building a railroad from La Paz to the coast and allowing Bolivia free port privileges in Antofagasta, Bolivians have never forgotten this devastating *enclaustromiento*, which left them without a seacoast. Even today, the government uses the issue as a rallying cry whenever it wants to unite the people behind a common cause.

During the years that followed, Peru, Brazil and Argentina each had their turn hacking away at Bolivia's borders. The next major loss was in 1903 during the rubber boom. Both Brazil and Bolivia had been ransacking the forests of the remote Acre territory, which stretched from Bolivia's present Amazonian borders to about halfway up Peru's eastern border. The area was so rich in rubber trees that Brazil engineered a dispute over sovereignty and sent in its army. Brazil convinced Acre to secede from the Bolivian republic, and promptly annexed it.

Brazil attempted to compensate Bolivia's loss with a new railway, this one intended to open up the remote northern reaches of the country and provide an outlet to the Amazon Basin by circumventing the rapids that rendered the Río Mamoré unnavigable below Guayaramerín. The Madeira to Mamoré line (nicknamed Mad María), however, never reached Bolivian soil. Construction ended at Guajará-Mirim on the Brazilian bank of the Mamoré, and it is now used only infrequently as a tourist novelty.

The boundaries between Bolivia and Paraguay had never been formally defined, and in 1932, a border dispute with Paraguay for control of the Chaco erupted into full-scale warfare. This time the conflict was caused partly by rival foreign oil companies that had their eye on concessions should their prospecting activities reveal huge deposits of oil in the Chaco. In a bid to secure

TERRITORY LOSS 1825–1935

ACRE To Brazil 251,000 km² 1867
To Brazil 188,704 km² 1903
PURUS
To Peru 250,000 km² 1909
BRAZIL
PERU
To Brazil 50,733 km² 1867
BOLIVIA
MATO GROSSO
PACIFIC OCEAN
CHILE
PUNA DE ATACAMA 4753 km²
To Paraguay 243,500 km² 1935
PARAGUAY
LITORAL
To Chile 120,000 km² 1879–1884
To Argentina 130,095 km²
CHACO BOREAL
To Argentina 1862 35,910 km² 1883
ARGENTINA
CHACO CENTRAL

favorable franchises, a quarrel was engineered, with Standard Oil supporting Bolivia and Shell siding with Paraguay.

Paraguay, badly beaten after taking on Argentina, Uruguay and Brazil in the War of the Triple Alliance, needed an outlet to avenge its loss. Victory in this respect would also guarantee a prosperous economic future – if the oil companies' theories regarding the prevalence of oil proved correct. Bolivia fell victim to Paraguayan pride and, within three years, lost another 225,000 sq km, 65,000 young men and a dubious outlet to the sea via the Río Paraguai before the dispute was finally settled in 1935 in Paraguay's favor. (Although it was not until 1938 that Bolivia formally ceded to Paraguay all land taken over and occupied by Paraguay during the 1932-35 war.) The anticipated reserves of oil were never discovered, but several fields in the area that remained Bolivian territory now keep the country self-sufficient in oil production.

Continuing Political Strife
During the 20th century, Bolivian farming and mining interests were controlled by tin barons and wealthy landowners, while the

peasantry was relegated to a non-feudal system of peonage known as *pongaje*. The beating Bolivia took in the Chaco War paved the way for the creation of reformist associations, civil unrest among the *cholos* (indigenous people who dress traditionally but live in larger cities; see Population & People later in this chapter), and a series of coups by ostensibly reform-minded military leaders.

The most significant development was the emergence of the Movimiento Nacionalista Revolucionario (MNR), which united the masses behind the common cause of popular reform. It sparked labor unrest and friction between peasant miners and absentee tin bosses. The miners' complaints against outrageous working conditions, pitifully low pay and the export of profits to Europe raised the political consciousness of all Bolivian workers. Under the leadership of Victor Paz Estenssoro, the MNR prevailed in the 1951 elections, but a last-minute military coup prevented it from actually taking power. The coup provoked a popular armed revolt by the miners, which became known as the April Revolution of 1952. After heavy fighting, the military was defeated and Victor Paz's MNR took the helm for the first time. He nationalized mines, evicted the tin barons, put an end to pongaje and set up COMIBOL (Corporación Minera de Bolivia), the state entity in charge of mining interests.

The revolutionaries were also concerned with agrarian and educational reform and universal suffrage. They pressed ahead with a diverse reform program, which included redistribution of land among sharecropping peasants and restructuring of the educational system to include primary education in villages. To open up the long-isolated and underrepresented Oriente lowlands, a road was constructed from Cochabamba to Santa Cruz.

All these social and economic reforms were aimed at ensuring political participation of all sectors of the population. In the end, the miners and peasants felt they were being represented, and the relatively popular MNR government lasted an incredible

12 years under various presidents. Victor Paz himself served three nonconsecutive terms of varying lengths. (It also spared Bolivia the populist guerrilla uprisings that later plagued Peru and Colombia.) Even with US support, however, MNR was unable to raise the standard of living or increase food production substantially, and its effectiveness and popularity ground to a standstill. As dissent increased within his ranks, Victor Paz was forced to become more and more autocratic. In 1964 his government, weakened by internal quarrels, was overthrown by a military junta headed by General René Barrientos Ortuño.

This fresh round of military rule was strongly opposed, and General Barrientos lashed back at his detractors. In 1967 the Argentine-born Marxist folk hero Ché Guevara, who attempted to foment a peasant revolt in southeastern Bolivia (see 'Ché Guevara – The Most Complete Man' in the Santa Cruz chapter), was executed by a US-backed military squad working with the Bolivian Armed Forces. In the same year, military forces massacred miners who had gathered at Catavi to form an antigovernment front.

Following the death of General Barrientos in a 1969 helicopter accident, one coup followed another and military dictators and juntas came and went with some regularity. Right-wing coalition leader General Hugo Banzer Suárez took over in 1971 and served a turbulent term, punctuated by reactionary extremism and human-rights abuses. In 1978, amid demand for a return to democratic process, he scheduled general elections. Although Banzer lost the elections, he ignored the results and accused the opposition of ballot-box tampering.

Shortly thereafter Banzer was forced to step down in a coup by General Juan Pereda Asbún. Pereda tenuously held power very briefly until the job was snatched from him by General David Perdilla, who at least had the support of the democratic opposition. Perdilla announced elections in 1979, but they failed, and then the National Congress appointed Walter

Guevara Arze as interim president. His government was overthrown, however, in the bloody 1979 coup by Colonel Alberto Natusch Busch, who stepped down after only two weeks in office owing to widespread lack of support.

That same year, Congress appointed Lidia Gueilar, a woman, as interim president, and the country enjoyed a brief respite from military mania. When elections were held the following year, no candidate achieved a majority, and it became apparent that Congress would select Hernán Siles Zuazo and his Unión Democrática y Popular (UDP) party. The appointment process, however, was interrupted by a military coup led by General Luis García Meza Tejada under the direction of cocaine traffickers and resident Nazi activist Klaus Barbie, known as the Butcher of Lyons. This hideous regime saw a rash of tortures, arrests and disappearances, as well as a substantial increase in cocaine production and trafficking.

By 1981, García Meza had lost control of the military and was forced to step down, to be replaced by General Celso Torrelio Villa. At this stage, the populace had had enough of military scuffling and called for democratic rule, but the Torrelio government resisted. In 1982, an attempted coup by García Meza led to the appointment of General Guido Vildoso Calderón to oversee a peaceful return to democratic rule. (García Meza fled the country, but in April 1993 was convicted in absentia of genocide, treason, human-rights abuses and armed insurrection, and sentenced to 30 years' imprisonment; in March 1995, the unrepentant 64-year-old former dictator was extradited from Brazil and brought back to Bolivia to serve his sentence.)

In 1982, Congress elected Dr Hernán Siles Zuazo, the civilian left-wing leader of the Communist-supported Movimiento de la Izquierda Revolucionaria (MIR). His term was beleaguered with labor disputes, ruthless government spending and monetary devaluation, resulting in a staggering inflation rate that at one point reached 35,000% annually!

When Siles Zuazo gave up after three years and called general elections, Victor Paz Estenssoro returned to politics to become president for the third time. He immediately enacted harsh measures to revive and stabilize the shattered economy: he ousted labor unions, removed government restrictions on internal trade, slashed the government deficit, imposed a wage freeze, eliminated price subsidies, laid off workers at inefficient government-owned companies, allowed the peso to float against the US dollar, and deployed armed forces to keep the peace.

Inflation was curtailed within weeks, but spiraling unemployment, especially in the poor mining areas of the Altiplano, caused enormous suffering and threatened the government's stability. Throughout his term, however, Victor Paz remained committed to programs that would return the government mines to private cooperatives and develop the largely uninhabited lowland regions of the north and east of the country. To encourage the settlement of the Amazon region, he promoted road building (with Japanese aid) in the wilderness and opened up vast Indian lands and pristine rain forest to logging interests.

Democracy Prevails

The 1989 presidential elections, free from the threat of military intervention, were characterized mostly by apathy. Hugo Banzer Suárez of the Acción Democrática Nacionalista (ADN) resurfaced, the MIR nominated Jaime Paz Zamora and MNR put forth mining company president and economic reformist Gonzalo Sánchez de Lozada ('Goni'). Although Banzer and Sánchez placed ahead of Paz Zamora, no candidate received a majority, so it was left to the National Congress to select one. Longtime rivals Banzer and Paz Zamora formed a coalition to prevail over Sánchez, and Congress selected Paz Zamora as the new president.

In the following election, on June 6, 1993, Sánchez returned to defeat Banzer. Sánchez and his Aymará running mate, Victor Hugo Cárdenas, appealed to campesinos and cholos, while European urbanites generally embraced his free-market economic policies. This opened the way for this administration to attack corruption and begin implementing *capitalización*, opening up state-owned companies and mining interests to overseas investment in hopes that private enterprise would prove more efficient and cost-effective than government. Officials had also hoped privatization would

The Drug War

If outsiders know one thing about Bolivia, Colombia, Peru and neighboring countries, it's their affiliation with the coca leaf and the refinement and trafficking of cocaine and other illicit coca derivatives. While this factor isn't as prevalent as the Western news media would have people believe, as recently as 1989, one third of the Bolivian work force was dependent on the illicit production and trafficking of cocaine. Far and away the most lucrative of Bolivia's economic mainstays, it was generating an annual income of US$1.5 billion, of which just under half remained in the country. Most of the miners laid off during Victor Paz's austerity measures turned to cocaine as a source of income, and ensuing corruption, terrorism and social strife threatened government control over the country.

As early as 1987, the US was sending Drug Enforcement Agency (DEA) squadrons into the Beni and Chapare regions, and by the early 1990s, US threats to cease foreign aid unless efforts were made to stop cocaine production forced Victor Paz to comply with a half-baked coca eradication program. Instead of eliminating the trade, however, the US eradication directive brought about the organization of increasingly powerful and vociferous peasant unions and interest groups. This, combined with lax enforcement, corruption and skyrocketing potential profits, actually resulted in an increase in cocaine production.

The Bolivian government refused to chemically destroy coca fields, and instead urged coca farmers to accept US$2000 per hectare to replace their crops with such alternative commodities as coffee, bananas, yucca, spices and cacao. In early 1990, price decreases brought about a temporary lull in coca production, and some farmers sold out to the government's crop substitution programs. Despite the millions of US dollars spent to develop processing plants for alternative crops, the markets for these products remained distant and difficult to reach. As a result, many coca farmers simply collected the money and moved farther north to replant. Not only did coca yield four crops per year, it was easier to cultivate and sell than alternative crops, and even if it failed, farmers could merely uproot the crop and collect another US$2000 per hectare!

Facing a weakened Bolivian economy, in May 1990 President Jaime Paz Zamora appealed for an increase in US aid to fund the crackdown on cocaine producers. In response, US President George Bush sent US$78 million in aid and stepped up US 'Operation Support Justice' activities in northern Bolivia. In June 1991, Bolivian police and DEA agents staged a daylight helicopter raid on Santa Ana del Yacuma, north of Trinidad, and seized 15 cocaine labs, nine estates, numerous private aircraft and 110kg of cocaine base; however, no traffickers were captured, having been given sufficient warning to escape. Several surrendered later under Bolivia's lenient 'repentance law.'

By 1992, US antinarcotic operations in South America operated on a budget of US$1.2 billion. The US forces' greatest fear was that peasant resistance would fuel leftist insurgencies and guerrilla groups, while the millions designated for drug enforcement operations would merely fatten corrupt military and government officials. At the same time, some US military personnel in Bolivia claimed that the ultimate winners would be the drug cartels; at least 85% of Bolivian antinarcotic trainees, many with family members involved in cocaine production and trafficking, served one-year stints.

stabilize and streamline companies, making them profitable. Overseas investors in formerly state-owned companies received 49% equity, total voting control, license to operate in Bolivia and up to 49% of the profits. The remaining 51% of the shares were distributed to Bolivians as pensions and through another scheme dubbed *Participación Popular*, which would channel spending away from cities and into rural

The Drug War

Once free of active duty, some used their expertise in US military operations to secure work as highly paid informants and security guards for cocaine producers and traffickers.

In mid-1992, Bolivia's senate voted to expel US troops participating in antinarcotic activities, but the USA was unwilling to resume aid without a role in a subsequent program. By early 1995, the US government had grown impatient with Bolivia's failure to destroy its coca crop in a timely manner, and set a deadline of June 30, 1995, for the eradication of nearly 2000 hectares of Chapare coca, and a further 3500 hectares by December 31. Threatening cuts in foreign aid and financing, it also demanded Bolivia's signature on an extradition treaty that would send drug traffickers to trial in the US.

All the while, the US government remained unwilling – at least outwardly – to consider that drug addiction and the resulting market for illicit substances might be a domestic problem, mainly because it seemed more politically expedient to lay the blame on distant countries than on its own voters. In April, a geographically challenged US Congressman, Dan Burton, suggested the US spray the Bolivian coca crop with herbicides to be dropped by planes based on an aircraft carrier 'off the Bolivian coast.' Once the laughter subsided, protests were launched against the US and Bolivian governments for even suggesting such military force, and the Coca Leaf Growers Association again pointed out that the trade was perpetuated not by the producers, but by a burgeoning US market.

In any case, Bolivia met the June 30 deadline by paying farmers US$2500 for each hectare destroyed; this placed heavy strains on government resources, and predictably, most farmers simply collected the money and moved elsewhere to replant. When violence erupted over UMOPAR (Anti-drug Mobile Rural Patrol Unit) eradication methods on public lands in Isiboro-Sécure National Park – resulting in 187 arrests, five deaths and eventually, a renewal of the state of siege – the US began moaning about human-rights abuses. Nevertheless, the US government set another deadline that required the eradication of an additional 5400 hectares by December 31, 1995. Although Bolivia managed to meet it, there was a negligible decrease in actual production – farmers merely planted more coca in order to collect the money for uprooting it – and the costs were borne mainly by Bolivian taxpayers.

In 1998, coca eradication programs were handed over to the Banzer government, which ambitiously pledged to eradicate the entire Chapare coca crop and all coca paste production by 2002 – if donor countries would supply at least US$750 million to finance the effort. At the same time, they ended compensation to farmers, which clearly wasn't working. Hugo Banzer Suárez' 'Dignity Plan' of 1999 promised alternative development schemes in exchange for eradication, but growers have yet to find markets for alternative crops. The election of long-standing cocalero leader Evo Morales to Congress in 1997 created a stir, but thus far he has achieved little on behalf of the growers.

Despite recent US-backed coca eradication measures that have resulted in violence on both sides, coca growing continues in Bolivia. At press time, officials claimed the amount of coca growing in the Chapare region was down from 80,000 acres in 1998 to 4000 acres and dwindling, but the actual number is probably higher. As long as cocaine remains illegal and demand continues, the potential profits will make it difficult for Bolivian farmers – or international drug traffickers or street-sellers – to give up the trade.

municipalities, to be used for schools, clinics and other local infrastructure.

Initially, Participación Popular drew widespread disapproval; city dwellers didn't want to lose their advantage, and rural people, who stood to benefit most, feared a hidden agenda or simply didn't understand the program. Most working-class people viewed it as privatization by another name, and concluded that it would lead to the closure of unprofitable operations that failed to attract investment, resulting in greater unemployment. They had a point – while potential investors clamored for the oil company YPFB and the huge agribusinesses of Santa Cruz department, the antiquated COMIBOL mining operations and the hopelessly inefficient ENFE railways drew little more than polite sneers (and many components of these operations have in fact closed down).

In early 1995, labor grievances over these new policies resulted in a 90-day state-of-siege declaration and the arrest of 374 labor leaders. By mid-year, measures were relaxed, but as the year progressed, reform issues were overshadowed by violence and unrest surrounding US-directed coca eradication in the Chapare (see the 'The Drug War' in this section). Even the establishment of a Spanish-managed private pension scheme and a subsequent payment of US$248 to each Bolivian pensioner – with the promise of future payments from the less-than-fluid plan – did little to boost the administration's popularity.

In the next election, held on June 1, 1997, voters upset by the reforms cast 22.5% of the ballot in favor of former dictator General Hugo Banzer Suárez over MNR's Juan Carlos Duran, former president Jaime Paz Zamora and Santa Cruz millionaire Ivo Kuljis. After cobbling together a disparate coalition – with little in common but a distaste for contender Jaime Paz Zamora – Congress deemed Banzer the victor, and he was sworn in on August 6 to a five-year term (thanks to a recent constitutional amendment that increased presidential terms from four to five years).

In the late 1990's, Banzer faced swelling public discontent with his coca eradication measures (see 'The Drug War,' earlier in this chapter), widespread government and police corruption, unrest in response to increasing gasoline prices, and a serious water shortage and economic downturn in Cochabamba department. During the first half of 2000, public protests over increasing gasoline prices versus government-controlled transport fares resulted in the blockade of the Yungas Highway for several weeks, and several issues inspired marches, demonstrations and occasional violence, which sporadically halted all traffic (in some cases even vendor and pedestrian traffic) in La Paz and other cities. Throughout much of the year 2000, public discontent continued to grow more vocal, and it remains to be seen whether it will escalate or simply run out of steam.

GEOGRAPHY

Bolivia currently encompasses 1,098,581 sq km, which makes it 3½ times the size of the British Isles, slightly smaller than Alaska, and just less than half the size of Western Australia. It's bordered on the west by Chile and Peru, on the north and east by Brazil, and on the south by Argentina and Paraguay. The country is shaped roughly like an equilateral triangle. At its greatest extents, it measures 1300km from east to west and 1500km from north to south.

Much of Bolivia's appeal for the visitor lies in its awesome geography. Physically, the land is divided into five basic and diverse regions: the high Altiplano, the highland valleys, the Yungas, the Chaco and the forested lowlands of the Amazon and Paraná basins.

The Altiplano

The Altiplano ('high plain') is Bolivia's most densely populated region, although it is by no means crowded. This great plateau, which is characterized by *puna* vegetation (high open grasslands), runs from the Peruvian border north of Lake Titicaca southward to the Argentine border, and spills over into neighboring Peru, Chile and Argentina.

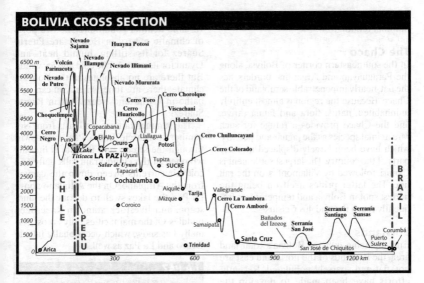

BOLIVIA CROSS SECTION

Despite its name, the Altiplano is anything but flat. Basin altitude ranges from 3500m to 4000m, but the snowcapped peaks of the Cordillera Real and the many isolated volcanic summits of the Cordillera Occidental reach much higher. Nevado Sajama, a volcano near the Chilean border and disputably Bolivia's highest peak, rises to an elevation of 6542m. The average elevation of peaks in the Cordillera Real near La Paz is 5500m.

Bolivia's 'great lakes' are also found on the Altiplano. Lake Titicaca, the largest and most beautiful, is South America's second largest lake. Lakes Uru Uru and Poopó, south of Oruro, are little more than immense puddles just a few meters deep. South of the lakes, where the land becomes drier and less populated, lie the sprawling Salar de Uyuni and Salar de Coipasa, which are remnants of two ancient lakes. These two salt deserts and the surrounding plains form eerie white expanses of salt deposited by leeching from the surrounding peaks.

Highland Valleys

The highland valleys south and east of the Altiplano boast the most hospitable living conditions in the country, with near-optimum climatic conditions and fertile soils. This is the Cordillera Central, an area of scrambled hills and valleys, fertile basins and intense agriculture. The cities of Cochabamba, Sucre, Potosí and Tarija support most of the population. With a very pleasant reversed Mediterranean climate – rain falls in summer instead of winter – the fertile land supports olives, nuts, wheat, maize and grapes, and wine is produced around the city of Tarija. Only the exposed and lofty city of Potosí experiences a chilly and relatively unfavorable climate.

The Yungas

North and east of Cochabamba and La Paz, where the Andes fall away into the Amazon Basin, are the Yungas – the transition zone between dry highlands and humid lowlands. Above the steaming, forested depths rise the near-vertical slopes of the Cordillera Real and the Cordillera Quimsa Cruz, which halt Altiplano-bound clouds, causing them to deposit bounteous rainfall on the Yungas. Vegetation is abundant and tropical fruit, coffee, sugar, coca, cacao, vegetables and tobacco grow with minimal tending.

The Chaco

In the southeastern corner of Bolivia, along the Paraguayan and Argentine borders, lies the flat, nearly impenetrable scrubland of the Chaco. Because the region is almost entirely uninhabited, native flora and fauna thrive, and the Chaco provides a refuge for such rare animal species as the jaguar and peccary, which have been largely displaced in other parts of the country. The largest settlement is Camiri, followed by Villamontes, on the rail line. The latter prides itself on being the hottest spot in Bolivia and temperatures frequently reach the mid 40s Celsius.

Lowlands

Encompassing 60% of Bolivia's total land area, the lowlands of the north and east are hot, flat and sparsely populated. Recently, efforts have been made to develop the forestry, agricultural and mineral potential of the region. The only breaks in the largely flat, green monotony of the Beni, Pando and northern and eastern Santa Cruz departments are the natural monoliths and ranges of low hills that rise from the Llanos de Moxos, Guarayos and Chiquitos.

Two great river systems drain this vast area. The Acre, Madre de Dios, Abunã, Beni, Mamoré, Ichilo, Ibare, Grande, Paraguá and a score of other rivers flow northward and eastward toward Brazil into tributaries of the Amazon. In the far southeast, the Río Paraguai flows southward into the Paraná Basin and eventually to the Atlantic via the Río de la Plata.

CLIMATE

Bolivia has as wide a range of climatic patterns as it has of elevation and topography, but the overall temperatures are probably cooler than most people expect. Even in the humid forest regions of the north, frosts are not unheard of during a *surazo*, a cold wind blowing from Patagonia and the Argentine pampa.

Although most of Bolivia lies as near the equator as Tahiti or Hawaii, its elevation

and unprotected expanses contribute to variable weather conditions. The two poles of climatic misery in Bolivia are Puerto Suárez for its stifling, humid heat, and Uyuni for its near-Arctic cold and icy winds. But there are no absolutes in the Bolivian climate; there are times when you can sunbathe in Uyuni and freeze stiff in Puerto Suárez!

The summer rainy period lasts from November to March. In La Paz, mists swirl through the streets and the city is literally wrapped in the clouds; rain falls daily and cold air currents sweep down the canyon from the Altiplano. On the Altiplano above La Paz, the lakes swell to devour the landscape, and livestock stand in knee-deep puddles. Of the major cities, only Potosí normally has snow, which occasionally falls in Oruro and La Paz as well.

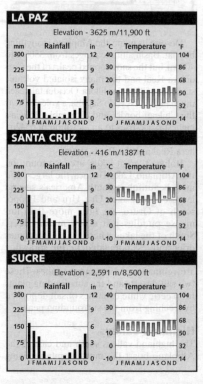

During the winter, the climate is drier and more pleasant. Throughout the country, nighttime temperatures drop dramatically, and on the high Altiplano, when a cloud passes over the sun, the temperature drops noticeably. Subzero temperatures are frequent, especially at night, and precipitation is possible at any time of year, but most of the rain falls during the summer months (December to March).

In Cochabamba, Sucre and Tarija, winter is the time of clear, beautiful skies and optimum temperatures, and there is hardly a healthier or more ideal climate on earth. The lowlands experience hot sunny days and an occasional 10-minute shower to cool things off and settle the dust. Because of their elevation variance, the Yungas may experience rainstorms on any day of the year.

ECOLOGY & ENVIRONMENT

The early 1990s saw a dramatic surge in international and domestic interest in ecological issues and environmental attitudes in the Amazon region. This was clearly demonstrated by the choice of Brazil as the venue for ECO-92, the UN's enormous environmental bash aimed at thrashing out priorities for the environment and economic development.

Little explored and for years relatively ignored, Bolivia's lowlands have only recently begun to figure in the consciousness of the Bolivian government. With the current push toward securing undeniable sovereignty of the lowland regions, and the potential fortunes to be made in minerals, agricultural opportunities and forest products, conservation isn't as convenient as it once was. With so many economic advantages, there's unfortunately little incentive to consider long-term effects.

Environmental problems have not yet reached apocalyptic proportions, but change is coming rapidly, and it is not being accompanied by the sort of careful thought required to maintain a sound ecological balance. Bolivia fortunately lacks the population pressures of Brazil, but it is nevertheless promoting indiscriminate development of its lowlands. With governmental encouragement, settlers are leaving the highlands to clear lowland forest and build homesteads. Though several local and international groups have found innovative ways to preserve selected spots, in other areas, insensitive development continues and many regions risk exhaustion of their forest and wildlife resources.

The Fate of the Amazon

Although books, magazines, TV shows and myriad international causes seem to be debating ecological issues, and the words 'fate of the Amazon' have begun to seem trite, it is appropriate to consider the issue a planetary concern. The Amazon is a very large, complex and fragile ecosystem that contains one tenth of the earth's total number of plant and animal species and drains one fifth of the world's fresh water – and it's increasingly endangered.

While resource development is necessary for Bolivia and other countries to meet their own needs, haphazard development is inappropriate in this sensitive region. The construction of roads is a prerequisite for exploitation of the region. New roads have created a swath of development across the former Beni wilderness from La Paz to Guayaramerín and Yucumo to Trinidad. The Riberalta-Cobija road is currently spreading the frenzy on into the Pando department.

These roads are the direct result of 'humanitarian aid' and earth-moving equipment donated by outside logging interests (Japan and the USA have seemingly insatiable appetites for forest products!), but similar projects throughout the Amazon have been encouraged and financed with collaboration from the World Bank, the International Monetary Fund (IMF), US and other international banks, and a variety of private corporations, politicians and military interests.

The inevitable conclusion is that new highway projects such as these will follow established patterns of development and open up the region for further decimation. According to calculations based on Landsat photos, the damming of rivers and the burning and clearing of the forests between 1970 and 1989 destroyed about 400,000 sq km, or about 10%, of the Amazon forest.

Economic Development of the Amazon

Most biologists doubt that the Amazon can support large-scale agriculture. The rain forest lushness is deceptive: The volcanic lands and flood plains can support continuous growth, but the forest topsoil is thin and infertile, and much of it is acidic and contains insufficient calcium, phosphorus and potassium for effective crop production.

Small-scale slash-and-burn, a traditional agricultural technique adopted by nomadic Indians, supported small populations on such fragile lands as those of the Amazon Basin with few ecological compromises. Indians would fell an approximately 12 or 24-hectare plot of land and burn off the remaining material. The resulting ash would support a few years of crops: squash, maize, manioc, plantains and beans. Clearings were small and few, and once the land was no longer productive, it was left fallow long enough for the forest to recover.

In contrast, modern agricultural interests in the region have emphasized cattle ranching, which does not give the land a rest. Ranchers clear enormous tracts of land – some larger than European nations – which are never left fallow, so once any nutrients or topsoil are gone, the land is permanently wasted.

Effects of Development The Amazon's indigenous population has borne the brunt of the destruction that has systematically decimated their lands and their forest habitat. New roads have attracted settlers and opportunists into the last refuges of tribes which, as a consequence, have suffered from introduced diseases, pollution, overhunting and violent confrontations. Similarly, careless development brings about the extinction each year of thousands of forest species. This loss reduces the genetic pool that is vital (as a source of foods, medicines and chemicals) for sustaining life.

Parts of the northern La Paz department are facing an environmental catastrophe. Owing to the presence of valuable minerals in the northern rivers, both commercial mining companies and maverick prospectors stream into the Alto Beni region to work the streams and rivers. Their principal technique involves the use of highly poisonous mercury to extract gold from ore, and large quantities of mercury are washed into the water and present a health hazard for local inhabitants and remaining wildlife.

Since the failure of its early-1950s attempt at agrarian reform on the Altiplano, the Bolivian government has officially encouraged both immigration and development in the vast lowland regions. The 1950s program entailed allotting each farmer with a plot of land known as a *minifundio*. These private plots made obsolete the communal *ayllu* system of shared responsibility and production practiced since Inca days. However, the minifundio parcels were too small to sustain life on the harsh Altiplano and, in the end, farmers were forced to somehow wrest a living from the land or relocate. For the past decade, the government has been actively promoting development in the lowland regions with promises of land and loans. Although it has meant a complete change in lifestyle, the advantages of migrating to the verdant and productive lowlands have been too inviting for many to pass up.

The theory that the Amazon forests are the prime source of the world's oxygen is no longer given much credence by the scientific community, but there is increasing concern over the regional and global climatic changes brought on by forest clearing. One of the most dramatic and disturbing developments is *el chaqueo* (see 'El Chaqueo' in the Amazon Basin chapter), the burning of immense tracts to clear forest for agriculture or cattle ranching, which in Bolivia amounts to up to 200,000 sq km annually. In September, the Altiplano skies are obscured by a dirty gray haze that obliterates the mountains and turns the sun into an egg yolk. In the northern lowlands, visibility can diminish to as little as 200m, and the smoke clouds may extend as far as Africa and Antarctica. Scientists generally agree that the torching of the forest on such a massive scale contributes to the greenhouse effect, but opinions differ regarding the scale of damage involved.

Currently, a proposed dam on the Río Beni would likely inundate 300,000 hectares, including a large swath of the fabulous Parque Nacional Madidi (see *National Geographic*, March 2000). However, international criticism has been vociferous and its construction is far from a foregone conclusion.

Remedies & Compromise Although Brazil's development policies in the Amazon Basin have been singled out for criticism, the region also includes vast tracts of six other countries – Bolivia, Colombia, Venezuela, Guyana, Ecuador and Peru. It's only fair to point out that many countries outside the region were once supporters of such development, and have been reminded only recently that their own treatment of the environment was hardly exemplary. Through the 1990s, a range of approaches to development were applied around the region in order to halt and/or remedy the destruction.

One example is debt-for-nature swaps – international agreements whereby a portion of a country's external debt is canceled in exchange for funding of conservation initiatives. Negotiation of such swaps requires that the sovereignty of recipient countries remains intact, and economic damage is avoided.

In August 1987, the US-based Conservation International kicked off the idea by agreeing to pay US$650,000 of Bolivia's foreign debt (which totals US$4 billion!) in exchange for permanent protection of the 334,200-hectare Reserva Biosférica del Beni, near San Borja. Bolivia retains management of the land but, theoretically, wildlife is protected, and haphazard development is curtailed.

Conservation International also succeeded in setting aside the 351,000-hectare Parque Regional Yacuma in the central Beni, as well as creating the 1.15 million-hectare

Reserva Forestal Chimane, which adjoins the Reserva Biosférica del Beni, for sustained development by local indigenous populations. Their most recent efforts have concentrated on the Parque Nacional Madidi, where they've worked with the community of San José de Uchupiamonas to establish and run the fabulous Chalalán Eco-Lodge. It now serves as both a tourist destination and a venue for rain forest researchers. Immediately east of the Parque Nacional Madidi, the Mapajo-Asociación Indígena has set aside the Reserva de la Biosfera Pilón Lajas, which reserves land for indigenous communities and promotes ecotourism focusing on the integration of indigenous peoples on their environment.

Another concept, which has been tried in Brazil, involves the creation of extractive reserves for the sustainable harvesting of Brazil nuts, rubber, and other nontimber products. The idea is to use the forest as a renewable resource without destroying it. These reserves gained worldwide attention when Chico Mendes, an enthusiastic advocate of the idea, was assassinated in Brazil's Acre state.

Alternatives have also been suggested to stop wasteful clear-cutting of timber and the wastage of huge tracts of forest in order to extract a few commercially valuable species, especially mahogany, or to clear land for cattle ranching. Proposed schemes included limiting the size of logging tracts and controlling the manner in which they were logged, as well as education for locals on the utilization and value of 'waste species' on the international market.

Ecotourism & Conservation Environmental conservation and carefully managed development must be achieved through the combined efforts of concerned individuals and groups both within Bolivia and abroad. Thus far, efforts have concentrated on education of the public, pressure on international financial institutions not to fund wasteful or destructive development projects, and encouragement of regional governments to adopt rational and sustainable rain forest plans.

Ecotourism provides a financial incentive to preserve the environments that attract tourist money, and Bolivia offers several successful community-based tourism projects. Currently, the Reserva Biosférica del Beni, the Chalalán project in Parque Nacional Madidi, the Pilón Lajas project near Rurrenabaque, the new FAN plan for Parque Nacional Noel Kempff Mercado, and the PROMETA administration of four new reserves in Tarija department all provide local communities with income and employment from ecotourism.

It's important that these organizations prove they are actively making progress toward the protection and preservation of the environment. One positive force in this direction is growing consumer pressure, which has the power to change economic trends on a global scale simply by changing purchasing patterns. For information, contact any of the following:

Asociación para la Protección del Medio Ambiente de Tarija – PROMETA (☎ 066-33873; fax 066-45865; prometa@olivo.tja.entelnet.bo; Alejandro del Carpio 0659, Casilla 59, Tarija)

Armonía (☎/fax 03-371005; armonia@scbbs-bo .com; Casilla 3081, Santa Cruz)

Conservación Internacional (☎ 02-434058; ci-bolivia@conservation.org; Calle Macario Pinilla 291, 2do Piso, Casilla 5633, La Paz), website www.ecotour.org

Fundación Amigos de la Naturaleza (☎ 03-337475; fax 03-329692; ecotourism@fan .scbbs-bo.com; Santa Cruz)

Instituto de Ecología (☎ 02-792416; fax 02-797511; insteco@zuper.net; Universidad Mayor de San Andrés, Calle 27, Campus Universitario Cotacota, Casilla 10077-Correo Central, La Paz)

Reserva de la Biosfera Pilón Lajas (☎/fax 0832-2524; Calle Bolívar at Tarija s/n, Casilla 935-4, Rurrenabaque) or (☎/fax 02-227337; Calle República Dominicana at Nicaragua, Miraflores, La Paz)

FLORA & FAUNA
Flora

Because of its enormous range of altitudes, Bolivia enjoys a wealth and diversity of flora rivaled only by its Andean neighbors.

In the overgrazed highlands, the only remaining vegetable species are those with some defense against grazing livestock or those that are unsuitable for firewood. Even this near the equator, there's little forest above 3000m elevation, although hardy dwarf trees such as the *queñua (Polylepis tarapana)* survive at altitudes of up to 5300m. Another oddity of the high Altiplano is the giant century plant *(Puya raimondii)*, which is found only in Bolivia and southern Peru. Several species of cactus and other succulents have adapted to the typically dry conditions of Bolivia's southwestern deserts and grow at altitudes between about 2000m and 3000m.

At lower elevations, the temperate highland hills and valleys support vegetation similar to that found in Spain or California, including date palms and cactus; there are few forests, and most of the trees are eucalyptus, which were transplanted to counter soil erosion. On the better-watered Chaco plains farther east, the vegetation increases in size and becomes more dense. Most of southeastern Bolivia is covered by a nearly impenetrable thicket of cactus and thorn scrub, which erupts into colorful bloom in the spring. Instantly recognizable are the hideously spiky *toboroche* (also known as *palo borracho)* and the red-flowering *quebracho* or 'break-axe' tree.

The moist upper slopes of the cloud and mist-soaked Yungas, which are exposed to moisture rising from the Amazon Basin, are characterized by dwarf forest composed mostly of small trees and shrubs, thick with moss and ferns. Descending farther, one enters the cloud forest, where the trees grow larger and the vegetation even thicker.

The lowland flats of northern Bolivia are characterized by true rain forest dotted with vast soaking wetlands and open savanna grasslands. The Amazon Basin contains the richest botanical diversity on earth, and botanists have spent their lives cataloguing the thousands of species endemic to the area. In the more humid regions, the land is comprised largely of swampland, low jungle scrub and rain forest. Although the northern grasslands are maintained by annual burning, there's evidence that this is the natural vegetation in these areas.

Fauna

Thanks to its varied geography, sparse human population and lack of extensive development, Bolivia is one of the best places on the continent for viewing South American wildlife. You'll need to venture beyond the cities, but that doesn't necessarily mean you'll have to slog through snow, swamp and rain forest to see something. A boat journey along a northern river or a rail trip through the far Southwest or the Oriente will probably present at least a glimpse.

The Altiplano Although llamas and alpacas are hardly wild, having been domesticated for centuries in the Andean highlands, you're bound to see plenty of them on the Altiplano. Despite their cute and cuddly appearance, they have a nasty reputation for biting and spitting, so beware when observing at close range. These ill-tempered camelid domesticates, cousins of the equally ill-tempered Arabian and Bactrian camels of Africa and Asia, also have cousins in the New World. Guanacos are quite rare in Bolivia, but the delicate little *vicuñas* are occasionally seen along the railway line between Uyuni and the Chilean border, as well as throughout the remote southwestern part of the country.

As for vicuñas, the problem is their soft and fuzzy hides, which fetch a bundle on the illicit market. As a result, vicuñas are declining in the wild, but in a couple of Bolivian reserves – the Reserva de Fauna Andina Eduardo Avaroa and Área Protegida Apolobamba – their numbers have been increasing. The best place to observe them is just across the Chilean border in Parque Nacional Lauca, which harbors thousands of zealously protected vicuñas. Other wild inhabitants of the Altiplano include Andean wolves, foxes, and *huemules* (Andean deer), but again, your best chance of seeing them is in Chile's Parque Nacional Lauca.

The Southern Altiplano is the exclusive habitat of the James flamingo; just look for any shallow lake and it will probably be full

of them. Also relatively common is the versatile *ñandú* or rhea (the South American ostrich), which inhabits the Altiplano to the Beni, the Chaco and the Santa Cruz lowlands. Then there's the *viscacha*, a longtailed rabbitlike creature that spends most of its time huddled under rocks.

In the highlands, lucky observers may see a condor or two; highly revered by the Inca, these rare vultures are the world's heaviest birds of prey. They have a wingspan of over 3m and have been known to effortlessly drag carcasses weighing 20kg.

Highland Valleys Unfortunately, the well-populated highland valleys are now nearly devoid of wildlife. The puma, which is native throughout the Americas and was once indigenous here, was considered sacred by many of the tribes conquered by the Inca, and the Inca capital at Cuzco was laid out in the shape of this feline deity. Even today, many Bolivians believe that eclipses are caused by hungry pumas nibbling at the sun or the moon, both of which are considered deities. On such occasions, the people stage noisy celebrations in the hope of frightening it away. After centuries of human interference, however, the puma is now wisely reclusive. Tracks are occasionally seen in the Cordillera de los Sombreros and other remote ranges, but there's little chance of spotting one without mounting a special expedition.

The Chaco The jaguar, tapir and *javeli* (peccary), which occupy the nearly inaccessible expanses of the Chaco in relatively healthy numbers, are quite elusive. Slightly more common, but still threatened with extinction, is the giant anteater, which exists in far eastern Bolivia near the Pantanal.

Amazon Basin The Amazon Basin – which contains the richest density of species on earth – features an incredible variety of lizards, parrots, monkeys, snakes, butterflies, fish and bugs (by the zillions!). River travelers are almost certain to spot capybaras (large amphibious rodents), turtles, alligators, pink dolphins and, occasionally, giant river otters. It's not unusual to see anacondas in the rivers of the Beni, and overland travelers frequently see armadillos, rheas, sloths and the agile, long-legged *jochis* (agoutis).

Many of the more common animals wind up in the stew pot. Locals roast turtles in the shell and eat their eggs. Jochi and armadillo are considered staples in some areas, and a great many of the latter are also turned into *charangos*, traditional Andean ukulele-type instruments.

Rarer still, but present in national parks and remote regions of the Beni, Pando and northern Santa Cruz and Cochabamba departments, are jaguars, peccaries, maned wolves, tapirs, giant anteaters and spectacled bears. Your best chances to see them are probably in Parque Nacional Noel Kempff Mercado.

Background Reading

Ecology & the Amazon Region
In *Amazonia* (1991), explorer and photographer Loren McIntyre photographically depicts the gradual demise of the Amazon region and its original inhabitants. For more on McIntyre's quest for the source of the Amazon – and his extraordinary psychic experiences with indigenous tribes – see *Amazon Beaming* (1991), by Petru Popescu. For a popularized vision of Amazonian wildlife and some good background material, see *Amazon Wildlife* (Insight Guides, 1992).

Wizard of the Upper Amazon – The Story of Manuel Córdova-Ríos (Houghton Mifflin, 1975) and the sequel *Río Tigre and Beyond*, by F Bruce Lamb, are worthwhile reading for insight into *yagé*, the hallucinogenic drug used by certain tribes of the upper Amazon.

The Fate of the Forest: Developers, Destroyers, and Defenders of the Amazon, by Susanna Hecht and Alexander Cockburn (Verso, 1989), provides one of the best analyses of the complex web of destruction of the Amazon, as well as recommendations for mending the damage.

The Rainforest Book, by Scott Lewis (Living Planet, 1990), is a concise analysis of rain forest problems and remedies. It's packed with examples that link consumer behavior with rain forest development, and

includes lists of conservation organizations and advice on individual involvement. A similar publication compiled by the Seattle Audubon Society and the Puget Consumers Co-operative is the booklet entitled *Rainforests Forever: Consumer Choices to Help Preserve Tropical Rainforests* (1990).

Emperor of the Amazon (Avon Bard, 1980) is by modern satirist Márcio Souza, who is based in Manaus (Brazil). His biting humor captures some of the greater horrors of the Amazon region and the absurdity of personal and governmental endeavors to conquer the rain forest. Both this and his other work, *Mad Maria* (Avon Bard, 1985), which deals with the abortive Madeira-Mamoré railway between Pôrto Velho, Guajará-Mirim (Brazil) and Riberalta, should be of interest to travelers around Bolivia's northern frontiers.

Field Guides *Rainforests – A Guide to Tourist and Research Facilities at Selected Tropical Forest Sites in Central and South America*, by James L Castner, is full of information and is especially worthwhile for researchers and rain forest visitors.

The beautifully illustrated *In Search of the Flowers of the Amazon Forest*, by Margaret Mee, comes highly recommended for anyone (not only botanists) interested in the Amazon.

Neotropical Rainforest Mammals: A Field Guide, by Louise Emmons & François Feer, contains color illustrations to identify mammals of the rain forest. For a reference work (as opposed to a field guide) consult *World of Wildlife: Animals of South America* by FR de la Fuente.

Bird-watchers in the Amazon region of Bolivia often use field guides for other South American countries – many species overlap. Amateur interests should be satisfied with titles such as *South American Birds: A Photographic Aid to Identification*, by John S Dunning; *A Guide to the Birds of Colombia*, by Stephen L Hilty & William L Brown; and *A Guide to the Birds of Venezuela*, by Rodolphe Meyer de Schauensee & William Phelps.

A more comprehensive tome is *A Guide to the Birds of South America*, by Rodolphe Meyer de Schauensee (Academy of Natural Science, Philadelphia). The high-priced reference work *The Birds of South America*, by RS Ridgley & G Tudor (University of Texas Press, 1989), comes in several extremely detailed and technical volumes. Also definitive is *Birds of the High Andes*, by Jon Fjeldsa & Niels Krabbe (Apollo Books, Denmark).

For some fascinating oddities, dip into *Ecology of Tropical Rainforests: An Introduction for Eco-tourists*, by Piet van Ipenburg & Rob Boschhuizen (Free University Amsterdam, 1990). This booklet is packed with intriguing and bizarre scientific minutiae about sloths, bats, the strangler fig and other extraordinary bits of rain forest ecology. It's available in the UK from J Forrest, 64 Belsize Park, London NW3 4EH; or in the USA from M Doolittle, 32 Amy Rd, Falls Village, CT 06031. Proceeds from its sales support the Tambopata Reserve Society, which funds rain forest research in southeastern Peru's Reserva Tambopata.

A useful book for botanists is the 1000-page illustrated guide, *Guía de Árboles de Bolivia (Guide to Bolivia's Trees)*, published in 1993 by the Bolivian National Herbarium and the Missouri Botanical Garden. It's available from the Instituto de Ecología, Casilla 10077, La Paz.

In Britain, these and thousands of other natural history titles are available from Subbuteo Natural History Books Ltd (☎ 01352-756551; fax 01352-756004; sales@subbooks.demon.co.uk), Pistyll Farm, Nercwys, near Mold, Flintshire, North Wales CH7 4EW. They also take international orders. See the website www.subbooks.demon.co.uk.

National Parks & Reserves

Bolivia boasts a number of national parks and reserves, some of which have only recently opened to visitors, that are the habitat of a myriad of plant, bird and animal species. Several other marginally protected areas might also one day become national parks. Following is a brief outline of the parks and reserves included in this book. For more information, see the relevant chapters (chapter titles follow in brackets).

Parque Nacional Aguaragüe (South Central Bolivia & the Chaco) This long, narrow park protects the transition zone between the Gran Chaco and the highlands of Tarija Department. Its best-known feature, the Cañón de Pilcomayo, is easily accessible from Villamontes.

Parque Nacional & Área de Uso Múltiple Amboró (Santa Cruz) Amboró, encompassing 430,000 hectares at the juncture of the highland, Chaco and Amazon ecosystems, is home to the rare spectacled bear, jaguars, capybaras, peccaries and an astonishing variety of bird life.

Área Protegida Apolobamba (Cordilleras & Yungas) Excellent hiking is possible in this remote park abutting the Peruvian border beneath the Cordillera Apolobamba. It was established in 1972 as a vicuña reserve and presently contains 2500 vicuñas and a large population of condors.

Reserva Biosférica del Beni (Amazon Basin) The 334,200-hectare Beni Biosphere Reserve, near San Borja in the Amazon Basin, exists in conjunction with the adjacent Reserva Forestal Chimane. It is home to at least 500 species of tropical birds, as well as more than 100 species of mammals.

Parque Nacional Carrasco (Amazon Basin) Attached to Parque Nacional Amboró, the Parque Nacional Carrasco attempts to protect some remaining stands of rain forest in the volatile Chapare region. The most accessible site is the Cuevas de los Pájaros Nocturnos.

Parque Nacional Cotapata (La Paz/Cordilleras & Yungas) This recently designated park includes the upper Zongo Valley and parts of the wild mountains and Yungas country along the La Cumbre to Coroico trek.

Reserva Privada de Patrimonio Natural de Corvalán Better known as just Corvalán, this small reserve protects a small but beautiful slice of the Gran Chaco, and is rich in wildlife. Access is via a long 4WD track from Villamontes.

Reserva Nacional de Fauna Andina Eduardo Avaroa (Southern Altiplano) This beautiful park in the southwestern corner of the country takes in steaming volcanoes, hot springs, geyser basins, and some of Bolivia's most colorful landscapes, as well as a range of Andean wildlife: flamingos, rheas, viscachas, vicuñas and numerous rare and unusual plant species.

Parque Nacional Isiboro-Sécure (Amazon Basin) Unfortunately, owing to a 1905 policy to colonize the Chapare, the Indian population of northern Cochabamba department has been either displaced or exterminated, and wildlife exists only in the most remote areas. Access is difficult and visitors are mostly limited to the Fremen Tours trips to Laguna Bolivia. Because of coca cultivation and cocaine processing and trafficking, independent visitors should exercise caution.

Parque Nacional Kaa-Iya del Gran Chaco (Eastern Lowlands) This 2 million-hectare national park – the largest in Latin America – protects a vast tract of the Gran Chaco, including the enigmatic Bañados del Izozog. It also serves as an indigenous reserve for the Guaraní and Ayoreo peoples.

Parque Nacional Madidi (Amazon Basin) This enormous new national park in northern La Paz department protects some of Bolivia's wildest remaining rain forest. With 1200 species of birds, it harbors the world's most dense concentrations of avifauna species, and is home to wildlife endemic to all Bolivian ecosystems, from tropical rain forest and tropical savanna to cloud forest and alpine tundra. Access is on foot from Apolo or, more conveniently, by boat from Rurrenabaque. You'll never forget a stay at the lodge at Chalalán, which sits beside a lovely lagoon deep in the rain forest.

Parque Nacional Noel Kempff Mercado (Amazon Basin) This remote park near the Brazilian border is named in honor of the Bolivian biologist who was murdered by renegades in 1986. It contains a variety of Amazonian wildlife and some of the most inspiring natural scenery in Bolivia, including the Sierra de Caparuch and the fabulous waterfalls of Arco Iris and Federico Alhfeld.

Reserva de la Biosfera Pilón Lajas (Amazon Basin) This reserve near Rurrenabaque protects six traditional communities and a large and relatively intact rain forest ecosystem.

Reserva de Vida Silvestre Ríos Blanco y Negro (Amazon Basin) This remote 1.4-million-hectare wildlife reserve consists of vast tracts of undisturbed rain forest. Wildlife includes giant anteaters, peccaries and tapirs, as well as over 300 bird species.

Parque Nacional Sajama (Southern Altiplano) This national park, which adjoins Chile's magnificent Parque Nacional Lauca, contains Volcán Sajama (6542m), Bolivia's highest peak. Tourist facilities include several private *alojamientos* (small inexpensive lodgings).

Reserva de la Biosfera Sama (South Central Bolivia & the Chaco) The Sama Biological Reserve features both the Altiplano and inter-Andean valley ecosystems. The most visited region in the highland portion is the mysterious Tajzara Lakes region, while the lowlands include rivers, waterfalls and lush vegetation.

Reserva Nacional de Flora y Fauna Tariquía (South Central Bolivia & the Chaco) This 247,000-hectare reserve takes in a large area of dense cloud forest on the eastern slopes of the mountains of Tarija department. It's relatively accessible, but may be explored only on foot.

Parque Nacional Torotoro (Central Highlands) This beautiful and unusual park boasts caves, ancient ruins and lovely wild landscapes, as well as lots of Cretaceous-era biped and quadruped dinosaur tracks.

Parque Nacional Tunari (Central Highlands) This park, right in Cochabamba's backyard, features pleasant mountain scenery and hiking around Cerro Tunari and the small lakes of Huarahuara.

GOVERNMENT & POLITICS

In theory, Bolivia is a republic, loosely modeled on the USA, with legislative, executive and judicial branches of government. The first two bodies convene in La Paz, the de facto capital, and the Supreme Court sits in Sucre, the constitutional capital. Politically, Bolivia is divided into nine departments, which are subdivided into 112 provinces. In turn, these are divided into 294 sections and the sections are subdivided into 1408 cantons.

The president is elected to a five-year term (up from four by a 1996 constitutional amendment) by popular vote and cannot hold more than one consecutive term. Once elected, the president appoints a cabinet of 15 members and also selects departmental and local government officers.

The Legislature consists of a Senate and a Chamber of Deputies that convenes in legislative session for 90 days per year. Each of the nine departments send three elected senators for terms of six years, with one third elected every two years. The Chamber of Deputies has 102 members who are elected to four-year terms.

Having said all that, Bolivia has had nearly as many governments and leaders as

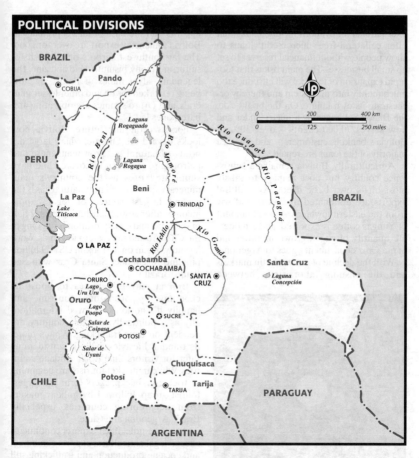

POLITICAL DIVISIONS

it has years of independence, and has in fact been ruled by military juntas for much of its existence. This may seem to make a mockery of the democratic processes outlined in the constitution, but since the late 1980s, Bolivia has seen peaceful and democratic transitions of government, and it's currently one of Latin America's most stable countries politically.

The current government is led by former military dictator General Hugo Banzer Suárez, who was elected by Congress in 1997 (with just 22.5% of the popular vote) after forming a loose coalition of disparate parties.

ECONOMY

Bolivia currently has the second lowest per-capita GNP (US$900 annually, after Guyana) in South America, and the third lowest in the Western Hemisphere (Haiti is the poorest). Fortunately, this is not as severe as it sounds, because most rural Bolivians operate outside the currency system and enjoy adequate subsistence lifestyles.

In late 1996, in hopes of tipping the scales toward a more international economy – and increased foreign investment – Bolivia joined the successful customs and trading block Mercosur, which aligned it with Argentina,

Brazil, Paraguay, Uruguay and Chile. Other international innovations include banks that offer collateral-free 'microcredit' loans to allow people without financial reserves to set up small businesses. The main risk is that too-rapid expansion of this tool will introduce too much money into the system and thereby orchestrate its own failure. On the bright side, the Banco Sol began as a micro-lender and now serves 70,000 clients – over 30% of Bolivia's banking customers – and the vast majority of the loans are repaid.

Agriculturally, Bolivia remains a subsistence country, but does manage to satisfy most of its own basic needs. Agricultural exports are dominated by cotton and soy from the eastern lowlands. A small amount of Yungas coffee is exported, and a moderate quantity of sugar, grown in Tarija and Santa Cruz departments, goes to Argentina.

With the decline of the world tin markets and the ensuing labor strife between miners' unions, cooperatives and the state, it appears that the days of tin's supremacy as Bolivia's mainstay export are over for good. The far Southwest harbors rich deposits of sulfur, antimony, bismuth, lead and zinc. The legendary silver mines of Potosí are now being reworked for tin and other lesser minerals, and Oruro's mines are operating at a bare-bones level.

For its economic future, Bolivia now looks toward the Oriente, where large deposits of natural gas, iron manganese and petroleum have been discovered and have supplanted ores as the country's main mineral exports. Currently, natural gas is the second largest source of legal export income (after soy), contributing nearly half of the total, and oil exploration is ongoing in the Chapare and the eastern lowlands. Work has now begun on a 3150km, US$1.9 billion pipeline to connect Santa Cruz with São Paulo, Brazil.

Bolivia currently hopes to boost its economy by promoting tourism, and happily, it's no longer viewed internationally as a politically unstable country dependent on drug trafficking. What's more, its tranquil lifestyles make it considerably safer for visitors than other Andean countries. While upmarket tourists are beginning to trickle in, backpackers form the largest tourist group, followed by holiday-makers from neighboring countries, especially Brazil, Argentina and Chile.

As a side note, illicit exports continue to exceed legal agricultural exports combined, and cocaine production and trafficking still account for up to 350,000 jobs. Despite eradication attempts (see 'The Drug War,' earlier in this chapter), the Chapare region alone cultivates much of the world's illicit coca, yielding up to 100,000kg of cocaine annually. (In contrast, most coca grown in the Yungas region is used domestically to chew or make tea.)

POPULATION & PEOPLE

With just eight million people, Bolivia is relatively thinly populated. Despite its cold, arid climate, the Altiplano supports 70% of the people and for centuries has been the

Bolivian miners still play an important role in the country's ecomomy.

ERIC WHEATER

country's most densely populated region. Most of these people are concentrated in the northern end of this region in the environs of La Paz, Lake Titicaca and Oruro.

Bolivia organized the first resistance to Spanish rule in South America, which included mestizo revolts in 1661 and 1780, and Indian insurrections that lasted from 1776 to 1780. Modern Bolivians are also generally a rugged and strong-spirited people. Many of the dispersed Altiplano communities of Aymará-speaking Indians fought historic battles against the cultural dominance and oppression of the expanding Inca Empire. In pre-Hispanic Bolivia, they flourished as one of the most influential cultures in the Andes.

Currently, between 50% and 60% of the total population is of pure Native American (Indian) stock; most of these largely traditional people speak either Quechua or Aymará as a first language and strongly resist cultural change. In the countryside, they're known locally as *campesinos* (or campesinas, if referring to an entirely female group), while indigenous people in urban areas who wear traditional dress are commonly known as *cholos/cholas*. In addition, about 35% Bolivia's population is of *mestizo* heritage, meaning they are of mixed Spanish and Native American descent. Nearly 1% of the population is of African heritage, mostly descended from the slaves conscripted to work in the Potosí mines.

Most of the remainder of Bolivia's people is of European extraction. Some are descendants of the early Spanish conquerors, but there are also colonies of Mennonites speaking Platt Deutsch (Low German), descendants of Jewish refugees from Nazi Europe, Eastern European refugees, and hordes of researchers, aid workers and missionaries. Small Middle Eastern and Asian minorities, consisting mainly of Palestinians, Punjabis, Japanese and Chinese, have immigrated. Most of these have opened restaurants in urban areas or settled in the rapidly developing lowlands of Santa Cruz department.

The standard of living of most Bolivians is low, and in places such as El Alto, on the plains above La Paz, housing, nutrition, education, sanitation and hygiene standards are appalling. The state of health care, particularly in rural areas, is also quite poor, and it's estimated that 8% of infants born in Bolivia will die before their first birthday. Similarly, the average life expectancy in the country is only about 60 years for men and 65 years for women, compared with 70 to 75 years in most developed nations.

EDUCATION

School attendance is theoretically compulsory for children from ages six to 14, and thanks to Participación Popular (see History, earlier in this chapter), schools have now been founded in most rural areas. Unfortunately, public schools are generally very poor in both quality and funding, and nearly all wealthy families send their children to private or church-run schools.

Overall, 87% of primary-school-aged children are enrolled in classes, but attendance isn't necessarily a high priority. As a result, Bolivia's official literacy rate of 75% is one of the lowest in Latin America. There are several universities in the country, the major ones being the Universidad de San Simón in Cochabamba and the Universidad Mayor de San Andrés (UMSA) in La Paz. Sucre and Santa Cruz also have large universities.

ARTS
Literature

As with most South American nations, Bolivia has developed a literature of its own. Unfortunately, two of the three Bolivian novels ever translated into English aren't very recent, and to really come to grips with Bolivian literature will require a knowledge of Spanish.

The main sources for information on Bolivian literature are Fernando Diez de Medina's literary history *Literatura boliviana* (4th edition, 1980); Adolfo Cáceres Romero's monumental *Nueva historia de la literatura boliviana* (1987); and the annual *Bio-bibliografía boliviana*, which lists all books published in Bolivia, published by Werner Guttentag Tichauer & M Rita Arze Ramirez. In addition, there is a fine article by Oscar Rivera-Rodas on the history of

Bolivian literature in the *Handbook of Latin American Literature* (Garland, 1992).

Bolivia's indigenous people had no written language, but the first volume of Cáceres Romero's study is devoted to the oral literature of the four indigenous cultures – Aymará, Quechua, Kallawaya and Guaraní. The slim collection *Quechua People's Poetry*, by Jesús Lara (Curbstone Press, 1986), includes some melodies.

Bolivia's most prominent colonial-era writer is Bartolomé Arzáns Orsúa y Vela (1676-1736), whose immense *Historia de la villa imperial de Potosí* relates the history of that city year by year from its founding in 1545 until the author's death in 1736. The emphasis was on what we would now call 'human interest stories' and grand narrative sweep. Some of these wonderful stories and anecdotes have been translated into English in *Tales of Potosí* (Brown University Press, 1975).

After Bolivian independence, the first literary movement was Romanticism, which spawned two prominent writers. Julio Lucas Jaimes (1840-1914), in contrast to conventional European Romanticism, rewrote history and oral narratives into short tales. He also founded the 'traditionalist' genre, which attempted to recover a local style and thereby create a national literature. In the works of Nathaniel Aguirre (1843-1888), also a traditionalist, the narrator plays an important role, and foreshadows a predominant construct in contemporary Latin American fiction.

Bridging the transition from Romanticism to modernism was the poet Adela Zamudio (1854-1928). The modernist writer Ricardo Jaimes Freyre (1866-1933) was the first Bolivian author to gain international recognition. His story *Indian Justice*, which dealt with the exploitation of the indigenous population, is translated in *The Spanish American Short Story – A Critical Anthology* (University of California Press, 1980). Other notable modernist writers include the poet Franz Tamayo (1879-1956) and Gregorio Reynolds (1882-1948).

The first and most influential of the new generation of realist Bolivian authors was the historian and novelist Alcides Arguedas. His sociological treatise *Pueblo Enfermo* ('sick nation'), published in 1909, and his novel *Raza de Bronce* (1919), emphasize the diversity of Bolivian culture and strongly criticize the predominant feudal system for its enslavement of the indigenous population.

Another writer of this generation was novelist, dramatist, poet and diplomat Adolfo Costa du Rels (1891-1980), who spent much of his career in Europe – as the president of the League of Nations Council, among other things – and some of his works were written in French. His drama *Les Étendards du Roi* has been translated as *The King's Standards* (1958) and his novel *Terres Embrasées* (1932) was rewritten in Spanish as *Tierras Hechizadas* and translated into English as *Bewitched Lands* (Knopf, 1945). This realistic novel describes the rivalry between an authoritarian mestizo Chaco landholder and his European-educated, democratically minded son, as seen by two Englishmen looking for oil. It's interlaced with evocative descriptions of the Bolivian rain forests and Chaco.

The Chaco War provided material for a range of novels. Augusto Céspedes published his collection of short stories *Sangre de Mestizos* in 1936, Jesús Lara published his diary-novel *Repete* in 1937, and Costa du Rels wrote *Laguna H-3* in 1967. Céspedes' *Metal del Diablo* ('devil's metal'), which appeared in 1946, depicts the wretched conditions of the workers in Bolivian tin mines and sharply attacks the wealthy owners and exploiters.

The Revolution of 1952 and the military dictatorship of General René Barrientos and subsequent guerrilla uprising ushered in the contemporary period and coincided with innovations in narrative technique.

In 1957, two influential books were published. Marcelo Quiroga Santa Cruz' (1931-1980) existentialist novel *Los Des-habitados* ('the vacant ones') was concerned with the meaninglessness of reality and experiences. Similarly, Oscar Cerruto's (1912-1981) collection of short stories, *Cerco de Penumbras* ('fence of shadows'), grapples with failure and the absurdity of existence.

One novel inspired by Ché Guevara's struggle was Renato Prada Oropeza's *Los Fundadores del Alba* (1969), 'founders of the dawn,' translated into English as *The Breach* (Doubleday, 1971). This novel, which won the 1969 *Casa de las Américas* prize in Cuba, revolves around the experiences of two young men, one a saintlike guerrilla modeled on Ché Guevara, and the other a soldier who lacks ideals and is fighting only because he has been drafted.

Three notable contemporary Bolivian poets are Jaime Sáenz (1921-1986), Pedro Shimose (born 1940) and Eduardo Mitre (born 1943). Sáenz' *Muerte por el Tacto* (1957), 'death by touch,' and *Obra Poética* (1975), 'poetic work,' are written in free verse and deal with love on an abstract level. Shimose's eight volumes of poetry, collected in *Poemas* (1988), are presented in colloquial idiom and controversially attack tyranny and social inequality. Five short poems by Mitre are translated into English in the *Anthology of Contemporary Latin American Literature, 1960-1984* (Fairleigh Dickenson University Press, 1986).

The Bolivian novel most recently published in English is Arturo von Vacano's *Morder el Silencio* (1980), which was translated as *The Biting Silence* (Avon, 1987). This autobiographical novel runs through the life, career and ultimate arrest of the journalist narrator, who has written an article critical of the military government and is accused of being a communist. The solution offered in the end is distinctively Maoist: to let the country die along with its government and start all over again from scratch.

A new and worthwhile Bolivian novel is the hard-to-find *Barriomundo* ('world neighborhood') by Jaime Nisttahuz. The characters are borrowed from classical Greek figures, but the story is told through the eyes of boys growing up in a La Paz neighborhood. It presents a refreshingly honest view of the world and presents the eternal conflict between childhood and endless political agendas. And why is it so hard to find? Because it's priced for the common reader – only US$2.20 – and no mainstream bookstore will accept such a low profit margin. (Try the La Paz Casa de la Cultura, at the corner of Potosí and Mariscal Santa Cruz.)

Painting

In the early colonial days, a number of artists worked on religious themes in Bolivia, among them Italian-born Bernardo Bitti, Gregoria Gamarra, Matías Sanjinés, Zurbarán and Leonardo Flores. Look for work by all of these early artists in Bolivian museums and churches.

Bolivia's major contribution to religious painting, however, is represented by the Escuela Potosina Indígena, which was inspired by the Potosí master Melchor Pérez de Holguín. Hallmarks of this tradition include gilded highlights and triangular representations of the Virgin Mary.

Holguín, who was born in Cochabamba, arrived in Potosí in 1670 and entered the workshop of Francisco Herrar y Velarde, a Spanish painter who had settled there. His earliest works were paintings of the saints, portrayed as gaunt and wrinkled, presumably from pious asceticism. Once his talents were known, commissions poured in and his reputation spread. His last signed canvas was completed in 1732, but his tradition was carried on by *potosino* students, including Gaspar Miguel de Berrio, Nicolás de los Ecoz, Joaquín Caraballo and Manuel Córdoba.

In the mid-1800s, Bolivian life was depicted in naive watercolors by Melchor María Mercado, the US-born son of Spanish parents living in Sucre. His work was clearly influenced by the French artist/explorer Alcides d'Orbigny, who spent three months in Sucre during Mercado's early years.

A distinctive modern artist was Alejandro Mario Yllanes, an Aymará tin miner from Oruro who turned to art in the 1930s as an engraver and muralist. He drew on themes from Andean mythology and pre-Hispanic history, which raised consciousness and a sense of identity among Aymará campesinos. The government of General Toro recognized the threat this represented and exiled him to the lowlands, where he absorbed the brilliant tropical colors that suffuse his later work. He somehow wound up in New York City, where he stayed until his death in 1960. His paintings, which depict the fiery side of the Aymará tradition, were first exhibited in New York in 1992, and they received favorable reviews. La Paz drives to bring his work home to Bolivia have so far been unsuccessful.

Also of note was Miguel Alandia Pantoja who, in the late 1940s, painted scenes of popular revolution – superimposed on industrial revolution – in the time leading up to the reforms instituted by Victor Paz Estenssoro in 1952. His scenes of good (the workers) versus evil (the establishment) are vibrant, angular and color-rich.

The modern Aymará artist Mamani Mamani, from Tiahuanaco village, strives to portray the true 'color' of the Altiplano – not the landscape but the images that inspire the people – and it is brilliant. The *paceño* artist Gil Imana brings out the stark, cold and isolated nature of life in the Andes, using only tiny splashes of color on drab backgrounds to hint at the underlying vibrancy of the culture.

Other names to watch for are Andrés Chambi, of La Paz, who's concerned with the hopes of Bolivia's working classes; Elsa Quintanilla, also from La Paz, who uses watercolors to interpret the female character in brilliant colors; Gilka Wara Libermann, who turns religious art into a modern riot of color; Alfredo La Placa, former Bolivian ambassador to the UN, with his surreal interpretations of his country, its mining heritage and its desire for order and progress; and Ricardo Pérez Alcalá, from Potosí, who eschews political and moral messages in favor of realistic whimsy, such as his preoccupation with Simón Bolívar or his painting of Leonardo da Vinci riding the bicycle he was never able to invent. Another realist is David Dario Antezana, whose watercolors of Bolivian rural life reflect obsession with detail and the rich red light of late afternoon; it's a stunning and evocative effect.

For more on Bolivian visual arts, see the book *La Pintura en los Museos de Bolivia*, by José de Mesa & Teresa Gisbert.

Music

Although the musical traditions of the Andes have evolved from a series of pre-Inca, Inca, Spanish, Amazonian and even African influences, each region of Bolivia has developed distinctive musical traditions, dances and instruments. The strains of the Andean music from the cold and bleak Altiplano are suitably haunting and mournful, while those of warmer Tarija, with its complement of bizarre musical instruments, take on more vibrant and colorful tones.

Although the original Andean music was exclusively instrumental, recent trends toward popularization of the magnificent melodies has inspired the addition of appropriately tragic, bittersweet or morose lyrics.

In the far eastern and northern lowland regions of Bolivia, Jesuit influences upon Chiquitano, Moxos and Guaraní musical talent left a unique legacy that is still in evidence and remains particularly strong in the musical traditions of neighboring Paraguay. In addition to economic ventures, the Jesuits promoted education and culture among the tribes. Extremely able artists and musicians, the Indians handcrafted musical instruments – the renowned violins and harps featured in Chaco music today – and learned and performed Italian baroque music, including opera! In the remotest of settings, they gave concerts, dances, and theater performances that could have competed on a European scale.

Artists & Recordings Although there is a wealth of yet-to-be-discovered musical talent in Bolivia, key players are influencing musical trends and tastes worldwide with their recordings and occasional performances abroad.

Many visitors to Bolivia, especially those who have attended *peñas* (folk music shows for locals and tourists) or fiestas, are taken with the music and set out in search of recordings to take home. While CDs and original recordings are available in larger cities, they're quite expensive, and most of the cassettes sold in shops or markets are bootlegged and are prone to rapid self-destruction. They cost only US$3 to US$5,

Traditional Andean Musical Instruments

Although the martial honking of tinny and poorly practiced brass bands seems an integral part of most South American celebrations, the Andean musical traditions employ a variety of instruments dating back to pre-colonial days.

Only the popular ukulele-like *charango*, based on the Spanish *vihuela* and *bandurria* – early forms of the guitar and mandolin – has European roots. By the early 17th century, Andean Indians had blended and adapted the Spanish designs into one that would better reproduce their pentatonic scale: a 10-stringed instrument with llama-gut strings arranged in five pairs and a *quirquincho* (armadillo carapace) soundbox. Modern charangos are scarcely different from the earliest models, but because of the paucity and fragile nature of quirquinchos, as well as efforts to improve sound quality, wood is nowadays the material of choice for charango soundboxes. Another stringed instrument, the *violín chapaco*, originated in Tarija and is a variation on the European violin. Between Easter and the Fiesta de San Roque (held in mid-August) it is the favored instrument (for information on other instruments unique to Tarija, see the South Central Bolivia & the Chaco chapter).

Prior to the advent of the charango, melody lines were carried exclusively by woodwind instruments. Best recognized are the *quena* and the *zampoña* (pan flute), which feature in the majority of traditional musical performances. Quenas are simple reed flutes played by blowing into a notch at one end. The more complex zampoñas are played by forcing air across the open ends of reeds lashed together in order of their size, often in double rows. Both quenas and zampoñas come in a variety of sizes and tonal ranges. Although the quena was originally intended for solo interpretation of musical pieces known as *yaravíes*, the two flutes are now played as part of a musical ensemble. The *bajón*, an enormous pan flute with separate mouthpieces in each reed, accompanies festivities in the Moxos communities of the Beni lowlands. While being played, it must be rested on the ground or carried by two people.

Other prominent wind instruments include the *tarka* and the *sikuri*, the lead instrument in the breathy *tarkeadas* and *sikureadas* of the rural Altiplano, and the *pinquillo*, a Carnaval flute available in various pitches.

Percussion also figures in most festivals and other folk musical performances as a backdrop for the typically lilting strains of the woodwind melodies. In highland areas, the most popular drum is the largish *huankara*. The *caja*, a tambourine-like drum played with one hand, is used exclusively in Tarija.

---

but copy them onto a better tape before giving them much play time.

Major artists to look for include charango masters Ernesto Cavour, Willy E Centellas, Alejandro Camara, Eddy Navia, Celestino Campos and Mauro Núñez; a good selection is available on the recording *Charangos Famosos*.

The Bolivian group that has been the most successful abroad is Los Kjarkas. They've recorded at least a dozen albums, and their superb 'Canto a la Mujer de Mi Pueblo' is unsurpassed in the Andean genre. The track entitled 'Llorando Se Fue' by the late Bolivian composer Ulisses Hermosa and his brother Gonzalo was recorded in Portuguese by the French group Kaoma in 1989 and became a worldwide hit as 'Lambada.' In June 1990, the Hermosa brothers finally received official recognition for their authorship of the ultra-popular song.

Other groups worth noting are Savia Andina, known for their protest songs, Chullpa Ñan, Inti Illimani, Rumillajta, Los Quipus, Grupo Cultural Wara, Los Masis and Yanapakuna.

In the USA, tapes of Bolivian music are available through the South American

Explorers Club (see Useful Organizations in the Facts for the Visitor chapter).

Dance

The pre-Hispanic dances of the Altiplano were celebrations of war, fertility, hunting prowess, marriage or work. After the Spanish arrived, some traditional European dances and those of the African slaves brought to work in the mines were introduced and massaged into the hybrid dances that characterize Bolivian festivities today.

If Bolivia has a national dance, it's the *cueca*. This heartfelt dance is derived from the Chilean cueca, which in turn is a Creole adaptation of the Spanish fandango. Its liberally interpreted choreography is rendered by whirling handkerchief-waving couples, called *pandillas*, to three-four time. Cuecas are intended to convey a story of courtship, love, loss of love and reconciliation. A favorite part of the dance comes with the shouting of *Aro, aro, aro*, which indicates that it's time for the couple to stop dancing for a moment and celebrate with a glass of spirits each.

The *auqui-auqui*, or 'old man' dance, parodies highborn colonial gentlemen by portraying them ludicrously with a top hat, gnarled cane and an exaggerated elderly posture. Another popular dance is the *huayño*, which originated on the Altiplano.

In the south around Tarija, where musical traditions depart dramatically from those of the rest of Bolivia, the festival dance is known as the *chapaqueada*. It is usually associated with religious celebrations, especially San Roque, and is performed to the strains of Tarija's host of unusual musical instruments. Also popular in Tarija is *la rueda* (the wheel), which is danced at fiestas throughout the year.

In San Ignacio de Moxos and around the Beni lowlands, festivities are highlighted by the dancing of the *machetero*, a commemorative folkloric dance accompanied by drums, violins and *bajones*. Dancers carry wooden machetes and wear elaborate crowns of brilliant macaw feathers, wooden masks, and costumes made of cotton, bark and feathers.

Other popular dances in the northern lowlands include the *carnaval* and the *taquirari Beniano*, both adapted from the Altiplano, and the *chovena*, indigenous to northeastern Bolivia.

Some of the most unusual and colorful dances are those performed at festivals on the high Altiplano, particularly during Carnival. *La Diablada* (The Dance of the Devils) fiesta at Oruro draws a large number of both foreign and Bolivian visitors.

The most famous and recognizable of the Diablada dances is *la morenada*, which is a reenactment of the dance of the African slaves brought to the courts of Viceroy Felipe III. The costumes consist of hooped skirts, shoulder mantles, and dark-faced masks adorned with plumes. Another dance with African origins is *los negritos*. Performers beat on drums, and the rhythm is reminiscent of the music of the Caribbean. In the *suri sikuri*, dancers gyrate wearing enormous hats decked with rhea feathers.

The *los llameros* dancers represent Andean llama herders, the *waca takoris* satirize Spanish bullfighters and the *waca tintis* represent the *picadores*, also of bullfighting fame. The *los Incas* commemorates the original contact between the Inca and Southern European cultures, and the *las tobas* is performed in honor of those Indian groups of the tropical lowlands (inaccurately called 'los apaches') that were conquered by the Inca and forcefully absorbed into the empire.

Potosí and La Paz both claim to be the birthplace of the *caporral de Potosí*, but it was almost certainly inspired by the harsh treatment of slaves in the Potosí mines. Caporrales were slave drivers, and the dance commemorates the slaves who were flogged with *latigos* (whips) and forced to wear leggings made of *cascaveles* (rattles) that prevented them from moving silently. Modern dancers wear strings of bottle caps to simulate the effect.

Another Potosí tradition is the *tinku*; although it resembles a kind of disorganized dance, it is actually a ritual fight that takes place primarily in the northern part of the department during festivals. Tinkus usually begin innocently enough, but near the end of the celebrations, they tend to erupt into drunken – and often rather violent – mayhem.

Cinema

Bolivian cinema has only recently gotten off the ground, thanks largely to filmmaker Jorge Sanjinés, who has made a dozen pictures and garnered 18 international awards with his popular, politically oriented works. Films such as *Ukamau* and *La Nación Clandestina* extol indigenous society in conflict with the prevailing imperialist values.

An early Bolivian film venture was the brilliant *Chuquiago*, by directors Oscar Soria and Antonio Equino, which appeared in the 1970s. Much of the dialogue is in Aymará and the theme concerns the enormous cultural and economic divides in modern La Paz – from El Alto to Calacoto – and is developed in four vignettes: the lives of Isico, a poor Aymará boy who has migrated to the city to find work, however meager; the *cholo* Johnny, who works as a bricklayer and dreams of migrating to the USA; Carlos, the tax inspector, whose main concerns seem to be crossword puzzles and soliciting bribes from the public; and the student Patricia, daughter of a wealthy entrepreneur, who idolizes Ché Guevara and joins an ill-fated revolutionary movement.

In 1988 Jac Ávila, who studied his trade in New York, came up with a semi-documentary shot in Haiti before the fall of Baby Doc Duvalier. In 1995, he master-minded a distinctly Bolivian murder mystery entitled *El Hombre de la Luna* (The Man in the Moon), a five-part miniseries that aired on Bolivian television. It was made on an extremely low budget but has attracted international attention. He now wants to draw on Bolivia's unique traditions in a planned feature film entitled *Pachamama*.

Another name to watch for is Juan Carlos Valdivia, who in 1992, produced an award-winning documentary for CNN about the unauthorized US military activities in Santa Ana del Yacuma. He also won an award from the Foundation for New Latin American Cinema for his screenplay of the Bolivian novel *Jonah and the Pink Whale*, a critique of the Santa Cruz 'new rich' in the chaotic and drug-ridden mid-1980s. Hopefully, it will attract sufficient funds to bring it to the screen.

With the 1995 release of the Latin 'road movie,' Marcos Loayza's *Cuestión de Fe*, Bolivian film was given a further boost internationally. This sensitive and original comedy tells the story of three bumbling friends charged with a religious quest that takes them from La Paz to Coroico and around the Yungas in a classic pickup truck called *Ramona*. The scenery is predictably inspiring and the story provides a revelation of Bolivian values.

For more, see the 1985 book *Adventures of Bolivian Film*, by Carlos Mesa.

Weaving

Spinning and weaving methods have changed little in Bolivia for 3000 years. In rural areas, girls learn to weave before they reach puberty, and women spend nearly all their spare time spinning with a drop spindle or weaving on heddle looms. Prior to Spanish colonization, llama and alpaca wool were the materials of choice, but sheep's wool is now the most readily available and least expensive medium.

Regional differences are manifest in weaving style, motif and use. Bolivian textiles have diverse patterns, and the majority display a degree of skill that results from millennia of experience. The beautiful and practical creations are true works of art, and away from major tourist haunts, you can find real quality for good prices.

Weavings from Tarabuco, near Sucre, are made into the colorful costumes (men wear a *chuspa* – or coca pouch – and a trademark red poncho) and zoomorphic patterns seen around the popular and touristy Sunday market in Tarabuco. Designs are typically arranged in orderly bands of proportionally sized figures – humans, animals and ordinary objects – and rendered in a rainbow of colors. Articles woven when in mourning are executed in a spectrum of blue hues. The most commonly decorated article is a rectangular women's overskirt that is known in Quechua as an *axsu*. This style is sometimes known as *Candelaria*, after a nearby village.

The most famous and celebrated of Bolivian weavings are the red or magenta and black zoomorphic designs from the Jalq'a region, which is centered on the village of Potolo, northwest of Sucre. Patterns range from faithful representations of *khurus*, wild animals that cannot be domesticated such as frogs, pumas, squirrels and owls, to creative and mythical combinations of animal forms: llamas, horses, dragons and a menagerie of avian aberrations. The patterns are typically asymmetrical, and the relative sizes of figures represented often don't conform to reality – for example, it isn't unusual for a gigantic horse to be depicted alongside a tiny building. Jalq'a

pieces are prized by weavings buffs and command relatively high prices.

Zoomorphic patterns are also prominent in the Cordillera Apolobamba country north of Lake Titicaca and in several areas in the vicinity of La Paz, including Lique and Calamarka. Some extremely fine weavings originate in Sica Sica, one of the many dusty and nondescript villages between La Paz and Oruro, and in Calcha, southeast of Potosí near the boundary of Chuquisaca. Some of Bolivia's best clothing textiles are produced here, with expert spinning and an extremely tight weave – over 60 threads per centimeter.

Anyone interested in Bolivian textiles should look for the books *A Travelers' Guide to Eldorado and the Inca Empire*, by weavings expert Lynn Meisch, or the hard-to-find *Weaving Traditions of Highland*

Chola Dress

The characteristic dress worn by many Bolivian Indian women was imposed on them in the 18th century by the Spanish king, and the customary center parting of the hair was the result of a decree by the Viceroy Toledo.

This distinctive ensemble, both colorful and utilitarian, has almost become Bolivia's defining image. The most noticeable characteristic of the traditional Aymará dress is the ubiquitous dark green, black or brown bowler hat that would seem more at home on a London street than in the former Spanish empire. You'd be hard pressed to find a chola or campesina without one.

The women normally braid their hair into two long plaits that are joined by a tuft of black wool known as a *pocacha*. The short *pollera* skirts they wear are constructed of several horizontal bands tucked under each other. This garment tends to make the women appear overweight (most actually aren't), especially when several skirts are combined with multiple layers of petticoats.

On top, the outfit consists of a factory-made blouse, a woolen *chompa* (sweater/jumper), a short vestlike jacket, and a cotton apron, or some combination of these. Usually, women add a woolen shawl known as a *llijlla* (sometimes spelled *llica*) or *phullu*.

Slung across the back and tied around the neck is the *ahuayo*, a rectangle of manufactured or handwoven cloth decorated with colorful horizontal bands. It's used as a carryall and is filled with everything from coca or groceries to babies.

The Quechua of the highland valleys wear equally colorful but not so universally recognized attire. The hat, called a *montera*, is a flat-topped affair made of straw or finely woven white wool. It's often taller and broader than the bowlers worn by the Aymará. The felt montera of Tarabuco, patterned after the Spanish conquistadores' helmets, is the most striking.

Bolivia, by Laurie Adelson & Bruce Takami, published by the Los Angeles Craft & Folk Art Museum. If you read Spanish, a good information source on the Chuquisaca traditions is *Los Diseños de los Textiles Tarabuco y Jalq'a*, by Veronica Ceveceda, Johnny Dávalos & Jaime Mejía; it's sold at ASUR (Antropólogos del Surandino) in Sucre. Another excellent booklet on Bolivian textile arts is *Bolivian Indian Textiles*, by Tamara E Wasserman & Jonathon S Hill, available through the South American Explorers (see Useful Organizations in the Facts for the Visitor chapter).

Architecture

The pre-Columbian architecture of Bolivia is represented primarily by the largely ruined walls and structures of Tiahuanaco and the numerous Inca remains scattered about the country. Restoration of these sites has not revealed much about the artistic values of the Inca or other groups. The only examples of the classic polygonal cut stones that dominate many Peruvian Inca sites are on Isla del Sol and Isla de la Luna in Lake Titicaca.

Surviving colonial architectural trends correspond with four major overlapping periods: renaissance (1550-1650), baroque (1630-1770), mestizo (1690-1790), which was actually a variation on baroque, and the modern period (post-1790). The beginnings of the modern period were marked by a brief experimentation with the neoclassical style, which was then followed by a return to the neo-Gothic.

Some Andean renaissance churches indicate *mudéjar* (Moorish) influences. Renaissance churches are simple in design. They were constructed primarily of adobe with courtyards, aisle-less naves and massive buttresses. One of the best examples is in the village of Tiahuanaco. The three classic examples of mudéjar renaissance design are found at San Miguel and San Francisco in Sucre, and at Copacabana on the shores of Lake Titicaca.

Baroque churches were constructed in the form of a cross with an elaborate dome and walls made of either stone or reinforced adobe. Late in the baroque period, mestizo elements in the form of whimsical decorative carvings were introduced and applied with what appears to be wild abandon. Prominent elements included densely packed Inca deities and designs, masks, Christian cherubs, sirens, gargoyles and a riot of tropical flora and fauna – vine leaves, frogs, pineapples, chirimoyas etc.

Neoclassical design, which dominated between 1790 and the early 20th century, can be seen in the church of San Felipe Neri in Sucre and the cathedrals in Potosí and La Paz.

Paralleling the mainstream church construction in the mid-18th century, the Jesuits in the Beni and Santa Cruz lowlands were designing churches reflecting Bavarian rococo and Gothic influences. Their most unusual effort was the bizarre mission church at San José de Chiquitos, whose design is unique in Latin America.

SOCIETY & CONDUCT
Meeting Bolivians

Making contact with Bolivians, particularly in the cities, will be no problem at all. Few people are shy about striking up conversations in shops, buses or micros, and your attempts at friendly interaction are almost certain to be reciprocated. Even if your Spanish is limited, people will be happy to tax your abilities as far as they'll go, and they will probably welcome the opportunity to dredge up their own English vocabulary, however meager it may be.

What may seem off-putting at first is that nearly everyone you meet – even total strangers – will be interested in subjects that are considered taboo in much of the West. You'll frequently be asked about your marital and reproductive status; if you appear to be of marriageable age and profess to be unmarried or childless, you're likely to be met with sympathy, further probing questions and advice about how to remedy your 'problems.' To avoid this sort of innocent but perhaps off-putting reaction, you may want to conveniently invent a spouse and children waiting for you in another city or back home.

People will also want to know your profession, how much you earn and what your trip costs. Many people believe all foreigners are wealthy beyond imagining, and because most foreigners they meet are on holiday – most Bolivians travel only to visit family or for some sort of economic gain – they also assume that little of this wealth is derived from work. If you're uncomfortable with this, perhaps explain your interest in their country and that you had to work, save and sacrifice to pay for your holiday in Bolivia. Talk about your profession and explain the prices of housing and staples back home. If you are involved in a project in Bolivia – even if it's a possible newspaper article to write when you get home – it's worth mentioning; this is a concept that will hit home and partially explain your mysterious globetrotting behavior.

Noise

Noise is a constant companion in Bolivian cities, and locals seem undisturbed by noise levels 50 decibels above anything most Europeans would willingly tolerate. Music blares in restaurants and buses, horns honk constantly, TVs are turned up to full volume, rusted-off mufflers (vehicle silencers) are rarely replaced, urchins holler destinations from every passing micro or trufi, vendors screech at potential customers or at each other, brass bands honk away at any opportunity, and people converse at a volume that would suggest a heated argument. To say it can be annoying doesn't mean it isn't colorful, but in any case, there isn't much you can do about it.

Time

Since the invention of the clock, the world has become a more organized place, but in Bolivia, the concept of time has taken hold only superficially. Time-related terminology does exist, but its interpretation isn't necessarily what visitors might expect. For example, *mañana*, 'tomorrow,' could mean almost any time in the indefinite future. In many places – particularly government offices – 'come back tomorrow' is the equivalent of 'go away and don't bother me with your problems.'

Bolivians invited to lunch on a Tuesday might arrive on a Wednesday and, by their understanding of time, may regard themselves as only a little late. You should not adopt local habits to this extent, but arriving a bit late is normal. If you're invited to a party at, say, 8 pm and you turn up at 9 pm, you're likely to be the first guest to arrive.

The same applies to meeting in the street. Arriving half an hour later than arranged will still give you time to read a newspaper before your friend arrives (if the friend arrives at all). If you become versed in this local custom, it can be a good idea to fix two or three meetings with different people at the same time and place – somebody will probably turn up!

Offices and institutions have a similarly flexible grasp of their advertised working hours. The rule seems to be that if money is directly involved, the hours are more likely to be adhered to. Banks, for instance, run like clockwork (Swiss, not Bolivian!) and shops and other commercial establishments are normally during open the hours stated.

Another problem word is *ahora*, 'now,' or its more common variation, *ahorita*, 'in a moment.' If, for example, you're waiting for a bus and ask a bystander when the bus should arrive, the answer will almost invariably be *ahorita* or more exasperatingly *ya viene*, 'it's already coming.' This probably means that the bystander has no idea when the bus is coming, but is hopeful that it will come and has taken an optimistic approach. The pessimist, on the other hand, might say that the bus you're waiting for *no existe, ya pasó* or *está plantado* – it 'doesn't exist,' 'already passed' or 'is broken down.' Don't give up and go away – get a second or third opinion and then consider a course of action. Most of the time, patience will pay off.

The moral is to adopt a relaxed and flexible travel schedule, and if things don't go according to plan, take it easy and try to appreciate the forced sense of uncertainty that's dictated by travel in this part of the world.

Things Go Better with Coca

Cocaine, marijuana, hashish and other drugs are illegal in Bolivia, but the coca leaf, which is the source of cocaine and related drugs, is chewed daily by many Bolivians and is even venerated by indigenous peoples. Mama Coca is revered as the daughter of Pachamama, the earth mother, and coca is considered a gift to the people to be used to drive evil forces from their homes and fields.

Both the Quechua and Aymará people make sacrifices of coca leaves when planting or mining to ensure a good harvest or lucky strike. The *yatiri* (traditional Aymará healer) use them in their healing and exorcising rituals, and in some remote rural areas leaves are often used in place of money. People embarking on a journey also place several leaves beneath a rock at the start as an offering to Pachamama in hopes that she'll smooth their way. Visitors walking or hiking in the mountains may want to hedge their bets and do the same, or at least carry some leaves as a gift for helpful locals (coca is always gratefully received).

Taking a coca break

The conquering Spanish found that laborers who chewed the leaf became more dedicated to their tasks, so they promoted its use among the peasants. Today, nearly all campesinos and cholos, men and women alike, take advantage of its benefits. It's also becoming popular among younger middle-class people, particularly those who sympathize with the causes of Indian peasants. Most Bolivians of European origin, however, still regard chewing coca as a disgusting 'Indian' habit and generally avoid its use.

Used therapeutically, coca serves as an appetite suppressant and a central nervous system stimulant. Indian people use it while working to lessen the effects of altitude and eliminate the need for a lunch break. They also chew it recreationally and socially in much the same way people smoke cigarettes or drink coffee. Among Bolivian miners, the 'coca break' is an institution.

The leaf itself grows on bushes that are cultivated in the Yungas and Upper Chapare regions at altitudes of between 1000m and 2000m. They are sold by the kilogram in nearly every market in Bolivia along with *legía*, an alkaloid usually made of mineral lime, potato and *quinoa* ash, which is used to draw the drug from the leaves when chewed. There are two kinds of legía: *achura*, which is sweet, and *cuta*, which is salty.

The effects of coca chewing are not startling. It will leave you feeling a little detached, reflective, melancholy or pleasantly contented. The Indians normally chew about 30 to 35 leaves at a time. If you want to try it, place a few leaves, say, five to 10, between your gums and cheek until they soften. Then repeat the process, placing a little legía between the leaves. Don't start chewing until you've stuffed in the desired amount. Once you've chewed it into a pulpy mess, you're meant to swallow the bitter-tasting juice, which will numb your mouth and throat. (In fact, novocaine and related anesthetics are coca derivatives.)

Litter

As with noise, litter is an integral part of Bolivian life, so prepare for it. Thanks perhaps to a long subsistence-oriented tradition and the notion that useless items might as well be discarded, Bolivians are accustomed to throwing things away wherever the usefulness of those items happens to expire – in the streets, on the floor, in buses, along the highway and in the countryside. In extreme cases, such as the bizarre community of Puerto Pailas near Santa Cruz, you'll wade through the streets ankle-deep in pastel plastic bags.

In time, you'll get used to the local standards and the general absence of trashcans. In La Paz, wastebaskets have been set up around the city bearing proud slogans about keeping the city clean, but the campaign is enjoying only limited success; people are just too accustomed to throwing things on the street. About all you can do is set an example, although you may be the only one on the street carrying plastic cups, tissues and greasy *salteña* napkins.

In budget hotels and restaurants you'll only rarely find an ashtray, and asking for one may embarrass the management, because they probably won't have one. Nobody will care at all if you throw your cigarette ash and butts on the floor, and you're keeping someone employed sweeping them up.

Dos and Don'ts

One thing to remember about Bolivia is that every part of the country is different, but generally, the higher the altitude or smaller the town, the more conservative and traditional the society.

The fiercely proud rural Aymará, for example, may sometimes appear as harsh and cold as the land they inhabit, and may understandably question the motives of visitors who venture in with what appears to be a lot of money and no visible means of support. These people who work hard at meager survival can't fathom someone trotting around the globe rather than attending to work and religious and family responsibilities at home (some of your relatives may

feel the same way!). With patience and diplomacy, however, you can break the icy barrier and catch a glimpse of their unimaginably harsh lifestyle. Generally, Quechua speakers in the central highlands are more open to outsiders, but they may still harbor suspicions.

In rural areas, very few people speak any Spanish and, in places, uninvited outsiders, particularly those who don't speak the local language or aren't familiar with the society's customs, are likely to be misconstrued. Off the trodden track, you'll probably be much happier with a local guide, who can smooth the way and reassure people that you mean no threat.

Religion plays a major role in the lives of most Bolivians, whether they follow Catholicism or animistic beliefs. Most people will be more comfortable if you profess some sort of religion – whether or not you actually practice or believe in it. Superstition is also deeply rooted and has a great deal of influence, and there's no point in attempting to explain it away using western logic.

Perhaps the most important advice is to remember that to traditional Bolivians, their own culture is a natural state of being. The best approach is to accept that things are done differently here and to resist the temptation to introduce your own notions or values. Respect peoples' beliefs and values, whether or not they coincide with your own, and avoid making light of anything, however unusual, that appears to be taken seriously by the local community. Don't assume that outsiders are welcome to join in local fiestas or dance in processions; wait until you're invited to do so.

Similarly, if you find something disturbing, bow out rather than criticize. Tinku fights, for example, can become extremely violent and, on occasion, may even result in deaths, but these rituals are an integral part of local life and any bloodshed is considered an offering to the earth mother Pachamama. To outsiders, llama sacrifices may represent animal cruelty, but to many Bolivians, it's an essential ritual to preserve a harmonious relationship with the elements.

If you find it impossible to tune out your cultural tendencies, it's probably best to avoid these scenarios.

RELIGION

Roughly 95% of Bolivia's population professes Roman Catholicism and follows it to varying degrees. However, the absence of Roman Catholic clergy in rural areas has led to the emergence of a hybrid Christian/folk religion in which the Inca and Aymará belief systems blend with Christianity into an interesting amalgamation of doctrines, rites and superstitions.

The most obvious aspect of native religion is the belief in natural gods and spirits, which dates back to Inca times and earlier. People are aware that the sun and the earth make human life possible, that lunar cycles are linked to human reproduction and that the mountains influence the weather and the availability of water. From these basic precepts emerge an array of benevolent and malevolent figures who regularly expect veneration by their devotees to keep the world on an even keel. Many Christians see no conflict between Christianity and homage to the gods of nature; they believe that God in his far-off heaven uses the mountains and the elements as his intermediaries.

Perhaps the most ubiquitous of these deities is the earth mother. Pachamama shares herself with human beings, helps bring forth crops and distributes riches to those she favors. She seems to have quite an appetite for coca, alcohol and the blood of animals, particularly llamas. If the earth must be disturbed – for plowing, construction or mining – an apology is offered in the form of a sacrifice. The bigger the wound, the greater the sacrifice expected; in the case of a mine or a building foundation, Pachamama expects a llama dressed in a silk jacket and adorned with gold, silver and valuable trinkets. Alcohol is considered an integral part of the procedure, and even the llama gets to imbibe heavily before it's given the chop.

Fortunately, Pachamama does have mercy on poorer campesinos, who can't spare a llama whenever they need a new adobe dwelling. The next best thing is a *mesa con sullo*, an aborted llama fetus that is smeared with fat, dressed in a jacket (preferably silk) and laid on white wool with a variety of tokens, including *confites* (ritual sweets), nuts, herbs, coca and bits of jewelry. When the sacrifice is ready, it's wrapped up and buried beneath the foundations of the building.

Talismans are also used in daily life to bring out the better elements of life, or to protect a person from evil. A turtle is thought to bring health, a frog or toad carries good fortune, an owl signifies wisdom and success in school and a condor talisman will ensure a good journey. For general good luck, people employ an image of the earth goddess Pachamama.

Another fundamental belief among the Aymará is in mountain gods, the *apus* and *achachilas*. The apus, mountain spirits who provide protection for travelers, are often associated with a particular *nevado* (snow-capped peak). Achachilas are the spirits of the high mountains, who are believed to be ancestors of the people and look after their *ayllu* (native group of people, loosely translated as 'tribe') and provide bounty from the earth. In La Paz, they're thought to be incarnated in the dogs that await handouts along the Yungas road! These are spirits that are propitiated in order to ensure sufficient water for a bountiful harvest, or to permit a safe journey through their ranks.

There are also other characters worth mentioning. Ekeko, which means 'dwarf' in Aymará, is the usually pleasant little household god of abundance, and because he's responsible for matchmaking, finding homes for the homeless and ensuring success for businesspeople, he's a good friend to have. He's also a symbol of the abundance a family has to share with its community. The Alasitas festival in La Paz is dedicated to Ekeko; see Special Events in the La Paz chapter for more information.

There are also negative forces. The evil and dreaded *Happiñuñoz*, for example, are personifications of beautiful women who seduce men, cause them to lose their powers of reason and eventually abscond with their souls. The inevitable result is death for their poor victims. Another unsavory lot is the *liquichiri*, harmful spirits who suck out a person's vitality, causing death for no visible reason.

If a person has a problem with a particular god, a *yatiri* (witch doctor) will often be able to help. To find out what dangers lie ahead in life, a visit to a *thaliri* (fortune-teller) is in order. This will tell the yatiri what should be prevented from happening and which god can be encouraged (or bribed) to prevent it. There is, however, a particularly insidious night phantom called Kharisiri who preys on sleeping humans, and once a person is on his bad side, not even the best yatiri will be able to help.

In the mines of Oruro and Potosí, a number of beliefs and superstitions have developed and persisted over the years. Luck, the miners assume, is procured by avoidance of certain 'unlucky' practices, and by propitiation of *El Tío* (the devil), the sovereign ruler of hell and owner of the minerals. He must be constantly appeased with gifts of alcohol, cigarettes, coca, incense and sweets. Miners' wives may not enter certain mines lest El Tío become jealous, and while underground, miners may not whistle, eat toasted *haba* beans, or season llama meat with salt. Breaking any of these taboos would bring down the wrath of El Tío, inviting bad luck and low mineral yield.

LANGUAGE

The official language of Bolivia is Latin American Spanish, but only 60 to 70% of the people speak it, and then often only as a second language. The remainder speak Quechua (the language of the Inca conquerors) or Aymará (the pre-Inca language of the Altiplano). In addition, a host of other minor indigenous tongues are used in limited areas throughout the country. For more information and a small Spanish-English glossary of useful terms, see the Language section toward the back of the book.

Facts for the Visitor

HIGHLIGHTS

If you have only limited time in Bolivia and can't do the sort of exploration the country so amply rewards, you'll probably want to seek out the highlights. Although taste is subjective, there are some sites and experiences that will appeal to most visitors.

Arts

Few visitors to Bolivia would argue that artesanía and music aren't exceptional. Bolivia has no bad music except, perhaps, that of unpracticed brass bands and traditional music that has been adapted for elevators and dentists' offices! Peñas – traditional folk music programs – are held at least weekly in most larger cities and towns.

You'll find a range of musical instruments, lovely woolen clothing and colorfully decorated bags at tourist shops around the country, but the best and least expensive are bought either directly from the artisan or around Calle Sagárnaga in La Paz. To see the origins of Bolivia's world-famous weavings, visit the smaller villages around Sucre, such as Potolo and Candelaria, or in the Cordillera Apolobamba north of Lake Titicaca.

Landscapes & Activities

The Bolivian landscape is awesome, offering everything from snow-capped peaks to colorful canyons and steaming rain forest. Particularly inspiring – and accessible – areas include the *salares* (salt pans), volcanoes and colorful lakes of the southwest, and the jungle and savanna lowlands around Rurrenabaque. If you're looking for a magical Amazon Basin experience, visit the Chalalán Eco-Lodge in Parque Nacional Madidi or travel by cargo boat along one of the northern rivers.

For excellent hiking or mountain biking, base yourself in La Paz or Sorata and set off into the Cordillera Real, where you can climb into the high passes or follow ancient Inca roads into the dramatic Yungas region. The more remote Cordilleras Apolobamba,

Quimsa Cruz and Los Frailes offer similarly attractive alternatives. Ideal for horse-riding are the Old West landscapes of the Butch & Sundance country around Tupiza.

When you feel like relaxing for a few days in a small, picturesque village – as many Bolivians like to do – some prime choices include Sorata, Coroico or Chulumani in the Yungas; Copacabana or Yumani (Isla del Sol) on Lake Titicaca; Uyuni on the Southern Altiplano; Samaipata west of Santa Cruz; and Rurrenabaque or San Ignacio de Moxos in the northern lowlands.

Food

Bolivian cuisine isn't world renowned, but some dishes and drinks are worth sampling. Some, including trout from Lake Titicaca; *jugos* and *licuados* (fresh fruit juices and fruit shakes) from market stalls; *salteñas* (Bolivia's favorite mid-morning snack); *sopa de quinoa* (quinoa soup); and *surubí* (an Amazonian catfish), are delicious. Sampling others – *charque kan* (jerked meat – often llama – with hominy); *yuca* (cassava); *masaco* (beef jerky with plantain) and the various types of *chicha* – will at least satisfy curiosity, and many people actually like them! For more information, see Food, later in this chapter.

Buildings & Sites

For church fans, the Jesuit Missions Circuit in the Eastern Lowlands will provide plenty of inspiration. Of particular interest are San Miguel, San Rafael, and San José de Chiquitos. The Moorish-style cathedral in Copacabana and the mestizo-influenced churches of San Francisco in La Paz and San Lorenzo in Potosí are all beautiful and inspiring. Other forms of colonial architecture are most in evidence around Sucre and Potosí, and La Paz also preserves a few colonial-era buildings.

There are also highly worthwhile historical and archaeological sites; among them are the ancient ruins of Tiahuanaco near

La Paz; the ruins on Isla del Sol in Lake Titicaca; the pre-Inca hilltop ritual site of El Fuerte near Samaipata; and remote Iskanwaya northwest of La Paz. A visit to the Potosí mines will provide an eye-opening perspective on the medieval conditions and hardships that endure in highland Bolivia.

Fiestas

Some of the best and most interesting annual fiestas include La Diablada, which takes place in Oruro during Holy Week; Phujllay, a commemoration of *campesino* resistance in Tarabuco; La Festividad de Nuestro Señor Jesús del Gran Poder, which takes place in La Paz in late May or early June; Alasitas, which is dedicated to Ekeko, the household god of abundance, in La Paz in late January; Tarija's Fiesta de San Roque, which is a week-long celebration in mid-August; the Fiesta del Santo Patrono de Moxos, a colorful Moxos Indian celebration in San Ignacio de Moxos, in the Beni; the Virgen de Candelaria, both a solemn and riotous bash in Copacabana in early February; Chu'tillos, an international dance and music festival held in Potosí in late August; and the Virgen de Urcupiña, the biggest festival in Cochabamba department, which occurs in Quillacollo around mid-August.

SUGGESTED ITINERARIES

Naturally, I recommend that you allow as much time as possible for a trip to Bolivia. Even after a couple of years traveling around the country, I've only scratched the surface of what there is to see and do. If you're traveling independently and your time is limited, the following suggestions might help you spend your time rewardingly.

One week Spend three or four days exploring La Paz and perhaps take a day trip to Tiahuanaco and an overnight excursion to Copacabana.

Two weeks Add two days trekking on Isla del Sol and an excursion to Sorata or Coroico in the Yungas; or a hike on the Taquesi, La Cumbre to Coroico (Choro) or Yunga Cruz routes.

Three weeks To the above, add any of the following: three days hiking around Sorata plus a couple of days hiking in the Zona Sur; a jungle

or pampas excursion around Rurrenabaque; or visits to Potosí and Sucre.

One month All of the above, plus an excursion from Uyuni through the Far Southwest. Alternatively, you can add Santa Cruz, Samaipata and the Jesuit Missions Circuit; Tupiza and Tarija; or a trek in the Cordillera Apolobamba.

Two months All options listed under one month plus one of the following: Parque Nacional Noel Kempff Mercado; Parque Nacional Amboró; a river trip on the Mamoré from Trinidad to Guayaramerín; or a trek in the Cordillera de los Frailes, near Sucre.

PLANNING
When to Go

The most important climatic factor to remember is that the weather is generally wet in the summer and dry in the winter. Remember, however, that Bolivia lies within the southern hemisphere, so winter lasts from May to October and summer from November to April.

On the Altiplano, winters can be icy but days are normally crystal clear and dry. Summers are warmer, but there's usually at least some rainfall every day, most often in the afternoon. In the highland valleys you can expect a comfortable climate at any time of year, with a bit more rain in the summer months.

For travel in the humid lowlands, winter is generally the best season, as the rainy season can be utterly miserable with mud, steamy heat, bugs and relentless tropical downpours. Travel is particularly difficult at this time of year, as transport services are often delayed or shut down altogether by mud or flooding. On the other hand, such conditions necessitate an increase in river transport, so it's normally the best time of year to look for cargo boats in northern Bolivia.

It's also worth considering that the high tourist season falls mainly from late June to early September. This is only partially due to climatic factors: not only is this the time of European and North American summer holidays, but it is also the season with most of Bolivia's major fiestas. This means that lots of Bolivians and other South Americans also travel during this period. This can be an advantage if you're looking for people to form a Southwest Circuit tour group, for example, but bear in mind that prices for food, accommodation, tours, transport and artesanía are generally higher than during the rest of the year.

What Kind of Trip

Your style of travel depends largely on your budget, available time and preparedness for unknowns. Even in inexpensive Latin America, low-budget travel requires sacrificing the security of structure and allowing time to accommodate infrastructural uncertainties. While backpacking travelers tend to take things as they come, some young, elderly or inexperienced travelers will appreciate organized tours because they minimize hassles and uncertainties. Those who are new to Latin America may have no idea which areas will appeal to them, and a quick 'scouting tour' will provide an overview for a more adventurous trip to follow! For such travelers, tours that concentrate the best of Bolivia into a one- or two-week holiday do have their merits. For suggestions, see Organized Tours in the Getting There & Away chapter.

If you decide to travel with others, bear in mind that travel can strain relationships more than any other experience. These discomforts can be minimized by either agreeing on a rigid itinerary beforehand or agreeing to remain flexible about everything. When planning your itinerary, you may want to just hole up for awhile in one place and get to know it well, observing local lifestyles and discovering lesser-known sites.

Maps

Internationally Distributed Maps For general mapping of South America with excellent topographical detail, it's hard to beat the sectional maps published by International Travel Map Productions (530 West Broadway, Vancouver, BC Canada V5Z 1E9, Canada). Coverage of Bolivia is provided in *South America – South* (1999); *South America – North East* (1997); *South America – North West* (2000); and *Amazon*

Basin (2000). Climbing maps of Illimani and Illampu at a scale of 1:50,000 are published in Germany by the Deutscher Alpenverein and are distributed internationally.

Also very worthwhile are Liam O'Brien Cartographic's *Cordillera Real* and *Bolivia* maps. The former is a particularly good resource for climbers and trekkers – or anyone wanting to get their bearings – between Ancohuma and Illimani. To order directly, contact Liam O'Brien Cartographics (obrien@batelco.com.bh; 28 Turner Terrace, Newtonville, MA 02160, USA). Either costs US$10 plus postage and packing. See also the website www.obriencartographics.com.

In the USA, *Maplink* (☎ 805-692 6777; fax 805-692 6787; custserv@maplink.com; 30 S La Patera Lane, Unit 5, Santa Barbara, CA 93117) is an excellent and exhaustive source for maps of Bolivia and just about anywhere else in the world. Their website is www.maplink.com. A similarly extensive selection of maps is available in the UK from *Stanfords* (☎ 020-7836-1321; 12-14 Long Acre, London WC2E 9LP).

In Bolivia Maps are available in La Paz, Cochabamba and Santa Cruz through Los Amigos del Libro. Government mapping topo sheets and specialty maps are available from the Instituto Geográfico Militar – IGM, whose head office is on Avenida Bautista Saavedra in Miraflores, La Paz. It's open weekdays from 9 to 11 am and 2:30 to 4:30 pm. The office is in a military compound, so you have to leave your passport at the entrance. More convenient is the small central La Paz outlet (Oficina 5, Calle Juan XXIII 100), on a dead end off Calle Rodríguez between Calles Linares and Murillo. Here you select and pay for maps, and they're ready for collection the following day.

Both offices sell good topographic sheets at a scale of 1:50,000 and 1:250,000, covering some 70% of the country for US$7.50 each. Unfortunately, they often run out of the more popular sheets, such as Cordillera Real treks and peaks, or Lake Titicaca. If the sheet you want is sold out, they'll provide photocopies for US$5.20, but these are typically poor quality and aren't recommended unless you're desperate. Notable areas that are unavailable (for security reasons) include the Tipuani Valley, the Cordillera Apolobamba and Parque Nacional Noel Kempff Mercado.

IGM also publishes a 1994 map of the entire country at a scale of 1:1,000,000. It comes in four sheets and shows communities, political divisions, transport routes and named physical features. This is the best national map available, but it still has serious problems – mainly missing road segments and marked roads that appear to run in circles. From IGM, it costs US$18.60. A more manageable alternative is IGM's *Mapa de Comunicaciones de la República de Bolivia*, at a scale of 1:3,000,000.

Earlier versions of IGM maps are also sometimes sold in bookstores. They're easily recognizable because they're attributed to the president who was in power when the map was commissioned. Check the publication date as there are still a lot of 1937 and 1952 maps floating around!

Bolivian geological maps are sold at Geobol, on Ortiz at Federico Zuazo, in La Paz; take your passport. For US$5, you can buy a four-sheet geologic map of the entire country.

For detailed trekking maps around the Cordillera Real and Sajama, look for the colorful contour maps produced by Walter Guzmán Córdova, which are most readily available at the Librería Olimpia in La Paz for US$5 to US$8.25 each. Titles include the 1:50,000 *Choro/Taquesi/Yunga Cruz*, *Murata/Illimani*, *Huayna Potosí/Cononiri* and *Sajama* and the 1:2,500,000 *Bolivia – Mapa Físico/Político/Rodoviario*. However, they are based on the IGM maps and contain many of the same errors. Climbing maps of major Bolivian peaks are available from Club Andino Boliviano (☎ 324682; Calle México 1638, Casilla 1346, La Paz).

Another map that's occasionally available is the *Red de Caminos* (Highway Network), which is more an optimistic highway commissioner's game of connect the dots than a serious guide to the country's road system.

The most recent edition was published in the early 1990s.

For more information about hiking and trekking maps, see Activities, later in this chapter.

What to Bring

When preparing for a trip, your packing list will depend on your intended budget, itinerary, mode of travel, time of visit and length of stay. While traveling as light as possible is always a good idea if you want to enjoy the trip, if you can't splash out, you'll have to bring certain items from home. For specific guidelines for hikers, trekkers and mountaineers, see Activities, later in this chapter.

Bags The type of luggage you should carry will depend largely upon your style of travel. Those on prearranged tours who are staying in finer hotels and using taxis around town will get by with traditional but strong suitcases or shoulder bags. For independent travelers, a backpack – or a pack that zips into a suitcase – is probably the most practical and useful carry-all. The most important factors to consider are comfort, strength, weight and manageability.

Essentials As always, the most important advice is to travel light: only take along that which is indispensable. Unfortunately, most everyone has a different idea about what indispensable means and when it comes to traveling light, I'm not the best authority. To help you avoid disdain for your belongings, the following checklist outlines items that either are difficult to obtain in Bolivia or will probably be used often enough to justify their weight.

- First-aid kit (see under Health, later in this chapter)
- Antimalarial tablets (for the lowlands – see your doctor for advice)
- Travel alarm clock
- Small flashlight (torch) and extra batteries
- Water bottle – aluminum or plastic
- Water purification tablets – iodine-based to kill amoebas

- Swiss Army-type pocketknife with bottle opener, corkscrew, scissors, etc
- Spare glasses or contact lenses and a copy of your optical prescription
- Towel
- Flip-flops (thongs) – for relaxing or coping with Bolivian plumbing
- Clothesline – 2 or 3m of cord is useful for all sorts of things
- Sewing kit
- Writing implements – few South American pens function well on airmail paper
- Spanish/English dictionary and possibly Lonely Planet's Quechua and Latin American Spanish phrasebooks
- Contraceptives
- Tampons – they're still not common outside major cities
- Any prescription medications you normally take, including a copy of the prescription

Amazon Basin Essentials For jungle trips in the northern lowlands, the following items should be included in your checklist: two sets of clothing, one for slogging through the forests, rivers and mud and an extra set to keep dry and wear in camp; extra shoes, also to keep dry; plastic bags for wet gear, shoes and for items that should never get wet; binoculars; camera and zoom or telephoto lens; gaiters; strong flashlight for night walks and animal spotting; *effective* insect repellent; sleeping bag; bathing suit (swimming costume); long-sleeved shirt for cool and/or bug-infested evenings; sunscreen; hat; and a large plastic bag for trash.

Clothing Without going overboard and lugging an entire wardrobe, it's wise to be reasonably prepared for Bolivia's climatic extremes. For the cold, you'll need a warm jacket suitable for freezing temperatures, several pairs of warm wool or polypropylene socks, a pullover, a pair of woolen gloves and a hat with ear coverings (the last three items are inexpensive and readily available in Bolivia). If you have the slightest tendency toward chills, thermal underwear won't go amiss on winter nights and a waterproof/

breathable rain outfit will be handy during the wet season or for mountain hiking.

For lowland travel, about all you need will be two sleeveless shirts, a pair of flip-flops or sandals and shorts. On the Altiplano and in the Andes, there is still a prejudice against women wearing shorts, so bring a light skirt or dress (see Women Travelers, later in this chapter). Men will encounter few cultural dress restrictions, but going shirtless is not acceptable unless you're swimming.

You'll also need two pairs of trousers – one to wash and one to wear; a long-sleeved, lightweight shirt to wear under itchy woolen or alpaca sweaters; underwear and socks; swimming gear – there are lots of waterfalls and hot springs; one pair of sneakers or comfortable walking shoes; and perhaps even a nicer set of clothing for evenings out or other occasions.

Fortunately, it's not difficult to find fairly inexpensive clothing in major Bolivian

CHRIS BEALL

Take a tip from the locals: wear a hat.

cities. However, most Bolivians are smaller than the average foreigner, and larger shoe and clothing sizes, as well as children's pullovers and gloves, are hard to come by.

TOURIST OFFICES

Although Bolivia's appeal should not be underestimated, much of its attraction lies in the fact that it has been largely ignored by large-scale tourism. While this is changing, the Bolivian tourist industry is still in its formative stages, and government tourist offices still concentrate more on statistics and bureaucratic spending than on promotion of the country's attractions. In fact, most real development and promotion have been courtesy of the private sector.

As a result, the tourist offices run by the Secretaría Nacional de Turismo (Senatur) and municipal tourism bodies range from helpful to worthless, but most can provide street plans and answer specific questions about local transport and attractions. The most worthwhile are those in Oruro, Cochabamba and Potosí, while those in La Paz, Sucre, Tarija, Uyuni and Santa Cruz seem to be considerably less useful.

In this book, tourist offices are marked on city maps where applicable. As with many Bolivian operations, posted opening hours are often superseded by the personal whims of their employees.

VISAS & DOCUMENTS
Passport

A passport is essential for all visitors to Bolivia, and if yours is within a few months of expiration, get a new one before you leave on a South American circuit, as many countries won't issue a visa or admit you at the border if your passport is about to expire. For Bolivia, passports must be valid for at least six months beyond the date of entering the country (some fussy officials – perhaps hoping for a bribe – may well insist on one year validity). Even if your passport isn't about to expire, make sure it has a few blank pages for visas and entry and exit stamps, or have extra pages added at home or at an embassy en route.

Although Bolivia currently lacks a market for passports, some neighboring countries have a thriving black market in Western passports, so keep a close eye on your document. Losing your passport is very inconvenient, and getting a replacement takes time and money (usually cash).

In Bolivia, everyone must carry proof of identification to avoid fines during police checks (this is most closely enforced in lowland regions). It also helps save time at the police station while paperwork is shuffled. Some travelers carry photocopies of their passport (preferably certified) and visa (if applicable) and leave the originals in a safe place. Carrying an expired passport can also be useful as backup ID to give to hotels if they demand your documents as 'security.'

If you're in Bolivia (or any foreign country) for a longer period, it helps to register your passport with your embassy. This will eliminate the need to send faxes to your home country to verify that you really exist. It's also wise to have a photocopy of your birth certificate or a driver's license, student card, or some form of photo identification, as most embassies require photo ID before they'll issue a replacement passport. Note that replacement US passports may be purchased only with US dollars cash.

Visas & Lengths of Stay

Currently, citizens of Argentina, Austria, Chile, Colombia, Ecuador, Israel, Paraguay, Switzerland, Uruguay, Scandinavian countries (including Finland and Iceland), the UK, Germany, France, Belgium, the Netherlands, Luxembourg, Switzerland, Italy, Portugal, Spain and the USA (except residents of Puerto Rico) do not require visas for stays of up to 90 days, but it's common practice at Bolivian borders to stamp passports with permission to stay only 30 days. However, for those who are allowed 90 days, extending lengths of stay to the full period takes only from the morning to the afternoon in La Paz and normally less than 24 hours at other immigration offices.

Citizens of Australia, New Zealand, Canada, South Africa and Japan are granted stays of 30 days without a visa. Note, however, that citizens of Ireland, South Korea, Andorra, Liechtenstein, Singapore and US nationals residing in Puerto Rico do require a visa issued by a Bolivian consulate, as do citizens of most countries in the Middle East, Caribbean, Central America, South and Southeast Asia, Africa, Eastern Europe and the former Soviet republics. Visa fees vary according to the consulate and nationality of the applicant, and can be as high as US$50 for a one-year multiple entry visa. To confuse matters, each consulate – particularly those in border towns – has its own tariff schedule for different nationalities. However, Bolivian visa requirements change with astonishing frequency and may even seem arbitrary.

In addition to a visa, citizens of many Communist, African, Middle Eastern and Asian countries require 'official permission' by cable from the Bolivian Ministry of Foreign Affairs before a visa will be issued. Details are available from Bolivian consulates and embassies.

Officially, everyone requires proof of onward transport and sufficient funds for their intended stay; in practice officials rarely scrutinize these items. Entry or exit stamps are free of charge and attempts at charging should be met with polite refusal.

Minors under 18 must be accompanied by their parents. Those traveling with only one parent may be required to produce a notarized letter from the other parent granting permission to travel and guaranteeing financial responsibility. An official-looking statement that the missing parent is deceased should obviate this requirement.

All business travelers must obtain a business visa. To apply, you'll need a passport, letter of intent and a financial guarantee from your employer. Business visas cost US$50 and are valid for visits of up to 90 days.

Visa & Length-of-Stay Extensions Visas and lengths of stay may be extended with little ado at immigration offices in major cities. If you don't need a visa, avoid confusion by requesting a length-of-stay extension rather than a visa extension. Length-of-stay-extensions are free to most nationalities, but US and EU passport holders must pay US$20 for each month over their original 90 days. Overstayers are fined US$1.10 per day at immigration in La Paz and US$5 per day at the airport, and even those who do pay up may face a measure of red tape at the border or airport when leaving the country.

Long-Term Visas Diplomatic, official, student and missionary visas are officially issued free of charge. Permanent-residence and work visas are extremely difficult to obtain (see 'The Lowdown on Getting a Bolivian Work Visa,' later in this chapter), so prepare for a complex stream of paperwork, expenditure and headaches. In any case, they're practically impossible to get unless you have a job lined up.

Travel Insurance
In general, all travelers need a travel insurance policy, which will provide some sense of security in the case of a medical emergency or the loss or theft of money or belongings. It may seem an expensive luxury, but if you can't afford a travel health insurance policy, you probably can't afford a medical emergency abroad, either. Travel health insurance policies (see Health, later in this chapter) can usually be extended to include baggage, flight departure insurance and a range of other options. It's sensible to buy your policy as early as possible. If you wait until the week of departure, you may find, for example, that you're not covered for delays caused by industrial action.

Some policies are very good values, but finding them will require shopping around. Long-term or frequent travelers can generally find something for under US$200 per year, but these will normally be from a general business insurance company rather than one specializing in travel. Note, however, that such inexpensive policies may exclude or limit coverage in the USA (where health care costs are extremely high) and may offer very limited baggage protection. Always read the fine print!

Claims on your travel insurance must be accompanied by proof of the value of any items lost or stolen (purchase receipts are the best, so if you buy a new camera for your trip, for example, hang on to the receipt). In the case of medical claims, you'll need detailed medical reports and receipts for amounts paid. If you're claiming on a trip cancelled by circumstances beyond your control (illness, airline bankruptcy, industrial action, etc), you'll have to produce all flight tickets purchased, tour agency receipts and itinerary and proof of whatever glitch caused your trip to be cancelled.

If you book an organized tour, the company will probably encourage you to purchase their own travel insurance policy, which may or may not be a good deal. Bear in mind that some unscrupulous companies – particularly in Europe – manage to keep their tour prices low and appealing by requiring overpriced travel insurance as part of the package.

Driver's License
Most car-rental agencies in Bolivia will accept your home driver's license, but if you're doing a lot of driving, it's wise to back up your credentials with an International Driver's License from your local automobile association. Bolivia doesn't require special motorcycle licenses, but neighboring countries do, so motorcycle travelers should ensure that their international driver's license is valid for motorcycles.

International Health Card
An international health card lists all current vaccines the bearer has received and will be provided by your doctor at the time of vaccination. It's not required for entry into Bolivia unless you're arriving from an area where yellow fever is endemic – which usually means Sub-Saharan Africa, some parts of Central America, the Caribbean and the Guianas – but it's still a good idea to have one. You'll also need proof of yellow-fever vaccination

to enter Brazil overland from Bolivia; this requirement is generally strictly enforced. Technically, you'll also need a yellow-fever vaccination for travel in Santa Cruz department, although visitors are rarely, if ever, asked to produce proof.

Copies
When it comes to passports, identification and other valuable documents, prepare for the worst. Even if your passport is registered with your embassy, it's wise to keep separate records of your passport number and issue date, and photocopies of the pages with the passport number, name, photograph, place issued and expiration date.

Also make copies of visas, birth certificate, traveler's check receipt slips, health and travel insurance policies and addresses, personal contact addresses, credit card numbers (along with emergency loss numbers) and airline tickets, and keep them separate from your passport and money (most hotels have safes for guests' valuables, but only those in finer hotels are likely to be truly safe). Keep one copy with you, one copy inside your luggage and, if applicable, deposit another with a traveling companion. As a hedge against disaster, slip US$100 or so into an unlikely place to use as an emergency stash.

EMBASSIES & CONSULATES
Bolivian Embassies Abroad
Here's a partial listing of Bolivian diplomatic representation abroad; for updated information on consulate and embassy addresses, see the website www.mypage .bluewin.ch/caccia/ or email Renato Caccia at embassies@bluemail.ch.

Australia (☎ 02-9235 1858; 74 Pitt St, Level 6, Sydney 2000, NSW)

Canada (☎ 613-236-5730; fax 613-236-8237; bolcan@iosphere.net; 130 Albert St, Suite 416, Ottawa, Ont K1P SG4); website www.iosphere .net/~bolcan/

France (☎ 01-45 27 84 35; fax 01-45 25 86 23; 12 Ave du President Kennedy, F-75016 Paris 16)

Germany (☎ 0228-362 038; Konstantinstrasse 16, D-5300 Bonn 2)

UK (☎ 020-7235 4248 or 020-7235 4255; 100746.1347@compuserve.com; 106 Eaton Square, London SW1 9AD)

USA

Consulate General: (☎ 212-687-0530 or 212-499-7401; fax 212-687-0532; 211 E 43rd St, Room 802, New York, NY 10017)

Embassy: (☎ 202-483-4410; fax 202-328-3712; embassy@bolivia-usa.org; 3014 Massachusetts Ave NW, Washington, DC 20008); website www.bolivia-usa.org

Embassies & Consulates in Bolivia

The following countries are among those with diplomatic representation in Bolivia. Note that holidays and opening hours of foreign embassies vary and some services are available only at specific hours, so it's wise to phone in advance. Australia and Canada have nominal consulates in La Paz, but citizens of New Zealand, which lacks diplomatic representation in Bolivia, should contact the British embassy for diplomatic or consular business.

Visas for neighboring countries – Chile, Peru, Brazil, Paraguay, Argentina and other Latin American countries – are issued at consulates in most large Bolivian cities and in smaller towns near frontiers. For details, see under individual cities and towns throughout the book.

All of the following are in La Paz; opening hours are weekdays only:

Argentina Calle Aspiazu 497, Casilla 64 (☎ 353233; fax 391083); 9 am to 4 pm

Australia Edificio Montevideo, Mezzanine, Avenida Aniceto Arce 2081, Casilla 7186 (☎ 440459; fax 440801; ch@wara.bolnet.bo); phone for an appointment

Brazil Calle Capitán Ravelo 2334, Edificio Metrobol, Casilla 429 (☎ 440202); 9 am to 1 pm

Canada Plaza Avaroa, Avenida 20 de Octubre 2475, Casilla 10345 (☎ 431215 fax 432330); 9 am to noon

Chile Avenida Hernando Siles 5843 at Calle 13, Obrajes, Casilla 286 (☎ 785275; fax 785046); 9 am to 1 pm and 3 to 5:30 pm

Colombia Calle 9 7835, Calacoto, Casilla 1418 (☎ 784491; fax 786510); 9 am to 1pm

France Avenida Hernando Siles 5390 at Calle 8, Obrajes, Casilla 717 (☎ 786114; fax 786746); 9 am to noon

Germany Avenida Arce 2395, Casilla 5265 (☎ 430850; 431297); 9 am to noon

Israel Avenida Mariscal Santa Cruz, Edificio Esperanza, 10th floor, Casilla 1309 (☎ 358676); 9:15 am to 4 pm

Italy Avenida 6 de Agosto 2575, Casilla 626 (☎ 361129; 391075); 9 am to 2 pm

Japan Calle Rosendo Gutiérrez 497 at Sánchez Lima, Casilla 2725 (☎ 373151; fax 391052); 9 am to noon

Netherlands Avenida 6 de Agosto 2439, Edificio Hilda 7th floor, Casilla 10509 (☎ 432020; fax 431004); 9 am to 1 pm

Paraguay Avenida 6 de Agosto at Pedro Salazar, Edificio Illimani II, Casilla 882 (☎ 432201); 8 am to 1 pm

Peru Avenida 6 de Agosto, Edificio Alianza 110 (☎ 352352; fax 378599); 9 am to 1 pm and 3:30 to 5:30 pm

South Africa Calle Rosendo Gutiérrez 482 (☎ 367754); 9 am to noon

Switzerland Avenida 16 de Julio, Edificio Petrolero, 6th floor, Office 1, Casilla 9356 (☎ 315617; fax 391462); 9 am to noon

UK Avenida Arce 2732, Casilla 694 (☎ 433424; fax 431073); 9 am to noon

USA Avenida Arce 2780 at Cordero, Casilla 425 (☎ 430251; fax 433854); 8:30 am to noon

Venezuela Avenida Arce 2678, Edificio Illimani, 4th and 5th floors, Casilla 960 (☎ 432023; fax 432348); 8:30 am to 12:30 pm and 2:30 to 6:30 pm

MONEY
Currency

Bolivia's unit of currency is the boliviano, divided into 100 centavos. After catastrophic inflation in the mid-1980s, austerity measures were undertaken and today the boliviano is one of Latin America's most stable currencies, with an annual inflation rate of less than 10%.

Bolivian bills (notes) come in denominations of five, 10, 20, 50, 100 and 200 bolivianos. Coins come in two (rare), five, 10, 20 and 50 centavos; and one and two bolivianos. Bolivian currency is practically worthless outside Bolivia, so don't change more than you'll need.

Exchange Rates

Exchange rates as of October 2000 were as follows:

country	units		bolivianos
Argentina	Arg$1	=	B$6.27
Australia	A$1	=	B$3.26
Brazil	R$1	=	B$3.26
Canada	C$1	=	B$4.13
Chile	Chil$100	=	B$1.00
Euro	€1	=	B$5.40
France	FFr1	=	B$0.79
Germany	DM1	=	B$2.65
Japan	¥100	=	B$6.00
New Zealand	NZ$1	=	B$2.50
Peru	S/1	=	B$1.78
Switzerland	SF1	=	B$3.45
UK	UK£1	=	B$9.01
USA	US$1	=	B$6.27

Exchanging Money

The black market in currency was abolished in 1985, and because the official exchange rate represents the currency's actual value, there's no need for a parallel market in currency. As a rule, visitors fare best with US dollars, which is the only foreign currency accepted throughout Bolivia. Currencies of neighboring countries may be exchanged in border areas and at *casas de cambio* (exchange offices) in major cities. The rate for cash varies little from place to place, although rates may be slightly lower in border areas. A few Bolivian banks offer currency exchange services, but it isn't the norm.

Casas de cambio usually open at about 9 am and close at 6 pm, with a two- to three-hour lunch break beginning at noon. In smaller towns, you can often change money in travel agencies, jewelry, photo or appliance shops, artesanía stores or other establishments that conduct international business.

Cash When exchanging money, ask for the cash in as small denominations as possible, as Bolivia has a chronic shortage of change. If the amount due you is small, you may receive your change in boiled sweets or other token items, but just *try* to use a B$10 or larger note to buy a B$2 bottle of soda!

'*¿No tiene sencillo?*' (Don't you have change?) has become a national mantra, and is invariably uttered whenever customers fail to produce exact change for their purchase.

There are several theories to explain the change shortage. The most plausible suggests that vendors hoard change in order to create an artificial shortage – and the opportunity to avoid giving change or charge a commission to change larger denomination notes.

Another problem concerns mangled bills. Banks refuse to accept worn-out small-denomination notes, which tend to disintegrate quickly, on the grounds that corrupt bank managers pocket them before they can be destroyed, thereby increasing inflation. Unless both halves of torn and repaired notes bear identical serial numbers, the note is worthless. Similarly, don't accept B$2 notes; they have been worthless for years.

Traveler's Checks American Express traveler's checks seem to be the most widely accepted brand, but you shouldn't have problems with other major brands. La Paz, Cochabamba, Santa Cruz and Sucre all have casas de cambio that change both notes and traveler's checks (at 3% to 5% lower than cash). In La Paz, some casas de cambio will even change US$ traveler's checks into cash dollars for a 1% to 3% commission. Smaller businesses that change traveler's checks usually offer 5% to 10% less than for cash. In smaller towns, don't count on being able to change traveler's checks at all; carry enough cash to get back to a larger city.

Credit & Debit Cards Major cards, such as Visa, MasterCard and American Express, are useful for regular purchases and in emergencies. They may be used in larger cities at first-rate hotels, restaurants and tour agencies. Because traveler's checks may be difficult to change in some places, there's a good case for carrying a Visa or MasterCard credit card. Visa, and often MasterCard, cash withdrawals of up to US$300 per day are available with no commission and a minimum of hassle, from branches of the Banco de Santa Cruz, Banco Mercantil and the Banco Nacional de Bolivia in La Paz, Sucre, Cochabamba and Santa Cruz. Banco de La Paz charges 1.75% commission on cash withdrawals.

Alternatively, credit card and debit card cash withdrawals are available at the very convenient ENLACE automatic teller machines (ATMs), which are found around La Paz and in all larger cities and towns. Service charges are imposed at the time of billing by the bank issuing the card. The exchange rate used is the one applicable on the date the transaction is posted.

Have on hand the number to call if you lose your credit card, and be quick to cancel it if it's lost or stolen. To guard against surreptitious duplication of your credit card, don't let it out of your sight. Carbonless credit-card slips offer some protection against misuse but old-style coupons are still in use, so ask for the carbon inserts and destroy them after use. Similarly, destroy any slips that have been filled out incorrectly.

Moneychangers Street moneychangers operate virtually around the clock in most cities and towns, but usually they only change cash dollars, paying roughly the same rates as the casas de cambio.

Most street moneychangers are legitimate, but there are some sleight-of-hand artists out there, so you must guard against rip-offs. The established method is to first say how much you want to change. They'll then tell you the rate, which should be slightly higher than in casas de cambio (unless it's after hours, in which case the rate will be lower).

If you agree with their rate, tell them you want the cash in as small denominations as possible. They'll count out the money, then hand it to you to be recounted. Only when you're satisfied should you produce your dollar bills and count them out. The changers will then recount the dollars and if they're happy, the transaction is complete.

Costs

Overall, prices for food, services, hotels and transportation are slightly higher than in Ecuador and Peru, but lower than in Brazil, Argentina and Chile. When converted to US dollars, prices for most items, including lodging, are now actually lower than they were a decade ago. Budget travelers can get by on as little as US$10 to US$15 a day, while most upmarket visitors won't have to spend more than US$150 a day.

If you encounter is 'gringo pricing,' a deliberate overcharging of foreigners, an approach somewhere between acceptance and paranoia is advised. In restaurants, ask for the Spanish version of the menu (if you can read it) and check the bill carefully; if you suspect a problem, request an itemized bill *(cuenta detallada* or *cuenta elaborada)*. Before hailing a taxi or setting off to buy something, try to ask locals for a ballpark idea of what you can expect to pay. To avoid unpleasant scenes, agree on food, accommodation and transport prices before the goods or services are consumed.

Tipping & Bargaining

Tipping Tipping is uncommon except in four- and five-star hotels and more expensive restaurants – and most formal restaurants add a 10% service charge to your bill anyway, so further tipping is unnecessary. As a rule, bus and taxi drivers are not tipped unless they really go out of their way to provide extra service.

Bargaining While prices in retail shops or finer restaurants are generally fixed, in most other places they're eminently negotiable – not only for artesanía, but also for food, transport and even lodging. Mid-range to top-end hotels may offer spontaneous price reductions of up to 20% during slow periods and on some buses, high competition or low demand may mean that discounts of up to 10% are available for the asking. In the case of artesanía and market goods, you'll normally wind up paying about 80% of what is initially quoted.

Bolivians expect to haggle over prices and much of the so-called 'gringo pricing' is inspired by foreigners who pay the first price asked. If you do – whether out of ignorance or guilt feelings about how much cash you have on hand relative to the local economy – you'll not only be considered silly, but you'll be doing fellow travelers a disservice by creating the impression that foreigners will pay any price named. What's more, in well-touristed areas, visitors who voluntarily pay higher than market value actually cause market price increases. They thereby put some items and services out of reach of locals who generally have less disposable cash. And who can blame the vendors; why sell to a local when foreigners will pay twice as much?

If you don't want to appear ripe for exploitation, play the game as the Bolivians do. Bargaining is normally conducted in a friendly and spirited manner. The vendor's aim is to identify the highest price you're willing to pay. Your aim is to find the price below which the vendor will not sell.

Even if you find precisely the item you're after, avoid becoming visibly attached to it or enthusiastic about it, as this will hinder your ability to bargain. Decide what you want to pay or what others have told you *they've* paid; your first offer should be about half this. At this stage, the vendor may laugh or feign outrage, but the price will quickly drop from the original quote to a more realistic level. When it does, begin making better offers until you arrive at a mutually agreeable price.

A distinctly Bolivian alternative to bargaining over small market items is to ask for *llapa*, a price that's agreeable if the vendor throws in additional goods. If you're haggling over a mound of oranges, for example, saying 'llapa' means that you want them to add an extra orange or two for the price. If you're buying a trinket or minor household item, they may throw in a few boiled sweets or other low-value extra.

Having said all that, no matter how adept your bargaining skills, you probably won't get things as cheaply as the locals can and there may be times when you cannot get a vendor to lower the price to anywhere near what you know the item should cost. This probably means that many tourists have passed through and if you refuse to pay the inflated prices, some other fool will.

There's no reason to lose your temper when bargaining. If the vendor appears intransigent or the effort seems a waste of time, politely take your leave. Sometimes vendors will change tack and call you back if they think their stubbornness may be losing a sale. If not, you can always look for another vendor or try again the following day.

POST & COMMUNICATIONS

All major and minor cities have both ENTEL (Empresa Nacional de Telecomunicaciones), the recently privatized national telephone company, as well as post offices run by ECOBOL (Empresa de Correos de Bolivia).

Postal Rates

Airmail postcards *(postales)* or letters weighing up to 20g cost US$0.15 locally, US$0.20 to elsewhere in Bolivia and US$0.40 to the rest of Latin America. To North America, they're US$0.65, to Europe, they cost US$1 and to anywhere else in the world, they are US$1.15. Letters between 20 and 40g to North America cost US$1.75 and to Europe they're US$2.40, meaning that anything up to 40g will be cheaper if it's sent in two envelopes!

A 1kg airmail parcel costs US$12.75 to North America, US$16 to Europe and US$20.50 elsewhere (certification is recommended – see below). Express mail service to all overseas destinations costs US$20 for the first 500g and US$4 for each additional kilogram. Within Bolivia, Express Mail (Expreso) is available for an extra US$0.20.

For US$0.20 extra, any piece of mail may be certified. Special precautions are taken to ensure these items aren't lost or pilfered and savvy locals reckon it's worth it.

Sending Mail

From major towns, the post is generally reliable, but when mailing anything important, it's still wise not to send anything you can't risk losing and send everything else by certified mail (see previous paragraph). The only mailboxes are inside post offices.

It's best not to mail anything from small town post offices; sacks of mail have been known to lie around for months awaiting vehicles to carry them to larger centers.

Parcels *Encomiendas* (parcels) to be sent overseas must weigh under 2kg and are a bit more tricky to send. Firstly, the unwrapped parcel must be taken to the *aduana* (customs office) for inspection. You'll have to wrap and seal the parcel in the presence of a customs official, so carry along a box, paper, tape, string and the address. Once the parcel is ready, the customs official stamps it and it's ready for the post office.

Some post offices have an in-house customs agent, but elsewhere, the customs office may be across town. The most straightforward procedures exist at the main post office in La Paz, where onsite inspectors check the parcel, oversee the wrapping and point you toward the proper window for mailing. The chances of a parcel's arrival at its destination are inversely proportional to its value and to the number of 'inspections' to which it is subjected.

Courier services, including FedEx, UPS and DHL, are found in larger cities. They ship parcels under 1kg to Europe or North America for around US$30.

Receiving Mail

Poste restante (occasionally called *lista de correos)* is available in larger cities and towns. Letters sent to poste restante should include the name of the addressee followed by 'Poste Restante, Correo Central,' then the city and country. Poste Restante letters are delivered to the city's main post office and are held for 90 days, more or less, before being returned to the sender. Recipients must present a passport when collecting mail.

Names in Bolivia, as in all Spanish-speaking countries, are constructed of any number of given and acquired names followed by the father's family name and the mother's maiden name. The *apellido*, or surname, is therefore not the 'last' name used. This can lead to confusion in receiving mail filed or listed alphabetically. For instance, a letter to the president of Bolivia, Hugo Banzer Suárez, would be filed under 'B' for 'Banzer.' Although most postal

clerks are aware of the Western convention of placing the surname last, a letter addressed to Mary Ann Smith may still end up in the 'A' pigeonhole. Given the way things tend to work, however, Mary would be wise to check under 'M,' as well. Although capitalizing and underlining the surname won't always alleviate the confusion, it may help.

If you're having anything shipped to you in Bolivia, it's wise to declare the lowest possible value at the point of origin. Otherwise, you'll find yourself in a quagmire of red tape and owing an import duty of up to 100% of the item's declared value.

Addresses

In this book, addresses often include both the mailing address (post office boxes are known as *casillas)* and the street address.

Telephone

National & Local Calls Local telephone calls can be made from ENTEL offices and only cost a few centavos; for calls in and around La Paz, you can also use the local carrier COTEL. Long-distance calls to locations within Bolivia are also relatively inexpensive; when using area codes, include the leading zero. The number for the operator is ☎ 101 and directory assistance is ☎ 118. Information on new and changed telephone numbers (and they're changing all the time!) is available at ☎ 104.

In major cities, you'll find pay telephone booths, and surprisingly, many tiny rural villages also have telephone booths that accept either coins or cards. In addition, small street kiosks and shops are equipped with telephones that may be used for brief local calls. These cost between US$0.20 and US$0.30. ENTEL produces telephone cards in denominations of B$10, B$20 and B$50, available at ENTEL or from kiosks and some street vendors.

To phone to another town within Bolivia, precede the telephone number with the relevant telephone code; in this book, codes are provided at the title for each town or city. If you're phoning from outside Bolivia, drop the leading zero in the telephone code. In this book, when the given phone number is in another city or town (eg, some rural hotels have La Paz reservation numbers), the telephone code is provided along with the number.

International Calls Bolivia's country code is 591 and the international direct dialing access code is 00. At ENTEL offices, a three-minute call to North America costs about US$8 station-to-station and US$10 person-to-person. To Europe and elsewhere, you'll pay at least 30% more.

Note that ENTEL offices do not accept reverse-charge/collect calls. From a private line, you can dial the International Operator (☎ 02-356700) and explain that the call is *por cobrar* (reverse charges) or dial 0-800 followed by the following operator numbers:

Argentina	0054
Brazil	0055
Canada	0101 or 0102
Chile	0056
France	0033
United Kingdom	0044
USA	1111, 2222, 3333 or 4444
Peru	0051

Fax
ENTEL offices in most major Bolivian cities have a fax desk, and despite some rough edges, it works surprisingly well. Oddly enough, *Entelitos* (small urban ENTEL offices) appear to offer more efficient fax services than main offices. Fax charges to Europe, Central America and the Caribbean are US$3 per minute; to the USA and Canada, US$2.50 per minute; and to Asia, Africa and Australasia, US$5 per minute.

Faxes may be received at public fax numbers in most cities. If the document includes the name, address and telephone number of the recipient's hotel, ENTEL will deliver the fax.

Email & Internet Access
All larger cities and towns now have I-café's offering email and Internet services, with machines set up for quick access to Hotmail,

Yahoo, Latinmail and other popular providers. In La Paz, which has at least 70 I-café's, you'll pay as little as US$1 or US$1.20 per hour, while the average charge in other places is US$1.50 to US$2.50 per hour (in some smaller towns, however, you'll pay as much as US$5). In most places, ENTEL offers high-speed connections for a standard US$2.50 per hour.

INTERNET RESOURCES
There are surprisingly few good websites relating to Bolivia. Lonely Planet's Destination Bolivia page (www.lonelyplanet.com/dest/sam/bolivia.htm) has an overview of Bolivian culture, general information, travel suggestions and much more. Another decent choice is bolivia.wwwdirectory.net. More than you'd ever like to know about the Bolivian government is available at www.congreso.gov.bo/principal.html. For facts and figures from the CIA perspective, see www.odci.gov/cia/publications/factbook/bl.html. You'll find the weather in scores of Bolivian cities and towns on www.weatherhub.com/global/bl.htm. More offbeat information, including a listing of Bolivian restaurants around the world, is found at www.boliviaweb.com.

BOOKS
Most books are published in different editions by different publishers in different countries. As a result, a book might be a hardcover rarity in one country while it's readily available in paperback in another. Fortunately, bookstores, libraries and online vendors search by title or author.

English-, German- and French-language publications are available from *librerías* (bookstores), such as Los Amigos del Libro, with outlets in La Paz, Cochabamba and Santa Cruz. Thanks to hefty import duties, they're quite pricey, but they do offer a selection of popular paperbacks, Latin American literature and nonfiction books, as well as magazines and glossy coffee-table books dealing with Bolivia's anthropology, archaeology and landscapes. Small local librerías normally concentrate on school texts and

Market, Sucre

Wood carver, La Paz

Shoe shiner, La Paz

Airplane mechanic, Amazon

Pants for sale!

Working at a tin mine, Oruro

JAMES LYON

Soccer break in the Altiplano

ERIC WHEATER

Playtime in the Cordilleras

stationery, but may also keep a stash of used English-language paperbacks, so it's worth asking.

Lonely Planet

The regularly updated *South America on a shoestring* (Lonely Planet, 1999) is a thoroughly researched general guide that contains lots of maps and information in a well-organized format. Language assistance is available in the Lonely Planet phrasebooks for *Latin American Spanish* and *Quechua*.

If you're traveling in other Latin American countries, Lonely Planet also has guides for *Brazil, Colombia, Peru, Ecuador & the Galápagos, Argentina, Uruguay & Paraguay, Chile & Easter Island, Venezuela* and others. If you're traveling overland, Lonely Planet's *Mexico* travel guide and *Central America on a shoestring* will be especially useful. For a full title list, see the back of this book.

Guidebooks

Hikers and trekkers will enjoy *Trekking in Bolivia – A Traveler's Guide*, by Yossi Brain, Andrew North and Isobel Stoddart (The Mountaineers, 1997), which describes most of the country's finest trekking routes. For serious alpinists, Yossi Brain also wrote *Bolivia – A Climbing Guide* (The Mountaineers, 1999), which details major climbs in the Cordillera Real, Cordillera Apolobamba and Cordillera Quimsa Cruz.

The 7th edition of *Backpacking and Trekking in Peru & Bolivia*, by Hilary Bradt (Bradt Publications, 1999) covers major hikes in the Cordillera Real and the Yungas, as well as snippets on the lowland regions. Bolivia gets second billing, but there's lots of good route information and advice for keen ramblers (and guinea pig fans).

A Traveler's Guide to El Dorado & the Inca Empire, by Lynn Meisch (Penguin Books, 1980), is a timeless treatise on Colombia, Ecuador, Peru and Bolivia, with details on their weaving and textiles traditions. It's highly recommended.

Travel

The classic *Exploration Fawcett* by Colonel Percy Harrison Fawcett (Century, 1988) haphazardly follows the quirky travels of the unconventional explorer, including details of his term as a surveyor for the Bolivian government. An intrepid sailor's journeys through landlocked Bolivia are recorded in *The Incredible Voyage*, by Tristan Jones (Sheed, Andrews & McNeel, Inc, 1977). It includes narrative about several months' sailing and exploring on Lake Titicaca and a complication-plagued haul across the country to the Paraguay River.

Sons of the Moon – A Journey in the Andes, by Henry Shukman (Charles Scribner & Sons, 1989), is a well-written account of a fairly unremarkable journey from northwestern Argentina, across the Bolivian Altiplano and on to Cuzco, Peru. It does, however, include superb observations of typically introverted Altiplano cultures.

Chasing Che – A Motorcycle Journey in Search of the Guevara Legend, by Patrick Symmes (Vintage Press, 2000), chronicles the author's motorcycle trip around South America, in a naïve but well-intentioned attempt to balance the legendary figure with the curious reality of this controversial character.

The humorous and well-written *Inca-Kola* by Matthew Parris (Orion Books, 1993) follows the ramblings of several Englishmen on a rollicking circuit through Peru and parts of Bolivia. It would be an excellent read on a journey through the region.

The Old Patagonia Express, by Paul Theroux (Pocket Books, 1980) recounts a rail odyssey from Boston to Patagonia. The author takes a sniffy attitude toward budget travelers and doesn't seem to enjoy his trip, but it's still an interesting tale, and anyone who traveled Bolivia's rail system prior to privatization will certainly recognize some of the misadventures.

The Cloud Forest, by Peter Mathiessen (Collins Harill, 1960), isn't exclusively about Bolivia, but this account of his 30,000km journey across the South American wilderness, from the Amazon to Tierra del Fuego, is well worth a read. The descriptions of the South American environment are especially adept.

Highways of the Sun – A Search for the Royal Roads of the Incas, by Victor W von Hagen (Victor Gollancz, 1956, or Plata Press, 1975) is an interesting account about a 1950s expedition along ancient Inca roads, and a treatise on pre-Columbian paving and Inca traditions.

An interesting and offbeat historical character is portrayed in *Lizzie – A Victorian Lady's Amazon Adventure*, by Tony Morrison, Ann Brown & Anne Rose (BBC Books, 1985), which was compiled mostly from letters. It chronicles the experiences of a Victorian woman, Lizzie Hessel, in the Bolivian Amazon settlement of Colonia Orton during the rubber boom. Characters in the book read like a litany of modern Amazonian history: Colonel Fawcett, Carlos Fermín Fitzcarrald ('Fitzcarraldo'), Dr Edwin Heath, Francisco and Nicolás Suárez, Henry Alexander Wickham and Dr Antonio Vaca Diez. The book is the companion volume to the BBC film production *Letters from Lizzie*.

The classic *Brazilian Adventure*, by Peter Fleming (Penguin, 1957), is the story of the author's 1930s expedition across the Mato Grosso and down the Amazon to find the missing explorer Colonel Percy Harrison Fawcett. It's not about Bolivia, but it's one of the funniest and most entertaining travel books around, and Fleming's descriptions and impressions of the Brazilian Amazon are equally applicable to the Bolivian rain forests. *Touching the Void*, by Joe Simpson (Pan Books, 1989), isn't about Bolivia, either, but this riveting tale of an ill-fated ascent of Peru's Siula Grande may well be the most (or, in a sense, least!) gripping climbing book ever written, and will affect both Andean alpinists and nonclimbers. The sequel, *This Game of Ghosts* (Vintage/ Random House, 1994), carries the story both forward and backward and has also become a climbers' classic.

History & Politics

The biography, *Ché Guevara*, Daniel James (Stein & Day, 1969), is a fascinating, slightly right-leaning biography of the folk hero, with emphasis upon his activities and ultimate demise in Bolivia. Perhaps better insight into Ché's thinking is available straight from the horse's mouth in *Bolivian Diary* by Ernesto 'Ché' Guevara (Jonathan Cape/Lorrimer, 1968). This book traces the revolutionary's ill-fated travels through Bolivia while unsuccessfully struggling to bring the campesinos to an awareness – and defiance – of their downtrodden status. His more upbeat *Motorcycle Diaries* removes some of the myth and replaces it with the confused humanity of this controversial figure.

The concise and extremely informative *Bolivia in Focus* by Paul van Lindert and Otto Verkoren (Latin American Bureau, 1994) provides an excellent synopsis of Bolivia's history, economics, politics and culture. It provides the best and most up-to-date background information available on the country and will be useful for familiarization before traveling to Bolivia.

The modern classic on Bolivian social issues is *Rebellion in the Veins*, by James Dunkerly (Verso Editions, 1984), which chronicles Bolivian political and social struggles from 1952 to 1982. It's heavy going but full of facts and insights that are unavailable elsewhere. If you can't find a copy, order it directly from the publisher: Verso Editions, 6 Meard St, London W1V 3HR, UK.

Economists will be particularly interested in *Silent Revolution – The Rise of Market Economics in Latin America* by Duncan Green (Latin America Bureau, 1995). It outlines the causes and effects – and particularly the hardships – imposed by the International Monetary Fund's economic structural adjustment programs in Latin America. Another interesting political/economic work is *Plowing the Sea*, by Michael Fairbanks and Stacy Lindsay (Harvard University Press), which examines Bolivian rural lifestyles and perceived poverty in the Andean region.

Despite its title, *The Great Tin Crash & the World Tin Market* by John Crabtree (Latin American Bureau, 1987) quite readably recounts the fascinating story of the Bolivian tin industry. It ties the current slump in tin prices to fluctuations in the valuation of the dollar and the pound, as well as poor infrastructure, lack of maritime access and the shortage of smelters.

Let Me Speak, by Domitila Barrios de Chungará, is a Bolivian's compelling and touching account of life in the Siglo XX mine. Another perspective is offered in *We Eat the Mines and the Mines Eat Us*, by June Nash (Columbia University Press, 1979). This anthropologist's study of life and death in the Bolivian tin mines is recommended for anyone interested in the harsh conditions faced by Bolivian miners.

If you can read Spanish, perhaps look for *Pueblo Enfermo*, by Alcides Arguedas (La Paz, 1996), which is a discourse on the corruption and the sick state of the Bolivian political system. No outsider would ever get away with saying such things! It sells for US$5 at Los Amigos del Libro in La Paz.

The Incredible Incas & Their Timeless Land, by Loren McIntyre (National Geographic Society Press, 1975), is an informal, easily digestible account of Inca history and a description of Inca lands in modern times by one of the last South American explorers.

The hard-to-find anthology, *Tales of Potosí*, edited by Bartolomé Arzáns de Orsúa y Vela (Brown University Press, 1975), chronicles colonial life and times in a city whose history reads more like fiction than fact. A more recent treatise on that subject is *I am Rich Potosí – The Mountain that Eats Men*, by Stephen Ferry (Monacelli Press, 1999).

For everything you've ever wanted to know about the Andean wonder drug – and more – see the cult classic *The History of Coca – The Divine Plant of the Incas*, by W Golden Mortimer (And/OR Press, 1974), originally published in 1901. A more up-to-date assessment of Bolivia's relationship with the coca leaf is found in *Bolivia and Coca – A Study in Dependency*, by James Painter (Lynne Reiner Publishers, 1994).

John Hemming's *The Conquest of the Incas* (Harcourt, Brace, Jovanovich, 1970), is the definitive work on the Spanish takeover of the well-established Inca empire. A good companion book is *Monuments of the Incas*, by John Hemming and Edward Ranney (University of New Mexico Press, 1990), with illustrations and explanations of major Inca-era sites. The same theme from the local perspective features in *La Venas Abiertas de América Latina*, by the Eduardo Galeano, which is available only in Spanish. The 16th-century work, *Royal Commentaries of the Incas*, by Garcilaso de la Vega, details the history, growth and influence of the Inca Empire, as well as a first-hand account of its decline and demise.

General

The novel *At Play in the Fields of the Lord*, by Peter Mathiessen, is a strong and well-written tale of missionaries in the Amazon rain forests.

The classic tale of South American life, *One Hundred Years of Solitude*, by Gabriel García Márquez, won the Nobel Prize for literature in 1982. Although it's considered by critics to reflect more fantasy than realism, it's actually based on acute observation and reflects South America's pervasive surrealism as much as the author's vivid imagination.

The Bridge of San Luis Rey, the fictional classic by Thornton Wilder (Grosset & Dunlap, 1927), describes the collapse of the renowned bridge over Peru's mighty Río Apurímac. It actualizes the greatest fears of anyone who ever crossed or relied on that bridge, while focusing on the characters of each victim and the values of traditional Andean society.

The rollicking science fiction tale, *The Lost World*, by Sir Arthur Conan Doyle (Buccaneer Books, 1977; originally published 1912), describes a prehistoric world in the rain-forested mountains of the Serranía de Huanchaca, in northeastern Bolivia's Parque Nacional Noel Kempff Mercado.

If you read German, you may want to check out the series of novels on Bolivia by German author Gudrun Pausewang: *Boliviänische Hochzeit* (Bolivian Wedding), *Die Freiheit des Ramón Acosta* (The Freedom of Ramón Acosta), *Plaza Fortuna*, *Guadelupe* and *Der Glückbringer* (The Luck-Bringer).

Some of the finest Bolivian literature is discussed in the Arts section of the Facts about the Country chapter.

Coffee-Table Books

Exploring South America, by Loren McIntyre, is the best of its kind, a compilation of photos from McIntyre's nearly 60 years in South America. A new coffee-table publication is the amazing *Bolivia – Images from an Aerial Journey*, by photographer and pilot Willy Kenning, which features surreal visions of Bolivia from aloft. It's available through the publisher, K-Edición y Fotografía (☎/fax 03-420891), Casilla 292, Santa Cruz.

Language

The *Latin American Spanish phrasebook* (Lonely Planet, 1991) is handy for travelers to most of Latin America. The *University of Chicago Spanish-English/English-Spanish Dictionary* (Pocket Books 1972), which emphasizes Latin American usage and pronunciation, is highly recommended.

The *Quechua phrasebook* (Lonely Planet, 1989) provides useful phrases and words in the Cuzco dialect, which is also spoken in the central Bolivian highlands.

NEWSPAPERS & MAGAZINES

The national daily newspaper is *La Razón*, but the major cities all have daily newspapers. They include *Presencia, El Diario, Hoy* and *Última Hora* in La Paz; *La Patria* in Oruro; *El Mundo* and *El Deber* in Santa Cruz; *El Correo del Sur* in Sucre; and *Los Tiempos* in Cochabamba. Of these, *Presencia, La Razón* and the two Santa Cruz papers generally provide the best coverage.

There's also an English-language weekly, the *Bolivian Times* (US$1), which is published on Friday and is sold at newsstands and bookstores in major cities. Yearly subscriptions cost US$40 in La Paz, US$48 elsewhere in Bolivia, US$74 elsewhere in Latin America, US$110 in North America, US$116 in Europe and US$130 in Australasia. Contact the Bolivian Times (☎ 392556; fax 390700; boliviantimes@latinwide.com; Pasaje Jáuregui 2248, Casilla 1696, La Paz).

Time, Newsweek, the *International Herald Tribune, The Economist*, the *Financial Times* and the *Miami Herald* are sold at some street kiosks in major cities and at Los Amigos del Libro in La Paz, Cochabamba and Santa Cruz.

A very useful publication is the monthly *Guía Boliviana de Transporte y Turismo*, which contains transport schedules and directories of services in major cities; they also produce the bimonthly *Guía Turística de Bolivia*, with information of particular interest for tourists. It's available for US$5 from GBT (☎ 434441; fax 432073; gbt@ceibo.entelnet.bo), Avenida 6 de Agosto entre Pinilla Y Gonsalvez, Pasaje Pascoe 5, La Paz. GBT also has branch offices in other major cities.

RADIO & TV

Bolivia has 125 radio stations broadcasting in Spanish, Quechua and Aymará. The seemingly inordinate number may be explained by the mountainous nature of the terrain – signals don't reach very far. Recommended listening includes FM-96.7 in La Paz, which plays classic American and English rock and pop music; FM-98.5 in La Paz, which plays folk music (without adverts!); and Radio Latina in Cochabamba, at the upper end of the FM band, which plays a mix of Andean folk music, salsa and local rock.

The country has two government and five private TV stations operating in La Paz, Cochabamba, Trinidad, Oruro, Potosí, Tarija and Santa Cruz, which are watched on the country's 650,000-odd TV sets. Most of the programming is foreign.

PHOTOGRAPHY & VIDEO

Photographers will find plenty of fodder in Bolivia. Points worth remembering include cold, heat, humidity, sand, and tropical sunlight and shadows. Don't leave your camera for long in direct sunlight, and don't store used film for long in the humid conditions as it could fade.

On sunny days or at high altitudes, the best times to take photos are the first two hours after sunrise and the last two before sunset. This brings out the best colors and takes advantage of the color-enhancing long red rays cast by a low sun. At other times, colors may be washed out by harsh sunlight and if you're shooting on sand or near water, it's important to adjust for glare. The worst of these effects can be countered by using a polarizing (UV) filter. It's always important to avoid exposing your photographic equipment to sand and water.

Film & Equipment

Cameras are sold in Bolivia but are subject to high import duties, so photographers should bring all necessary equipment from home. Polaroid film is difficult to find, but some Fujichrome, Agfachrome and print film are available at reasonable prices in some markets and from street vendors.

If you're shooting slides, you'll probably get the best results with Fujichrome Sensia 100 (about US$6 per 36-exposure roll), Velvia 50 (US$10 for 36 exposures), Agfachrome (US$4 to US$5 for 36 exposures) or Kodachrome 64 (around US$6 for 36 exposures). La Paz is generally the best place to pick up film; for information on the best photo shops, see Film in the La Paz chapter. Film prices sometimes include processing and you can mail the exposed film to the labs in the envelopes provided. It's wise, however, to rewrap the package to disguise it and send it via registered mail.

Useful photographic accessories include a small flash, a cable release, a polarizing filter, a lens-cleaning kit, and silica-gel packs to protect against humidity (especially if you're traveling in the lowlands). Also, take spare batteries for cameras and flash units and make sure your equipment is insured.

Repairs & Processing Reliable camera repair is best found in La Paz; for information, see Film in the La Paz chapter. Film processing in Bolivia is generally poor; your best option is probably Foto Linares in La Paz, which offers decent European standards at good European prices. Prints cost around US$1 for a 36-exposure roll, plus US$0.20 per print. You may want to pay only for the negatives and wait to have the prints done at home. To keep costs down on

slide processing, ask for *solo revelado*, which means the slides are developed but not mounted. This costs between US$2 and US$2.50 for one 36-exposure roll. For mounted slides, you'll pay US$7 to US$8, including scratches. Alternatively, you can buy your own slide mounts at Casa Kavlin for US$7.50 per 100.

Photographing Scenery

Bolivian landscapes swallow film, so don't be caught without a healthy supply of film. Keep in mind, however, that the combination of high-altitude ultraviolet rays and light reflected off snow or water will conspire to fool both your eye and your light meter. A polarizing filter is essential when photographing the Altiplano and will help to reveal or emphasize the dramatic effects of the exaggerated UV element at high altitude. Unless there's a haze to filter sunlight, avoid taking photos during the brightest part of the day, when the rays are short, the light is harshest and the shadows are blackest.

In the lowland rain forests, conditions include dim light, humidity, haze and leafy interference. For optimum photos, you need either fast film (200 or 400 ASA) or a tripod for long exposures.

Photographing People

As in most places, the quest for the perfect 'people shot' will prove a photographer's greatest challenge. The average Bolivian doesn't indulge in photography as a hobby but does recognize the inherent value of camera equipment. If you carry a camera, especially a swanky model, you'll inevitably be branded with the 'wealthy foreigner' label. This isn't necessarily a problem, but it does set you apart and those who are superstitious about photography may well react differently toward you than toward someone without photographic aspirations.

While some Bolivians are willing photo subjects, others – especially traditional women – may be superstitious about your camera, suspicious of your motives, or simply interested in whatever economic advantage they can gain from your desire to photograph them.

Whatever the case, be sensitive to the wishes of locals, however photogenic. Ask permission to photograph if a candid shot can't be made; if permission is denied, you should neither insist or snap a picture anyway.

Often, people will allow you to photograph them provided you give them a copy of the photo, a real treasure in rural Bolivia. Understandably, people are sometimes disappointed not to see the photograph immediately materialize. If you don't carry a Polaroid camera, take their address and make it clear that you'll send the photo by mail once it's processed – and then be sure to follow through with your promise!

Photographing Wildlife

For serious wildlife photography, you'll need a single-lens reflex camera and telephoto or zoom lenses. If all you have is a little 'point and shoot' camera, don't bother. The more sophisticated cameras may have a maximum focal length of 70mm or so, but that's still not sufficient for decent wildlife shots.

Zoom lenses work best for wildlife photography since you can frame your shot easily and work out the optimum composition; this is particularly useful for wildlife on the move. You'll need at least 200mm for good close-up shots; 70-to-300mm zoom lenses are popular. The main problem with long lenses is that the excess of glass inside absorbs about 1.5 f-stops and necessitates higher ASA film (200 to 400) for photos in anything but broad, bright daylight.

A straight telephoto lens will yield better results and greater clarity than zoom lenses, but you're limited by having to carry a separate lens for each required focal length. A 400 or 500mm lens will bring the action up close but you'll still need fast film.

Another option is a 2x teleconverter, a small adapter that fits between the lens and camera body and doubles the focal length of the lens. This is a good, cheap way of getting a long focal length without having to purchase expensive lenses. It does, however, have a couple of disadvantages: it requires fast film and, depending on the camera and lens, can be difficult to focus quickly and

precisely, which is naturally a major drawback when it comes to wildlife photography.

When using long, heavy lenses, tripods are very useful, and they're essential for anything greater than about 300mm unless you have an exceptionally steady hand.

TIME

Bolivian time is four hours behind Greenwich Mean Time. When it's noon in La Paz, it's 4 pm in London, 11 am in New York, 8 am in San Francisco, 4 am the following day in Auckland and 2 am the following day in Sydney.

ELECTRICITY

Bolivia uses a standard current of 220 volts at 50 cycles except in La Paz and a few selected locations in Potosí, which use 110 volts at 50 cycles. Ask before you plug in. In some areas, particularly smaller towns and villages, demand for power exceeds the power stations' ability to supply it and water and power services are routinely turned off at certain times of day and/or at night. Night owls will need to have a flashlight (torch) on hand.

Most plugs and sockets in use are of the two-pin round-prong variety, but in some places (particularly La Paz), you may encounter American-style two-pin parallel flat-pronged sockets.

WEIGHTS & MEASURES

As in all of South America, Bolivia uses the metric system except, strangely, when weighing vegetables at the market; these are sold in *libras* (pounds, 0.45kg). Uniquely South American measurements, which are used occasionally, include the *arroba*, which is equal to 11.25kg, and the *quintal*, which equals four arrobas.

For converting between metric and imperial units, refer to the table at the back of the book.

LAUNDRY

While Bolivia has very few coin-operated launderettes, small and inexpensive private laundry services exist around larger cities. Most budget hotels in Bolivia offer rudimentary laundry facilities – normally just a sink and a cold-water supply. Most other places to stay (excluding upmarket hotels) have staff members who will scrub up your togs for a good rate. Those using laundry services at high-priced hotels will generally pay international rates to return their clothing to socially acceptable cleanliness.

TOILETS & PLUMBING

Much Bolivian plumbing is jerry-built or poorly installed and inferior to what you're probably used to. Bathtubs and hot and cold running water are rare outside upmarket tourist hotels, but you can still have hot (or tepid) showers, thanks to a deadly looking device that attaches to the shower head and electrically heats the water as it passes through. Bare wires run from the ceiling into the shower head (if they're dangling from the ceiling, you won't have a hot shower because the device is broken).

On the wall, you'll find a lever that suspiciously resembles an electrocutioner's switch, sometimes known as a 'Frankenstein switch.' Fortunately, later models of the device allow the switch to remain permanently engaged, so you don't actually have to flip it when the water is running. When the water is turned on – leave your shoes on for this – the heater is activated, and will begin to emit an electrical humming sound. Normally, the lights in the room will dim or go out altogether due to the great deal of electricity required to operate the contraption effectively.

The water temperature can then be adjusted by increasing or decreasing the flow. However, because a large volume of water cannot be adequately heated in the time it spends passing through the shower head, a shower of a bearable temperature may be little more than a pressureless drip. Don't touch the metal valves during your shower; few of these devices are properly grounded (earthed) and you may get an electric shock. When you're finished, don't touch the valves until you're dry and have your shoes on. (This may be tricky, especially if the shower cubicle is small.)

The toilet or WC is commonly called *el baño*, or it may be misnamed *servicio sanitario* or *servicios higiénicos* (often abbreviated to SSHH). Usually neither sanitary nor hygienic, facilities may well be unspeakable, but in markets or transport terminals, you'll pay US$0.10 to US$0.20 to use them. This investment typically yields two sheets of one-ply toilet paper, which – if you're normal – won't do the job. Most Bolivians carry a roll of toilet paper wherever they go and travelers would be advised to do the same.

Thanks to typically low water pressure, few toilets can even choke down shit, let alone toilet paper, so a wastebasket is usually provided. If there's no receptacle or if it's full, toss the used paper on the floor. In rural areas, toilets tend to be more basic – for example, a hole in a corner of the pigsty.

HEALTH

General travel health depends on predeparture preparations, day-to-day attention to health-related matters, and the correct handling of medical emergencies if they do arise. Although the following health section may seem like a who's who of unpleasant diseases, your chances of contracting a serious illness in Bolivia are slight. You will, however, be exposed to environmental factors, foods and sanitation standards that are probably quite different from what you're used to, but if you take the recommended jabs, faithfully pop your antimalarials and use common sense, there shouldn't be any problems. However, people with a history of cardiac, pulmonary or circulatory problems should consult a physician before traveling to Bolivia, as they may be at risk of experiencing acute mountain sickness.

Travel Health Guides

There are a number of books on travel health, and if you intend to get anywhere off the beaten track on your travels, you should prepare yourself by referring to a selection of these.

Healthy Travel – Central & South America by Dr Isabel Young (Lonely Planet, 2000). Provides all the information you'll need to minimize risks and stay fit and healthy in Latin America.

Where There is No Doctor by David Werner (Macmillan, 1994). A very detailed guide intended for longer-term volunteers working in undeveloped areas.

Wilderness Medical Society Practice Guidelines for Wilderness Emergency Care by William W Forgey (ICS Books, 1995). Includes excellent wilderness medical guidelines, especially for dealing with natural hazards: altitude, frostbite, water impurities, animal hazards, lightning and a host of other problems.

Mountain Sickness: Prevention, Recognition and Treatment by Peter Hackett (AACP, 1992). This practical and easy-to-carry field guide is indispensable for alpinists and high-altitude trekkers.

For general direction, you may want to contact the International Association for Medical Assistance to Travellers (IAMAT, ☎ 1-716-754-4883; 417 Center St, Lewiston, NY 14092-3633, USA); their website is www.sentex.net/~iamat.

Predeparture Preparations

Health Insurance A wide variety of travel insurance policies are available; ask your travel agent for recommendations. The international student travel policies handled by STA Travel or other student travel organizations are usually good values. It's always important, however, to check the small print (see also under Planning, earlier in this chapter):

• Some policies specifically exclude 'dangerous activities,' which can include white-water rafting, motorcycling, climbing with a rope (as if it would be less dangerous without a rope!), or even trekking. If these activities are on your agenda, such a policy would be of limited value.

• You may prefer a policy that pays doctors or hospitals directly rather than requiring you to pay first and claim later. If you must claim after the fact, however, be sure you keep all documentation. Some policies ask you to phone (reverse charges) to a center in your home country where an immediate assessment of the problem will be made.

• Check on the policy's coverage of emergency transport or evacuation back to your home country. If you need to stretch out across several airline seats, someone has to pay for it!

Health Preparations & Optical Prescriptions Make sure you're healthy before embarking on a long journey, have your teeth checked, and if you wear glasses or contacts, bring a spare pair and a copy of your optical prescription. Losing your glasses can be a real problem, although in larger Bolivian cities, you can have a new pair made with little fuss. Soft contact lenses are also readily available, but hard/gas permeable lenses are extremely expensive in Bolivia and delivery may take up to six weeks.

At least one pair of good quality sunglasses is essential, as the glare can be terrific, particularly on the Altiplano, and dust and blown sand can get into the corners of your eyes. A hat, sunscreen lotion and lip protection are also important.

When buying drugs anywhere in South America, check expiry dates and storage conditions. Some drugs available there may no longer be recommended, or may even be banned, in other countries.

Immunizations Vaccinations provide protection against diseases you may be exposed to during your travels. Currently yellow fever is the only vaccine subject to international health regulations, and a yellow-fever vaccination and related documentation are strongly recommended for travelers in Bolivia. It's technically required for travel in Santa Cruz department, and Brazilian authorities will not grant entrance from Bolivia without it. The vaccination remains effective for 10 years.

Seek medical advice about vaccinations at least six weeks prior to your departure; some vaccinations require an initial shot followed by a booster, and some should not be given together.

The possible list of vaccinations includes:

Cholera Although some border officials may ask to see evidence of this vaccine – often unofficially as a means of extracting bribes – it is of limited effectiveness, lasts only three to six months and is not recommended for pregnant women. There have been no recent reports of cholera vaccine requirements in Bolivia or neighboring countries.

Infectious Hepatitis Hepatitis A is the most common travel-acquired illness but it may be prevented fairly reliably by vaccination. Protection can be provided in two ways – either with the antibody immune globulin or with the vaccine Havrix. Havrix provides long-term immunity (up to 10 years or more) after an initial dose and a booster at six or 12 months.

Polio A booster of either the oral or injected vaccine is required every 10 years to maintain immunity.

Smallpox Smallpox has now been wiped out worldwide, so immunization is no longer necessary.

Tetanus DPT Boosters are necessary at least every 10 years and are highly recommended as a matter of course.

Typhoid Available as either an injection or a course of capsules. Protection with the injectable vaccine lasts three years; capsules require boosting annually. Useful if you are traveling for long periods in rural, tropical areas.

Yellow Fever Protection, which is available from yellow-fever vaccination centers, lasts for 10 years and is highly recommended. Vaccination is is not advised during pregnancy, but if you will be traveling to a high-risk area it is probably advisable.

Basic Rules

Bolivia is not a particularly unhealthy country, but sanitation and hygiene are generally poor, so pay attention to what you eat. Stomach upsets are the most common travel health problem (30% to 50% of people traveling abroad for two weeks or less can expect to experience them) but most upsets are minor. Don't be paranoid about sampling local foods – it's all part of the travel experience and shouldn't be missed. If an inexpensive restaurant or market stall is popular with locals, chances are it's a good choice.

Medical Kit Check List

It's wise to carry a small, straightforward medical kit, which may include:

❏ **Aspirin or paracetamol** (acetaminophen in the USA) – for pain or fever.

❏ **Antihistamine** – (such as Benadryl) – useful as a decongestant for colds and allergies, to ease itching from insect bites, or to prevent motion sickness. Antihistamines may cause sedation and interact with alcohol, so care should be taken when using them.

❏ **Antibiotics** – useful if you're traveling off the beaten track. Most antibiotics are prescription medicines, so carry the prescription along with you. Some individuals are allergic to commonly prescribed antibiotics such as penicillin or sulfa drugs. It is sensible to always carry this information when traveling.

❏ **Bismuth subsalicylate preparation** (such as Pepto-Bismol) – for stomach upsets and loperamide (eg, Imodium or Lomotil) to bung things up in case of emergencies during long-distance travel.

❏ **Rehydration solution** – for treatment of severe diarrhea; particularly important when traveling with children. These preparations are available from Bolivian pharmacies.

❏ **Antiseptic liquid** or cream and antibiotic powder – for minor injuries.

❏ **Calamine lotion** or Stingose spray – to ease irritation from bites and stings.

❏ **Bandages** and band-aids (plasters).

❏ **Scissors, tweezers, and a thermometer** – note that mercury thermometers are not permitted on airlines.

❏ **Insect repellent**, UV-protection factor 15+ sunblock (sunscreen), chapstick with sunblock, and water-purification tablets (or iodine).

❏ **Sterile syringes** – have at least one large enough for a blood test as those normally used for injections are too small.

❏ **Contraceptives** and any prescription medicines you normally take, plus a prescription with the generic name of any drugs required. If you're carrying syringes or any sort of powdery preparation, be sure to carry a doctor's letter (preferably in Spanish) stating the purpose of and reason for carrying them.

Water Purification Some Bolivian tap water is safe to drink, but much of it isn't. The simplest way to purify suspect water is to boil it for eight to 10 minutes, but remember that at high altitudes water boils at a lower temperature and germs are less likely to be killed. Simple filtering won't remove all dangerous organisms, so if you can't boil suspect water, treat it chemically. Chlorine tablets (eg Puritabs or Steritabs) will kill many, but not all, pathogens. Micro-Pure and other silver-based tablets don't kill giardia. Iodine is very effective and is available in tablet form (such as Potable Aqua) but follow the directions carefully and remember that too much iodine is harmful.

If you can't find iodine tablets, use either 2% tincture of iodine or iodine crystals. Add four drops of tincture of iodine per liter or quart of water and let it stand for 30 minutes. (Preparation of iodine crystals is a more complicated and dangerous process, as you first must prepare a saturated iodine solution.) Iodine loses its effectiveness if exposed to air or damp, so store it in a tightly sealed container. Flavored powder will disguise the normally foul taste of iodine-treated water and is especially useful when traveling with children.

Reputable brands of bottled water or soft drinks are usually fine, although mineral water bottles are sometimes refilled and resold, so check the seals before buying. The most widely available brand is Viscachani, but its main mineral content appears to be salt and it tastes foul. Better choices are Vertiente from Cochabamba or Salvietti from Sucre.

In rural areas, take care with fruit juices and licuados, since water may have been added. Milk should be treated with suspicion as it is often unpasteurized. Boiled milk is fine if it's kept hygienically and yogurt is always good. Tea or coffee should also be OK because the water used was probably boiled.

Food Vegetables and fruit should be washed with purified water or peeled where possible. Ice cream is usually OK but beware of ice cream – especially that sold by street vendors – that has melted and been refrozen. Thoroughly cooked food is safest but not if it has been left to cool or if it has been reheated. Take great care with shellfish or fish, and avoid undercooked meat. If a place looks clean and well run and the vendor also looks clean and healthy, then the food is probably all right. In general, places that are packed with travelers or locals will be fine. Busy restaurants mean the food is being cooked and eaten quite quickly with little standing around and is probably not being reheated.

To clean fruit and vegetables without adding undesirable flavors, you can use Bolivia's own choice, D-6 germicide, which is available at local pharmacies. Mix 25 to 30 drops in 1L of water and place the vegetables in the solution for 20 minutes.

Nutrition If your food is poor or limited in availability, if you're traveling hard and fast and therefore missing meals, or if you simply lose your appetite, you can soon start to lose weight and place your health at risk.

Make sure your diet is well balanced. Eggs, tofu, beans, lentils and nuts are all safe ways to get protein. Fruit you can peel (bananas, oranges or mandarins for example) is always safe and a good source of vitamins. Try to eat plenty of grains (maize, rice, quinoa, etc) and bread. Remember that although food is generally safer if it is cooked well, overcooked food loses much of its nutritional value. If your diet isn't well balanced or if your food intake is insufficient, it's a good idea to take vitamin and iron supplements.

Everyday Health It's wise to learn how to assess both body temperature and pulse rate. A normal body temperature is 98.6°F or 37°C; more than 2°C (4°F) higher is a 'high' fever. A normal adult pulse rate is 60 to 80 per minute (children 80 to 100, babies 100 to 140). As a general rule the pulse increases about 20 beats per minute for each 1°C (2°F) rise in fever.

An abnormal respiration rate is also an indicator of illness. Count the number of breaths per minute: between 12 and 20 is normal for adults and older children (up to 30 for younger children, 40 for babies).

People with a high fever or respiratory illness breathe more quickly than normal. More than 40 shallow breaths a minute may well indicate pneumonia while short, gasping breaths may indicate an asthma attack.

Medical Problems & Treatment

Self-diagnosis and treatment can be risky, so seek qualified help wherever possible. Although we do give treatment dosages in this section, they are for emergency use only, and medical advice should be sought where possible before administering any controlled drugs.

Embassies, consulates and five-star hotels can usually recommend English-speaking doctors and reputable clinics. In some areas, however, standards of medical attention are so low that for serious illnesses, the best advice is to get on a plane and head for La Paz or Santa Cruz, or in extreme cases, Miami or home!

Pharmacies & Medications Pharmacies in Bolivia are known as *farmacias* and medicines are called *medicamentos*. The word for doctor is *médico* and medicine tablets are known as *comprimidos*. *Farmacias de turno* are pharmacies that take turns staying open 24 hours a day. Those currently on duty are listed in daily newspapers.

It's unnecessary to carry remedies for every illness you might conceivably contract during your trip, as most drugs are available in Bolivian pharmacies without a prescription. However, most pharmacies are a bit lax about storage, so be sure to check expiry dates before buying. It's also wise to take a supply of vitamin tablets and any prescriptions that you must take habitually, including contraceptive pills.

Environmental Hazards

Altitude Sickness (Soroche) Much of Bolivia lies at high altitude and most of the country's population lives above 3000m. The atmospheric density at Potosí, the most lofty city at 4070m, is less than two-thirds its value at sea level; and at 5345m Chacaltaya, near La Paz, it's only about half. Water in La Paz boils at 88°C (as opposed to 100°C); the

stall speed for planes landing in La Paz is nearly twice that for Santa Cruz, at just 427m; and drivers from Santa Cruz to La Paz must let air out of their tires (in the opposite direction, they must add air).

The human body is also affected by an increase in altitude, and in much of the highland and Altiplano regions of Bolivia, travelers may experience altitude-related sickness. On a rapid ascent to high altitude, say a flight from Lima at sea level to El Alto airport in La Paz at 4010m, your body lacks time to adapt to the lower pressure and consequent lack of oxygen. In an attempt to compensate for the decreased oxygen and air pressure, the heart and lungs must work harder.

Symptoms of altitude sickness include breathlessness, a racing pulse, lethargy, tiredness, insomnia, loss of appetite, headache and dehydration. These symptoms are sometimes accompanied by nausea and vomiting. Newly arrived visitors invariably experience a condition locally known as *soroche* (altitude sickness), and should take it easy for the first few days until they've had time to acclimatize.

There is no medical evidence that the traditional remedy of chewing coca leaves or drinking *mate de coca* (coca leaf tea) does more than provide liquids and deaden some of the body's senses, but numerous testimonials suggest that it does help with the acclimatization process. Rural Bolivians also make tea from other high-altitude plants – the leaves of *pupusa* and *chachakoma* and the flower of *flor de puna* – to counter soroche. The best remedy, however, is a day or two of rest while the body begins its acclimatization process. In any case, it's essential to drink large quantities of water – up to 3L or more daily.

For altitude-related discomfort, especially on brief ascents to over 4500m, mild painkillers can be taken. For headache, a nonaspirin pain-reliever such as acetaminophen (paracetamol, Tylenol) may be used.

Some local soroche remedies, such as Micoren (or the popular Sorojchi – a blend of Micoren, caffeine and aspirin), actually slow the heart rate, forcing you to breathe more deeply and thereby promoting acclimatization. Using this rather drastic approach can do more harm than good – it's akin to stopping your car by hitting a wall. Rather than take chances with your health, it's probably better to allow your body to make its own adjustments.

If you're ascending quickly to high altitudes (eg, from Lima to La Paz), acetazolamide (Diamox) – available only by prescription – is sometimes used as a prophylactic to help with acclimatization. It should be taken in 250mg doses four times daily starting 24 to 48 hours before your arrival at high altitude. Note, however, that acetazolamide can mask the warning signs of acute mountain sickness, and because it's a diuretic, it may cause dehydration. To compensate loss of liquid, drink at least 3 to 4L of water daily. Another side effect is tingling in the fingers and toes. People with sulfa allergies should not take acetazolamide.

Acute Mountain Sickness (AMS) Acute mountain sickness (AMS), a more serious condition than soroche, is experienced by climbers and hikers who climb too high too quickly, and it can also strike visitors to La Paz. There are two forms of malignant AMS: high-altitude pulmonary edema (HAPE), and high-altitude cerebral edema (HACE), both of which are fatal if untreated. The only treatment is immediate descent to a lower altitude.

Susceptibility to AMS varies greatly between individuals. Some people start feeling ill at altitudes as low as 2450m; others feel fine at 6000m. In general, AMS is rare below 2450m. To ascend to altitudes of over 5000m for any length of time (longer than a few hours at Chacaltaya), first spend a week at the altitude of La Paz or the Altiplano. Climbers and hikers going seriously high should seek medical advice and be familiar with expedition rules and methods for dealing with AMS.

Even with acclimatization you may still have trouble adjusting. Breathlessness; a dry irritative cough (which may produce pink, frothy sputum); severe headache; loss of appetite; nausea; and sometimes vomiting, are

all danger signs. Increasing tiredness, confusion, lack of coordination and balance, vision problems (including blindness), speech difficulties and irrational behavior indicate even more advanced problems. Any of these symptoms individually, even just a persistent headache, can be a warning; if it persists or grows worse, get the sufferer down to a lower altitude immediately – even in the middle of the night! Every minute counts and it is easier to assist an unwell person who can still walk than to carry an unconscious victim. If someone is unconscious and vomiting, place them on their side to prevent the vomit entering their lungs. For anyone suffering from severe AMS in La Paz or elsewhere on the Altiplano, seek hospital treatment or descend to a lower altitude immediately.

Minimizing Risk The best way to minimize the risk of AMS is to ascend slowly. There's normally little problem ascending to around 3000m, but above that, the body needs time to acclimatize. A gain of about 300m per day is recommended but since that may be impractical (using that guideline, it would take three days to cross La Paz, from the Zona Sur to El Alto!), the best advice is to follow the climbers' adage: climb high, sleep low.

Dehydration can result from increased sweating and loss of moisture through accelerated respiration in cold, dry air, so when you trek at high altitude, increase your intake of liquids. Eat light meals high in energy-rich carbohydrates and avoid smoking, which reduces the amount of oxygen the blood can carry. Alcohol should also be avoided since it increases urine output and results in further dehydration. You should also avoid sedatives, as they may mask symptoms of AMS.

Most importantly, do not trek alone. AMS reduces good judgment and symptoms are often ignored or not perceived by the victim. If you are suffering from any symptoms of AMS, don't go higher, and avoid exertion until the symptoms have disappeared. Light outdoor activity is better than bed rest.

Doctors and climbers who want to keep up with the latest research on high-altitude medicine can contact the International Society for Mountain Medicine (fax 41-36-553852; Membership Secretary, Arztpraxis, CH-3822 Lauterbrunnen, Switzerland). Its newsletter is available by subscription for SF50 per year. In Bolivia, contact the Clínica del Instituto de Patología en la Altura or IPPA (☎ 02-245394; fax 02-229504; zubieta@ oxygen.bo; Avenida Saavedra 2302, Casilla 2852, La Paz) for information or physicals before climbing to high altitude. You can also see their website www.geocities.com/capecanaveral/6280.

Hypothermia Hypothermia is a dangerous lowering of the body temperature. It is caused by exhaustion and exposure to cold, damp, wet or windy weather, which can occur anywhere in Bolivia. Hypothermia is a threat whenever a person is exposed to the elements at temperatures below 10°C.

Symptoms of hypothermia include exhaustion, numbness (particularly of the toes and fingers), shivering, slurred speech, irrational or violent behavior, lethargy, stumbling, dizzy spells, muscle cramps and violent bursts of energy. Irrationality may take the form of sufferers claiming they are warm and trying to take off their clothes.

The best treatment is of course to get the sufferer to shelter and give them warm drinks and a hot bath if possible (which it probably won't be in Bolivia). Wet clothing should be changed or removed – no clothing at all is better than wet garments. The sufferer should lie down, wrapped in a sleeping bag or blanket to preserve body heat. Another person may lie down with them in order to provide as much warmth as possible. If no improvement is noticed within a few minutes, seek help but don't leave the victim alone while doing so. The body heat of another person is of more immediate importance than medical attention.

Sunburn The Altiplano and much of the highland regions of Bolivia lie within the tropics at elevations greater than 3000m. In many areas, the atmosphere there is too thin to screen out much of the dangerous ultraviolet radiation that is absorbed and deflected at lower altitudes. The use of a strong sunscreen is essential; serious burns can occur after even brief exposure. Don't neglect to apply sunscreen to any area of exposed skin, especially if you're near water or snow. On Lake Titicaca and in the high mountains, reflected rays can burn as severely as direct rays.

Sunscreen is unfortunately quite expensive in Bolivia, and it's also difficult to find one with a rating high enough for fair skin, so you may want to bring some from home. A hat is also essential to shade your face and protect your scalp, and sunglasses will prevent eye irritation (especially if you wear contact lenses). At higher altitudes (above about 2500m), you'll need sunglasses such as those used by mountaineers, which screen 100% of incoming UV.

Some people also experience a rash caused by photosensitivity in high altitudes. This can be treated with light applications of cortisone cream to affected areas (never use cortisone near your face, however).

Prickly Heat Prickly heat is an itchy rash caused by excessive perspiration trapped under the skin. It usually strikes those newly arrived in a hot climate whose pores have not opened enough to accommodate profuse sweating. Frequent baths and application of talcum powder will help relieve the itch.

Heat Exhaustion In the tropical lowlands, Yungas and Chaco regions, heat combined with humidity and exposure to the sun can be oppressive and leave you feeling lethargic, irritable and dazed. A cool swim or lazy afternoon in the shade will do wonders to improve your mood. You'll also need to drink lots of liquids and eat salty foods in order to replenish what you've lost during sweating.

Serious dehydration or salt deficiency can lead to heat exhaustion. Take time to acclimatize to high temperatures, and make sure you drink sufficient liquids – don't rely on feeling thirsty to indicate when you should drink. Always carry a bottle of water with you on long trips. Salt deficiency, which can be brought on by diarrhea or nausea, is characterized by fatigue, lethargy, headaches, giddiness and muscle cramps. Salt tablets will probably solve the problem.

Fungal Infections Hot weather fungal infections are most likely to occur on the scalp, between the toes or fingers (athlete's foot), in the groin (jock itch) and on the body (ringworm). You get ringworm (which is a fungal infection, not a worm) from infected animals or by walking on damp areas, such as shower floors.

To prevent fungal infections wear loose, comfortable clothes, avoid artificial fibers, wash frequently and dry carefully. If you do get an infection, wash the infected area daily with a disinfectant or medicated soap and water, and rinse and dry well. Apply an antifungal medication (eg, Tinaderm). Try to expose the infected area to air or sunlight as much as possible and change your towels and underwear often, washing them in hot water.

Motion Sickness If you're susceptible to motion sickness, come prepared, because Bolivian roads and railways aren't exactly velvety smooth. If an antihistamine such as Dramamine works for you, take some along. Eating very lightly before and during a trip will reduce the chances of motion sickness. Try to find a place that minimizes disturbance, near the wing on aircraft or near the center on buses. Fresh air almost always helps but reading or cigarette smoking (or even being around someone else's smoke) normally makes matters worse.

Commercial motion sickness preparations (eg, scopolamine or Dramamine), which can pupil dilation and cause drowsiness, have to be taken before the trip; after you've begun to feel ill, it's too late. Ginger can be used as a natural motion-sickness preventative and is available in capsule form.

Infectious Diseases

Diarrhea Sooner or later – unless you're exceptional – you'll get Montezuma's (or Atahuallpa's) Revenge, Turista or any of a dozen other names for plain old travelers'

diarrhea, so you may as well accept the inevitable. The problem is caused not so much by poor sanitation or 'bad' food as by dietary changes and lack of resistance to local strains of bacteria. Your susceptibility will depend largely on how much you've been exposed to foreign bacteria and what your guts are used to.

The first thing to remember is that every case of diarrhea is not dysentery, so don't panic and start stuffing yourself with pills. A few rushed toilet trips with no other symptoms isn't usually indicative of a serious problem. Moderate diarrhea, involving half-a-dozen loose movements in a day, is more of a nuisance. Dehydration is the main danger with any diarrhea, particularly in children, where dehydration can occur quite quickly.

Fluid replacement remains the mainstay of management. Try to starve out the bugs. If possible, eat nothing, rest and avoid traveling. Weak black tea with a little sugar, soda water, or flat soft drinks diluted 50% with bottled water are all good. If you can't hack that, keep to dry toast, biscuits and black tea.

With severe diarrhea a rehydration solution is necessary to replace minerals and salts. Commercially available oral rehydration salts (ORS) are very useful; add the contents of one sachet to a liter of boiled or bottled water. In an emergency you can make up a solution of 8 teaspoons of sugar to a liter of boiled water and provide salted cracker biscuits at the same time. Stick to a bland diet as you recover; try some yogurt but stay away from other dairy products, sweets and fruit.

Loperamide (Lomotil or Imodium) can be used to temporarily 'plug the drain' but they do not actually cure the problem. Only use these drugs if absolutely necessary (for example, if you *must* travel) and under all circumstances, remember that fluid replacement is the most important thing. In certain situations antibiotics may be indicated:

• Watery diarrhea with blood and mucus

• Watery diarrhea with fever and lethargy

• Persistent diarrhea for more than 48 hours

• Severe diarrhea, if it is logistically difficult to stay in one place

The recommended drugs (adults only) would be either norfloxacin 400mg twice daily for three days or ciprofloxacin 500mg twice daily for three days. Bismuth subsalicylate (as in Pepto-Bismol) has also been used successfully (it's unavailable in Australia). The dosage for adults is two tablets or 30ml and for children it is one tablet or 10ml. This dose can be repeated every 30 minutes to one hour, with no more than eight doses in a 24-hour period.

The drug of choice in children would be co-trimoxazole (Bactrim, Septrin, Resprim). A five-day course is given but dosage is dependent on weight. Ampicillin has been recommended in the past and may still be an alternative.

If you don't recover after a couple of days, it may be necessary to visit a doctor to be tested for other problems that could include giardiasis, dysentery, cholera and so on.

Giardiasis The parasite causing this intestinal disorder is present in contaminated water. 'Giardia' is prevalent in tropical climates and is first characterized by a swelling of the stomach, pale-colored feces, diarrhea, frequent gas, headache and later by nausea and depression. Symptoms will appear after a 14-day incubation period, but may later disappear for a few days and then return; this can go on for several weeks.

Many doctors recommend 250mg metronidazole (Flagyl) twice daily for three days. Metronidazole however, can cause side effects and some doctors prefer to treat giardiasis with two grams of tinidazole (Fasigyn or Tinaba), taken in one fell swoop to knock the bug out hard and fast. If it doesn't work the first time, the treatment can be repeated for up to three days.

Dysentery This serious illness is caused by consumption of contaminated food or water and is characterized by severe diarrhea, often with blood or mucus in the feces, and painful gut cramps. There are two types: bacillary dysentery, which is uncomfortable but not enduring, and amoebic dysentery, which, as its name suggests, is caused by amoebas. This variety is much more difficult to treat and is more persistent.

Bacillary dysentery is characterized by a high fever and rapid onset; symptoms include headache, vomiting and stomach pains. It doesn't generally last more than a week, but it is highly contagious, and because it's caused by bacteria, it responds well to antibiotics.

Since the symptoms of bacillary dysentery themselves are actually the best treatment – diarrhea and fever are both trying to rid the body of the infection – you may just want to hole up for a few days and let it run its course. If activity or travel is absolutely necessary during the infection, you can take either Imodium or Lomotil to keep things under control until reaching a more convenient location to R & R (rest and run).

Often recommended is norfloxacin, which should be taken in 400mg doses twice daily for seven days, or ciprofloxacin, 500mg twice daily for seven days. If you're unable to find either of these drugs, an alternative is co-trimoxazole (Bactrim, Septrin, Resprim) twice daily for seven days. This is a sulfa drug (each tablet contains 400mg sulphametoxozole and 160mg trimethoprim) and must not be used in people with a known sulfa allergy. For children, co-trimoxazole is a reasonable first-line treatment.

Amoebic dysentery, or amoebiasis, builds up more slowly and is more dangerous. It is caused by protozoans, or amoebic parasites (*Entamoeba histolytica*), which are also transmitted through contaminated food or water. Once they've invaded, they live in the lower intestinal tract and cause heavy and often bloody diarrhea, fever, tenderness in the liver and intense abdominal pain. If left untreated, ulceration and inflammation of the colon and rectum can become very serious. If you see blood in your feces over two or three days, seek medical attention.

A stool test is necessary to diagnose which kind of dysentery you have, so you should seek medical help urgently. In case of an emergency, norfloxacin or ciprofloxacin (for doses, see the Diarrhea section above) can be used as presumptive treatment for bacillary dysentery, and metronidazole (Flagyl) for amoebic dysentery.

For amoebic dysentery, the recommended adult dosage of metronidazole is one 750mg to 800mg capsule three times daily for five to 10 days. Children from eight to 12 years old should have half the adult dose; the dosage for younger children is one-third the adult dose. Metronidazole should not be taken by pregnant women. An alternative is tinidazole (Tinaba or Fasigyn), taken as a 2-gram daily dose for two to three days. Alcohol must be avoided during treatment and for 48 hours afterwards.

The best method of preventing dysentery is, of course, to avoid eating or drinking contaminated items.

Cholera The bacteria responsible for cholera are waterborne, so attention to the rules of eating and drinking should protect you. The cholera vaccine is between 20 and 50% effective and short-lived (three to six months) according to most authorities, and it can have some side effects. Vaccination is recommended, but is not legally required by Bolivian authorities. The risk is low to moderate.

Cholera is characterized by a sudden onset of acute diarrhea with 'rice water' stools, vomiting, muscular cramps and extreme weakness. You need medical attention but your first concern should be rehydration. Drink as much water as you can – if it refuses to stay down, keep drinking anyway. If there is likely to be an appreciable delay in reaching medical treatment, begin a course of tetracycline, which, incidentally, should not be administered to children or pregnant women (be sure to check the expiry date, since old tetracycline can become toxic). An alternative drug would be Ampicillin. Remember that although antibiotics might kill the bacteria, a toxin produced by the bacteria causes the massive fluid loss. Fluid replacement is by far the most important aspect of treatment.

Viral Gastroenteritis This is not caused by bacteria but, as the name implies, a virus. It is characterized by stomach cramps, diarrhea, and sometimes by vomiting and a slight fever. All you can do is rest and keep drinking as much water as possible.

Hepatitis This incapacitating disease is caused by a virus that attacks the liver. Hepatitis A, which is the most common strain in South America, is contracted through contact with contaminated food, water, cutlery, toilets or individuals. It is a very common problem among travelers to areas with poor sanitation.

Symptoms include fever, chills, headache, fatigue, feelings of weakness and aches and pains, followed by loss of appetite, nausea, vomiting, abdominal pain, dark urine, light colored feces and jaundiced skin; the whites of the eyes may turn a sickly yellow. You should seek medical advice, but in general there is not much you can do apart from rest, drink lots of fluids, eat lightly and keep to a diet high in proteins and vitamins. Avoid fatty foods, alcohol and cigarettes. People who have had hepatitis must forgo alcohol for six months after the illness, to allow the liver time to recover.

If you contract hepatitis A during a short trip to South America, you might want to make arrangements to go home. If you can afford the time, however, and have a reliable traveling companion who can bring food and water, the best cure is to stay where you are, find a few good books and only leave bed to go to the toilet. After a month of so, you should feel like living again.

The best preventative measures available are either the recently introduced long-term hepatitis A vaccine (Havrix); or a immune globulin jab before departure and booster shots every three or four months thereafter (beware of unsanitary needles!). A jab is also in order if you come in contact with any infected person (that is, if you haven't had a hepatitis A vaccine); and if *you* come down with hepatitis, anyone who has been in recent contact with you should have a shot too. However, if symptoms of hepatitis are already present, do not get a shot.

Hepatitis B, formerly known as serum hepatitis, can only be caught by sexual contact with an infected person, unsterilized needles, blood transfusions or by skin penetration – such as tattooing, shaving or having your ears pierced. If type B is diagnosed, fatal liver failure is a real possibility and the victim should be sent home and/or hospitalized immediately. Immune globulin is not effective against hepatitis B.

The symptoms of type B are much the same as type A except that they are more severe and may lead to irreparable liver damage or even liver cancer or fatal liver failure. Although there is no treatment for hepatitis B, an effective prophylactic vaccine is readily available in most countries. The immunization schedule requires two injections at least a month apart followed by a third dose five months after the second. If you anticipate contact with blood or other bodily secretions, perhaps as a health-care worker or through sexual contact with the local population, you should get a hepatitis B vaccination.

To avoid other strains of hepatitis, such as hepatitis C, it's probably best to follow the same precautions as for hepatitis A and B.

Typhoid Contaminated food and water are responsible for typhoid fever, another gut infection that travels the fecal-oral route. Vaccination against typhoid isn't 100% effective. Since it can be very serious, medical attention is necessary.

Early symptoms are like those of many other travelers' illnesses – you may feel as though you have a bad cold or the flu combined with a headache, sore throat and a fever. The fever rises slowly until it reaches 40°C or more, while the pulse slowly drops, unlike a normal fever, in which the pulse increases. These symptoms may be accompanied by nausea, diarrhea or constipation.

In the second week, the fever and slow pulse continue and a few pink spots may appear on the body. Trembling, delirium, weakness, diarrhea, weight loss and dehydration set in. If there are no further complications, the fever and symptoms will slowly fade during the third week. Medical attention is essential, however, since typhoid is extremely infectious and possible

complications include pneumonia, peritonitis or perforated bowel.

When feverish, the victim should be kept cool. Watch for dehydration. The drug of choice is ciprofloxacin at a dose of 1 gram daily for 14 days, but it's expensive and may not be available. The alternative, chloramphenicol, has been the mainstay of treatment for many years. In many countries it's still the preferred antibiotic but Ampicillin has fewer side affects. The adult dosage for chloramphenicol is 500mg, four times a day for 14 days. Children aged between eight and 12 years should have half the adult dose; younger children should have one-third the adult dose. People who are allergic to penicillin should not be given Ampicillin.

Tetanus This potentially fatal disease is found in undeveloped tropical areas and is difficult to treat, but it's easily prevented by vaccination (which is highly recommended). Tetanus occurs when a wound becomes infected by a bacterium that lives in soil and in human or animal feces. Clean all cuts, punctures and bites. Tetanus is also known as lockjaw and the first symptom may be difficulty in swallowing, a stiffening of the jaw and neck followed by painful convulsions of the jaw and whole body.

Rabies This is a fatal viral infection. A prophylactic rabies vaccination should be considered if you intend to travel to places more than two days away from medical help, or if you anticipate spending a lot of time around animals.

Throughout Bolivia, but especially in the humid lowlands, rodents and bats carry the rabies virus and pass it on to larger animals and humans. Avoid any animal that appears to be foaming at the mouth or acting strangely. Stray dogs are particularly notable carriers, as are bats, especially vampire bats, which are common in the Amazon Basin. Make sure you cover all parts of your body at night, especially your feet and scalp.

Any bite, scratch or even lick from an unfamiliar mammal should be cleaned immediately and thoroughly. Scrub with soap and running water for at least five minutes and then clean with iodine or an alcohol solution. This greatly reduces your risk of contracting rabies, but if there's any possibility that the animal is infected with rabies, you must still seek medical help. (Even if the animal isn't rabid, all bites should be treated seriously as they can become infected or result in tetanus.)

If you're bitten or scratched by a suspect animal, you must have a booster or, if you're not immune, a course of vaccine and immunoglobulin. The virus is incurable and fatal if it reaches the brain and the symptoms appear, but it moves very slowly; although you should seek medical treatment as quickly as possible, there's no reason to panic.

Rabies vaccinations and treatment are available at the Centro Epidemiológico Departamental La Paz (see Medical Services in the La Paz chapter).

Meningococcal Meningitis This very serious disease is spread by close contact with people who carry it in their throats and noses. They probably aren't aware they are carriers and pass it on through coughs and sneezes. Meningococcal meningitis attacks the brain and can be fatal. A scattered blotchy rash, fever, severe headache, sensitivity to light and stiffness in the neck preventing forward bending of the head are the first symptoms. Death can occur within a few hours, so immediate treatment with large doses of penicillin is vital. If intravenous administration is impossible, it should be given intramuscularly. Vaccination offers reasonable protection for over a year, but you should check for reports of recent outbreaks and try to avoid affected areas.

Tuberculosis If you will be traveling for more than three months in South America, you should consider TB risk. As most healthy adults do not develop symptoms, a skin test before and after travel to determine whether exposure has occurred is recommended. Vaccination for children who will be traveling for more than three months is recommended.

Insect-Borne Diseases

Malaria This serious disease is spread by mosquito bites, but it's curable, as long as you seek medical help when symptoms occur, either during your travels or at home. The areas of greatest risk include the Amazon Basin, the Chaco and the eastern lowlands. Symptoms include loss of appetite, fever, chills and sweating, which may subside and recur. Without treatment malaria can develop more serious, potentially fatal effects.

There are a number of different types of malaria. The one of most concern is *Plasmodium falciparum*, which is responsible for the very serious cerebral malaria.

Prevention The most effective form of malaria prevention, of course, is to avoid being bitten by mosquitoes. The mosquitoes that transmit malaria bite from dusk to dawn but you can avoid bites by covering bare skin with trousers and long-sleeved shirts. Also, avoid strongly scented perfumes or aftershave, and sleep under a mosquito net. During the day, it helps to wear light-colored clothing, and use a repellent containing DEET (diethylmetatoluamide) on

AREA OF MALARIA RISK

Guayaramerín
Riberalta
Cobija
Trinidad
Rurrenabaque
Puerto Villarroel
Santa Cruz

Area of Malaria Risk

exposed areas of skin. Note, however, that DEET is a strong toxin and high concentrations may be especially harmful to children; an alternative would be Mosi-Guard Natural, which matches the efficacy of DEET but isn't so harsh on the skin.

Next best – but hardly 100% effective – is a course of antimalarials, which is normally taken two weeks before, during and several weeks after traveling in malarial areas. The drug-resistant status of different malarial strains is constantly in flux. Expert advice should be sought regarding your choice of antimalarials. Factors to consider include the risk of exposure to malaria in areas to be visited, your medical history, and your age and pregnancy status. You should also discuss with your doctor the potential side effects of any prescribed prophylaxis, and work out the ratio of the benefits versus the risks. It's also worth noting that the use of prophylaxis often results in mutation and resistance in the parasites that cause malaria, thus affecting the efficacy of the drugs locally used for malaria treatment.

A commonly recommended prophylaxis for lowland areas of South America is chloroquine, although local strains are growing increasingly resistant to it. As a result, many doctors are recommending some newer drugs, such as doxycycline (Vibramycin, Doryx), tetracycline and mefloquine (Lariam). Don't switch to chloroquine, however, if you've previously been taking mefloquine, as they make a potentially dangerous combination. Note also that Lariam has been associated with serious and distressing side effects, and should only be used in conjunction with a doctor's advice.

Diagnosis & Treatment Malarial symptoms include (in this order) gradual loss of appetite, general disinterest in one's surroundings, malaise, weakness, diarrhea, periodic fever (lasting four or five hours), severe headache, vomiting and – if it reaches the potentially fatal cerebral stage – hallucinations and periodic paralysis. If you develop malarial symptoms, seek medical advice immediately. Diagnosis is confirmed by a simple blood test, preferably during the fever stage, when the parasite is active in the bloodstream.

Chagas' Disease There is very little possibility of contracting this disease, which is caused by a parasite *(Trypanosoma cruzi)* transmitted through the bite of the ominously named assassin bug – locally known as the *vinchuca* beetle. This beetle mainly inhabits thatch and daub huts from the tropical lowlands up to 2800m elevation.

The parasite causes progressive constriction and hardening of blood vessels, swelling of internal organs and increasing strain on the heart. At present there is no cure and Chagas' is fatal over a period of years. Mind-boggling estimates suggest that at least 25% of Bolivia's population suffers from this disease.

The best prevention is to avoid thatched-roof huts and to use a mosquito net or a hammock if you sleep in a thatched building; insecticides and repellents will also help to minimize risks. Bites are generally painful, and may cause a slight, hard violet-colored swelling at the site of the bite or around the eyes. If you are bitten, wash the affected area well and don't scratch the bite or the parasite may be rubbed into the wound. The disease is only treatable if caught early, so if you are bitten, seek medical attention or perhaps even visit the Chagas Institute at the University of San Simón in Cochabamba. A blood test six weeks after the bite will confirm whether or not the disease is present.

Dengue Fever Incidences of dengue fever have been reported in low-lying jungle areas, especially in Beni and Pando departments. There is no pharmaceutical prophylaxis for this disease, which is transmitted by the *Aecdes aegypti* mosquito. As usual, the main preventative measure is to avoid mosquito bites. Unlike the malarial *anopheles* mosquito, the species carrying dengue is active during the day and found mainly in urban areas, in and around human dwellings. A sudden onset of fever, headaches, nausea, vomiting and severe joint and muscle pains are the first signs; about four days after exposure, a 'pinprick' rash – which is in fact capillary hemorrhaging – may appear on the trunk of the body and spreads to the limbs and face (At this stage, the disease may have begun to progress into potentially fatal hemorrhagic fever, or DHF, which is characterized by heavy capillary bleeding; avoid using aspirin, as it will only increase hemorrhaging.) Normally, the immune system will kick in and the fever will subside, signaling recovery. If not, however, professional attention, preferably in a hospital, should be sought immediately.

Leishmaniasis This disease – which can become truly horrible if untreated – is a protozoan transmitted at night in the bite of the Amazonian blood-sucking sandfly. This fly – known in Bolivia as the mariguí – is ubiquitous throughout lowland Bolivia, particularly in moist forest. The best prevention is to avoid sandfly bites by covering up and using repellents. The first symptom is a bug bite that won't heal (it's easy to confuse with an infected tick bite). The external version of the disease, cutaneous leishmaniasis, attacks the skin and may leave severe scarring; the internal form, known as *kala-azar*, or visceral leishmaniasis, attacks the liver, spleen or bone marrow and can cause infection, organ enlargement and anemia.

If left untreated, the infection may become systemic and begin to attack the body's cartilage, and eventually lead to death by gangrene – not pleasant at all. The prescribed treatment is a course of drugs containing antimony.

Worms Worms are common throughout the humid tropics. They can live on unwashed vegetables or in undercooked meat, or you can pick them up through your skin by walking barefoot. Infestations may not be obvious for some time and although they aren't generally serious, they can cause health problems if left untreated. If there's a chance you have contracted them, take a stool test when you return home. Once confirmed, over-the-counter medication is available to clear it out.

Myiasis This very unpleasant affliction is caused by the larvae of tropical flies, which lay their eggs on damp or sweaty clothing. One of the most common offenders in lowland Bolivia is the botfly. The eggs of this fly hatch and the larvae burrow into the skin, producing a painful lump (or, if it becomes infected, an ugly boil) as they develop. To kill the invader, place drops of hydrogen peroxide, alcohol or oil over the boil to cut off its air supply, then squeeze the lump to remove the bug. However revolting the process, at this stage the problem is solved.

Yellow Fever Yellow fever is endemic in much of South America, including the Amazon Basin and southern lowland areas. This viral disease, which is transmitted to humans by mosquitoes, first manifests itself with fever, headache, abdominal pain and vomiting. There may appear to be a brief recovery before it progresses into its more severe stages when liver failure becomes a possibility. There is no treatment apart from keeping the fever as low as possible and avoiding dehydration. The yellow-fever vaccination, which is highly recommended for every traveler in South America, offers good protection for 10 years.

Cuts, Bites & Stings

Cuts & Scratches The warm, moist conditions of the tropical lowlands invite and promote the growth of 'wee beasties' that would be thwarted in more temperate climates. As a result, even a small cut or scratch can become painfully infected and lead to more serious problems.

The best treatment for cuts is to frequently cleanse the affected area with soap and water and apply an antiseptic cream. Where possible, avoid using band-aids and bandages, which keep wounds moist. If, despite your ministrations, the wound becomes tender and inflamed, then use of a mild, broad-spectrum antibiotic may be warranted.

Snakebite Although threat of snakebite is minimal in Bolivia, you may wish to take precautions if you're walking around the forested northern areas. The most dangerous snakes native to Bolivia are the bushmaster and the fer-de-lance, which inhabit the northern and eastern lowlands. To minimize chances of being bitten, wear boots, socks and long trousers when walking through undergrowth. A good pair of canvas gaiters will further protect your legs. Don't put your hands into holes and crevices and be careful when collecting firewood. Check shoes, clothing and sleeping bags before use.

Snakebites do not cause instantaneous death and antivenins are usually available, but it is vital that you make a positive identification of the snake in question, or at the very least, have a detailed description of it. Keep the victim calm and still, wrap the bitten limb as you would for a sprain and then attach a splint to immobilize it. Tourniquets and suction on the wound are now comprehensively discredited and should not be applied. Seek medical help immediately, and if possible, bring the dead snake along for identification (but don't attempt to catch it if there is even a remote chance of being bitten again). Bushwalkers and hikers who are (wisely) concerned about snakebite should carry a field guide with photos and detailed descriptions of the possible perpetrators.

Insects Ants, gnats, mosquitoes, bees and flies – especially the vicious sandfly known as the mariguí – are just as annoying in Bolivia as they are anywhere. Cover yourself well with clothing and use insect repellent on exposed skin. Burning incense and sleeping under mosquito nets in air-conditioned rooms or under fans also lowers the risk of being bitten. When walking in humid or densely foliated areas, wear light cotton trousers and shoes rather than shorts and sandals. Regardless of temperature, never wear shorts or thongs in the forest, and use an effective insect repellent. Astringent Australian tea-tree oil works remarkably well on noninfected bites, to dry up the bite and minimize the itching.

Unless you're allergic, bee and wasp stings are more painful than dangerous. Calamine lotion offers some relief and ice packs will reduce pain and swelling. Anyone with bee-sting allergy should avoid parts of the Amazon Basin – particularly Noel Kempff Mercado National Park – during the enormous bee hatch-outs, which can occur anytime between September and December.

Scorpion and centipede stings are normally more painful than dangerous, and large, hairy spiders – as well as several smaller black ones – may deliver an agonizing bite. If you're camping in the northern bush, check your socks, shoes, hat and sleeping bag before inserting any part of your body.

Body lice and scabies mites are also common, and a number of shampoos and creams are available to eliminate them. In addition to hair and skin, clothing and bedding should be washed thoroughly to prevent further infestation.

Sexually Transmitted Diseases

Gonorrhea & Syphilis Sexual contact with an infected partner can spread a number of unpleasant diseases. Abstinence is the only guaranteed preventative measure, but if this isn't for you, use of a condom will considerably lessen your risks. Gonorrhea and syphilis are the most common of these diseases; in men they first appear as sores, blisters or rashes around the genitals and pain or discharge when urinating. Symptoms may be less marked or not evident at all in women. The symptoms of syphilis eventually disappear completely but the disease continues and may cause severe problems in later years. Antibiotics are used to treat both syphilis and gonorrhea.

HIV/AIDS HIV, the Human Immunodeficiency Virus, may develop into AIDS, Acquired Immune Deficiency Syndrome. Although HIV/AIDS hasn't yet reached staggering proportions in Bolivia, it is prevalent in neighboring Brazil to a degree unfamiliar to most Western travelers, and should be a concern to all visitors.

Any exposure to blood, blood products or bodily fluids may put the individual at risk. Although in developed countries it's most commonly spread through intravenous drug abuse and male homosexual activity, in South America the virus is transmitted primarily through heterosexual activity. Apart from abstinence, the most effective preventative is always to practice safe sex using condoms. It is impossible to detect the HIV-positive status of an otherwise healthy-looking person without a blood test.

HIV/AIDS can also be spread through infected blood transfusions. If you must have an emergency transfusion, private clinics are generally a better option than public hospitals but if you're able, you should still try to make absolutely certain that the blood in question is safe.

HIV is also spread by dirty needles – vaccinations, acupuncture, tattooing and ear or nose piercing are potentially as dangerous as intravenous drug use if the equipment isn't clean. If you do need an injection, ask to see the syringe unwrapped in front of you, or buy a new syringe from a pharmacy and ask the doctor to use it. You may also want to carry a couple of syringes, in case of emergency.

Fear of HIV infection should never preclude treatment for serious medical conditions. Although there may be a risk of infection, it is very small indeed.

Women's Health

Gynecological Concerns Poor diet, lowered resistance due to use of antibiotics, and even contraceptive pills can lead to vaginal infections when traveling in hot climates. To prevent the worst of it, maintain good personal hygiene, wear cotton underwear and skirts or loose-fitting trousers.

Yeast infections, characterized by a rash, itch and discharge, can be treated with a vinegar or lemon juice douche or with yogurt. Nystatin, miconazole or clotrimazole suppositories are the usual medical prescription. Trichomoniasis and gardnerella are more serious infections that cause a smelly discharge and sometimes a burning sensation during urination. If a vinegar and water douche is not effective, medical attention should be sought.

Metronidazole (Flagyl) is the most frequently prescribed drug. Male sexual partners must also be treated.

Pregnancy Most miscarriages occur during the first trimester of pregnancy, so this is the most risky time to be traveling. The last three months should also be spent within reasonable reach of good medical care since serious problems can develop at this stage as well. Pregnant women should avoid all unnecessary medication, but vaccinations and malarial prophylactics should still be taken where possible. Additional care should be taken to prevent illness and particular attention to diet and proper nutrition will significantly lessen the chances of complications.

WOMEN TRAVELERS

Bolivia is still very much a man's country, and for a woman traveling alone, this can prove frustrating. Things are changing – Bolivia has had a woman president, Lidia Gueiller Tejada (1979-80), and from 1993 to 1995, Mónica Medina de Palenque served as mayor of La Paz. Even so, the machismo mind-set remains and the mere fact that you appear to be unmarried and far from your home and family may cause you to appear suspiciously disreputable.

Because many South American men have become acquainted with foreign women through such reliable media as girlie magazines and North American films and TV, the concept of *gringa fácil* ('loose foreign woman'), has developed. Since Bolivia has cultural roots in southern Europe, it has been subjected to over four centuries of machismo and many men consider foreign women – especially those traveling alone – to be fair and willing game. Fortunately, the recent increase in tourism to Bolivia has meant that locals are becoming more accustomed to seeing Western travelers, including unaccompanied women. This has significantly reduced the incidence of sexual harassment, but in some places, you may still face unwanted attention.

It may be useful to remember that at least some of the time, problem behavior is the consequence of simple ignorance.

Unequivocal insults or blatant arrogance on a woman's part may derail obnoxious suitors, but more often, it will simply amuse them and may even reinforce the undesirable behavior. If you can't ignore the comments – as well-bred Bolivian women would be expected to do – it may help to convey (in Spanish) that you expect to be treated with more respect. Uttering a thinly veiled insult, such as '*hombres civilizados respetan más a las mujeres*' ('civilized men have more respect for women') may hit the mark.

For your part, bear in mind that modesty is expected of women in much of Spanish-speaking Latin America. Short sleeves are more or less acceptable but hemlines shouldn't be above knee level and trousers should be loose-fitting. In general, the lower the altitude in Bolivia, the more liberal the dress code. The best advice is to watch the standards of well-dressed Bolivian women in any particular area and follow their example.

A 100% effective alternative is to find a male traveling companion, but then you may have to contend with being ignored while Bolivians direct their comments to your companion – even if you speak Spanish and he doesn't! In any case, if you prefer to travel alone, it's wise to avoid such male domains as bars, sports matches, mines, construction sites and the like. It's all right to catch a lift on a *camión* (truck), especially if there are lots of other people waiting, but otherwise, women shouldn't hitch alone.

GAY & LESBIAN TRAVELERS

Naturally, homosexuality exists in Bolivia and is fairly widespread among rural indigenous communities. It's also perfectly legal (though the constitution does prohibit same-sex marriages), but the overwhelmingly Catholic society tends to both deny and suppress it, and to be openly gay in Bolivia limits vocational and social opportunities and may cause family ostracism. The Bolivian government merely defines homosexuality as 'a problem.' Bolivia currently has three active gay rights lobby groups: MGLP Libertad, Casilla 10471, La Paz; Dignidad, in Cochabamba; and UNELDYS, in Santa Cruz. They are working to launch a national newspaper and take their cause to the government.

Gay bars and venues are limited to the larger cities, but due to bashings and police raids, they come and go with some regularity. The only one I'm currently aware of is Cherry, in La Paz, but I suspect there must be several in liberal Cochabamba and cosmopolitan Santa Cruz. As for hotels, sharing a room is no problem as long as you don't request a double bed. The bottom line is that discretion is in order – at least for a while!

DISABLED TRAVELERS

Bolivian businesses and services make very few concessions to disabilities; wheelchair ramps are available only at a few upmarket hotels and restaurants, and most Bolivian public transport will be especially challenging for anyone with limited mobility.

Disabled travelers may also want to prepare for image problems. The relatively enlightened attitudes toward disability that prevail in most Western countries haven't yet taken hold in Bolivia. Here, as in much of the developing world, people with visible disabilities may be expected to turn to professional begging or selling telephone tokens, and are often exploited by unscrupulous characters. Launching a personal crusade to set everyone straight probably won't do much good, but disabled travelers who can discuss their jobs, educational background, opportunities – and even problems – at home may well inspire some Bolivians to rethink their society's attitudes toward disability.

Organizations

In the US, Mobility International (☎ 541-343 1284; fax 451-343 6812; PO Box 1076, Eugene OR 97440) advises disabled travelers on mobility issues. It primarily runs educational exchange programs, including South American travel. For assistance and advice specific to individual needs, disabled travelers in the USA can contact the Society for the Advancement of Travel for the

Handicapped (☎ 212-447-7284; fax 212-725-8253; 347 Fifth Ave, Suite 610, New York, NY 10016). A one-year subscription to its quarterly magazine, *Access to Travel*, costs US$13. In the UK, a useful contact is the Royal Association for Disability & Rehabilitation (☎ 0207-250-3222; fax 0207-250-2112; radar@radar.org.uk; 12 City Forum, 250 City Rd, London EC1V 8AF). See also their website at www.radar.org.uk/.

On the Internet, you can also check out www.acess-able.com.

SENIOR TRAVELERS

There are few discounts or special deals for older travelers, and few facilities for those with limited mobility, but older travelers are generally treated with respect and courtesy, and those with a reasonable fitness level will have few problems in Bolivia. However, it's wise to have a physical exam before setting out, as Bolivia's altitudes may present serious problems for anyone – and especially older people – with cardiac, respiratory or circulatory problems.

Some US organizations may be able to provide advice. The AARP (toll-free ☎ 800-424-3410; 601 E St NW, Washington, DC 20049) is an advocacy group for Americans over 50 years of age and a good source of travel bargains. Non-US residents can get one-year memberships for US$10. For details, see the website www.aarp.org.

Grand Circle Travel (☎ 617-350-7500; toll-free ☎ 800-350-7500; 347 Congress St, Boston, MA 02210) offers escorted tours and travel information in a variety of formats. It also distributes a useful free booklet, *Going Abroad: 101 Tips for Mature Travelers*.

TRAVEL WITH CHILDREN

Few foreigners visit Bolivia with children, but those who do are usually treated with great kindness. While there aren't many attractions or facilities designed specifically for kids, transport, food and lodging are all quite manageable and a widespread local affection for the younger set opens up all sorts of social interaction for traveling families. Children with fair hair are especially likely to receive local attention.

Civilian airlines allow children under 12 to fly at half fare, but on long-distance buses, those who occupy a seat will normally have to pay the full fare. Most hotels have some rooms with three or four beds, and some even have dedicated *habitaciones familiares* – family rooms – at a special rate. Restaurants rarely advertise children's portions, but will often offer a child-sized serving at a lower price, or will allow two kids to share an adult meal. For light, cheap meals, bring some cups, plates and utensils and go to the supermarkets for cereals, soft drinks and sandwich fixings.

Children may well enjoy Bolivian video arcades – which are ubiquitous – as well as outdoor activities, such as horseback riding, river trips and light hiking. It's a good idea to alternate adult activities (museums, galleries, shopping and tours) with things the kids will enjoy.

For travel with very young children, it's useful to carry a baby-backpack, but note that prams/strollers will normally be difficult to push over the typically rough and broken pavement. Older children may enjoy having their own small backpacks to carry favorite toys or teddies, books, crayons and paper. For more information, advice and anecdotes, see Lonely Planet's *Travel with Children*.

USEFUL ORGANIZATIONS

One of the most useful resources for visitors to South America is the South American Explorers (formerly the South American Explorers Club) (☎ 607-277-0488; 800-274-0568; fax 607-277-6122; explorer@samexplo.org; 126 Indian Creek Rd, Ithaca, NY 14850, USA). This organization provides information and support to travelers, researchers, mountaineers and explorers; offers trip-planning services; sells a wide range of books, guides and maps for South America; and publishes a catalog and the quarterly *South American Explorer* magazine. Considering the package of benefits offered, membership is quite a bargain at US$40 (US$70 per couple) per year, plus US$10 for addresses outside the USA. This includes four issues of the magazine.

The organization maintains clubhouses in Quito, Ecuador (☎/fax 02-225228; explorer@saec.org.ec; Jorge Washington 311 y Leonidas Plaza, Mariscal Sucre, Apartado 17-21-431, Eloy Alfaro, Quito); in Lima, Peru (☎/fax 01-425 0142; memberlima@amauta.rcp.net.pe; República de Portugal 146, Breña, Casilla 3714, Lima 100) and in Cuzco, Peru (☎/fax 084-223102; saec@wayna.rcp.net.pe; El Sol 930; Apartado 500, Cuzco). You can also check out their website at www.samexplo.org.

The Latin American Travel Consultants, (fax 02-562566; rku@pi.pro.ec or lata@pi.pro.ec; Apartado 17-17-908, Quito, Ecuador) publishes a quarterly news bulletin, *The Latin American Travel Advisor*, which features news on travel, public safety, health, climate, costs and so on for travelers in the region. Books, maps and videos are available by mail order. See also the website www.amerispan.com/lata.

A useful contact in the UK is the Latin American Bureau (☎ 020-7278-2829; fax 020-7278 0165; 1 Amwell St, London EC1R 1UL), which keeps up to date with all Latin American happenings, and publishes a growing list of titles dealing with regional politics, culture and travel. It's also an active proponent of political fairness and human rights.

Hostelling International

For information about Bolivia's hosteling organization, Asociación Boliviana de Albergues Juveniles, contact Valmar Tours (☎ 02-361076; fax 02-328433; valmar@waranet.com or penaloza@ceibo.entelnet.bo; Edificio Alborada, 1st floor, Oficina 105, Juan de la Riva 1406, Casilla 4294, La Paz).

DANGERS & ANNOYANCES
Security

Although many visitors are apprehensive about security in Bolivia, it is in fact one of the safest – if not *the* safest – of Latin American countries. Bolivians habitually refer to their country as *muy tranquilo* ('very calm') and serious or violent crime is relatively rare – and almost always perpetrated by foreigners (most often Peruvians) who

regard Bolivians as naïve about security. In fact, violent crime elicits the same incredulous lament in Bolivia that it does in some Western countries.

As a traveler, the biggest worries you're likely to encounter will be petty thievery and the odd crooked official, especially if you're unfamiliar with the turf. Even if you consider yourself an impecunious traveler, people may assume you're carrying an expensive camera and lots of money. However, paranoia is unwarranted and a few guidelines – as well as an understanding of local scams and awareness of what's going on around you – should ensure a minimum of problems.

If you have something stolen, report it to the police. No big investigation is going to occur, but you will get a police statement for your insurance company. Unfortunately, Bolivian police often attempt to extract 'fees' for such statements, especially from foreigners who they think may be trying to scam their insurance companies.

Predeparture Precautions If you work on the elements of vulnerability, risks can be minimized. For starters, only take items you are prepared to lose or replace. Travel insurance is essential for replacement of valuables, and the cost of a good policy is worthwhile if it limits disturbance to or abrupt termination of your travel plans. Loss through violence or petty theft can be an emotional and stressful experience, and an insurance policy can relieve some of the sting. Also, the less you carry, the less you have to lose. Don't travel with jewelry, gold chains or expensive watches.

On the Road Before arriving in a new place, have a map or at least a rough idea about orientation. Plan your schedule so you don't arrive at night, and use a taxi if you're unsure about security. Most of all, stay observant and learn to move like a street-smart local. Your style of dress should be casual and inexpensive. If you carry a day pack, secure the zips with safety pins and wear it on your front. Whenever you have to put your day pack down, put your foot through the strap.

Avoid wandering around with a camera dangling over your shoulder or around your neck – keep it out of sight as much as possible. It's also unwise to keep it in a swanky camera bag as this will attract attention. It may help to carry your camera gear in a sturdy plastic bag from a local supermarket.

When carrying all your valuables – such as to the bus station – distribute them about your person and baggage. A money belt will provide some measure of protection only if it's worn *under* clothing; external pouches attract attention and are easy prey. An alternative would be to use cloth pouches sewn into trousers or attached under clothes with safety pins. Other methods include belts with concealed zipper compartments, and bandages or pouches worn around the leg.

Keep small change and a few banknotes in a shirt pocket, to pay for bus tickets and small expenses without having to extract large amounts of money. Keep wallets zippered or buttoned inside a pocket and don't take them out on public transport or in crowded places.

When changing money on the street, follow the advice given in the Money section earlier in this chapter.

Favorite Scams Scams are continuously being developed and transmuted across borders. Stay aware of changes by talking to other travelers, but don't let the stories get to you. Theft and security are sources of endless fascination for travelers; some of the stories are true, some are incredible, and some are taller than Illimani!

Distraction is a common tactic employed by street thieves. The simple 'cream technique' is now ubiquitous throughout South America, including Bolivia. The trick commences when you're on the street or standing in a public place, and someone surreptitiously slops a substance on your shoulder, back or day pack. It can be anything from mustard to chocolate or even dog muck. An assistant (young or old, male or female) then taps you on the shoulder and amicably offers to clean off the mess… if you'll just put down your bag for a

second. If you foolishly agree, the bag disappears. Ignore any such attempt or offer and simply endure your mucky state until you can find a safe place to wash.

Druggings have been reported in neighboring countries, but are thankfully rare in Bolivia. You may still want to be wary of cigarettes, beer, sweets, etc, proffered by strangers. If the circumstances appear suspicious, the offer can be gently refused by claiming medical concerns.

If someone 'accidentally' drops a packet of money (or jewelry or white powder or whatever) at your feet, don't touch it. You may be accused of having stolen it and then asked to pay to avoid arrest. Alternatively, you may be offered the opportunity to share the 'spoils' with another, and then have your own money taken in a deft sleight of hand.

Also beware of scams involving travelers claiming to have had all their money and belongings stolen, and asking for handouts from other travelers. One Canadian woman has been successfully working the streets of La Paz and Santa Cruz for nearly a decade now. Don't give her anything but a lecture about moral behavior and perhaps try to get a photo of her (and take it to the *Bolivian Times*!)

There is also a series of scams associated with police and characters purporting to be police or other law-enforcement officials. Foreigners may be stopped by someone claiming to be a police officer who asks to see their money and passport, or search their bags for 'drugs.' This often happens shortly after they've made the acquaintance of a stooge, a 'fellow traveler' from Peru, Chile or elsewhere. The 'fellow traveler' immediately complies with the police officer's request as if it were routine. When the foreigner follows suit, the accomplices clean them out and disappear. This 'friendly fellow tourist' scam is a current favorite and is popping up all over South America (one wonders if there's a training school for this sort of thing).

A similar scenario proceeds as follows: A traveler is stopped on the street by a 'plainclothes police officer' with a fake ID, who asks the traveler to accompany them in a taxi to the police station. Once inside the taxi, the traveler's belongings are 'inspected' and valuables 'confiscated.' If you're stopped, insist upon full proof of their identity and *never* get into a taxi with anyone claiming to be a police officer, as it will invariably be a setup. If they don't back off, make a note of their ID and insist on phoning the police station or going on foot. At this stage, they'll probably take off in search of an easier target.

In most parts of Bolivia you can contact the Radio Patrulla (Police Radio Patrol) by dialing 110.

Streets & Public Transport Thieves watch for tourists leaving hotels, bus terminals, railway stations, banks, casas de cambio, or tourist sights, then follow their targets. If you notice you're being followed or closely observed, it may help to pause and look straight at the person involved or simply point them out to a traveling companion. The element of surprise favored by petty criminals will then have been lost.

Long-distance bus and train travel is usually well organized. When giving your luggage to baggage-handlers, make sure you receive and keep your receipt and ensure that it actually goes into the hold or onto the roof – and that it stays there. On my recent visit to Villazón a baggage-handler, who assumed that I'd already boarded the bus, was caught trying to disappear with my pack into a warehouse across the street. It may help to padlock two or more items together, making them awkward to carry off. Also, avoid placing luggage on overhead racks; if you must, try to padlock it to the rack.

Taxis Although Bolivian taxi drivers are no different than their counterparts worldwide when it comes to arbitrary fare augmentation, more serious taxi problems are very rare in Bolivia.

Set fares are standard in Bolivia, and a disinterested party, such as a shopkeeper, will naturally provide better information than a taxi driver. Around large hotels or bus and railway stations, quoted fares are likely to be triple the actual standard rates.

It's better to walk 200m down the road and start your haggling there.

When entering or leaving a taxi, keep a passenger door open while loading or unloading luggage – particularly if this is being done by someone other than the driver. This minimizes any temptation to drive off with the luggage, leaving the passenger behind. If there's space, try to fit luggage inside the taxi rather than in the trunk (boot). If you're not traveling alone, one person should remain near the open passenger door or inside the taxi whenever luggage is still inside.

Hiking & Trekking While most hikes in Bolivia can be considered safe, some popular routes have become less than perfectly safe. Fortunately, most trail robberies involve relatively innocuous techniques – mainly tent-slashing – that occur while the victims are asleep. The best prevention is to carry only essentials, keep everything inside your tent and camp well off the trail and out of sight. Potential troublemakers know all the best campsites and the only way to foil them is to select an improbable spot.

In the unlikely event you do meet with threatening demands on the trail (in the absence of a serious weapon, of course), it may help to feign ignorance of Spanish – just shrug your shoulders and keep on walking – or simply ignore the crisis at hand and do something totally unexpected: laugh or ask for the time, pick up three stones and start to juggle, start babbling in Spanish about some unrelated topic or simply smile and extend your hand in friendly greeting. Unless the would-be perpetrator is a real professional, they'll probably be thrown off balance long enough for you to make a polite exit.

Hotels If you consider your hotel to be reliable, place valuables in the hotel safe, note the contents and get a receipt. Pack your valuables in a small zippered bag and padlock it, or use a signed seal that will easily reveal tampering. In dodgy hotels, check the door, doorframe and windows of your room for signs of forced entry or unsecured access.

Although you'd be ill advised to leave valuables in your hotel room, some travelers padlock baggage to room fixtures or tape items in concealed places. If you take the tape route, however, don't leave your valuables behind as a windfall for the cleaner!

Border Crossings Travelers crossing the Peru-Bolivia border at Yunguyo/Copacabana have reported that their Bolivian entry stamp had been dated one day *ahead* of the day of entry. This was simply a set-up for a 'fine' later in the day. The obvious advice is to check your date stamp carefully at the border and, if it is incorrect, insist that it be corrected.

Villazón is particularly notorious for uniformed police who stop foreigners, alleging that they must confiscate any 'illegal' US dollars the travelers may be carrying. (Of course, dollars are not illegal anywhere in Bolivia.) Hide your cash well, leave it in your hotel or tell the offender you only carry traveler's checks.

Drugs

Bolivia may be the land of cocaine, but rumors that a cheap and abundant supply is readily available to the general public are unfounded. Refined cocaine is highly illegal in Bolivia – the standard sentence for possession of cocaine in Bolivia is eight years – so it's clearly best left alone.

The big guys get away with processing and exporting because they're able to bribe their way around the regulations. Backpackers and coca farmers become statistics to wave at foreign governments as proof, if you will, that Bolivia is doing something about the drug problem. Although foreign travelers are rarely searched, it's still unwise to carry drugs of any kind, as the consequences are just too costly.

If the worst happens – you're caught with drugs and arrested – the safest bet is to pay off the arresting officer(s) before more officials learn about your plight and want to be cut in on the deal. It's best not to call the payoff a bribe per se. Ask something like: '*¿Cómo podemos arreglar este asunto?*' ('How can we put this matter right?'). They'll understand what you mean.

If the officer refuses, then you're on your own, as foreign embassies are normally powerless and in most cases, they simply don't want to know.

Begging

For many, one of the most disconcerting aspects of travel in Bolivia is the constant presence of beggars. With no social welfare system to sustain them, elderly, disabled, mentally ill and jobless people take to the streets, hoping to arouse sympathy.

Since donating even a pittance to every beggar encountered would be financially impossible for most visitors, each traveler has to make an individual decision about what constitutes an appropriately humanitarian response. Some choose to give only to the most pathetic cases or to those enterprising individuals who provide some value for money, such as by singing or playing a musical instrument. Others simply feel that contributions only serve to fuel the machine that creates beggars, and ignore the whining cries that haunt Bolivian streets.

The best I can offer on this issue is a couple of guidelines. Mentally indigent or elderly people who would appear to have no other possible means of support may be especially good candidates. For anyone who appears truly hungry, an offer of food will go a long way. The physically disabled are always underemployed, often relegated to selling lottery tickets or telephone tokens, but they do manage to earn something. Keep in mind, however, that many families simply set their older members on the pavement with a tin bowl hoping to generate extra income.

One ethnic group in Potosí department has even organized a begging syndicate that sends brown-clad older women into larger cities around the country, provides accommodation, and supplies them with suitably grubby-looking children. If I could make only one recommendation, it would be against fueling this scam machine when there are so many genuinely needy individuals out there. You'll know who these people are; they're always dressed in brown and accompanied by children, and often become obnoxious and difficult to ignore.

Gift Giving

When traveling around Bolivia, particularly rural areas, some visitors may be shocked by the apparently backward and often primitive living conditions they encounter. In response, some are moved to compare the locals' lot with their own, and experience pangs of conscience and outrage at inequalities. In an attempt to salve the guilt or inspire goodwill, many indiscriminately distribute gifts of sweets, cigarettes, money and other foreign items to local children and adults.

What people from Western societies may not realize is that in Bolivia and many other developing countries, the lack of money, TV, automobiles, modern conveniences or expensive playthings does not necessarily indicate poverty. The people of rural Bolivia have crops, animals and homes that provide sufficient food, clothing and shelter. They work hard with the land and it, in turn, takes care of them.

While it may be difficult for Westerners to become accustomed to this lifestyle, the proud and independent highland Bolivians have known nothing else for well over 1000 years and are as comfortable with it as foreigners are in their own element. When short-term visitors hand out sweets or cigarettes, they cause dental and health problems that cannot be remedied locally; when they give money, they impose a foreign system of values and upset a well-established balance.

It's undoubtedly well meaning, but the long-term consequences of indiscriminate gift giving are undeniable. As more visitors venture into traditional regions, proud and independent people come to associate the outside world with limitless bounty – which appears to be theirs for the asking. Visitors are pestered with endless requests, and locals become confused as once-generous foreigners begin to regard them with contempt. Communication breaks down and the meeting of cultures becomes a strain on everyone.

If you wish to be accepted by local people, you can perhaps share a conversation, teach a game from home, or show a photograph of your friends or family. If you wish to make a bigger difference, you can donate money and supplies to organizations working to improve rural conditions. Alternatively, bring a supply of bandages, rehydration mixture or other medicines and leave them with the local health-care nurse (larger rural villages have a clinic), or buy a handful of pens and a stack of exercise books and give them to the schoolteacher. When a personal gift becomes appropriate – if you're invited for a meal, for example, or someone goes out of their way to help you – share something that won't disrupt or undermine the local culture or lifestyle, such as a piece of fruit, a bread roll or a handful of coca leaves.

Street children who must beg for a living will stand out clearly from those who have been taught to beg by well-meaning foreigners. If you hand out money, it stokes the begging tendency and leads to exploitation by unscrupulous adults; it also creates dissatisfaction with their own society and gives the impression that foreigners can always be tapped for goodies. Bolivians often complain that money given to child beggars too often winds up in the video-game parlors. For a child who appears truly hungry, a piece of fruit or other healthy snack will be appreciated. If they refuse such gifts and demand money,

it should be fairly obvious what's really going on.

Incorrect Information

If you're in need of information or directions, be aware that some Bolivians prefer to provide incorrect answers or directions rather than give no response at all. They're not being malicious; they merely want to please you and appear helpful and knowledgeable. It's therefore best not to take spontaneous answers at face value. Ask several people the same question and if one answer seems to prevail above the others, it's probably as close to correct as you'll find.

BUSINESS HOURS

Business hours in Bolivia are dictated largely by age-old southern European traditions, and while they can often be inconvenient for travelers accustomed to Australasian, North American or even northern European opening hours, they provide incentive for travelers to synchronize with the local rhythms.

Although more and more places serve breakfast, many of these still don't roll up their aluminum doors before 9 or 9:30 am. In smaller towns, those desperate for a caffeine fix will usually find joy at the market food stalls. Similarly, shops, travel agencies and financial institutions open at about 9 or 10 am. Early morning shopping is limited to the markets, where dribbles of activity begin as early as 6 am.

At noon, cities virtually close down, with the exception of markets and restaurants serving lunch-hour crowds. The afternoon resurrection begins at around 2 pm but in some towns, businesses may remain closed until as late as 4 pm. While a few places close at 5 or 6 pm, most stay open until 8 or 9 pm. Many bars and restaurants close at 10 pm, although some serve until midnight and beyond.

On Saturdays, shops, services and even some eateries close down at noon but street markets remain open at least until midafternoon, and often into the evening. On Sundays, nearly everything – except those businesses and snack restaurants catering to families – remains dead until evening, when a few places open.

Most post offices are open from 9 am (8:30 am for some services) to noon and 2:30 to 7 pm. Some also open on Saturday mornings and the GPO in La Paz is open for some services from 9 am to noon on Sundays. Most banks are open from 9 to 11:30 am and 2:30 to 5 pm.

PUBLIC HOLIDAYS & SPECIAL EVENTS

Bolivian public holidays include: New Year's Day (January 1); Carnaval (February/March); Semana Santa (Easter Week: March/April); Labor Day (May 1); Corpus Christi (May); Independence Days (August 5-7); Columbus Day (October 12); Día de los Muertos (All Souls' Day: November 2); and Christmas (December 25).

In addition, each department has its own holiday: La Paz (July 16); Tarija (April 15); Cochabamba (September 14); Santa Cruz (September 24); Pando (September 24); Beni (November 18); Oruro (February 22); Chuquisaca (May 25).

Special Events

Bolivian fiestas are invariably of religious or political origin, usually commemorating a Christian or Indian saint or god, or a political event such as a battle or revolution. They can be lots of fun and they're a chance for a homegrown experience of Bolivian culture. Fiestas typically feature lots of folk music, brass bands, dancing, processions, food and ritual, as well as generally unrestrained merrymaking involving alcohol, water balloons (tourists are especially vulnerable!) and fireworks.

Bolivian towns stage fiestas whenever an excuse arises – mainly in the winter months. The entire month of August seems to be devoted to one fiesta or another, so at that time, you'll probably catch two or three during even a short stay. The following is a partial list of the major Bolivian festivals; listed dates are subject to change.

January 6
Día de los Reyes 'Kings' Day' (Epiphany) is celebrated as the day the three wise kings visited the baby Jesus after his birth. The largest celebrations are in Reyes (Beni); Sucre; Tarija; and rural villages in Oruro, Cochabamba and Potosí departments.

January 24
Alasitas The Festival of Abundance dates from Inca times and is dedicated to Ekeko, the little household god of abundance. It's celebrated in La Paz.

February (first week)
La Virgen de Candelaria This weeklong festival is held in honor of the Virgin of Candelaria in Aiquile (Cochabamba); Samaipata (Santa Cruz); Angostura (Tarija) and Cha'llapampa (Oruro). The biggest celebration, however, is at Copacabana in La Paz department.

February/March (week before Lent)

Carnaval celebrations are held nationwide, but the most spectacular event is *La Diablada*, which is staged in Oruro. Elsewhere, celebrations start with enthusiastic processions and booming brass bands, but – with the addition of alcohol – eventually crescendo into madness. Participants are subject not only to harmless water balloons, but increasingly, to indelible paint, sugar water, urine and even less agreeable substances (foreign women are favorite targets). If you have an expendable change of clothing, you can head for the streets and partake of the music and merry-making; others may well want to hole up inside a mild hotel or guest house and wait until the insanity passes (or passes out)! In most parts of the world, the whole thing grinds to a halt with the dawning of Ash Wednesday, but in Bolivia, hair-of-the-dog celebrations may continue for several days later than the Catholic Church would consider appropriate.

March (date varies)

Fiesta de la Uva This Tarija festival is dedicated to grapes, wine and the spirits derived from them.

March (2nd Sunday)

Phujllay The name of this festival, which takes place in Tarabuco (Chuquisaca), means 'play' in Quechua. Phujllay (pronounced **'pookh**-yai') commemorates the Battle of Lumbati. It's one of Bolivia's most prominent festivals.

March or April

Semana Santa One of the most impressive of the nationwide Holy Week activities is the Good Friday fiesta in Copacabana, when hundreds of pilgrims arrive on foot to Copacabana from La Paz.

April 15 & 16

Efemérides de Tarija & Rodeo Chapaco; Tarija's town anniversary celebrations commemorate the battle of La Tablada and culminate in a rodeo recalling the city's gaucho and Argentine connections.

May 3

Fiesta de la Cruz Commemorates the cross on which Christ was crucified, and despite the somber theme, the celebrations are quite upbeat. The greatest revelry takes place in Tarija, with 15 days of music, parades, and alcohol consumption. The fiesta is also held in Vallegrande (Santa Cruz), Cochabamba and Copacabana (both in La Paz).

May 27

Día de la Madre Mother's Day celebrations are held nationwide. In Cochabamba, the festivities are known as *Heroínas de la Coronilla* in honor of the women and children who defended their cities and homes in the battle of 1812.

May/June

Festividad de Nuestro Señor Jesús del Gran Poder This animated festival, one of Bolivia's most lively, is held in La Paz in late May or early June. It's dedicated to the 'great power of Jesus Christ.'

June (date varies)

La Santísima Trinidad The festival of the Holy Trinity takes place in Trinidad with music, dancing and a bullfight.

June 24

San Juan Bautista Held nationwide, but the largest bash takes place in Santa Cruz.

July 31

Fiesta del Santo Patrono de Moxos This unique local festival in the lovely Indian community of San Ignacio de Moxos is lively, colorful and highly worthwhile.

August 6

Independence Day Fiesta This event provides inspiration for excessive raging nationwide! The largest celebration is held at Copacabana.

August 10-13

San Lorenzo Tarija department's largest fiesta is celebrated in San Lorenzo. It features traditional Chapaco dances and musical instruments.

August 15-18

La Asunción de la Virgen de Urcupiña This festival, the largest held in Cochabamba department, is staged at Quillacollo. Other celebrations commemorating the Assumption of the Virgin Mary into heaven are held around the country, including the famous *Virgen de Chaguaya*, which is held in Chaguaya (Tarija department).

August (last week)

Chu'tillos This festival in Potosí is dedicated to the wealth of music and dance traditions from around Bolivia and throughout South America. In recent years, music and dance troupes have come from as far away as China and the USA.

September (1st Sunday)

San Roque Although San Roque's feast day is August 16 (when canine revelers honor San Roque, the patron saint of dogs), the main Tarija celebration begins a couple of weeks later. Participants wear brightly colored clothing, feathers and belts, and the unique Chapaco music features prominently.

October (1st week)

Vírgen del Rosario This celebration is held on different days in different locations, including Warnes (Santa Cruz); Tarata, Morochata and Quillacollo

(Cochabamba); Tarabuco (Chuquisaca); Viacha (La Paz) and Potosí.

November 1 & 2

Día de Todos los Santos Cemetery visits and decoration of graves nationwide.

December 25

Christmas Christmas is celebrated throughout Bolivia, but some of the most unique and colorful festivities take place in San Ignacio de Moxos (Beni) and Sucre.

ACTIVITIES
Hiking & Trekking

Hiking and trekking are among the most rewarding ways to gain an appreciation for the Andes and their many moods. Although Bolivia rivals Nepal in trekking potential, it has only recently been discovered by trekking enthusiasts.

Because so much of the country is rural, lightly populated and far from main transport routes, opportunities for trekking through wild or little-visited areas are practically limitless. A glance at a topographical sheet of any highland area will reveal a host of crisscrossing footpaths. These often beautiful routes, some ancient, are used by rural people as links with the outside world.

As with the Himalaya, the mountain backbone of South America is not a wilderness area and has been inhabited for thousands of years by farmers and herders. Most of the popular hikes and treks in Bolivia begin near La Paz, traverse the Cordillera Real along ancient Inca routes, and end in the Yungas, but many other areas of the country are also suitable for hiking. This book includes most of the popular alternatives, but doesn't begin to exhaust the possibilities.

Few of the possible routes are ever traversed by outsiders, and people living along them may be surprised – and perhaps even frightened – at the sight of foreign trekkers. In remote areas, a Quechua- or Aymará-speaking guide is essential in order to reassure the campesinos that you mean no harm. A good guide doesn't necessarily have to know the terrain in question; once you've made contact, locals will almost invariably be friendly and happy to help with directions.

If you're looking for pure Andean culture and interaction with the locals, choose your trip carefully. In the more popular trekking areas, many well-meaning visitors who have passed before have indiscriminately bestowed gifts, and as a consequence, foreigners are often pestered with persistent and sometimes threatening demands for material goods by both adults and children. For guidelines, see 'Gift Giving' earlier in this chapter.

For details on major trekking routes, see the Cordilleras & Yungas chapter; trekking guides are described under Books, earlier in this chapter. Maps are discussed under Mountaineering, later in this section, and under Planning, at the beginning of this chapter.

Skiing

For information on Bolivia's very limited skiing possibilities, see Chacaltaya, in the La Paz chapter.

Mountaineering

Climbing in Bolivia, like the country itself, is an exercise in extremes. In the dry southern winter (May to September), temperatures may fluctuate as much as 40°C in a single day, but the weather is better than can be expected in any other mountain range in the world (at other times, conditions can be as uncomfortably wet as in any range in the world). Another plus point is ease of access; although public transport may not always be available, roads pass within easy striking distance of many fine peaks.

Most people who wish to explore Bolivia's mountains will find that the 160km-long Cordillera Real northeast of La Paz offers the easiest access and most spectacular climbing in the country. Providing delightful contrasts, it separates the stark Altiplano on its west from the fertile green Yungas falling away to the Amazon on its east. Six of its peaks rise above 6000m and there are many more gems in the 5000m range. Owing to the altitude, glaciers and ice or steep snow, few of the peaks are 'walk-ups,' but most are well within reach of the average climber and many can be done by beginners with a competent guide.

During the winter dry season, the Cordillera Real is blessed with stable weather,

Baby capybaras partying in the pampas

Nose bear hangout

Pint-sized monkey, Beni

Lurking in the Río Yacuma

Flamingos on Laguna Colorada

Did someone say *sopaipillas*?

WOODS WHEATCROFT

Climbing Huayna Potosí

SANDRA BAO

You in the shades! Give a hand, will ya?

JANE SWEENEY

Piranha fishing

GRANT DIXON

Time for some trail mix, Parque Nacional Sajama

DAVID PHILLIPS

Only two chances a week to catch the Río Grande to Oruro train!

High Highways

Many of the finest hiking and trekking routes in the Bolivian Andes – Taquesi, La Cumbre to Coroico, Yunga Cruz, El Camino del Oro, Chataquila to Chaunaca – follow ancient routes laid down by the Inca and their predecessors. At the height of the Inca empire, the mountain landscape was crossed with a network of routes that radiated out from Cuzco and provided administrative, trade and communications links with the rest of the empire.

For their day, these roads were marvels of engineering. In fact, explorer Alexander von Humboldt said, 'The roads of the Incas were the most useful and stupendous works ever executed by humanity.' They snaked up and down over some of the most rugged terrain imaginable, striking a balance between the shortest and easiest routes. Across flat or open ground, they were often wide, paved thoroughfares. On steep land, they narrowed into stone stairways or followed cobbled switchbacks up the slope. Great river gorges were spanned by spindly suspension bridges, which were constructed with the twisted fibers of the cactuslike maguey plant and maintained by nearby villages. The most famous was, of course, the bridge over the roiling and fearsome Río Apurímac in Peru, which was built around 1350 and allowed the empire to expand northward. Its cables reportedly had the thickness of a man's body, and it was supported by great stone towers erected on either rim. Over the 500 years that it hung across that deep abyss, millions of people crossed over in terror of plunging to the roaring waters below. In 1927, the bridge – and the fears – were immortalized in *The Bridge of San Luis Rey*, by Thornton Wilder.

Along the roads there was a series of wayside inns known as *tambos* (the New World counterpart of the caravanserai), which were built every 20km or so. These roads weren't used only by travelers and soldiers; because the Inca lacked the wheel or a written language, communications were handled by long-distance relay runners called *chasqui* who carried messages to and from the emperor in Cuzco. These robust lads were normally sons of officials and had to run for 14 days per month for up to a year as a portion of their taxes to the empire. A strong chasqui could run from one relay station to the next, a distance of just over 3km, in under 20 minutes, which meant that even faraway Quito lay only five days from the capital at Cuzco. In *Highway of the Sun*, Victor W von Hagen wrote, 'At his palace in Cuzco, the Inca dined off fresh fish delivered from the coast, a distance of 200 miles (320km) over the highest Andes, in two days.'

As a chasqui approached a station, he'd blow a conch shell, warning the next runner to prepare to receive the message and carry it on. Messages were handed over either verbally or on chains of knotted and colored wool known as *quipus*. This system, developed and standardized by the record-keeping caste, the *quipucamaya*, became quite sophisticated over time and facilitated communications throughout the empire. With only colored, knotted wool, they kept records of disputes, mines, population, taxes, tribute, land distribution, and so forth.

Von Hagen's *Highway of the Sun* (Plata Press, 1975), though hard to find, is full of information on this subject. It chronicles a research journey through Peru following and studying the ancient roads.

minimal precipitation and mild winds. Daytime highs can exceed 30°C, while at night, temperatures above 5000m may plunge as low as -15°C. This ideal climate leads to relatively stable snow conditions, making these peaks excellent for honing snow-climbing skills.

To the north of the Cordillera Real lies the less accessible Cordillera Apolobamba, and to the south, the Quimsa Cruz, which boasts Bolivia's best climbing rock.

The dangers of climbing in Bolivia mainly relate to the altitude and the difficulties in mounting any sort of rescue, as

well as the small but potentially serious avalanche danger. For information on dealing with potentially fatal altitude problems, it's wise carry the practical and easily transportable *Mountain Sickness*, by Peter Hackett, whenever you ascend to high altitude (these guidelines could prove to be lifesavers for those whose judgment is compromised by mountain sickness).

Those who've spent some time in the highlands will have a head start on acclimatization, but newly arrived climbers should spend a week in La Paz or on the Altiplano, including some hiking (staying as high as possible), before attempting their climb. Once you're acclimatized to the Altiplano's relatively thin air, remember there are still 2500m of even thinner air lurking above, so climb smart. Drink plenty of fluids, sleep as low as possible, and descend at any sign of serious altitude sickness *before* a headache, troubled breathing or lethargy turn into life-threatening pulmonary or cerebral edema (see Health, earlier in this chapter).

Bolivia still lacks a reliable mountain rescue service (rescues/recoveries are often conducted by local mountaineers), so emergency help cannot be expected. What few helicopters Bolivia possesses generally cannot fly above 5000m. While help may sometimes be available on the frequently climbed routes up Huayna Potosí and Illimani, transport difficulties and the lack of phones mean any rescuers not already on the mountain will take many hours to arrive. The bottom line is that climbers should prepare to get themselves out of trouble.

Mountaineering insurance is essential to cover the high costs of rescue and to ensure medical evacuation out of the country in the event of a serious accident.

Maps Historically, maps of Bolivian climbing areas have been of poor quality and difficult to obtain. Even now, elevations of peaks are murky, with reported altitudes varying as much as 600m.

Liam O'Brien's excellent new map, *Cordillera Real* (see Internationally Distributed Maps in the earlier Planning section), at a scale of 1:135,000, shows mountains, roads and pre-Hispanic routes. It uses Aymará names according to the current official orthography, which can be confusing (for example, the peak commonly known as Ancohuma may be labeled 'Janq'uma' or 'Chearoco Ch'iyaruq'u').

Roughly 70% of Bolivia is covered by 1:50,000 topo sheets produced by the Instituto Geográfico Militar (IGM). Notable exceptions include the areas north of Sorata, the Cordillera Apolobamba and Parque Nacional Noel Kempff Mercado. IGM maps are relatively accurate on altitudes and topographical details, but spellings may be inconsistent and locations inaccurate. When you're route-finding, bear in mind that on most maps, only major paths are marked, while other perfectly feasible routes are omitted (this is often due to the lack of map updating).

Walter Guzmán Córdova has produced 1:50,000 color maps of *Choro-Takesi-Yunga Cruz*, *Muru-rata-Illimani*, *Huayna Potosí-Condoriri* and *Sajama*, which are most reliably found at Librería Olimpia in La Paz for US$7.50 per sheet.

The Deutscher Alpenverein (German Alpine Club) produces the excellent and accurate 1:50,000-scale maps *Alpenvereinskarte Cordillera Real Nord (Illampu)*, which includes the Sorata area, and *Alpenvereinskarte Cordillera Real Süd (Illimani)*, which centers on Illimani. Both are occasionally available in La Paz.

For further map information, see Planning, earlier in this chapter.

Guidebooks & Magazines The best mountaineering guide is *Bolivia – a Climbing Guide*, by Yossi Brain (The Mountaineers, 1997); the late author worked as a climbing guide in La Paz and also served as secretary of the Club Andino Boliviano. In Bolivia, it's sold at América Tours in La Paz (see Organized Tours in the Getting Around chapter).

Michael Kelsey's *Guide to the World's Mountains* (310 East 950 South, Springville, UT 84663, USA) includes helpful maps and trip descriptions. The *American Alpine Club Journal* and *Alpine Journal* are essential reading for detailed and new route information. *Mountaineering in the Andes*, by Jill Neate (2nd edition), published by the Expedition Advisory Service of the Royal Geographic Society, London, lists every mountain in Bolivia for which there is a written record. *Summit* magazine also has some useful features, especially in the July-August 1982 to July-August 1983 issues.

La Cordillera Real de los Andes, Bolivia, by Alain Mesili (Los Amigos del Libro, La Paz, 1984), in Spanish, is currently out of print, but you may be able to scare up a photocopied edition (try the Librería Don Bosco in La Paz). In German, there's *Die Königskordillere – Berg-und Ski-wandern in Bolivien*, by Robert Pecher & Walter Schmiemann (C & M Hofbauer-Verlag, Jutastrasse 41, 8000 Munich, 1983), which concentrates on trekking, climbing and skiing on the main peaks of the southern Cordillera Real.

For alpine history, look in the library for the classic, *The Bolivian Andes: a record of climbing and exploration in the Cordillera Real*, by W M Conway, first published in 1901.

Equipment & Clothing Scrambling in the Bolivian Andes can be done with little more than what the average traveler normally carries – a sturdy pair of shoes, a good layering of clothes, hat and gloves, daypack, sturdy water bottle etc. Loose-fitting layers are best for the constantly changing temperatures. A sturdy windbreaker that can take the abuse of buses, camiones, mules and the constant dust is important. Bolivia is one of the few places in South America where down is practical.

If higher peaks beckon, however, more serious equipment is essential. Bring your own climbing gear, as that found in Bolivia is generally expensive or of poor quality, or what you can pick up secondhand from other climbers and hikers. Remember, you'll have to carry this stuff on the plane, bus, camión, mule or on your back, so 'light is right.' When you're not climbing, your gear can be left with your tour agency or a reliable hotel. The following is a list of general recommendations for clothing and gear:

Camping Gear

- sleeping mat – important for insulating from cold or rocky ground
- sleeping bag – down or synthetic, good to -5°C (you can always put on more clothes if it gets colder!)
- tent – useful for occasional snotty weather; adds warmth
- backpack – a large capacity (60L plus), internal frame (external frames exposed to Bolivian buses don't last long)
- water bottles – at least two 1L containers. Avoid aluminum bottles, as they crack at subfreezing temperatures
- headlamp – important for those predawn starts; bring an adapter as round-cell batteries are available everywhere, while flat batteries are available only at a couple of specialist shops and are expensive

Food

Dried foods such as soups, rice and instant coffee can be bought locally. If you're visiting Bolivia only for a few weeks climbing, you may want to bring freeze-dried food; otherwise, buy your food at the markets. Instant rice and packet pasta meals are available in La Paz at ZATT, on Avenida Sánchez Lima near Plaza Avaroa.

Cooking

For cooking stoves, leaded gas, kerosene and methylated spirits (alcohol antiséptico, sold in pharmacies, works in Trangia stoves) are available in Bolivia. White gas (shellite/Coleman fuel) is sold in portable quantities only at the YPFB in Cochabamba; in La Paz, you must buy a minimum of 250L. Epigaz and Camping Gaz canisters are expensive but available in La Paz, but note that no type of stove fuel or canister may be carried on aircraft anywhere in the world, and not even clean, empty aluminum fuel bottles are permitted on flights originating or stopping in the USA. Currently, flights originating or passing through New Zealand restrict both fuel bottles and camp stoves. Useful utensils include a large pot for melting snow and another for cooking, and a nonstick frying pan is a nice luxury for frying up the ubiquitous eggs and potato.

Water Purification

Remember that giardia, dysentery, hepatitis and their ilk lurk in the mountains, too, and llamas are perfectly happy up to 5000m. Be sure to treat your water with a suitable filter or with iodine- or chlorine-based purifiers. When collecting snow or ice to melt for water on popular routes such as Huayna Potosí and Illimani, try to stay away from popular campsites, and keep your eyes open for human waste. For further guidelines, see Health, earlier in this chapter.

Climbing Gear

The amount and type of gear you'll need (and need to know how to use!) will obviously depend on just how serious you want to get, but the following recommended equipment would suffice for the standard routes on almost any peak in the Cordillera Real. Most routes include some technical climbing and pass over snow and/or glaciers. Climbing and camping gear can often be sold to locals or other travelers for more than you could get at home.

- plastic ice boots – heavy and expensive but how much do you value your toes?
- crampons and protectors
- ice axe and protector
- harness
- three to five carabiners, at least one locking
- 9 or 11mm rope
- two or three ice screws and snow pickets, flukes or stakes (essential earlier in the season)
- ice hammer – particularly for the more difficult climbs (Cabeza del Cóndor, Illampú, Ancohuma)
- prusiks – and practice in using them – for crevasse rescue
- sun protection – top-quality sunscreen and 100% UV-proof glasses are essential (don't scrimp here!) and aren't readily available in Bolivia; a baseball hat with bandanna makes an effective 'Lawrence of Arabia' sun shield

Buying & Renting Equipment Condoriri (☎/fax 02-319369; Calle Sagárnaga 345, La Paz), run by mountaineering guides, offers a wide selection of new and secondhand climbing and camping equipment: clothing, ropes, backpacks, tents, boots, paragliders, compasses, Camping Gaz, Epigaz, headlamp batteries and climbing hardware. It also rents out equipment and has a repair service. The agency also offers mountaineering and paragliding trips.

If you can't carry everything you'll need from home – or you don't have it – you can rent climbing equipment and clothing from specialist agencies in La Paz. Colibri (Calle Sagárnaga 309, La Paz), has a good selection, but the employees can't offer much assistance so you'll have to know exactly what you want. Some examples of daily rental charges: plastic ice boots US$3.80, crampons US$2.70, ice axe US$2.50, two-person tent US$5.70. New equipment, including headlamp batteries, ropes, backpacks and clothing can be bought at several La Paz shops; see Camping Equipment under Information in the La Paz chapter.

Agencies & Guides Many La Paz travel agencies offer to organize climbing and trekking trips in the Cordillera Real and other areas (see Organized Tours in the Getting Around chapter). Not all, however, are all they claim to be. Some have gotten lost, even on Huayna Potosí, and others have strung 10 or more climbers on the same rope (more than four climbers on one rope is extremely dangerous). These sorts of things aren't uncommon, so it's worth sticking to reputable specialist climbing agencies.

Specialist agencies in La Paz can do as much or as little as you want – from just organizing transport to a full service with guide, cook, mules, porters, and so forth, providing a full itinerary. Trekking guides generally charge US$25 per day, plus their food. Mountain guides cost US$50 per day and also must be fed. In addition, you need your food, technical equipment and clothing and – often the most expensive part of any trip – transport to and from the base camp or start of the trek to the mountain. Some people do resort to public transport or hitching on camiones, but this requires more time and logistics, so it's wise carry an extra couple of days' food in case of glitches.

In addition to the agencies, mountain guide information is available from the Club Andino Boliviano (☎ 02-324682; Calle México 1638, Casilla 1346, La Paz), which is mainly a ski organization and runs the piste at Chacaltaya but also has a number of top climbers as members. Alternatively, try the national guiding association, the Bolivian Association of Mountain Guides (☎/fax 02-317497; Andean Summits, Local 27, Galería Doryan, Calle Sagárnaga 189, Casilla 6976, La Paz). Note, however, that not all competent Bolivian mountain guides belong to this association.

Mountain Biking

Bolivia is blessed with some of the most dramatic mountain-biking terrain in the world, seven months every year of near-perfect weather, and relatively easy access to mountain ranges, magnificent lakes, pre-Hispanic ruins and trails, and a myriad of ecological zones. However, mountain biking is relatively new to the country; generally speaking, many areas have yet to be explored properly by bike, and as yet, there's no guidebook dedicated specifically to mountain biking.

Travelers with their own mountain bikes need to consider several factors. During the December to February wet season, some roads become mired in muck, and heavy rain can greatly reduce visibility, creating hazardous conditions (even in the dry season, conditions on some roads could be considered abusive). Also worth noting are Bolivia's lack of spare parts and shortage of experienced mechanics. While some bike shops in larger cities do have competent mechanics, most lack experience with complicated systems, such as hydraulic and disk brakes and newer suspension systems. In short, independent cyclists will have to carry all essential spares from outside and know how to make their own repairs.

While mountain bikes aren't suited to all parts of Bolivia, most highland areas and some lowland regions present great potential. Hard-core, experienced, fit and acclimatized riders can choose from a huge range of possibilities; either work out a route on a map and take a gamble on it, or find a guide and tackle some really adventurous rides. The Bolivian highlands are full of long and thrilling descents, as well as challenging touring possibilities, such as the Apolo road, which descends from the Cordillera Apolobamba to Apolo. In addition, one of the world's longest downhill rides will take you from Sajama National Park down to the Chilean coast at Arica, for a total descent of over 5000m. In the dry season, you can even tackle the mostly level roads of the vast Amazonian lowlands.

Some rides from La Paz can be done by riders of any experience level. The best known is the thrilling 3600m descent down 'The World's Most Dangerous Road' from La Cumbre to Coroico. Other popular routes from the highlands into the Yungas include the descent into the lush, green Zongo Valley and the twisting route from near Lake Titicaca to Bolivia's 'Trekking Capital,' Sorata. Alternatively, you can opt for a descent from the 5300m summit of Chacaltaya, which winds up in central La Paz! For descriptions of these routes, see 'Mountain Biking in Bolivia' in the Cordilleras & Yungas chapter.

Choosing an Operator Currently, no one rents safe, high-quality bikes, so if you prefer not to drag along your own mountain bike, you'll need to take a guided trip with a reputable agency. These are concentrated in La Paz, which is close to several fabulous and relatively accessible downhill routes. However, you'll have to choose your agency carefully, because many companies use cheap, inappropriate and potentially dangerous bicycles, inexperienced guides and insufficient guide-to-client ratios, and offer little or no instruction or advice during the ride. The potential for disaster on some routes – particularly The World's Most Dangerous Road – is great if the bicycle fails, if unsupervised clients become lost, if clients aren't aware which side of the road they need to use, or if there's a crash without rapid attention from the guide.

When selecting an agency, make sure they use good-quality brand-name bicycles (normally US-made) with decent front suspension (quality fork manufacturers include Rock Shox, RST, Manitou, and Mazzochi). Rear suspension is a plus. Reliable bicycle brands currently available in Bolivia include Trek, Cannondale, Kona and Raleigh (make sure these names aren't just painted over a less-reputable brand name!) As a general rule, good bikes will be equipped with Shimano STX-RC, Deore, LX, or XT derailleurs (the mechanism that moves the chain from gear to gear on the cogs). If you aren't being offered one of these models, be warned that the quality of the construction and parts is likely to be questionable at best.

You should also make sure the guides are experienced, and will communicate instructions, advice and coaching both before and during the ride. Also, make sure that groups don't exceed 15 to 20 people and that they are closely supervised, including one guide in front of the group and one taking up the rear, especially if there are more than seven or so cyclists in the group. Remember also that if you don't speak Spanish and your guide doesn't speak your language, it's unlikely that he or she will be able to communicate vital information, such as braking and cornering techniques, directions or emergency information.

One reliable and recommended operator is Gravity Assisted Mountain Biking; see Organized Tours in the Getting Around chapter for contact details.

Rafting & Kayaking

One of Bolivia's greatest secrets is the number of white-water rivers that drain the eastern slopes of the Andes between the Cordillera Apolobamba and the Chapare. Here, thousands of rivers and streams await to provide thrilling first descents for avid rafters and kayakers. While access will normally require long drives and/or treks – and considerable expense – several fine rivers are relatively accessible. For descriptions of several possible white-water trips, see 'Rafting & Kayaking in Bolivia' in the Cordilleras & Yungas chapter.

LANGUAGE COURSES

It's relatively easy to learn Spanish in Bolivia, and keener language students may also want to tackle Quechua. The best courses are generally found in Sucre, Cochabamba and La Paz, in that order. For specifics, see the Central Highlands and La Paz chapters.

WORK

There are a vast number of volunteer and nongovernmental organizations at work in Bolivia, and quite a few international companies have offices there, but travelers looking for paid work on the spot probably won't have much luck. Medical students usually have no problem picking up work experience, but it's likely to be on a volunteer basis. Geologists probably have the best chance of paid work through La Paz's many mining and exploration companies, but it's wise to scope out possibilities and arrange contracts before you arrive. (Also see 'The Lowdown on Getting a Bolivian Work Visa,' later in this chapter.)

Teaching English

Qualified English teachers interested in working in La Paz and several other cities may want to try the professionally run

Centro Boliviano Americano, with centers in La Paz and other major cities. Be aware, however, that you'll be required to forfeit two months' salary in order to pay for your training whether you're already qualified or not. La Paz also has numerous other English-language schools and universities – ask working teachers for guidelines and recommendations.

Volunteer Organizations

If you want to pay for a working holiday with an emphasis on environmental protection, contact Earthwatch (☎ 978-461-0081, 800-776 0188; fax 978-461-2332; info@ earthwatch.org; 3 Clock Tower Place, Suite 100, PO Box 75, Maynard, MA 01754, USA). It sponsors a project to study forest habitats in the Reserva Biosférica del Beni. In the UK contact Earthwatch Europe (☎ 01865-311600; fax 01865-311383; info@ uk.earthwatch.org; 57 Woodstock Rd, Oxford OX2 6HJ, UK). In Australasia, contact Earthwatch Australia (☎ 03-9682 6828; fax 03-9686 3652; earth@earthwatch .org; 126 Bank St, South Melbourne 3205, Vic). The Earthwatch website is www.earthwatch.org.

Another worthwhile volunteer option is the Street Kids Project operated by ENDA Bolivia, a Swiss-sponsored project that provides food and shelter for street children while offering an education and teaching useful skills. Among its more successful endeavors is a highly acclaimed street theater troupe. Potential volunteers should contact Señor Hugo Montecinos (☎ 811695; fax 811446; Casilla 9772, La Paz).

US citizens might want to consider volunteer service with the Peace Corps (☎ 800-424-8580; 1111 20th St NW, Washington, DC 20526), which is quite active in Bolivia. Accepted volunteers may request specific postings, and while nothing is guaranteed, those who speak Spanish and/or have requisite skills may well be fortunate enough to wind up in Bolivia.

ACCOMMODATIONS

In general, the prices and value of accommodations are not uniform throughout Bolivia. The cheapest lodging is found in Copacabana, and the Amazon region is generally the most expensive area. Note that in most places, rates are negotiable, especially during slow periods.

In this book, Places to Stay sections are divided into budget, mid-range and top-end categories. Anything charging under US$15 for a double is typically considered budget. Mid-range accommodations run from approximately US$15 to US$40 for two people, whether the rate is charged per person or per room. Top-end places typically start at US$40 for a double and include most places rated with three or more stars on the Bolivian rating scale. This scale may be adjusted slightly to account for regional differences. Hotels that are recommended or represent a particularly good value for the money – or are frequented by budget-conscious travelers – are identified as such.

Camping

Bolivia offers excellent wild camping, especially along trekking routes and in remote mountain areas. There are only a handful or organized campgrounds, but with the right gear – a tent, sleeping bag, light source and perhaps even a stove and fuel – you can set up camp almost anywhere outside population centers. Remember, however, that highland nights get very cold indeed. Although there are often places where you can melt into the hills near larger cities, they're not likely to have a safe and reliable water supply.

Along mountain trekking routes, camping is possible just about anywhere except in someone's pasture or potato field. Ask around in villages – locals may put travelers up or allow them to camp in their garden for a small fee. Rural schools are also good – and normally clean – alternatives. If you're sleeping in thatched huts, particularly in the lowlands or the highland valleys, see the Health section for warnings about Chagas' disease.

Hotels

The Bolivian hotel rating system divides accommodations into categories that, from bottom to top, include *posadas*, *alojamientos*,

The Lowdown on Getting a Bolivian Work Visa

All the required statements and basic form letters described in the following discussion, which must be printed on officially sealed paper with your name inserted in all the right places, can be most economically purchased from Office No 5 in the building adjacent to and just uphill from the PTJ (pronounced pay-tay-hota) on Calle Landaeta in La Paz.

Getting the one-month work visa, which is a prerequisite for the one-year visa, is pretty easy; just supply the Migración office on Camacho in La Paz with the following documents:

1. Passport
2. Photocopy of passport
3. Photocopy of work contract on letterhead paper
4. Photocopy of RUC (Value Added Tax document) of the company giving you the work contract
5. *Memorial* (statement) to Director de Migración describing your intent and purpose
6. US$136 (B$815), as of March 2000 (prices are subject to increase, of course…)

This buys you a month to do the nitty-gritty task of applying for the one-year visa, which is slightly more formidable. Here are the items you'll need (this cumbersome process must be repeated if you subsequently apply for a two-year visa):

1. Statement to the Director of Immigration soliciting 'Permanencia Temporal de Un Año' (or two years, if applicable)
2. Passport
3. Photocopy of passport, with date of issue and Bolivian entry stamp
4. Original of work contract on letterhead paper.
5. Notarized photocopy of the business RUC (VAT authorization)
6. PTJ certificates with a description of 'Antecedentes' and 'Domiciliario'
7. Interpol certificate certifying that you're not a foreign spy
8. INSO medical certificate certifying that you're not suffering from socially unacceptable ailments
9. US$167 (B$1000)/US$250 (B$1500) for a one-/two-year work visa

To get the Interpol Certificate, go to the Interpol office on Calle Colón, where you'll have to present a passport-photo and a local address. You'll have to submit to fingerprinting, which should verify that you're not a spy and don't have a criminal record. Getting this certification may well take up to two months, but you'll always find someone who can cut this time to 24 hours for US$17 (B$100). US Citizens can circumvent some of this by applying to the US Embassy for an official document stating that you're not a criminal or undesirable character.

residenciales, *casas de huéspedes*, *hostales* and *hoteles*. This rating system reflects the price scale and, to some extent, the quality.

Fortunately for travelers, most Bolivian hotel owners are friendly, honest people and demand the same of their staff. Unless you're staying in a hotel with a dodgy reputation, your belongings should be relatively safe, at least in upper budget to top-end places.

It's still wise to use common sense. Don't leave valuables in sight; decide whether you can trust the proprietor to keep an eye on

things while you're away. Money or jewelry may be checked at the hotel desk, but package it well and get a receipt; in the end, it may be just as secure stashed in some obscure corner of a locked pack. In some lower priced hotels, doors don't lock from either side and there may even be a window beside the door that can be easily opened from the outside. If you'll be away for a few days, most hotels will watch luggage free of charge. This service ranges from an informal area behind the counter

The Lowdown on Getting a Bolivian Work Visa

The certificates from the PTJ office, on Calle Landaeta, may take a bit more time, because you must supply them with the following:

1. A rental agreement with your current local address.
2. A copy of your most recent water and electric bills, which must bear your name and the same address as that of your official residence.
3. Photocopies of the *carnetes de identidad* (front and back) of two Bolivians who are willing to serve as witnesses to your application.
4. Verification sheet from the PTJ lawyer with these two witnesses' statements (see No 3, above). Both witnesses must sign this document.
5. 'Valores' (notarized documents) on 'papel sellado,' one documenting Antecedentes (stating that you have no criminal record in Bolivia, which costs US$4.50), and the other for Domicilio (stating that you live in Bolivia, which costs US$1.20). The forms for these must be purchased from the ground floor of the PTJ.
6. One photocopy of each of these Valores.
7. A statement to the PTJ director requesting Antecedentes and Domiciliario checks. Don't be too surprised if a staff member requests an additional US$3 to US$4 for a 'taxi' in order to process your application in a timely manner. The lawyer in the office adjacent to the 'Oficina Contra la Corrupción' will ironically also request a contribution in order to encourage the Chief of Police to sign your form sometime within the current millennium.
8. The medical certificate is obtained at INSO, next to Hospital Torax in Miraflores. You need to arrive at INSO between 8 and 11 am with a doctor's certificate (US$4.50 or B$25), which can be purchased around the corner at the Hospital Militar on Avenida Saavedra. The basic checkup (US$25 or B$150) consists of a blood test, urine sample (don't eat breakfast), chest X ray and brief doctor's interview. You get the results in two days' time.
9. The RUC can only be legitimized at La Renta (the tax department). Your prospective boss will have to take care of that, and remind him or her to get on it early, as the process may take a number of days.
10. The latest twist at Migración is that they won't return your passport (replete with your new visa stickers) until you pay US$43.50 (B$260) to process your Bolivian Carnet de Identidad. For that, they need the money plus two 4cm by 4cm photos (either color or black & white) and two weeks' time. Once all this paperwork has been completed, you'll (hopefully) receive your carnet.

to a locked baggage room; naturally, the latter is preferable.

Note that in some establishments, *simples* (single rooms), are unavailable, or cost only slightly less than a *doble* (double room). In some cases, if you're given a double you'll be expected to pay for both beds. In cheaper places, *camas matrimoniales* (double beds), are also scarce. Triple or quadruple rooms are frequently available, but they cost the same per bed as smaller rooms unless you can negotiate a high-occupancy discount.

Water and electric utilities throughout the country can be sporadic, and some inexpensive hotels only turn on the water and power for several hours in the morning and evening (see Toilets & Plumbing, earlier in this chapter). Some establishments expect you to advise them when you want a shower so that they can make the necessary arrangements.

Some final advice – never accept a room without inspecting it first. The most cheery reception areas can shelter some pretty dank and dingy rooms, some without windows.

Most proprietors are eager to please, so if you're not satisfied with the room you're first shown, ask to see another.

Posadas When you think 'posada' in Bolivia, don't envision those posh and lovely country estates that dot rural Spain! Here, posadas are the bottom end – the cheapest basic roof and bed available – and are frequented mainly by country folk visiting the city. They cost between US$1 and US$2.50 per person and vary in quality, normally from bad to worse. In most places, you could scrape off the scum with a putty knife, and hot water is unknown. In fact, most lack any sort of bathing facilities.

Alojamientos A step up are the alojamientos, which are also generally quite basic, but are considerably better and cost only a little more. However, the value varies greatly – some are clean and tidy while others are disgustingly seedy. Plumbing facilities are almost always communal, but some do provide hot showers. Double beds are rare and rates are normally charged per person rather than per room so there's no advantage in turning up as a group. Prices range from US$1.20 per person in Copacabana to US$6 in some Amazon Basin towns.

Residenciales, Casas de Huéspedes & Hostales These all serve as finer budget hotels, but their quality also varies and some alojamientos have taken to calling themselves 'residenciales' to improve their image. Most, however, are very acceptable, and you'll often be able to choose between a *baño privado* (private bathroom with a sink and flush toilet, and a shower with a hot water attachment), or a *baño común* (shared toilet and shower). Many places also provide a laundry sink or reasonably priced laundry services, and there's often a restaurant or snack bar where you can buy coffee, breakfast or sandwiches. These places charge US$8 to US$20 for a double with private bath, and about 30% less without; some places even include a basic continental breakfast in the room rate.

Other Hotels Moving upmarket, there's a whole constellation of hotels, which vary in standard from literal dumps to five-star luxury. The lower-range hotels can be amazingly cheap while the most expensive hotels top US$100 per person.

In general, Bolivia is not a country for accommodation snobs. There are only a handful of five-star hotels in the country, and some of these would rate only three or four stars on an international scale. Nevertheless, you can expect clean rooms, acceptable restaurants with bars, entertainment, room service, laundry service (albeit expensive), hot and cold running water, a telephone, bar fridge and all the usual amenities – for about half the price you'd pay in New York, London or Sydney.

A one-star hotel, on the other hand, may offer only cold water – possibly with a hot-shower attachment, a snack bar, shabby but clean linen and often a rather seedy appearance. Two- to four-star hotels, of course, fall somewhere in between. No stars indicate that the establishment is called a hotel but may actually belong in a lower category. Heating or air-con are unheard of below the three-star level.

Reservations

Although most top-end hotels expect guests to make room reservations, room availability is normally only a problem during major fiestas or holiday periods, when prices may double or triple and there's a local demand. At such times – for example, during Oruro's La Diablada carnival or Tarabuco's Phulljay – private homeowners will often rent rooms to out-of-town visitors. On weekends, it may also be difficult to find rooms in Bolivian resort areas, such as Coroico. During the winter months, Uyuni may also experience accommodation shortages.

FOOD

Bolivian cuisine is as diverse as its regions and climatic zones. The fare of the Altiplano tends to be starchy and loaded with carbohydrates, while in the lowlands, vegetables, fish and fruits feature more prominently.

While the national cuisine may not win any international awards, an admirable versatility has been derived from a few staple foods. Meat invariably dominates the typical Bolivian meal, and is usually accompanied by rice, potatoes (or another starchy tuber such as oca) and shredded lettuce. Often the whole affair is drowned in *llajhua*, a hot salsa made from tomatoes and *locotos* (small, hot pepper pods) or another spicy sauce. In the lowlands, the potato and its relatives are replaced by steamed or fried plantain or *yuca* (cassava). Other fresh vegetables are also more prevalent than in the highlands.

If you're interested in attempting classical Bolivian recipes at home, call up the websites www.bolivia.co.uk/recipes.htm or www.bolivian.com/cocina/platos.html.

Meals

Breakfast is known as *desayuno* and often consists of little more than coffee and a bread roll or some kind of pastry. Around mid-morning, many Bolivians eat a snack of *salteñas*, *tucumanas* or *empanadas* (see Fast Foods, later in this section).

Lunch is the main meal of the day and most restaurants offer an *almuerzo*, which means simply 'lunch,' but here it refers to a set lunch served at midday (à la carte lunches aren't usually called almuerzos). For almuerzo, restaurants ranging from backstreet cubbyholes to classy establishments offer bargain set meals consisting of soup, a main course, and tea or coffee. In some places, a salad starter and a simple dessert are included. Depending on the class of the restaurant, almuerzos cost anywhere from US$1.50 to US$3. If you don't want the almuerzo, you can order something from the à la carte menu for roughly twice the price of the special.

The evening meal, *la cena*, is similar to lunch, but normally less elaborate. It's invariably eaten after 7 pm. While you'll occasionally find cena specials, dinner is most often served à la carte.

Fast Food

For a mid-morning snack, Bolivians eat *salteñas*, delicious football-shaped meat and vegetable pasties that originated in Salta (Argentina). The baked shell is stuffed with beef or chicken, olives, eggs, potatoes, onions, peas, carrots, raisins and assorted other things. They're guaranteed to dribble all over the place and make a mess on your clothing, so have a supply of napkins (serviettes). A similar juicy incarnation is the *tucumana*, a puff-pastry shell packed with spicy egg, potatoes, chicken and onions. Both varieties are normally heavily spiced and are absolutely delicious. They're most often sold by street vendors, who supply a range of condiments to spice them up, and between 10 and 11 am, salteña stands along city streets become the scenes of informal social gatherings.

Empanadas, ubiquitous throughout South America, are filled with varying quantities of beef *(empanadas de carne)*, chicken *(empanadas de pollo)* or cheese *(empanadas de queso)*, and are either baked or deep-fried. Sometimes other ingredients, such as those used in salteñas, are added to the meat varieties. A variation is the *pukacapa*, a circular empanada filled with cheese, olives, onions and *ají* (hot pepper sauce) and baked in an earth oven.

The name of the *llaucha paceña*, a type of doughy cheese bread, would imply that it's a specialty of La Paz, but in fact, it appears to be more popular in Cochabamba. *Papas rellenas*, stuffed potatoes, are also delicious, especially served piping hot. They're a specialty in the central highlands around Cochabamba and Sucre.

Tamales are cornmeal dough filled with spiced beef, vegetables and potatoes. They're wrapped in a maize husk and fried, grilled or baked. *Humintas* (sometimes spelled *humitas*), which are similar, are filled with cheese only and are normally quite dry. A related concoction, called a *relleno*, resembles a corn fritter.

A popular way of preserving vegetables – mainly carrots, onion and peppers – is to pickle them in vinegar; the result is called *escabeche*. It's eaten as a snack or an accompaniment to meals. In some markets and stands, you'll find *chola* sandwiches, which are bread rolls filled with meat, onion, tomato and escabeche.

A common snack that is an acquired taste is *pasankalla*, puffed *choclo* (maize) with caramel, which normally sits out long enough to go sticky and very chewy.

Soup

Every Bolivian almuerzo or cena is prefaced by a large bowl of soup, which comes in three main varieties. *Chupe* is a thick meat, vegetable and grain soup with a clear broth flavored with garlic, ají, tomato, cumin or onion. *Chaque* is similar, but is much thicker and contains more grain. *Lawa* has a broth thickened with corn starch or wheat flour. Two delicious popular soup bases are quinoa and peanuts *(maní)*.

The type and amount of meat that appears in the soup will depend on where you get it. In markets, small eateries and bus stops, you'd be lucky to get more than a scrap of bone and gristle, usually beef or llama, in the bottom of the bowl. In more upmarket restaurants, you may get chicken or a bit of bone with some tough but edible meat attached. Look at the positive side – it's easy to remove this item and turn any Bolivian soup into a marginally vegetarian dish.

Meat & Fish

Most Bolivian dishes are derived from beef, chicken or fish and every region has its own cuisine and specialties. Poorer campesinos eat *cordero* or *carnero* (mutton), *cabrito* or *chivito* (goat) or llama.

Pork *(carne de chancho)* is considered a delicacy and is usually eaten only on special occasions; *lechón* (suckling pig) is a specialty of Cochabamba, but may also be served elsewhere as a fiesta dish. Another pork delicacy is *fritanga*, spicy hot pork with mint and hominy.

Typical beef dishes include barbecued or grilled beef *(parrillada* or *asado)* in various cuts *(lomo, brazuelo* and *churrasco)*. Jerked beef, llama or other red meat is called *charque*; on the Altiplano, it's often served with mashed hominy in a dish known as *charque kan*. In the lowlands, llama charque with mashed plantain and/or yuca is known as *masaco*. In the Beni, beef may be served as *pacumutus*, enormous chunks of grilled meat accompanied by yuca, onions and other trimmings.

Other meat variations include *thimpu*, spicy lamb and vegetable stew, and *falso conejo* (which, oddly enough, means 'false rabbit'), a greasy, glutinous substance that appears to be animal-based. Another popular way to serve meat or chicken is in *milanesa*, a greasy schnitzel. When the meat is pounded even thinner and allowed to absorb even more grease, the result is known as *silpancho*, which is a specialty of Cochabamba department and other areas. It's said that a properly prepared silpancho could be used to view a solar eclipse!

The dish called *pique a lo macho* – chunked grilled beef and sausage served with french-fried potatoes, lettuce, tomatoes, onions, capsicum and locoto – is popular in central Bolivia. *Rostro asado*, or sheep's head, is a favorite in Oruro. *Anticuchos* (beef-heart kebabs) and *fricasés* (pork or chicken stews with maize grits) are specialties in La Paz and Cochabamba. Other Cochabamba favorites include *jolque* (kidney soup), *ranga* (potato soup with chopped liver), *witu* (beef stew with pureed tomatoes), *chajchu* (beef with *chuño* – freeze dried potatoes – hard-boiled egg, cheese and hot red pepper sauce) and *tomatada de cordero* (lamb stew with tomato sauce).

Then there's the combination known as El Intendente, after the finicky Oruro official who always requested that restaurant owners prepare for him a bizarre combination of steak, chicken, blood sausage, chorizo, tripe, kidneys, and whole potatoes.

Chicken is normally either fried *(pollo frito)*, cooked on a spit *(pollo al spiedo)* or broiled *(pollo asado* or *pollo dorado)*, or any combination of the above (yielding *pollo a la broaster, broasted* or even *broasterd)*. It's commonly served as *pollo a la canasta:* 'chicken-in-a-basket,' with mustard, fries or yuca, and ají. A more sophisticated chicken concoction is Potosí's own (bizarrely named) *ckocko* – spicy chicken cooked in wine or chicha and served with choclo, olives, raisins, grated orange peel and other aromatic condiments.

On the Altiplano, the most popular *pescado* (fish) is *trucha* (trout) from Lake

Titicaca. The lowlands have a wide variety of other freshwater fish, including *sábalo*, *dorado* and the delicious *surubí*. Surubí, a catfish caught throughout the lowlands, is arguably the best of the lot.

In addition, *tatú* (armadillo), *jochi* (or agouti), monkeys, alligators and other endearing rain-forest critters have been eaten to the brink of extinction in some lowland areas.

Dairy Foods

Fresh milk is available through agencies of the national dairy PIL in most cities and towns, but in smaller places, it may be difficult to find. Any shop displaying a picture of a happy cow licking its lips will have milk for sale. Some markets also sell raw (unpasteurized and unhomogenized) milk.

Sheep's milk cheese is made all over the Altiplano and is delicious provided it doesn't contain too much salt. Vendors will usually let you sample it before buying. It's cheaper and arguably better than cow's milk cheese, which is considered more prestigious among campesinos.

Chaco cheese from eastern Tarija and western Santa Cruz departments is coveted all over Bolivia as the finest produced in the country. The Mennonite colonies of Santa Cruz department also produce some excellent European-style cheeses.

Tubers

Tuberous plants make up a large percentage of most Bolivians' vegetable diet. Potatoes come in nearly 250 colorful varieties. Freeze-dried potatoes, known as *chuños* or *tunta*, are made by leaving potatoes out in the winter cold for four consecutive nights. They're then pressed to extract the water, peeled and dried. Tunta, or bleached chuño, is a little more complicated and requires the chuño to be packed in straw and left in running water for at least a month before drying. They're then rehydrated, cooked and eaten as snacks or as accompaniment to meals. Few foreigners find them particularly appealing, mainly because they have the appearance and consistency of polystyrene when dry and are tough and tasteless when

cooked. A favorite dish featuring chuños is *chairo*, a mutton or beef soup with chuños, fresh potatoes and *mote* (dried maize, prepared in the same way as the chuños).

Ocas are tough, purple, potato-like tubers. They taste pretty good fried or roasted, but boiled ocas will take some getting used to – the flavor has been described as a cross between potato and skunk spray. Another tuber sold in markets everywhere is the *añu*, a tiny purple, yellow and white stalagmite-shaped thing that tastes like a cross between a rutabaga (swede) and a parsnip, and is usually served boiled.

In the lowlands, the potato and its relatives are replaced by plantain or the root of the ubiquitous yuca (manioc or cassava), which is good – if rather bland – provided it has been sufficiently cooked.

Cereals

Two other common foods include choclo, a large-kernel maize that is eaten everywhere on the Altiplano, and *habas*, the beans of the *palqui* plant, which grow wild and are eaten roasted or added to stews. They are also used to make a coffee-like beverage. In Potosí and Sucre, a particularly appealing dish is *kala purkha*, a delicious soup made from maize that is cooked in a ceramic dish by adding a steaming chunk of heavy pumice. Another popular legume is *tarhui*, which is grown in diminishing quantities mainly around Sucre.

Quinoa, a grain unique to the area, is high in protein and is used to make flour and thicken stews. It's similar in most respects to sorghum or millet, but grows on a stalk and resembles caviar when it's in the field. Quinoa was first cultivated in the Andes several thousand years ago but the Spanish conquistadors forced the Indians to adopt European grains and thereafter, quinoa was rarely used. This nutritious grain has been rediscovered, however, and analysis has revealed that it contains a unique balance of fat, oil and protein. It is the only edible plant that contains all essential amino acids in the same proportions as milk, making it especially appealing to vegans. Among the best strains are *quinoa blanca*, or *quinoa real*, which is produced on the Southern Altiplano in Potosí and Oruro departments.

Fruit

In addition to familiar fruits such as oranges and bananas, many other varieties are cultivated, some of which are unfamiliar outside South America. *Chirimoya*, or custard apple, is a green, scaly fruit sold in markets around the country. The flesh looks and tastes like vanilla custard. The fruit of the prickly pear cactus *(tuna)* is eaten in the highlands. *Maracuya* (passion fruit) is a sweet and delicious fruit; unripe maracuya is known as *tumbo* and makes an excellent juice. Variations on the banana – *plátanos* (plantains) and *guineos* (finger bananas) – are available practically everywhere.

In the lowlands, the range of exotic tropical fruits defies middle-latitude imaginations; among the more unusual are *ambaiba (Cecropia sp)*, which is shaped like a human hand; the small, round, green-and-purple *guaypurú (Myrciaria cauliflora)*; the spiny yellow *ocoro (Rheedia madruno)*; lemon-like *guapomo (Silacia elliptica)*; bean-like *cupesi (Prosopis chilensis)*; the *marayau (Batris major)*, which resembles a bunch of giant grapes; the *nui (Pesudolaredia laevis)*, a berry that is similar to the currant; the *sinini (Annoru muricata)*, which resembles a scaly onion; and the stomach-shaped *paquio (Hymenaea courbaril)*. A good place to sample more exotic fruits is Mercado Los Pozos in Santa Cruz.

Sweets

Perhaps the most interesting Bolivian sweets are *confites*, which are associated with holidays and offerings. These festive candies may only be made by traditional rural confectioners after performing a *cha'lla* (offering) to Pachamama, the earth mother. The candies are made of blue, pink, red or green boiled sugar syrup, hardened around a filling of nuts, aniseed, fruits, biscuit or desiccated coconut. Ceremonial confites are intended as religious offerings and are not meant to be eaten.

Another sweet popular with children is *tojorí*, an oatmeal-like concoction of mashed corn, cinnamon and sugar. In Potosí, you can get *tawa-tawas* (a type of doughnut) and delicious *sopaipillas*, sweet fried breads. The similar *buñuelos* are available around Bolivia, normally in conjuction with *api* (see Drinks, later).

For a real treat, Bolivia's own Breick chocolate rivals that of Switzerland and some say it's better than Cadbury. Judge for yourself!

Restaurants

Food stalls in the market *comedores* (dining halls) sell cheap and filling – and usually tasty meals. They're found in every city and town, and are viable and convenient if you're traveling on limited funds or enjoy sampling a bit of local culture. Keep in mind, however, that your internal plumbing may need time to adjust; don't give up on market food just because you got the runs the first time you tried it.

Local restaurants range from street stalls selling quick bites to classy sidewalk cafés where you can sit beside a palm-lined boulevard and eat steak. Every city and town also has numerous backstreet cubbyholes, greasy-spoon truckstops and family-run operations of varying quality. Smaller informal establishments describe the day's offerings on a blackboard posted at the entrance; this is normally derived from whatever seemed a bargain at the morning market. When there is a menu, it normally reflects what the propietor wishes were available more than a true representation of what's cooking. In some cases, it's more efficient to ignore the menu and ask what's actually on offer. This is the sort of place where wall space is shared by Swiss chalets, Jesus Christ, the Pope, and bikini-clad babes suggesting you enjoy a beer with your lunch.

Confiterías and *pastelerías* normally sell little more than some snacks and coffee. *Heladerías*, or ice-cream parlors, are becoming increasingly sophisticated, offering pizza, pasta, doughnuts, salteñas, coffee specialties and even full meals, in addition to ice cream. They're open daily, including Sunday afternoons, and are very popular with Bolivian youth.

There are also several fast-food joints in La Paz, Cochabamba and Santa Cruz, including McDonald's, Burger King and Subway. Restaurants serving typical European or North American foods are often found around larger hotels or in middle-class districts of larger cities. Italian restaurants are increasingly popular, *chifas* (Chinese restaurants) exist in most major cities, and even more exotic cuisines, such as vegetarian, Mexican, Swiss and Japanese, are represented.

DRINKS
Nonalcoholic Drinks
Beyond the usual black tea, coffee and chocolate, typical local hot drinks include *mate de coca* (coca leaf tea), *mate de manzanilla* (chamomile tea) and *api* (see Chicha, later in this section). A favorite that you'll find at bus stops and railway stations is *refresco* (refreshment), an anonymous fruit-based juice, often with a fuzzy ball in the bottom of the glass. The fuzzy ball, known as *despepitado* or *mocachinchi*, is actually a dried and shriveled peach.

Common soft drinks are available, as are locally produced soft drinks of varying palatability. Locals have also been known to enjoy a Peruvian sugar rush known as Inca Kola (immortalized in the book by Matthew Parris), a piss-yellow soft drink that tastes like liquefied bubble gum. It's too disgusting for words.

Other favorite drinks include *tostada* (known as *aloja* in southern Bolivia), which is made of corn, barley, honey, cinnamon and cloves. A delicious walnut-based drink, which was originally made popular in Central America, is known as *horchata*. Many markets and restaurants serve up *licuados*, delicious fruit shakes made with either milk or water. *Batidas* are whipped up with milk, sugar and a nonalcoholic beer known as *bi-cervecina*.

Alcoholic Drinks
When imbibing stronger alcoholic beverages, remember that altitude intensifies their effects. In La Paz, you can be good and laid out after three bottles of beer and practically unconscious after the fourth. Also remember that when Bolivians gather to drink alcohol – whether it's beer, wine, *chicha* or whatever – it's serious; they intend to get plastered. Before accepting an invitation to drink with locals, consider that you'll be expected to do the same. In fact, Bolivians seem to take offense if any person in their party is able to walk out of a bar under their own steam.

Beer Bolivian lagers generally aren't bad. Popular brands include the fizzy and strange-tasting Huari, and the good but rather nondescript Paceña, both from La Paz; the pleasant but weak-flavoured Sureña from Sucre; refreshing Taquiña from Cochabamba; Astra, from Tarija, which is available as lager or malt; robust Potosina from Potosí; and the slightly rough Ducal, and cold and tasty Tropical Extra – arguably the best of the lot – both from Santa Cruz. Note that at higher altitudes, beer (particularly Huari) tends to froth more than you're probably used to.

Wine & Singani Most of Bolivia's *vino* (wine) is produced around Tarija with varying degrees of success. The best – and most expensive – is Concepción San Bernardo de la Frontera, which sells for about US$5 for a 750ml bottle. San Pedro, which is produced in beautiful Camargo, also costs US$5 a bottle and isn't too bad.

The same wineries also produce *singani*, a spirit obtained by distilling poor-quality grapes and grape skins, and in fact, some products labeled as 'wine' are actually singani mixed with grape juice. The three main brands of singani – San Pedro, Rujero and Casa Real – all employ grading systems. The finest-quality singani are San Pedro de Oro, Rujero Etiqueta Negra and Casa Real Etiqueta Negra Merillada. Cheaper and harsher are San Pedro de Plata and Casa Real Etiqueta Negra Común. For the real rotgut stuff, go for San Pedro Cinteña, Rujero Etiqueta Roja or Casa Real Etiqueta Roja.

A favorite singani-based cocktail is *chuflay*, a pleasant blend of singani,

Spirits for the Spirits

The world of the Andean Indians – Quechua and Aymará – is populated by hosts of well-respected spirits, the *apus* and *achachilas* (mountain spirits believed to be ancestors of the people). They mainly pervade wild areas and are prone to both favorable behavior and fits of temper. The people also believe they themselves are literally descended from the earth mother, Pachamama, who is also respected and venerated.

In order to demonstrate respect and keep on the better side of all these entities, people take them into consideration in facets of everyday life. Before a person takes the first sip of alcohol from a glass, it is customary to make an offering, or *t'inka*, to Pachamama. This is done by spilling a few drops from the glass onto the floor or ground, thus demonstrating to Pachamama that she takes precedence over her human subjects. When an object such as a home or vehicle needs to be blessed by Pachamama, the apus and/or achachilas, a glass of alcohol is splashed over the object. This is known as a *cha'lla*. When it's sprinkled with the fingers, it's called a *chu'ra*.

These rituals are readily observed by visitors on weekends in front of the cathedral in Copacabana, when cars and trucks are blessed with a cha'lla, and at La Cumbre near La Paz, in preparation for the treacherous descent into the Yungas.

lemon-lime soda, ice and lemon. Around Cochabamba, you can sample such alcoholic concoctions as *guarapo*, a specialty in Sipe-Sipe, and *garapiña*, which is popular in Quillacollo.

Imported wines are also available, and if you buy them at small street stalls, *tiendas* or *almacenes*, they can be excellent value. The popular Chilean wine, Undurraga (white or red), costs only US$2 for a 750ml bottle in La Paz. Even better is the Argentine Toro Viejo, which costs from US$1.50 to US$2.50 for a 750ml bottle; the red is particularly good.

More-expensive wines – mainly Chilean, Argentine and Californian – are also available for considerably less than you'd pay in Europe or North America.

Chicha The favorite alcoholic drink of the Bolivian masses is a maize liquor known as *chicha cochabambina*, obtained by fermenting maize. It's quite good and is guaranteed to produce an effect, but there are a lot of rumors flying around Bolivia concerning additional ingredients, which are best ignored if you plan to drink it. Although chicha is made all over Bolivia, production is concentrated in the Cochabamba region. Those white plastic flags you see flying on long poles indicate a *chichería*, a place where chicha is sold.

Considerably milder are the numerous other incarnations of chicha, which are made from a variety of items and may or may not contain alcohol. In Copacabana and La Paz, *api* is served at breakfast or after meals. Usually served hot, api is a very syrupy form of chicha made from *kulli* or *maíz morada* (sweet purple maize), lemon, cinnamon and staggering amounts of white sugar. A less sweet and lightly alcoholic form of *chicha de maíz* is made from *maíz blanco* (white maize). *Chicha de maní* is made from peanuts. In the Amazon region, a favorite drink is *chicha de yuca*, a light and refreshing yuca beverage that tastes like an Indian lassi. In San Ignacio de Moxos, *chicha de camote* (sweet potato chicha), is served as an accompaniment to meals. It's both rich and not too sweet, and tastes much better than it sounds.

Poorer campesinos rarely consider such trifles as taste or personal health when looking for a cheap and direct route to inebriation, and many favor an especially head-pounding swill known simply as *alcoól potable* or *aguardiente* (fire-water). This fiery, gut-wrenching stuff is essentially pure alcohol, so if you're offered a glass, you may wish to make a particularly generous offering to Pachamama (see 'Spirits for the Spirits').

ENTERTAINMENT
Cinemas

Every Bolivian city has at least one cinema. Most films are shown in English with

Spanish subtitles, but sound systems are poor and crackly and nobody bothers to keep quiet for the foreign dialogue, anyway, so a knowledge of Spanish will help. In larger towns, you'll be able to catch first-run films less than a month after their debuts in North America and Europe. In smaller towns, you'll need to appreciate the likes of *Girls' Dorm, Ninjas from Space* and *Rocky Meets Rambo*.

Admission to a film or double feature averages US$1.50, although in some places, you can sit on the concrete bleachers in the *galería* for a 30% reduction.

Theater

Bolivia's most renowned theater group is Sucre-based Teatro de los Andes, which was begun in 1991 by Argentine-born César Brie. Brie studied and worked in Italy and Denmark before returning to South America and settling in Bolivia because of its rich indigenous traditions. His aim is to combine modern European theater with Andean themes and traditions. The troupe now consists of seven members – Argentine, Bolivian and Italian – who are based at Brie's *finca* (country retreat) in Yotala, occasionally offering theater workshops.

Over the past few years, the group has performed a range of European, Bolivian and original works, from *Don Quixote* and *Romeo and Juliet* to *Ubu* and *Legend of a People who Lost the Sea*. They perform not only in the cities – which pays the expenses – but also in rural areas, where they hope to spread an appreciation of theater not only to the urban middle classes, but to the campesinos as well.

Folk & Traditional Music

For a taste of Bolivian folk music, you can attend a peña, an Andean or highland Bolivian folk music show that may include dancing. The music is usually played on typical Andean instruments such as *quenas*, *zampoñas* and *charangos*. Shows featuring only guitars, singing, comedy or a combination of these are also common. In all cases, the music gets better as the bottles get emptier, and to get you started the admission charge will generally include your first drink. Although most peñas ambitiously advertise action six or seven nights a week, when there aren't enough patrons they scale them back to two or three nights a week, most often Thursday to Saturday.

Pubs & Bars

In Bolivia, as elsewhere, drink tends to bring out a measure of brutal honesty and intense emotion in people, and things may become uncomfortable. Reactions toward foreigners may go either way, but will rarely be neutral. If you're a male, there's a chance you'll have an interesting experience, but you'll also run the risk of being regarded in a less-than-friendly manner. For example, just try to reason with someone who's been seized with the notion that all foreigners are Drug Enforcement Agency (DEA) agents. Unaccompanied women would be wise to avoid local male bars altogether, lest they be misconstrued.

Don't expect much from local bars in Bolivian cities. They're frequented almost exclusively by men who go there not to dance or carry on conversation, but to drink and get drunk. Once that goal is met, anything can happen. Most patrons are already past sobriety by 6 pm, and the next six hours until closing do nothing to improve their condition (to avoid trouble, most local bars stop serving at midnight or earlier).

Classier drinking dens are sometimes known as *wiskerías*, and there's also a growing selection of reputable bars in La Paz, Cochabamba, Sucre and Santa Cruz catering to middle-class Bolivians and the substantial expatriate communities.

SHOPPING

Although prices for artesanía (handicrafts) are generally lower at the point of original production, in La Paz and Copacabana you'll find a range of work from all over the country. All sorts of clothing – including ponchos, *chompas* (jumpers), *chullos* (woolen hats), vests, jackets and mufflers – is available in wool, llama and alpaca (which is the finest). Some pieces are hand-dyed and woven or knitted while others are mass-produced by machine. Learn to tell the difference and never take an overzealous shopkeeper's word for it. Some would tell you it was made of solid gold if it would result in a sale!

Prices vary depending on quality, but expect to pay about US$15 to US$17 for a passable alpaca sweater and up to US$25 for a good one. A chullo costs about US$3 and a very nice poncho from US$16 to US$18. Prices for most things will be slightly higher in La Paz than in Puno or Cuzco (Peru), or directly from the artisans around

the country, but this is normally justified by the quality and variety of items available.

Each town or region has its own specialty. For traditional musical instruments, head for Tarija or check out the Calle Sagárnaga area of La Paz. For weavings, head for the Cordillera Apolobamba or the environs of Sucre, where you'll find some of the world's finest work. Ceramics are a specialty around Cochabamba and lowland arts in tropical woods are sold in Santa Cruz, Trinidad and other towns of the Amazon Basin.

Getting There & Away

AIR

South America isn't exactly a hub of international travel, nor is it an obvious transit point along the major international routes. This is often reflected in high airfares to or from Europe, North America and Australia. You may find bargain fares to Quito (Ecuador), Lima (Peru), Santiago (Chile) or Rio de Janeiro (Brazil), where you can travel overland or find decent short-haul flight deals to La Paz or Santa Cruz.

You'll also get some relief with low-season fares, and fortunately, the low season partially coincides with the best times to visit the region. Low- and shoulder-season fares from Europe and North America typically apply from April to June. High season is from July to September and the weeks around Christmas. The rest of the year falls into the shoulder-season category.

Airports & Airlines

Bolivia's two main international airports are El Alto (also known as John F Kennedy Memorial Airport), in La Paz, and Viru-Viru, in Santa Cruz. Note that owing to altitude concerns, flying into La Paz is generally more expensive than into Santa Cruz. Alternatively, many travelers choose to take discounted flights into larger urban centers, such as Lima (Peru), Santiago (Chile), Buenos Aires (Argentina), Rio de Janeiro or São Paulo (Brazil), then fly on local airlines or travel overland to Bolivia.

The Peruvian airline AeroContinente has flights between La Paz and Cuzco, Peru (US$100), on Monday, Thursday and Saturday; Colombia's Avianca flies between Lima and La Paz (US$234) four times weekly; Iberia flies daily to and from Madrid (from US$1157) via Buenos Aires, São Paulo, Miami or Lima; LanChile connects La Paz with Arica (US$90), Iquique (US$123) and Santiago (US$410), all in Chile, once daily; Varig has flights between La Paz and Rio de Janeiro (US$445), via São Paulo (US$445), daily except Sunday; and LanPeru flies daily

to Lima (US$203), with connections to Cuzco and Arequipa. See the Getting There & Away section in the La Paz chapter for contact details on airlines serving La Paz.

From Santa Cruz, Lloyd Aéreo Boliviano (LAB; ☎ 03-344159; fax 03-344709), on Warnes at Chuquisaca, offers international service to Santiago via La Paz and direct flights to Manaus, São Paulo, Belo Horizonte, Rio de Janeiro, Caracas, Panama City and Miami (from US$434/810 one-way/ roundtrip). The Paraguayan airline TAM Mercosur (☎ 03-371999) flies three times weekly to Asunción (US$312/512), with connections to Miami, Buenos Aires and several Brazilian cities. VARIG (☎ 03-349333; toll-free ☎ 0800-8484; fax 03-341114; Edificio Nago, Celso Castedo 39) flies to Rio de Janeiro (US$445/890) and São Paulo (US$445/890); American Airlines (☎ 03-341314; Beni 202) has daily flights to Miami (US$533/810); and Aerolíneas Argentinas

---

Warning

The information in this chapter is particularly vulnerable to change: Prices for international travel are volatile, routes are introduced and canceled, schedules change, special deals come and go, and rules and visa requirements are amended. Airlines and governments seem to take a perverse pleasure in making price structures and regulations as complicated as possible. You should check directly with the airline or a travel agent to make sure you understand how a fare (and ticket you may buy) works. In addition, the travel industry is highly competitive and there are many lurks and perks.

The upshot of this is that you should get opinions, quotations and advice from as many airlines and travel agents as possible before you part with your hard-earned cash. The details given in this chapter should be regarded as pointers and are not a substitute for your own careful, up-to-date research.

(☎ 03-339776; Plaza 24 de Septiembre) flies daily to Buenos Aires (US$347/533).

Buying Tickets

Your plane ticket will probably be the single most expensive item in your travel budget, and it's worth taking some time to research the current state of the market. Start early; some of the cheapest tickets must be purchased well in advance, and some popular flights sell out quickly. Speak with recent travelers, watch for ads in newspapers and magazines, and look for special offers, remembering to check the press aimed at the citizens of the country you plan to travel to.

Inexpensive tickets are available in two distinct categories: official and unofficial. Official ones have a variety of names, including advance purchase tickets, advance purchase excursion (APEX) fares, super-APEX and simply budget fares. Unofficial tickets are discounted tickets that the airlines release through selected travel agents and are usually not available through the airline offices. Airlines can, however, supply information on routes and timetables and book official tickets; their low-season, student and senior citizens' fares can be competitive. Also, normal, full-fare airline tickets sometimes include one or more en-route stopovers free of charge, which can make them a good value.

Roundtrip tickets usually work out to be cheaper than two one-way fares – often much cheaper. Be aware that immigration officials may ask to see return or onward tickets, and that if you can't show either, you might have to provide proof of 'sufficient means of support,' which means you have to show a lot of money or, in some cases, valid credit cards.

Phone travel agencies to find discounted tickets. You may discover that those impossibly cheap flights are 'fully booked, but we have another one that costs a bit more…' Or that the flight is on an airline notorious for its poor safety standards and leaves you in the world's least favorite airport in mid-journey for 14 hours – where you're confined to the transit lounge because you don't have a visa. Or the agent claims to have the last two seats available for that country for the whole of August, which he will hold for you for a maximum of two hours as long as you come in and pay cash. Don't panic – keep calling around.

If you're coming from the USA, southeast Asia, or the UK, you'll probably find the cheapest flights are being advertised by obscure agencies whose names probably haven't even reached the telephone directory. Many such firms are honest and solvent, but there are a few rogues who will take your money and disappear – only to reopen elsewhere a month or two later under a new name.

If you feel suspicious about a firm, don't give them all the money at once – leave a deposit of 20% or so and pay the balance when you get the ticket. If they insist on cash in advance, go somewhere else or be prepared to take a very big risk. And once you have the ticket, call the airline to confirm that you are actually booked on the flight.

You may decide to pay more than the rock-bottom fare by opting for the safety of a better-known travel agent. Firms such as STA Travel, which has offices worldwide, Council Travel in the USA and elsewhere or Travel CUTS in Canada offer good prices to most destinations, and won't disappear overnight leaving you clutching a receipt for a nonexistent ticket.

Once you have your ticket, copy down the ticket number, the flight number and other details, and keep the information safe and separate from the ticket. If the ticket is lost or stolen, this will help you get a replacement. It's sensible to buy travel insurance as early as possible. Travel insurance purchased the week before you fly may not cover flight delays caused by industrial action.

Use the fares quoted in this book as a guide only. They are approximate and based on the rates advertised by travel agents at the time of research, but they're subject to change at any time.

Buying Tickets Online Purchasing tickets online is a growing trend. Many airlines now have their own websites that allow you to book and purchase tickets with a credit card. There are also several websites that specialize in discounted tickets, including www.lowestfare.com, www.travelocity.com and www.priceline.com; with the latter, you bid on available tickets and can sometimes score very good deals. In most cases, you can choose between electronic tickets, which are issued at the time of check-in at the airport, and paper tickets, which will be delivered by post or courier at an additional cost.

There are glitches, however. On Priceline, for example, you're limited to routings that include three or fewer legs, so if you're traveling to South America from Asia or Africa – or even from smaller centers in North America, Europe or Australasia – you can forget it. Travelocity does very well with domestic US routes, but seems to have less success with international itineraries, especially when they include relatively obscure destinations (such as Bolivia).

With Lowestfare, some very weird things can happen: When I attempted to purchase a roundtrip ticket to La Paz, Bolivia, the itinerary that came up included one-way from Anchorage to La Paz, Bolivia, but the return flight departed from La Paz, Mexico – despite the fact that I'd keyed in the airport code (LPB) and not just the city name! In Bolivia, I met several US travelers who'd jumped at the apparently excellent fare offered and were understandably unimpressed when they landed in La Paz, Mexico. Only with a great deal of unpleasant wrangling – and additional expense – did they eventually arrive in Bolivia.

Travelers with Special Needs
If you have special needs of any sort – you're vegetarian, diabetic, halaal- or kosher-observant, or allergic to peanuts; traveling in a wheelchair; using a guide dog; taking the baby; terrified of flying; or whatever – let the airline staff know as soon as possible so that they can make the necessary arrangements. Remind them when you reconfirm your booking (at least 72 hours before departure) and again when you check in at the airport. It may also be worth calling around before you make your booking to find out which airline can best handle your particular requirements.

Children aged under two travel for 10% of the full fare – or free on some airlines – as long as they don't occupy a seat. They don't get a baggage allowance in this case. 'Skycots,' baby food and diapers (nappies) should be provided by the airline if requested in advance. Children aged two to 12 can usually occupy a seat for half to two-thirds of the full fare, and are allowed a standard baggage allowance.

Departure Tax
Travelers who have spent fewer than 90 days in Bolivia are charged a US$20 departure tax on international flights. Those staying longer than 90 days must pay an additional US$30. The tax is payable to the aviation authority, AASANA, after check-in. In addition, most Bolivian airports levy domestic AASANA departure taxes, plus miscellaneous surcharges to fund various community projects.

The USA
Flights originating in the USA are subject to numerous restrictions and regulations because of governmental red tape in determining fare structures, in addition to competition between carriers. This is especially true of bargain tickets; anything cheaper than the standard tourist or economy fare must be purchased from 14 days to a month prior to departure. From the USA, open tickets, which allow an open return date within a 12-month period, are generally not available, and penalties of up to 50% are imposed if you change the return booking. Departure and return dates must be booked in advance, and tickets are normally subject to minimum and maximum stay requirements: usually seven days and three to six months, respectively.

The major carrier gateway cities from the USA are New York, Los Angeles and Miami. For South America, the best deals are out of Miami, with some departures from Los Angeles.

The best way to find cheap flights in the USA is by checking the Sunday travel sections in major newspapers such as the *New York Times*, *Chicago Tribune*, *Los Angeles*

Air Travel Glossary

Bucket Shops These are unbonded travel agencies specializing in discount airline tickets.

Cancellation Penalties If you have to cancel or change a discounted ticket, heavy penalties are often involved; insurance can sometimes be taken out against these penalties. Some airlines impose penalties on regular tickets as well, particularly against 'no-show' passengers.

Courier Fares Businesses often need to send urgent documents or freight securely and quickly. Courier companies hire people to accompany the package through customs and, in return, offer a discount ticket that is sometimes a phenomenal bargain. However, you may have to surrender all your baggage allowance and take only carry-on luggage.

Full Fares Airlines traditionally offer 1st-class (coded F), business-class (coded J) and economy-class (coded Y) tickets. These days, so many promotional and discounted fares are available that few passengers pay full economy fare.

Lost Tickets If you lose your airline ticket, an airline will usually treat it as a traveler's check and, after inquiries, issue you another one. Legally, however, an airline is entitled to treat it like cash: If you lose it, it's gone forever. Take good care of your tickets.

Onward Tickets An entry requirement for many countries is a ticket out of the country. If you're unsure of your next move, the easiest solution is to buy the cheapest onward ticket to a neighboring country or a ticket from a reliable airline that can later be refunded if you do not use it.

Open-Jaw Tickets These are roundtrip tickets that permit you to fly into one place but return from another. If available, these tickets can save you backtracking to your arrival point.

Overbooking Because almost every flight has some passengers who fail to show up, airlines often book more passengers than they have seats. Usually excess passengers make up for the no-shows, but occasionally somebody gets 'bumped' onto the next available flight. Guess who it is most likely to be? The passengers who check in late.

Promotional Fares These are officially discounted fares, available from travel agencies or direct from the airline.

Reconfirmation If you don't reconfirm your flight at least 72 hours prior to departure, the airline may delete your name from the passenger list. Call to find out if your airline requires reconfirmation.

Restrictions Discounted tickets often have various restrictions – for example, they may need to be paid for in advance, or altering them may incur a penalty. Other restrictions include minimum and maximum periods you must be away.

Round-the-World Tickets RTW tickets give you a limited period (usually a year) in which to circumnavigate the globe. You can go anywhere the carrying airlines go as long as you don't backtrack. The number of stopovers or total number of separate flights is decided before you set off, and these tickets usually cost a bit more than a basic roundtrip flight.

Transferred Tickets Airline tickets cannot be transferred from one person to another. Travelers sometimes try to sell the return half of a ticket, but officials can ask you to prove that you are the person named on the ticket. On an international flight, tickets are compared with passports.

Travel Periods Ticket prices vary with the time of year. There is a low (off-peak) season and a high (peak) season, and often a low-shoulder season and a high-shoulder season as well. Usually the fare depends on your outward flight – if you depart in the high season and return in the low season, you pay the high-season fare.

Times or *San Francisco Examiner*. All these papers produce weekly travel sections in which you'll find any number of travel agents' ads for airfares to South America. The *Travel Unlimited* newsletter (PO Box 1058, Allston, MA 02134) publishes the cheapest airfares and courier possibilities for destinations around the world. Alternatively, see the *Air Courier Bulletin* published by the International Association of Air Travel Couriers (☎ 561-582 8320; PO Box 1349, 220 South Dixie Hwy, Lake Worth, FL 33460). The student travel bureaus – STA Travel or Council Travel – are also worth a try, but you may have to produce proof of student status and, in some cases, be under 26 years of age to qualify for their discounted fares.

North American consolidators are relative newcomers to the bucket shop traditions of Europe and Asia, so ticket availability and restrictions should be weighed against what is offered on the standard APEX or full economy (coach) tickets; note that it's often cheaper to purchase a roundtrip ticket and trash the return portion than to pay the one-way fare. North Americans won't get the great deals that are available in London and elsewhere, but a few discount agencies keep a lookout for the best airfare bargains. To comply with regulations, these are sometimes associated with travel clubs:

Airtech (☎ 800-575-8324) 584 Broadway, suite 1007, New York, NY 10012

Cheap Tickets, Inc (☎ 800-377-1000)

Council Travel (☎ 800-226-8624)

Educational Travel Center (☎ 800-747-5551) 438 N Frances St, Madison, WI 53703

High Adventure Travel (☎ 800-428-8735, 415-912-5600; fax 415-912-5606; airtreks@highadv.com; www.highadventure.com) 353 Sacramento St, suite 600, San Francisco, CA 94111

Interworld Travel (☎ 800-468-3796) 800 Douglass Rd, Miami, FL 33134

Last Minute Travel Services (☎ 800-527-8646)

Skylink (☎ 800-247-6659) 265 Madison Ave, 5th floor, New York, NY 10014

STA Travel (☎ 800-777-0112) 10 Downing St, New York, NY 10014

Uni Travel (☎ 314-569-2501) PO Box 12485, St Louis, MO 63132

Canada

As with US-based travelers, Canadians will probably find the best deals traveling to South America via Miami or Los Angeles. Travel CUTS has offices in all major Canadian cities. Scan the budget travel agents' ads in the *Toronto Globe & Mail*, *Toronto Star* and *Vancouver Province* (see also the USA section for publications listing courier flights from North America). The following sometimes offer good airfare deals:

Flight Centre (☎ 604-739-9539) 3030 Granville St, Vancouver, BC V6H 3J8

Nouvelles Frontières (☎ 514-526-8444) 1001 Sherbrook East, suite 720, Montreal, PQ H2L 1L3

Travel CUTS (☎ 888-838-2887, 416-979-2406) 187 College St, Toronto, Ontario M5T 1P7

Australia & New Zealand

Travel between Australasia and South America is not cheap, so it makes sense for Australasians to think in terms of a RTW ticket or a roundtrip ticket to Europe with a stopover in the USA, Rio de Janeiro, Buenos Aires or Santiago. RTW tickets are still available for as little as A$2100, but these tend to include only Northern Hemisphere stopovers, with surcharges for stops in Latin America, Africa or the South Pacific.

STA Travel and Flight Centres International are major dealers in cheap airfares, but it doesn't hurt to check the travel agents' ads in the Yellow Pages and call around. The Saturday travel sections of the *Sydney Morning Herald* and *Melbourne Age* include ads offering cheap fares to South America, but don't be surprised if they happen to be 'sold out' when you contact the agents: They're usually low-season fares on obscure airlines with conditions attached. With Australia's large and well-organized ethnic populations, it may also pay to check special deals in the periodicals aimed at citizens of the country.

One option is to use Qantas' or Air New Zealand's APEX fares between Sydney or Auckland and the US west coast, which are about US$1600 roundtrip (US$2630 roundtrip to Miami) with up to three stopovers. From Los Angeles or San Francisco you can travel overland to Miami or find a cheap APEX ticket. Qantas and Air New Zealand fly over the South Pole between Auckland or Sydney and Buenos Aires or Santiago for US$1170 roundtrip, with specials as low as US$985 roundtrip. The Rio de Janeiro route from Sydney via Johannesburg or Bangkok costs around US$2500.

The main discount agency in Australasia is STA Travel, which is represented in most cities and on university campuses; roundtrip fares to South America on mainstream airlines cost between US$1000 and US$1500.

Affordable South America (☎ 03-9600 1733) 288 Queen St, Melbourne, Victoria

South American Adventure Travel (☎ 07-854 1022) 132 Wickham St, Fortitude Valley, Brisbane, Qld

South American Tour Specialists (☎ 03-9725 4655) 344 Main St, Croydon, Victoria

South American Travel Centre (☎ 02-264 6397) 49 Castlereagh St, Sydney, NSW

STA (☎ 02-9212 1255) 855 George St, Ultimo, NSW

(☎ 08-8223 2426) 234 Rundle St, Adelaide, SA

(☎ 07-3221 3722) 111-117 Adelaide St, Brisbane, Qld

(☎ 03-9349 2411) 224 Faraday St, Carlton, Victoria

(☎ 08-9430 5553) 53 Market St, Fremantle, WA

(☎ 0800-100 677) 10 High St, Auckland, NZ

The UK

You'll find the latest deals listed in the travel sections of the Saturday and Sunday editions of London newspapers. Prices for discounted flights between London and Rio de Janeiro start at around UK£300 one way or UK£550 roundtrip – bargain hunters should have little trouble finding even lower prices. A word of warning, however: Don't take travel agency advertised fares as gospel truth. To comply with advertising laws in the UK, companies must be able to offer *some* tickets at the cheapest quoted price, but they may only have one or two of them per week. If you're not one of the lucky ones, you may be looking at higher fares. Start looking for deals well in

advance of your intended departure so you can get a fair idea of what's available.

When buying discounted tickets, make sure the agent you select belongs to some sort of traveler-protection scheme, such as the Association of British Travel Agents (ABTA). If you have bought a ticket through an ABTA-registered agent who subsequently folds, ABTA guarantees a refund or an alternative. Unregistered bucket shops may be cheaper but are often riskier. The following London agencies offer some of the most discounted deals:

Bridge the World (☎ 020-791 0900; fax 020-7813 3350) 47 Chalk Farm Rd, London NW1 8AN

Journey Latin America (☎ 020-8747 8315; sales@ journeylatinamerica.co.uk)

STA Travel (☎ 020-7581 4132) 86 Old Brompton Rd, London SW7 3LQ

Trailfinders (☎ 020-7937 5400) 215 Kensington High St, London W8 6BD

Travel Bug (☎ 020-7835 2000) 125 Gloucester Rd, London SW7 4SF

Europe

The cheapest fares from Europe to South America will be via Miami. On whatever bargain-basement transatlantic carrier is currently operating, you can normally hop to New York for as little as US$150 in the low season, and APEX roundtrip fares between New York and Miami can be as low as US$99. If you're pressed for time, Delta, United, British Airways, Virgin Airways and others offer direct flights between London and Miami for as little as US$400 roundtrip, but getting this fare will require vigilance and flexibility.

Passengers through New York (JFK) or Miami normally must pass through US customs and immigration procedures, even if they won't be visiting the USA. That means you'll either need a US visa or be eligible for the Visa Waiver Program, which is open to Australians, New Zealanders and most Western Europeans unless they're traveling on a non-accredited airline (which includes most Latin American airlines). For information on flights between Miami and South America, see The USA, earlier in this chapter.

UK Travel Publications

The following publications will provide guidance for prospective travelers, and most are happy to post copies to overseas clients who may want to study current offers before deciding on a course of action:

Globe (BCM Roving, London WC1N 3XX) This newsletter, published for members of the Globetrotters' Club, covers obscure destinations and can help in finding traveling companions.

The Star & SA Times (☎ 020-7405 6148; fax 020-7405 6290; satimes@atlas.co.uk; Tower House, Sovereign Park, Market Harborough, Leics LE16 9EF, UK) Published mainly for South African visitors and expats in London, this paper contains a lot of good travel advertising.

Time Out (☎ 020-7836 4411; Tower House, Southampton St, London WC2E 7HD) London's weekly entertainment guide also contains travel information and advertising, and is available at bookstores, newsagents and newsstands. Subscription inquiries should be addressed to Time Out Subs, Unit 8, Grove Ash, Bletchley, Milton Keynes MK1 1BZ, UK.

TNT Magazine (☎ 020-7937 3985; 52 Earls Court Rd, London W8, UK) This publication is available free at most London Underground stations and on street corners around Earls Court and Kensington. It caters to Aussies and Kiwis working in the UK, so it's full of travel advertising. You'll find discounted fares to Lima, Quito and Rio de Janeiro, as well as other parts of South America, often with Varig.

Trailfinder (☎ 020-7603 1515; fax 020-7938 3305), 42-48 Earls Court Rd, London W8 6EJ, UK) This magazine is free in London, but if you want it mailed it costs UK£6 for four issues in the UK or Ireland and UK£10 or the equivalent for four issues elsewhere (airmail). The affiliated travel agency, Trailfinders, can organize ticketing, as well as injections, anti-malarials, visas and travel publications. It also has a library of information for prospective travelers. It's been in business for years and the staff is friendly; see The UK for contact information.

Wanderlust Magazine (☎ 01753-620426; fax 01753-620474; PO Box 1832, Windsor, Berks SL4 6YP, UK) This excellent travel magazine includes articles, advertising, fare and package-tour information, guidebook reviews and pointers for both independent and tour-group travelers. It's available by subscription all over the world.

There are bucket shops by the dozen in Paris, Amsterdam, Brussels, Frankfurt and other places. Many travel agents in Europe have ties with STA Travel, where you'll find cheap tickets that may be altered once without charge. STA and other discount outlets in major transport hubs include:

Alternativ Tours (☎ 030-881 2089) Wilmersdorferstrasse 94, Berlin

Council Travel (☎ 01-42 66 20 87) rue St Augustine, Paris

Council Travel (☎ 01-44 55 55 44) 22 rue des Pyramides, Paris

CTS (☎ 06-46791) Via Genova 16, off Via Nazionale, Rome

Kilroy Travel (☎ 030-310 0040) Hardenbergstrasse 9, D-10623 Berlin

International Student & Youth Travel Service (☎ 01-322 1267) Nikis 11, 10557 Athens

Malibu Travel (☎ 020-623 6814) Damrak 30, Amsterdam

NBBS (☎ 020-624 0989) Rokin 38, Amsterdam

SSR (☎ 01-261 2956) Leonhardstrasse 5-10, Zürich

STA Travel (☎ 069-70 30 35) Bergerstrasse 118, 60325 Frankfurt

USIT (☎ 01-679 8833) 19 Aston Quay, Dublin

Voyages Wasteel (☎ 01-43 43 46 10) 2 rue Michel Charles, 75012 Paris

Asia

From Asia, the hot tickets are on Japan Airlines (JAL) and Singapore Airlines. On JAL, cheap fares are available between Tokyo, Rio de Janeiro and São Paulo (from US$1616 one way), via Los Angeles; JAL also offers reasonable fares to Rio from the US west coast.

South America

For more on flights and fares between Bolivia and neighboring South American countries, see also Airports & Airlines, earlier in this chapter.

Argentina Traveling between Buenos Aires and Santa Cruz (US$347/533 one-way/roundtrip), LAB flies three times weekly and Aereolíneas Argentinas (in La Paz ☎ 375711; fax 391059) flies daily.

Brazil LAB has flights between Rio de Janeiro (US$445), São Paulo (US$445) and La Paz, via Santa Cruz, four times weekly, and Varig (☎ 02-314040) flies the same route daily. There's a US$18 departure tax on international flights originating in Brazil.

Chile LanChile (☎ 02-358377) and LAB both fly daily between La Paz, Arica, Iquique and Santiago. Passengers departing Chile are subject to a departure tax of US$20, and Australians, Canadians and US citizens landing in Santiago must pay an 'entry tax' of US$40 per person.

Paraguay Between La Paz, Santa Cruz and Asunción, you can fly TAM Mercosur (☎ 02-443442) three times weekly, with connections to and from Buenos Aires and cities all over Brazil. One-way fares from Asunción to La Paz start at US$312.

Peru Airlines: LAB, LanPeru (☎ 02-358377), Avianca (☎ 02-375220) and Lufthansa (☎ 02-372170) all fly between Lima and La Paz several times weekly for US$205 one way. To Cuzco (US$100), Aero Continente (☎ 02-310707) flies three times weekly and LanPeru flies daily. Peru levies an air-ticket tax of 21% for Peruvian residents and 7% for nonresident tourists.

LAND

Many travelers enter Bolivia from Peru or Chile as part of a journey along the 'Gringo Trail.' This popular and inexpensive route between North and South America includes eight fascinating countries between the Río Grande (Mexico-US border) and the Colombian border.

Travelers intending to follow this route should know the Pan-American Highway (Carretera Panamericana) is broken in eastern Panama, so they'll be obliged to either fly into Colombia or travel overland past the Darién Gap (Panama) using a combination of rather risky methods, all of which include at least a seven- to 14-day slog through the rain forest. For details on this route, see Lonely Planet's *Central America on a shoestring* or *South America on a shoestring*.

Argentina

There are two major land crossings between Bolivia and Argentina – at Pocitos and between Villazón and La Quiaca – as well as a minor crossing between Bermejo and Aguas Blancas. Argentine officials are extremely vigilant about drugs and no one entering from Bolivia escapes suspicion. Expect thorough searches by customs and police both at the frontier and 20km down the road, inside Argentina.

Several daily international bus services now connect Buenos Aires with the main terminals in La Paz (72 hours, US$110/120 regular/reclining sleeper), Tarija (32 hours, US$98), Cochabamba (72 hours, US$120), and Santa Cruz (36 hours, US$108).

Via La Quiaca From Salta or Jujuy in northwestern Argentina, buses leave several times daily for La Quiaca, opposite the Bolivian town of Villazón. It takes about 20 minutes to walk between the Argentine and Bolivian bus terminals, excluding immigration procedures, but taxis are available.

From Villazón, buses run to Tupiza and Potosí, and trains leave for Tupiza, Uyuni and Oruro. See Villazón in the Southern Altiplano chapter for details.

Via Pocitos The border crossing at tiny Pocitos is just a short distance south of Yacuiba (Bolivia) and north of Tartagal (Argentina). The walk across the border between Pocitos (Argentina) and Pocitos (Bolivia) takes about 10 minutes. There are taxis between Pocitos and Yacuiba and buses to and from Tartagal.

From Tucumán in north central Argentina, take a bus to Embarcación and Tartagal, and from there to Pocitos, on the Bolivian border. Trains and buses connect Yacuiba with Santa Cruz, and there are buses between Yacuiba and Tarija. See Pocitos and Yacuiba in the South Central Bolivia & the Chaco chapter.

Via Orán The minor border crossing between Bermejo and the Argentine hamlet of Aguas Blancas lies one hour by bus from Orán; access across the river is by bridge or ferry. From Bermejo, several bus companies do daily runs to Tarija. See Bermejo in the South Central Bolivia & the Chaco chapter for details about these routes.

Brazil
Via Corumbá Corumbá, opposite the Bolivian border town of Quijarro, is the busiest port of entry between Bolivia and Brazil, and has both train and bus connections from São Paulo, Rio de Janeiro, Cuiabá and southern Brazil. Between Corumbá and Quijarro, buses cost around US$2. Trains travel regularly between Santa Cruz and Quijarro, but they may be less than comfortable, and in the wet season you may face delays of up to several days. From Cáceres, southwest of Cuiabá, you can cross to San Matías in Bolivia and from there either take a bus to San Ignacio de Velasco or fly to Santa Cruz (via Roboré).

See the Eastern Lowlands chapter for further information.

Via Northern Brazil From Brasiléia, in Acre state, you can cross into Cobija, Bolivia, where you'll find a dry-season road and unreliable year-round flights to Riberalta and on to La Paz. A more popular crossing is by ferry from Guajará-Mirim, across the Río Mamoré in Brazil, into Guayaramerín, which is on the Bolivian bank of the river. From there, you can fly to Trinidad, Santa Cruz or La Paz, or travel the long and dusty bus routes to Riberalta and on to Cobija, Rurrenabaque or La Paz.

From Guayaramerín, it's also possible to take a six-day river trip up the Río Mamoré and Río Ichilo to Trinidad, or a 10-day trip to Puerto Villarroel; both destinations have highway links to Santa Cruz or Cochabamba. When the water is high, you may even find transportation up the Río Beni to Rurrenabaque.

See the Amazon Basin chapter for details about these routes.

Chile
It's worth noting that meat, fruit and vegetables cannot be carried from Bolivia into Chile and will be confiscated at the border. You will, however, be issued a receipt. Owing to the high altitudes, warm clothing is essential for any land crossing between Bolivia and Chile!

Via Arica Several *flotas* (long-distance buses) leave the main La Paz bus terminal daily for Arica, Chile (eight hours, US$16), traveling via Tambo Quemado and Lauca National Park. Thanks to the new tarred highway, this once troublesome trip now takes only eight or nine hours. For more information, see Getting There & Away under La Paz and Oruro.

Via Iquique Several companies also offer direct services to Iquique (24 hours, US$20), but it's a much rougher route. Buses usually reach the Colchane border in the wee hours, and passengers must endure typically icy conditions until immigration opens at 7:30 am. Fortunately, coffee and *empanada* (meat or cheese pasty) vendors and moneychangers arrive early.

Via Antofagasta/Calama Coming from Antofagasta, you must first take a bus from the Tramaca bus terminal to Calama (two hours, US$3). From there, a Wednesday evening train goes to Ollagüe on the Bolivian border, eight hours uphill from Calama. In Ollagüe, passengers cross the border to Avaroa on foot to connect with the Bolivian train to Uyuni and Oruro. Although this connection does work occasionally, it may also entail waits of up to 12 hours for the Bolivian train to arrive (as one reader put it 'time enough to get to know all the pigs in Ollagüe by their first names'). As on all routes between Chile and Bolivia, warm clothes are vital. For details, see the Southern Altiplano chapter.

Paraguay

The three-day overland route between Bolivia and Paraguay is extremely rough and sandy, but the trip is now negotiated by hardy *camiones* (flatbed trucks) and buses during the winter dry season. For information on specific routes, see Getting There & Away under Santa Cruz in the Santa Cruz chapter or 'The Chaco Road' in South Central Bolivia and the Chaco chapter.

For the easiest route between Paraguay and Bolivia, cross from Pedro Juan Caballero, in Paraguay, to Ponta Porã, in Brazil, and then travel by bus or train to Corumbá (18 hours with a change at Campo Grande), on the Bolivian border (for more information, see Lonely Planet's *Brazil* guide). From Quijarro, on the Bolivian side, trains run regularly to Santa Cruz.

Peru

Via Puno There are two routes from Puno, which is Peru's main access point for Bolivia. The quicker but less interesting route is by microbus from Puno to the frontier at Desaguadero (two hours, US$2), where you can connect with several daily micros to La Paz (3½ hours, US$2.50).

The more scenic and interesting route is via Copacabana and the Estrecho de Tiquina (Straits of Tiquina). Micros leave from Avenida Ejército in Puno and enter Bolivia at Kasani (2½ hours, US$2), 10km from Copacabana. Tour buses, such as those run by Colectur (Calle Tacna 221), in Puno,

are also a convenient option; they'll even wait while you exchange money at the border. Bolivian visas are available from the consulate at Calle Arequipa 120 in Puno. At Copacabana, you can readily connect with buses, micros or minibuses to La Paz. The entire run from Puno to La Paz can be done in a day, but the Copacabana area merits a couple of days' exploration. See the Lake Titicaca chapter for more information.

If you're headed straight to Cuzco, check out any of the five or six Copacabana travel agencies offering tickets on the daily buses (they can also arrange efficient bus journeys to Arequipa, Lima and other Peruvian destinations). The least expensive seems to be Thunupa Tours (☎ 784130; Calle Oruro 555), which charges US$10 for the 12-hour trip (most others charge anywhere from a negotiable US$12 to US$16). All require a two-hour layover in Puno, which allows time to change money. Note that Peruvian time is one hour behind Bolivian time.

For further information on travel to and around the Peruvian portion of Lake Titicaca – and beyond – see Lonely Planet's *Peru* guide.

Via Puerto Acosta It's also possible to use the obscure border crossing near Puerto Acosta, north of Lake Titicaca. See The Northeastern Shore in the Lake Titicaca chapter for information.

Via Puerto Heath Adventurous travelers can opt for the rain forest route, along the rivers of the north. For around US$80, you can hire a boat at the Madre de Dios dock in Puerto Maldonado (Peru) to take five or so passengers to the Peruvian-Bolivian border at Puerto Pardo/Puerto Heath. With time and luck, however, you may find a cargo boat that's going anyway and will allow you to ride along for a much lower rate, say US$5 per person. Peruvian and Bolivian border guards will stamp you in or out of their respective countries, but they see few foreign travelers and will probably enjoy a good chat, some fruit, a few cigarettes and news of the outside world!

From Puerto Heath, it's possible to continue down the Río Madre de Dios to the balsa crossing at Conquista (road transport passes here only during the dry season) or all the way to Riberalta. However, it can take several days (or weeks!) to organize transportation and will be most affordable if you have a group to share the costs. It's wise to avoid the June to September dry season, when the river is often too low for cargo boats.

Car & Motorcycle

Details on how to take your own vehicle to South America are beyond the scope of this book. Suffice it to say that you can enter Bolivia by private vehicle from any of the neighboring countries – Chile, Peru, Brazil, Argentina or Paraguay. The routes from Brazil and Chile are poor, and the one from Paraguay should be considered only with 4WD and careful preparation. For details about driving in Bolivia, see Car & Motorcycle in the Getting Around chapter.

RIVER
Brazil

Information on boats between Asunción (Paraguay) and Corumbá (Brazil), just over the Brazilian border from Quijarro, is available at the Porto Geral in Corumbá. Now that the regular riverboat service is in mothballs and no longer runs between Asunción and Corumbá, river transport between Paraguay and Bolivia is likely to involve a series of adventurous shorter river journeys and informal arrangements with individual boat captains.

Paraguay

From Asunción, there's a regular river service to Concepción (Paraguay), which costs US$8 in a hammock on deck and US$11 for a cabin. Make arrangements with the captain of the boat, which moors one long block west of the main port area in Asunción. To travel from Concepción on to Corumbá by river will involve making informal arrangements with boat owners. You'll probably wind up doing it in two stages:

Concepción to Bahía Negra (northern Paraguay) and then Bahía Negra to Corumbá.

ORGANIZED TOURS

There are literally hundreds of tour companies out there, and a growing number are adding South America to their itineraries. There are basically two types of tour companies. Overseas agents book transport and hotels, and cobble together a range of itineraries, and locally based operators actually provide the tours. Within Bolivia, there are quite a few of these tour companies, most of which run their trips in small coaches, minibuses or 4WD vehicles.

These all-inclusive tours are less prevalent in Bolivia than in neighboring Peru, where 'checklist sites' such as Cuzco and Machu Picchu serve as mass tourism magnets. A typical Bolivia package tour booked entirely overseas will probably include some sort of hydrofoil excursion on Lake Titicaca, a stop on Isla del Sol, a visit to the Tiahuanaco ruins, perhaps a drive into the Cordillera Real, and museum visits and shopping in La Paz. Some tours also include Sucre or Potosí and increasingly, a circuit through Rurrenabaque and/or the far Southwest. Although this is a comfortable way to check off the sights, it's also a confining and expensive way to travel, and it isn't for everyone.

Most people find adventure tour packages considerably more appealing; these feature activities more than sightseeing and are usually designed with some sort of ecotourism in mind. These trips may include anything from treks in the Cordillera Real or ascents of 6000m peaks to wildlife expeditions in the Bolivian Amazon. Such options are advertised mainly in hiking, mountaineering and wildlife magazines.

If you're taking either type of pre-booked package, it always pays to shop around for deals; especially in Europe, it's becoming increasingly popular to look for late bookings, which are available at a fraction of the normal price. The best place to start looking is the travel sections of weekend newspapers. In some cases, there are special late bookings counters at international airports.

If you prefer not to organize all your time beforehand, you can always book just your flights and your first few nights' accommodations, then take your chances on joining a tour locally (see Organized Tours in the Getting Around chapter). Naturally, time flexibility is essential, but you'll often find some very good deals.

The following list provides an idea of what's available, including some of the more creative and offbeat offerings:

USA

Destination Wilderness (☎ 541-549-1336, 800-423-8868; fax 541-549-1297; destwild@bendnet.com; PO Box 1965, Sisters, OR 97759) This company offers 10-day trips that feature trekking around Sorata and kayaking on Lake Titicaca for US$1870, including gear, meals and accommodations, but not airfares from the USA. For details, see the website www.wildernesstrips.com/bolivia.htm.

Exito Travel (☎ 800-655-4053; fax 510-655-4566; exito@wonderlink.com; 1212 Broadway suite 910, Oakland, CA 94612) This agency specializes in travel to Latin America and has access to inexpensive consolidator airfares. The website is www.exitotravel.com.

Explore Bolivia (☎ 303-545-5728, 877-708-8810; fax 303-545-6239; xplorbol@ix.netcom.com; 2510 N 47th St, suite 207, Boulder, CO 80301) This highly recommended Bolivian-run company provides the most adventurous organized tours you're likely to find. A 12-day trekking and whitewater adventure on the Río Tuichi costs US$1995 and five days of kayaking on Lake Titicaca costs US$990. They also run wonderful trips to Noel Kempff Mercado (from US$1695), trekking and climbing in the Cordillera Real (rates are contingent on the length and difficulty of the trips), nine/14 days of mountain biking in the Andes (US$1395/2240) and 14-day bird-watching tours in the Bolivian Amazon (US$2660). Rates are per person in groups of three to five people. See the website at www.explorebolivia.com.

Focus Tours (☎ 505-466-4688; fax 505-466-4689; focustours@aol.com; 103 Moya Rd, Santa Fe, NM 87505-8360) This group operates bird-watching tours from the Andes to the Amazon, and other natural-history excursions in Bolivia and other countries. See the website at www.focustours.com.

Away.ComTravel (☎ 202-518 7743; fax 202-518-2179; gcohn@away.com; 1611 Connecticut Ave NW 4-C, Washington, DC 20009) This company's adventurous offerings include a 16-day llama trek (US$2435), mountain biking from the highlands to the Amazon Basin (US$2725), hiking in the Apolobamba (US$2775), 10-day cultural tours to the Kallawayas country (US$1656), cultural tours around Lake Titicaca (US$3062), trekking on the Inca Trails (US$3395) and 23-day hiking, trekking and cultural tours in Peru and Bolivia (US$2595). The website is www.away.com.

Myths & Mountains (☎ 800-670-6984; fax 775-832-4454; travel@mythsandmountains.com; 976 Tee Ct, Incline Village, NV 89451) This company organizes small-group tours that focus on natural folk medicine, archaeology and indigenous arts and crafts. It aims to emphasize socially and ecologically responsible tourism, uses local guides and encourages cultural interaction. Offerings include a Cultures & Crafts tour (US$2325), a Folk Medicine tour in the Cordillera Apolobamba (US$1345), ruins tours through central Bolivia and the far Southwest (US$2450), and cruises in the Amazon Basin (US$1345). See the website at www.mythsandmountains.com.

Rainforest Expeditions (☎/fax 530-478-1957; rainfrst@netshel.net; PO Box 2242, Nevada City, CA 95959) This company (which shouldn't be confused with Rainforest Expeditions in Peru) conducts exciting small-group non-motorized camping, canoeing and kayaking trips in the rain forests of northern Bolivia – including Parque Nacional Madidi – for US$2300 to US$3000. It's a good choice if you really want to get off the trampled track.

Mountain Travel Sobek (☎ 510-527 8100, 888-687-6235; fax 510-525-7710; 6420 Fairmount Ave, El Cerrito, CA 94530) This well-known adventure travel company operates a range of climbing and trekking trips in the Cordillera Real. See the website at www.mtsobek.com.

Southwind Adventures (☎ 800-377-9463; fax 303-972-0708) This one offers hiking and trekking in the Cordillera Real; the website is at www.southwindadventures.com.

Wilderness Travel (☎ 800-368-2794 ext 155; 801 Allston Way, Berkeley, CA 94710) The specialty of this firm is guided hiking, trekking and other adventure activities in the Cordillera Real and beyond. The website is www.wildernesstravel.com.

Canada

Great Adventure People (☎ 416-260 0999 ext 114, 800-465 5600; fax 416-260 1888; natalie@gap.ca; 19 Duncan St, suite 401, Toronto, Ontario M5H 3H1) GAP features seven-day adventures at Chalalan Eco-Lodge in Madidi National Park for US$765, plus US$150 for the flight from La Paz to Rurrenabaque. They also do a Bolivian highlights tour from La Paz for US$935, taking in La Paz, Sucre, Potosí and Uyuni. See the website at www.gap.ca for more details.

Australia

Inca Tours (☎ 02-4351 2133, 800-024955; 3 Margaret St, Wyong 2259, NSW) The website for this South America specialist is www.southamerica .com.au.

World Expeditions (☎ 02-9261 1974, 800-803688; 377 Sussex St, Sydney 2000, NSW) For information on this adventure specialist, see the website at www.worldexpeditions.com.au.

UK

Austral Tours (☎ 020-7233 5384; fax 020-7233 5385; info@latinamerica.co.uk) This company hits the Bolivian highlights; see the website at www.latinamerica.co.uk.

Exodus Walking Holidays (☎ 020-8673 0859; sales@exodustravels.co.uk; 9 Weir Rd, London SW12 0LT) Exodus, which is better known for its overland trips, also does hiking and trekking excursions. Its best Bolivian program is probably the seven-day Inca Llama Trek, which traverses the northern end of the Cordillera Real. The website is www.exodus.co.uk.

Explore Worldwide (☎ 01252-344161; fax 01252-343170; 1 Frederick St, Aldershot, Hants GU11 1LQ) This company specializes in adventurous trips all over Latin America.

High Places Ltd (☎ 0114-275 7500; fax 0114-275 3870; wl@highpl.globalnet.co.uk; Globe Works, Penistone Road, Sheffield S6 3AE) This hiking and trekking specialist offers walking itineraries around Lake Titicaca and the Cordillera Apolobamba. The website is at www.highplaces.co.uk.

Himalayan Kingdoms (☎/fax 0114-2763322; expeditions@hkexpeds.demon.co.uk; 45 Mowbray St, Sheffield S3 8EN) This renowned company offers climbs of Huayna Potosí and Illimani, plus a visit to Rio de Janeiro, for UK£2350, including airfare from the UK.

Journey Latin America (☎ 020-8747 8315, 0161-832 1441; fax 020-8742 1312; 12 & 13 Heathfield Terrace, Chiswick, London W4 4JE) This popular company is better known for good airline deals, but it also organizes highlights trips around Latin America. In Bolivia, the focus is on La Paz, Potosí, Lake Titicaca and the Yungas. See the website at www.journeylatinamerica .co.uk for details.

Magic of Bolivia (☎ 020-7221 7310; fax 020-7727 8746) These folks take in the main sights – the Salar de Uyuni, Lake Titicaca, La Paz, Rurrenabaque – and also cobble together custom tours. See also their website at www.bolivia.co.uk.

South American Experience (☎ 020-7976 5511; fax 020-7976 6908; sax@mcmail.com; 47 Causton St, Pimlico, London SW1P 4AT) Basic tours all over the continent are offered here, with catchy names including the Llama, the Potato and the Coffee Bean; several of these include Bolivian highlights. A plus point is the airfare portion of the tour; it's likely to be the lowest available. The website is at www.sax.mcmail.com.

Wildwings (☎ 0117-984 8040; fax 0117-961 0200; wildinfo@wildwings.co.uk; International House, Bank Rd, Kingswood, Bristol BS15 2LX) If you've always wanted a bird-watching holiday in the mountains and rain forests, here's your opportunity. Wildwings concentrates on birds, and if you see larger animals as well, they're frosting on the cake! The website is www.wildwings.co.uk.

Overland Trips

Overland trips are very popular, especially with UK and Australasian travelers. They're designed mainly for first-time travelers who feel uncomfortable striking out on their own or for those who prefer guaranteed social interaction to the uncertainties of the road. If you have the slightest inclination toward independence or would feel confined traveling with the same group, think twice before booking yourself on something like this.

For information or a list of agents selling overland packages in your home country, contact one of the following South America overland operators, all of which are based in the UK (Exodus and Encounter also have offices in Australia, New Zealand, the USA and Canada, and may be contacted through the UK offices).

Dragoman (☎ 01728-861133; fax 01728-861127; Camp Green, Kenton Rd, Debenham, Stowmarket, Suffolk IP14 6LA)

Encounter Overland (☎ 020-73706845; 267 Old Brompton Rd, London SW5 9JA) The website is www.encounter-overland.com.

Exodus Overland Expeditions (☎ 020-8673 0859; sales@exodustravels.co.uk; 9 Weir Rd, London SW12 0LT) The company's website is www.exodus.co.uk.

Guerba Expeditions (☎ 01373-826689; fax 01373-838351; 101 Eden Vale Rd, Westbury, Wiltshire BA13 3QX)

Overland Latin America (☎ 01926-650166) Phone for a brochure or call up the website www.ola-adventure.com.

South American Safaris (☎ 07713-639627) A five-week Andean tour from La Paz to Quito costs £595 plus a food kitty. See the website www.southamericansafaris.com.

Top Deck (☎ 020-7244 8641; fax 020-7373 6201; Top Deck House, 131/135 Earls Court Rd, London SW5 9RH)

Getting Around

AIR

Air travel in Bolivia is inexpensive and is the quickest and most reliable means of reaching out-of-the-way places. It's also the only means of transportation that doesn't wash out during the wet season, and although weather-related schedule disruption does occur, planes can normally get through even during summer flooding in northern Bolivia.

Bolivia's national carrier is Lloyd Aéreo Boliviano (LAB), which connects major cities and remote corners of Bolivia, as well as international destinations. It offers quite reasonable fares and – during the dry season – flights that run more or less on schedule. Although service is rudimentary, LAB is quite proud of its skilled pilots, who are familiar with Bolivia's difficult terrain, and its near-perfect safety record (a DC-6 did go down in the Cordillera Quimsa Cruz in 1969, but this was due to a politically motivated bombing). LAB has ticket offices in every town it serves and, except around holidays, seats are usually available the day before the flight. However, it's essential to reconfirm your reservations 72 hours before the flight (this cannot be stressed strongly enough!), preferably at the airport of departure, or your reservations will be canceled. For their current fares, see their website www.labairlines.com.

Bolivia's other domestic airline, AeroSur, generally offers better service than LAB, including snacks and in-flight meals on longer flights. In general, AeroSur covers the profitable runs (eg, La Paz-Cochabamba and La Paz-Santa Cruz) and also fills gaps in LAB's schedules, but it doesn't serve Tarija. Between major cities, it charges about 20% more than LAB, but to Trinidad, fares are notably higher. The only special deal available is a free flight for every five full-fare roundtrip flights flown (say that five times fast!).

Both major airlines allow 20kg of luggage per passenger, excluding hand luggage, without additional charges, but if your flight isn't full, you might get away with a bit more.

The military airline, Transportes Aéreos Militares (TAM), also operates domestic flights. (Its logo – a lost pelican in a thunderstorm over Illimani – isn't so much a comment on the operation as a political statement on Bolivia's lost seacoast.) TAM uses small planes, such as Fairchild F27s, which fly closer to the landscape than the big jets. Unfortunately, the windows are normally so scratched that you'll be unable to appreciate the stunning scenery below. As military operations go, TAM is remarkably reliable, but schedules can change without notice, flights may be canceled by bad weather or muddy runway conditions, and reservations may be made only in the town of departure. TAM is currently the preferred carrier from La Paz to Rurrenabaque, the popular tourist center, but note that it's strict with its 20kg baggage limit and passengers are charged a whopping US$2 for each additional 5kg.

Air Passes

LAB offers a special 30-day Visite Bolivia (VIBOL) air pass, which includes five flight coupons for a circuit through four different Bolivian cities; you can choose between La Paz, Cochabamba, Sucre, Santa Cruz, Tarija and Trinidad, but may pass through each city only once. If you're flying into Bolivia with LAB, it costs US$150; those traveling on other airlines pay US$225, and a change to a ticketed itinerary costs US$10 per flight. It's available from LAB offices and travel agents abroad. Within Bolivia, both LAB and local travel agents sell the LABpass, which offers the same deal for US$231. There's also a 30-day Benipass, which includes five flight coupons to visit four of the following Amazon Basin towns: Trinidad, San Joaquín, Cobija, Magdalena, Guayaramerín and Riberalta. It also costs US$231 and is sold only in Bolivia.

Domestic Departure Tax

AASANA, the government agency responsible for airports and air traffic, charges a US$1.20 to US$2 domestic airport departure tax *(derecho del aeropuerto)* on domestic flights, which is payable at the AASANA desk on check-in for the flight. Some airports also charge a municipal airport tax on internal flights, which is not included in the ticket price and must also be paid when checking in.

See Departure Tax in the Getting There & Away chapter for international departure taxes.

BUS

For the most part, bus travel in Bolivia is the favored form of transportation among the Bolivian middle classes, and for anyone interested in meeting the Bolivian people, their children, their luggage and sometimes even their animals, buses are the way to go. Long-distance bus lines in Bolivia are called *flotas*, large buses are known as *buses* (**boo**-sehs) and small ones are called *micros* (**mee**-cros). If you require directions to a bus terminal, ask for *la terminal terrestre* or *la terminal de buses*.

Compared with the highway systems of other South American countries, Bolivia's is rather poor, but given their inhospitable terrain and limited resources, the Bolivians have done an admirable job of highway construction. Although the Bolivian government is currently upgrading several main routes, work progresses slowly and construction crews convert main routes into sand traps and mud holes. During the November-March rainy season, and particularly in lowland regions, any or all modes of public transportation, including airlines, may suspend service for weeks at a time.

Bolivian buses range from sagging, sputtering, dilapidated wrecks to large, modern and increasingly comfortable coaches with VCRs, pullman (reclining) seats and ample leg room for the average foreigner. The good news is that the vast majority of flotas now operate the latter type. Gone are the days when a Bolivian bus trip almost invariably meant a long, stiff journey aboard an ancient Bluebird school bus salvaged from a US scrapyard after 500,000km of faithful service. Some Bolivian roads, however (such as the route between Uyuni and Tupiza), remain so wretched that companies will run only expendable equipment over them, providing these older buses with a continued sense of purpose.

That said, even the plushest Bolivian coaches are subjected to hard usage, and true to local standards, they enjoy only a

Bolivian travel is not for stick-in-the-muds.

SANDRA BAO

minimum of nonessential repairs. This leaves many with sprung seats, jammed windows and nonfunctioning heaters – and a conspicuous (and perhaps merciful) absence of on-board toilets, which would require more maintenance that anyone is prepared to commit to. In years of experience on Bolivian buses, I've never encountered a reading light that actually worked or a window that would remain in the position I wanted it. However, most flotas do proudly keep video machines in tip-top repair, and a few companies even offer *bus cama* (sleeper bus) services, which are normally more comfortable than normal buses, with reclining seats, functional heaters, toilets and often even an attendant who serves refreshments.

Between any two cities, you should have no trouble finding at least one bus leaving every day. On the most popular routes, such as La Paz-Oruro, La Paz-Cochabamba or Cochabamba-Santa Cruz, you can choose between dozens of departures daily.

There are, however, a few bus-travel guidelines to consider. If you can manage to travel by daylight, you'll be treated to an eye-level view of the spectacular Bolivian landscapes. Unfortunately, many flotas depart in the evening and travel through the night to arrive in the wee hours of the morning. Except on the most popular runs, most companies' buses depart at roughly the same time, regardless of the number of competitors.

Although most buses travel at night, conditions aren't optimal for sleeping. If you have a seat – and fortunately, most flotas do accept advance seat reservations – you'll soon discover that buses were designed with capacity rather than comfort in mind. Even if a flota limits the number of passengers to the number of seats available, children aren't counted as passengers, and wind up wherever they find room to stretch out: on the floor, on the luggage, on the laps of their parents or sprawled across other passengers.

On buses where the seating capacity is ignored, the floors, racks and roof may be packed to overflowing with bags, boxes, tins, animals and Bolivians. Because the average Bolivian travels with 16 pieces of luggage – often bundles of trade goods to be sold at distant markets – there's pitifully little room for anyone's feet. Then there's the obligatory radio, tape player or video machine that typically blares insipid Latin pop music at concentration-shattering volumes through the night. Add to that the screaming children, the stops at highway *trancas*, the meal and toilet breaks, the icy blasts pouring in through broken windows and, of course, the inevitable breakdowns, and you'll be lucky even to close your eyes.

A good rule of thumb is that any bus journey over unpaved roads, even under optimum conditions, can take up to a quarter again as long as scheduled. During the rainy season, anticipate spending at least double the time.

Note that drunken driving is as serious a problem in Bolivia as it is elsewhere. It's officially prohibited (of course), but don't be surprised to see drivers swill an alcoholic beverage or six during rest stops.

The Journey

The first thing to remember is to keep your baggage receipt, as you'll need it to retrieve your bags at your destination. On longer trips, it's wise to take along food and something to drink, especially if you're traveling through remote areas. Rest stops are unscheduled and depend largely upon the whims and bodily necessities of the driver. When you do stop, ask the driver or assistant when the bus will leave; stops rarely allow time for a leisurely meal and passengers are expected to attend to ablutions and eat their food as quickly as the driver does, or risk being left behind.

On some overnight routes, there may be no rest stops at all; on the infamous 12-hour run from Santa Cruz to San Ignacio de Velasco, the only stop is at Cotoca, just an hour outside Santa Cruz. The obvious advice is to use the toilet before you leave and drink as little as possible along the way.

A few years ago, at any sort of stop – trancas, intermediate stations and toll posts – buses were invaded by vendors selling anything from parrots to shampoo. These days, touts still ply their wares at the outset of the journey, but most of the ambulatory vendors must remain outside the buses and carry on their awkward business through the windows. At stops, you can choose among anything from soft drinks, bread, *empanadas* (meat or cheese pasty), *humintas*, fruit or potatoes to complete meals.

Changes in altitude often necessitate addition and subtraction of clothing, and even in lowland areas, nights get surprisingly cold. Even if you're suffocating from lack of air or stifling from heat exhaustion, people will insist on trying to keep the windows shut tight, lest they invite the swirling Sahara outside into the bus. Once darkness descends or you climb into the highlands, you'll quickly work out why the Bolivians seemed so overdressed when they boarded the bus in 30°C heat, and you'll sorely miss that fuzzy alpaca pullover packed safely away on the roof of the bus. Don't be lulled into a false sense of security by flotas that advertise heating systems; I've yet to see one actually working, and buses are usually rattled so badly on the unpaved roads that it's impossible to keep the windows latched anyway.

Major Routes

Flotas offer long-distance services between the following: La Paz and Oruro, Copacabana, Cochabamba, the Yungas (Coroico, Chulumani and Sorata), Rurrenabaque, Riberalta and Guayaramerín; Cochabamba and Sucre, Santa Cruz and Oruro; Potosí and Sucre, Uyuni, Oruro, Tupiza and Tarija; Tupiza and Villazón, Uyuni and Tarija; Tarija and Yacuiba; Santa Cruz and Trinidad, Camiri, Yacuiba and the Jesuit Missions; Guayaramerín and Riberalta; and Riberalta and Cobija. Other long-distance routes are constructed with connections between one or more of these and may require waits and changing buses.

CAMIÓN

Much of the Bolivian population, especially the lower economic classes, uses the *camión* (flatbed truck) as its primary means of long-distance transport, while camión owners/drivers use passengers as a means of lowering their costs. Often the number of passengers loaded onto the camiones far exceeds the practical – and the comfortable – capacity of the vehicle, but if you want to get off the main routes, camiones may well be your only option.

For their part, drivers usually charge about 75% of the standard bus fare on the same run, but it's still wise to ask fellow passengers what a reasonable fare would be. Drivers may assume that foreigners have access to unimaginable wealth and adjust the price accordingly, apparently unaware that wealthy people rarely climb onto rattle-trap trucks loaded with chickens, goats, oil drums, 500 cases of beer, noodles and 42 other passengers.

Every town has a market, street or plaza where camiones await passengers. When they're full by the driver's definition, they leave, and it can be quite a contest. Once a few passengers have assembled, the driver announces that the vehicle will leave *ahorita* – 'right away.' If the passengers feel that ahorita isn't soon enough, they may shift to another waiting vehicle. At this point, other passengers in other waiting vehicles also shift to this vehicle. The lucky driver of the nearly 'full' vehicle keeps trying to recruit a few more for as long as the passengers will tolerate it. As soon as they begin to climb down, imminent departure is announced and, wonder of wonders, the vehicle begins to move. After a spin around the block, however, the vehicle returns to the spot where it was waiting before the 'departure.' When the collective patience again begins to wear thin, the vehicle actually departs.

A less trying way to catch a camión is to take a taxi or micro to the tranca, the highway police post outside every entrance to every town. All vehicles are required to stop at these posts, and they're convenient places to ask drivers where they're headed. The drawback to this method is that at this point you've lost the option of choosing a place to sit.

While most Bolivians ride in the back of camiones because of the economic savings, foreigners (especially women) may be accorded VIP treatment and invited to ride in the cab. Failing that, you can pay 30% or so more and ride inside anyway. This isn't nearly as interesting as riding *atrás* (in the bed of the camión), but if it's raining, you'll appreciate the option.

This brings up another point: Rain damages cargo, so every camión carries a large sheet of heavy canvas tarpaulin known as *la carpa*, which is draped over the truck bed during rainstorms. Passengers are required to either bear the weight of it on their heads or hunker down in the dark, claustrophobic and fume-filled space below. When diesel exhaust and carbon monoxide have turned the experience into a literal hell on wheels, your only option is to confront the elements face on and escape to the rear bumper of the vehicle to contemplate the joys of independent travel.

Even if you're sitting atop your luggage, it may be wedged inaccessibly beneath cargo, luggage and other passengers. When riding atrás, have a variety of clothing at hand, especially on journeys that involve altitude gain.

TRAIN
Bolivia's 4300km of rail lines were formerly owned by Empresa Nacional de Ferrocarriles (ENFE), which was a government railway formed in 1964. During its useful life, ENFE suffered from chronic inefficiency, mainly as a result of top-heavy administration, outdated equipment, political interference, and a lack of focus; whenever the government changed, an entirely new staff came on board. Recently, however, the system was sold to the Chilean-based company Empresa Ferroviaria Andina, better known as Ferrocarriles Andinas (FCA), which hopes to solve some of these problems without eliminating passenger services or placing rail fares out of reach of the people.

The Red Occidental (Western Network) has its nerve center in Oruro, with services to Uyuni, Atocha, Tupiza and, on the Argentine border, Villazón, and to Avaroa on the Chilean border. The Red Oriental (Eastern Network) focuses on Santa Cruz, with lines going to Quijarro on the Brazilian border and to Yacuiba on the Argentine border.

Reservations & Tickets
Estaciones ferroviarias (railway stations) officially operate on railway timetables, but in reality, arrival and departure times may be written on a chalkboard as soon as it appears something may happen. In smaller stations – where things rarely happen – tickets may not be available until the train has arrived. Larger intermediate stations are allotted only a few seat reservations, and tickets go on sale quite literally whenever employees decide to open up. Normally, the only sense of urgency comes from the prospective passengers clamoring to buy tickets. Even in major towns along the routes, tickets can be reserved only on the day of expected departure. The best information is usually available from the *jefe de la estación* (stationmaster).

The obvious result of this 'efficiency crisis' has been a move by the general public away from rail travel and toward the more convenient bus and airline services. In turn, lower demand has led to a decrease in the frequency of rail services. While this has decreased competition for tickets at a perpetually closed *boletería* (ticket window), you may still be faced with a bit of scuffling to secure and defend your place in a ticket line. When buying tickets, make sure you have on hand the personal documents of each person for whom you're buying tickets (this is a remnant from the days when ticket scalping was profitable).

If you do get a seat reservation and the train does arrive, the trip itself will be a continuation of the adventure. Tracks are in a poor state of repair and especially on the Red Oriental, rail cars leap down the tracks like bucking broncos. Rainy periods may bring about delays, but in most cases, washouts are repaired as soon as railway crews can attend to them.

Classes & Trains
For the Red Oriental, the privatized services include flashy pullman (1st-class) carriages, and those used on the Red Occidental have

also improved in recent years. They still lack compartments or any sort of sleeping berths, but the seats are relatively comfortable. Note, however, that pullman seats numbered 27 to 30 or 57 to 60 are up against the walls and do not recline.

If you don't mind the crowded 2nd-class carriages, you can avoid lining up and purchase tickets from the conductor, who sells them for 10% to 20% more than ticket window price. However, 2nd-class tickets don't normally include seat reservations, so some passengers inevitably wind up on the floor or in the *bodegas* (boxcars).

The nicest rail conveyance is the *ferrobus*, a bus on bogies, which is currently available only between Santa Cruz and Quijarro. It's more expensive than other trains, so you need to reserve as early as possible. Next are the *Expreso del Oriente* (between Santa Cruz and Quijarro) on the Red Oriental and the *Expreso del Sur* on the Red Occidental (between Oruro, Uyuni, Tupiza and Villazón), which are less expensive but generally quite reliable. They normally carry relatively new and comfortable carriages with 1st-class seats, as well as more crowded 2nd-class carriages and a dining car. The *Tren Wara Wara*, which operates between Oruro and Villazón, provides slightly slower, cheaper and less comfortable transport.

The *tren mixto*, which is mainly a goods/freight train, offers 2nd-class transport in bodegas. Due to the low fares, it's used mainly by *campesinos* (peasants or common folk) and all their attendant children, luggage and animals. These trains don't run on a fixed schedule and may well hold the low speed record for the continent.

CAR & MOTORCYCLE

The advantages of using a private vehicle are, of course, schedule flexibility, access to remote areas and the chance to seize photographic opportunities. However, only a few Bolivian roads are sealed and others are in varying stages of decay, so high-speed travel is impossible (unless, of course, you're a Bolivian bus driver), and the typically narrow and winding mountain roads meander along

contours and rocky riverbeds rather than following the shortest route.

The undaunted should prepare their expeditions carefully. Bear in mind that auto parts are a rare commodity outside cities and that many Bolivian mechanics simply jerry-rig repairs well enough to render the vehicle functional by the local definition. A 4WD high-clearance vehicle is essential for travel off major routes. You'll need a set of tools, one or two good spare tires, a puncture repair kit, extra gas, oil and water, and as many spare parts as possible – as well as the expertise to diagnose problems and install the parts. For emergencies, carry camping equipment and plenty of food and drinking water.

Low-grade (85-octane) gasoline and diesel fuel are available at *surtidores de gasolina* (gas dispensers) – also known as *bombas de gasolina* (gas pumps) – in all cities and major towns. At the time of writing, gasoline cost about US$0.50 per liter.

Road Rules

Foreigners entering Bolivia from another country need a circulation card, or *hoja de ruta*, which is available from the Servicio Nacional de Tránsito at the frontier or in the Bolivian city where your trip begins. This document must be presented and stamped at all police posts, variously known as trancas, *tránsitos* or *controles*, spaced along highways and just outside major cities.

Peajes or 'tolls' are sometimes charged at these checkpoints and vehicles and luggage may be searched for contraband, although fortunately this practice is becoming quite rare. Unfortunately, the poorly paid police may not be able to resist stopping obvious foreigners, so expect to pay a few bogus fines for alleged infringements.

Traffic regulations don't differ greatly from those in North America or Europe. Speed limits are infrequently posted, but in most cases, the state of the road will prevent you from exceeding them anyway. As in most of the Americas, Bolivians keep to the right. On the Yungas road between La Paz and Coroico, however, downhill vehicles are required to keep to the outside, whichever side of the road that happens to be. For the nail-biting lower half of the trip (the half nearest Coroico), this means traffic must pass on the left side of oncoming traffic. This way the driver, who sits on the left side of the vehicle, has the best view of the outside tires.

In the cities, most of the cacophonous horn-honking isn't to get traffic moving or to intimidate pedestrians; when two cars approach an uncontrolled intersection (ie, one with no police officer or functioning signal) from different directions, the driver who honks first has right of way if intending to pass straight through. Turning vehicles, of course, must wait until the way is clear before doing so. Keep in mind that this system doesn't always work in practice. While timidity may cost some time, it may be better for your sanity until you're accustomed to local driving habits.

When two vehicles meet on a mountain road too narrow for both to pass, the downhill vehicle must reverse until there's room for the other to pass. Again, this works better in theory than in practice.

Rental

Given the state of roads and services and the convenience of public transportation, few travelers in Bolivia rent self-driven vehicles. Although things are improving, it's best not to put much faith in Bolivian rental vehicles. Only the most reputable agencies service vehicles regularly, and insurance bought from rental agencies may cover only accidental damage. This means that breakdowns may be considered the renter's problem, but even where they are covered, the logistics of having repairs done must be handled by the driver. Sort out the policy and get details in writing before accepting the vehicle!

The minimum age for most rental agencies is between 21 and 25 years. You need a driver's license from your home country (or in some cases, an international driver's license, so it's wise to have one issued from your automobile club), a major credit card or cash deposit (typically around US $1000) and, usually, accident insurance. You'll be charged a daily rate and a per-kilometer

rate (some agencies allow a set number of free kilometers, after which the rate applies). They'll also want you to leave your passport or *cédula de identidad* (identity document for Bolivian residents) as a deposit.

Prices vary widely between agencies and areas. The average daily rate for a small Volkswagen or Toyota starts at US$25, plus an additional US$0.35 per kilometer. Many agencies also offer up to 100km per day for a slight discount on the per-kilometer rate. For its least expensive 4WD vehicle, companies charge as little as US$40 per day plus US$0.45 per kilometer. Lower daily rates are available for rentals of a week or more and in most cases, collision damage waiver insurance is included in the rental fees.

If you plan on a lot of driving, go with an agency that offers unlimited or a generous number of free kilometers. Weekly rates with Localiza Rent-a-Car, with 980 free kilometers, start at US$238 for a compact and US$448 in a 4WD Mazda pickup.

Here's a listing of some better-known agencies (note that inclusion here doesn't constitute a recommendation):

American Rent-a-Car
La Paz (☎/fax 02-361666 or 02-328635; mobile ☎ 012-35167; Mariscal Sucre 1423 or Camacho 1574)

Barron's Rent-a-Car (toll-free ☎ 0800-8880)
Santa Cruz (☎ 03-420160; mobile ☎ 013-97511; fax 03-423439; rentacar@netmail.tfnet.org; Avenida Alemana 50), at Tajibo
Cochabamba (☎ 04-222774; mobile ☎ 014-98050; Calle Sucre E-0727)
Tarija (☎ 066-36853; mobile ☎ 018-60363; Calle Ingavi E-339)

International Rent-a-Car
La Paz (☎ 02-342406; mobile ☎ 012-95181; fax 02-357061; Calle Federico Zuazo 1942)
Cochabamba (☎ 04-26635; mobile ☎ 017-20091; fax 04-26635), Ayacucho at Colómbia
Santa Cruz (☎/fax 03-344425; mobile ☎ 016-25218), Avenida Uruguay at Pedro Antelo

Kolla Motors (website www.waranet.com /kollamotors.htm)
La Paz (☎ 02-419141; mobile ☎ 015-66185; fax 411344; kollamotors@zuper.net; Avenida Sánchez Lima 2321; Casilla 7152)
Santa Cruz (☎ 03-338535; Calle Colon 456/1er Anillo 2648)

Localiza Rent-a-Car (toll-free ☎ 0800-2050)
La Paz (☎ 02-414890; mobile ☎ 012-98765; Plaza
    España 7)
Cochabamba (☎ 04-283123; mobile ☎ 014-99099;
    airport ☎ 04-96098; Avenida Pando 1199)
Santa Cruz (☎ 03-372223; mobile ☎ 016-29576;
    airport ☎ 03-852190; Independencia 365)

SH Car Rental (toll-free ☎ 0800-2886)
La Paz (☎ 02-414890; mobile ☎ 012-98765; fax 02-
    415188; shteam@ceibo.entelnet.bo; Casilla 300)

Drivers

Many people just want transportation to
trailheads or base camps rather than a tour.
Examples of one-way transport prices from
La Paz with a private driver, regardless of
the number of passengers, include the fol-
lowing: Refugio Huayna Potosí – US$70;
Estancia Una (for Illimani climb) – US$140;
Curva, for the Cordillera Apolobamba
trek – US$325; Chuñavi or Lambate, for the
Yunga Cruz trek – US$150; Sajama –
US$300; and Rurrenabaque – US$325. For
roundtrip rates, double these figures. Private
Salar de Uyuni and Southwest Circuit tours
cost from US$180 per day.

Several recommended La Paz drivers
offer a worthwhile value. Carlos Aguilar
(☎ 352111, 352112; mobile ☎ 015-25897; fax
392934; caguilar@travelinexpeditions.com;
Edificio Cámara de Comercio, Traveline
Tours, Mariscal Santa Cruz 1392, La Paz)
speaks some English and provides safe, informative and inexpensive jeep trips. He
also works as a climbing guide and is especially popular with mountaineers. Oscar L
Vera Coca (☎ 230453; mobile ☎ 019-61283)
also speaks some English and is known as an
excellent driver, which means that he's very
busy. You can choose between Toyota Landcruisers or 12-passenger minibuses. Another
recommended driver is Romero Ancasi
(☎ 831363; mobile ☎ 019-18376), who offers
experienced driving in well-maintained
Toyota Landcruisers.

Another option is Minibuses Yungueña
(☎ 213513), which contracts out 2WD
minibuses, with drivers. Book through
América Tours (see Organized Tours later
in this chapter).

Motorcycle

In lowland areas, where temperatures are
hot and roads are scarce, motorbikes
(they're far too light to actually be called
motorcycles) are popular for buzzing
around the plazas, as well as exploring areas
not served by public transportation. They
can be rented for around US$18 per 24
hours from motorbike taxi stands on or near
the main plazas in Trinidad, Riberalta,
Guayaramerín and other northern Bolivian
towns. In Sucre, a new agency offers motorcycle tours through the area's rugged highland terrain (see Organized Tours under
Sucre in the Central Highlands chapter).

Motorbike taxi drivers can make a lot
more money by renting out their bikes than
by working, and while you're using their
bike, they have the day off. As a result,
there's lots of competition, so negotiate the
price – which should be payable upon
return of the vehicle.

No special licenses or permits are required, but you do need a driving license
from your home country. Bear in mind that
many travel insurance policies will not cover
you for injuries arising from motorbike accidents, so check your policy carefully.

BICYCLE

For cyclists who can cope with the chal-
lenges of steep terrain, cold winds, poor road
conditions and high altitude, Bolivia is a paradise. In this vast and breathtaking country
of back roads and remote villages, a mountain bike will bring within reach culture and
magnificent scenery inaccessible to travelers
confined to public transportation.

Fortunately, traffic isn't a serious problem
because there's so little of it. On main
routes, however, large, loud and intimidating buses and camiones may leave cyclists
lost in clouds of dust and sand, or embedded
in mud. Where there's a parallel rail line,
you may prefer to abandon the road and
follow the typically less-used footpath
alongside the tracks. On minor roads and
tracks, however, apart from foot and animal
traffic, cyclists will have the roads largely to
themselves.

Naturally, finding supplies – particularly off the beaten track – may prove difficult. Few small villages have even a tiny provisions shop, so cyclists in remote areas must carry ample food and water to reach the next city or town.

Transporting a Bicycle

Almost all international airlines accept bikes as checked baggage. Some airlines may charge a standard rate – say US$25 – to transport a bike, but most will simply apply their excess baggage charge if you're over your allowed weight limit. You'll probably have to decrease the space required (and the risk of damage to the bike) by removing the pedals and handlebars, and locking the front wheel. You should also deflate the tires to prevent an explosion in the event of depressurization. Usually, it isn't strictly necessary to pack your bike in a bike bag or encase it in plastic or cardboard, but either process would serve as a thin line of protection against the inevitable bumps and scratches it will receive in the care of underconscientious baggage handlers.

In Bolivia, there's no problem transporting bikes on camiones (unless the camión is already packed to the gills with passengers and/or cargo). Most flotas are equally amenable, which isn't surprising considering that a bicycle takes up much less space than the luggage carried by the average Bolivian. Similarly, Lloyd Aéreo Boliviano and AeroSur are not averse to carrying bikes as checked baggage provided they don't exceed your 20kg weight limit.

Equipment

Outside La Paz, bicycle spares and tools are for the most part unavailable, although most towns do have bicycle repair shops that can manage emergency or jerry-rigged repairs. However, not even in La Paz will you find parts for state-of-the-art or complicated brake and gearing systems, or nonstandard-sized tires (most sell only 27- and 28-inch tires). The best place for cycle parts is the lowly shop at Avenida Buenos Aires 606 in La Paz.

Unless you're willing to forgo familiarity, versatility and durability, think about carrying your equipment from home. Although some people do purchase bikes in Latin America, those available in Bolivia generally won't stand up well to the rigors of cycle touring. To minimize maintenance, you'll need a strong but stable traditional mountain bike. For the hills, you'll fare best with full-suspension, cantilever brakes and a low gear ratio.

For advice and recommendations on equipment options – bike models, features, panniers, spare parts, tools, clothing and so on – a good source of information is *Latin America by Bike* by Walter Sienko (The Mountaineers, Seattle, 1993). It contains gear and parts checklists, offers hints on bicycle security and even contains a handy Spanish-English vocabulary of cycle parts.

HITCHHIKING

Thanks to relatively easy access to camiones and a profusion of buses and other long-distance public transport, hitching isn't really popular in Bolivia (although it could be argued that passengers riding in the backs of camiones are in fact hitchhikers). Still, it's not unknown and drivers of *mobilidades* – *carros* (cars), *camionetas* (pickup trucks), NGO vehicles, gasoline trucks and other vehicles – are usually happy to pick up passengers when they have space. Always ask the price, if any, before climbing aboard; if they do charge, it should amount to about half the bus fare for the equivalent distance.

Please note that hitchhiking is never entirely safe in any country in the world. If you decide to hitch, you should understand that you are taking a small but potentially serious risk. Travel in pairs and let someone know where you're planning to go.

BOAT
Cargo Boats

The most relaxing way to get around in the Amazon region is by river. You can lie in a hammock for days on end and read, sleep, relax and watch the passing scene. Adventurous types may even build a raft or hire a dugout canoe to explore under their own steam, but they'd need either a local river guide or a measure of expertise in wilderness survival and familiarity with navigation along multichanneled tropical waterways.

There's no scheduled passenger service in the Bolivian Amazon, so river travelers almost invariably wind up on some sort of cargo vessel, but the quality, velocity and price will largely depend on luck. Passenger comfort is probably the last thing Amazonian cargo-boat builders have in mind, but accommodation standards in Bolivia are still superior to those on many of the 'cattle-boats' that ply the Amazon proper.

While the riverside scenery can be mesmerizing, it changes little, so bring along a couple of books, but don't expect to be bored. Shipboard acquaintances develop quickly, and on some routes you'll have good chances of seeing wildlife both in the water and on the riverbanks.

Wildlife Viewing Bolivia's portion of the Amazon Basin is probably more interesting than the Amazon proper. For a start, the rivers are narrower, so the boats can travel nearer the shore, allowing better observation. The area is also relatively less developed and has a much lower population density, so wildlife viewing is considerably better than along the heavily populated Brazilian rivers.

The Río Beni isn't much of a wildlife river – nor is it a route well covered by cargo vessels – but along the Mamoré and Ichilo you'll almost certainly see sloths, monkeys, capybaras, rheas, turtles and hundreds of species of birds and butterflies. On the Mamoré, you have a good chance of seeing giant river otters, alligators, anacondas, countless pink river dolphins, and if you're very lucky, even a tapir or an anteater.

Food & Accommodations River passages typically include food, and although onboard cooks tend to show little imagination, the fare is life sustaining. Breakfast invariably consists of *masaco* – a mash of yucca, plantain, *charque* (dried meat), oil, maize and salt – which is definitely an acquired taste.

Other meals usually consist of rice or noodles, more charque and fried or steamed plantains. Many boats transport lemons, bananas, grapefruits and oranges, so fruit is often plentiful. Coffee is made from river water and sugar is added unsparingly until it reaches a syrupy consistency. Take along a supply of goodies to complement your diet and relieve your taste buds.

Occasionally, passengers may be offered turtle eggs or soup made from turtle meat. In the interest of the turtles, which are threatened throughout the Bolivian Amazon, you may wish to avoid partaking and express concern about their diminishing numbers. This won't stop anyone from eating turtles or turtles' eggs, but it may introduce an entirely new perspective.

On some boats, you'll need a hammock for sleeping. On others, you can roll out a sleeping bag on the deck, the roof or even on the cargo. On one trip between Puerto Barador and Guayaramerín, the decks were full and I was permitted to sleep on the roof of the boat, witness to the sunset, stars and the raucous night-long jungle symphony. All these magical things were missed by passengers sleeping under the roof, nearer the noisy engines.

Even the jungle gets chilly at night, and there's always a heavy dew, so you do need a sleeping bag. Some sort of mosquito protection (a net or a good repellent) is also essential, especially if your boat ties up at night. If you must spend a lot of time outside, use a strong sunscreen. You're also advised to carry either bottled drinking water or water purification tablets, preferably iodine-based, to treat the murky water, which is typically drunk straight from the river.

Most boats are equipped with toilet facilities, but bathing and laundry are done in the river. Piranhas and alligators appear to pose little threat – everyone swims – but just the same, check with locals before jumping in.

Routes The most popular routes are from Puerto Villarroel to Trinidad and Trinidad to Guayaramerín. Both of these require three days downstream and five or more days upstream. There are also less frequented routes from Rurrenabaque or Puerto Heath to Riberalta.

Lake Titicaca

Water travel is not limited to the rivers. Lake Titicaca, which straddles Bolivia's boundary with Peru, is traditionally known as the highest navigable lake in the world. At an altitude of 3810m, it bustles with all sorts of watercraft including a rapidly decreasing number of the world-famous totora reed boats, which Thor Heyerdahl used on his Ra II Expedition from North Africa. These sturdy canoes have plied the waters of Titicaca since pre-Columbian times.

In the more recent past, steamers, which were carried piece by piece from the sea to landlocked Bolivia, ferried passengers between Guaqui and the Peruvian ports, linking the railroad terminals of the two countries. This service was discontinued in 1985, however, when its home port of Guaqui disappeared under the waters of the rising lake.

Currently, the only public ferry service operates between San Pedro and San Pablo, across the narrow Estrecho de Tiquina (Straits of Tiquina). This is along the well-traveled route between La Paz and Copacabana, Puno and Cuzco (these last two are in Peru, of course).

To visit the several Bolivian islands of Lake Titicaca, you can travel by launch or rowboat. To the Huyñaymarka islands in the lake's southernmost extension, boats and tours are available in Huatajata. To visit Isla del Sol, you can take a tour, hire a launch or catch a scheduled service in Copacabana, or look for a rowboat in Yampupata.

Cruises by motorboat or hydrofoil are provided by the tour companies Crillon and Transturin. See Organized Tours later in this chapter for more information.

LOCAL TRANSPORTATION

Micros

Micros – half-size buses – are used in larger cities and serve as Bolivia's least expensive form of public transport, ranging in price from US$0.10 (B$0.50) per ride in Sucre to US$0.18 (B$0.90) in La Paz. Few micros are in optimum condition – at least from the exterior – but mechanically, they seem to go on forever and make remarkably easy work of steep hills.

Micros follow set routes, and the route numbers or letters are usually marked on a placard behind the windshield. This is often backed by a description of the route, including the streets that are followed to reach the end of the line. They can be hailed anywhere along their routes. When you want to disembark, move toward the front and tell the driver or assistant where you want them to stop.

Minibuses & Trufis

Colectivos (minibuses) and *trufis* (which may be either cars or minibuses) are prevalent in both La Paz and Cochabamba and follow set routes that are numbered and described on placards either in the front window or on the roof. For the benefit of nonreaders, they often employ a child who calls (or screams) out the destination whenever the vehicle passes a group of potential customers. They are always cheaper than taxis and they're nearly as convenient. As with micros, you can board or alight anywhere along their route.

Taxis

Urban taxis in Bolivia are relatively inexpensive. Few are equipped with meters, but in most cities and towns there are standard per-person fares for short hauls. When you first arrive in a city, ask a merchant or other local what the usual taxi fare is to your destination before you agree on a price with the driver. Outside bus terminals, railway stations and larger hotels, taxi drivers will initially quote inflated fares, particularly if you appear to be a newly arrived foreigner. In these cases, walk down the street 200m or so before hailing a taxi.

In some places, taxis are collective and behave more like trufis, charging a set rate per person. However, if you have three or four people all headed for the same place, you may be able to negotiate a reduced rate for the entire group. Radio taxis, on the other hand, always charge a set rate for up to four people; if you squeeze in five people, the fare increases by a small margin. When using taxis, try to have enough change to cover the fare; drivers often like to plead a lack of change in the hope that you'll give them the benefit of the difference. As a general rule, taxi drivers aren't tipped, but if an individual goes beyond the call of duty, a tip of one or two bolivianos wouldn't be amiss.

Taxis may also be chartered for longer distances. They're particularly handy if, as a group, you want to visit places near major cities that are outside local transportation areas but too near to be covered by long-distance bus networks.

ORGANIZED TOURS

A growing number of foreign and Bolivian tour operators are cashing in on the country's appeal and organizing excursions to places that would otherwise be difficult to reach. Note, however, that most operators will run a tour only if a specified minimum number of people are interested. If you can't muster a group of the requisite size, you may have to pay at least partial fares for the number lacking.

Options range from half-day familiarization tours in or near major cities to fully guided, multiweek excursions that include food, transport, accommodations, transfers etc. The latter are 'classical' tours, which include organized excursions by bus, jeep or boat to the classic tourist sites and circuits, and take the uncertainties out of accommodation, transport and sightseeing. Such tours are usually purchased outside Bolivia.

Shorter tours, on the other hand, are typically organized locally through hotels or agencies. If you're short on time, they provide a convenient way to quickly visit a site you'd otherwise miss, or allow you to do a popular circuit, such as the Jungle and Pampas tours around Rurrenabaque or the Southwest Circuit from Uyuni. These options are typically less than luxurious, but are also quite inexpensive, averaging around US$25 per person per day.

Most of Bolivia's tour operators are concentrated in La Paz and other large cities. The most popular short options from La Paz, for example, include city sightseeing and half-day or full-day tours to nearby attractions, such as Chacaltaya or Tiahuanaco (where an English-speaking guide can turn the ruins into more than an impressive heap of rocks!). Inexpensive tour-agency transfers to Puno or Cuzco provide the most straightforward access to Peru, and longer excursions to hard-to-reach destinations, such as the Southwest Circuit or the Cordillera Apolobamba, are most conveniently done through agencies. These tours are more comfortable than crowded local buses, but they do encourage you to pack more sights into less time.

For those who are more adventurous but don't want to strike out into the wilderness alone, there are lots of outfits offering adventure tours, including mountaineering, trekking, mountain biking, jungle tours, kayaking, parapente, extreme skiing, canyoning, sailing on Lake Titicaca, and any other hands-on or adrenaline-inducing activity you can name. Prices vary between agencies, but well-established companies generally charge considerably higher prices. The best agencies will be able to organize specialty tours and draw up customized itineraries for you or your group. On request, they'll also be able to provide English-, French- or German-speaking guides (but often at a higher price).

For mountain trekking or climbing in the Cordilleras, tour operators mainly offer customized expeditions, and can arrange anything from just a guide and transport right up to camping and mountaineering equipment, porters and even a cook.

If you have only a short time in Bolivia, don't set out on a whirlwind circuit through the main cities without first checking out adventure offerings. If you're up to it, a trek through the Cordillera Apolobamba or a climb up Illimani or Huayna Potosí would almost certainly be more rewarding than Oruro, Cochabamba and Santa Cruz combined!

Note that many Bolivian travel agencies concentrate only on flights or external tourism and earn their keep by selling airline tickets and Disney World tours to

Bolivian holiday-makers. The following La Paz agencies and operators (along with a couple in other cities) run or cobble together organized tours around Bolivia. Agencies in most other towns are listed in their respective chapters.

América Tours (☎ 02-328584, fax 02-374204; Avenida 16 de Julio 1490, ground floor, Casilla 2568, La Paz) This highly recommended agency specializes in tours to the fabulous Chalalán Eco Lodge in Madidi National Park, as well as trips to Lake Titicaca, the Southwest Circuit and Rurrenabaque. It also handles rock climbing at Amor de Dios in the Zona Sur (US$29 per person with two or three people, including gear) and the popular Gravity Assisted Mountain Biking tours (see the entry later in this list). English-, French- and German-speaking guides are available. Their website is www.america-ecotours.com.

Andean Summits (☎/fax 02-317497; andean@ latinwide.com; Doryan Centre Local 27, Calle Sagárnaga 189, first floor, Casilla 6976, La Paz) This company offers mountaineering and trekking in all parts of Bolivia, plus rock climbing, mountain biking, jungle trips, paragliding and archaeological tours. It's run by experienced English- and French-speaking Bolivian mountain guides. They have one of the best selections of new climbing and camping equipment for sale, including head-lamp batteries, Camping Gaz, Epigaz etc. Their website is at www.andeansummits.com.

Andes Expediciones (☎ 02-319655; fax 02-392344; andesexp@ceibo.entelnet.bo; Avenida Camacho 1377, Casilla 12287, La Paz) This company runs a climbing school and conducts medical examinations for prospective climbers and visitors to high altitudes.

Balsa Tours (☎ 02-440620; fax 02-440310; turismo_balsa@megalink.com or balsa1@ megalink.com; Calle Capitán Ravelo 2104, PO Box 5889, La Paz) Balsa concentrates on the Lago Huyñaymarka part of Lake Titicaca, where it operates the Complejo Nautico Las Balsas, and also organizes tours to the far Southwest and the Amazon Basin.

Bolivian Journeys (☎/fax 02-357848; mobile ☎ 015-39803; boljour@ceibo.entelnet.bo; Calle Sagárnaga 363, La Paz) This company specializes in hiking and climbing trips around the Cordillera Real, and the owner speaks good English.

Camel Expeditions (☎/fax 02-433202; camel _expeditions@boliviatrek.com; Pedro Salazar 2485, PO Box 8057, La Paz) Camel claims to run

trekking, climbing, glacier hikes, ice-climbing instruction, paragliding and other outdoor activities in the Cordilleras Real, Apolobamba and Quimsa Cruz. A unique option is rock climbing near Curahuara de Carangas, on the Southern Altiplano.

Colibri (☎ 02-371936, fax 02-355043; acolibri@ ceibo.entelnet.bo; Calle Sagárnaga 309, Casilla 7456, La Paz) This is a comprehensive adventure travel service, including trekking and climbing and 4WD tours. French and English are spoken, and it also has German- and Italian-speaking guides. It also offers a good selection of climbing and trekking gear for rent. However, for trips that include meals, discuss in advance what you'll be eating, as groups have complained about 'meals' of coca tea and powdered soup.

Crillon Tours (☎ 02-337533; fax 02-391039; titicaca@caoba.entelnet.bo; Avenida Camacho 1223, Casilla 4785, La Paz) Bolivia's most popular tour company features upmarket hydrofoil trips between Huatajata and Puno on Lake Titicaca (three hours). It also runs a five-star hotel in Huatajata and a luxury lodge at Yumani on Isla del Sol and does transfers between La Paz and Puno by bus and hydrofoil for US$160 each way. A rushed roundtrip day tour from La Paz to Huatajata, Isla del Sol (which includes a quick run up and down the Escalera del Inca) and Copacabana ('packaged right down to the campesino paid to stand with his llamas on the dock for the tourists to take photos') costs US$130.

Diana Tours (☎ 375374; fax 360831; hotsadt@ ceibo.entelnet.bo; Hotel Sagárnaga, Calle Sagárnaga 328, La Paz) This popular agency does city tours and tours to Tiahuanaco, Valle de la Luna, Chacaltaya and the Yungas. The guides certainly aren't top quality, but it does have some of the cheapest transfers to Copacabana (US$4) and Puno (US$8).

Fremen Tours, La Paz (☎ 02-414069; fax 02-417327; vtfremen@caoba.entelnet.bo; Pedro Salazar 537, Casilla 9682); Cochabamba (☎ 04-259392; fax 04-259686; Calle Tumusla 245, Casilla 1040); Santa Cruz (☎ 03 338535; fax 03-360265; Cañoto at 21 de Mayo); Trinidad (☎/fax 046-21834, 6 de Agosto 140) Fremen is one of Bolivia's best agencies and provides tours of the Amazon area as well as around Cochabamba, including Torotoro, Incallajta and Cerro Tunari. For more information, see the Central Highlands chapter, and Villa Tunari and Trinidad in the Amazon Basin chapter. The website is www.andes-amazonia.com.

Gravity Assisted Mountain Biking (☎ 02-374204; gravity@unete.com; 1490 Avenida 16 de Julio, Edificio Avenida, La Paz) If you'd appreciate a thrilling and safe adrenaline rush through some of the world's most spectacular landscapes, how about hopping on a mountain bike and heading down the World's Most Dangerous Road (the Yungas highway), for a total elevation loss of 3500m in just 62km? It costs US$70 per person if four people are booked and US$55 with eight or more, including a guide and top-notch equipment. Alternatively, you can ride down from Chacaltaya to La Paz, from Milluni into the Zongo Valley and even down the scenic road to Sorata. The website is www.gamb.acslp.org.

Hidalgo Tours (☎ 062-25186; fax 062-22707; uyusalht@ceibo.entelnet.bo; Bolívar at Junín, Casilla 314, Potosí) This upmarket agency specializes in tours to Southwestern Bolivia and runs the Hotel Palacio de Sal on the Salar de Uyuni and the Hospedaría Hidalgo on Laguna Colorada. The website is at www.salar-uyuni.com.

Huayna Potosí Tours (☎ 02-456717; bolclimb@ mail.cafe-monet.com; Hotel Continental, Calle Illampu 626, Casilla 731, La Paz) This agency operates the Refugio Huayna Potosí mountain hut at Paso Zongo, at the foot of Huayna Potosí (US$7 per night), and also organizes trekking and climbing expeditions, including Huayna Potosí climbs.

Incaland Tours (☎ 02-457908; incaland@ceibo .entelnet.bo; Hotel Pando, Avenida Pando 252, La Paz) This is a basic travel agency offering inexpensive day tours from La Paz to Lake Titicaca, Chacaltaya, Tiahuanaco and other sights.

Neblina Forest (☎/fax 03-438231; mobile ☎ 016- 44732; neblinaforest@daitec.scz.com; Calle Las Maras 2318, Casilla 5598, Santa Cruz) This recommended operator specializes in birdwatching and natural-history tours throughout Bolivia, especially Noel Kempff Mercado, Amboro and Madidi National Parks, along with the Beni region and the Pantanal. See its website at www.neblinaforest.com.

Pachamama Tours (☎ 02-319740; mobile ☎/fax 0811-3179; pachamama@megalink.com; Calle Mercado 1362, Galería Paladium Mezzanine Oficina M, La Paz) Pachamama specializes in soft adventure tours, including bird-watching, trekking, cultural tours, 'mystical' trips and of course, the ubiquitous Southwest Circuit.

Paititi (☎ 02-336061; fax 329625; paititi@ceibo .entelnet.bo; Calle Hermanos Manchego 2469, La Paz or ☎/fax 02-342759; Camino Real Aparthotel, Calle Capitán Ravelo 2123, La Paz) Paititi does tours and treks around La Paz, in the Yungas, Amazonia and the far Southwest. Recommended trips include the four-day trek through the little-known Ciudad de Piedra (US$224) and white-water rafting on the Río Coroico (US$67). They also offer three-day treks on the Choro (US$109) and Taquesi (US$128) trails, and can arrange rental of camping and mountaineering gear.

Sky Bolivia (☎/fax 02-460750; skyinter@kolla.net; Calle Linares 880, Galería El Pueblito, La Paz) For very reasonable rates you can visit Tiahuanaco or Chacaltaya (US$12), trek the Choro Trail (US$120), raft the Río Coroico (US$65), visit Isla del Sol (US$79) and even climb Huayna Potosí (US$130). Rates include only transportation, guide and gear.

Tauro Tours (☎ 02-335834; fax 02-392549; tauro@ ceibo.entelnet.bo; Avenida 16 de Julio 1566, Edificio Mariscal Ballivián, 1st floor, Casilla 11142, La Paz) This operator combines classical tourism with a range of upmarket adventures, including 4WD tours to the far Southwest, Lake Titicaca, Rurrenabaque, Pando, the Beni, archaeological trips, and 'total adventure tours' that combine fast-paced 4WD tours with rafting, climbing and parapenting. Mountaineering, trekking and adventure activities are run by the experienced guide Carlos Aguilar, who is qualified with the German Alpine Club.

TAWA Tours (☎ 325796; mobile ☎ 019-33300; fax 391175; tawa@caoba.entelnet.bo; Calle Sagárnaga 161, Casilla 8662, La Paz) TAWA focuses on adventure tourism in the southwestern deserts (including Parque Nacional Sajama), as well as trekking and 4WD tours through the Cordilleras Real and Apolobamba and stays at Santa Rosa (US$40 per day), on the Río Tuichi in Bolivian Amazonia. Guides are available who speak French, English, Italian or German.

Terra Andina (☎ 02-422241; terra-andina@ mail.zuper.net; Calle Chaco 738, Dpto 5B, Edificio Colores, La Paz) This newish company is run by a mining engineer, a geophysicist and a geologist who speak Spanish, English and French. They've traveled the length and breadth of Bolivia and share their experience with travelers: the Southwest Circuit and Altiplano tours, as well as customized mountain trekking, sailing on Lake Titicaca in a traditional fishing boat, flying tours to remote parts of Bolivian Amazonia, trekking in the Sajama National Park, geology tours, mountain biking to the sea at Arica (Chile) and so on. They also book upmarket hotels for discounted rates. The website is www.terra-andina.com.

Toñito Tours (☎ 02-336250; mobile ☎ 019-22725; tonitotours@yahoo.com; Sagárnaga 213, Galería

Chuquiago, La Paz) Toñito concentrates on the Southwest Circuit and always runs its own tours, so you won't be handed over to an unknown agency. They're currently setting up a solar energy project on Isla de Pescado in the Salar de Uyuni.

Transturin (☎ 310545 or 320445; fax 391162 or 310647; transturin@megalink.com; Avenida Mariscal Santa Cruz 1295, 3rd floor, Casilla 5311, La Paz) Transturin offers enclosed catamaran cruises around Lake Titicaca, including Copacabana, Isla del Sol and Puno, Peru. The focus is on responsible tourism and they provide visitors with an appreciation of local culture. La Paz to Puno, with stops at Copacabana and Isla del Sol, costs US$129. Roundtrips to Isla del Sol are US$70 and to Copacabana, US$90. Isla del Sol with an overnight at Hotel Titicaca costs US$130. Prices include meals. The website is at www.turismo-bolivia.com.

Transamazonas (☎ 350411; fax 360923; Office 3C, 3rd floor, Edificio V Centenario, Avenida 6 de Agosto, Casilla 14551, La Paz) This outfit covers the top end of the adventure tourism market, offering well-organized hiking, climbing and 4WD expeditions. English, French, German and Spanish are spoken.

TrekBolivia (☎ 02-317106; fax 02-460566; trekbo@ ceibo.entelnet.bo; Sagárnaga 392, La Paz) This company offers standard tours around La Paz, as well as extended trips to Cuzco and Machu Picchu.

Turisbus (☎ 451341; fax 451991; turisbus@ caoba.entelnet.bo; Residencial Rosario, Calle Illampu 704, La Paz) Turisbus runs day tours to Chacaltaya (US$10), Tiahuanaco (US$10) and Lago Huyñaymarka (US$41), as well as tours to Copacabana and Isla del Sol; weekend specials with transport fro m La Paz, sightseeing in Copacabana, a day tour of Isla del Sol and accommodations at the Hotel Rosario del Lago cost from US$48/72 per person for two/three days. See the website www.travelperubolivia.com.

La Paz

• **elev 3632m** ☎ **02**

The home of more than a million Bolivians, over half of whom are of Indian heritage, La Paz is the country's largest city and its center of commerce, finance and industry. Although Sucre remains the judicial capital,

Highlights

- Admire the mestizo architecture of Iglesia San Francisco
- Discover Bolivian history, art and culture in La Paz's many museums
- Catch a traditional *peña* for a taste of traditional folk music
- Shop for *artesanía* on and around Calle Sagárnaga
- Stroll through the Mercado Negro and other sprawling markets to see and experience the indigenous side of La Paz
- Spend a day exploring the ancient ruins of Tiahuanaco
- Walk through the bizarre formations of Valle de la Luna, hike into the dramatic Cañón de Palca or climb to the impressive Muela del Diablo

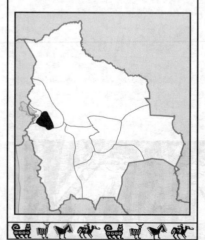

La Paz has usurped most government power and is now the de facto capital.

A visitor's first view of La Paz (except for those sneaking in from the Amazon Basin via the Yungas) will never be forgotten. La Paz is in the same scenic league as Rio de Janeiro, Cape Town, San Francisco and Hong Kong, but you wouldn't know it as you approach through the gray, littered and poverty-plagued sprawl of El Alto, on muddy streets that appears to have escaped attention since Inca times. Once a La Paz suburb, an ongoing influx of immigrants from the countryside has caused El Alto to swell into a separate entity. In the untidy, rapidly growing city, unkempt children play in potholes, Indian women pound laundry in a sewage-choked stream, streets are lined with vendors and sparsely stocked stalls, and every other business seems to be an auto repair shop or scrapyard.

At the edge of El Alto, however, the earth drops away, obliterating all the poverty and ugliness and revealing, 400m below, the grand city of La Paz, which fills the bowl and climbs the walls of a gaping canyon nearly 5km from rim to rim. On a clear day, the snowcapped triple peak of Illimani (6402m) towers in the background. If you're fortunate enough to arrive on a clear, dark night, La Paz will appear like a mirrored reflection of the glittering night sky.

Since La Paz is nearly 4km above sea level, warm clothing is needed through much of the year. In the summer, the climate can be harsh: Rain falls on most afternoons, the canyon may fill with clouds, and the steep streets may become torrents of runoff. In the winter, days are slightly cooler, but the crisp, clear air is invigorating. Occasionally, rain and even snow fall during spring and autumn.

HISTORY

La Paz was founded on October 20, 1548, by a Spaniard, Captain Alonzo de Mendoza (under orders of Pedro de la Gasca, to whom the Spanish king had entrusted rule over the former Inca lands), and named La

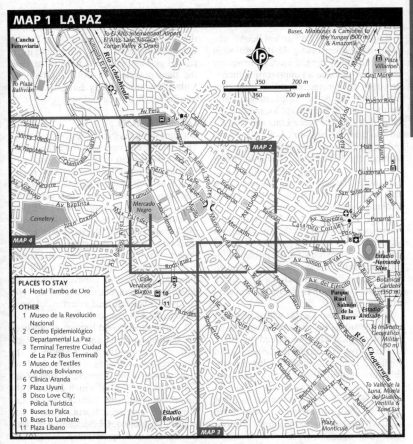

MAP 1 LA PAZ

0   350   700 m
0   350   700 yards

PLACES TO STAY
4 Hostal Tambo de Oro

OTHER
1 Museo de la Revolución
 Nacional
2 Centro Epidemiológico
 Departamental La Paz
3 Terminal Terrestre Ciudad
 de La Paz (Bus Terminal)
5 Museo de Textiles
 Andinos Bolivianos
6 Clínica Aranda
7 Plaza Uyuni
8 Disco Love City;
 Policía Turística
9 Buses to Palca
10 Buses to Lambate
11 Plaza Líbano

Ciudad de Nuestra Señora de La Paz – The City of Our Lady of Peace. The first site chosen by Mendoza was at present-day Laja on the Tiahuanaco road. Shortly after its founding, La Paz was shifted to its present location, the valley of the Chuquiago Marka (now called the Río Choqueyapu). Until then, the site had been occupied by a community of Aymará miners and goldsmiths.

The 16th-century Spanish historian Cieza de León remarked of the new city:

This is a good place to pass one's life. Here the climate is mild and the view of the mountains inspires one to think of God.

In spite of León's rather lofty assessment (perhaps he mistakenly got off at Cochabamba), the reason behind the city's founding was much more terrestrial. The Spanish had always had a weakness for shiny yellow metal, and the now-fetid Río Choqueyapu, which these days flows beneath La Paz, seemed to be full of it. The Spaniards didn't waste any time in seizing the gold mines, of course, and Mendoza was installed as the new city's first mayor. The conquerors also imposed their religion and lifestyle on the Indians, and since most colonists were men, unions between Spanish men and Indian women eventually gave rise to a primarily mestizo population.

If the founding of La Paz had been based on anything other than gold, its position in the depths of a rugged canyon probably would have dictated an unpromising future. However, the protection this setting provided from the fierce Altiplano wind and weather – and its convenient location on the main trade route between Lima and Potosí – did also offer the city some hope of survival and prosperity once the gold had played out. Much of the Potosí silver bound for Peruvian ports on the Pacific passed through La Paz, and by the time the railway lines were built, the city was well enough established to continue commanding attention.

On November 1, 1549, Juan Gutiérrez Panaigua was given the task of designing an urban plan. He laid out plazas and public lands and designated sites for public buildings. La Plaza de los Españoles, now known as Plaza Murillo, was selected as the future site of the cathedral, royal homes and government buildings.

Spain controlled La Paz with a firm grip and the Spanish king had the last word in all matters political. He once denied the job of La Paz mayor to a certain petitioner named Miguel Cervantes de Saavedra. It was probably just as well; the rejected candidate stayed in Spain and wrote *Don Quixote* instead. Some Bolivians, however, feel that given the opportunity, he would have written it anyway, but to the glory of Bolivia rather than Spain.

In spite of its name, the City of Our Lady of Peace has seen a good deal of violence. Twice in 1781, for a total of six months, a group of Aymará under the leadership of Tupac Katari laid siege to La Paz, destroying public buildings and churches before the uprising was quelled. Another period of unrest erupted 30 years later when Altiplano Indians laid a two-month siege on La Paz. Since Bolivian independence in 1825, Plaza Murillo (the main square in La Paz) has been center stage for other revolutions and protests.

An abnormally high mortality rate once accompanied high office in Bolivia, and with

the job of president came a short life expectancy. In fact, the presidential palace on the plaza is now known as the Palacio Quemado (Burned Palace), owing to its repeated gutting by fire. As recently as 1946, the then president of Bolivia, Gualberto Villarroel, was publicly hanged in Plaza Murillo by 'distraught widows.'

ORIENTATION

It's almost impossible to get lost in La Paz. There's only one major thoroughfare, and it follows the canyon of the Río Choqueyapu (fortunately for your olfactory system, the river flows mostly underground these days). The main street changes names several times from the top to bottom: Avenidas Ismael Montes, Mariscal Santa Cruz, 16 de Julio (the Prado) and Villazón. At the lower end, it splits into Avenida 6 de Agosto and Avenida Aniceto Arce. Away from the Prado and its extensions, streets climb steeply uphill, and many are cobbled or unpaved. Above the downtown skyscrapers, the adobe neighborhoods and the informal commercial areas climb toward the canyon's rim.

Contrary to US and European practices, the business districts and wealthier neighborhoods occupy the lower altitudes. The most prestigious suburbs are found far down in the canyon in the generically named Zona Sur (Southern Zone), which includes the suburbs of Achumani, Calacoto, Cotacota – sometimes rendered 'Cota Cota' – San Miguel, La Florida, Obrajes and a growing throng of other upmarket *barrios*, while above, cascades of cuboid mud dwellings and makeshift neighborhoods spill over the canyon rim and down the slopes on three sides. Numbered streets (Calles 1, 2, 3 and up) run perpendicular to the main road in the Zona Sur, making navigation easier; the numbers increase from west to east (see the Around La Paz section for a map of Zona Sur.) In the poorer barrios if you become disoriented and want to return to the center, you need only head downhill.

On Sunday afternoon, when traffic is minimal, the lower Prado hosts promenading families, and the sidewalks fill up with balloon, cotton-candy and soft-drink sellers,

MAP 2 CENTRAL LA PAZ

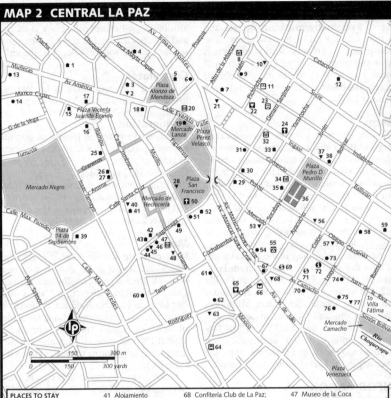

PLACES TO STAY	41	Alojamiento	68	Confitería Club de La Paz;	47	Museo de la Coca
1 Hostería Florida		El Viajero (El Lobo)		Restaurant/Peña	50	Iglesia de San Francisco
3 Alojamiento La Scala	42	Hotel Sagárnaga		Los Escudos	51	Galería Doryan:
4 Alojamiento Universo	43	Hotel Alem	77	Wall St Café I		Restaurant/Peña Parnaso;
5 Hotel Oruro	49	Hotel Happy Days				Sarañani Camping Hire;
7 Hostal Ingavi	52	Hostal Naira	OTHER			Andean Summits
12 Alojamiento Carretero	58	Hotel Viena	6	TAM	54	Galería Handal: Camping
15 Hotel Andes	59	Hostal República	8	Calle Jaén Museums; Museo de		Caza y Pesca; Librería Olimpia
16 Hotel Continental	60	Hotel Milton		Instrumentos Musicales	55	Main ENTEL Telephone Office
17 Hotel Italia			9	Peña Marka Tambo	61	Casa del Corregidor;
18 Tiquina Palace Hotel	PLACES TO EAT		11	Cinemateca Boliviana		Bodegón de Cinti
19 Hostal La Valle	2	El Gran Palacio	13	Lavandería por Kilo	62	IGM Office
25 Hostal Dinastía	10	Casa de los Paceños		(Laundry by the kg)	64	Plaza Belzu (Micros to
26 Hostal Rosario;	21	Vigor	14	Booze & Wine Stalls		Bolsa Negra)
La Fuente; Tambo Colonial	28	Profumo di Caffe	20	Museo Tambo Quirquincho	65	La Luna
27 Residencial	37	Heladería Napoli	22	Nameless Bar	66	Central Post Office
Copacabana	40	El Lobo	23	Teatro Municipal	67	El Obelisco
29 Hotel Presidente	45	100% Natural Fruit &	24	Iglesia de Santo Domingo	69	Casa de Cambio América
30 Hotel Gloria;		Salad Bar	31	El Calicanto Peña	70	Óptica Paris
Café Pierrot	48	Ángelo Colonial;	32	Museo de Etnografía	71	Casa de Cambio Sudamer
33 Hostal Austria		Internet Café		y Folklore	72	Senatur Tourist Office
35 Hotel Torino;	53	Pollo Copacabana	34	Museo Nacional del Arte	73	Los Amigos del Libro
Café Torino	56	Pollo Copacabana	36	Cathedral; Museo de Arte Sacro	74	Unitours
38 Gran Hotel Paris		& Chocolate Shop	44	Condoriri; Bolivian Journeys	75	Immigration
39 Hotel Galería	57	Boutique del Pan	46	Peña Huari; Snack El	76	LAB
Virgen del Rosario	63	Acuario II		Montañés		

and people renting kites, bicycles and little toy cars. Especially when the sun shines, there's a pleasantly festive atmosphere, and it may recall a bit of lost childhood. The best-preserved colonial section of town is near the intersection of Calles Jaén and Sucre (see Map 2), where narrow cobbled streets and colonial churches offer a glimpse of early La Paz.

Maps

The best city map, bar none, is the Journey map entitled *Guía de Atractivos Turísticos y Rutas La Paz*, but it's unfortunately scarce; you'll occasionally find it in the kiosks in the main bus terminal. An outdated alternative is *La Paz Información*, which is sold at the municipal tourist office and several bookstores. The same tourist office also sells simple route maps of hiking areas in the valley below La Paz.

Another useful map is the typically up-to-date Polyjake map, available from Polyjake (☎ 211164; polyjake@zuper.net; Casilla 9224) as well as at several hotels. It includes maps of the Center, Sopocachi, Miraflores and Calacoto and features museums, galleries, embassies and ENTEL offices (including Entelitos). For information on buying topo sheets and climbing maps, see Planning in the Facts for the Visitor chapter.

INFORMATION
Tourist Offices

The national tourist office Senatur (Map 2; ☎ 367463; fax 374630; Edificio Mariscal Ballivián, Calle Mercado 1328) is open weekdays from 8:30 am to noon and 2:30 to 6:30 pm. The more convenient municipal tourist office (☎ 371044; gmlp@hotmail.com; Plaza del Estudiante) is open weekdays 8:30 am to noon and 2:30 to 7 pm and on Saturday from 9:30 am to 12:30 pm (they also run a small tourist kiosk on Plaza Alonzo de Mendoza). They distribute brochures in English, French and German, but the original Spanish versions may make more sense than the often amusing translations.

A reliable alternative is the privately run tourist office at Ángelo Colonial (Map 2; ☎ 360199; fax 0811-2866; angelo@ angelocolonial.com; Calle Linares 922-924). Housed in an old colonial mansion, it also has a post office, café, book exchange and Internet access. For more information, see the website www.angelocolonial.com.

Consulates

Embassies and consulates in La Paz are listed in the Facts for the Visitor chapter.

Immigration

Extensions to visas and lengths of stay are normally processed in a few hours at the immigration office (☎ 370475), at Avenida Camacho 1433 (see Map 2). For length-of-stay extensions, you can drop off your passport at the top-floor office in the morning and pick it up in the afternoon. The office is open weekdays from 9 am to 4 pm.

Money

Most of the *casas de cambio* (exchange offices) are found in the central area (see Map 2). Recommended choices include Casa de Cambio Sudamer, at Calle Colón 206; Casa de Cambio América, on Avenida Camacho; and Unitours, on Calle Mercado, all of which change traveler's checks for around 1% commission. They also sell currency from neighboring countries (when it's available).

Some casas de cambio also change traveler's checks into US dollars for around 1% commission, which is generally worthwhile, considering that outside La Paz you'll get 3% to 10% less for checks than for cash. However, check carefully for counterfeit US bills, which surface frequently, and don't accept US currency with even the tiniest rips or tears (they won't be accepted anywhere else in Bolivia).

During the week, casas de cambio are open regular business hours, and on Saturday, in the morning only. To change traveler's checks on Sunday or after hours, try the Hotel Gloria, the Hostal Rosario or El Lobo Restaurant. Around the intersections of Calle Colón, Avenida Camacho and Mariscal Santa Cruz, *cambistas* (street moneychangers) change cash for slightly lower than casa de cambio rates. Stay attentive during the transaction and never hand over your cash until you're holding the correct number of bolivianos.

Visa and Mastercard cash withdrawals of up to US$300 daily are available with no added commission and a minimum of hassle from the Banco de Santa Cruz, at Calle Mercado 1077; Banco Mercantil, on the corner of Calles Mercado and Ayacucho; and Banco Nacional de Bolivia, on the corner of Calle Colón and Avenida Camacho. Banco de La Paz charges 1.75% commission on credit card withdrawals. Cash withdrawals on Visa cards and in some cases, Cirrus and/or Plus System debit (ATM) cards, can be made at ENLACE automatic teller machines, which are concentrated along and near the Prado.

The American Express representative is Magri Turismo (Map 3; ☎ 442727; fax 443060; magri-emete@megalink.com; Capitán Ravelo 2101, Casilla 4469).

Post & Communications

The central post office, on the corner of Avenida Mariscal Santa Cruz and Calle Oruro (see Map 2), is open Monday to Friday from 8:30 am to 8 pm, Saturday from 9 am to 7 pm and Sunday from 9 am to noon. Poste restante is free, but you must present your passport when collecting mail. It's sorted into foreign and Bolivian stacks, so those with a Latin surname may want to check both stacks.

To mail an international parcel, take it downstairs to the customs desk and have it inspected before sealing it up and going to the parcels desk. Parcels to Bolivian destinations should be taken to the desk marked 'Encomiendas.' A large notice board in the main hall lists airport departure times for mail to various destinations.

The main ENTEL telephone office, at Calle Ayacucho 267 (see Map 2), is open daily from 7:30 am to 10:30 pm for national and international telephone calls. Public telephones are found in the ENTEL lobby and in hotels, restaurants, street stalls and in telephone boxes along the Prado. There is also an increasing number of convenient Entelitos (little ENTELs) scattered around

the city. ENTEL also provides telegram and telex services and a convenient but rather inefficient fax service; the public fax number at the main ENTEL office is 0811-9121.

La Paz has caught on to email and the Internet in a big way, and there are now around 70 Internet cafés scattered around the city. Most of these charge between US$1 and US$1.50 per hour. The best is probably in the café Ángelo Colonial, at Calle Linares 922-924 (see Map 2), which charges US$1.20 per hour for good fast satellite connections. Another good choice is Web Bolivia (Map 3; Avenida 16 de Julio 1764), which has dozens of machines and charges US$1.20 per hour, with discounts in the morning.

Bookstores

La Paz has quite a few bookstores but most sell only comics, trashy novels or Bolivian school texts. Los Amigos del Libro (gutten@amigol.bo.net) has outlets at Calle Mercado 1315 (Map 2; ☎ 204321), in the Edificio Alameda on 16 de Julio beside the Hotel Plaza (Map 3; ☎ 358164), on Avenida Montenegro in San Miguel in the Zona Sur (☎ 793934), and at El Alto Airport. Each one has a selection of popular English-, German- and French-language paperbacks and souvenir books, as well as dictionaries, Spanish-language books and foreign newsmagazines, such as *Time*, *Newsweek* and the *Economist*. Gisbert & Compañía, at Calle Comercio 1270, sells Spanish-language literature and maps. For a good selection of national and local maps, see the Librería Olimpia (Map 2; ☎ 353833), in the Galería Handal, Local 14, on Avenida Mariscal Santa Cruz; and at Calle Ingavi 151 (☎ 351781).

For popular used paperbacks in English, check out the stalls in the booksellers' section of the Mercado Lanza.

Cultural Centers

Several international centers offer cultural programs and reading rooms with films, magazines, books and news from their sponsoring countries. All the following are on Map 3. The British Council (☎ 431240; fax 431377; bcouncil@ceibo.entelnet.bo), at Avenida

Arce 2708, features British newspapers and magazines and the pleasant Mongo's Café (see Places to Eat); in the morning, they do an especially fine English breakfast. The Centro Boliviano-Americano (☎ 431342), on Avenida Aniceto Arce at Parque Zenón Iturralde 121, is open weekdays except at lunchtime. The Goethe Institut (☎ 325022 or 391950; goethe@caoba.entelnet.bo) is at Avenida 6 de Agosto 2118, and is also open on weekdays and offers German-language videos, magazines and newspapers. The Alliance Française (☎ 324075; fax 391950; alflapaz@ceibo.entelnet.bo) is on Fernando Guachalla 399 near Avenida 20 de Octubre and shares space with Café Montmartre. It provides French-language publications and occasionally screens French films.

Laundry

Most middle- and high-range hotels offer laundry services. A recommended laundry is Express Lavandería, at Aroma 720, near the Hostal Rosario. There are also several lavanderías around Plaza Isabel la Católica, such as Lavaya (Avenida Arce 2529), as well as on upper Calle Muñecas. At any of these places, plan on paying around US$1.40 per kilogram. There's also a self-service launderette, Lavandería Vicky, in the San Antonio building, at the corner of Fernando Guachalla and Ecuador in Sopocachi.

Film

Fujichrome color slide film is widely available for about US$6 per roll; be cautious about buying film at street markets where it is exposed to strong sun all day. Fujicolor is the most widely available print film and costs as little as US$3 for a roll of 36 exposures. Lots of film and photo shops cluster around the intersection of Calle Comercio and Avenida Mariscal Santa Cruz. In the street stalls along Buenos Aires, you'll find Fujichrome Sensia 100 for around US$4.50 and Kodak Gold 100 print film for US$2.50. Only occasionally will you find anything over 400 ASA, and even then, it will probably be outdated. For relatively inexpensive cameras and equipment, try the small shops

at Calle Eloy Salmón 849 and 959, off the west end of Calle Santa Cruz.

For processing of both slide and print film, two reliable laboratories are Casa Kavlin (☎ 369286; Calle Potosí 1130), which is the only place to find Kodak Elite II film, and Foto Linares (☎ 327703; Edificio Alborada), at the corner of Loayza and Juan de la Riva. The latter is an excellent choice for specialist processing. If you have camera problems, the man to see is Rolando Calla. You'll find him at Foto Linares between 10:30 am and 12:30 pm, and at his home (☎ 373621 or 411154; rolando_calla@ megalink.com; Avenida Sánchez Lima 2178) from 3 to 7:30 pm. For camera cleaning, he charges US$29. Alternatively, try AGFA Bolivia (Calle Loayza 250).

Outdoor Equipment

A good selection of new and secondhand climbing, trekking and camping equipment is at Condoriri (Map 2; ☎/fax 319369; Calle Sagárnaga 343). It sells everything from ropes and backpacks to boots, compasses and headlamp batteries, plus a selection of climbing hardware. It also rents out equipment and has a repair service. Bolivian Journeys, just a few meters up the hill, sells maps, climbing gear, camping equipment and stove fuel, and rents stoves, tents and sleeping bags.

You'll find one of Bolivia's widest ranges of camping equipment at Camping Caza y Pesca (Map 2; ☎ 379207; Galería Handal, Local 9), near the corner of Socabaya and Mariscal Santa Cruz. This is a good place to pick up gas canisters for Bleuet stoves. Alternatively, check out King Sport at Calle Graneros 364.

If you prefer to rent equipment, visit Sarañani (Map 2; Galería Doryan, Local 25), at Sagárnaga and Murillo. Outdoor adventurers will also find an excellent selection of climbing, camping and trekking equipment, as well as a good range of climbing hardware for sale or rent, at Andean Summits (☎/fax 317497; Galería Doryan), two doors from Sarañani. See also their website www.andeansummits.com.

For all kinds of backpack protection – wire mesh, plastic sacks, chains, padlocks, and so on – check the street stalls along Calle Isaac Tamayo.

Medical Services

The Centro Epidemiológico Departamental La Paz (Map 1; ☎ 450166; Avenida Vásquez 122), near the brewery just off upper Avenida Ismael Montes, is open from 8:30 am to noon and 2:30 to 6:30 pm. Here, rabies vaccinations are available for US$1, and those heading for the lowlands can pick up yellow-fever vaccinations and chloroquine to be used as a malaria prophylaxis (avoid chloroquine if you've previously been taking Lariam – also called mefloquine – as they make a potentially dangerous combination).

Alternatively, for blood tests, use the more convenient Laboratorio/Clínica Hematológico (☎ 328821; Edificio Alameda, Avenida 16 de Julio, 2nd floor).

The rather marginal Clínica Americana (☎ 783509), also known as the Hospital Metodista, is at Avenida 14 de Septiembre 78, at Calle 9, in Obrajes (Zona Sur). The Clínica Alemana (☎ 329155; Avenida 6 de Agosto 2821) offers very basic services. Other options include the Clínica Aranda (Map 1; ☎ 243683; Plaza Uyuni 1351, Miraflores), Clínica Cemes (☎ 430350; cemessrl@ceibo.entelnet.bo; Avenida 6 de Agosto 2881), and Trauma Klinik (☎ 771819; Calle Claudio Aliaga 12, San Miguel, Zona Sur). English-speaking doctors who have been recommended include Dr Fernando Patiño (☎ 794614) and Dr Raúl Pinto Campero (☎ 322058; Avenida Arce 2342).

A recommended dentist is Dr Mario H Humesez Pérez (☎ 420596; mobile ☎ 015-61109; fax 420716; mdecabecera@hotmail .com; Edificio ANIBAL Mezzanine, Sánchez Lima 2520). The best optical outlet, which can provide optical exams, glasses and contact lenses, is Óptica Paris (Map 2), on Avenida Camacho.

Some pharmacies, known as *farmacias de turno*, take turns opening at night, on weekends and on public holidays. The current ones on duty are listed in the newspaper *El Diario*.

Emergency

Robberies and other problems may be reported to the Policía Turística (Map 1; ☎ 225016), beside the Disco Love City on Plaza del Estadio in Miraflores. They won't recover any stolen goods but will take an affidavit *(denuncia)* for insurance purposes. The phone number for Radio Patrulla (Radio Patrol), as in all major Bolivian cities, is 110.

Dangers & Annoyances

La Paz is a great city to explore on foot, but don't be in too much of a hurry or the altitude might take its toll, especially when you're walking uphill. If you're arriving in La Paz from the lowlands, see Altitude Sickness in the Health section of the Facts for the Visitor chapter.

La Paz may be an incredibly safe city by South American standards, but there are still a number of scams aimed at tourists. Read the rundown of the most popular ploys under Dangers & Annoyances in the Facts for the Visitor chapter and stay aware of what's going on around you.

CHURCHES
Iglesia de San Francisco

The hewn stone basilica of San Francisco (Map 2), on the plaza of the same name, reflects an appealing blend of 16th-century Spanish and mestizo trends. The church was founded in 1548 by Fray Francisco de los Ángeles, and construction began the following year. The original structure collapsed under heavy snowfall in about 1610, but it was reconstructed between 1744 and 1753. The second building was built entirely of stone quarried at nearby Viacha. The façade is decorated with stone carvings of natural themes such as *chirimoyas* (custard apples), pinecones and tropical birds.

After looking at the church, turn toward the bizarre and ambitious sculpture on the upper portion of Plaza San Francisco. This mass of rock pillars and stone faces in suspended animation is intended to represent and honor Bolivia's three great cultures – Tiahuanaco, Inca and modern.

Cathedral

Although it's a recent addition to La Paz's collection of religious structures, the 1835 cathedral (Map 2) on Plaza Murillo is an impressive structure – mostly because it is built on a steep hillside. The main entrance on Plaza Murillo is 12m higher than its base on Calle Potosí. The sheer immensity of the building, with its high dome, hulking columns, thick stone walls and high ceilings, is overpowering, but the altar is relatively simple. Inside, the main attraction is the profusion of stained-glass work throughout; the windows behind the altar depict a gathering of Bolivian generals and presidents being blessed from above by a flock of heavenly admirers.

Beside the cathedral is the Presidential Palace, and in the center of Plaza Murillo, opposite, stands a statue of President Gualberto Villarroel. In 1946, he was dragged from the palace by vigilantes – in this case, widows of his victims – and hanged from a lamppost in the square. Interestingly enough, Don Pedro Domingo Murillo, for whom the plaza was named, had met a similar fate there in 1810.

Iglesia de Santo Domingo

Like the Iglesia de San Francisco, the exterior of the Iglesia de Santo Domingo (Map 2), a block northwest of Plaza Murillo, shows evidence of Baroque and mestizo influences. The rest of the structure, however, is of limited interest.

MUSEUMS

La Paz, as Bolivia's de facto capital, has its share of cultural and historical museums. Most are closed over the Christmas holiday (December 25 to January 6).

Calle Jaén Museums

Four interesting museums (Map 2) – the Museo de Metales Preciosos Pre-Colombinos, the Museo del Litoral, the Museo Casa

Murillo and the Museo Costumbrista Juan de Vargas – are clustered together along Calle Jaén, a beautifully restored colonial street, and can easily be bundled into one visit. The museums are open Tuesday to Friday from 9:30 am to noon, 12:30 to 2:30 pm and 3 to 7 pm, and on weekends from 10 am to 12:30 pm. For admission to all four, foreigners pay US$2 for a combination ticket, which is sold at the Museo Costumbrista. On Saturday, admission is free for everyone.

Museo de Metales Preciosos Pre-Colombinos Also known as the Museo del Oro, this museum (☎ 371470; Calle Jaén 777) houses three impressively presented salons of pre-Columbian silver, gold and copper works. A fourth salon in the basement has examples of ancient pottery.

Museo del Litoral Sometimes called Museo de la Guerra del Pacífico, this small exhibit at Calle Jaén 798 incorporates relics from the 1884 war in which Bolivia became landlocked after losing its Litoral department to Chile. The collection consists mainly of historical maps that defend Bolivia's emotionally charged claims to Antofagasta and Chile's Segunda Región.

Casa de Don Pedro Domingo Murillo Once the home of Pedro Murillo, a leader in the La Paz Revolution of July 16, 1809, the house now displays collections of colonial art and furniture, textiles, medicines, musical instruments and household items of glass and silver that once belonged to Bolivian aristocracy. Other odds and ends include a collection of Alasitas miniatures (see Special Events later in this section). Murillo was hanged by the Spanish on January 29, 1810, in the plaza now named after him. One of the paintings on display in the house is entitled *The Execution of Murillo*.

Museo Costumbrista Juan de Vargas This museum (☎ 378478), on Calle Sucre at Jaén, contains art and photos of old La Paz, as well as some superb ceramic

MAP 3 LOWER PRADO & SOPOCACHI

PLACES TO EAT
3 Las Velas
11 Unicornio; Eli's Pizza Express II
13 Special Empanadas & Tucumanas
15 Café Alexander
18 Eli's Pizza Express I
19 Denny's
20 McDonald's
24 Café Ciudad
26 La Bodeguita Cubana
27 Restaurant Vienna
31 Café Oro
39 Sergio's
40 Andrómeda
41 Wall St Café II
45 Crêperie La Bohême
46 Café Montmartre; Alliance Française
47 Pronto Ristorante
51 Chifa Emy
54 Pronto Pettirosso
55 Kuchen Stube
56 La Québecoise
57 Café en Azul
60 Mongo's Rock Bottom Café
61 ZATT

63 Gringo Limón
64 El Arriero
65 Ketal Hipermercado
66 Jalapeños
67 Wagamama
70 Taquería Los Nopalitos
74 Supermercado X-Tra
75 New Tokyo

OTHER
2 Templete Semisubterráneo
7 San Pedro Prison
9 América Tours; Gravity Assisted Mountain Biking
10 AeroSur
12 Club Andino Boliviano
14 Web Bolivia Internet Café
16 Museo del Deporte Nacional
17 Municipal Tourist Office
21 Los Amigos del Libro
23 Hotel Europa (Swimming pool, Sauna)
25 Museo Nacional de Arqueología (Tiwanaku)
28 Planetario Max Schreier

29 Museo Kusillo
32 Universidad Mayor de San Andrés (UMSA)
33 Pig & Whistle
34 Australian Consulate
35 Magri Turismo
38 Goethe Institut
39 Peruvian Embassy
43 Museo Marina Núñez del Prado
44 Thelonius Jazz Bar
48 El Loro en su Salsa
49 German Embassy
50 Brazilian Embassy
52 Empresa Ferroviaria Andina (EFA)
53 Coyote Bar
58 Cambrinus
59 Dead Stroke Billiards Bar
62 Canadian Consul
68 Parque Zenón Iturralde; Centro Boliviano-Americano
69 GBT
71 British Council; Mongo's Café
72 British Embassy
73 US Embassy

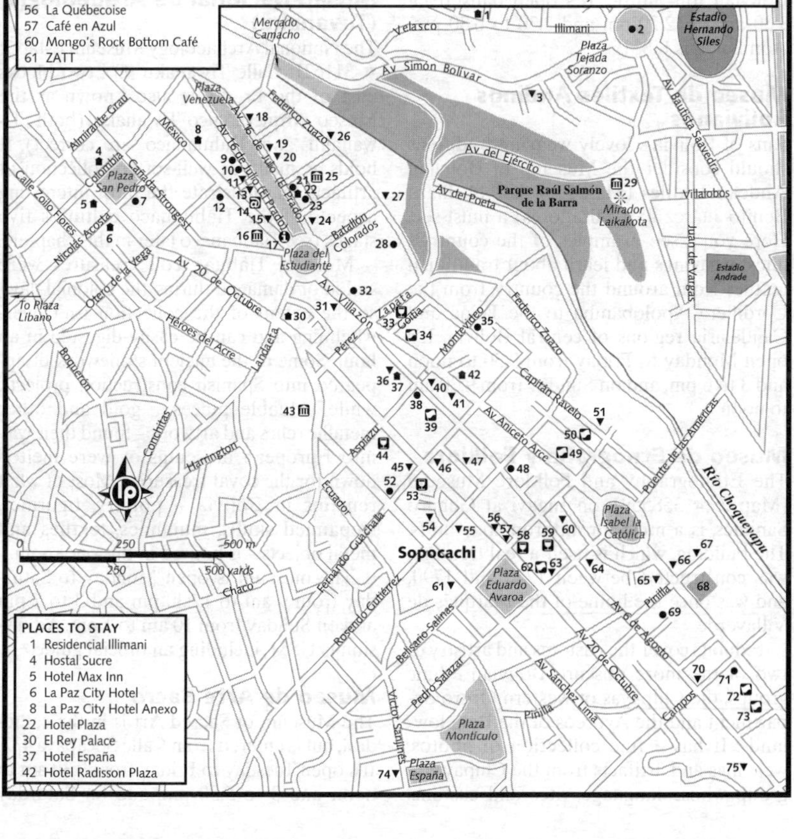

PLACES TO STAY
1 Residencial Illimani
4 Hostal Sucre
5 Hotel Max Inn
6 La Paz City Hotel
8 La Paz City Hotel Anexo
22 Hotel Plaza
30 El Rey Palace
37 Hotel España
42 Hotel Radisson Plaza

figurine dioramas of old La Paz. One of these is a representation of *akulliko*, the hour of coca-chewing; another portrays the festivities surrounding the Día de San Juan Bautista on June 24; another depicts the hanging of Murillo in 1810. Also on display are colonial artifacts and colorful dolls wearing traditional costumes.

Museo de Instrumentos Musicales

Also known as the Museo de Instrumentos Nativos, this small museum (Map 2; ☎ 331077; Calle Jaén 711) is the brainchild of *charango* master Ernesto Cavour; it displays all possible incarnations of charangos and other indigenous instruments used in Bolivian folk music. It's open daily from 9:30 am to 12:30 pm and 2:30 to 6:30 pm. Admission is US$1.

Museo de Textiles Andinos Bolivianos

Fans of Bolivia's lovely weaving traditions should consider the Museum of Bolivian Andean Textiles (Map 1; ☎ 223114; Plaza Benito Juárez 488, Miraflores) a must-see. Here you'll see examples of the country's finest weavings and learn about traditional textiles from around the country, from the Cordillera Apolobamba to the Jal'qa and Candelaria regions of central Bolivia. It's open Monday to Friday from 9:30 to noon and 3 to 6 pm, and on Sunday from 9:30 am to noon.

Museo de Etnografía y Folklore

The Ethnography and Folklore Museum (Map 2; ☎ 358559), on Ingavi at Genaro Sanjinés, is a must for anthropology buffs. The building, which is itself a real treasure, was constructed between 1776 and 1790, and was once the home of the Marqués de Villaverde.

Exhibits cover the customs and artistry of two of the more obscure Bolivian ethnic groups: the Chipayas of western Oruro department and the Ayoreos of the Beni lowlands. It has a fine collection of photos, weavings and artifacts from the Chipayas, a group whose language, rites and customs differ greatly from those of neighboring cultures. Some anthropologists have suggested that the Chipayas are descendants of the vanished Tiahuanaco culture. The museum is open Tuesday to Friday from 9 am to 12:30 pm and 3 to 7 pm, and on weekends from 10 am to 12:30 pm. Admission is free.

Templete Semisubterráneo

Also known as the Museo al Aire Libre (Map 3), this open pit opposite the stadium is a replica of the Templete Semisubterráneo at Tiahuanaco. It contains restorations of statues found at Tiahuanaco, and if you aren't visiting the actual site, it's worth a quick look.

Museo Nacional de Arqueología (Tiwanaku)

The National Archaeology Museum (Map 3; ☎ 311621; Calle Tiwanaku 93), two blocks east of the Prado, is also known as the Museo Arqueológico Tiwanaku (both 'Tiwanaku' and 'Tiahuanaco' are correct). It holds a small but well-sorted collection of artifacts that illustrate the most interesting aspects of the Tiahuanaco culture's five stages (see Tiahuanaco later in this chapter).

Most of Tiahuanaco's treasures were stolen or damaged during the colonial days, so the extent of the collection isn't overwhelming and can be easily digested in an hour. Some of the ancient stonework disappeared into Spanish construction projects, while valuable pieces – gold and other metallic relics and artwork – found their way into European museums or were melted down for the royal treasuries. Most of what remains in Bolivia – pottery, figurines, trepanned skulls, mummies, textiles and metal objects – is housed in this one room.

The museum is open Monday to Saturday from 9 am to 12:30 pm and 3 to 7 pm and on Sunday from 10 am to 1 pm. Admission is US$1, including an official guide.

Museo de Arte Sacro

The Museum of Sacred Art is in the cathedral, but is entered from Calle Socabaya 432. It's open Tuesday to Friday from 9:30 am to noon and 3 to 5:30 pm, and on Saturday from 10 am to 12:30 pm. Foreigners pay US$1 admission. The museum consists mostly of typical religious paraphernalia, but there are two unusual mother-of-pearl coffins and well-executed portraits of the 12 Apostles.

Museo Tambo Quirquincho

This museum (Map 2), on Evaristo Valle near Plaza Alonzo de Mendoza, once served as a *tambo*, which is the Quechua word for a wayside inn and market. It now houses an exhibit of weird and colorful Diablada masks, drawings of 1845 Bolivia by Neman Regendas, old-time clothing, silverware, paintings, sculptures, photos and festive items. It's open Tuesday to Friday from 9:30 am to 12:30 pm and 3 to 7 pm, and on weekends from 10 am to 12:30 pm. Admission is US$0.50 on weekdays and Sunday, and free on Saturday.

Museo Kusillo & Cerro Laikakota

This little museum (Map 3), also known as Museo del Niño (Children's Museum), lies on Avenida del Ejército and features science-oriented displays and hands-on experiments of interest to children. It also holds children's workshops, games, music, theater and dance programs. It's opposite the park known as the 'Ex-Zoológico' and is open Monday to Sunday from 10:30 am to 6:30 pm. Admission is US$1.50 (US$1 on Tuesday).

The *mirador* (lookout) in nearby Parque Raúl Salmón de la Barra, on Cerro Laikakota, affords a spectacular view over the city; admission to the mirador is US$0.20.

Museo de la Coca

This tourist-oriented museum (and who isn't interested in coca?) at Linares 906 (Map 2), operated by the Netherlands' International Coca Research Institute (ICORI; ☎ 791758; icori@ xs4all.nl), will reveal all you ever wanted to know about the sacred leaf that

Coca

has kept many Andean people in a resigned stupor since time immemorial. And then there's the effect it has had on the rest of the world! It's open weekdays from 10 am to 1 pm and 2 to 6 pm. Admission is US$1.50.

Museo de la Historia Natural

La Paz's Natural History Museum (☎ 795364; Calle 26, Cotacota), on the university campus in the Zona Sur, has exhibits on Bolivia's geology, paleontology, botany and zoology. The location is a bit inconvenient, but it's worthwhile if you're in the area. It's open Tuesday to Sunday from 8:30 am to 4 pm, and admission for foreigners costs US$0.50. From Calle México or the Prado, take *micro* 'Ñ' or *colectivo* 21 or 260 (or any downhill colectivo marked 'Cotacota').

Museo Nacional del Arte

The National Art Museum (Map 2; ☎ 371177), on Calle Comercio at Socabaya, near Plaza Murillo, is housed in the former Palacio de Los Condes de Arana. The building was constructed in 1775 of pink Viacha granite, and was restored to its original grandeur by Bolivian architects Teresa Gisbert and José de Mesa.

In the center of a huge courtyard, surrounded by three stories of pillared corridors, is a lovely alabaster fountain. The various levels are dedicated to contemporary artists: Marina Núñez del Prado, the late-Renaissance works of Melchor Pérez de Holguín and students of his Potosí school, and works of other Latin American artists. Visiting exhibitions are shown in the outer salon.

It's open Tuesday to Friday from 9 am to 12:30 pm and 3 to 7 pm, and on weekends from 10 am to 1 pm. Admission is US$0.50.

Museo Marina Núñez del Prado

This museum (Map 3; ☎ 324906; Avenida Ecuador 2034) is dedicated to the work of the late sculptor, whose works focus on subjects from the Quechua and Aymará cultures. Located in her former home in Sopocachi, it contains her personal collection of cultural paraphernalia and numerous examples of her work.

Marina Núñez del Prado

Bolivia's foremost sculptor, Marina Núñez del Prado, was born on October 17, 1910 in La Paz. From 1927 to 1929, she studied at the Escuela Nacional de Bellas Artes (National School of Fine Arts) and from 1930 to 1938 worked there as a professor of sculpture and artistic anatomy.

Her early works were in cedar and walnut, and represented the mysteries of the Andes: indigenous faces, groups and dances. From 1943 to 1945, she lived in New York and turned her attentions to Bolivian social themes, including mining and poverty. She later went through a celebration of Bolivian motherhood with pieces depicting indigenous women, pregnant women and mothers protecting their children. Other works dealt largely with Andean themes, some of which took appealing abstract forms. She once wrote, 'I feel the enormous good fortune to have been born under the tutelage of the Andes, which express the richness and the cosmic miracle. My art expresses the spirit of my Andean homeland and the spirit of my Aymará people.'

During her long career she held over 160 exhibitions, which garnered her numerous awards and received international acclaim from the likes of Pablo Neruda, Gabriela Mistral, Alexander Archipenko and Guillermo Niño de Guzmán. In her later years, Marina lived in Lima, Peru, with her husband, Peruvian writer Jorge Falcón. She died there in September 1995 at the age of 84.

It's open Tuesday to Friday from 9:30 am to 1 pm and 3 to 7 pm, and Saturday through Monday from 9:30 am to 1 pm. Phone ahead if you wish to visit at any other time.

Museo del Deporte Nacional

If you really love sports, at this museum (Map 3; ☎ 320221; Calle México 1710) you can learn about Bolivian sports history and examine all sorts of sporting paraphernalia – prizes, medals, trophies, photos and other items. It's open Monday to Friday from 8:30 am to noon and 2:30 to 6:30 pm.

Museo Histórico Militar

Military sorts may appreciate examining the arms, uniforms and ideologies that starred in Bolivia's war for independence and numerous territorial squabbles (and, incidentally, the seemingly countless revolutions) that have characterized Bolivian history. This museum (☎ 795863; Irpavi Calle 13, Calacoto) is housed in the Colegio Militar del Ejército and is open Monday to Friday from 9 am to noon and 3 to 6 pm.

Museo de la Revolución Nacional

The first question to ask when approaching this museum, on Plaza Villarroel at the end of Avenida Busch (Map 1), is 'Which Revolution?' (Bolivia has had over 100 of them). The answer is in fact the one of April 1952, the popular revolt of armed miners that resulted in the nationalization of Bolivian mining interests. It displays photos and paintings from the era and describes the creation of the government mining corporation COMIBOL, which was an economic failure and was recently transferred to private interests. The museum is open Tuesday to Friday from 9:30 am to 12:30 pm and 3 to 7 pm.

PLANETARIO MAX SCHREIER

La Paz's simple but interesting planetarium (Map 3; ☎ 359522; Federico Zuazo 1976) is great for an hour of astral entertainment. On weekdays, shows run at 9, 10, and 11 am and 3, 4 and 5 pm, and on Saturday, at 4 and 5 pm.

CEMETERY DISTRICT (MAP 4)

As in most Latin American cemeteries, bodies are first buried in the traditional way or placed in a crypt, then within 10 years, they're disinterred and cremated. Families then purchase or rent glass-fronted spaces in the cemetery walls for the ashes and affix plaques and mementos of the dead, and place flowers behind the glass door. Each wall has hundreds of these doors, and some of the walls have been expanded upward to

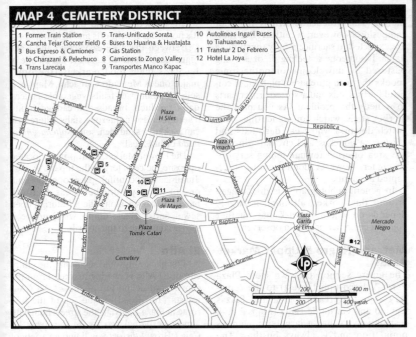

MAP 4 CEMETERY DISTRICT

1 Former Train Station
2 Cancha Tejar (Soccer Field)
3 Bus Expreso & Camiones
   to Charazani & Pelechuco
4 Trans Larecaja
5 Trans-Unificado Sorata
6 Buses to Huarina & Huatajata
7 Gas Station
8 Camiones to Zongo Valley
9 Transportes Manco Kapac
10 Autolíneas Ingavi Buses
    to Tiahuanaco
11 Transtur 2 De Febrero
12 Hotel La Joya

such an extent that they resemble three- or four-story apartment blocks. As a result, the cemetery is an active place, full of people passing through to visit relatives and leave or water fresh flowers. On November 2, the Día de los Muertos (Day of the Dead), half the city turns out to honor their ancestors.

There are also huge family mausoleums, as well as sections dedicated to mine workers and their families, and common graves for soldiers killed in battle. You may even see the black-clad professional mourners who provide suitable wails and tears during burials.

MARKETS

If you want to meet people or just observe the rhythms of local life, an ideal place would be one of the city's dozen or so markets. There's an artisans' market, a witchcraft market, a flower market, a black market and several food markets. Anything from cassette tapes and washtubs to tooth-paste and strawberry jam is available some-where in the markets of La Paz.

Mercado de Hechicería

The city's most unusual market (Map 2) lies along Calle Jiménez and Calle Linares between Sagárnaga and Santa Cruz, amid lively tourist *artesanía* shops. In Spanish, it's known as the Mercado de Hechicería or Mercado de los Brujos (the Witches' Market), and in Aymará, it's called *lak-i'asina catu*. What they're selling isn't exactly witchcraft as depicted in horror films and Halloween tales; the merchandise is mainly herbs and folk remedies as well as a few more unorthodox ingredients in-tended to manipulate and supplicate the various malevolent and beneficent spirits that populate the Aymará world.

If you're constructing a new home or office building, for example, you can buy a llama fetus to bury beneath the corner-stone as a *cha'lla* (offering) to Pachamama, encouraging her to inspire good luck therein. This practice is strictly for poor campesinos, however; wealthier Bolivians are expected to sacrifice a fully functioning llama. If someone is feeling ill, or is being pestered by unwelcome or bothersome spooks, they can purchase a plateful of colorful herbs, seeds and assorted critter parts to remedy the problem. As you pass the market stalls, watch for wandering *yatiri* (witch doctors) who wear dark hats and carry coca pouches, and circulate through the area offering fortune-telling services. Foreigners, however, don't seem to be accepted as clients.

In general, photography is discouraged around this market, although it largely depends on whom you ask and whether you're a customer or just an observer.

Mercado Negro & Upper Market Areas

The entire section of town from Plaza Pérez Velasco uphill (west) to the cemetery – past Mercado Lanza and Plazas Eguino and Garita de Lima (Maps 2 & 4, respectively) – has a largely indigenous population and is always bustling. The streets are crowded with traffic honking its way through the narrow cobbled streets, cholas rushing about socializing and making purchases, and pedestrians jostling with sidewalk vendors. The market stalls sell all manner of practical items from clothing and fast foods to groceries, healthcare products and cooking pots. The focus of activity is near the intersection of Calles Buenos Aires and Max Paredes, especially on Wednesday and Saturday.

The Mercado Negro, or 'Black Market,' along upper Calle Graneros and Eloy Salmón, is the place to pick up undocumented merchandise and just about anything else you may hope for. Most of it isn't stolen, exactly, although some of it is bootlegged, and in the case of music tapes, vendors make no effort to conceal the fact; the covers are merely photocopied. It's also good for electronics, imitation designer clothing and inexpensive Fuji and Agfa film,

including slide film. Be especially careful when wandering around this part of town; it's notorious for rip-offs and light fingers.

Between Plaza Pérez Velasco and Calle Figueroa is Mercado Lanza (Map 2), one of La Paz's main food markets (the other major one is Mercado Camacho; Map 3). It sells all manner of fruits, vegetables, juices, dairy products, breads and canned foods. There are also numerous stalls where you can pick up a sandwich, soup, *salteña*, *empanada* or full meal.

The Flower Market, appropriately located opposite the cemetery at the top of Avenida Tumusla, is a beautiful splash of color amid one of the city's drabber areas. Unfortunately, it also sits alongside a festering open sewer and garbage dump, which make it rather confusing to the nostrils.

El Alto

At first glance, it would seem that the entire city of El Alto is one big market. From the canyon rim at the top of the El Alto Autopista (Toll Road) or the top of the free route at Plaza Ballivián, the streets hum with almost perpetual activity. In the lively La Ceja ('Brow') district you'll find a variety of small electronic gadgets, such as tape recorders, and mercantile goods. Try the Thursday and Sunday Mercado La Ceja (also known as Mercado 16 de Julio), which stretches along the main thoroughfare and across Plaza 16 de Julio. If you keep your wits about you, speak Spanish and bargain politely, you're sure to have an excellent time, meet some friendly, down-to-earth Bolivians, and find some great deals. The activity starts at about 6 am and peters out after 3 pm.

BOTANICAL GARDENS

The most convenient botanical garden is on Calle Lucas Jaimes between Nicaragua and Villalobos in Miraflores. Displaying the vegetation of the Altiplano and Yungas, it's open to the public Monday to Saturday from 8 am to noon and 2 to 6:30 pm, and on Sunday from 10 am to 3 pm.

There's another botanical garden in Cotacota, in the Zona Sur (see the map in

The World's Highest Street Kids

You'll see street kids everywhere in La Paz – shining shoes, selling sweets, yelling out minibus destinations or doing any other work they are offered, including both those who've been abandoned by their families and those who must work to support their families. Sadly, their numbers are increasing because of Bolivia's poor economic situation – it is the third poorest Latin American country after Haiti and Guyana and, according to UNICEF, 80% of its population lives below the poverty level.

One survival strategy employed by Bolivian families is to send as many children as possible to work as early as possible. Many children begin working at the age of five, and often bring home more money than both their parents. According to the Bolivian Institute of Statistics, an average El Alto family earns about US$31 per month, which doesn't cover 10% of basic living costs. Meanwhile each working child – who will typically work up to 12 hours a day – can earn up to US$60 a month.

While struggling to survive, they soon realize that one job isn't enough to support themselves, and therefore grab every moneymaking opportunity offered; some resort to theft and organized crime.

Of the children living on the street, 80% are male. Girls are usually kept at home to do the housework and look after their younger sisters and brothers, or are given to wealthy families to work as maids. Those who wind up in the street survive mainly by prostitution – which is the easiest way to get (pathetically little) money quickly. Pregnancy is common, and they either attempt to get an abortion (which is illegal) or they have the children and are unable to provide them with basic necessities. This merely perpetuates the vicious cycle of destitution.

There are several private and state institutions in La Paz that provide street kids with food, dormitories and bathrooms. Only a few, however, offer psychological help, workshops and a route back to 'normal' life. One of these is HAPMA (Hogar Albergue Para Menores Abandonados – 'Home Hostel for Abandoned Children'), the main aim of which is to teach the children self-esteem and help them to take responsibility for their own lives. For more information contact HAPMA, Casilla 9343, El Alto, La Paz.

– Ulli Schatz, Germany

Around La Paz). Set around an artificial lake, it was established in 1991 and includes mainly Andean vegetation, as well as sections with cacti and medicinal herbs.

SAN PEDRO PRISON

The 1500 prisoners in La Paz's main prison (Map 3) engage in various activities to find the money they need to survive. The prisoners are expected to pay for their own upkeep, and those whose families choose to live in the prison (numbering about 500 women and children) are obliged to provide for them. The prison has five classes of cells; the most successful (or ruthless) prisoners are esconced in comfortable cells with all the conveniences of a good hotel, while the poorer ones inhabit much less amenable quarters. One profitable enterprise for an English-speaking inmate is to conduct escorted tours of the prison, resulting in one of the world's most bizarre visitor attractions. If you're interested, approach the main gate (preferably between Thursday and Sunday) between 11 am and 3 pm and tell the attendant that you'd like a tour. These cost around US$5, but you'll also need US$1 to pay the guard, a few bolivianos for the messenger and perhaps another US$20 or so in small bills to buy any of the toys or handicrafts made and sold by the prisoners.

Be sure to carry identification, but no cameras or other valuables.

ACTIVITIES
Hiking & Climbing
Established in 1939, the Club Andino Boliviano (Map 3; ☎ 324682; Calle México 1638, Casilla 1346) is an organization of climbers, skiers and other outdoor enthusiasts. It's responsible for organizing club mountaineering trips and running the Chacaltaya ski area. The club offers climbing advice and weekend trips as well as special monthly activities – off-piste skiing, climbing, slide shows and so on – that are open to anyone. From January to March the club organizes ski competitions, and in April and May it runs snow-climbing courses.

Rock Climbing
The rocky Amor de Dios area in the Choqueyapu valley near La Florida (Zona Sur) offers excellent day climbing and bouldering, and the several bolted routes are graded from IV to VII-C on the French scale. To get there, take a *trufi* or micro from the lower Prado going to La Florida, Aranjuez or Mallasa and get off at the Amor de Dios bridge over the Río Choqueyapu. The most easily accessible rock, El Peñón (literally, 'large rock') sits behind the Amor de Dios soccer field.

You can rent shoes, ropes, harnesses, carabiners and the like from several places in town; see Outdoor Equipment under Information, earlier in this chapter. Amateurs will probably want to secure the services of a professional guide. If you're a beginner or prefer an organized trip, try América Tours (see Organized Tours in the Getting Around chapter), which maintains a safe guide-to-climber ratio and offers rock-climbing courses and day tours from May to September. Climbing costs US$29 per person per day (minimum two people; single climbers pay US$45), including transport, equipment and a teacher/guide.

Golf, Tennis & Swimming
Golf and tennis buffs interested in some high-altitude practice must join a club because public facilities do not exist. For tennis, racquetball and swimming in a lovely setting, try the Strongest Club at Achumani Complejo in the Zona Sur (take any micro or minibus labeled 'Achumani Complejo'). On weekdays, they charge US$3.50 per person, and on weekends, US$5.

If you'd like to hone your driving and putting skills at the world's highest golf course, in Malasilla (Zona Sur map), you'll pay about US$10 for a caddie and a round of 18 holes. Bring your own equipment.

At the Hotel Europa (Map 3, in OTHER key), off the Prado (Avenida 16 de Julio), nonguests can use the swimming pool and sauna for US$10 from 3 to 10 pm daily; afterward, you can opt for a massage for an additional US$10. The Hotel Plaza (Map 3) also lets you use the pool for the same price, but the facilities aren't quite as nice.

Skiing
Skiing is possible at Chacaltaya during the season; for information, contact the Club Andino Boliviano. See Around La Paz in this chapter for details.

COURSES
Spanish language courses are available at the Centro Boliviano Americano (see Cultural Centers under Information in this chapter). There's also the Instituto de la Lengua Española (ILE; ☎ 799685; fax 799682; ilebol@latinwide.com; Calle Aviador 180, Achumani; Casilla 12205); check www.latinwide.com/ilebol.html, the website.

Note that not everyone advertising language instruction is accredited or even capable of teaching Spanish, however well they speak it, so seek local and personal recommendations and examine credentials before signing up. Private teachers who have been recommended by readers and others include: William Ortiz (☎ 310795; williamor@ hotmail.com; Pasaje General Gonzales 1273, San Pedro), Señora María Isabel Daza

Vivado (☎/fax 360769; maria_daza@ hotmail.com; Avenida Mariscal Santa Cruz 2150, ground floor 13), Cecilia C de Ferreira (☎ 365428; José María Camacho 1664, San Pedro), and Señora Zenaida Gutiérrez (☎ 226749; zenaidagutierrez@hotmail.com; Mercedes Torre Sur, Piso 6B, Calle Cuba, Miraflores, Casilla 11134). Plan on paying US$4 to US$6 per hour. Prospective students – particularly women – should approach with caution any La Paz 'Fastalk' courses advertised by Gonzalo, Dodi, Rasta Dude and a host of other pseudonyms.

For musical instruction (in Spanish) on traditional Andean instruments – zampoña, quena, charango, and so on – see Professor Heliodoro Niña at the Academía de Música Helios (☎ 362749; helios@caoba.entelnet.bo; Murillo 744). He charges about US$5 per hour.

ORGANIZED TOURS

Most of Bolivia's tour agencies are based in La Paz, and the city has at least 100 of them. Some are clearly better than others and many specialize in particular interests or areas. Lots of agencies, including Diana Tours, Turisbus, Crillon Tours, and América Tours, run day tours in and around La Paz, Lake Titicaca, Tiahuanaco and other sites. For details and contact information, as well as information on tours farther afield – for example to the Cordillera Apolobamba, the Far Southwest (these tours are more economically arranged in Uyuni), Rurrenabaque, Potosí, Sucre and so on – see Organized Tours in the Getting Around chapter.

Most day tours are moderately priced and provide easy sightseeing in the city's environs, including such popular destinations as Tiahuanaco, Copacabana, Zongo Valley, Chacaltaya and Valle de la Luna. Inexpensive agency transfers to Puno are the most straightforward way of getting to Peru, and they allow a stopover in Copacabana en route. Tour operators can also take you climbing in the snowcapped cordillera peaks, and if you lack hiking or trekking equipment, many will rent out whatever is

necessary. For information on specialist operators – those doing hiking, climbing, rafting, mountain biking, and such – see Activities in the Facts for the Visitor chapter.

SPECIAL EVENTS

La Paz enjoys several local festivals and holidays during the year. Of particular interest for visitors are Alasitas, held in late January, and El Gran Poder, which takes place in late May or early June.

Alasitas

The origin of the festival of abundance, or Alasitas (oddly, 'buy from me' in Aymará), dates back to Inca times when it coincided with the spring equinox on September 21. The date underwent some shifts in the colonial period until arriving at the current January 24.

Traditionally, the Alasitas Fair was intended to demonstrate the abundance of the fields. The campesinos weren't pleased with the changes or with the January date imposed by the Spanish, and in effect, decided to turn the celebration into a corny mockery of the original. 'Abundance' was redefined to apply not only to crops, but also to homes, tools, cash, clothing and lately, cars, trucks, airplanes and even 12-story buildings. The little god of abundance, Ekeko, made his appearance and the modern Alasitas traditions began.

Ekeko, whose name means 'dwarf' in Aymará, is the household god and the keeper and distributor of material possessions. During the Alasitas Fair, his devotees collect miniatures of those items they'd like to acquire during the following year and heap them on small plaster images of the god. He's loaded down with household utensils, baskets of coca, airline tickets, wallets and trunks full of miniature US dollars, lottery tickets, liquor, chocolate and other material goods. The more optimistic devotees buy buses, Toyota 4WDs, airline tickets to Miami, Volkswagen beetles and three-story suburban homes! Once purchased, all items must be blessed by a certified yatiri before they can become real.

If this apparent greed seems not to be in keeping with Aymará values – the community and balance in all things – it's worth noting that Ekeko is also charged with displaying that which a family is able to share with the community.

El Gran Poder

La Festividad de Nuestro Señor Jesús del Gran Poder began in 1939 as a candle procession led by an image of Christ through the predominantly campesino neighborhoods of upper La Paz.

The following year, the local union of embroiderers formed a folkloric group to participate in the event. In subsequent years, other festival-inspired folkloric groups joined in and the celebration grew larger and more lively. It has now developed into a strictly *paceño* festival (a paceño is a resident of La Paz), with dancers and folkloric groups participating from around the city. The embroiderers prepare elaborate costumes for the event and the performers practice for weeks in advance.

El Gran Poder is a wild and exciting time in La Paz and offers a glimpse of Aymará culture at its festive finest. A number of dances are featured, such as the *suri sikuris*, in which the dancers are bedecked in ostrich feathers, the lively *kullasada*, and the *inkas*, which duplicates Inca ceremonial dances.

If you'd like to catch the procession, go early to stake out a place along the route, keeping a lookout for stray or unruly water balloons. The tourist office can provide specific dates and details about a particular year's celebration.

PLACES TO STAY – BUDGET

La Paz has dozens of low-cost hotels and *residenciales*, the vast majority of which lie in the area between Calle Manco Capac and Avenida Ismael Montes, but others are scattered around the city. Most bottom-range hotels have a midnight curfew.

A cheap, clean, secure and friendly place, with hot showers, is the very simple *Alojamiento Universo (Map 2; ☎ 340431, Calle Inca Mayta Capac 175)*, which charges just US$2.50 for dormitory beds and only

US$3.50/5.50 for single/double rooms. Ground-floor rooms are nicer than those upstairs. Another very inexpensive favorite is the *Alojamiento Carretero (Map 2; ☎ 285271; Calle Catacora 1056)*. Here you'll pay US$3/5 for singles/doubles with shared bath and access to a simple kitchen, laundry facilities and a book exchange.

A former Peace Corps favorite – and very friendly place – is the *La Paz City Hotel (Map 3; ☎ 322177; bebahappy@hotmail.com; Calle Nicolás Acosta 487)*, at Héroes del Acre near Plaza San Pedro (also known as Plaza Sucre). Singles/doubles cost US$5/10. It also has an *Anexo* (annex) *(☎ 368380; Calle México 1539)* nearby. A more upmarket choice in the same neighborhood is *Hostal Sucre (Map 3; ☎ 328414; Plaza San Pedro)*, which has singles/doubles with private bath for US$11.50/18.60 and US$7.20/12.50 without bath.

If being central is a concern, the convenient *Hotel Torino (Map 2; ☎ 341487; Calle Socabaya 457)* isn't too bad, but its demeanor has grown quite surly – an unfortunate by-product of its former reputation as *the* travelers' crash pad. Services for guests only include a book exchange and a free luggage-storage service. The attached bar/restaurant serves almuerzos for under US$2 and offers live music on weekends, but it's mainly synthesized pop that most people would rather be without. Singles/doubles without bath cost US$5/8.50; doubles with bath are US$13.50. In the same building, you'll find an interesting exhibition of Native American art and history.

A friendlier option is the centrally located *Hostal Austria (Map 2; ☎ 351140; Calle Yanacocha 531)*, which offers safe gas-heated showers – but not enough of them. One- to four-bed rooms with shared bath cost US$6.50/10.50 single/double. Although several basic rooms lack windows, it's frequently crowded.

In the same area is the recommended *Hostal Ingavi (Map 2; ☎ 323645; Ingavi 727)*, which charges a negotiable US$7.50/13.50 for singles/doubles with bath and US$6/12 without. Although it gets a bit noisy, it's a good, clean central option. The similarly recommended but slightly more upmarket **Hostal La Valle** (Map 2; ☎ 456085; Evaristo Valle 153) has singles/doubles with bath for US$10/15.

An increasingly popular choice is the **Alojamiento La Scala** (Map 2; ☎ 350725; Unión 425), between Calle Chuquisaca and Avenida América. Here you'll find safe, clean rooms· for as little as US$5/6. However, the nearby disco can render it noisy on weekends.

From the outside, the one-star **Hotel Italia** (Map 2; ☎ 456710; Manco Capac 303) looks more expensive than it is. The toilets aren't the best and the nicer rooms at the front are subject to lots of street noise. Almuerzos in its restaurant are a bargain at US$0.80 and there's a folk music peña on Friday night at 9 pm. Singles/doubles with shared bath cost US$5.20/8; with private bath, they're US$9.30/11.20.

Just over the street is the **Hotel Andes** (Map 2; ☎ 455327; Avenida Manco Capac 364), with large rooms and rarely functioning elevators. It's friendly, however, and somewhat popular with budget travelers. A single/double room costs US$8/12 with bath or US$5.50/9 without; all rates include a continental breakfast. Hostelling International members receive a 20% discount. The most pleasant rooms are 402 to 405, which have balconies.

A fine option is the friendly, relatively elegant and very clean **Hotel La Joya** (Map 4; ☎ 453841; fax 453946; joyahot@ceibo .entelnet.bo; Max Paredes 541), near Plaza Garita de Lima amid the bustle of the Mercado Negro. The official single/double rates of US$13/17 without bath and US$21/28 with place it in the three-star mid-range, but when space is available (especially in low season), backpackers can stay for US$6.50 per person. It's away from the center of town but it's on numerous micro and trufi lines.

A pleasant inexpensive place is the quiet and friendly **Residencial Illimani** (Map 3; ☎ 325948; Illimani 1817), not far from the stadium. There's hot water a few hours a day, a laundry sink and a patio sitting area where cooking is allowed. The señora will pleasantly admit you if you arrive or return after

lock-up time at midnight. It's away from the center of action but it's quiet, friendly and popular with laid-back travelers. Singles/doubles without bath cost US$4.50/9.

Handy to the bus terminal is the pleasantly quiet, cozy and colonial-looking **Hostal Tambo de Oro** (Map 1; ☎ 281565; fax 282181; Avenida Armentia 367; Casilla 93). Nice carpeted single/double rooms with private bath are a good value at US$10.50/14.50; without bath they're US$6.20/8.30.

Also acceptable is the rather aloof **Hostería Florida** (Map 2; ☎ 363298; Viacha 489). The street outside unfortunately smells of piss, but the hotel rooms are clean and comfortable, and cost only US$5 per person with a continental breakfast and private bath. Upper-floor rooms may offer excellent views of the city and proximity to the TV lounge, but the elevator is (apparently permanently) broken.

One of the city's best options is the bright, friendly and very comfortable **Hotel Happy Days** (Map 2; ☎ 314759; fax 355079; happydays@zuper.net; Sagárnaga 229), a very yellow place right in the heart of the tourist district. Single/double rooms with both breakfast and television cost just US$7.50/15 with bath and US$7/13.50 without bath.

On Calle Illampu south of Plaza Eguino is the recently upgraded **Residencial Copacabana** (Map 2; ☎ 367896; fax 364712; Illampu 734). With private bath, it's US$9 per person, and with shared bath, US$6.50 per person. Rates include a continental breakfast. A few doors away, the popular **Alojamiento El Viajero** (Map 2; ☎ 453565), also known as 'El Lobo,' charges just US$3.50 per person in a single or double and US$2.75 in a four-bed dormitory. It's especially popular with Israeli travelers.

PLACES TO STAY – MID-RANGE

It seems the much-lauded **Hostal Rosario** (Map 2; ☎ 325348, fax 375532; Calle Illampu 704) has let success go to its top floor. The staff have become a bit blasé, prices have risen and all available space has been converted into a rabbit warren of stairways and passages to accommodate its enormous popularity. Still, it remains ultra-clean and pleasantly quiet: a sort of travelers' capsule with Bolivia just outside the door. Pluses include a sunny courtyard, a sauna (open Tuesday to Sunday from 3 to 9 pm), a travel agency on the ground floor and an excellent café and restaurant serving such gringo-trail specialties as crêpes, oatmeal, granola, cream of asparagus soup and banana pancakes.

Advance booking is essential these days, but the reservation system has a few holes – don't even think about getting a double bed. Singles/doubles/triples without bath cost US$14/18/25. Rooms with private bath are reserved primarily for tour groups and are priced accordingly at US$24/30/38.

On the same street, the more budget-oriented *Hostal Dinastía* (Map 2; ☎ 379096; *Illampu 684; Casilla 11171*) has clean carpeted single/double rooms for US$7.50/14 with shared bath and US$9/15.50 with private bath. Breakfast is available for an additional charge.

The sparkling and friendly *Hostal República* (Map 2; ☎ 356617; fax 370592; *marynela@ceibo.entelnet.bo; Calle Comercio 1455*) occupies a lovely historic building that was once home to a Bolivian president. It has two large courtyards, a garden and a warm reception area with a small library of foreign-language books for guests' use; try to get a newer and quieter room at the back. The staff really aim to please. Singles/doubles cost US$15/25 with private bath and US$10/16 without. Triple and quadruple rooms are also available.

On Plaza Eguino rises the two-star *Hotel Continental* (Map 2; ☎/fax 451176; fax 378226; h.continental@kolla.net; *Calle Illampu 626*), which offers a good value at US$13.50/17.50 for singles/doubles without bath and US$21/28 with bath. However, take a room away from the raucous disco on the 2nd floor.

The clean *Hotel Milton* (Map 2; ☎ 368003, fax 365849; *Calle Illampu 1224*) is a two-star hotel in the heart of the market area. This place is an excellent value and the gas showers are an attraction for any who fear the standard Frankenstein switch system. Singles/doubles with

bath, telephone and TV cost US$10/15, including breakfast, with discounts for more than two nights; without bath they're US$7/12. Laundry services and *cajas de seguridad* (safe boxes) are available.

Another good mid-range choice is the *Tiquina Palace Hotel* (Map 2; ☎ 315247; fax 322609; hoteltiquina@hotmail.com; *Pasaje Tiquina 150*), at Evaristo Valle, in the heart of La Paz's traditional action. For US$18/20, you'll get a nice, carpeted single/double room with bath, TV and a buffet breakfast. With 24 hours' notice, they'll also provide free transportation to or from the airport.

On Plaza San Pedro, a relatively quiet part of town, is the recommended three-star *Hotel Max Inn* (Map 3; ☎ 374391; fax 341720). For large, bright rooms with bath, it charges US$30/42. The attached restaurant serves marginal meals.

Overlooking 'artesanía alley' on steep and bustling Calle Sagárnaga is the recommended *Hotel Sagárnaga* (Map 2; ☎ 350252; fax 360831; hotsadt@ceibo.entelnet.bo; *Calle Sagárnaga 326*). Rooms cost US$20/27 with bath, breakfast and cable TV, and US$7/12 without bath. All rates include a continental breakfast; 10% discounts are available during periods of low occupancy. Peñas are held on Wednesday and Sunday from 8 to 11 pm. Next door is the pleasant *Hotel Alem* (Map 2; ☎ 367400; fax 350579; *Calle Sargánaga 334*), with rooms for US$6/12.50 without bath and US$10/15 with bath; all rates include breakfast. It's so clean that the floors squeak and it smells of disinfectant!

At the bottom of Calle Sagárnaga, near Plaza San Francisco, there's the repeatedly recommended *Hostal Naira* (Map 2; ☎ 355645; fax 327262; *Calle Sagárnaga 161*), a clean place that is quite popular with tour groups. Here you'll pay US$25/32 for a comfortable room with breakfast.

On Plaza Alonzo de Mendoza, opposite the trufi terminus, is the *Hotel Oruro* (Map 2; ☎ 325893). It's nothing special, but at US$7/12 without bath and US$12.50/15 with a private bath and television, it's a decent value for the money.

An interesting lower-mid-range place is *Hotel Viena* (Map 2; ☎ 321444; *Calle*

Loayza 420), a Baroque-style building with immense high-ceilinged rooms; it could be the set for a horror film. Apart from that, the ambience is rather bland, but room 113 is especially pleasant. Rooms with shared bath cost US$7/10; with bath, they're US$9.50/12.50. Be warned that disco activity makes it quite noisy at times.

At the lower end of the center, you'll find the comfortable *Hotel España (Map 3; ☎ 354643; fax 342329; Avenida 6 de Agosto 2074)*, a friendly hotel with a lovely courtyard that receives direct sun most of the day and is ideal for relaxing. It's also within an easy stroll of many of the city's best restaurants. Rooms, with breakfast and private bath, cost US$22/32; for a shared bath, including breakfast, you'll pay US$15/25. The attached restaurant also offers inexpensive breakfasts and à la carte meals.

The novel and very pleasant *Hotel Galería Virgen del Rosario (☎ 371565; fax 316857; Calle Santa Cruz 583)* rises above the bustling streets at the edge of the Mercado Negro area. The interior, which loosely resembles a cathedral, features lots of greenery and a lovely mezzanine café. Rooms with bath, TV and phone cost US$20/35, including breakfast.

See also *Hotel La Joya* under Places to Stay – Budget.

PLACES TO STAY – TOP END

The number of top-end options in La Paz is growing all the time. If you're after a bit of luxury, they're bargains considering the prices of comparable accommodations in most other world capitals! Expect such amenities as health clubs, spas, swimming pools, pubs, coffee shops and discos.

At the bottom of the top end is *Hotel Gloria (Map 2; ☎ 370010; fax 391489; gloriatr@datacom-bo.net; Calle Potosí 909)*, towering above the snarling traffic of the Prado. Singles/doubles cost US$49/58. A very basic breakfast is included, but the hotel standards make this place an excellent value.

Another recommended place is popular *El Rey Palace (☎ 393016; fax 367759; hotelrey@caoba.entelnet.bo; Avenida 20 de Octubre 1947)*. This pleasant four-star hotel

offers all European-standard services, including telephones, air-con and cable TV. All rooms from the 4th floor up have private jacuzzis. The 80-seat restaurant serves à la carte dishes and does executive almuerzos for US$6, and the bar is open from 7 pm to 2 am nightly. Singles/doubles cost US$70/80, which is a very good value given what's offered. Additional beds are US$15 and suites cost US$85 to US$105.

The *Gran Hotel Paris (☎ 319170; toll-free ☎ 0800-7799; fax 362547; hparis@caoba.entelnet.bo; Plaza Murillo)* sits on the corner of La Paz's main plaza. This relatively small hotel has the elegant Café Paris, which offers full restaurant service. Rooms are US$80/100, including an American breakfast and cable TV.

The *Hotel Plaza (Map 3; ☎ 378311; fax 378318; plazabolivia@usa.net; Avenida 16 de Julio 1789)* is one of the few places that still employs a dual pricing system in which foreigners pay considerably more than Bolivian residents. For singles/doubles with cable TV, a continental breakfast and use of the swimming pool, gym and jacuzzi, foreigners pay US$130/150 and Bolivians pay US$99/119. Nonguests may use the pool and fitness facilities for US$10 per day.

The *Hotel Radisson Plaza (Map 3; ☎ 441111; fax 440593; radissonbolivia@usa.net; Avenida Aniceto Arce 2177)* is a contender for La Paz's most upmarket option. It has everything you'd expect in a five-star hotel, including cable TV, but the cold and impersonal atmosphere isn't for everyone. Standard singles/doubles with breakfast cost US$130/150, but there is also a range of more luxurious options, from executive suites for US$150/170 up to the presidential suite for US$550. The top-floor restaurant affords a superb view over the city and surrounding mountains.

The *Hotel Presidente (Map 2; ☎ 368601; fax 354013; hpresi@caoba.entelnet.bo; Calle Potosí 920)* bills itself as the highest five-star hotel in the world, which is accurate since the equally five-star Hotel Plaza and Hotel Radisson Plaza are a few meters lower, farther down the Prado. Standard singles/doubles, including a buffet breakfast and airport transportation, cost US$125/155, and executive suites with private jacuzzi cost US$175/190. Weekend specials are available, and the hotel also has a couple of fine restaurants, including La Bella Vista on the 16th floor, and the simpler La Kantuta, on the mezzanine. The website is at www.htlpresidente-bolivia.com.

PLACES TO EAT

La Paz has a good variety of eateries – from street kiosks to fine dining – of generally high quality. All are reasonably priced compared to what you'd probably pay at home.

In the cheapest ranges, don't expect much variation from the local standards. Nearly all specialize in – or serve exclusively – some sort of beef or chicken. Most offer set meals (mainly almuerzo but sometimes also cena) and a short list of the most common dishes, with the occasional regional specialty.

The mid-range and upmarket restaurants are concentrated at the lower end of town: in the Sopocachi area around Avenidas 20 de Octubre and 6 de Agosto, on the lower Prado around Avenida 16 de Julio (it's easy to remember historical dates in La Paz!), and in the Zona Sur (see the Zona Sur map in the Around La Paz section).

Markets

If you don't mind the hectic settings, your cheapest food scene is the markets. Unfortunately, the most central, **Mercado Lanza** (Map 2), off Plaza Pérez Velasco, has a rather dirty and unpleasant comedor, but you will find a range of delicious fruit juices. Better is the **Mercado Camacho** (Map 3), at Camacho and Bueno, where takeout stalls sell empanadas and chicken sandwiches, and comedores dish up filling meals of soup, main course, rice, lettuce and oca or potato for around US$1. In **Mercado Uruguay**, off Calle Max Paredes, one particularly hygienic stall serves fresh *pejerrey* (a tasty freshwater fish) with vegetables and sauce for around US$1.50. It's the only one serving the fish, so you're sure to find it eventually. You'll find other cheap and informal meals in the street market areas around Calle Buenos Aires and the cemetery.

Breakfast

Few places that serve breakfast open before 8 or 9 am, but early risers desperate for a caffeine jolt before they can face the day will find bread rolls and riveting coffee concentrate at the markets for about US$0.40.

One exception to the late-opening rule is **La Fuente**, at the Hostal Rosario (Map 2), and nothing beats its fresh fruit, juices, delicious bread and all the other elements of continental and American breakfasts: ham, eggs, cheese, pancakes and excellent cocoa and cappuccino. An alternative breakfast spot is the **Café Torino** (Map 2) – beside the Hotel Torino – which opens at 7:30 am every day and serves breakfasts of rolls, salteñas and fruit juices. Both almuerzos and cenas are also available.

On the weekends, why not treat yourself to the fabulous **La Terraza** (☎ 795696; *Avenida Montenegro Bloque B5, San Miguel*), in the Zona Sur. It's a long minibus ride from the center, but here you'll find memorable espresso and other coffee treats, as well as incredible chocolate pie and cooked breakfasts that include North American-style pancakes and huevos rancheros. **Mongo's Café** (*Map 3; ☎ 431240; Avenida Arce 2708*), behind the British Council, prepares excellent English breakfasts and set lunches for US$3.25. It's run by the folks who operate Mongo's Rock Bottom Café, and as well as serving food they also have a book exchange, host art exhibitions and provide English-language newspapers.

The salteñas and tucumanas sold in the markets and on the streets – for a third of what they cost in sit-down cafés – are normally excellent; particularly good are the street stalls near Plaza Isabel la Católica and those opposite the cemetery, where you'll pay just US$0.15 for a hearty snack.

For just a quick coffee and a roll or salteña, go to **Confitería Club de La Paz** (*Map 2; mobile ☎ 019-26265; Camacho 1202*), a literary café and haunt of politicians (and formerly, of Nazi war criminals – I've reluctantly dined alongside Klaus Barbie here) at the sharp corner of Avenidas Camacho and Mariscal Santa

Cruz. It's known especially for its strong espresso and lemon meringue pie.

Coffee & Snacks

Near Plaza del Estudiante is the wonderful *Café Alexander (Map 3; ☎ 327123; Avenida 16 de Julio 1832)*, which is renowned for its excellent espresso and cappuccino, as well as fruit juices and tasty snacks, from pastries to vegetarian quiche. Fine coffee is also served up at *Café Oro (Map 3; ☎ 338918; Avenida Villazón 1694)*, below Plaza del Estudiante, and at the friendly *Pierrot (Map 2; ☎ 370018)*, on the ground floor of Hotel Gloria. Especially if you can imagine that Plaza San Francisco is the Piazza San Marco, you'll really enjoy *Profumo di Caffe (Map 2; ☎ 354115; Plaza San Francisco 502)*, a very Italian coffee shop where you'll find excellent coffee specialties as well as tiramisu, tramezzini, cakes, pastries and other snacks. For a real caffeine-oriented treat, head to *La Terraza* in the Zona Sur (see Breakfasts, earlier in this section).

On Avenida Simón Bolívar is *Las Velas*, a warren of smoky cubicles where vendors whip up everything from burgers to kebabs, sausages, sandwiches and other fast delights for an utter pittance. It's very good and is open until late. In the morning, empanada and tucumana aficionados should head for the first landing on the steps between the Prado and Calle México, where US$0.50 buys an enormous and excellent beef or chicken *empanada especial* smothered in your choice of sauces.

Opposite Hostal Ingavi on Calle Ingavi you'll find great fruit shakes and yogurt drinks at *Vigor* (Map 2). The *Boutique del Pan* (Map 2) on Calle Obispo Cárdenas (near where it becomes Calle Potosí) is a bakery selling any imaginable bread concoction: brilliant fruit bread, rolls, sweet breads, brown bread and so on. A convenient spot for healthy snacks is the *100% Natural Fruit & Salad Bar (Map 2; Calle Sagárnaga 345)*, opposite the Hotel Alem. The hole-in-the-wall *Snack El Montañés (Map 2; Sagárnaga 323)*, near Peña Huari and opposite Hotel Sagárnaga, serves excellent sandwiches, fruit juices and light meals and desserts.

If you're a cookie fan, make a pilgrimage down to *The Hutch* near Calle 21, just below the Ketal Supermarket in San Miguel (Zona Sur). One could wax poetic about the soft chocolate chips and awe-inspiring peanut butter cookies. The Hutch also does American-style burgers and especially generous portions of other fast foods. It's open daily except Sunday from 10:30 am to 9 pm.

For a reasonable burger, *Denny's (Map 3; 16 de Julio 1605)* is a possibility. Alternatively, you can take the international option and go for the very popular *McDonald's (Map 3; ☎ 311414; Avenida 16 de Julio 1607)*. Here the Big Mac is called a McNífico and they also invented the McPalta, an avocado burger designed for the Bolivian market. There's also a *Burger King (Map 2; ☎ 334893)* at Socabaya and Mercado. Either could compete for the 'cleanest toilet in La Paz award,' but the Burger King exceeds all competitors for bad taste in ambient music. Both of these fast-food giants also have outlets in San Miguel, in the Zona Sur.

The first North American pizza chain to appear in Bolivia is *Domino's Pizza (☎ 444888; Avenida Arce 2314)*, which does deliveries; there are also two outlets in the Zona Sur (☎ 771771 in San Miguel and 786888 in Obrajes).

For quick chicken, try *Pollo Copacabana*, where you'll find roasted chicken, french fries and fried plantain smothered in ketchup, mustard and ají for US$2. There are locations on Calle Potosí (Map 2), Calle Comercio and in the Zona Sur. Beside the one on Calle Potosí is a wonderful *chocolate shop* selling Bolivia's own Breick chocolates.

El Palacio de los Helados, near the cemetery, is locally popular for ice cream and has some strange and colorful murals. A good choice for Italian ice cream is *Heladería Napoli* (Map 2) on Plaza Murillo. In addition to ice-cream concoctions, it serves breakfasts, pastry, cakes and other snacks. There are also several popular ice-cream parlors along the Prado, such as the circus-like *Unicornio* (Map 3). A favorite for sweet snacks is *Kuchen Stube (Map 3; ☎ 361689; Calle Rosendo Gutiérrez 461)*;

here you can stuff yourself with decadent European coffee, pastries, biscuits and other sweets.

Lunch

Lunch options are numerous and limited only by what you're prepared to pay. For the strictest budgets, the markets are naturally the cheapest options (see earlier in this section).

In addition, there are plenty of family-run cubbyhole restaurants displaying blackboard menus at their doors; you can assume that these places are really cheap. As a general rule, the higher you climb from the Prado, the cheaper the meals will be.

There are lots of acceptable budget restaurants on Evaristo Valle, where an almuerzo or cena can cost as little as US$1; also cheap are the several places along the lower (eastern) end of Calle Rodríguez, which offer almuerzos for about US$0.50.

Calle Rodríguez also boasts a handful of excellent ceviche places, where a bowl of Peruvian-style ceviche costs about US$1.50. The best is *Acuario II* (Map 2; no sign), opposite the Acuario I (which does have a sign). A bit more sophisticated is the nearby *Portales*, on Avenida Mariscal Santa Cruz, a block uphill (northwest) from the post office. An often-recommended place is the *Playa Brava Cevichería* on Fernando Guachalla two blocks above (southwest of) Avenida 6 de Agosto, opposite Sopocachi market.

La Fuente (Map 2) at the Hostal Rosario is recommended, especially for the cream of asparagus and french onion soup, breaded chicken and pasta dishes.

A convenient fast-food venue with two central locations is *Eli's Pizza Express* (both Map 3; ☎ 319295; Avenida 16 de Julio 1491 and ☎ 318171; Avenida 16 de Julio 1800). You can choose among pizza, pasta, pastries and some rather unusual tacos. The food is not great – but there's no wait.

A fabulous little café (and travelers' nirvana) is the renowned *Ángelo Colonial* (☎ 360199; fax 0811-2866; angelo@ angelocolonial.com; Calle Linares 922-924), which is housed in an old colonial mansion and is tastefully stuffed with Bolivian

antiquities. The coffee is excellent, the sandwiches are inexpensive and enormous, and all the food is very well presented. In addition, they offer a book exchange, a tourist information office, a post office and the fastest Internet connections in La Paz.

Another good lunch choice is the French-oriented *Café Montmartre* (Map 3; ☎ 320801; cafemont@kolla.net; Fernando Guachalla 399), at the Alliance Française. Lunch specials, with some veggie choices, cost US$3. There's a range of crêpes and salads, and coq au vin becomes pollo al vino. It's open Monday to Friday for lunch and dinner. Just opposite is *Crêperie La Bohème* (Map 3; ☎ 326798; Fernando Guachalla 443), which serves up fine French cuisine and light lunches; it specializes in crêpes.

Another excellent lunch choice is *Andrómeda* (Map 3; ☎ 354723; Avenida Arce 2116), at Aspiazu in the Edificio Santa Teresa. It serves almuerzos every day, including both meat and vegetarian options and an excellent salad bar. On Friday, the almuerzo is always a fish dish. In the evening, they also do pastas and Bolivian dishes. It's open Monday to Saturday from 9 am to midnight.

At *Café Ciudad* (Map 3; ☎ 341527; Plaza del Estudiante), service is slow and the food ordinary – the Coke is warm and the fettuccine alfredo (which is actually carbonara) is cold – but the full menu of burgers (from US$2.50), pasta (US$4.50), steak, trout, pizza and other dishes is available 24 hours a day, every day, and you're free to linger over its two redeeming features, coffee and apple pie.

The renowned *El Lobo* (Map 2), on Illampu at Santa Cruz, offers a novel buffet for US$4.50 per kilogram (minimum US$1.50), full breakfasts or set lunches for US$2, and a menu with several Israeli dishes and pasta, pizza as well as other plates from US$3. The curry and chicken are particularly nice but the french fries should come with a grease warning. If you want to find out where Israeli travelers are going or avoiding, or which places are turning into travelers' ghettos, take a look at their books of travelers' recommendations in both English and Hebrew.

A highly recommended vegetarian restaurant – which claims to be the most popular eatery on the Gringo Trail – is at *Hotel Gloria (Map 2; Calle Potosí 909)*. Lunch buffets cost US$2.50 and run from noon to 3 pm, but arrive before 12:30 pm or you risk missing out on the best dishes. They also do a US$2.50 vegetarian dinner buffet from 7 to 10 pm.

The informal *Gringo Limón (Map 3; ☎ 418097; Plaza Avaroa 2497)*, near the corner of Salazar and 20 de Octubre, is run by a gentleman who prepares Bolivian and European specialties, including lunch and dinner buffets with a salad. Food is sold by the kilogram, and can be served as takeout.

Many of the following dinner spots also serve lunch and the descriptions include lunch details.

Dinner

Note that many of the lunch spots suggested in the previous section also serve dinner.

The *Tambo Colonial* (Map 2), in the Hostal Rosario, is known for its salad bar and excellent dishes such as trout in white wine sauce, and steak with bacon and mushroom sauce, as well as assorted pasta dishes. Afterward, indulge in what may be the best chocolate mousse south of the equator. There are live music performances on Thursday, Friday and Saturday nights.

In the evening, arguably the best pizzas in town come from *Sergio's (Map 3; Avenida 6 de Agosto 2040)*, a hole-in-the-wall place near the Aspiazu steps. In addition to pizza, you'll find gyros, chili and lasagna. For pizza, however, its reputation is being challenged by *Minuteman (Map 3; ☎ 245995; Simón Bolívar 1882)*, west of the stadium in Miraflores, which is owned by a true-blue Yankee from Boston and serves up an economical 'pizza of the day.' It's open weekdays from 5:30 to 10 pm and on weekends until midnight.

The repeatedly recommended *Pronto Ristorante (Map 3; ☎ 355869; Pasaje Jáuregui 2248)*, in a small alley off Fernando Guachalla near Avenida 6 de Agosto, serves delicious homemade pasta. Although fairly posh, it's a good value and there's no fuss about appearances. It's a bit hard to spot, being down a set of stairs from the street.

Bolivia may be landlocked, but there are several decent places for fish and seafood. At *Restaurant Gran Palacio (Map 2)*, on Avenida América, you'll pay about US$4 for *surubí, pacu, trucha,* pejerrey, *sábalo,* and other local fish dishes. More upmarket seafood options include the *Cevichería Mi Perú (not on map; ☎ 227578; Edificio Italia, ground floor, Avenida Saavedra 1983)*, in Miraflores, which offers a range of soups, fish and shellfish dishes, including Spanish paella and Peruvian ceviche.

An exceptional choice is *Casa de los Paceños (Map 2; ☎ 318018; Sucre 856)*, near Pichincha. In addition to set almuerzos for US$1.50, this friendly family-run place serves typical La Paz dishes, including *saíce, sajta, fricasé, chairo paceño* and *fritanga* (fried pork). It's open for lunch daily except Monday, and for dinner from Tuesday to Friday. Almuerzos cost just US$2 and à la carte dinners range from US$3.50 to US$6.

La Québecoise (Map 3; ☎ 361782; 20 de Octubre 2355) features Canadian and American cuisine. It's not cheap, at about US$7 per person, but the food and atmosphere are top quality.

Anyone who once knew the famous Casa del Papaco in Sorata will want to head down to its new location in the Zona Sur and experience the *Ristorante Pizzeria Italiana (☎ 792675)*. It's on Avenida Reyes Muñoz on the northern shore of Laguna Cotacota between Calles 29 and 30. The new location also features a pleasant garden and you'll find some of the finest and most genuine Mediterranean cooking in all of South America. For a more upmarket ambience, try the *Pronto Pettirosso (Map 3; ☎ 324853; Pasaje Gustavo Medinacelli 2282, Sopocachi)*, with its orange and blue décor and a wealth of original Botero paintings. You'll pay around US$25 per person for a fine Italian meal with wine.

The mega-popular *Mongo's Rock Bottom Café (Map 3; ☎ 440714; Hermanos Manchego 2444)*, west of Plaza Isabel la Católica, is open every day of the week. Its specialties include onion rings, chili, ceviche, nachos, burgers, pasta, vegetarian dishes, sweets and other international dishes, especially the delicious *crêpe de pollo*. Set almuerzos cost US$3.25, and they screen all major sporting events and stage free live music on Tuesday nights.

Sophisticated Cuban cuisine is the specialty at the friendly *La Bodeguita Cubana* (Map 3; ☎ 310064; *Federico Zuazo 1653*), which dishes up rich Caribbean-style meat and chicken dishes. Don't miss their signature drink, the *mojito*, which is a rum-based favorite. It's open Monday to Saturday for lunch and dinner.

For a strange Middle Eastern-Bolivian-New York hybrid, try the *Wall Street Café*, with two locations (Map 2; ☎ 316090; *Avenida Camacho 1363* and Map 3; ☎ 441619; *Avenida Arce 2142*). They're open from 8 am to midnight Monday to Saturday. Specialties include cooked breakfasts, Greek gyros, kepi, felafels, burgers, a range of sandwiches (including a Philly cheesesteak sandwich!), sweets and numerous incarnations of Yungas coffee beans.

The *New Tokyo* (Map 3; ☎ 433654; *Avenida 6 de Agosto 2932*) serves excellent Japanese cuisine, and the chef works wonders with what's on hand in Bolivia. So how about a sushi combination, featuring trout from Lake Titicaca? For a full meal with wine, you'll pay from US$10 per person. It's open Monday to Saturday from noon to 2:30 pm and 6 to 11 pm, and on Sunday from noon to 3 pm. An alternative Japanese place is *Wagamama* (☎ 434911; *Pinilla 2257*), just behind Jalapeños, offering friendly service and a nice atmosphere.

Ostensibly the best Chinese choice in town is *Chifa Emy* (Map 3; ☎ 440440; *Capitán Ravelo 2361*), near Belisario Salinas, which features all sorts of rice, pork, chicken, beef, shrimp dishes and other Oriental standards. On Wednesday, Thursday and Friday, they offer sophisticated live music performances and stay open until 2 am.

Big beef fans will want to try *El Arriero* (Map 3; ☎ 440880; *Avenida 6 de Agosto 2535*), which features Argentine cuisine – always heavy on the beef – as well as fine South American wines.

Restaurant Vienna (Map 3; ☎ 441660; *Federico Zuazo 1905*), which is a strong contender for La Paz's best restaurant, serves traditional central European cuisine in an antique atmosphere. It does both lunch and dinner, and the chocolate mousse has entered the realms of legend. It's open Monday to Friday from noon to 2 pm and 6:30 to 10 pm and on Sunday from noon to 2 pm.

La Paz also has a growing number of Mexican options. *Rumors*, on Avenida Ballivián at Calle 9 in Calacoto (in the Zona Sur), is on the expensive side, but serves excellent Mexican dishes in a US-style bar setting. The atmosphere is very North American, and perhaps that's why it's so popular with the trendy youth of Zona Sur. Also in Calacoto is *Super Mex* (☎ 795696; *Avenida Montenegro 5B*), which is owned and run by people from Guanajuato, Mexico. As the name suggests, it's a super Mexican restaurant. A small Mexican place is *Taquería Los Nopalitos* (Map 3), on Avenida 6 de Agosto at Daniel Campos. Perhaps the most popular Mexican option is the very nice *Jalapeños* (Map 3; ☎ 369876; *Avenida Arce 2549, San Jorge*), just below Plaza Isabel la Católica. At lunchtime, they offer an excellent three-course Mexican almuerzo for US$4, and on Friday, a Mexican lunch buffet. Dinner is served from 6:30 pm.

The *Café en Azul* (Map 3; ☎ 433872; *Avenida 20 de Octubre 2371*) does excellent submarine sandwiches and Mexican specialties, and for vegetarians, a mixed-vegetable-and-cheese sandwich that's a real delight. The most expensive meal costs around US$3.50. It's open Sunday to Thursday from 5 pm to 2 am and on Friday and Saturday until 3 am. Films are screened nightly at around 8 pm.

In Calacoto, between Calles 15 and 16 in Zona Sur, is *Abracadabra* (☎ 791880; *Avenida Ballivián 969*), accessible by micro or minibus trufi. It's good, but unfortunately falls short of its aim to turn standard American fare – steaks, ribs, pizza and salads – into trendy haute cuisine. Check your bill carefully, especially if you're in a large group.

For more dinner options – with live folk programs – see Peñas, under Entertainment, later in this chapter.

Self-Catering

The markets – Mercado Lanza and Mercado Camacho – are the place to find staple foods at good prices (see Markets at the beginning of Places to Eat). If you're after sweet snacks, go to Calle Isaac Tamayo (Map 2), near Manco Capac. On Sánchez Lima, above Belisario Salinas near Plaza Avaroa is *ZATT* (Map 3), an enormous and expensive US-style supermarket. For more variety, head for a *Ketal Hipermercado*; the most convenient one (Map 3) is on Avenida Arce, just below Plaza Isabel la Católica, but there's also a well-stocked outlet on Avenida Ballivián at Calle 15 in Calacoto, Zona Sur. It sells just about everything you'd find at home, including dehydrated pasta meals for trekking. There's also the decent but more basic *Supermercado X-Tra* (Map 3), on Plaza España in Sopocachi.

If you're just looking for a bottle of booze or good wine buys – Chilean Undurraga and Argentine Toro Viejo are both recommended and cost just US$2 for 750ml – head for the numerous *street stalls* (Map 2) on Calle Manco Capac, just above the Isaac Tamayo stairway.

ENTERTAINMENT
Peñas

Typical of La Paz (and most of Bolivia) are folk-music venues known as peñas. Most present traditional Andean music, rendered on zampoñas, quenas and charangos, but also often include guitar shows and song recitals. Some peñas play six days a week, while others have shows only on Friday and Saturday nights. Most start at 9 or 10 pm and last until 1 or 2 am. Admission ranges from US$5 to US$6 and usually includes the first drink.

The best known is *Peña Huari* (Map 2; ☎ 316225; Calle Sagárnaga 339), which is aimed at foreign tourists and Bolivian businesspeople. It plays nightly from 9 pm until late and costs US$5. The attached restaurant specializes in Bolivian cuisine, including llama steak, Lake Titicaca trout, *charque kan* and salads.

At the nearby *Peña Parnaso* (Map 2; ☎ 316827; Galería Doryan, Calle Sagárnaga 189) you can sample all sorts of local specialties, including various llama dishes – charque kan, shish kebab and even llama fondue. As well as these and Lake Titicaca trout, *pique a lo macho*, thimpu and sajta, a unique Andean breakfast is offered. It bills itself as 'a space for art,' and the peña at 9 pm nightly features Andean music and dancing. Admission is US$4.50.

Another fine restaurant/peña is *El Calicanto* (Map 2; Genaro Sanjinés 467), housed in an old colonial home two blocks from Plaza Murillo. It consists of the café El Molino, which does coffee and lunches, a bar with a nightly peña, and the Restaurant Las Tres Parrillas. Despite the very reasonable prices, the food is excellent, especially if you like parrillada; the broiled steaks are cooked over steaming volcanic rocks.

In the same neighborhood is *Salón Cecis* (☎ 350252; Calle Sagárnaga 328), at Hotel Sagárnaga, where the peña operates from 8 to 10 pm, Wednesday to Sunday.

A less expensive – and some claim more traditional – peña is the *Marka Tambo* (Map 2; ☎ 340416; Calle Jaén 710). Although the food is poor, the music is great and costs only US$5. Performances are staged on Thursday, Friday and Saturday from 10:30 pm. Another popular peña is that of *La Casa del Corregidor* (Map 2; ☎ 363633; Calle Murillo 1040), housed in a beautiful colonial building. It costs US$5, but come before the show to enjoy a meal of trout, chicken or vegetarian dishes at its recommended lunch and dinner restaurant, El Horno. Dinners average about US$6.

The peña at *Los Escudos* (☎ 322028), on Avenida Mariscal Santa Cruz in the same building as Confitería Club de La Paz, rounds out the list of larger tourist peñas. It plays Monday to Saturday and the cover charge is US$5, including the first drink. The set meal costs US$10.

You may also want to check the La Paz paper for advertisements and details about

LA PAZ

smaller unscheduled peñas and other musical events.

Pubs & Bars

There are scores of inexpensive local drinking dens scattered around the city, where local men go to drink *singani*, play dice and, eventually, pass out. Unaccompanied women should steer clear (even accompanied women may have problems) and no one should sit down to drink with Bolivians in one of these places unless they intend to pass out later in the evening. A great local drinking den in the center is *La Luna* (Map 2), at the corner of Murillo and Oruro, uphill from the post office. Another good choice is the *Nameless Bar* (Map 2; yes, it really is nameless!) on Calle Pichincha, just off Ingavi (opposite the obvious Mormon church). Its rustic interior, retro photographs from the '20s and '30s, Western pop music and pitchers/jugs of beer make it a favorite with middle-class locals.

You'll also find lots of more elegant bars, which are frequented by foreigners and middle-class Bolivians. Two British-style pubs come recommended by the La Paz expatriate community. The *Pig & Whistle* (Map 3; ☎ 390429; Calle Goitia 155), near Avenida Arce, is a pleasant but slightly-too-refined Tudor-style pub where you can drink, snack and chat. It also offers darts, backgammon, pub meals and a variety of imported European beer, but purists may be disappointed by the lack of British ales or bitters on tap. The *Britannia* between Calles 15 and 16 in Calacoto, Zona Sur, is the place to go if you can't live without a game of darts or a bottle of imported (and expensive!) Bateman's bitter. During the Friday happy hour (7 to 8 pm) it's crowded with Bolivians and foreigners taking advantage of the free pub snacks and half-price drinks. It's open Tuesday to Sunday night.

Café Montmartre (Map 3; ☎ 320801; Fernando Guachalla 399), at the Alliance Française, stages live bands on weekend evenings and is a good place to begin a cruise around the Sopocachi bar scene, since everything else opens later. On Calle

Montículo, near Calle Ecuador, is the agreeably tame *Juan Sebastián Bar*. The brightly lit and desert-themed *Coyote Bar* (Map 3; Avenida 20 de Octubre 2228), at Guachalla, features tequila, Corona beer and other Mexican elements. It's open Monday to Saturday from 7 pm.

In case you were wondering, yes, La Paz does have a microbrewery bar, the *Cambrinus* (Map 3; ☎ 430913; Plaza Avaroa, 20 de Octubre 2453). However, the brewing process is pretty hit or miss at this altitude, so ask for a sample before you order a whole pint! They also offer live piano music.

Those who can't get enough salsa music might want to trudge down to Achumani in the Zona Sur to visit the *Salsoteca Cayo Coco* (mobile ☎ 012-37831; Avenida García Lanza 510), at Calle 13. There's live music most nights and between 9 pm and midnight you'll get three drinks for the price of one. They also offer a free taxi service from the center with Servisur (☎ 799999 or 797777).

Mongo's Rock Bottom Café (Map 3; ☎ 440714; Calle Hermanos Manchego 2444) once served as the miners' bar in La Paz (hence the mining décor and the mineralogical map of Bolivia on the wall), but it's now one of the city's most popular venues, and it attracts crowds of Bolivians, expatriates and visiting foreigners with its rich food and lively music, dancing and ambience. On Friday from 5 to 7 pm and Saturday from 6:30 to 8:30 pm, happy hours feature half-price drinks.

The nearby billiards bar *Dead Stroke* (Map 3; ☎ 434784; Avenida 6 de Agosto 2460) is a happy – and only marginally sleazy – nightspot with cable TV. It attracts lots of night owls with pool, snooker, darts, chess and dominoes and also serves standard bar meals: chili, burgers, hot dogs and buffalo wings. It's open daily, but you may well need reservations to snag a table on the weekends.

Jazz fans will love the charmingly low-key *Thelonious Jazz Bar* (Map 3; ☎ 337806; 20 de Octubre 2172), which features smooth music and a great atmosphere for conversation. On weekends, live performances require a cover charge of around US$3.50. It's open from 8 pm to 3 am nightly.

A more upmarket choice is **El Bodegón de Cinti** *(Calle Murillo 1040)*, in La Casa del Corregidor; it's open from 10 pm. The Chuquisaqueño theme dictates southern specialties and drinks based on singani from Cinti province in Chuquisaca department.

Discos

La Paz has several discos that appeal to the young and restless at heart. **Forum** *(Calle Victor Sanjinés 2908)*, just south of Plaza España in Sopocachi, offers a different musical theme each night of the week. Also in Sopocachi is **El Loro en su Salsa** *(Map 3; ☎ 342787)*, at Rosendo Gutiérrez and Avenida 6 de Agosto. Yes, the name means 'the parrot in his own sauce,' and it features two-for-one drinks from Tuesday to Saturday between 8:30 and 10:30 pm. The dancing gets pretty riotous. Other discos include the optimistically named **Disco Love City** *(Map 1; ☎ 222626)*, a local teenage favorite near the stadium.

Cinemas

Your best chances of catching a quality film are at the **Cinemateca Boliviana** *(Map 2; ☎ 325346)*, at Calle Pichincha and Indaburo, which shows subtitled foreign films daily at 4 and 7:30 pm for US$1.50. French and German films are regularly shown by the Alliance Française and the Goethe Institut (see Cultural Centers under Information), respectively. The numerous other La Paz cinemas screen first-run films (many of which deserve to be last-run) for US$3.50; most are presented in English with subtitles.

Theater

The **Teatro Municipal** (Map 2), on the corner of Sanjinés and Indaburo, has an ambitious program of folklore shows, folk-music concerts and foreign theatrical presentations. It's a great old restored building with a round auditorium, elaborate balconies and a vast ceiling mural. The newspapers and tourist office have information about what's on. The average ticket price is about US$4.

SPECTATOR SPORTS

The popularity of *fútbol* (professional soccer) in Bolivia is comparable to that in other Latin American countries. Matches are played at Estadio Hernando Siles (Map 3) on Sunday year-round, as well as on Thursday evening during the winter. You can imagine what sort of advantage the local teams have over mere lowlanders; players from elsewhere consider La Paz games a suicide attempt! Check newspapers for times and prices.

SHOPPING
Souvenirs, Clothing & Artesanía

La Paz is a shopper's paradise; not only are prices very reasonable, but the quality of what's offered can be astounding. The main tourist shopping area, which features both artesanía and tourist kitsch, lies along the very steep and literally breathtaking Calle Sagárnaga between Avenida Mariscal Santa Cruz and Calle Isaac Tamayo, and spreads out along adjoining streets. Here, expensive shops compete with street vendors, and as a general rule, the lower their elevation, the higher their prices. Shopkeepers are normally less willing to haggle over prices than are street vendors, who charge less as a matter of course.

Some shops specialize in woodcarvings and ceramics from the Oriente and silver items from Potosí. Others deal in rugs, wall-hangings, woven belts and pouches. In the Mercado de Hechicería, you'll find all sorts of figurines, including such Aymará good-luck charms as toads and turtles, from US$0.15 for a small one to US$5 for a large and elaborate carving. Music recordings are available in small shops and stalls along Calle Evaristo Valle and in several more reputable places on Calle Linares. Quite a few shops also sell tourist kitsch, an art form unto itself, and amid the lovely weavings and other items displaying real craftsmanship, you'll find ceramic ashtrays with Inca designs, fake Tiahuanaco figurines, costume jewelry, T-shirts and all manner of mass-produced woolens.

If you'd prefer to find llama or alpaca sweaters, bowler hats and other clothing

Buying a Charango

Although it's rumored that Bolivia's best charango makers hail from Aiquile in central Bolivia, La Paz offers the widest variety of fine instruments. Once you eliminate the made-for-tourist charangos, two classes of instruments remain.

In the US$100 to US$200 category, you can purchase the work of the masters. Juan Achá Campos specializes in one-piece constructions of fine materials and consistent quality; you'll find his work at La Casa de Charangos, Calle Nicolas Ortiz 2417, San Antonio. At Calle Manco Capac 311, René Gamboa sells his own charangos, which play well despite their two-piece construction. Another master charango maker is Sabino Orosco, Calle Sagárnaga 217, 1st floor, Local 4.

With less money and more time, you can commission a charango directly from the makers, who charge as little as US$35 to US$50 for a two-piece construction (however, it may lack the durability of a one-piece instrument made by masters such as Juan Achá Campos). The brothers Bernardino and José Torrico work at Calle Linares 818 (Arte Aiquileño) and 820 (Yachay) in La Paz. José produces the most amazing small charangos, called *hualaichos*, as well as fine larger instruments. Bernardino's charangos are built of some of the most beautiful woods to be found, but watch their intonation. Bernardino carves interesting and elaborate designs on the backs of some of his soundboxes, and both brothers are also adept at charango repair and reconstruction.

Only 30m away at Calle Santa Cruz 270 is the shop of Phuju Pampa. Sadly, most of his instruments are constructed from *quirquinchos* (armadillos), which are an endangered species in Bolivia. This type of instrument is less sonorous and more fragile than the wooden ones, so try out Phuju Pampa's wooden charangos; his work may appear sloppy but the charango I tested had exceptional voice.

The most common complaint with smaller shops is their reluctance to tune instruments. Most artisans prefer building instruments to tuning them, and because new strings stretch so much, tuning them is very time-consuming. The conventional tuning is D (re), G (sol), B (ti), E (mi) and B (ti). The B strings are tuned one octave apart. Once a charango is in tune, you'll have to listen carefully to determine whether the frets are placed at proper intervals.

– Daniel Harvey, USA

items that weren't produced specifically for tourists (and are therefore less expensive), stroll around the informal street stalls that line Calles Graneros and Max Paredes.

Musical Instruments

Many La Paz artisans specialize in quenas, zampoñas, *tarkas* and *pinquillos*, among other traditional woodwinds. There's a lot of low-quality or merely decorative tourist rubbish around; visit a reputable workshop where you'll pay a fraction of gift-shop prices and contribute directly to the artisan rather than to an intermediary. Clusters of artisans work along Calle Juan Granier near Plaza Garita de Lima. Other recommended shops in La Paz include those on Calle Isaac

Tamayo near the top of Calle Sagárnaga, and those at Calle Linares 855 and 859.

GETTING THERE & AWAY
Air

El Alto airport sits on the Altiplano at 4018m, 10km from the city center. It's the world's highest international airport; larger planes need 5km of runway to lift off and must land at twice their sea-level velocity to compensate for the lower atmospheric density. Stopping distance is much greater, too, and planes must be equipped with special tires to withstand the extreme forces involved.

Airport services include a newsagent, souvenir shops, a tiny bookstore, a coffee shop and an upstairs bistro. The currency exchange facilities offer poor rates on traveler's checks – if possible, wait until you're in town. The duty-free shop is available to passengers departing internationally.

Most domestic flights are serviced by LAB and AeroSur. LAB has both the lower fares and the wider network, and flies to just about every corner of the country. Some sample fares are Cochabamba (US$49), Sucre (US$69), Santa Cruz (US$107), Puerto Suárez (US$172), Yacuiba (US$172), Tarija (US$108), Trinidad (US$67), Guayaramerín (US$150) and Cobija (US$159).

TAM is quite a bit cheaper but because they use small planes, they're more weather-dependent than most and flights may be postponed for several days. Most people use TAM to fly to Rurrenabaque (US$54), but they also fly to Cochabamba (US$29), Tarija (US$76), Sucre (US$50), Santa Cruz (US$50), Trinidad (US$50) and numerous smaller places, including Puerto Suárez (US$100), Guayaramerín (US$100) and Riberalta (US$100).

The following is a list of some airline offices in La Paz. Specific schedules and fares change regularly so it's best to contact individual carriers for details. For information on international flights, see the Getting There & Away chapter.

Aerolíneas Argentinas Reyes Ortiz 73, at Federico Suazo, Torres Gundlach, 2nd floor (☎ 351711; fax 391059)

AeroSur Edificio Petrolero, Avenida 16 de Julio (Map 3; ☎ 369292, 313233; toll-free ☎ 0800-3030)

American Airlines Plaza Venezuela 1440, Edificio Herrmann P Busch (☎ 351360; fax 391080)

British Airways Capitán Ravelo 2101, at Montevideo (☎ 443255; fax 0811-2702; discover@ceibo.entelnet.bo)

Iberia Calle Ayacucho 378, Edificio Credinform, 5th floor (☎ 324378; fax 391192)

KLM Plaza del Estudiante 1931 (☎ 441595; fax 443487)

LanChile Edificio 16 de Julio, Suite 102, ground floor (☎ 315832; fax 392051; lanbol@ceibo.entelnet.bo)

LAB (Lloyd Aéreo Boliviano) Avenida Camacho 1460 (Map 2; ☎ 371020; toll-free ☎ 0800-3001 or 0800-4321)

LanPeru Edificio 16 de Julio, Suite 102, ground floor (☎ 315832; fax 392051)

Lufthansa Edificio Illimani II, Avenida 6 de Agosto 2512 (☎ 431717; fax 431267)

TAM (Transportes Aéreos Militares) Avenida Ismael Montes 738 (Map 2; ☎ 379285 or 379286; TAM airport ☎ 842226; fax 390705)

TAM Mercosur Plaza del Estudiante 1931 (☎ 443442; fax 443487)

Varig/Cruzeiro Edificio Cámara de Comercio, Avenida Mariscal Santa Cruz 1392 (☎ 314040; fax 391131)

Bus

The main bus terminal (Map 1; ☎ 367275), the Terminal Terrestre Ciudad de La Paz, is at Plaza Antofagasta, a 15-minute walk north of the city center. Bus fares are relatively uniform between companies, but competition on most routes is such that discounts are available for the asking. This terminal serves all destinations south and east of La Paz, as well as international destinations. Other destinations – among them Copacabana, Sorata, Tiahuanaco, the Yungas and Amazonia – are served only by operators whose terminals are scattered around the cemetery and Villa Fátima districts; most of these companies run micros or minibuses.

Southern & Eastern Bolivia
Buses to Oruro run about every half hour (three hours, US$1.50), and several of these continue from Oruro to Llallagua. To Uyuni (14 hours, US$6.20), buses depart on Tuesday and Friday at 5:30 pm. Plenty of *flotas* (bus lines) go to Cochabamba (seven hours, US$3.50), leaving either in the morning or between 8 and 9 pm, and many of these continue on to Santa Cruz (17 hours, US$7.20) or connect with a Santa Cruz bus in Cochabamba. A good direct service is with El Dorado.

Most buses to Sucre (14 hours, US$12) pass through Potosí (10 hours, US$5 to US$7), and some require a layover there. Have warm clothes handy for this typically chilly trip. Some Potosí buses continue on to Tarija (24 hours, US$15), Tupiza (20 hours, US$10) or Villazón (23 hours, US$12).

Lake Titicaca & Peru Both Transportes Manco Kapac (Map 4; ☎ 350033; Calle José María Aliaga 670) and Transtur 2 de Febrero (Map 4; ☎ 377181; Calle José María Aliaga 287) run to Copacabana (3½ hours, US$2.20) four to six times daily. They are just off Avenida Baptista near the cemetery and quite a long way from the hotel areas. At Copacabana, you'll find camiones and colectivos to Puno and beyond.

Alternatively, for US$6 there are more comfortable tourist micros and minibuses, which provide the easiest way to Peru; you can book them at any La Paz tour agency. Most companies offer daily services to Puno (with a change in Copacabana) for about US$10, including hotel pickup. The trip takes nine to 10 hours, including lunch in Copacabana and the border crossing. If a company doesn't fill its bus, passengers may be shunted to another company so no one runs half-empty buses. All companies allow stopovers in Copacabana.

For those in a big hurry to reach Cuzco (17 hours, US$20), Flota Trans Litoral and Cruz del Sur offer direct services three times weekly from the main bus terminal.

Autolíneas Ingavi (Map 4; ☎ 328981) has at least four buses daily along the relatively uninteresting southern route to Desaguadero (three hours, US$1.50), on the Peruvian border, via Tiahuanaco and Guaqui.

Buses and micros to Huatajata (1½ hours, US$1) and other eastern Lake Titicaca towns and villages leave daily approximately every half hour from 4 am to 5 pm. The terminal (Map 4) is near the corner of Calles Manuel Bustillos and Kollasuyo. To return to La Paz from Huatajata (or any place along the route), just flag down the bus.

The Yungas & the Amazon Basin From about 1km uphill from Plaza Gualberto Villarroel (Map 1), in Barrio Villa Fátima (from Avenida Camacho, take any micro marked 'Villa Fátima'), several flotas offer daily bus and minibus services to the Yungas and beyond. Flota Yungueña (☎ 213275) has two offices; the one on Yanacachi, behind the gasoline station, serves Coroico and the one on Avenida Las Américas, just north of the gasoline station, serves Amazonian routes. Nearby Trans Totaí (☎ 219811 or 212391), on San Borja, and Trans San Bartolomé, on Ocobaya, go to Chulumani. Other companies serving the region are clustered along Virgen del Carmen, just west of Avenida Las Américas. Except for Rurrenabaque, most Amazon Basin routes only operate during the dry season. For all services, it's wise to reserve seats in advance. Camiones to the Yungas and Amazonia leave from behind the gasoline station.

Sample fares include Coroico (four hours, US$2.50), Chulumani (five hours, US$2.50), Caranavi (seven hours, US$3), Rurrenabaque (18 hours, US$10), Reyes (19 hours, US$10), Santa Rosa (19 hours, US$10), Riberalta (35 to 60 hours, US$28.50), Guayaramerín (35 to 60 hours, US$28.50) and Cobija (50 to 80 hours, US$40).

From Calle Ángel Babia (Map 4), Trans Larecaja and Trans-Unificado Sorata operate frequent buses to Sorata (four hours, US$1.50); the latter is recommended. Although it's possible to reserve seats, departures are frequent and if you just turn up, you'll probably get a seat. Be sure to watch your bags in this area, especially as you're boarding or leaving buses.

International Services From the main bus terminal, you'll find several flotas with daily buses to Arica (eight hours, US$16) and Iquique (24 hours, US$20), both in Chile; to Cuzco, Peru (17 hours, US$20), with connections to Lima, Arequipa and other places; and even to Buenos Aires, Argentina (72 hours, US$110/120 normal/bus cama), via either Yacuiba or Villazón. For more information, see the Getting There & Away chapter.

Train

The La Paz train station (Map 4) is now defunct (although a sporadic ferrobus service may resume between Arica and La Paz), and rail services to Chile and the Argentine border, via Uyuni and/or Tupiza, all leave from Oruro (which is readily accessible by bus). For information and bookings, contact the Empresa Ferroviaria Andina (Map 3; ☎ 416546 or 416545; fax 418516; Fernando Guachalla 464), also called FCA (Ferrocarriles Andinas), near the corner of Sánchez Lima. For information on the status of ferrobus travel to and from Arica, see the Administradora de Ferrocarriles Arica-La Paz (☎ 771881; Calle 21 No 8517, Calacoto), in the Zona Sur.

Tickets for rail services within Peru are available at ENAFER, the Empresa de Ferrocarriles del Perú (☎ 353648), on the 15th floor of the Edificio Litoral, Avenida Mariscal Santa Cruz. The tourist-class (one step above 1st-class) fare from Puno to Cuzco is US$22. From Puno to Arequipa costs US$19. For slightly more, you can opt for the even more plush Inca class.

Car & Motorcycle

Driving the steep, winding one-way streets of La Paz may be intimidating for the uninitiated, but for longer day trips into the immediate hinterlands, renting a car isn't a bad idea. For information on agencies and prices, see Car & Motorcycle in the Getting Around chapter.

GETTING AROUND
To/From the Airport

El Alto International Airport, in the sub-city of El Alto, sits on the Altiplano 10km from La Paz center. There are two access routes: the autopista toll road, which costs US$0.50, and the sinuous free route, which leads into Plaza Ballivián in the city of El Alto.

The cheapest but least convenient way to El Alto airport is on a La Ceja micro (US$0.20), which will drop you at the brow of the canyon; from there, it's a level 2km walk to the airport. Much easier is the minibus trufi 212, which runs between Plaza Isabel la Católica (Map 3) and the airport and costs US$1. Heading into town from the airport, this service will drop you anywhere along the Prado.

Radio taxis for up to four passengers cost from US$7 to US$8 from the city center to the airport and will pick you up at your door; confirm the price with the dispatcher when booking or ask the driver to verify it

when you climb in. Coming from the airport, some taxi drivers lie in wait, hoping to score unrealistic fares from unwitting arrivals (especially those heading for top-end hotels!); the current standard fare is around US$7 (B$40) for up to four passengers; for a fifth person, they charge an additional US$1.

TAM flights leave from the military airport in El Alto, accessible on the micro marked 'Río Seco,' which you can catch on the upper Prado. Taxi fares are the same as for the main El Alto airport.

Around Town

La Paz is well served by its public transport system. Basically, you can choose between micros (buses), which charge US$0.15 (B$1 to B$1.20); trufis – either cars or minibuses – which charge US$0.20 (B$1.80) around town, US$0.80 (B$5) to the airport and US$0.40 (B$1.70) to Zona Sur; taxis, which charge US$0.40 (B$1.80) per person around the center, although this may be a bit more for long uphill routes; and radio taxis, charging US$1 (B$6) around the center, US$1.40 (B$8) to the cemetery district, US$2 (B$12) to Zona Sur and US$7 (B$40) to the airport. Radio taxi charges are for up to four passengers and include pickup, if necessary, while other taxis charge a per-person rate.

Any of these vehicles can be waved down anywhere, except near intersections or in areas cordoned off by the police. In the case of micros and trufis, destinations are identified on placards on the roof or windscreen.

Micro La Paz's sputtering and smoke-spewing micros mock the law of gravity and defy the principles of brake and transmission mechanics as they grind up and down the city's steep hills. You'd be forgiven for assuming they somehow missed their appointment with the scrap dealer, but they do provide cheap, coronary-free transport for the city's masses.

In addition to a route number or letter, micros plainly display their destination and route on a signboard posted in the front window. You'll see micro stops, but they're superfluous; micros will stop wherever you wave them down.

Trufi & Colectivo Trufis and colectivos are small cars or minibuses that ply set routes and provide reliable and comfortable transport that falls somewhere between the taxis and micros. For the benefit of nonreaders, colectivos often carry small urchins with big lungs who cry out the destinations.

Taxi Although most things worth seeing in La Paz lie within manageable walking distance of the center, both the rail and bus terminals are rather steep climbs from the main hotel areas. Especially considering the altitude, struggling up the hills through traffic beneath a heavy pack isn't fun.

Fortunately, taxis aren't expensive, but if the journey involves lots of uphill travel, drivers may expect a bit more. Most regular taxis – as opposed to radio taxis, which carry roof bubbles advertising their telephone numbers – are actually collective taxis. Don't be concerned if the driver picks up additional passengers and don't hesitate to flag down a taxi already carrying passengers. If you're traveling beyond the city center or your journey involves a long uphill climb, arrange a fare with the driver before climbing in, and if possible, pay the fare in exact change.

Taxi drivers may not always be well versed in city geography, so have a map handy to explain roughly where you want to go.

Long-distance taxis gather at the Centro de Taxis on Avenida Aniceto Arce near Plaza Isabel la Católica. Prices are negotiable; as a general rule, plan on US$40 to US$50 per day.

Around La Paz

VALLE DE LA LUNA

The Valle de la Luna (Valley of the Moon) is a pleasant and quiet half-day break from urban La Paz and may be visited easily in a morning or combined with another outing such as a hike to Muela del Diablo to fill an entire day. It isn't a valley at all, but a bizarre eroded hillside maze of canyons and pinnacles technically known as badlands. It lies about 10km down the canyon of the Río Choqueyapu from the city center. The

desert-like landscape and its vegetation inspire the imagination and invite exploration. Several species of cactus grow here, including the hallucinogenic *choma*, or San Pedro cactus.

The route is badly eroded and unconsolidated silt makes it slippery and dangerous; the pinnacles collapse easily and some of the canyons are over 10m deep. Be cautious, carry drinking water and wear a good pair of hiking shoes.

Getting There & Away

If you visit Valle de la Luna as part of an organized tour, you'll have only an unimpressive five-minute photo stop. On your own, however, you'll have time to explore the intriguing formations on foot.

From the Prado, catch minibus 231 or 273 (or anything marked 'Mallasa' or 'Zoológico') toward Mallasa. Continue past Calacoto and Barrio Aranjuez and up the hill to the fork in the road; the right fork goes to Malasilla Golf Course. Get off at the first soccer field on your left (unfortunately, it's now surrounded by a brick wall and difficult to see, so you may have to ask the driver), where a sign announces 'Hotel Oberland 3km.' The Valle de la Luna is just downhill from this sign.

Alternatively, catch micro 11 (marked 'Aranjuez') and get off at Barrio Aranjuez, cross the Río Choqueyapu bridge to your right and follow the road up the hill. After 45 minutes, you'll reach the *cactario*, or cactus garden. It's not marked as such but is easily identifiable as a slightly artificial-looking stand of cacti. From there, a badly eroded and dangerous walking track winds up through Valle de la Luna to emerge at the aforementioned soccer field. Since the rains drastically alter this fragile landscape, portions of the track may wash out in coming years and the route may change. Alternatively, you can keep following the road and you'll eventually reach the top of Valle de la Luna.

For a taxi from the center, you'll pay around US$12 for up to three people, and the driver will wait for an hour or so while you look around.

MALLASA

After a traipse around Valle de la Luna, you can also visit the blossoming resort village of Mallasa. La Paz's spacious Vesty Pakos Zoo (☎ 795992), just east of Mallasa, is open daily from 10 am to 5 pm. Admission is US$1. Guides are available only on weekends.

From the overlook immediately east of the zoo is a clearly marked walking track that passes the rubbish dump, then descends to and crosses the fetid Río Choqueyapu before beginning a lung-bursting 600m climb to the Muela del Diablo (see later in this chapter).

Places to Stay & Eat

The Swiss-run *Hotel Oberland (☎ 745818; fax 745389; oberland@usa.net; Casilla 9392, La Paz)* is a well-designed country-style hotel 30 minutes by trufi from the center of La Paz. It sits at an altitude of just 3200m, so it's a good 5°C warmer than central La Paz. Cacti grow in the garden, which is frequented by butterflies and dragonflies. The hotel has a swimming pool and sauna; squash, racquetball, and volleyball courts; and table tennis. It also offers guests Internet access and cable TV. Single/double rooms

are US$30/38 (plus US$10 per person for transfers from the center); honeymoon suites cost US$50, including transfers. They also have a special backpackers' rate of US$15 per person, but only when rooms are available; no reservations are possible. All rates include a full American breakfast buffet. The à la carte restaurant is also lovely, with tables in the garden – try the *pacu*, a large freshwater fish from the Beni. Also see their website www.h-oberland.com.

Several shops in Mallasa sell snacks, beer and soft drinks; the restaurant at the zoo serves meals only on weekends.

Getting There & Away

From La Paz, take minibus 231 or 273, or anything marked 'Mallasa' or 'Zoológico.' From the top of Valle de la Luna, you can either hop on one of these or simply continue on foot; it's only about 1km.

MUELA DEL DIABLO

The prominent rock outcrop known as the Muela del Diablo (Devil's Molar) is actually an extinct volcanic plug rising between the exceedingly smelly Río Choqueyapu (or 'Omo River,' after the quantity of Omo

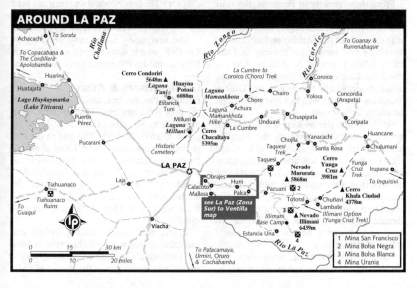

AROUND LA PAZ

The Río Choke

If recent statistics are anything to go by, the name of the Río Choqueyapu, which flows through La Paz, might as well be shortened to the Río Choke. This fetid stream, which provided the gold that gave La Paz its present location, is now utterly dead and beyond help. According to one source, 'the Río Choqueyapu receives annually 500,000 liters of urine, 200,000 tons of human excrement and millions of tons of garbage, animal carcasses and industrial toxins.' These include cyanide from tanneries and a cocktail of chemicals and dyes from textile and paper industries, which cause the river to flow bright orange in places, or red topped with a layer of white foam.

The Choqueyapu fortunately flows underground through the city, but as it emerges in the Zona Sur, it's used by campesinos, who must make their way around heaped trash and animal carcasses to take water for washing, cooking and drinking. Most people heat the water before drinking it, but few boil it, and even boiling wouldn't eliminate chemical pollutants from industrial wastes. The potential for health problems is staggering.

Currently, no one can be fined or cited for dumping waste into the river because – incredibly – the city has no laws or regulations against it. In 1994, the Municipal Environmental Office outlined 48 projects aimed at controlling water pollution, vehicle emissions, rubbish dumping and noise. As always, the problem with implementation has been funding, and still the foul stream continues to flow.

laundry soap flowing in it) and the recently established outer suburb of Pedregal. A hike to its base makes a pleasant half-day trip from La Paz, and can be easily combined with a visit to Valle de la Luna.

From the cemetery in Pedregal, the trail climbs steeply (several times crossing the new road that provides access to the hamlet near the base of the Muela) and affords increasingly fine views over the city and the surrounding tortured landscape. After a breathless hour or so, you'll reach a pleasant grassy swale where the Muela del Diablo comes into view, as well as some precarious pinnacles farther east.

At this point, the walking track joins the road and descends through the hamlet. About 300m farther along, a side route branches off to the left and climbs toward the base of the Muela. With extreme caution, from the end of this route you can pick your way up to the cleft between the double summit, where a large cross was planted in 1994. Without technical equipment and expertise, however, it's inadvisable to climb farther.

After descending to the main track, you can decide whether to return the way you

came or follow the steep track that circles the Muela in a counterclockwise direction and descends to the Río Choqueyapu before climbing up the other side of the valley to the zoo in Mallasa (see earlier in this chapter). The latter option will turn this hike into a full-day trip, as it takes about six hours for the hike between Pedregal and Mallasa.

The marginally useful map *Trekking en La Paz*, which shows both routes, costs US$1 at the La Paz municipal tourist office.

Getting There & Away

From La Paz, the best access to the start of the hike is on minibus 288, marked 'Comunidad Pedregal,' from Calle Murillo or the lower Prado (US$1.50). The end of the line is the parking area about 100m downhill from the cemetery in Pedregal. Alternatively, take micro 21, marked 'Los Rosales,' which will drop you at a murky rivulet (the ambitiously named Río Lakha Khollu), from where it's 600m to the cemetery, all uphill.

If you don't mind walking farther, you can take any micro or minibus trufi headed for Cotacota, Chasquipampa or Ovejuyo from Calle Murillo, near the corner of Calle

Sagárnaga, or anywhere on the lower Prado. Get off at the sign identifying Calle 34, where the main road swings sharply to the left, and head downhill, through the apparently half-constructed village. After crossing the aforementioned Río Lakha Khollu, follow the maze of well-worn trails uphill, bearing left up the slope, until you strike the main road. This road climbs straight to the Pedregal cemetery, where the hike begins.

Coming from Valle de la Luna, you can board these micros or minibuses at Plaza Humboldt or follow the difficult walking track from near the zoo in Mallasa, which involves a descent to the Río Choqueyapu and then a stiff 600m ascent to the eastern side of the Muela.

VALLE DE LAS ÁNIMAS
The name 'Valle de las Ánimas' (Valley of Spirits) is used roughly to describe the eerily eroded canyons and fantastic organpipe spires to the north and northeast of the barrios of Chasquipampa, Ovejuyo and Apaña (which are rapidly being absorbed into the Zona Sur neighborhoods of La Paz). The scenery resembles that of Valle de la Luna, but on a grander scale.

There are two walking routes through the Valle de las Ánimas; for either, you need an early start from La Paz.

Río Ovejuyo Route
The Río Ovejuyo route begins at Calle 50, near the Instituto de Biología Animal in Chasquipampa. This point is accessible on micro Ñ or minibuses 288 or 203, marked 'Chasquipampa' or 'Ovejuyo.' From the northern side of the road, the route descends slightly through desultory development. When you reach the diminutive Río Ovejuyo, turn right and follow its southern bank northeast past the spectacularly eroded formations.

After about 6km, the river valley turns to the north. If you don't want to return the way you came, you'll need a compass, the 1:50,000 topo sheet *5944-II* and, for a very short section along the upper Río Ovejuyo, topo sheet *5944-I*. Traverse up the slope to your right and head south, over Cerro Pararani, until you arrive at the head of Quebrada Negra. Here, you can follow the Quebrada Negra route (described below) either back to Ovejuyo or down to the village of Huni. This option can be challenging, especially because of the altitude, and you have to carry enough water for the entire day, as there's no drinkable surface water along the way.

Quebrada Negra Route
The 7km route up Quebrada Negra, over Cerro Pararani and down to Huni is a demanding day hike that requires six to seven hours. It begins at the obvious Quebrada Negra ravine, which crosses the road at the upper (eastern) end of Ovejuyo village. Micros and trufis marked simply 'Ovejuyo' stop about half a kilometer short of this ravine, but micro 'Ñ' and minibus 385, marked 'Ovejuyo,' or minibus 42, marked 'Apaña,' all continue right past the ravine mouth.

The easy-to-follow 4km route up Quebrada Negra will take you through the most dramatic of the eroded Valle de las Ánimas pinnacles. Near the head of the ravine, you need to traverse southeast around the northern shoulder of Cerro Pararani until you strike the obvious route that descends steeply to Huni village (*not* Huni chapel, which is also marked on the topo sheet). In fine weather, you'll have good views of Illimani along this section.

To return to La Paz, follow the road for 2km up over Paso Huni and thence another 1.5km downhill to Apaña, where you'll catch up with regular micros and trufis returning to the city.

For this route, you'll need a compass and either the tourist office's *Trekking en La Paz* map, or the 1:50,000 topo sheets *5944-I* and *6044-III*.

CAÑÓN DE PALCA (QUEBRADA CHUA KERI)
The magnificent Cañón de Palca (marked on the topo sheet as Quebrada Chua Kheri) brings a slice of grand canyon country to the dramatic badland peaks and eroded amphitheaters east of La Paz. Although it's

LA PAZ (ZONA SUR) TO VENTILLA

1 Rumors
2 Britannia & Abracadabra
3 Super Mex
4 Ketal Supermarket & The Hutch
5 Ristorante Pizzería Italiana

now a motorable track, a walk through this wonderful gorge makes an ideal day hike from La Paz.

The Route

At Paso Huni, about 2km above Ovejuyo, you'll pass a small trash-rimmed lake where the road begins to descend the other side. Several hundred meters past the summit, on your left you'll see some magnificent 'church choir' formations – rows of standing pinnacles that resemble an ensemble in song.

About 2km beyond the pass, take the right (south) fork of the road into the village of Huni. After less than 1km, the road begins to descend in earnest. Just a few years ago, much of this route followed an ancient Inca road, with good examples of pre-Hispanic paving, but that was ripped up to make it passable to vehicles.

With sensational views all along, the route drops slowly toward the gravelly canyon floor. The approach to the canyon is

dominated by a 100m-high natural obelisk, and in the opposite wall is the rock formation Ermitaño del Cañón, which resembles a reclusive human figure hiding in an enormous rock niche. The route then winds along the usually diminutive Río Palca for about 2km between spectacular vertical walls. Upon exiting the canyon, you'll have a gentle 3km climb through green farmland to the former gold-mining village of Palca.

If you don't find transport back to La Paz on the same day, you can stay at the alojamiento in Palca or camp around Palca or nearby Ventilla. However, beware of the badly polluted surface water and ask permission before you set your tent up in a field or pasture.

Getting There & Away

For the start of this hike, you need to reach Huni, which is served only by micros and minibus trufis headed for Ventilla and Palca. These leave at least once daily from near

LA PAZ (ZONA SUR) TO VENTILLA

the corner of Boquerón and Lara, two blocks north of Plaza Líbano in the San Pedro district of La Paz. There's no set schedule, but most leave in the morning. You'll have the best luck on Saturday and Sunday, when families make excursions into the countryside. Alternatively, take micro 'Ñ' or minibus 385, marked 'Ovejuyo/ Apaña,' get off at the end of the line, and slog the 1.5km up the road to Paso Huni.

From Palca back to La Paz, you'll find occasional camiones, micros and minibuses, particularly on Sunday afternoon, but don't count on anything after 3 or 4 pm. Alternatively, you can hike to Ventilla, an hour uphill through a pleasant eucalyptus plantation, and try hitching from there.

If you arrive in Palca geared up for more hiking, you can always set off from Ventilla along the Taquesi Trek, a two-day route over a pre-Hispanic road into the Yungas. For a map and description of this hike, see the Cordilleras & Yungas chapter.

CHACALTAYA

The world's highest developed ski area (the term 'developed' is used loosely) is at an altitude of over 5000m, atop a dying glacier on the slopes of 5395m Cerro Chacaltaya. The name comes from the Aymará words *chaka*, or 'bridge,' and *thaya*, meaning 'cold.' It's only a 90-minute ride from central La Paz, and the accessible summit is an easy hike from there.

Those who fly into La Paz from the lowlands will want to wait a few days before visiting Chacaltaya or other high-altitude places. For guidelines on avoiding or coping with altitude-related ailments, see Health in the Facts for the Visitor chapter.

Snacks and hot drinks are available at the lodge; if you want anything more substantial, bring it from town. Also bring warm (and windproof) clothing, sunglasses (100% UV proof) and sunscreen.

Most La Paz tour agencies take groups to Chacaltaya. For prospective skiers, Club Andino Boliviano is the best bet.

Skiing

The steep, 700m ski piste runs from 5320m (75m below the summit of the mountain) down to about 4900m. The ski season is February to April, but it's often possible to ski on snow rather than ice even later in the year. There is no 'bunny hill,' but beginners who can cope with bumps can have a good time. The major problem is the lift; real beginners often spend the entire day at the bottom of the hill because they can't come to grips with the utterly confounding cable tow. The club has long intended to replace it, but the project has been less than successful

(see 'Skiing in Bolivia – Thin Air & Thin Ice'). Wear expendable clothing; it will suffer if you do manage to hook up to the cable.

The Club Andino Boliviano (☎ 324682; Calle México 1638, La Paz) organizes transport to Chacaltaya on Saturday and Sunday throughout the year, as long as there are sufficient takers to justify sending a minibus, but the ski lift operates only when snow conditions are favorable. To reserve a spot, call or drop by the office, which is open weekdays from 9:30 am to noon and 3 to 7 pm. Ski trips leave from the club office at 8:30 am and arrive at Chacaltaya sometime

---

Skiing in Bolivia – Thin Air & Thin Ice

The improvement of the Chacaltaya ski lift, the highest in the world, has been on the Club Andino Boliviano agenda for almost as long as the club has been in existence (since 1939). Built in 1940, it was South America's first ski lift, and it hasn't changed much since then. An automobile engine in an aluminum hut turns a steel cable loop. Skiers clip on to the cable at the bottom of the slope using a length of steel fashioned into a hook (gancho), which is attached to a short length of rope and bit of wood. This fits between the skiers' legs and acts as a seat that theoretically drags them to the top of the hill, where they disengage from the cable. As you can imagine, there's lots of scope for complications.

In 1994, a retired – but still relatively modern – ski lift (25 years old) was shipped to Chacaltaya from the ski resort of Sestriere in northern Italy. Until two engineers were flown over from Sestriere to install it nearly a year later, it languished in an El Alto warehouse as a rather large and formidable jigsaw puzzle. The engineers determined that, yes, the jigsaw puzzle could be reassembled but, because the piste was on a glacier (that is, slowly moving ice), the lift would have to be re-erected every year to make adjustments for glacial motion. It was decided that this would make it uneconomical, and in 1995 the old steel cable was replaced and bits of the Sestriere lift were cannibalized to improve the existing lift.

More bad news for Chacaltaya lies in global warming, which is causing the glacier to recede at a rate of 6 to 10m per year. Glacial shrinkage is not new at Chacaltaya – Club Andino Boliviano helped pay to construct the road to the piste by selling chunks of the glacier – but this time it's probably terminal. According to current estimates, unless there's a change in the current climatic trends, the Chacaltaya glacier will completely disappear within 30 years. In fact, the bottom of the ski lift is now below the snow line, which will require some engineering if skiing is going to continue there.

As a result, the search is on for another piste, but all of Bolivia's glaciers are shrinking (as they are all over the world – only the Patagonian ice cap is expanding) and there's very little permanent ice left on any Bolivian peak under 5000m. Higher glaciers still have a long way to go before the big meltdown, but they're so high that day-trippers from La Paz would risk cerebral or pulmonary edema. The future of skiing in Bolivia looks bleak – owing to glacial melting, it probably won't continue past 2005 – so enjoy it while you can.

– Yossi Brain

before 11 am. You ski until 4 pm and are back in La Paz by 6:30 pm.

Transport alone costs US$10 to US$20 per person; equipment rental is an additional US$7, including a *gancho* (hook) for the ski tow. Admission for nonskiers is US$2. The equipment rental shop is in the warm-up hut. When you're choosing equipment, make sure that your gancho has a complete U-shaped curl, otherwise it won't clip onto the cable tow.

Hiking
For nonskiers or out-of-season visitors, a trip to Chacaltaya can still be rewarding. The views of La Paz, Illimani, Mururata and 6088m Huayna Potosí are spectacular, and it's a relatively easy (but steep) 1km high-altitude climb from the lodge to the summit of Chacaltaya. Remember to carry warm clothing and water and take plenty of rests, say a 30-second stop every 10 steps or so and longer stops if needed, even if you don't feel tired. If you begin to feel light-headed, sit down and rest until the feeling passes. If it doesn't, you may be suffering from mild altitude sickness and the only remedy is to descend.

From Chacaltaya it's possible to walk to the Refugio Huayna Potosí, at the base of Huayna Potosí, in half a day. Climb to the second false summit above the ski slope and then wind your way down past a turquoise lake, to meet up with the road just above the nearly abandoned mining settlement of Milluni. Turn right on the road and follow it past Laguna Zongo to the dam, where you'll see the refugio on your left and the trail-head for Laguna Mamankhota on your right (see Milluni & the Zongo Valley later in this section).

Mountain Biking
It's a long way down from Chacaltaya, and Gravity Assisted Mountain Biking, at América Tours in La Paz (see Organized Tours in the Getting Around chapter), takes advantage of the potential energy by running riveting full-day rides downhill along the sinuous route. For US$55, they offer a variety of itineraries, depending on the weather and skill level of the participants. You reach Chacaltaya by 4WD, which provides the opportunity to savor the view before you're assaulted by a serious adrenaline rush on the downhill route to the Prado in La Paz.

Places to Stay
For overnight stays at Chacaltaya, you can crash in Club Andino's well-ventilated mountain hut, which has recently been renovated to include beds with linen. A private room costs US$10 per person and dormitory beds are US$5. Austrian-style meals are available for US$3 to US$5. Alternatively, at the heated La Paz UMSA research laboratory, about 200m downhill from the warm-up hut, the friendly scientific personnel welcome visitors.

A warm sleeping bag, food, and some sort of headache/soroche relief are essential for an overnight stay in either location.

Getting There & Away
There's no public transport to Chacaltaya; you'll have to go with either Club Andino Boliviano or a La Paz tour operator (see Organized Tours in the Getting Around chapter). Especially from March to May, the Chacaltaya road may become impassable to 2WD vehicles, so check the situation before choosing a tour that can't arrive at its destination or you'll have a long, uphill slog at high altitude. Self-drivers shouldn't attempt this road without a good 4WD vehicle and excellent driving skills.

If you go with Club Andino Boliviano on Saturday, you should be able to catch a lift back to La Paz with their Sunday trip, if the bus isn't full. On other days, tour groups may have space for extra people; they'll normally charge about half the tour price for the one-way trip.

MILLUNI & THE ZONGO VALLEY
Dramatic Zongo Valley plunges sharply down from the starkly anonymous mining village of Milluni – from 4624m to 1480m within 33km. At its head, between Chacaltaya and the spectacular peak of Huayna Potosí, is the glacial blue Laguna Zongo,

which was created to run the Zongo hydro-electric power station.

Laguna Mamankhota Hike

Once upon a time, a lovely set of ice caves high above the valley floor provided a good excuse for day hikes and tours, but in 1992 they melted away, leaving not even an ice cube. Now, the best excuse to climb to the former site is the impressive views of Huayna Potosí across ice-blue Laguna Mamankhota (also known as Laguna Cañada).

To reach the trailhead, continue for about 5km northeast of Milluni, which will be visible downhill on your left, stopping along the way to have a look at the interesting and unusual miners' cemetery on the roadside, overlooking Milluni. If you're traveling by vehicle, you'll reach Laguna Zongo, an artificial lake with milky blue-green water, and the Compañía Minera del Sur gate a few minutes later. On your right you'll see a trail climbing up the hillside. From there, the road winds steeply downward into Zongo Valley.

The hike begins at 4600m. From the parking area, strike off uphill to the right. After about 100m, you'll reach an aqueduct, which you should follow for about 50 minutes along a rather treacherous precipice. Watch on your left for the plaque commemorating an Israeli's final motorbike ride along this narrow and vertigo-inspiring route. The plaque marks the spot where he plunged over the precipice.

About 20m after you cross a large bridge, turn right along a vague track leading uphill, following the cairns that mark the way. After a short climb, you'll reach Laguna Mamankhota, and stunning views of Huayna Potosí, Tiquimani, Telata and Charquini – if the peaks aren't shrouded in clouds. A further 25 minutes up the vague trail will bring you to the site of the former ice caves.

Mountain Biking

For a thrilling day, hop on a mountain bike with the tour company Gravity Assisted Mountain Biking and wind your way downhill into the Zongo Valley, from the bleak highlands to the lush rain-forested lowlands. The full day costs US$55 per person, including transport from La Paz, guides and quality equipment.

Places to Stay & Eat

At Paso Zongo, above the dam at the head of Zongo Valley, the mountain hut *Refugio Huayna Potosí* provides accommodations for US$7/10 per person in the low/high season, including breakfast; other meals are also available. Hikers will find an incredible number of day hikes and long-distance trekking possibilities in the area. Contact Huayna Potosí Tours (see Organized Tours in the Getting Around chapter) in La Paz for information or reservations. Further information on Huayna Potosí is found under Climbing in the Cordillera Real, in the Cordilleras & Yungas chapter.

At the seismic station on the western end of Laguna Zongo, the friendly Miguel and Yolanda Altimarana offer *camping sites* and *basic meals* for US$1.

Getting There & Away

Camiones leave for Zongo Valley, via Paso Zongo, from Calle Kollasuyo in the La Paz cemetery district and from Plaza Ballivián in El Alto around midday on Monday, Wednesday and Thursday, and usually return the following day. Micros (one hour, US$1) leave daily when full from the same places, normally between 5 and 7 am.

By hired taxi, the half-day trip costs about US$40 for up to five people. Make sure the driver understands that you want the Zongo Valley via Milluni, as drivers may expect you to ask for Chacaltaya and try to take you there anyway. At the trailhead, the driver will wait while you walk up the mountain to the lake; allow a minimum of three hours for the walk.

To hire a 4WD and driver from La Paz to Paso Zongo costs about US$70 for up to nine people. For suggestions, see the Getting Around chapter.

LAJA

The tiny village of Laja, formerly known as Llaxa or Laxa, lies about midway between

La Paz and Tiahuanaco. In 1548, the Spanish captain Alonzo de Mendoza was charged with founding a city and rest stop along the route from Potosí to the coast at Callao, Peru. On October 20, 1548, he arrived in Laxa and declared it his chosen location. He soon changed his mind, however, and the site was shifted to the gold-bearing canyon where La Paz now stands.

Over Laja's plaza towers a grand church built in commemoration of Spanish victories over the Incas. The interior is ornamented with colonial artwork, including lovely wooden carvings adorned with gold and silver. The mestizo-style façade even bears the indigenized visages of King Ferdinand and Queen Isabella.

Most organized Tiahuanaco tours make a brief stop here.

TIAHUANACO

Little is actually known about the people who constructed the great Tiahuanaco ceremonial center on the southern shore of Lake Titicaca over 1000 years ago. Archaeologists generally agree that the civilization which spawned Tiahuanaco rose around 600 BC. Construction on the ceremonial site was under way by about AD 700, but around AD 1200 the group had melted into obscurity, becoming another 'lost' civilization. Evidence of its influence, particularly in the area of religion, has been found throughout the vast area that later became the Inca empire.

The treasures of Tiahuanaco have literally been scattered to the four corners of the earth. Its gold was looted by the Spanish, and early stone and pottery finds were sometimes destroyed by religious zealots who considered them pagan idols. Some of the work found its way to European museums; farmers destroyed pieces of it as they turned the surrounding area into pasture and cropland; the church kept some of the statues or sold them as curios; and the larger stonework went into Spanish construction projects, and even into the bed of the La Paz-Guaqui rail line that passes just south of the site.

Fortunately, a portion of the treasure has been preserved and some of it remains in

Bolivia. A few of the larger anthropomorphic stone statues have been left on the site, and others are displayed in the Museo al Aire Libre and the Museo Arqueológico de Tiwanaku in La Paz. Pieces from the earliest Tiahuanaco periods are kept in an onsite museum, which is opened infrequently to the public. Pieces from the three later epochs may be found scattered around Bolivia, but the majority are housed in archaeological museums in La Paz and Cochabamba. The ruins themselves have been so badly looted, however, that much of the information they could have revealed about their builders is now lost forever.

Tiahuanaco is open daily from 9 am to 5 pm. Foreigners pay US$2.50 admission, which includes the site and visitors center. Admission to Puma Punku and the nearby museum costs an additional US$2.50. People selling cheap clay trinkets (fortunately all fake; don't pay more than about US$0.20 for a small one) are no longer permitted inside the ruins area. Neither are clientless guides; guides can be hired only outside the fence. They can take you around the site for around US$2, but you'll have to bargain.

Note that beginning in 2000, a major three-year excavation and research project will be conducted at Tiahuanaco, which means that some of the main features may well be closed to the public during your visit.

History

Although no one is certain whether it was the capital of a nation, Tiahuanaco undoubtedly served as a great ceremonial center. At its height, the city had a population of as many as 20,000 inhabitants and encompassed approximately 2.6 sq km. Although only a very small percentage of the original site has been excavated – and what remains is less than overwhelming – Tiahuanaco represents the greatest megalithic architectural achievement of pre-Inca South America.

The development of the Tiahuanaco civilization has been divided by researchers into five distinct periods, numbered Tiahuanaco I

LA PAZ

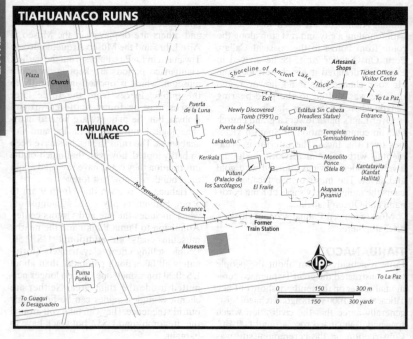

TIAHUANACO RUINS

through V, each of which has its own outstanding attributes.

The Tiahuanaco I period falls between the advent of the Tiahuanaco civilization and the middle of the 5th century BC. Significant finds from this period include multicolored pottery and human or animal effigies in painted clay. Tiahuanaco II, which ended around the beginning of the Christian Era, is hallmarked by ceramic vessels with horizontal handles. Tiahuanaco III dominated the next 300 years, and was characterized by tricolor pottery of geometric design, often decorated with images of stylized animals.

Tiahuanaco IV, also known as the Classic Period, developed between AD 300 and 700. The large stone structures that dominate the site today were constructed during this period. The use of bronze and gold is considered evidence of contact with groups farther east in the Cochabamba valley and farther west on the Peruvian coast. Tiahuanaco IV pottery is largely anthropomorphic;

pieces uncovered by archaeologists include some in the shape of human heads and faces with bulging cheeks, indicating that the coca leaf was already in use at this time.

Tiahuanaco V, or the Expansive Period, is marked by a decline that lasted until Tiahuanaco's utter disappearance around AD 1200. Pottery grew less elaborate, construction projects slowed and stopped, and no large-scale monuments were added after the early phases of this period.

When the Spanish arrived in South America, local Indian legends recounted that Tiahuanaco had been the capital of the bearded white god called Viracocha, and that from his city Viracocha had reigned over the civilization.

For further information on the rise and fall of Tiahuanaco, you may want to pick up the English translation of the book *Discovering Tiwanaku*, by Hugo Boero Rojo, which is now unfortunately rather hard to find.

Visiting the Ruins

Scattered around the Tiahuanaco site, you'll find heaps of jumbled basalt and sandstone slabs weighing as much as 175,000kg each. Oddly enough, the nearest quarries that could have produced the basalt megaliths are on the Copacabana peninsula, 40km away over the lake. Even the sandstone blocks had to be transported from a site more than 5km away. It's no wonder, then, that when the Spanish asked local Aymará how the buildings were constructed, they replied that it was done with the aid of the leader/deity Viracocha. They could conceive of no other plausible explanation.

Tiahuanaco's most outstanding structure is the **Akapana pyramid**, which was built on an existing geological formation. At its base, this roughly square 16m hill covers a surface area of about 200 sq m. In the center of its flat summit is an oval-shaped sunken area, which some sources attribute to early, haphazard Spanish excavation. The presence of a stone drain in the center, however, has led some archaeologists to believe it was used for water storage. Because much of the original Akapana went into the construction of nearby homes and churches, the pyramid is now in a rather sorry state.

North of the pyramid is **Kalasasaya**, a ritual platform compound with walls constructed of huge blocks of red sandstone and andesite. It measures 130m by 120m. The blocks are precisely fitted to form a platform base 3m high. Monolithic uprights flank the massive entrance steps up to the restored portico of the enclosure, beyond which is an interior courtyard and the ruins of priests' quarters.

Other stairways lead up to secondary platforms, where there are other monoliths including the famous **El Fraile**. At the far northwest corner of Kalasasaya is Tiahuanaco's best-known structure, the **Puerta del Sol** (Gateway of the Sun). This megalithic gateway was carved from a single block of andesite, and archaeologists assume that it was associated in some way with the sun deity. The surface of this fine-grained, gray volcanic rock is ornamented with low-relief designs on one side and a row of four deep niches on the other. Some believe these may have been used for offerings to the sun, while others maintain that the stone served as some kind of calendar. The structure is estimated to weigh at least 44,000kg.

There's a smaller, similar gateway carved with zoomorphic designs near the western end of the site that is informally known as the **Puerta de la Luna** (Gateway of the Moon).

Near the main entrance to Kalasasaya, a stairway leads down into the **Templete Semisubterráneo**, a red sandstone pit structure measuring 26m by 28m with a rectangular sunken courtyard and walls adorned with small carved stone faces.

West of Kalasasaya is a 55m by 60m rectangular area known as **Putuni** or Palacio de los Sarcófagos, which is still being excavated. It is surrounded by double walls and you can see the foundations of several houses.

The heap of rubble at the eastern end of the site is known as **Kantatayita**. Archaeologists are still trying to deduce some sort of meaningful plan from these well-carved slabs; one elaborately decorated lintel and some larger stone blocks bearing intriguing geometric designs are the only available clues. It has been postulated – and dubiously 'proven' – that they were derived from universal mathematical constants, such as *pi*; but some archaeologists simply see the plans for a large and well-designed building.

Across the railway line south of the Tiahuanaco site, you'll see the excavation site of **Puma Punku** (Gateway of the Puma). In this temple area, megaliths weighing over 440,000kg have been discovered. Like Kalasasaya and Akapana, there is evidence that Puma Punku was begun with one type of material and finished with another; part was constructed of enormous sandstone blocks, and during a later phase of construction, notched and jointed basalt blocks were added.

Special Events

On June 21, when the rays of the rising sun shine through the temple entrance on the eastern side of the complex, the Aymará New Year is celebrated at Tiahuanaco, and up to 5000 people – including a large contingent of New Agers – descend on the place from all over the world. Locals don colorful ceremonial dress and visitors are invited to join the party, drink singani, chew coca and dance. Special buses leave La Paz at 4 and 5 am to arrive in time for sunrise, but bundle up, because the pre-dawn hours are bitterly cold at this time of year. Local artisans also hold an annual *feria de artesanía* (crafts fair) to coincide with this celebration.

Organized Tours
Dozens of La Paz tour agencies offer reasonably priced guided full- and half-day tours to Tiahuanaco. Day trips are remarkably inexpensive – about US$12 per person, including transport and guide – and are probably worth it to avoid the crowded local buses. A list of tour agencies is found in the Organized Tours section in the Getting Around chapter.

Places to Stay & Eat
You'll find several basic eateries around the entrance to the ruins, and Tiahuanaco village, 1km west of the ruins, has several marginal restaurants and an incredibly colorful Sunday market. As a tour participant, you may want to carry your own lunch; otherwise, you'll be herded into a restaurant, such as the overpriced El Turista, and charged three times the going rate to cover the tour guide's kickback.

For overnight stays, the basic *Hostal Wiracocha* has overpriced rooms at US$10 for a double with breakfast. The reasonable *Hostal Puerta del Sol*, at the La Paz end of the village, charges US$3 per person. Here you'll hear some bizarre stories about Tiahuanaco, including tales of UFOs over the site. Both hostales do simple meals in an attached restaurant from US$1.50. The restaurant *Kalasasaya*, on Calle Bolívar, also offers informal sleeping possibilities.

Getting There & Away
Most tourists and travelers visit Tiahuanaco on a guided day tour from La Paz (see Organized Tours in the Getting Around chapter). For those who prefer to go it

alone, Autolíneas Ingavi leaves for Tiahuanaco (1½ hours, US$1) – some buses continue to Guaqui and Desaguadero (see the Lake Titicaca chapter) – about eight times daily from Calle José María Asín (Map 4) in La Paz. Buses are crowded beyond comfortable capacity – even when passengers are hanging out the windows and doors, drivers are still calling for more.

In the past, buses dropped passengers north of the ruins, but thanks to the new road, they now pass the museum near the southern entrance to the complex. To return to La Paz, just flag down a micro along the road south of the ruins. However, they'll already be overflowing, so it may be worth catching one in Tiahuanaco village. Micros to Guaqui and the Peruvian border leave from the plaza in Tiahuanaco village, or may be flagged down just west of the village. Again, expect crowds.

Taxis to Tiahuanaco from La Paz cost from US$30 roundtrip for two people, US$40 for four.

URMIRI
Urmiri lies at an elevation of 3800m, in the Valle de Sapahaqui 30km east of the La Paz-Oruro highway and three hours southeast of La Paz. Here, the Hotel Gloria (see Places to Stay under La Paz) runs the simple but charming resort-style Hotel Gloria Urmiri. It owes its existence to the mineral- and ion-rich Termas de Urmiri (Urmiri Hot Springs), which emerge from the ground at 72°C. It boasts two outdoor pools, which have both been allowed to cool to a comfortable temperature.

Places to Stay & Eat
Camping is possible in the countryside outside the village, and although it can get chilly, those luscious hot springs are never far away. At the *Hotel Gloria Urmiri* (☎ 02-370010; fax 02-391489; gloriatr@ceibo .entelnet.bo), rooms with a private bath cost US$15 per person, including breakfast and use of the hot springs and eucalyptus saunas. Rooms with their own private Roman bath, fed by the hot springs, are US$20 per person. Lunch and dinner cost

US$6 each and nonguests may use the pools for US$3 per person. Make accommodation and transport reservations at least two days in advance through the Hotel Gloria in La Paz, and note that the pools are closed on Monday for cleaning. For further information, see www.gloria-tours-bolivia.com, the website.

Getting There & Away

The easiest way to reach Urmiri from La Paz is with Hotel Gloria's shuttle (☎ 02-370010), which leaves the hotel daily in the morning and costs US$8 roundtrip per person (with a minimum of seven people).

To attempt reaching Urmiri independently, take a bus or camión from La Paz toward Oruro and get off near the bridge in Villa Loza, 70km south of La Paz and 15km north of Patacamaya. Here, turn east along the unpaved road and pray for a lift, because if nothing is forthcoming, you're in for a very long walk. About 5km along, the road passes a cluster of *chullpas*, and farther on, views of the Valle de Sapahuaqui will open up ahead as the road winds into the fruit-producing Valle de Sapahaqui. After 20km (a five-hour walk), you'll reach the junction at Lurjavi, where you should turn right for the final 3km into Urmiri.

The Cordilleras & Yungas

The 200km-long Cordillera Real, Bolivia's most prominent range, is also one of the loftiest and most imposing in the Andes. Not only is it Bolivia's best mountaineering venue, it's also popular as a trekking destination, and the bulk of the country's popular walking routes follow ancient roads connecting the high Altiplano with the steamy Yungas (valleys).

Highlights

- Follow the pre-Inca paving on the Choro, Taquesi or Yunga Cruz treks
- Lounge, hike and eat your fill in cloud-wreathed Coroico
- Pump adrenaline while mountain-biking down the world's most dangerous road!
- Explore medieval-looking Sorata and enjoy its fabulous hiking opportunities
- Climb to over 6000m on the straightforward glaciated peak of Huayna Potosí – this option is for fit mountaineers only!
- Hike over the five high passes between Curva and Pelechuco, in the wild Cordillera Apolobamba

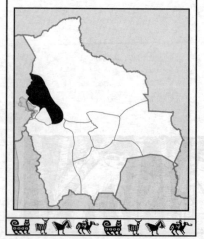

North of Lake Titicaca lies the remote Cordillera Apolobamba, with scores of little-known valleys and traditional Aymará villages. Here live the renowned Kallawaya healers who employ a blend of herbs and magic to cure ailments. This area also includes the Área Protegida Apolobamba (formerly Parque Nacional Ulla Ulla), a vicuña reserve abutting the Peruvian border. Access to this region is difficult – and often uncomfortable – but the lonely landscapes, looming peaks and wonderful trekking possibilities make it worthwhile for an increasing number of visitors.

The wild and even-less-visited Cordillera Quimsa Cruz, the beautifully glaciated southern outlier of the Cordillera Real, also holds promise as a trekking and mountaineering destination. It has long been a major tin-mining area, but only recently has it been discovered by anyone else.

To the north of the Cordilleras, the misty, jungle-filled valleys and gorges, or 'Yungas,' descend dramatically toward the Amazon Basin, forming a distinct natural division between the cold, barren Altiplano and northern Bolivia's rain-forested lowlands. The Yungas is composed of two provinces in La Paz Department, Nor and Sud Yungas (oddly, most of Sud Yungas lies well to the north of Nor Yungas!), as well as bits of other provinces. Transport, services, commerce and administration focus on Coroico and Chulumani, while such outlying towns as Yanacachi, Sorata, Caranavi and Guanay function as regional commercial centers.

The Yungas' physical beauty is astonishing, and although the hot, humid and rainy climate may induce lethargy, it's nevertheless more agreeable to most people than that of the chilly Altiplano. Winter rains are gentle, and the heavy rains occur mainly between November and March. The average year-round temperature hovers around 18°C, but summer daytime temperatures in the 30s aren't uncommon, especially in the Alto Beni. As a result, the region provides a balmy lowland retreat for chilled highlanders, and is also a favorite of foreign travelers.

History

The first settlers of the Yungas were inspired by economic opportunity. In the days of the Inca empire, gold was discovered in the valleys of the Río Tipuani and Río Mapiri, and the gold-crazed Spanish immediately got in on the act. To enrich the royal treasury, they forced local people to labor for them along the Yungas streams, and the region became one of the continent's most prolific sources of gold. Today, the rivers of the lower Yungas are being ravaged by hordes of wildcat prospectors as well as a growing number of multinational mining concerns that have apparently perfected the art of large-scale environmental devastation. A distressing side effect is water pollution from the mercury used to recover fine particles from gold-bearing sediment; in parts of Brazil, the water pollution is so extensive it poses a major health hazard and could also affect northern Bolivia.

Agriculture has also played a part in the development of the Yungas. Today, most of the farmland in the Yungas occupies the intermediate altitudes, roughly between 600m and 1800m. Sugar, citrus fruits, bananas and coffee are grown in sufficient quantities to supply the highlands with these products, and transport is plentiful even if the route is difficult. The area centered on the village of Coripata and extending south toward Chulumani is also major coca-producing country. The sweet Yungas coca is mostly consumed locally, while leaves from the Chapare region farther east generally serve more infamous purposes.

Unfortunately, Yungas coca is also coming under fire and is slated to be the target of an upcoming eradication scheme, jointly promoted and financed by the Bolivian government and foreign-sponsored (mainly US) programs. It's only hoped that this lovely region will be able to avoid the unrest and violence suffered by the Chapare region since eradication programs first came on line in the early 1990s.

THE CORDILLERAS & YUNGAS

TREKS
1 Curva to Pelechuco Trek
2 Mapiri Trail
3 Illampu Circuit
4 El Camino del Oro
5 La Cumbre to Coroico Trek
6 Taquesi Trek
7 Yunga Cruz Trek
8 Mina Caracoles to Viloco Trek

CORDILLERAS & YUNGAS

LA CUMBRE TO COROICO (CHORO) TREK

The La Cumbre to Coroico (or Choro) trek, northeast of La Paz, is now Bolivia's premier hike. It begins at La Cumbre, the highest point on the La Paz-Coroico highway, and climbs to Abra Chucura (Chucura Pass) at 4859m before descending 3250m into the steaming Yungas to the village of Chairo. Along the route, you'll note distinct differences in the people and their dress, herds, crops and dwellings.

Energetic hikers can finish the trek in two days, but it's more comfortably done in

The World's Most Dangerous Road

Yes, it is now confirmed: The road between La Paz and Coroico has been officially dubbed 'The World's Most Dangerous Road,' and given the number of fatal accidents that occur on it, the moniker is well deserved. Despite the number of apparently daring (and, some would say, lucky) readers who've written to complain that I've exaggerated the dangers of this route, an average of 26 vehicles per year disappears over the edge into the great abyss – that's one every two weeks – and a report from the Inter-American Development Bank listed it as the most risky route on the planet.

Those up for an adrenaline rush will be in their element, but if you're unnerved by a gravel track just 3.2m wide – just enough for one vehicle – sheer 1000m drop-offs, hulking rock overhangs and waterfalls that spill across and erode the highway, your best bet is to bury your head and not look until it's over. Conventional wisdom asserts that minibuses are safer than the larger camiones or buses.

The trip starts off innocuously enough. Upon leaving La Paz to cross La Cumbre, you'll notice a most curious phenomenon: Dogs stand like sentinels at 100m intervals, presumably awaiting handouts. Camión drivers feed them in the hope that the achachilas (ancestor spirits who dwell in the high peaks) will encourage gravity to be merciful during their trip down. At La Cumbre, drivers also perform a cha'lla for the apus (ambient mountain spirits) and achachilas, sprinkling the vehicle's tires with alcohol or methylated spirits before beginning the descent.

A number of crosses – described as 'Bolivian Caution signs' – line the way and testify to the frequency of vehicular tragedies. The most renowned took place on July 24, 1983, when driver Carlos Pizarroso Inde drove his camión over the precipice, killing himself and more than 100 passengers. It was the worst accident in the history of Bolivian transport.

Accidents along this route stem from several causes. Drunken driving is probably the most prevalent, followed by carelessness and disputes for the right of way when passing oncoming traffic. However, these human weaknesses pale in comparison to the undeniable weakness of the soil beneath the precarious turnouts that must be used by downhill traffic. In early 1999, an attempt was made to mitigate the dangers by allowing only downhill traffic in the morning and uphill traffic in the afternoon. However, Yungas residents complained that it limited access to their supplies and their markets, and the plan was scrapped after only a few months, despite a drastic drop in fatal accidents on the road.

Largely owing to general international dissatisfaction with such safety hazards, this road is currently being replaced by a new route on the opposite wall of the valley, thanks to a loan of US$120 million from the Inter-American Development Bank. However, the additional costs involved in tunnel building (US$28 million) to connect the two completed ends of the road have delayed its opening for at least several years, so for now, the Yungas road follows the same old unnerving route.

The good news is that the risks of traveling from La Paz to Coroico and beyond are balanced by some of South America's most rewarding vertical scenery. Those who prefer to remain under their own power all the way down (with only a little help from gravity) might want to hike the La Cumbre to Coroico Trek or attempt it on a mountain bike (see Getting There & Away in Coroico, later in this chapter).

Note: Although Bolivian traffic normally keeps to the right, downhill traffic on the Yungas road passes on the outside, whether that's the right or the left side of the road. That is, vehicles heading downhill must maneuver onto the sliver-like turnout ledges bordering the big drop and wait while uphill traffic squeezes past, hugging the inside wall. In fact, this makes sense, as it ensures that the risk is taken by the driver with the best possible view of the outside tires.

three days, and many people allot even more time to appreciate the incredible variety of landforms and vegetation across the various altitude zones.

Prepare for a range of climates. On the first day you'll need winter gear, but on the second and third days, it will be peeled off layer by layer. For the lower trail, light cotton trousers or something similar will protect your legs from sharp vegetation and biting insects.

Dangers & Annoyances

Over the past decade, this route has seen a marked increase in begging, which is more of an annoyance than anything else. Fortunately, the incidence of robbery has now declined greatly, but petty theft is still a possibility, so it's wise to camp out of sight if possible and not leave anything outside your tent. Most reported thefts seem to occur between Achura and Choro.

Organized Tours

A growing number of companies offer organized treks along this route for very reasonable prices. Most include meals, guides and camping equipment, and some also include the services of pack animals or porters. For suggestions, see Organized Tours in the Getting Around chapter.

Access

The La Cumbre to Coroico trek is easy to access and follow. From the Villa Fátima area of La Paz, take any Yungas-bound camión, bus or minibus. If there's space (Yungas-bound passengers naturally take first priority), you'll pay US$1 in a bus or minibus or US$0.75 in a camión to be dropped at La Cumbre, the high point of the Yungas road, where the trek begins.

The road climbs steeply out of Villa Fátima, and less than an hour out of La Paz at the 4725m crest of the La Paz-Yungas road is La Cumbre, marked by a statue of Christ. This is the trailhead. For the best chance of good clear views of the stunning scenery, start as early as possible, before the mist rises out of the Yungas.

The Route

From the statue of Christ, follow a well-defined track to your left for about 1km. There you should turn off onto the smaller track that turns right and passes between two small ponds. Follow it up the hill until it curves to the left and begins to lose altitude.

At this point, follow the light track leading up the gravelly hill to your right and through an obvious notch in the barren hill before you. This is Abra Chucura, and from here, the trail trends downhill all the way to its end at Chairo. At the high point is a curious pile of stones called Apacheta Chucura. For centuries, travelers have marked their passing by tossing a stone atop it (preferably one that has been carried from a lower elevation) as an offering to the mountain apus. An hour below the abra lie the remains of a *tambo* (wayside inn) dating from Inca times.

The best first-night campsites are found along the river, an hour's walk below the village of Achura (also known as Chucura). Tentless travelers can ask the schoolteacher about accommodations in the school, which should be about US$1 per person. If an 'official' appears later and demands a tribute for village 'hospitality,' tell them you've already agreed on a price and that the matter should be taken up with the schoolteacher. At Cha'llapampa, between Achura and Choro, Señora Juana has established a campsite (US$1 per person) and basic guest accommodations in a smoky and sooty little hut for US$1.50 per person.

Above Choro, many stretches of the trail consist of pre-Columbian paving, which is at once beautiful and difficult to negotiate, especially when it's wet. Near the bridge in Choro, Doña Rosalia sells beer, soda and biscuits, and has beds for US$1. Unfortunately, the river crossing at Choro is an uncertainty; a 'sturdy' suspension bridge was destroyed in a flood in the late 1980s, and after several twig-and-vine structures also headed downstream, a tenuous cable-and-pulley contraption was installed to ferry people and cargo across the river. Subsequent bridges have also proven less than

LA CUMBRE TO COROICO TREK

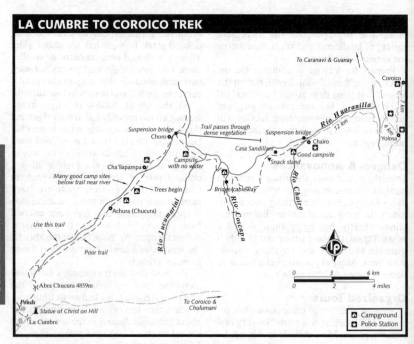

reliable, so depending on your timing, you may need to choose between a precarious bridge or that cable crossing, which will cost whatever the folks at Choro want to charge.

Past the crossing, bear left. After a few meters, the route begins to climb steeply to the ridge above town, then enters dense trail-swallowing vegetation. There are several dry campsites between this point and Chairo, but you'll have to carry water from elsewhere. Because of security risks, it's wise to set up camp as far from Choro as possible.

From the ridge above Choro, the trail plunges and climbs alternately from sunny hillsides to vegetation-choked valleys, crossing streams and waterfalls. You'll have to ford the Río Jucumarini, which may be rather intimidating in the wet season; the steep gradient necessitates crossing with a good, stout stick and careful steps. Farther along, the trail crosses the deep gorge of the Río Coscapa, where you can choose between

a cableway (US$1 to US$2) or a very treacherous suspension bridge (which may well have collapsed by the time you read this).

Near the trail's end, about 2½ hours from Chairo, you'll encounter the curious Casa Sandillani, a Japanese-style home surrounded by beautifully manicured gardens. The friendly owner, Mr Tamiji Hanamura de Furio, is full of trail news and enjoys having visitors stop by to chat and sign his guestbook. He's happy to let you camp in his garden; you may want to bring some stamps or postcards from home to augment his now extensive collections. In this area, you'll also encounter several snack and soft-drink stalls set up by enterprising locals for hungry and thirsty hikers.

From Casa Sandillani, it's an easy 7km downhill to Chairo; here you can sleep on the verandah of the school or camp near the trail across the suspension bridge. Meals and supplies are available from the friendly shop on the main street.

Camiones and other intermittent traffic leaves from Chairo to Yolosa or Coroico (if the road hasn't been cut by mud, falling boulders or landslips, as it frequently is), but don't count on hitching. The relatively level 12km walk from Chairo to the highway isn't difficult, but it does involve a river ford that can be especially worrying after rain. For when the water is too high, there is a spindly suspension bridge that's just as dangerous as the river crossing. Minibuses for the 23km to Coroico now charge around US$50 per group.

Once on the main road, it's easy to find a camión to Yolosa, 4km away (7km from Coroico). There's also lots of traffic heading either uphill to La Paz or down toward Caranavi, Guanay and the Amazon lowlands.

YOLOSA

Traveling between La Paz and the Beni – or from anywhere to Coroico – you'll pass through Yolosa, which guards the Coroico road junction. The tranca at Yolosa closes between 1 and 5 am, impeding overnight traffic between the Yungas and La Paz. Pickup trucks awaiting passengers to Coroico (10 minutes, US$0.40) line up at the corner by the police checkpoint.

Places to Stay & Eat

If you're planted overnight here, you can crash at *Alojamiento El Conquistador*, which charges US$1.50 per person. Rows of stalls along the street sell inexpensive snacks, *almuerzos* (set lunches) and *cenas* (set dinners) to passing truckers. There's also the slightly more formal *Spaguetti Restaurant*, which doesn't serve spaghetti, but cooks up roughly the same stuff as the cheaper food stalls outside.

Near Chairo, and about 5km from the end of the La Cumbre to Coroico trek, is the *Río Selva Resort* (☎ 02-411561, 412281 or 411818; fax 02-411754; rioselva@ d-concepts.com; Calle Romecín Campos 696, Sopocachi, La Paz), a posh five-star place, right on the riverside. Rooms cost US$57 to US$70, and cabañas for up to six people cost from US$100 to US$110. Peripheral amenities include racquetball

courts, aerobics, a sauna and a swimming pool. Three-day river rafting packages cost from US$155 to US$220, including two nights accommodation, four meals and one day's rafting on the Río Huarinilla; you can choose from three runs, which are ranked from beginner to expert. The resort also organizes four-day trekking packages along the Choro Trail (US$165 to US$225), with a big finish at the resort and transport back to La Paz. See the website www.rioselva.com.

El Camino de las Cascadas

An adventurous reader has recently reported on an alternative walking route past the worst of the Yungas road:

I did the Camino de las Cascadas from the Chuspipata truck stop to Yolosa. It's an easy trek, following an old 4WD route built by Paraguayan POWs during Bolivia's war with that country. You can't get lost, but you should probably bring a machete, as it was pretty overgrown. In any case, you'll have a good 'Look-at-me-I'm-in-the-jungle-with-a-machete' sort of experience. There are countless waterfalls along this route, including the 100m monster that the trail curls above.

Begin by getting off the La Paz to Coroico transport at Chuspipata and follow the old 4WD track downhill. Past the power station the road begins to be overgrown. For the next two to three days, the track, cut into the hillside (in one 30m stretch, it's quite exposed but still passable), gradually loses altitude, then crosses a ridge into the valley above Yolosa. When the town is clearly visible below, you can cut down through the fields and save several hours.

You can't get lost, there was no trash along the trail, and it was the only place in the Yungas where I heard monkeys in the trees.

Rafting & Kayaking in Bolivia

One of Bolivia's greatest secrets is the number of white-water rivers that drain the eastern slopes of the Andes between the Cordillera Apolobamba and the Chapare. Here, thousands of rivers and streams await, providing thrilling first descents for avid rafters and kayakers. Although access will normally require long drives and/or treks – and considerable expense – several fine rivers are relatively accessible.

Organizing rafting and kayaking trips would prove difficult for individual travelers, but most La Paz tour agencies can organize day trips on the Río Coroico and Río Huarinilla. For real adventure trips – which will require a great deal of planning and expense – a good operator to use is Explore Bolivia (see Organized Tours in the Getting There & Away chapter for contact details). Within Bolivia, their trips can be organized through América Tours, in La Paz (see Organized Tours in the Getting Around chapter).

Río Coroico

The most convenient rafting river to La Paz is the Río Coroico, which flows through the Nor Yungas about three hours from town. This pool-drop river is the country's most popular commercially rafted river, with well over 30 rapids, great surfing holes, dramatic drops and challenging technical maneuvers (most of these can be scouted from the river and from several bridges). It alternates between calm pools and 50m to 900m rapids, with sharp bends, boils, mean holes, undercurrents, sharp rocks and rather treacherous undercuts. The white water normally ranges from Class II to IV, but may approach Class V during periods of high water (when it becomes too dangerous to raft). Although trips run year-round, conditions are normally optimal from mid-March to mid-November. There are few spots to take out and rest, so stay focused and be prepared for quick surprises.

Access is from the highway between Yolosa and Caranavi; the best put-ins lie about 20 minutes north of Yolosa and near the confluence with the Río Santa Bárbara, 50 minutes by road north of Yolosa. Just look for any track that winds down from the road toward the river and find one that provides suitable access. Trips average three to five hours. For the take-out, look on the river right for a devastated steel bridge (destroyed in a 1998 flood) across a normally diminutive creek. Don't miss it, because the road stays high above steep, jungled and practically unclimbable slopes, and it's a long, long way to the next possible exit.

Río Huarinilla

The Río Huarinilla flows from Huayna Potosí and Tiquimani down into the Yungas to meet the Río Coroico near Yolosa, and is best accessed from Chairo, at the end of the La Cumbre to Coroico trek. Although it's normally Class II and III, high water can swell it into a much more challenging Class IV to V. The full-day trip is best suited to kayaks and narrow paddle rafts. The new Yungas Highway will pass right by the take-out at the confluence of the Ríos Huarinilla and Coroico.

Río Unduavi

The road to Chulumani follows part of another good white-water river, the Río Unduavi. The upper section ranges from essentially unnavigable Class V to VI, with steep chutes, powerful currents, large boulder gardens, blind corners and waterfalls. Beyond this section, it mellows out into some challenging Class IV white water followed by Class II and III rapids. Access is limited, but the Chulumani road does offer several put-ins and take-outs. The best access points have been left by construction crews who've mined the riverbanks for sand and gravel. A good take-out point is Puente Villa, which lies three to four hours below the best put-ins.

Rafting & Kayaking in Bolivia

Río Tuichi

Parque Nacional Madidi is one of the world's most diverse and magical spots, encompassing everything from the Andean glaciers to the Amazon rain forest, and right through its heart flows the wild Río Tuichi, which features rapids up to Class V. From its source high in the Cordillera Apolobamba, it flows southeastward through some of South America's wildest terrain until it meets with the great Río Beni in the vast Amazonian rain forests.

Access isn't straightforward, but it's worth the effort if you're up for 10 to 14 adventurous days. The trip to the Tuichi is divided into three parts: the drive, the trek and the river-running itself.

The first day's drive takes you from La Paz to the Río Kamata hot springs in the Cordillera Apolobamba. From there, you follow the road down into the Yungas, passing jungled mountains, misty waterfalls and powerful white-water rivers. This section requires low-range 4WD, good strong tires and excellent driving skills. Once at Santa Cruz del Valle Ameno, beyond Apolo, you'll have to travel for three days on foot – with horses or mules to carry the gear – along muddy, rocky trails used by rubber-tappers a century ago. Note that this stretch also includes several thigh-deep stream crossings. From a prominent plateau, the track continues over grass-covered ridges and then down desert slopes to the put-in site on the Río Tuichi.

The Tuichi is characteristically a pool-drop river, with powerful rapids and numerous obstacles, requiring technical skills to negotiate. From the put-in, the river narrows, then opens up before narrowing again and slipping into the wild Cañón de San Pedro. From this point, you're in for three days of fast water, sharp bends, steep, powerful rapids and keeper holes; this stretch includes countless Class IV rapids and two Class V's, which have proven fatal to inexperienced loggers and locals who've underestimated their power. Any mistakes are rewarded by a long, frightening swim in roiling waters.

Along the way you'll see lots of howler and spider monkeys and a myriad of tropical bird species, as well as collared peccaries, capybaras and tapirs, and perhaps even a jaguar (or at least jaguar tracks).

Beyond the canyons, the Tuichi mellows out into Class II and III waters, then widens and slows as it enters flatter rain-forested country. It's wise to arrange to be met by a motorboat in San José de Uchupiamonas to take you back to civilization. En route, be sure to stop off at Chalalán (see the Amazon Basin chapter) for a few days of relaxing before heading three hours downstream to Rurrenabaque.

Chapare

The Chapare region offers great white water, with numerous penetration-standard trips awaiting real adventurers. The terrain is similar to the Yungas, but with lower elevations, a warmer climate and great white water. There are few roads, however, so access to the best rivers is quite difficult and will almost certainly require lots of jungle-bashing.

COROICO

☎ 0811

Serene little Coroico, the Nor Yungas provincial capital, sits at the pleasantly tropical altitude of 1750m. Perched aerie-like on the shoulder of Cerro Uchumachi, it commands a far-ranging view across forested canyons, cloud-wreathed mountain peaks, patchwork agricultural lands, citrus orchards, coffee plantations and dozens of small settlements. When the weather clears, the view stretches to the snow-covered summits of Mururata, Huayna Potosí and Tiquimani, high in the Cordillera Real. The

name is derived from *coryguayco*, which is Quechua for 'golden hill.'

The town's most appealing attraction is its tranquility and slow pace, which allow plenty of time for relaxing, swimming, lying in the sun or walking in the surrounding hills. Coroico stays relatively warm year-round, but summer storms can bring some mighty downpours. Because of its ridgetop position, fog is common, especially in the afternoon, when it rises from the deep valleys and swirls up through the streets and over the rooftops.

Although Coroico seems just perfect for lounging by the swimming pool and

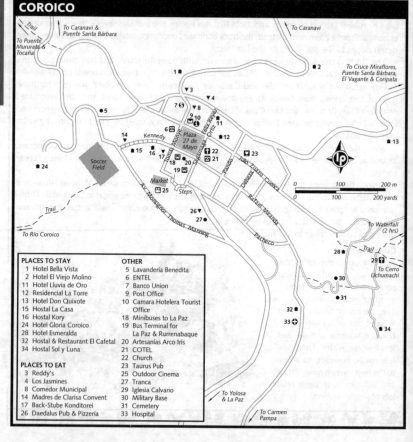

COROICO

To Caranavi & Puente Santa Bárbara
To Caranavi
To Puente Mururata & Tocaña
To Cruce Miraflores, Puente Santa Bárbara, El Vagante & Coripata
Trail
Soccer Field
Kennedy
Plaza 27 de Mayo
Market
Steps
Trail
To Río Coroico
To Waterfall (2 hrs)
To Cerro Uchumachi
Trail
To Yolosa & La Paz
To Carmen Pampa

0   100   200 m
0   100   200 yards

PLACES TO STAY
1 Hotel Bella Vista
2 Hotel El Viejo Molino
11 Hotel Lluvia de Oro
12 Residencial La Torre
13 Hotel Don Quixote
15 Hostal La Casa
16 Hostal Kory
24 Hotel Gloria Coroico
28 Hotel Esmeralda
32 Hotel & Restaurant El Cafetal
34 Hostal Sol y Luna

PLACES TO EAT
3 Reddy's
4 Los Jasmines
8 Comedor Municipal
14 Madres de Clarisa Convent
17 Back-Stube Konditorei
26 Daedalus Pub & Pizzeria

OTHER
5 Lavandería Benedita
6 ENTEL
7 Banco Union
9 Post Office
10 Camara Hotelera Tourist Office
18 Minibuses to La Paz
19 Bus Terminal for La Paz & Rurrenabaque
20 Artesanías Arco Irís
21 COTEL
22 Church
23 Taurus Pub
25 Outdoor Cinema
27 Tranca
29 Iglesia Calvario
30 Military Base
31 Cemetery
33 Hospital

relaxing, be aware that it is inhabited by some especially vicious biting insects. While they don't carry malaria, the bites itch for days (or weeks!), so don't forget the repellent.

Information

The Cámara Hotelera information office on the north side of the plaza distributes a useful town map, as well as hotel and restaurant brochures. They can also provide basic information on walks and sites of interest.

Money You can change traveler's checks at the Hotel Esmeralda or Hotel Gloria Coroico, and at several other businesses around town. The Banco Unión, opposite the Comedor Municipal, also changes cash and traveler's checks.

Post & Communications Officially, the post office is open Tuesday to Saturday from 8 am to noon and 2 to 6 pm, but in fact, it's often closed for no apparent reason.

The ENTEL office on the plaza can make direct-dial connections anywhere in the world, and is open from 8 am to 10 pm daily. The local telephone network, COTEL, keeps these same hours, and enables you to phone La Paz at local call rates.

Laundry Cleaning services are available at Lavandería Benedita (Avenida Monsignor Thomas Manning), near the Hotel Gloria Coroico; look for the very small sign.

Hiking

Women especially should avoid hiking alone in this area, as there have been incidents, including one well-publicized disappearance. It can get extremely hot, so carry plenty of water.

Cerro Uchumachi For a good panoramic view of Coroico and the surrounding countryside, walk up to the Iglesia Calvario (Calvario Church) on the hill. From the red and white antenna, a track climbs for about 30 minutes, then enters a dense woodland dotted with voodoo images used in local *hechicería* (traditional Aymará witchcraft –

don't touch them!). From here, you can keep climbing up the ridge through intermittent woodlands right to the summit of the extinct crater of Cerro Uchumachi. Wait for a sunny day, however, or the spectacular view will be irrelevant.

Waterfall Walk Alternatively, turn left at Iglesia Calvario and follow the trail that contours along the flowery hillside, following an aqueduct and plunging occasionally into mini rain forests. After 5km – about two hours – you'll reach a waterfall with lovely views down the valley. Since the stream supplies water to the picturesque village below, bathing is forbidden. If you climb higher up, you'll reach two more waterfalls. Wear sturdy shoes and long trousers, as the track is overgrown in places.

Río Coroico The tracks leading down to the Río Coroico are more complicated and difficult to follow because part of the trip involves road walking. The easiest one leads from the northwest corner of the plaza, down the steps, and across the soccer field. From the northwest corner of the field, the track that winds downhill will take you to the main road at Yolosita, 9km from Yolosa toward Caranavi. Turn right on the road and continue along it until you reach Puente Mururata, which features some lovely swimming holes just upstream from the bridge.

You can also continue walking up to the African-Bolivian village of Tocaña. Cross Puente Mururata and follow the road for about 500m to the Tocaña track, which turns off to the left. The village is a winding 2.5km uphill from there.

For this hike you'll need long trousers and insect repellent against the nasty yellow flies that can make your life miserable for several days after an encounter. On the brighter side of the insect world are the blue morphos and other butterfly species that are frequently observed here. Watch also for toucans and other colorful tropical birds.

El Vagante A good day's walk will take you to El Vagante, an area of natural stone swimming holes in the Río Santa Bárbara.

Downhill Thrills in the Cordillera Real

The vertical scenery in the spectacular Cordillera Real will prove a sort of nirvana for mountain bikers who prefer sitting back and letting gravity do the work! The following descriptions of the most prominent rides should start your wheels spinning. For further information on mountain biking in Bolivia, as well as choosing an operator, see Activities in the Facts for the Visitor chapter.

La Cumbre to Coroico

Quite deservedly, this ride is Bolivia's most popular, made so by travelers wishing to combine a long and thrilling downhill run with a very appealing destination. It features an incredible range of scenery and a spectacular 3600m descent from the Altiplano, down between snowcapped peaks into the steaming Yungas. Part of the route follows the dramatic and scenic Yungas Highway, which in 1995 the Inter-American Development Bank deemed The World's Most Dangerous Road (see boxed text earlier in this chapter). After this thrilling day trip, riders can relax poolside in the quiet Yungas town of Coroico. From here, it's possible to continue to Rurrenabaque, in the Amazon Lowlands, or return to La Paz on public transport.

For information on reaching La Cumbre from La Paz, see Getting There & Away under the La Cumbre to Coroico Trek, earlier in this chapter.

Sorata

Sorata is not only Bolivia's 'Trekking Capital,' but it's also saturated with mountain-biking opportunities, and the fun begins with a descent into the town from the mountains astride Lake Titicaca. From La Paz, take a Sorata-bound bus to the pass north of Achacachi and then choose either the main road or any of the downhill routes along unpaved roads. Most routes eventually lead to Sorata – or at least in view of it (but some don't, so it's wise to have a map). Throughout the ride you're presented with superb views of towering snowcapped peaks, plunging valleys and tiny rural villages.

Zongo Valley

This ride includes a descent from the base of spectacular 6088m Huayna Potosí, past Zongo Dam, and then along a fun and dramatic 40km, 3600m descent into the lush and steaming Yungas. This is a dead-end road that lacks a great destination at its finish, but there's little vehicular traffic, making it more suitable for nervous beginners or intrepid speed demons than the Coroico ride. For further information, including access to the start of this route, see Milluni & the Zongo Valley, in the La Paz chapter.

Chacaltaya to La Paz

This trip begins with a drive up to the world's highest developed ski slope at 5345m. After taking in the incredible view across the Cordillera Real, riders descend along abandoned mine roads. Along the way, you'll have marvelous vistas across the mountain ranges, the Altiplano and the city of La Paz, nestling in the bottom of the Choqueyapu canyon. This route is nearly all downhill, descending over 2000m from Chacaltaya back to central La Paz.

For more on Chacaltaya, including access from La Paz, see the La Paz chapter.

Follow the road toward Coripata to Cruce Miraflores, 750m beyond the Hotel Don Quijote. Here you should turn left at a fork in the road and head steeply downhill past Hacienda Miraflores; at the second fork, bear right (the left fork goes to Santa Ana).

After two hours along this route, which features a stretch with some pre-Columbian terraces, you'll reach a cement bridge. Turn right before the bridge and follow the river downstream for 20 minutes to a series of natural swimming holes and waterfalls. The water isn't drinkable, so carry water or purification tablets – and bear in mind that the return route is uphill all the way!

Organized Tours

For organized walks and trips into the Coroico hinterlands, contact Martín Carranza (☎ 0792-1014), who has a 4WD and speaks some English. Other individuals also offer guided walking tours; watch for their notices in the tourist-oriented cafés and the ENTEL office.

Two French guys, Philippe and Ivan (mobile ☎ 019-20104), conduct daylong white-water rafting trips for US$35 per person, with a minimum of five people. El Relincho (019-23814) offers guided horseback riding to the waterfalls and Carmen Pampa for US$6 per hour, but don't accept horses that appear to be less than fit and healthy.

Places to Stay

Budget On weekends from June to August, hotels are often booked out. Although it's possible to make advance reservations, there's no guarantee that all hotels will honor them. On holiday weekends, prices may increase by as much as 100%, but on Mondays, the town utterly closes down and most shops and restaurants don't reopen until Tuesday morning.

Secluded camp spots may be found near the church on the hill above town. The cheapest acceptable accommodations are in the clean and sunny *Residencial la Torre*, which charges US$2.50 per person. *Hostal & Restaurant El Cafetal*, which includes a superb French eatery, also has several clean, secure rooms with good views and access to the swimming pool and hammocks for US$4 per person.

Although its standards are sliding downhill, the *Hotel Lluvia de Oro* just hangs in there with its sundeck, patio, green pool, mediocre restaurant and faded garden. Rooms cost US$4 per person (US$6 with private bath).

One of Bolivia's most appealing backpackers' haunts is the *Hotel Esmeralda* (☎ 6434; fax 6017; esmeralda@latinwide.com),

a family-run place that sits high in the clouds about 300m from the center. Rooms, some of which afford spectacular views, cost anywhere from US$7 to US$18 per person. The cheaper rooms lack private baths, but the pricing is based on a somewhat complicated assessment of the view (as well as, one might suspect, the phases of the moon). Peripheral amenities include a pool, hammocks, tropical garden, video lounge, email and Internet access (US$3.25 per hour) and a sunny patio overlooking the universe. If you'd rather not climb the hill with luggage, look around the plaza for their free pickup jeep; if they aren't there, phone from the ENTEL office, and they'll pick you up. Note that they hold reservations only until 3 pm. For more information, see their website www.latinwide.com/esmeralda/.

The popular and clean *Hostal Kory* (☎ 015-64050) – the name means 'gold' in Quechua – is also a good bet. Singles/doubles with shared baths cost US$5/8, doubles with private baths cost US$6.50 per person, and there's a large clean swimming pool (nonguests can use it for US$1 per person). The fantastic view from the deck takes in everything from the valleys to the Cordillera peaks. To book from La Paz, call ☎ 02-431311 or fax 02-431234.

The *Hostal La Casa*, down the stairs from the Hostal Kory, is as clean and tidy as you'd expect from a German-run establishment. They have a few small rooms with shared/private baths for US$3.50/4 per person, including use of the swimming pool. Email and Internet access costs US$3.25 per hour.

Another German-run favorite is the friendly and quiet *Hostal Sol y Luna* (mobile ☎ 015-61626), which occupies an extensive and luxuriant garden setting high on the hillside, a 20-minute walk from town (follow the road to Hotel Esmeralda and watch for the small painted sun and moon signs, which indicate the way). Sol y Luna has a range of accommodations, from tent sites (US$2 per person) and basic singles/doubles in the 'White House' for US$5/8 to lovely self-contained cabañas for US$5 to US$10 per person. Plus points include the novel – if a bit temperamental – open-air showers, the diminutive swimming pool, the breezy vegetarian restaurant, inviting hammocks, and the homegrown, home-roasted Yungas coffee. For US$12, owner Sigrid Fronius will provide 50 minutes of Japanese massage (nirvana for weary bones coming off the La Cumbre to Coroico trek or a downhill mountain bike ride!). To book from La Paz, contact Chuquiago Turismo (☎ 02-362099; fax 02-359227).

Mid-Range Downhill from town, just below the soccer fields, is the distinctive red-roofed *Hotel Gloria Coroico* (☎ /fax 6020; mobile ☎ 019-29327; glocoroi@ceibo.entel-net.bo)*, with some of the finest views in Coroico. Since it was recently renovated, it boasts a number of pleasant lounges, as well as a video room and a games room with billiards and Ping-Pong tables. While the high ceilings and grandiose halls foster a colonial ambience, it's animated only on weekends. Singles/doubles with shared baths cost US$10/20; with private baths, US$15/26. All rates include a continental breakfast, and other meals are available from the attached restaurant. Book ahead if you want a double bed.

The friendly and good-value *Hotel Don Quijote* (☎ 6007), 1km from the plaza, is popular with Bolivians. It looks more expensive than it is and makes an excellent alternative to staying in town. Ultra-clean single/double rooms with all the amenities of a solid mid-range option – including a nice pool and breakfast – cost only US$12/16. In La Paz, you can book at ☎ 360007 or 721254.

The sparkling new *Bella Vista* (mobile ☎ 015-69237) lacks a swimming pool, but features modern clean rooms and some stunning views from the verandahs. There is also a racquetball court and some basic bicycles to rent. Singles or doubles with baths cost US$21, and singles with a shared bath cost US$5.

Top End The top end in Coroico is represented by the overpriced *Hotel El Viejo Molino* (☎/fax 6004), 1km from the center on the road toward the Rio Santa Bárbara. Standard single/double rooms with TVs and private baths cost US$50/75, including a buffet breakfast. Nominally, this includes access to the sauna and jacuzzi, which may or may not be functional, as well as the swimming pool, which may or may not be salubrious.

Places to Eat

For its size, Coroico offers a boggling variety of excellent eateries; in fact, few visitors can stick around long enough to exhaust the possibilities.

The plaza is ringed by a number of relatively inexpensive local places – *Vico's Planet*, *Uchumachi* and *Don Lucho* – all with ordinary menus, acceptable fare and a typically tropical sense of urgency and service. If you're in a rush or on a strict budget, the many food stalls around the Comedor Municipal (a market-style public dining hall) can fill the empty spaces in your stomach, but you'll need a bit of gastric stamina.

The indisputable favorite with travelers is the French-run *Hostal & Restaurant El Cafetal* (☎ 019-33979 or 015-10570), where you can enjoy an incredible meal in a verdant setting, accompanied by an inspiring view and mellow music. This little place, expertly run by Dany and Patricio Nguyen, is consistently rated by travelers as the best in all of Bolivia – and they're not far off the mark. The menu includes crêpes (how about banana with chocolate sauce?), curries, soufflés, soups, pasta, curry, sandwiches, burgers, vegetarian lasagna, superb Yungas coffee, chocolate mousse, cakes and other goodies. It's near the hospital, a 15-minute walk uphill from the town center.

Hotel Esmeralda and *Hostal Kory* also offer recommended restaurants with fantastic views. The former offers a good range of meals, including pizza and various vegetarian options. The one at Hostal Kory is now run by an Argentine chef who rustles up classy meals, including Argentine *parrillada* (barbecue) and other meat dishes for US$7 to US$9, as well as pasta and pizza.

Los Jasmines, one street north of the plaza, has an extensive menu and good food. Two notable pizzerias are *Reddy's*, just below the main plaza, and the ***Daedalus Pub & Pizzeria***. The former is also excellent for pasta dishes and cakes, and has live music on weekends. The funky ***Taurus Pub*** is fun for a drink or snack.

The ***Back-Stube Konditorei*** (mobile ☎ 019-26759), run by friendly Hans and Claudia Hellenkamp, serves excellent European-style breakfasts with Yungas coffee from 6:30 to 11:30 am. The homemade muesli and the 'Mexican' breakfast are fantastic. The rest of the day, they do unbeatable pizza, pasta, soups, omelettes, vegetarian dishes and German-style cakes and pastries. Importantly, most meals are accompanied by their incredible home-baked bread.

European cuisine is also available at the German/Bolivian-run ***Hostal La Casa*** (☎ 6024), down the stairs from the main plaza. They do a great range of breakfasts, fondues, coffee, hot chocolate, pancakes, and local or continental dishes. If you're planning on a fondue, you'll need a minimum of two people and an advance booking. A wonderful fondue bourguignonne or raclette costs only US$5 per person, including a range of salads and appetizers. Like most things in Coroico, La Casa is closed on Monday.

An extraordinary treat if you have a group – or can muster one – is the *luna llena*, an Indonesian buffet for eight to 20 people at the ***Hostal Sol y Luna*** on the hill. It costs an affordable US$3.50 per person, but must be booked a day in advance.

The ***Madres de Clarisa Convent***, opposite La Casa, is renowned for its delicious brownies, orange cakes, biscuits (chocolate, vanilla, coconut, honey and peanut butter!) and local wine and port wine. It's open from 8 am to 10 pm; knock on the door to get into the shop area.

Entertainment
Coroico's novel outdoor cinema, near the market, screens films nightly at 9 pm. Take a warm jacket and a pillow to cushion your backside on the hard benches.

Shopping
For quality handmade jewelry, visit Artesanías Arco Irís, on the plaza. It isn't cheap, but you'll find some very nice items. The plaza is increasingly frequented by itinerant South American craftspeople selling a dazzling array of cheap and novel jewelry; after a couple of laps around, you're sure to find something that catches your eye.

Getting There & Away
Bus From the barrio Villa Fátima in La Paz, buses and minibuses leave for Coroico; given the road conditions (see 'The World's Most Dangerous Road,' earlier in this chapter), minibuses are the best way to go. Most weekday departures are in the morning, starting at 7:30 am, with extra runs on weekends. Minibuses Yungueña (☎ 213513; La Paz) is experienced and reliable. From Yolosa, 7km downhill from Coroico, you can catch buses and camiones north to Guanay, Rurrenabaque and farther into Bolivian Amazonia.

Camión Camiones from La Paz to Coroico leave until mid-afternoon from the street behind the Villa Fátima gasoline station. Given the road's terrifying reputation, the US$1 saved by taking this option may not be all that economical; although most journeys end safely, the stress can be taxing!

To travel from Coroico into the Amazon Basin, you must first get to Yolosa. Drivers always stop for a snack in Yolosa, and all downhill vehicles must pass through the tranca there, so it's a good place to wait for a lift. When the roads are open, there should be no problem finding transport to Caranavi, Guanay, Rurrenabaque or La Paz.

To reach Chulumani from Coroico, head back toward La Paz and get off at Unduavi to wait for onward transport. Alternatively, you can make a trip through Bolivia's main coca-growing region: Take a camión from Coroico to Arapata, another from Arapata to Coripata, and yet another to Chulumani. It's a pleasant adventure, but don't be in too much of a hurry, and don't try it during rainy season, as this road features some of the deepest mud ever.

Walking Many people walk into the Yungas from La Cumbre, the summit of the

Yungas road, near La Paz (see La Cumbre to Coroico, earlier). It is also possible to walk the Camino de las Cascadas from Chuspipata (see 'El Camino de las Cascadas,' earlier); allow two or three days and bring a machete.

Bicycle An exhilarating yet (arguably) safe option is to mountain bike from La Paz to Coroico. Gravity Assisted Mountain Biking (see Organized Tours in the Getting Around chapter) guides safe and thrilling one-day downhill mountain-bike tours to Coroico several times weekly during the February to November high season (also see 'Downhill Thrill in the Cordillera Real,' earlier). This company uses US-made mountain bikes and provides an experienced English-speaking guide for every six bikers, as well as a support vehicle, helmets, gloves, snacks and the all-important free T-shirt.

TAQUESI TREK

Also known as the Inca Trail or Inca Road, the Taquesi trek is one of the most popular and impressive walks in the Andes. The route was used as a highway by the early Aymará, the Inca and the Spanish, and it still serves as a major route to the humid Yungas over a relatively low pass in the Cordillera Real. Nearly half the trail's 40km consists of expertly engineered pre-Inca paving, more like a highway than a walking track. The walk itself takes only 12 to 15 hours, but plan on several days owing to transport uncertainties to and from the trailheads. It's now hiked by around 5000 people annually.

Naturally, the May to October dry season is best for this trip. In the rainy season, the wet and cold combined with ankle-deep mud may contribute to a less-than-optimal experience. Since the trail's end is in the Yungas, however, plan on some rain at any time of year.

As for maps, you're in luck here, because the entire route appears on a single 1:50,000 IGM topo sheet: *Chojlla – 6044-IV*. A good source of information is the NGO known as Fundación Pueblo (☎ 413031; pueblo@ceibo.entelnet.bo), in La Paz, which supports

rural development projects and develops tourism infrastructure, thereby reducing rural poverty and increasing local economic opportunity. Currently, the group is working with villagers along the Takesi Trail to develop bridges, hikers' huts and access to well water. In Takesi and Kakapi, they've developed huts and campsites costing US$1 per person, as well as places to buy meals and soft drinks.

Access

On public transportation, your first destination will be Ventilla. A daily micro leaves La Paz (three hours, US$1.50) from the market area above Calle Sagárnaga, at the corner of Calles Rodríguez and Luis Lara. Another option for groups is to charter a minibus to the Choquekhota trailhead. Most La Paz tour agencies can organize this for you; alternatively, contact Fundación Pueblo.

You can also take an urban micro or minibus trufi from La Paz's center to Chasquipampa or Ovejuyo, then either hitch along the road or trek through the beautiful Palca Canyon (and the Valle de las Ánimas, if you like) to Palca and then to Ventilla. This will add at least one extra day to the trip, but will be a fitting run-up to the longer trek. For details, see Around La Paz in the La Paz chapter.

There are also minibus trufis going from La Paz's Calles Rodríguez and Luis Lara to Ventilla and Palca at least once daily on weekdays and several times daily on weekends. There is now a billboard announcing your arrival in Ventilla – which is little more than a road junction – that includes a rough map of the local area. Make sure the driver – and anyone else you may care to tell – knows that that's where you want to get off. Transport between Ventilla and the San Francisco mine, where the trek begins, is sparse. If you're extremely lucky, a vehicle may pass and offer a lift, but otherwise, you should probably resign yourself to paying a negotiable US$15 for a taxi or slogging four hours uphill to the trailhead.

Long-distance taxis from the taxi center near Plaza Isabél la Católica in La Paz charge about US$50 for up to four people

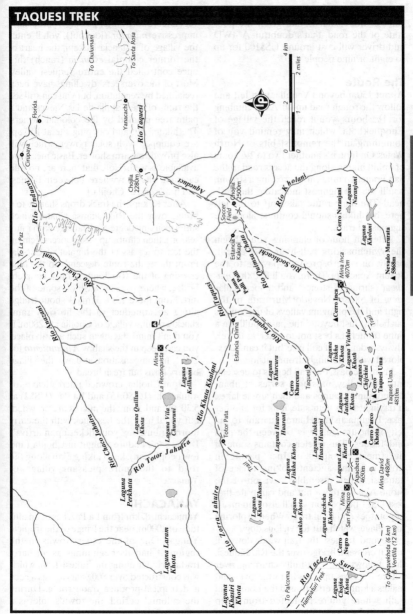

TAQUESI TREK

to the San Francisco Mine trailhead – if they can get there, that is, and given the poor state of the road, that's doubtful. A 4WD and driver will cost around US$100 for up to eight or nine people.

The Route

About 150m beyond Ventilla, turn left and follow the rough road uphill. After climbing for 1½ hours, you'll reach the village of Choquekhota, which may remind you of something in the remotest bits of North Wales. On foot, it's another two to 2½ hours of uphill hiking along the access road to the San Francisco mine; after crossing a stream, you'll see the signpost indicating the trailhead. The mine route takes off to the left here, but hikers should continue along the signposted track.

After an hour of climbing, you'll begin the switchbacking half-hour final ascent, partly on superb pre-Inca paving, to the 4650m Apacheta. There, you'll find the *apacheta* (shrine of stones) and a spectacular view of 5868m Nevado Mururata to the right and the plunging valleys of the Yungas far below. Just beyond the pass you'll see a mine tunnel; it's best not to enter, as there's always a danger of collapse, but it can be explored with a flashlight from outside.

From the pass, the trail begins to descend into the valley, passing a series of abandoned mining camps and high alpine lakes. If daylight is on your side, look for another lake, Laguna Jiskha Huara Huarani, to the left of the trail midway between the pass and Taquesi. This stretch contains some of the finest examples of Inca paving in Bolivia. At the ancient-looking village of Taquesi, which resembles a vision of the Stone Age, there's a hut and campsite that cost US$1 per person; you'll also find meals of potatoes and local trout. When exploring the village, watch out for vicious dogs.

Beyond Taquesi, the trail winds downhill until it crosses a bridge over the Río Taquesi, then follows the beautifully churning river before it moves upslope from the river and makes a long traverse around the Loma Palli Palli, where you're protected from steep drop-offs by a pre-Columbian wall. As you descend, the country becomes increasingly vegetated. Shortly after passing a particularly impressive *mirador* (lookout), you'll enter the village of Estancia Kakapi, the heart of the former colonial *estancia* (ranch) that once controlled the entire Taquesi valley. Most of the overseers' dwellings have been reclaimed by vegetation, but you can still see the ruins of the Capilla de las Nieves and a palm tree planted by the colonial owners. The hikers' hut and camping site at Kakapi are equipped with solar power, which will also provide a warm shower. Basic meals are available as well. (Note that there are no wild camping sites anywhere between Taquesi and trail's end at Chojlla.)

After Kakapi, the track drops sharply to a bridge over the Río Quimsa Chata (which suffers varying degrees of damage each rainy season), then climbs up past a soccer field on the left to a pass at the hamlet of Chojila. From there, the route descends to the final crossing of the Río Taquesi, on a concrete bridge, where you can wash off some of the dirt. From there, it's a 3km, 1½-hour trudge along an aqueduct to the horridly ramshackle mining village of Chojlla at 2280m. If you don't mind staying in such a drab place, you can sleep in the shabby *Alojamiento* for US$1. In compensation, at dawn, the village bakery turns out fresh bread.

From Chojlla, crowded micros leave for Yanacachi (US$0.15) and La Paz (US$2) at 5:30 am and 1 pm; the micros are crowded, but you'll have the best luck with the early morning bus; buy your ticket upon arrival! If you can't endure a night in Chojlla (and few people can), keep hiking 5km along the road to the more pleasant village of Yanacachi.

YANACACHI

Yanacachi, 87km from La Paz, lies at an altitude of 2000m, near the fringe of the tropical Yungas. One of the oldest towns in the region, it had its beginnings as an early trading center along the Takesi Trail, which was constructed over 800 years ago as a coca and tropical-produce trade route. During the colonial period, the town's role as a commercial center expanded as hacienda owners settled there. By 1522, they'd already constructed the Iglesia de Santa Bárbara, which is the oldest existing church in the Yungas. The bells in the tower date from 1735 and 1755, and in the lower part of town you can still see traces of the colonial heritage in the thick stone walls and colonial balconies.

Modern amenities include a COTEL telephone office on the plaza, as well as a health clinic. For information, contact Fundación Pueblo, which can help you with trekking and transportation information, as well as guides and mule hire.

Places to Stay & Eat
The recommended place to stay is *Alojamiento Don Tomás*, which has a pool and pleasant gardens. You'll pay US$2.75 per person. The more comfortable *Hotel San Carlos* charges US$6 per person. Both places serve food, and there are also quite a few pensiones on the plaza. A couple of recommended ones are *Don Edgar* and *Doña Yolla*.

Getting There & Away
Buses leave Mina Chojlla for La Paz (US$2) daily at 5:30 am and 1 pm and pass through Yanacachi, stopping at the Hotel San Carlos at 6 am and 1:30 pm. You can buy the tickets in Chojlla, and there's usually little problem getting a seat on the morning bus. Minibuses to La Paz (US$2) leave the plaza in Yanacachi on Friday and Sunday at 2 pm and on Monday at 5 pm. For information on space or tickets, see Doña Yolla at her pensión on the plaza. If you're unable to find space or you wish to go to Chulumani, you can walk 30 minutes along the track out to the main road, where you'll readily find transportation to either La Paz or Chulumani.

From their office at Ocabaya 495, Villa Fátima, in La Paz, Veloz del Norte buses leave for Yanacachi daily at 9 am and 2 pm.

YUNGA CRUZ TREK
This is a relatively little-trodden trek with good stretches of pre-Hispanic paving that connects the village of Chuñavi with the Sud Yungas provincial capital of Chulumani. There are a couple of variations to the standard trek, including a pass over the northern shoulder of Illimani to get you started, as well as an alternative – and considerably more spectacular – route over Cerro Khala Ciudad, which starts beyond Lambate. Expect to see lots of condors, eagles, hawks, vultures and hummingbirds along the route.

The map in this book is intended as a route-finder only; you'll need to carry the 1:50,000 topo sheets *Palca – 6044-I*, *Lambate – 6044-II* and *Chulumani – 6044-III*. The walk takes at least four days, not including the Illimani option or transport time to and from the trailheads.

Access
There's a good case for laying out the money to hire a 4WD and driver to take you to the trailhead at Tres Ríos, Chuñavi or Lambate. On your own, you'll first have to get to Ventilla (see Taquesi Trek, earlier), which is a bit of a transport cul-de-sac. Beyond Ventilla, the road is poor and vehicles are scarce.

The Bolsa Negra micro from Plaza Belzu in La Paz will get you all the way to Tres Ríos, 40km from Ventilla, where the vehicle turns north toward the Bolsa Negra mine. From Tres Ríos, you can either continue walking (or hitching) along the road toward Chuñavi or walk over the northern shoulder of Illimani to Estancia Totoral (not to be confused with Totoral Pampa, 3km west of Tres Ríos). See the Illimani Option, later in this section.

Alternatively, you can go straight to Chuñavi by micro, which is an all-day trip from La Paz. Buses leave from Calle Venancio Burgoa, near Plaza Líbano, at least twice weekly at 9 am. Advance information is hard to come by, and no reservations are taken; you'll just have to turn up early (around 7 to 7:30 am) and see if a micro is leaving. Friday is a good day to try. Failing those options, go to Ventilla and wait for an eastbound camión, or begin walking along the road, over the 4524m Abra Pacuani.

Taxi access from La Paz isn't good owing to the distance and condition of the road;

YUNGA CRUZ TREK

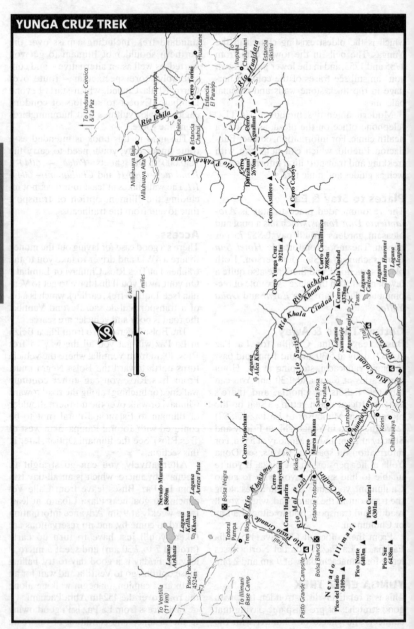

it's at least five hours to the Chuñavi trail-head and six or more to Lambate. It would be preferable to hire a 4WD and driver from La Paz (see Drivers in the Getting Around chapter).

The return to La Paz is straightforward; just catch one of the many daily camiones from the tranca at Chulumani or go with one of the flotas.

The Route

Illimani Option If you're taking the Illimani option and have made it as far as Tres Ríos, cross the bridge over the Río Khañuma and follow the Río Pasto Grande uphill toward Bolsa Blanca mine, on the skirts of Illimani. After 2km, a track leads downhill and across the river (it traverses around the northernmost spur of Illimani), but it's better to continue along the western bank of the river to the Pasto Grande campsite, at some abandoned buildings at the head of the valley. Here begins a steep and direct huff-and-puff up the valley headwall to the 4900m pass below Bolsa Blanca mine, which is overlooked by the triple-peak of Illimani. It takes the better part of two hours to get from the valley floor to the pass.

From the pass, the route becomes more obvious as it descends steeply into the Quebrada Mal Paso. Once you've entered the valley, cross to the southern bank of the Río Mal Paso as soon as possible and follow it steeply down to the village of Estancia Totoral, back on the Lambate road, where there's a *tienda* (small shop).

Even strong hikers will need two days from Tres Ríos to Estancia Totoral, owing to the altitude as well as the several exhausting climbs and treacherous descents. The best campsite is at the Pasto Grande valley headwall below Bolsa Blanca.

Chuñavi Trailhead Approximately 5km east of Estancia Totoral, turn northeast (left) along the track that descends through the village of Chuñavi. Beyond the village, the track traverses a long steady slope, high above the Río Susisa, and keeps to about 4200m for the next 30km. It passes the west-

ernmost flank of Cerro Khala Ciudad, but the spectacular views of the mountain's cirques and turrets are hidden from view.

Just 2km beyond Cerro Khala Ciudad the track joins up with the Lambate Trailhead route, and 4km later, skirts the peak of Cerro Yunga Cruz before trending downhill along a ridgeline through heavy cloud forest. Just below the tree line is a prominent campsite – the last before the trail's end – but unfortunately it's dry, so fill your water bottles at every opportunity. Despite the dampness and vegetation, the track stays above the watershed areas, and running water is scarce unless it has been raining. In 1990, a massive landslide blocked this section. An alternative route around cuts to the right past a stagnant pool, but it's difficult to follow.

After the track narrows and starts to descend steeply, the vegetation thickens and often obscures the way. Three hours below the tree line, the trail forks in a grassy saddle between two hills. The right fork climbs up the shoulder of Cerro Duraznuni before descending anew. After approximately two hours, you'll pass through a steep plantation to the hillside village of Estancia Sikilini, a citrus estate across the Huajtata Gorge from Chulumani. When you hit the road, turn left and continue along it for about two hours into Chulumani.

Lambate Trailhead This route is more difficult but also more beautiful than the Chuñavi route. Lambate is approximately 2½ hours on foot east of Estancia Totoral, and 2km beyond the Chuñavi cutoff. Lambate, which enjoys a commanding view, has a tienda – the last place to buy a soft drink or pick up snacks.

Follow the continuation of the road from La Paz toward the village of San Antonio until you reach a small house on the left, set on a precipice. Descend to the house on any of the small paths, and just beyond it, turn right to follow a path between some bean fields to an opening in a stone wall. If you take the left fork beyond the wall, you'll descend to a footbridge over the dramatic Río Chunga Mayu. Here, you should turn downstream onto a path beside a small house with a cross on top. After crossing the Río Colani (collect water here!), head uphill into the village of Quircoma (Ranchería).

Follow the main track up through Quircoma; above the village, you'll reach the last possible campsite, but it's waterless. Ascend the only path out of the village; when you reach a gate, cross the cow pasture – the track continues on the other side. From here, the route is fairly straightforward but a real struggle – it's a 10km, 2000m climb past Laguna Kasiri to the pass.

After the first couple of hours the heat will back off a bit, and two hours later, you'll reach a well-watered meadow with good campsites beside the Río Kasiri, which you've been following. At this point, the track makes a steep ascent up the prominent mountain spur to the west, then levels off before the final short climb to Laguna Kasiri, which is said to be haunted by an evil spirit. This lovely and mysterious spot lies in a cirque surrounded by the snowy peaks of Cerro Khala Ciudad.

Skirt around the right side of the lake; here the path crosses the stream, then switchbacks upward for about 2½ hours to the 4300m pass on Cerro Khala Ciudad, where there's an apacheta and a predictably incredible view from the Cordillera Real right down into the Yungas. Immediately after the pass, bear left and pass a narrow section of trail with a vertical drop to the right. After this section, 20 to 30 minutes beyond the pass, you should take the left fork between two large rocks over the ridge or you'll descend into the wrong valley.

After this fork, the trail descends and deteriorates. About 2km beyond the pass, you'll meet up with the Chuñavi Route, where you should turn right. There's a good campsite just after a small stream crossing; fill up with water here, because it will probably be the last water available.

From this point the increasingly forested route, now marked by green arrows, trends downhill most of the way to Chulumani. When you reach a small meadow before Cerro Duraznuni, continue directly across

it, then take the right fork, which climbs the hill but skirts the right side of the peak.

At this point, you begin a long and occasionally steep descent through increasingly populated countryside to the citrus farm at Estancia Sikilini. You can either follow the shortcut across Huajtata Gorge – which will seem an excruciating prospect at this stage – or just lumber along the longer but mercifully level road into Chulumani.

CHULUMANI
☎ 0811

Chulumani, the capital of Sud Yungas, is another relaxing town with a view. It lies at a subtropically warm and often wet altitude of 1700m, and is a center for growing coffee, bananas and Yungas coca.

Rebels during the 1781 La Paz revolt escaped to the Yungas and hid out in the valleys around Chulumani until things calmed down. There is a large population of African-Bolivians living in the Chulumani area, descendants of the slaves brought to work in the Potosí mines. Locals claim the town's name is derived from *cholumanya* (tiger's dew), to commemorate a jaguar's visit to the town well; it's a good story, anyway.

Increasing political pressure on coca growers has recently heated up in this area – never mind that the local crop is used almost exclusively for domestic consumption – and it's likely that an earnest attempt at eradication will commence in late 2001.

Information
Although Chulumani has a nominal tourist office, it's inactive (to say the least), and local hotel owners will be your best source of information. There's also a marginal area map painted just inside the church doors. The telephone service is provided by ENTEL.

Things to See & Do
Chulumani sees few visitors, but it is a good base for several worthwhile excursions, and when the going gets too hot, you can cool off in the municipal pool for US$0.20.

The most interesting day trip is probably to the **Apa Apa Ecological Forest** (locally

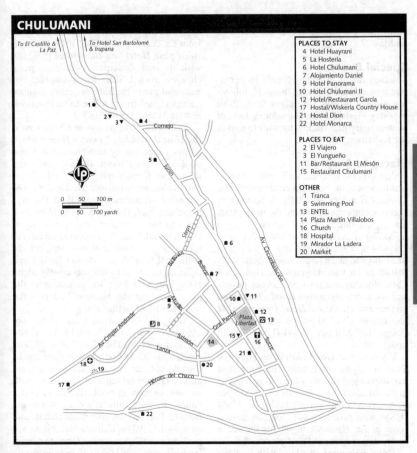

CHULUMANI

To El Castillo &
La Paz

To Hotel San Bartolomé
& Irupana

PLACES TO STAY
4 Hotel Huayrani
5 La Hostería
6 Hotel Chulumani
7 Alojamiento Daniel
9 Hotel Panorama
10 Hotel Chulumani II
12 Hotel/Restaurant García
17 Hostal/Wiskería Country House
21 Hostal Dion
22 Hotel Monarca

PLACES TO EAT
2 El Viajero
3 El Yungueño
11 Bar/Restaurant El Mesón
15 Restaurant Chulumani

OTHER
1 Tranca
8 Swimming Pool
13 ENTEL
14 Plaza Martín Villalobos
16 Church
18 Hospital
19 Mirador La Ladera
20 Market

0   50   100 m
0   50   100 yards

Cornejo
Junín
Steps
Balsián
Bolívar
Av. Circunfalación
Murillo
Av. Crispín Andrade
Salmón
Lanza
Héroes del Chaco
Gral Pando
Plaza
Libertad
Sucre

CORDILLERAS & YUNGAS

pronounced 'Apapa'), 8km from Chulumani. The 800-hectare forest is the last
remnant of primary humid montane forest
in the Yungas, and is rich in tree, orchid and
bird species. In fact, a 10-year scientific
study revealed the presence of 16 previously unknown plants. It's a beautiful place
for day hikes and overnight camping. For information and to arrange transportation,
contact Señor Ramiro Portugal (% 6106) in
Chulamani, or the forest administration
(% 790381; Casilla 10109, Miraflores, La
Paz) in La Paz. Admission, guide and transportation from Chulumani cost US$25 for

groups of up to about five people. From La
Paz, you can book through Apa Apa Trek
Rainforest Expeditions (%/fax 02-333991;
aptrekad@ceibo.entelnet.bo; Calle Safár-
naga 189, La Paz).

The area offers numerous lovely **hiking**
opportunities. A five-hour one-way walk
will take you to the clean and swimmable
Río Solacama; perhaps catch a micro down
and walk back. In three to four hours, you
can also walk to the lovely village of
Ocabaya, which claims to have Bolivia's
second-oldest church. Nearby Chicaloma is
home to lots of African-Bolivian residents,

and their traditional *saya* dance is widely performed during the annual town festival on May 27.

Special Events

The only time Chulumani breaks its pervasive *tranquilidad* is during the week following August 24, when it stages the riotous four-day Fiesta de San Bartolomé. Lots of winter-weary highlanders turn up to join in the festivities.

Places to Stay

Unless otherwise noted, accommodations in Chulumani can be booked through the Cámara Hotelera (☎ 6109). A number of cheap options cluster around the main plaza. The good-value **Hostal Dion** charges US$3.76 per person on the lower floor and US$4.10 upstairs. The entrance is through a paint shop. To make reservations, phone ☎ 02-361048 in La Paz. **Alojamiento Daniel**, on Calle Bolívar, charges US$2.50 per person and also serves almuerzos. **Hotel Chulumani**, on the same street, and **Hotel Chulumani II** also charge US$2.50 per person. **La Hunin** charges US$2.50 per person (US$4.10 with private bath).

If you stay at **Hotel García** on Friday or Saturday night, you'll either have to wear earplugs or join the noisy fun and go dancing in the attached disco. Rooms cost US$3 per person (US$4 with private bath). For US$4 (US$6 with private bath), you can have a room at **La Hostería**; highlights include a lovely dining room and roof garden.

Hotel Huayrani (☎ 6117), with its large manicured garden, is a complex of kitchen-equipped apartments, offering a large manicured garden and a small pool. It's run by the friendly and knowledgeable Ricardo and Angelica Sacermote. Rates are US$6.20 per person on weekdays, US$10.50 on weekends. The friendly **Hotel Panorama**, on Murillo at Andrade, has a nice garden, restaurant and swimming pool, and charges US$6.50 per person in rooms with baths. In La Paz, you can book by calling ☎ 02-783899.

The mid-range **Hotel Monarca** (☎ 6121) – formerly Hotel Prefectural – is laid out like a holiday camp and lacks character, but it has an enormous swimming pool to help you cope with the subtropical stickiness. To book from La Paz, phone ☎ 02-351019. The relatively posh **Hotel San Bartolomé** (☎ 6114), with its odd Z-shaped swimming pool, charges from US$50 for a double. For weekend guests, the hotel organizes minibus transportation from La Paz. In La Paz, book at ☎ 02-316161; fax 02-316302.

The nicest place to stay in Chulumani is the **Hostal Wiskería Country House**, which enjoys a cozy, homey ambience, as well as a pool and dining room. To give you some idea about the atmosphere, it's run by Javier Sarabia Sardon, who once lived in the USA, attended Woodstock and hiked the Appalachian Trail. The bar is open 24 hours a day, and the swimming pool appears to be less than full. Local sightseeing and adventure trips are available. Rooms with private baths cost US$7.50 per person for the first night and US$6 for each subsequent night. It's a 1km walk from the center; from the plaza, head for the Mirador Ladera – the hotel lies 100m farther along.

Along the Chulumani road, 20km from Unduavi at an altitude of 1934m, is the idyllic two-star **El Castillo** (☎ 02-410579 or 359881; fax 02-340866). This private castle, Castillo el Chaco, now functions as a hotel and restaurant (albeit moth-plagued), with its own swimming pool, riverbank and a couple of waterfalls. It's only two hours from La Paz, and its subtropical climate and oxygen-rich 1934m altitude make it an appealing weekend getaway from the highlands. Rooms cost US$12.50 per person on weekdays, including breakfast, and slightly more on weekends. To get there, take a Chulumani minibus from La Paz and get off 20km past Unduavi.

Places to Eat

Chulumani's market may well be the cleanest in Bolivia. It's especially good for breakfast, local coffee and delicious cocoa.

Those arriving from nosh-rich Coroico may well feel deprived. The best place for almuerzos is probably the **Restaurant Chulumani**, on the plaza, which charges US$1.20. Another good option that's on the plaza is *El Mesón*, which overlooks a pastoral slice of the Yungas and charges just US$0.80 for almuerzos. The restaurant in the *Hotel García* has a similar view and charges the same price. *El Viajero* and *El Yungueño*, near the tranca, are also good but simple little eateries. *La Bodega de La Tía* is scheduled to open soon, and should offer good set almuerzos and cenas, as well as pastries and snacks.

Apart from the Hotel San Bartolomé, the only choice with a varied menu is the *restaurant* in La Hostería (see Places to Stay); it's also your only hope of finding any vegetarian options. Main courses range from US$3 to US$4.

Entertainment
On Friday and Saturday nights, *Hotel Garcia* and *El Mesón* provide karaoke and a cacophonous disco. On weekends, a small cinema near the tranca plays second-string films, but don't expect much.

Getting There & Away
The beautiful route from La Paz to Chulumani, which extends on to Irupana, is wider, less unnerving and statistically safer than the road to Coroico. Trekkers on the Yunga Cruz trek from Lambate or Chuñavi finish up in Chulumani, and the town is readily accessed from Yanacachi, at the end of the Taquesi trek. From Yanacachi, walk down to the main road and wait for transport headed downhill; it's about 1½ hours to Chulumani.

Buses, micros and minibuses from Villa Fátima, in La Paz (four hours, US$3) leave several times daily. Camiones (eight to nine hours, US$1.50) leave from roughly the same area between 5 am and 2 pm. From Chulumani, buses leave regularly and minibuses irregularly from Plaza Libertad. To assure a seat, book with Trans San Bartolomé or Minibuses Yungueña. Camiones also run irregularly to neighboring villages; your best bet is to wait beside the appropriate road in the morning.

If you're coming from Coroico or Guanay, get off at Unduavi and wait for another vehicle. Be sure to have access to a range of clothing, in order to accommodate the tropical to highland climactic ranges along this route. Between Unduavi and Chulumani, watch for the wispy Velo de la Novia (Bridal Veil Falls) beside the road, and the unusual Castillo El Chaco, a castlelike hotel 20km from Unduavi.

SORATA
☎ 0811

Lovely, medieval-looking Sorata, with its steep stairways and maze of narrow cobbled streets, may well have the finest setting of any town in Bolivia. Perched on a hillside at an elevation of 2695m, in a valley beneath the towering snowcapped peaks of 6362m Illampu and 6427m (more or less) Ancohuma, it's a popular getaway for urban Bolivians and also attracts growing numbers of hikers and mountaineers.

Tourists aren't the only ones enchanted with Sorata. Bolivian writer Don Emiterio Villamil de Rada was so inspired by the bountiful greenery and clear rivers that he used Sorata as the setting for the Garden of Eden in *La Lengua de Adán* (Adam's Tongue). Aymará, he postulated, was the language of Adam, and Cerro Illampu was the true Mt Olympus.

In colonial days, Sorata provided a link to the gold fields and rubber plantations of the Alto Beni and a gateway to the Amazon Basin. In 1791 it was the site of a distinctly unorthodox siege by indigenous leader Andrés Tupac Amaru and his 16,000 soldiers. They constructed dikes above the colonial town, and when these had filled with runoff water from the slopes of Illampu, they opened the floodgates and the town was washed away.

Now that commercial traffic moves into the Yungas from La Paz, Sorata has slipped into comfortable obscurity. Today, it's best known to travelers and paradise-seekers who've re-routed the Gringo Trail to include this formerly off-the-beaten-track destination. For mountaineers, it's the base to use for scaling Illampu (also called Kun-Tixi-Wiracocha, 'the giver of water,' or Hualpacayo, 'the hen's foot' in Aymará), and Ancohuma, which can also be spelled

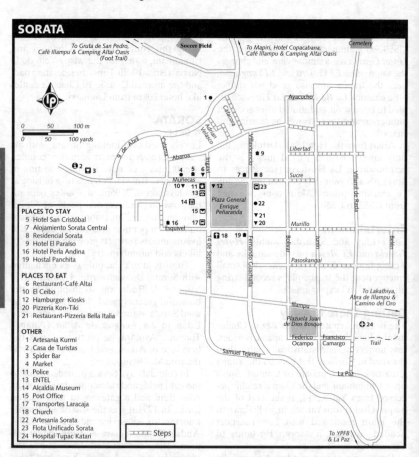

SORATA

To Gruta de San Pedro,
Café Illampu & Camping Altai Oasis
(Foot Trail)

Soccer Field

To Mapiri, Hotel Copacabana,
Café Illampu & Camping Altai Oasis

Cemetery

Ayacucho

Catacora

Adrián Velasco

9 de Abril

Calatini

Abaroa

Muñecas

Esquivel

Libertad

Sucre

Murillo

Bolívar

Villavicencio

Villamil de Rada

Belén

Plaza General
Enrique
Peñaranda

14 de Septiembre

Fernando Guachalla

Illampu

Pasoskanqui

Plazuela Juan
de Dios Bosque

Samuel Tejerina

Federico
Ocampo

Francisco
Camargo

To Lakathiya,
Abra de Illampu &
Camino del Oro

To YPFB
& La Paz

La Paz

Trail

0   50   100 m
0   50   100 yards

PLACES TO STAY
5 Hotel San Cristóbal
7 Alojamiento Sorata Central
9 Residencial Sorata
9 Hotel El Paraíso
16 Hotel Perla Andina
19 Hostal Panchita

PLACES TO EAT
6 Restaurant-Café Altai
10 El Ceibo
12 Hamburger Kiosks
20 Pizzería Kon-Tiki
21 Restaurant-Pizzería Bella Italia

OTHER
1 Artesanía Kurmi
2 Casa de Turistas
3 Spider Bar
4 Market
11 Police
13 ENTEL
14 Alcaldía Museum
15 Post Office
17 Transportes Laracaja
18 Church
22 Artesanía Sorata
23 Flota Unificado Sorata
24 Hospital Tupac Katari

:::: Steps

Jankhouma and a variety of other ways.
You'd be hard-pressed to find anyone who
doesn't like the place.

Information
Sunday is Sorata's market day, and Tuesday,
when many businesses are closed, is considered as the *Domingo Sorateño* (Sorata's
Sunday). Tourist information is available at
the Restaurant-Café Altai and other visitor-
oriented businesses.

While some shops and tourist businesses
may change cash, the place to change traveler's checks is Artesanía Sorata, which pays
15% less than official bank rates. Just below
the Spider Bar, the alpine climbing guide
Peter Ruckner and his partner Ursula have
set up the Casa de Turistas. They provide
tourist information, email and Internet
access, a beer garden with a great view
down the valley, and technical climbing trips
(see Organized Tours later in the Sorata
section).

Things to See
There isn't much of specific interest in
Sorata itself – its main attractions are its
medieval ambience, which is accentuated

when the mists roll in, and its narrow cobbled streets, which are suitable only for foot traffic. It's worth taking a look at Casa Günther, a historical mansion that now houses the Residencial Sorata. It was built in 1895 as the home of the Richters, a quinine-trading family. It was later taken over by the Günthers, who were involved in rubber extraction until 1955.

The main square, Plaza General Enrique Peñaranda, is Sorata's showcase. With the town's best view of the *nevados*, it's graced by towering date palms and immaculate gardens. Unfortunately, it's fenced off and is open to the public only on Wednesday, Saturday and Sunday. Upstairs in the *alcaldía* (town hall), on the plaza, there's a small town museum containing artifacts from the Inca Marka site near Laguna Chillata (see Hiking) and an exhibit of old festival clothing. It's open on weekdays (except Tuesday) from 8 am to noon and 2 to 5 pm.

Sorata is best known, however, as a convenient base for hikers and climbers pursuing some of Bolivia's finest landscapes.

Hiking

The Sorata area offers fit and enthusiastic trekkers some of Bolivia's finest hiking and trekking. Options range from half-day jaunts to Gruta de San Pedro (San Pedro Cave) to 24-day expeditions to Rurrenabaque, following in the footsteps of the early-20th-century explorer, Colonel Percy Harrison Fawcett. Independent trekkers will find maps, suggestions, directions and freelance guides at the Residencial Sorata and Sorata Guides & Porters (see Organized Tours, later in this section). Formal trekking tours are available through the Hotel Copacabana.

Hikers should carry the *Alpenverein-skarte Cordillera Real Nord (Illampu) 1:50,000* for all routes except the Gruta de San Pedro, which is off the map; for that walk, the map in this book should suffice. Alternatively, there's the outdated 1:50,000 IGM sheet *5846-I* or the schematic map distributed by the Restaurant-Café Altai. Basic information on climbing Illampu and Ancohuma is included under Climbing in the Cordillera Real, later in this chapter.

Most popular hikes – especially the Illampu Circuit – pass through traditional areas, so stay tuned to local sensitivities. Unless you're invited, don't set up camp anywhere near a village, and if you feel unwelcome, move on as quickly as possible.

Gruta de San Pedro Most visitors make a day trip of the 12km, 2½-hour (five-hour roundtrip) hike to the Gruta de San Pedro near the village of San Pedro. Begin by descending the Calle Catacora steps and turn down the track past the soccer field to the river to meet up with the road to San Pedro, a village about 10km away, where there's a church and soccer field. The cave is 15m above the end of the road, less than 1km beyond the village and just past the cutoff toward Consata. There was once an alternative route along the river, but it has been obliterated by impassable landslides.

Bolivians/foreigners pay US$0.80/1.20 admission to the cave, and there's usually someone on hand to crank up the generator that powers the lights (although given the cave's current condition, it may be better left in the dark). About 200m past the entrance, a cold underground lake impedes further exploration, but it makes a novel swimming hole (however, swimming isn't wise, as the water is quite chilly). With luck, you'll see some of the cave's batty residents.

It's worth continuing 10 minutes along the track past the cave, then turning right on the steep uphill track. After another 20 minutes, you'll reach a prominent ridge where there's a great lunch spot, a campsite and excellent views down the valley. There's also a decent campsite on the riverbank, accessed by a track leading directly down from the cave.

Lakathiya & Abra de Illampu A hike to the village of Lakathiya (elevation 3950m), high above Sorata, makes a good grunt of a day hike for the very fit. For a longer overnight trek, you can climb up into the Abra de Illampu, a dramatic pass on the northern shoulder of Cerro Illampu. This route is also the start of the Illampu Circuit and provides convenient access to Ancoma,

CORDILLERAS & YUNGAS

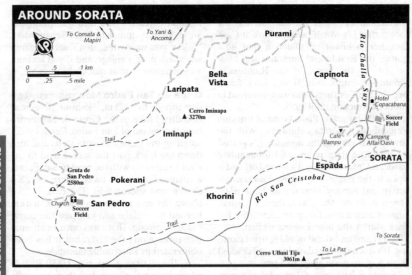

AROUND SORATA

To Consata & Mapiri

To Yani & Ancoma

Purami

Río Challa

Suyu

Bella Vista

Capinota

Hotel Copacabana

Laripata

Cerro Iminapa
▲ 3270m

Café Illampu

Soccer Field

Iminapi

Camping Altai Oasis

SORATA

Trail

Gruta de San Pedro 2580m

Pokerani

Espada

Church   Soccer Field

San Pedro

Khorini

Río San Cristobal

Trail

To Sorata

Cerro Ulluni Tija 3061m ▲

To La Paz

at the start of the Camino del Oro trek, detailed later in this chapter (obviating the need to hire a 4WD in Sorata).

To get started, take the track uphill at the northern end of the hospital to the aqueduct, where you should turn right and follow the aqueduct. The route slopes uphill to the left, away from the aqueduct after 500m. (Don't be tempted to take the trail that turns left immediately after the first ridge, which is a longer and more difficult route to Lakathiya.) After about 1km, there's a trail fork just below the crest of an obvious ridge. Don't cross the ridge, but follow the route to the left, which traverses the ridge and crosses it a few minutes later.

Two hours farther along, you'll pass through the tiny village of Quilambaya, which you should exit on the track up the slope to the north. Then follow the obvious route up and over a ridge and along the slope to cross the Río Lakathiya before zigzagging uphill into the village of Lakathiya, about 2½ hours beyond Quilambaya.

You can camp in a large open meadow 100m uphill from the village. Three hours and 800m of climbing will take you to the 4741m Abra de Illampu, where you can make a cold and windy camp.

Laguna Chillata If you have only limited time, an exhausting but recommended 12-hour roundtrip hike will take you to the beautiful Laguna Chillata, with views up to the surrounding peaks and glaciers. Several decades ago, this eerie and mysterious-looking lake was the focus of an irrigation project, and elicited all sorts of offerings to the traditional Bolivian earth-mother deity Pachamama in the hope of inspiring her to provide abundant water for fields lower down. The lake water is now quite clean and safe to drink.

The route to Laguna Chillata begins the same as the Laguna Glacial route, but instead of crossing the Río Tucsa Jahuira into Kolani, continue upstream along the northern bank of the river for about 1.5km and cross on the bridge about 300m below the confluence of the Río Lakathiya. From there, the path climbs through some trees, trending east along the southern slopes of the Tucsa Jahuira valley and through the village of Tucsa Jahuira itself.

About 1.5km above the village, beyond the Río Milluni Jahuira, the route bears sharply uphill and climbs very steeply to an abandoned mine at 4000m, where you'll cross the river. For those not doing the trip as a day hike, this area offers adequate campsites. Laguna Chillata is about 1km away, in a hollow over the next ridge to the south. Near the top of the ridge above the lake is a warm spring and several ruins, which include an old house foundation. This may have been used as a ceremonial center and is believed to date from pre-Inca times, but was probably also used by the Inca.

From Laguna Chillata, you can conveniently continue to Laguna Glacial or return via the Kolani route, which is described under Laguna Glacial.

Laguna Glacial The generically named Laguna Glacial lies at an altitude of 5038m, below a glacier separating Cerros Ancohuma and Illampu. The route begins on the same track as the one to the village of Lakathiya and Abra de Illampu, but when you reach the fork 1km above the aqueduct, just below the obvious ridge, bear right rather than left. The route continues to climb, following the northern slopes of the Río Tucsa Jahuira valley for another 1.5km before crossing the river and climbing through the village of Kolani, at 3000m elevation.

At the junction about 500m beyond Kolani, take the left turn and follow the steadily climbing route. At 3600m, about 2.5km from Kolani, note the field of dug-out tombs. This is Inca Marka, which is believed to belong to the Tiahuanaco-period Mollu culture. Although the site has suffered at the hands of amateur ceramics scavengers, it remains an important burial site, so avoid camping in the area.

From the trail fork 4km above Kolani, the left-hand road passes some ruins en route to Laguna Chillata while the right fork heads toward the Titisani Khollu tin mine and, eventually, Laguna Glacial. Beyond the mine, follow the stock tracks southward for about 2.5km, roughly following the 4450m contour, or take the shortcut over a prominent rocky

ridge. When you reach the obvious gravel moraine, turn left uphill; the lake lies about 1.75km up this moraine.

Most people take three days for this trip, which involves a very taxing 2500m elevation gain from Sorata. The first day is a climb to the Titisani mine, where there's good camping at 4450m elevation. There are also two natural caves at the 4300m level, about 30 minutes before Titisani mine, but you'll probably need a guide to find them. They're suitable for camping – one sleeps three people and the other accommodates one person.

On the second day, most people hike from Titisani to the lake and back, to avoid having to spend the night at over 5000m in a very exposed area subject to glacial winds. The final day is for the descent to Sorata.

Cerro Istipata & Untuma Warm Springs A walk along the ridge opposite Sorata, across the Río San Cristóbal, makes

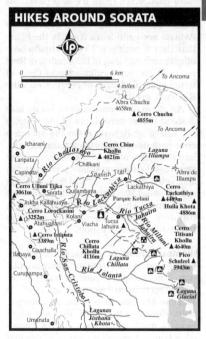

HIKES AROUND SORATA

To Ancoma

Abra Chuchu
4658m

Cerro Chuchu
4855m

To Ancoma

Icharani

Cerro Chiar
Khollu
4021m

Laguna
Illampu

Laripata

Chillkani

Capinota

Spanish Trail

Abra de
Illampu

Cerro Ulluni Tjika
3061m

Sorata

Quilambaya

Lackathiya

Cerro
Luckathiya
4449m

Jiskha Kallahuaya

Parque Kolani

Huila Khota
4886m

Cerro Lorockasini
3252m

Kolani

Atahuallani

Viacha

Tucsa
Jahuira

Cerro Istipata
3389m

Cerro
Chillata
4116m

Cerro
Titisani
Khollu
4640m

Ilabaya

Guachalla

Laguna
Chillata

Pico
Schulzel
5943m

Curupampa

Umanata

Lagunas
Jisthana
Khota

Laguna
Glacial

0   3   6 km
0   2   4 miles

an excellent day hike, and may be extended to include two sets of warm springs in the Chilabaya Valley. From Sorata, the walk begins at the YPFB station just south of town; take the obvious downhill path to reach a bridge over the Río San Cristóbal, then climb up the other side, following established footpaths to the ridge.

An easier alternative is to start by taking a La Paz-bound bus and get off at the road crest just south of the 3061m peak of Cerro Ulluni Tijka, which bears a statue of Christ. From there, you can start your walk south along the prominent ridge (this ridge adds a good 10km of road distance along the main route to La Paz). The next summit you reach will be 3252m Cerro Lorockasini, which once bore a large cross on its summit. It was removed when Ilabaya residents blamed a spate of crop failures on the fact that the cross faced Sorata and not Ilabaya.

Continuing south, roughly following the main ridge, you'll reach the next peak, flat-topped Cerro Istipata, which rises to 3389m. On its summit, locals make offerings to Aymará gods and leave coins, in the belief that they'll multiply. Cerro Istipata also offers excellent views of the Cordillera Real peaks. From there, walking tracks descend to the main road, near where it crosses the Río San Cristóbal.

An alternative route back to Sorata is to descend the western slopes of the ridge to the village of Ilabaya. From the village, a clear path descends through terraced fields into the valley of the Río Chilabaya. After you cross the river on stones, turn upstream and you'll reach the 32°C Untuma warm springs about 50m later. There's also a set of 35°C springs about 1km upstream, along a tributary stream. These now serve as popular local laundry spots.

Illampu Circuit To get started on this rewarding seven- or eight-day circumambulation of the Illampu-Ancohuma massif, follow the instructions to Lakathiya and Abra de Illampu. The best map is the *Alpenvereinskarte Cordillera Real Nord (Illampu)*, which includes much of the route. To my knowledge, however, there's no map available that

covers the entire trek. For general route finding, you can refer to the Illampu Circuit map in this book, but it's not detailed enough to use as a sole source of direction.

A short but interesting diversion on the third day of this route is to Laguna Subirana Khota, at 4433m, which serves as the climbers' base camp for 5760m Pico Esperanza. There's a particularly beautiful campsite and a bizarre legend that the lake is responsible for swallowing both people and their cattle.

The biggest worry along this route is the two-day stretch on either side of Laguna San Francisco, where the locals seem to take less kindly to strangers than most Bolivians do. Hikers have reported numerous problems here – mainly stone-throwing and unrealistic demands for money. With a guide, you'll have much more success mitigating such encounters; a guide is imperative for the shortcut between Laguna Chojña Khota and the warm spring near Laguna San Francisco. Avoid camping in this area if at all possible.

Organized Tours

While it's possible to hike independently, some hikes, such as the Illampu Circuit and the Mapiri Trail, are best done with a guide, mainly owing to local sensibilities and difficult route finding. The most economical option is to hire an independent guide from Sorata Guides & Porters (Calle Sucre 302), opposite the Residencial Sorata. Guides belonging to this local cooperative charge US$12 per group per day. Clients must also provide the guide's meals; according to one reader, this also extends to 'anyone who happens to pop out of the woodwork around mealtime,' so it's probably wise to draw the line when organizing the trek. The group also rents out sleeping bags, tents and stoves.

The Club Sorata Travel Agency (☎/fax 5042) at Hotel Copacabana organizes a range of trekking options from Sorata with minimums of two to five people: three-day treks to Lakathiya/Laguna Chillata or Laguna Glacial (US$60), the Illampu Circuit (US$160), the Mapiri Trail (US$190), Camino del Oro (US$140) and a hike from

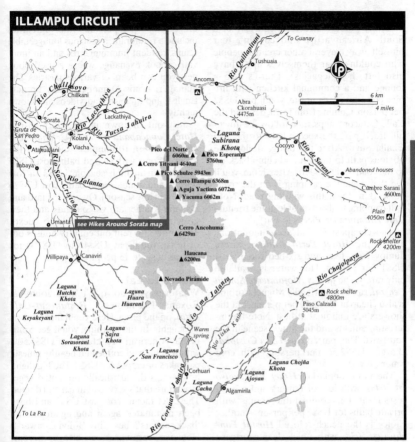

ILLAMPU CIRCUIT

To Guanay

Rio Quillapituni

Tushuaia

Ancoma

Rio Challasoyo

Chillkani

Abra
Ckorahuasi
4475m

0   3   6 km
0   2   4 miles

Cocoyo

Rio de Sarani

Sorata

Rio Lackathiya

Lackathiya

Rio Tucsa Jahuira

To
Gruta de
San Pedro

Kolani

Viacha

Atahualpani

Laguna
Subirana
Khota

Pico del Norte
6060m ▲ ▲ Pico Esperanza
5760m

Abandoned houses

Cumbre Sarani
4600m

Imbaya

Rio San Cristobal

▲ Cerro Titisani 4640m

▲ Pico Schulze 5943m

Rio Jalanta

▲ Cerro Illampu 6368m

▲ Aguja Yactima 6072m

▲ Yacuma 6062m

Plain
4050m

Umanta

see Hikes Around Sorata map

Cerro Ancohuma
▲6429m

Rock shelter
4200m

Rio Chajolpaya

Millipaya

Canaviri

Haucana
▲6200m

▲ Nevado Pirámide

Rio Uma Jalanta

Laguna
Hutchu
Khota

Laguna
Huara
Huarani

Rock shelter
4800m
Paso Calzada
5045m

Laguna
Keyakeyani

Laguna
Sajra
Khota

Rio Jisku Kenu

Laguna
Sorasorani
Khota

Warm
spring

Laguna
San Francisco

Corhuari

Rio Corhuari Jahuira

Laguna
Cacha

Laguna
Ajoyan

Algamirila

Laguna Chojña
Khota

To La Paz

Rio Chajolpaya

CORDILLERAS & YUNGAS

Sorata to Carabuco (US$100). Longer tours requiring a minimum of six people include 12 days of walking the length of the Cordillera Real (US$260); a 24-day route from Carabuco to Rurrenabaque via Sorata, Mapiri and Apolo (US$900); or just Apolo to Rurrenabaque (US$240). Rates include a guide, transport, porters, mules, muleteers, food and any hotel costs.

If you prefer some technical climbing on Illampu, Ancohuma or other big peaks, see Peter Ruckner at the Casa de Turistas (☎ 5244; pruckner@ceibo.entelnet.bo). Peter has been climbing since 1974 and

working in the Sorata area since 1989. The office is just downhill from the Spider Bar. For additional information, see the website www.skysorata.com/english.

Special Events
Sorata's main annual fiesta, which can be a riotous affair, is held on September 14.

Places to Stay
Visitors to Sorata are spoiled for choice in both accommodation and culinary matters! Campers will love the beautiful riverside *Camping Altai Oasis*, and in the high

season, a coffee shop operates in a most bizarrely painted structure, courtesy of a South African artist who couldn't tear himself away (several other creative people who couldn't tear themselves away have also left their legacies). There's also a lounge and a communal kitchen with fire pits. For a lovely campsite, you'll pay US$2 per person. Coming from town, descend the Calle Catacora steps, then follow the downhill track past the soccer field to the Río Challa Suyu. After the bridge, follow the obvious path to the left and climb back up to the road and turn left. After 150m, you'll see their sign; the camping is on the riverbank 1km down this winding road. Note that camping is also available at the friendly *Café Illampu* (see Places to Eat).

The cheapest formal accommodations are in the *Hotel Perla Andina*, where dumpy two-, five- and six-bed rooms cost US$1 per person. Hot water is available only rarely. The quirky *Alojamiento Sorata Central*, run by the friendly Miguel Coromi, is also cheap at US$1.50 per person, but the showers are marginal at best. Note the interesting shields and the jungle scene in the courtyard. The spartan *Hotel San Cristóbal* charges US$2.50 per person, with cold water only.

The more upmarket *Hotel El Paraíso* (☎ 5043), with lots of flowers and a good restaurant, has comfortable rooms with private baths for US$6 per person. Another choice is the peach-colored *Hostal Panchita* (☎ 5038), with a nice clean courtyard and a rather aloof atmosphere. Pleasant single/double rooms cost US$3/5.

For its clean, friendly atmosphere and brilliant flower garden, the Canadian-run *Residencial Sorata* (☎ 5044; fax 5218; resorata@ ceibo.entelnet.bo) is an accommodations highlight. As one *Bolivian Times* journalist said, 'It's as if someone had thrown slipcovers over the furniture, locked up the place and then returned 100 years later...the place is filled with a strange blend of periods and motifs that float like forgotten spirits through the hallways.' Grand antique rooms in this colonial-style mansion, known as Casa Günther, cost US$4.50 per person (US$6

with private bath); smaller rooms at the back are US$3.50 per person. Other amenities include a restaurant, a spacious lounge, table tennis, resident hummingbirds and an innovative book exchange where a used book nets you two beers or various pastries. The manager, Louis Demers, speaks French, English and Spanish, and videos are shown nightly.

Just out of town is the German-run *Hotel Copacabana* (☎/fax 5042; landhaus@ khainata.com), 10 minutes' walk from the plaza. Rooms with shared baths cost US$5 per person in high season, US$3 in low season, and doubles with baths cost US$26 (US$18 in low season). Owners Eduard and Dayana Kramer are video fiends, and their growing collection is available to guests. They now also rent out country houses out of town; you'll pay US$45 to US$100 for groups of six to 13 people.

Places to Eat

Whatever you do, don't miss Johny & Roxana Resnikowsi's *Restaurant-Café Altai*, on the plaza. Here you'll find all sorts of delights. In the morning, you'll get continental/American breakfasts for US$1.50/2 with real brewed coffee and healthy muesli, pancakes or crêpes for US$2. The highlight, however, is the artistically presented vegetarian fare that's served at lunch and dinner. These set menus cost just US$2 and have been nominated again and again for the 'backpackers' best in Bolivia' award! However, carnivores can also be accommodated with burgers (US$1.80), steak (US$4.50), goulash, borscht and other Eastern European specialties. In case you're wondering, the curious name of this place is indeed derived from that of the remote Mongolian range. There's a book exchange and a happy hour from 4 to 6 pm. During the winter months, they also run a very popular restaurant and coffee shop at their campsite outside of town (see Places to Stay).

When the unforgettable Casa de Papaco Italian restaurant left for La Paz, the staff headed for the plaza and opened the *Restaurant-Pizzería Bella Italia*. The very Italian menu matches that of its predecessor, under whose tutelage the methods were learned, so it can be very good. Specialties include pizzas (US$4 for a small one and US$7 to US$10 for a medium), pastas, vegetarian dishes, beef dishes and sweets. The spinach and ricotta cannelloni (US$4.20) comes especially recommended, and the homemade gelato is superb. You can choose between good quality Chilean or Bolivian wines for US$1.20 per glass, and the background music isn't bad either.

Out in the campo, you can also visit the lovely Alpine-like *Café Illampu* which, not surprisingly, is Swiss-run. The owner, Stephan Anders, is a master baker who produces sandwiches on home-baked bread, as well as cakes, pies and coffee. Other features include good music, a book exchange and assorted four-footed farmyard types. Passing visitors have left their own marks in the form of artwork, carvings and mosaics. It's an obligatory stop en route back from the San Pedro Cave hike, but camping is also available.

For a decent budget lunch, there are a couple of small and inexpensive places near the plaza. *El Ceibo (Muñecas 339)* serves breakfasts, vegetarian dishes, sandwiches, grilled food and typical Bolivian dishes; on Sunday you can get salteñas and tucumanas. It's open daily from 7 am to 11 pm. You'll find Bolivian-style pizzas at the *Pizzería Kon-Tiki*, next door to the Bella Italia on the plaza. For a quick burger, you can't beat the *kiosks* at the northwest corner of the plaza, where women do fry-ups until the wee hours of the morning.

The decent restaurant at the Residencial Sorata serves breakfast as well as set lunches and dinners. The US$3 evening set menu at the Hotel Copacabana includes salad, soup, main course, dessert and a hot drink.

Entertainment

The only place to see and be seen in Sorata is the British-run Spider Bar, a cozy and rustic little watering hole just downhill from the market. Musicians often turn up and play on weekend evenings, and the fabulous view is marred only by the cascade of rubbish just up the hill.

Shopping

A great place to look for local handiwork is the friendly Artesanías Kurmi, in a rustic two-story white house at Avenida Ernesto Gunther 107. Here Wilma Velasco sells wonderful homemade and hand-dyed clothing, hats, dolls, bags and wall-hangings for excellent prices; also ask to try the homemade orange wine! There's no sign, but if you knock on the door, she'll open up.

Diane Bellamy's Artesanía Sorata (☎ 5061; cnsorata@ceibo.entelnet.bo), on the plaza, sells a range of locally produced crafts and material arts, including unique hand-knitted woolens dyed with natural materials, as well as dolls, wall-hangings, carved wooden articles and other traditional gifts.

Getting There & Away

Sorata is a long way from the other Yungas towns, and there's no road connecting it directly with Coroico, so you must go through La Paz. The route is now being tarred, but at the current pace the project could extend well beyond 2000.

From La Paz (four hours, US$2), Transportes Larecaja and Flota Unificado Sorata leave every hour or so between 6 am and 2 pm. The terminals are on Calle Ángel Babia, near the cemetery in La Paz. To return to La Paz, micros leave from the plaza in Sorata at any time after 5 am; the last departure may be as late as 5 pm. To travel from Copacabana to Sorata or vice versa, alight at Huarina and wait for the next bus going the right way.

The only road route between Sorata and the lowlands is a rough 4WD track that leads to the gold-mining settlement of Mapiri. It strikes out from Sorata and passes through Quiabaya, Tacacoma, Itulaya and Consata, roughly following the courses of the Ríos Llica, Consata and Mapiri all the way to Mapiri. The biggest drawbacks are horrendous mud, road construction and some river crossings that are passable only with 4WD. Camionetas leave Sorata every couple of days for the grueling journey to Consata (seven hours, US$10) and on to the Sorata Limitada mine (11 hours, US$12).

From Sorata Limitada, you'll find camionetas on to Mapiri, which is another three hours away.

EL CAMINO DEL ORO (THE GOLD TRAIL)

If the current road-building trend continues, the popular trek between Sorata and the Río Tipuani goldfields may last only a few more years. This Inca road has been used for nearly 1000 years as a commerce and trade link between the Altiplano and the lowland goldfields. Indeed, the Tipuani and Mapiri valleys were major sources of the gold that once adorned the Inca capital, Cuzco.

Today, however, the fields are worked primarily by bulldozers and dredges owned by mining cooperatives. They scour and scrape the landscape for the shiny stuff and dump the detritus, which is picked over by out-of-work Aymará refugees from the highlands. Squalid settlements of plastic, banana leaves and sheet aluminum have sprung up along the rivers, the banks of which are staked out for panning by wildcat miners. It's projected that gold will soon replace tin as Bolivia's greatest source of mineral export income.

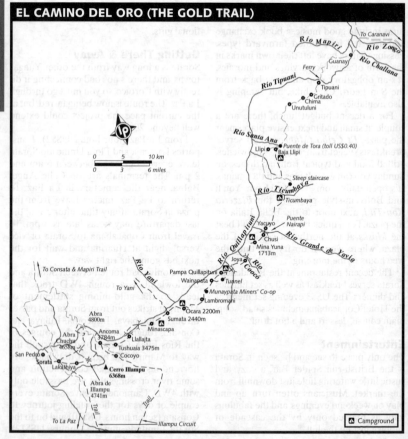

EL CAMINO DEL ORO (THE GOLD TRAIL)

To Caranavi
Río Mapiri
Río Zongo
Río Challana
Guanay
Ferry
Río Tipuani
Tipuani
Gritado
Chima
Unutuluni
Río Santa Ana
Llipi
Puente de Tora (toll US$0.40)
Baja Llipi
Steep staircase
Río Ticumbaya
Ticumbaya
Puente
Nairapi
Yacuyo
Río Quillapituni
Río Grande de Yavia
Chusi
Mina Yuna 1713m
Joya
Río Coocó
Pampa Quillapituni
To Consata & Mapiri Trail
Río Yani
Wainapata
Tunnel
To Yani
Munaypata Miners' Co-op
Lambromahi
Abra 4800m
Ocara 2200m
Ancoma 3784m
Sumata 2440m
Minascapa
Abra Chuchu 4658m
Lllajta
Tushuaia 3475m
San Pedro
Cocoyo
Sorata
Lakathiya
Cerro Illampu 6368m
Abra de Illampu 4741m
To La Paz
Illampu Circuit
Illampu Trail

0   5   10 km
0   3   6 miles

⛺ Campground

Huayna Potosí from La Paz

La Paz cemetery

La Paz street scene

La Paz at dusk

Huayna Potosí after a storm

Street in misty Sorata

Ski station, Chacaltaya

Coroico

Fortunately, the upper part of the route remains magnificent, and nearly everything above Chusi has been left alone, including some wonderfully exhausting Inca staircases and dilapidated ancient highway engineering. This trek is more challenging than the Taquesi, La Cumbre to Coroico, or Yunga Cruz routes; if you want to get the most from it, plan on six or seven days to walk between Sorata and Llipi, less if you opt for a jeep to Ancoma. At Llipi, find transport to Tipuani or Guanay to avoid a walking-pace tour through the worst of the destruction.

Although it's unlikely the road will reach as far up the valley as Ancoma, the aesthetics of the lower valley have already been scarred and eroded by large-scale mining and road building.

Access

Nearly everyone does the route from Sorata down the valley to Tipuani and Guanay, simply because it trends downhill. It's a shame, because the final bits pass through devastated landscapes and some of the ugliest settlements imaginable. Nevertheless, tradition demands describing the walk from the top down.

There are three options for the route between Sorata and Ancoma. First, you can rent a 4WD in Sorata and cut two days off the trek. After bargaining, you'll pay US$5 per person or US$50 to rent the entire vehicle. A challenging alternative is the steep route that begins near the cemetery in Sorata. It roughly follows the Río Challasuyo, passing through the village of Chillkani and winding up on the road just below the 4658m Abra Chuchu (this is also the access to the Mapiri Trail), which is four hours walking from Ancoma. The third option, which is shorter and more scenic, is to follow the route through the village of Lakathiya and over the 4741m Abra de Illampu to meet up with the road about 1½ hours above Ancoma (see Lakathiya & Abra de Illampu in Sorata). Foreigners are charged US$2 per person to camp anywhere in the vicinity of Ancoma, and US$0.50 to cross the bridge there.

Allow two days for either of the abras, and before setting out, see the Residencial Sorata or Hotel Copacabana for advice on routes and conditions.

The Route

Once you're in Ancoma, the route is fairly straightforward. Leave the 4WD track and follow the southern bank of the Río Quillapituni (which eventually becomes the Río Tipuani). At a wide spot called Llallajta, about 4½ hours from Ancoma, it crosses a bridge and briefly follows the north bank before recrossing the river and heading toward Sumata. Another Inca-engineered diversion to the north bank has been avoided by bridge washouts, forcing hikers to follow a spontaneously constructed but thankfully brief detour above the southern bank.

Just past the detour is the village of Sumata, and just beyond it, a trail turns off to the north across the river and heads for Yani (which is the start of the Mapiri Trail). A short distance farther along is Ocara, where there's a small shop. From here, the path goes up the slope – don't follow the river. After 1½ hours, you'll reach Lambromani, where a local has set up a toll gate and demands that foreigners pay US$0.40 per person to pass. Here you can camp in the schoolyard.

An hour past Lambromani you reach Wainapata, where the vegetation grows thicker and more lush. Here, the route splits (to rejoin at Pampa Quillapituni); the upper route is very steep and dangerous, so the lower one is preferable. A short distance along, the lower route passes through an interesting tunnel drilled through the rock. There's a popular myth that it dates from Inca times, but it was actually made with dynamite and probably blasted out by the Aramayo mining company early in the 20th century to improve the access to the Tipuani goldfields. At Pampa Quillapituni, half an hour beyond, is a favorable campsite. Just east of this spot, a trail branches off to the right toward Calzada Pass, several days away on the Illampu Circuit.

Four hours after crossing the swinging bridge at the Río Coocó, you'll reach the little settlement of Mina Yuna, where the trail is routed through an uninspiring mine pit. Here you can pick up basic supplies, and it's possible to camp on the soccer fields.

An hour farther down is Chusi, which lies just four hours before your first encounter with the road. There's no place to camp here, but you can stay in the school for US$0.80 per person. Puente Nairapi, over the Río Ticumbaya, is a good place for a swim to take the edge off the increasing heat.

Once you reach the road, the scene grows increasingly depressing. For a final look at relatively unaffected landscape, follow the shortcut trail, which begins with a steep Inca staircase and winds up at Baja Llipi and the Puente de Tora toll bridge (US$0.40; B$2) over the Río Santa Ana. In 1992, Llipi experienced one of Bolivia's worst-ever natural disasters when a massive mudslide broke loose from the hillside and killed 74 people. The US$200,000 of foreign aid money intended for disaster relief mysteriously disappeared before hitting its mark, and the village remains less than aesthetically appealing.

After crossing the bridge, climb up the hill and hope for a camioneta or 4WD to take you to Tipuani and Guanay. Camionetas between the Río Santa Ana bridge and Unutuluni cost about US$1 per person; to continue on to Tipuani or Guanay costs an additional US$3.

You can pick up basic supplies at Ancoma, Wainapata, Mina Yuna, Chusi and Llipi, as well as all the lower settlements along the road. Spartan accommodations may be found in Unutuluni, Chima (more rough-and-ready than most and not recommended!), Tipuani and Guanay, all of which are along the road.

MAPIRI TRAIL

A longer and more adventurous alternative to the Camino del Oro trek is the six-day pre-Hispanic Mapiri Trail, which was upgraded 100 years ago by the Richter family in Sorata to connect their headquarters with the *cinchona* (quinine) plantations of the upper Amazon Basin.

While the trailhead is technically at the village of Ingenio, you can also begin this unspoiled route by climbing from Sorata over the 4658m Abra Chuchu, then ascending

and descending through the open grassy flanks of the Illampu massif to Ingenio. For the next three days, it descends along one long ridge through grassland, dense cloud forest and pampa to the village of Mapiri. With the Sorata approach, the entire route takes anywhere from six to eight days, depending on the weather, your fitness and whether you reach the trailhead at Ingenio on foot or by motor vehicle.

An excellent side trip before you get started will take you from Ingenio up to the lovely and medieval cloud-wrapped village of Yani, where there's a basic alojamiento. Bolivia doesn't get much more enigmatic than this (see Colonel Fawcett's experience in 'The Mapiri Experience') and adventurers won't regret a visit.

Unfortunately, owing to mining sensitivity in the area, no government mapping is available for this trek. The sketch map in this book (which is derived from several sources) will head you in the right direction, but independent trekkers should ask at the Residencial Sorata or the guides' office in Sorata for the most up-to-date details. Guides for this trek charge around US$100 per group, and porters, US$70 each.

Access

The Mapiri Trail begins at the village of Ingenio, which has two basic alojamientos. It can be reached either by 4WD from Sorata (five to seven hours, US$60 to US$80 for five people) or on foot over the 4658m Abra Chuchu. For the latter, start at the cemetery in Sorata and follow the track up past the tiny settlements of Manzanani and Huaca Milluni to the larger village of Chillkani, about three hours from Sorata. From there, you have five hours of fairly relentless climbing up the semi-forested slopes to the Abra Chuchu. You'll meet up with the road a twisting 4km below the pass.

Shortly after the crest, take the left turn (the route straight on leads to Ancoma and the Camino del Oro trek) down toward a small lake. This route will take you over the 4750m Paso Pechasani Pass and down past the Mina Suerte to Ingenio and the start of the Mapiri Trail at 3550m elevation.

The Route

Past Ingenio, you'll cross the Río Yani. Here the trail starts downstream, but half an hour later cuts uphill along a side stream; there's a good campsite where it crosses the stream. The way then twists uphill for 1½ hours over a 4000m pass. In the next two hours, you'll cross three more ridges, then descend past a cave known as Cueva Cóndor, which is a good campsite, to a small lake. From the lake, the route ascends to the 3940m Paso Apacheta Nacional, then twists down El Tornillo, a corkscrew-like track that drops 150m. In under an hour, you'll cross the Río Mamarani, where a good campsite is protected by large rocks.

The next campsite lies three hours farther along, beside a stream crossing at the foot of the next big ascent. At the next stream, half an hour later (collect water here!), is another campsite. Here the trail climbs a long staircase, then descends into another valley before climbing to the next pass, Abra Nasacara, at 4000m. At this stage, you're on the ridge that dominates most of the Mapiri Trail route, with great views of the Illampu massif. For the next three days, you'll follow this ridge up and down, slowly losing altitude and passing through mostly lush jungle vegetation; fill your water bottles at every opportunity here. The first water along this stretch is at Tolapampa, which would also make a nice campsite.

The next stretch passes through thick forest, and may require a bit of bush-bashing with a machete; plan on getting good and wet from all the soaked vegetation. Six

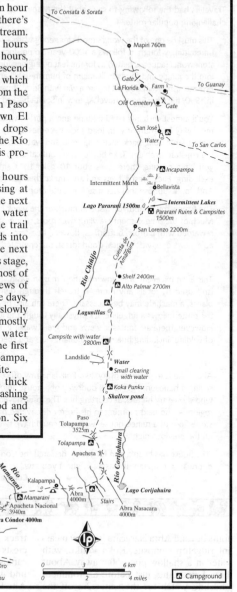

CORDILLERAS & YUNGAS

CORDILLERAS & YUNGAS

The Mapiri Experience

Travelers had the following to say about the Mapiri Trail, which is often considered Bolivia's most challenging popular route:

This must be one of the world's most staggering walks – in every sense. It is wildly beautiful and unremittingly tough. It follows a 1000-year-old pre-Inca track, remarkable not so much for its stonework (Taquesi is better) as for the feat of engineering that accommodated this 3000m drop into the jungle and for its millennium of human uphill and downhill traffic. In 1903, the entire Bolivian army went down it to lose a war with Brazil. It has been overgrown since the 1950s, but in 1990, the Club Sorata Travel Agency in Sorata hacked back the worst obstructions.

You'll almost certainly need a guide and a porter, which can be arranged in Sorata. Believe me, every kilogram of your load soon becomes a very personal matter. Travel light – never more than a 10kg pack, including food and water. Water is available in places en route, but is a constant problem. Take bottles and purification for at least three liters per person (unless you have porters, there goes your 10kg limit!). Camps must be waterproof and insect-excluding: Flies, wasps, bees and ants make themselves very much a part of the experience. And don't suppose that because the route drops overall, there aren't many arduous climbs!

The way is rough and you'll spend much of the week cursing yourself, your guide and God. Much of the time is spent crawling over rocks, along branches and under logs, but you'll be rewarded with parrots, butterflies, flowers, tree-ferns, millions of tons of moss and unbelievable views over vast vertical cloud forest, unpenetrated by humans but for this single trail.

– Matthew Parris, UK

This is an excellent way down to the Amazon Basin. The track is completely deserted as it isn't used by locals any more. It travels through dense cloud forest for two days and in places, a machete may be necessary. There can also be problems obtaining water as most of the route follows a ridgeline. It's physically tough and it can rain a lot (it certainly did on us). However, there are fantastic views and great walking, and there's the chance of seeing a lot of wildlife, including huemules (Andean deer) and spectacled bears.

– James A Lind, UK

About the turn of the century, two Bolivian army officers arrived here late one night . . . and seeing a handsome girl in the doorway of a house adjoining the tambo, tossed up to decide who should try his luck at courting her. The loser stayed with the village headman – the Corregidor – and next morning to his horror discovered his brother officer dead on the broken stone floor of a ruined house, which he could have sworn was not only whole but occupied on the previous night.

'The house has been a ruin for years,' declared the Corregidor. 'There was no maiden and no doorway, mi capitán. It was a . . . ghost you saw.'

– Colonel Percy Harrison Fawcett, Yani, 1906

hours beyond Abra Nasacara is a very pleasant ridgetop campsite, Koka Punku, with water in a shallow pond 50m away. About three hours later, just before a prominent landslide, watch for the water 3m off the track to the right. Four hours and three crests later is a permanent water source and campsite at Lagunillas. An hour later, you'll find good (but dry) campsites on the hill Alto Palmar.

From Alto Palmar, the trail tunnels through dense vegetation along the Cuesta de Amargura (Bitterness Ridge, so-called for its lack of water sources). After three hours, the jungle gives way to merely thick bush. Six hours later, you'll reach Pararaní at 1900m, where there's water (it needs to be purified) in a small pond near the ruins of an old house. An hour later, there's a semi-permanent lake, and just beyond it, the trail leaves the dense vegetation and issues onto a grassy ridge flanked by thick forest. It's then 4½ hours to Incapampa, with a semi-permanent marsh and a campsite. Along this stretch, wildlife is rife – mainly in the form of bees, ants, ticks, flies and mosquitoes, as well as plenty of flittering butterflies.

About three hours beyond Incapampa, you'll reach the hamlet of San José at 1400m, where there's a campsite and a view over the village of Santiago. Water can be found 300m down to the right of the route. After an open area that's in fact an old cemetery, the left fork provides the faster track to Mapiri.

Four to five hours of walking from San José brings you to Mapiri, which is visible 1½ hours before you arrive. Here you'll find several decent alojamientos charging US$2 per person (avoid the Alojamiento Sorata) and motorized canoes downstream to Guanay (three hours, US$5 to US$6), which is on the bus routes. Boats leave around 9 am, but arrive an hour earlier to get a place. Alternatively, catch a camioneta along the 4WD track first to Santa Rosa (don't attempt to walk, because there are two large river crossings), which has two small alojamientos, and then 175km uphill, back to Sorata (12 hours, US$6 to US$10).

CONSATA

The semi-abandoned gold-mining town of Consata, which looks like a holdover from the Old West, is accessible every couple of days by vehicle from Sorata (seven hours, US$10). This lovely village, characterized by rambling tropical gardens, hasn't yet been discovered by tourists. The place to stay is the cheap and rather charming *Hotel de Don Beto*.

AUCAPATA & ISKANWAYA
☎ 0811

The tiny and remote village of Aucapata is truly an undiscovered gem. Perched on a ledge at 2850m, on the shoulder of a dramatic peak, it's a great place to hole up for a couple of days' reading, hiking and relaxing. While most of Aucapata's very few visitors want to see Iskanwaya – somewhat optimistically dubbed 'Bolivia's Machu Picchu' – they may well take one look at the 1500m descent to the ruins (and corresponding climb back up!) and seek out the small Iskanwaya museum, containing artifacts from the site. Admission is free but donations are expected.

Iskanwaya

The major but near-forgotten ruins of Iskanwaya, on the western slopes of the Cordillera Real, sit in a cactus-filled canyon, perched 250m above the Río Llica. The site is attributed to the Mollu culture and is thought to date from between 1145 and 1425.

While Iskanwaya isn't exactly another Machu Picchu, the 13-hectare site is outwardly more impressive than Tiahuanaco. This large city-citadel was built on two platforms and flanked by agricultural terraces and networks of irrigation canals. It contains more than 100 buildings, plus delicate walls, narrow streets, small plazas, storerooms, burial sites and niches.

Note that it's a 1500m descent from Aucapata to Iskanwaya, and there's no accurate map of the area. In the rainy season, hiking is dangerous on this exposed route and not recommended.

For more information, ask around for Señor Jorge Albaracin, or look for the book *Iskanwaya: La Ciudadela que Solo Vivía de Noche*, by Hugo Boero Roja (Los Amigos del Libro, La Paz, 1992), which contains photos, maps and diagrams of the site, plus background on area villages.

Places to Stay & Eat

Aucapata has one smart-looking little *Hotel* with clean rooms and hot showers. There's also a small *Alojamiento* behind the church charging US$2 per person. For meals, there's just a small eatery on the corner of the plaza where you'll get whatever happens to be available. They'll probably also be happy to cook up your own supplies. Be sure to bring small change or you're likely to clean out the town!

Getting There & Away

Aucapata lies about 20km northeast of Quiabaya and 50km northwest of Sorata. From Calle Reyes Cardona in the cemetery district of La Paz, a weekly camión leaves on Friday and returns on Sunday. You'll probably pay around US$4.50 for this spectacular (and grueling) trip, which may well take more than 24 hours.

There's also a rather difficult access from Sorata, which involves a four-day hike via Pulliyunga. Another option is to find transport from Sorata to Consata and get off above the Boca del Lobo bridge over the Río Llica, where you should descend, then cross the river and climb up the other side to Iskanwaya. Guides and recommendations are available from Sorata Guides and Porters. One other access route, which is quite challenging and spectacularly interesting, is a little-known trek from the village of Amarete, in the Cordillera Apolobamba. A guide is essential for this route; you may be able to hire one in Amarete, Curva or Charazani, but there are a lot of would-be guides out there who've never ventured more than 5km from their birthplace. Make absolutely sure your chosen leader is more familiar with the terrain than you are!

GUANAY

Isolated Guanay makes a good base for visits to the gold-mining operations along the Río Mapiri and Río Tipuani. If you can excuse the utter rape of the landscape for the sake of gold, the down-to-earth miners and panners, known as *barranquilleros*, can make a visit to Guanay a singularly interesting experience. This area and points upriver are frontier territory, and you may be reminded of the USA's legendary Old West. Gold is legal tender in shops, and saloons, gambling, prostitutes and large hunks of beef appear to form the foundations of local culture.

Information

There's no place to change traveler's checks, but everyone displaying *Compro Oro* signs (which is just about everyone in town) changes US dollars cash. The ENTEL office is in the entrance to the Hotel Minero.

River Trips

Access to the mining areas is by jeep along the Llipi road, or by motorized dugout canoes up the Río Mapiri. The Mapiri trip is easier to organize because boats leave more or less daily. The trip to Mapiri takes five hours upstream and costs about US$7 per person. The exhilarating three-hour downstream run back to Guanay costs US$5. Although the forest has been largely decimated, bugs are still a nuisance, so you'll need repellent. If you want to spend the night, Mapiri has several *alojamientos* that will put you up for US$2 per person.

Places to Stay & Eat

The *Hotel Pahuichi*, a block downhill from the plaza, is by far the best value in town, and also has Guanay's best and most popular restaurant. A good, friendly alternative is the *Hotel Minero* next door. Both these places charge US$2 per person. *Alojamiento Plaza* and *Alojamiento Santos*, both on the plaza, are also recommended and charge just US$2 per person.

For large steaks and fresh juices, try *Las Parrilladas*, on the road leading to the port. The *Fuente de Soda Mariel*, on the plaza, does empanadas, cakes, ice cream, licuados and other snacks.

Getting There & Away

For information on walking routes from Sorata, see the Camino del Oro and Mapiri trek descriptions earlier in this chapter. A 4WD track now connects Mapiri with Sorata, via Consata, but the route is rough and the availability of vehicles to hire isn't terribly reliable.

Bus & Camión The bus offices are all around the plaza, but buses actually depart from a block away, toward the river. Four companies offer daily runs both to and from La Paz (11 hours), via Caranavi (four hours) and Yolosa (eight hours), leaving at around 8 am or between 4:30 and 5 pm. At around 7 am, micros heading for Caranavi cruise through town, honking wildly in search of passengers. To reach Coroico, you'll have to alight at Yolosa (unfortunately, most buses pass in the wee hours of the morning) and catch a camioneta up the hill. In the dry season, there's an overnight bus to Rurrenabaque, or you can reach Rurrenabaque, Trinidad or Riberalta by alighting in Caranavi and connecting with a northbound bus.

Camiones to Caranavi, Yolosa and La Paz are also plentiful and cheaper, but the trip takes longer.

Boat Alternatively, you may be able to organize a canoe along the Río Beni to or from Rurrenabaque. While this mode of transport was quite popular only a few years ago, boat operators' demands for unreasonable prices and the practice of filling canoes to dangerous levels with cargo and nonpaying passengers have just about destroyed the option. Canoes comfortably hold 10 people and their luggage, and initial asking prices for the trip to Rurrenabaque will be around US$250. However, that price may or may not get you to Rurrenabaque, and there's little chance you'll arrive without all sorts of extraneous goods and passengers. If that doesn't bother you, then don't complain that you haven't been warned! In this one respect, Guanay seems happy to pass up an opportunity to create a potentially lucrative economic base by promoting relatively unobtrusive tourism.

If you do manage to negotiate a reasonable rate, the upper Beni offers plenty of interest. For the first three hours from Guanay, you'll pass through mining-ravaged landscapes, dotted with toiling barranquilleros amid heaps of tailings and mining detritus. At one point, the river squeezes between two large rocks and drops over a 2m waterfall, which is quite a rush in a large wooden canoe. In several places, you pass between high and narrow canyon walls, including the dramatic Beú Gorge. Three hours above

Rurrenabaque, a more lethargic Río Beni slides past the Campamento de Papagayos, the nesting site of the brilliant and now endangered scarlet macaw. Because of the creation of the Parque Nacional Madidi, most of the *cazadores* (hunters), *pescadores* (fisherfolk) and *madereros* (woodcutters) who once exploited the region's natural resources have moved on to other pickings.

CARANAVI

All buses between La Paz and the lowlands pass through uninspiring little Caranavi, midway between Coroico and Guanay. Travelers love to dis this place – and the reason is pretty obvious – but those who find themselves stuck here can take a look at the Untucala suspension bridge, which spans a crossing used since Inca times.

Caranavi has several inexpensive hotels; among them are the *Hotel Avenida*, *Residencial México*, and the basic but economical *Residencial Caranavi*. The nicer *Hotel Landivar*, with a pool, charges US$7 per person. More sophisticated is the recommended *Caturra Inn* (☎ 02-374204; fax 02-328584), which has single/double rooms with private baths, hot showers and fans for US$13/22. It's set in lovely gardens and has a good restaurant and clean pool. *El Tigre* does basic meals for around US$1.

There are two bus terminals ten minutes' walk apart; one is for La Paz and Rurrenabaque services, and the other for Guanay.

Climbing in the Cordillera Real

The Cordillera Real has more than 600 peaks over 5000m, all of which are relatively accessible. They're also free of the growing bureaucracy attached to climbing and trekking in the Himalayas. The following section is a rundown of the more popular climbs in the Cordillera Real, but this is by no means an exhaustive list. There are many other peaks to entice the experienced climber, and whether you choose one of those described here or one of the lesser known and less traveled ones, climbing in the Bolivian Andes is always an adventure.

Note that the climbs described here are technical and require climbing experience, a reputable climbing guide and proper technical equipment. For information on Bolivian mountaineering, see Activities in the Facts for the Visitor chapter.

HUAYNA POTOSÍ

Huayna Potosí, at 6088m, is the most popular major peak in Bolivia because of its imposing beauty and ease of access, as well as the fact that it is over the magic 6000m figure (but 26 feet under the magic 20,000-foot figure). It's also appealing because it can be climbed by beginners with a competent guide and technical equipment.

Some people attempt to climb Huayna Potosí in one day, but this cannot be recommended. It's a 1500m vertical climb from the Paso Zongo and 2500m vertical altitude gain from La Paz to the summit, and to ascend in one day would pose a great risk of potentially fatal cerebral edema.

Access

Access is by taxi, which costs about US$40, with haggling – make sure your driver knows the way – or by the camión from Plaza Ballivián in El Alto at around midday on Monday, Wednesday and Friday. It may be difficult to squeeze on, and the ride is dusty and uncomfortable, but it's cheap at US$1 as far as Paso Zongo. A 4WD from La Paz to the trailhead costs about US$50 for up to about five people.

As Huayna Potosí is so popular, lots of climbers are headed out that way during the climbing season. If you only want a lift, check with specialist climbing agencies. Someone will probably have a 4WD going on the day you want, and you can share costs for the trip.

The Route

From the refugio, cross the dam and follow the aqueduct

until you reach the third path taking off to your left. Follow this to a glacial stream where a useful signpost points the way to the 'Huayna Potosí Glaciar.' Take this path through and across the rocks to reach the ridge of a moraine. Near the end of the moraine, descend slightly to your right and then ascend the steep scree gullies. At the top, you should bear left and follow the cairns to reach the glacier. If you got a late start, it may be wise to stop at Campamento Rocas, on dry land at the base of the glacier.

The glacier is crevassed, especially after July, so rope up while crossing it. Ascend the initial slopes, then follow a long, gradually ascending traverse to the right before turning left and climbing steeply to a flat area between 5500 and 5700m known as Campo Argentino. It will take you about four hours to reach this point. Camp on the right of the path, but note that the area farther to the right is heavily crevassed, especially later in the season.

The following morning, you should leave between 4 and 6 am. Follow the path/trench out of Campo Argentino, then head uphill to your right until you join a ridge. Turn left here and cross a flat stretch to reach the steep and exposed Polish Ridge (named in honor of the Pole who fell off it and died while soloing in 1994). Here, you cross a series of rolling glacial hills and crevasses to arrive below the summit face. Either climb straight up the face to the summit or cross along the base of it to join the ridge that rises to the left. This ridge provides thrilling views down the 1000m-high West Face. Either route will bring you to the summit in five to seven hours from Campo Argentino.

Descent to Campo Argentino from the summit takes a couple of hours; from there, it's another three hours or so back to the refugio at Paso Zongo.

Places to Stay

Dr Hugo Berrios runs the refugio in Paso Zongo and also guides climbs on the mountain. Accommodations cost US$10; meals are extra. Dr Berrios can also organize transportation to the hut, mountain guides and food rations, as well as porters to carry your kit up to first camp. Contact him at Huayna Potosí Tours in La Paz (see Organized Tours in the Getting Around chapter).

ILLIMANI

Illimani, the 6439m giant overlooking La Paz, is probably the most renowned of Bolivia's peaks. It was first climbed by a party led by W M Conway, a pioneer 19th-century alpinist. Although it's not a difficult climb technically, the combination of altitude and ice conditions warrants serious consideration and caution. Technical equipment is essential above the snow line; caution is especially needed on the section immediately above Nido de Cóndores where six Chileans died on the descent in 1989.

Access

The easiest way to reach the Illimani first camp, Puente Roto, is via Estancia Una, a three-hour trip by 4WD from La Paz (about US$160). From there, it's three to four hours' walk to Puente Roto. In Estancia Una you can hire mules to carry your gear to Puente Roto for around US$6. You can hire porters in Estancia Una or Pinaya for US$10 to carry rucksacks from Puente Roto to the high camp at Nido de Cóndores.

A daily 5 am bus (US$2) goes from near La Paz's Mercado Rodríguez to the village of Quilihuaya, from which you'll have a two-hour slog to Estancia Una – complete with a 400m elevation gain. In theory, buses return from Quilihuaya to La Paz several days a week at around 8:30 am, but those relying on public transportation should still carry extra food to tide them over for at least a couple of days.

An alternative route to the base camp is via Cohoni. In theory, buses and camiones leave La Paz for Cohoni (four hours, US$2) in the early afternoon Monday to Saturday from the corner of General Luis Lara and Calle Boquerón. They leave Cohoni to

return to La Paz around 8:30 am and may take anywhere from four hours to all day, depending on which route is followed.

The Route

The normal route to Pico Sur, the highest of Illimani's five summits, is straightforward but heavily crevassed. You'll have to either have technical glacier experience or hire a competent professional guide.

The route to Nido de Cóndores, a rock platform beside the glacier, is a four- to six-hour slog up a rock ridge from Puente Roto. There's no water at Nido de Cóndores, so you'll have to melt snow – bring sufficient stove fuel.

From Nido de Cóndores, you need to set off at about 2 am. Follow the path in the snow leading uphill from the camp; this grows narrower and steeper, then flattens out a bit before becoming steeper again. It then crosses a series of crevasses before climbing up to the right to reach a level section. From here, aim for the large break in the skyline to the left of the summit, taking care to avoid the two major crevasses, and cross one steep section that is iced over from July onwards. After you pass through the skyline break, turn right and continue up onto the summit ridge. The final three vertical meters involve walking 400m along the ridge at over 6400m elevation.

Plan on six to 10 hours for the climb from Nido de Cóndores to the summit and three to four hours to descend back to camp.

If possible, continue on from Nido de Cóndores to Puente Roto on the same day. The 1000m descent is not appreciated after a long day, but your body will thank you the following day and will recover more quickly at the lower altitude. You'll also avoid having to melt snow for a second night. On the fourth day, you can walk from Puente Roto back out to Estancia Una in about two to three hours.

CONDORIRI MASSIF

The massif known as Condoriri is actually a cluster of 13 peaks ranging in height from 5100 to 5648m. The highest of these is Cabeza del Cóndor (literally, 'head of the condor') which has twin winglike ridges flowing from either side of the summit pyramid. Known as Las Alas (The Wings), they cause the peak to resemble a condor lifting its wings on takeoff.

Cabeza del Cóndor is a challenging climb following an exposed ridge and should only be attempted by experienced climbers. However, a number of other peaks in the Condoriri Massif, including the beautiful Pequeño Alpamayo, can be attempted by beginners with a competent guide.

Access

There is no public transportation to Condoriri. A 4WD to the start of the walk-in at the dam at Laguna Tuni costs US$70. If you don't want to use a 4WD transfer, you can trek the 24km from Milluni into Laguna Tuni dam on the road to Paso Zongo (see Huayna Potosí earlier in this section).

From Laguna Tuni, follow the rough road that circles south around the lake and continues up a drainage trending north. Once you're in this valley, you'll have a view of the Cabeza del Condor and Las Alas.

It isn't possible to drive beyond the dam because there's a locked gate across the road. Some drivers know a way around it, but if you need to hire pack animals you'll have to do so before the dam, anyway. Locals charge US$8 per day for mules, and for llamas, which can carry less, they charge US$6 per day.

The Route

From the end of the road, follow the obvious paths up along the right side of the valley until you reach a large lake. Follow the right shore of the lake to arrive at the base camp, which is three hours from Laguna Tuni.

Leave base camp at about 8 am, following the path up the north-trending valley through boulders and up the slope of a moraine. Bear to the left here and descend slightly to reach the flat part of the glacier, above the seriously crevassed section. You should reach this point in about 1½ hours from base camp.

Here you should rope up and put on crampons. Head left across the glacier

before rising up to the col (lowest point of the ridge), taking care to avoid the crevasses. Ascend to the right up the rock-topped summit called Tarija – which affords impressive views of Pequeño Alpamayo – before dropping down a scree and rock slope to rejoin a glacier on the other side. From there, either climb directly up the ridge to the summit or follow a climbing traverse to the left before cutting back to the right and up to the summit. The summit ridge is very exposed.

ANCOHUMA

Ancohuma is the highest peak in the Sorata massif, towering 6427m on the remote northern edge of the Cordillera Real. It was not climbed until 1919 and remains very challenging.

No one seems to know how high Ancohuma is. At present, the generally accepted height is 6427m, but the *Times World Atlas* has it at 7012m, the maps in early 1900s editions of the *South American Handbook* says it's 7014m high, and various tourist board publications put it at 7002m. In 1994, a satellite picture suggested it was in fact nearly 7000m high. If that's correct, Ancohuma would not only be higher than the 6542m volcano Sajama (which is currently believed to be Bolivia's highest peak) but also the highest peak in the world outside the Himalayas. It would also mean that all those climbers who've slogged up Argentina's Aconcagua believing it to be South America's highest summit would have to come to Bolivia and try again.

A 1995 attempt to make an accurate measurement with two Global Positioning Systems could not establish the height after one of the GPSs failed. However, the expedition leader, Dennis Moore, is certain that Ancohuma is over 6500m high and is determined to climb it again and settle the matter conclusively.

Access

The peak is accessed via Sorata, which is accessible by public transport. From this lovely little town, you can hire a 4WD for the long traverse to Cocoyo, where the fun begins.

(It's also possible to hire a 4WD all the way from La Paz to Cocoyo, which is convenient but expensive.) If you have a serious amount of gear, you can hire a mule train to carry it from Sorata to base camp, which is in the lake basin east of the peaks at about 4500m. Plan on at least two days for these various transport arrangements to get you to the lakes. Alternatively, Ancohuma can be climbed from the west, using Laguna Glacial as a base camp (see Hiking in Sorata). Further advice and information are available in Sorata (earlier in this chapter).

The Routes

From the lakes, head west up to the glacier following the drainage up through loose moraine. Make camp below the north ridge, the normal route. After a circuitous path through a crevasse field, a steep pitch or two of ice will gain the north ridge. An exposed but fairly easy ridge walk will take you to the summit.

If you've opted for the more easily accessed western route, hike from Sorata to base camp at Laguna Glacial. From there, the route climbs the obvious moraine and then ascends the glacier, over fields of extremely dangerous crevasses to a bivouac at 5800m. From there, it climbs to the bergschrund and across a relatively level ice plateau to the summit pyramid. This is most easily climbed via the north ridge; the first part is quite steep and icy, but it gets easier toward the summit.

Cordillera Apolobamba

The remote Cordillera Apolobamba, flush against the Peruvian border north of Lake Titicaca, is gradually opening up as a popular hiking, trekking and climbing venue. Mountaineers, in particular, will find a wonderland of tempting peaks, first ascents and new routes to discover.

Despite the number of foreign researchers and anthropologists passing through, only a few locals – mostly men – speak Spanish, and sensitivity to local culture is requisite in this highly traditional area (most people in the region speak Aymará, but there is a Quechua-speaking enclave around Charazani, Pelechuco, and farther down at Apolo). It must be stressed that although things are changing rapidly, this region remains remote and isn't set up for tourism. There are few services, transport isn't reliable and the people maintain a fragile traditional lifestyle. Sensitivity to local sentiments will help keep its distinctive character intact.

Every town and village in the region holds an annual festival, most of which fall between June and September. One very worthwhile one takes place in Italaque, northeast of Escoma, around August 5: the Fiesta de La Virgen de las Nieves. It features a potpourri of traditional Andean dances, including: Quena Quenas, Morenos, Llameros, Choquelas, Kapñis, Jacha Sikuris, Chunchos etc.

Organized Tours

Individualized tours may be organized through any of the La Paz travel agencies that know the Cordillera Apolobamba. For suggestions, see Organized Tours in the Getting Around chapter and Activities in the Facts for the Visitor chapter.

CHARAZANI
☎ 0813

Charazani, also known as Villa General José Pérez, is the administrative town, commercial center and transport axis of Bautista Saavedra province. The surrounding area of the upper Charazani valley is the home of the Kallawaya (also spelled Kallahuaya or Callawaya), the wandering 'medicine men' who are versed in the art of natural healing with herbs, potions, amulets and incantations.

Services in Charazani have increased exponentially in recent years, and numerous organizations are working with the local community in the area on sustainable development projects, including solar power, textile production and the promotion of sensible tourism. There are now two telephones, in the alcaldía (☎ 2002)

CORDILLERAS & YUNGAS

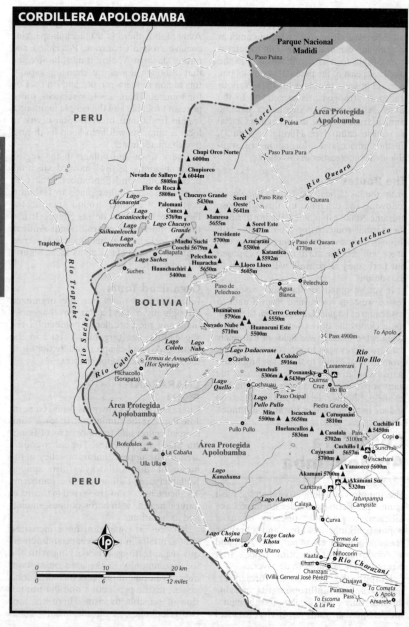

CORDILLERA APOLOBAMBA

Parque Nacional Madidi

Paso Puina

PERU

Río Sorel

Puina

Área Protegida Apolobamba

Paso Pura Pura

Río Queara

Queara

Chupi Orco Norte
▲ 6000m

Chupiorco
▲ 6044m

Nevada de Salluyo
5808m
Flor de Roca
5808m

Chucuyo Grande
▲ 5430m

Sorel Oeste
▲ 5641m

Paso Rite

Palomani Cunca
▲ 5769m

Manresa
▲ 5655m

▲ Sorel Este
5471m

Lago Chocnacota

Lago Cacanicoche

Lago Chuyuyo Grande

Presidente
5700m

Azucarani
▲ 5580m

Lago Saihuanlcocha

Lago Churococha

Machu Suchi
Coochi 5679m

▲ Katantica
5592m

Paso de Queara
4770m

Río Pelechuco

Trapiche

Calliapata

Pelechuco
Huaracha ▲
5650m

▲ Lloco Lloco
5605m

Pelechuco

Lago Suches

Suches

Huanchuchiri
5400m

Paso de Pelechuco

Agua Blanca

BOLIVIA

Huanacuni
5796m

Cerro Cerebro
▲ 5550m

Río Suches

Río Trapiche

Nevado Nube ▲
5710m

Huanacuni Este
5500m

Pass 4900m

To Apolo

Lago Cololo

Lago Nube

Lago Dadacorane

Río Illo Illo

Termas de Antaquilla
(Hot Springs)

Quello

▲ Cololo
5916m

Lavaererani

Río Cololo

Hichacollo
(Sorapata)

Lago Nube

Sunchuli
5306m

Posnansky
▲ 5430m

Quimsa
Cruz

Illo Illo

Cochauau

Paso Osipal

Piedra Grande

Área Protegida Apolobamba

Lago Quello

Lago Pullo Pullo

Mita
5500m

Iscacuchu
▲ 5650m

▲ Coruqunini
5810m

Cuchillo II
▲ 5450m

Copi

Pullo Pullo

Huelancallos
5836m

▲ Casalala
5702m

Pass
5100m

Sunchuli

Cuchillo I
5657m

Viscachani

Bofedales

La Cabaña

Área Protegida Apolobamba

Cayayani
5700m

▲ Yanaorco 5600m

Ulla Ulla

PERU

Lago Kanahuma

Akamani 5700m ▲

▲ Akamani Sur
5320m

Carizaya

Jatunpampa
Campsite

Lago Alueta

Calaya

Curva

Lago Chojna Khota

Lago Cacho Khota

Termas de Charazani

Kaata

Niñocorin

Río Charazani

Phujro Utano

Chari

Charazani
(Villa General José Pérez)

Chajaya

To Comata & Apolo

Pumasani
Pass

To Escoma & La Paz

Amarete

0   10   20 km
0   6   12 miles

The Kallawaya

The origins and age of the Kallawaya tradition are unknown, although some Kallawaya claim to be descended from the apparently vanished Tiahuanaco culture. The Kallawaya language, however, which is used exclusively for healing, is derived from Quechua, the language of the Inca. Knowledge and skills are passed down through generations, although it's sometimes possible for aspiring healers to study under acknowledged masters.

The early Kallawaya were known for their wanderings and traveled all over the continent in search of medicinal herbs. The most capable of today's practitioners will have memorized the properties and uses of 600 to 1000 different healing herbs, but their practices also involve magic and charms. They believe that sickness and disease are the result of a displaced or imbalanced *ajallu* (life force). The incantations and amulets are intended to encourage it back into a state of equilibrium within the body.

Hallmarks of the Kallawaya include the *huincha*, the woven headband worn by women, and the *alforja* (medicine pouch) carried by the men. The Kallawaya of Charazani region are known for their colorful weavings, which typically bear natural designs, both zoomorphic and anthropomorphic, and for their *llijllas*, striped women's shawls with bands of color representing the landscape of the village of origin.

The Kallawaya's legacy has been recorded by several anthropologists and medical professionals; German university psychiatrist Ina Rössing has produced an immense four-volume work called El Mundo de los Kallahuaya about her ongoing research, and Frenchman Louis Girault has compiled an encyclopedia of herbal remedies employed by the Kallawaya, entitled Kallahuaya, Curanderos Itinerantes de los Andes.

and in the office of Transportes Altiplano (☎ 2003), and the new Nawirywasi library has local maps, books on medicinal plants and the Kallawaya culture, and information that's of use to hikers, trekkers and climbers.

Termas de Charazani

Along the river about 10 minutes' walk upstream from town, you'll pass the Termas de Charazani, a hot spring where you can bathe for US$1 per person. Along the way, you'll follow a surprisingly lush, green valley that bursts into flower in September and October. Other natural thermal baths, complete with a steaming hot waterfall, are found two hours' hike down the valley from Charazani along the Apolo road.

Special Events

Two large fiestas are held around July 16 and August 6, and there's a wonderful children's dance festival that takes place around November 16.

Places to Stay & Eat

Charazani now has no fewer than five lodgings, three of which are relatively comfortable. The *Hotel Akamani*, less than a block from the plaza, offers probably the highest standards and charges US$2 to US$3.50 per person. Just off the plaza on the Curva road is the *Inti Wasi* on your right and the *Hotel Charazani* on your left. The former, arranged around a cobbled courtyard, provides a nice traditional atmosphere and also charges US$2.50. The Hotel Charazani affords a fabulous view over the valley, along with Doña Sofia's fine Bolivian cooking, for US$2.25 per person.

There are several pensiones; for an excellent traditional almuerzo, try the unnamed one beside the Cornejo tienda, just off the plaza. Here the dueña cooks up soup, a main course and coffee over an open fire for just US$0.80. The aforementioned efficient and quick-tempered Doña Sofia at the Hotel Charazani serves almuerzos at 12:30 pm and cenas at 7 pm; reserve a spot early, don't arrive late, stay humble and be sure to clean your plate!

Essentials – wheat, oats, tinned fish, pasta, rice, bread and a few fruits and vegetables – can be purchased in tiendas surrounding the plaza; try Don Francisco's store, which is located opposite the church. Trekkers, however, will probably want to bring their supplies from La Paz.

Getting There & Away

From La Paz (eight hours, US$4.50), Provincias del Norte (☎ 02-382239) and the more reliable Trans Altiplano (☎ 02-383079) leave daily at 6:30 am from along Calle Reyes Cardona, four blocks up Avenida Kollasuyo from the cemetery. To ensure a favorable seat, it's wise to purchase tickets in advance and turn up early. On Tuesday, Friday and Saturday, the Trans Altiplano bus continues to Curva (two hours, US$1.20), to arrive around 6 pm (and occasionally, it even dares to attempt the road down to Apolo!) From Curva, it leaves for La Paz, via Charazani, on Wednesday, Saturday and Sunday at around 4 pm. Provincias del Norte continues to Chari on Tuesday and Friday. From Charazani, both flotas leave for La Paz from the plaza daily between 6:30 and 8:30 pm.

From Mercado El Tejar, opposite the cemetery in La Paz, a weekly camión leaves for Charazani (15 to 20 hours, US$3) on Tuesday at 2 pm. As you can imagine, it isn't the most pleasant journey on earth – you'll be cold and rattled – and you'll still face a long day's walk to Curva.

Alternatively, you can take the Pelechuco micro (see Pelechuco, later in this section) and get off at Abra Pumasani (the Charazani turnoff). From there, you can look for an unlikely lift to Charazani or walk the long and winding 30km.

From Charazani, a 4WD route winds down from the heights to Apolo, which is in the Yungas at the edge of the Amazon Basin. It's occasionally negotiated by camiones, but several serious stream crossings and landslide risks mean it's strictly a

fair-weather route and is well suited to mountain bikes or foot traffic.

AMARETE
☎ 0813

Amarete, the largest community in the Apolobamba region, is known for its textiles, ceramics and Kallawaya heritage, and both men and women here wear bright traditional dress featuring white, orange, red and black. A good time to visit is during the annual festival, which takes place the first week in August. This valley has been worked for hundreds of years, and its ancient terraces are spectacular monuments to its agricultural history. With individual transportation, Amarete makes a nice side trip en route back to La Paz from Charazani. It's also the start of a fabulous trek to Iskanwaya (see earlier in this chapter).

Amarete has two satellite telephones (☎ 2000 and 2001), and a hotel is now being developed.

CHARI
☎ 0813

The village of Chari, 1½ hours' walk from Charazani, is a center of Kallawaya culture and a lovely blend of terraces, flowers and vegetable gardens. A German anthropologist has worked for many years here on the Tuwans textile project, which is designed to market the lovely local hand-dyed weavings. The town is also home to a Kallawaya cultural museum. This stone and thatch structure holds exhibits pertaining to medicinal plants and the area's unique and lovely weavings.

About an hours' walk outside the village is an impressive site of pre-Inca ruins. To get there, walk through the town and turn left at the enormous boulder that creates a small cave. Follow this path to the cemetery, where you should keep to the left until you gain the ridge. The ruins lie about 200m up this ridge. Because of local suspicion, please advise locals where you're headed before setting off on this track.

Accommodations in Chari are limited to a simple *Alojamiento*, attached to the museum, but several local families also have rooms to rent.

ÁREA PROTEGIDA APOLOBAMBA

In the late 1990s, the Parque Nacional Ulla Ulla was renamed the Área Natural de Manejo Integrado Apolobamba – more conveniently, the Área Protegida Apolobamba or ANMI-Apolobamba – and was expanded from 200,000 hectares to nearly 484,000 hectares. It now includes the entire Cordillera Apolobamba and most of the renowned Curva to Pelechuco trek on the eastern slopes of the range. At its northern end it abuts the Parque Nacional Madidi to form one of the most extensive protected areas in the Western Hemisphere.

The original park – a loosely defined vicuña reserve along the Peruvian border – was established in 1972, and was upgraded by UNESCO in 1977 into a Man and the Biosphere Reserve. Later that same year, the Instituto Nacional de Fomento Lanero (INFOL) was created to represent wool producers and charged with researching, monitoring and preventing habitat degradation of the reserve's camelids. INFOL has now been transformed into the Instituto Boliviano de Tecnología Agropecuaria (IBTA), which concentrates more on agricultural development and social services.

The modern park is home to at least 3000 vicuñas and also to Bolivia's densest condor population. In addition to the popular hiking routes, you'll find excellent wild trekking around Lagos Cololo, Nube, Quello, Kanahuma and Pullopullo, all of which enjoy snow-covered backdrops and populations of waterbirds: black ibises, flamingos and several species of geese.

Information

For predeparture information, contact the Servicio Nacional de Áreas Protegidas, or SERNAP (☎ 02-430881 or 434420; fax 02-434540; 20 de Octubre 2782, La Paz); see the website: www.rds.org.bo/miembros/ongs/sernap/index.htm. In an emergency, contact them by radio on frequency 8335 USB.

At Charazani, a cabaña is being constructed that will contain exhibits on the park and local traditional medicine. See Curva to Pelechuco Trek, below, for a description of that trek.

Places to Stay & Eat

Noncampers can normally find accommodations in local homes for US$2 per person – just ask around – and there's a tienda in Ulla Ulla village. At La Cabaña, 5km from Ulla Ulla village, IBTA has a small hostel where you may be able to hole up, but they want you to reserve from La Paz (see Information). In addition, ranger stations have recently been added at Charazani, Curva, Pelechuco, Pullo Pullo, Suches and Hichacollo; the last three were designed by a La Paz architect and blend adobe construction, domed thatched roofs and passive solar walls to reflect both modern and traditional styles. Hikers can camp at any of these sites – or can even stay inside, space permitting.

Getting There & Away

The micro to Pelechuco passes through Ulla Ulla. See Getting There & Away under Pelechuco, later in this section.

CURVA

The village of Curva, near the sacred mountain, Akamani, has a few basic tiendas, but no hotels or restaurants. If you need to stay the night, hunt up Sr Daniel Lizarraga or Sr Andres Quispe, who rent out rooms in their homes. The main festival here is a colorful affair that takes place on June 29.

CURVA TO PELECHUCO TREK

A fantastic hike through splendid and largely uninhabited wilderness is the five-day trek from Curva to Pelechuco, which stays mostly above 4000m and includes five high passes. There's arguably no better scenery in the Andes, and along the way you're sure to see llamas and alpacas, as well as more elusive Andean wildlife, such as viscachas, vicuñas, condors and perhaps even a spectacled bear (there's now a bear research center five hours on foot from Pelechuco, where two individual bears have been tagged and are occasionally observed).

The trek may be done in either direction, as both Charazani and Pelechuco have relatively reliable – albeit very limited – public transportation. Most people do the route from south to north, but starting in Pelechuco would mean an additional day of downhill walking and a grand finish at the hot springs near Charazani.

Pack animals are available in both Curva and Pelechuco for the following prices: Llamas cost US$4.50 to US$5 per day, mules are US$6.50 to US$7 per day, and guides/muleteers are US$8.50 per day. Clients must carry their own stove and food, and also provide meals for their guides, porters and muleteers.

If possible, bring all your trekking food from La Paz, as Curva and Pelechuco have only basics: fresh fruit and vegetables, bread, canned goods, pasta and drinks.

Access

For information on public transportation, see Getting There & Away under Charazani, earlier in this section, or under Pelechuco, later in this section.

A more expensive but considerably easier and more comfortable way to go is by 4WD. A vehicle and driver from La Paz to Curva (seven hours, US$300) or Pelechuco (10 hours, US$350) may be worthwhile because it allows daylight travel through the incomparable scenery. Be sure to fit in a diversion to the tidy Valle de Amarete, where the scenery takes on Himalayan proportions, and the locals wear some of the most colorful dress to be found anywhere in Bolivia.

Alternatively, you can pay to leave the logistics to someone else and do the trek with a tour agency (see Organized Tours in the Getting Around chapter).

The Route

Because most people do the trek from south to north, from Curva to Pelechuco, that's how it's described here. If you're coming from Charazani, you can either follow the long and winding road for four to five hours or take the 3½- to four-hour shortcut. Cross the river at the thermal baths, then climb up the other bank and back to the road. After about an hour, you should follow a path that climbs to a white and yellow church on your left. Beyond the church, descend the other side of the hill, to just above the community of Niñocorín. After a short distance, you'll strike an obvious path; turn left onto it and follow it as it contours through the fields and then descends to cross a river, where it then starts its climb up into Curva.

From Curva, head toward the cross on the hill north of the village and skirt around the right side of the hill. About an hour from Curva, you'll cross a stream. Continue uphill along the right bank of the stream. At a cultivated patch about 200m before the valley descending from the right flank of the snow peak, cross the stream to join a well-defined path entering from your left. If you continue along this path, you'll reach an excellent campsite in a small flat spot beside a stream. Alternatively, you can keep following this trail for another 1½ hours to the ideal 4200m-high campsite at Jatunpampa.

From Jatunpampa, head up the valley and across a small flat area to the col with a cairn, which takes about two hours. From this 4700m pass, you'll have fabulous views of Akamani off to the northwest. One to two hours farther along, you'll arrive at a nice camping spot near the Incacancha (also called Incachani) waterfall at 4100m.

The ascent that will face you the next morning may appear a bit daunting, but it isn't that bad. Cross the bridge below the Incacancha waterfall and take the zigzag path up the scree gully. As you ascend, you'll have distant views of Ancohuma and Illampu, and after two hours or so, you'll reach the pass at 4800m.

From the pass, traverse gently uphill to the left until you gain the ridge, which affords great views of Ancohuma, Illampu and the Cordillera Real to the south and Cuchillo II to the north. At this point, the obvious trail descends past a small lake before arriving at a larger lake with a good view of Akamani.

Climb from here up to the next ridge before descending to the small mining settlement of Viscachani, where you'll strike the 4WD track toward Illo Illo ('Hilo Hilo' in some sources). This takes about an hour. In another hour, this road ascends to a 4900m pass, which also provides superb views of the Cordillera Real to the south and Cuchillo II and the Sunchuli Valley to the north and west.

At the pass, the road drops into the valley; at the point where it bears right, look for a path turning off to the left. This will take you to a point above the Sunchuli gold mine, which reopened in 1992 and is worked by up to 100 miners. From Sunchuli, follow a contour line above the aqueduct for about an hour, until you see an ideal 4600m-high campsite below Cuchillo I.

The fourth day of the hike is probably the finest, as it includes sections that have been used for centuries by gold miners and campesinos. From the campsite below Cuchillo I, the road ascends for about two hours to a 5100m pass via a series of switchbacks. From the pass, you can scramble up to a cairn above the road for excellent views dominated by Cololo, the highest mountain in the southern Cordillera Apolobamba.

Descend along the road for a few minutes, then turn right down a steep but obvious path, which crosses a stream opposite the glacier lake below Cuchillo II before descending to the valley floor. If you follow the valley floor, you'll rejoin the road a couple of minutes above the picturesque stone-and-thatch village of Piedra Grande. It takes about three hours to get from the pass to Piedra Grande.

Keep on the road for an hour or so; follow the pre-Hispanic road turning off downhill to your right. After you cross a bridge, you should follow the obvious path to the right, which will conduct you up into the village of Illo Illo in about an hour. Here you'll find small shops selling beer and basics – biscuits, pasta, tuna, soft drinks and even candles and batteries.

When leaving Illo Illo, don't be tempted onto the path to the left, which leads west to Ulla Ulla and the Altiplano (although this is also a viable trek). The correct route leaves the village above the new school, between the public facilities and the cemetery. From there, cross the fields and llama pastures until the path becomes clear again. After crossing a bridge (about one hour out of Illo Illo) and beginning up a valley with a sharp rock peak at its head (if it's too overcast to see the rock, look for several small houses on your left and turn there), you'll stumble onto an ideal campsite. It lies at a bend in the valley, where there are a number of large fallen rocks.

From the campsite, head up the valley for about 1½ hours until you reach a bridge over the stream. At this point, the route begins to climb up to the final pass at 4900m, which you should reach in another 1½ hours. From the pass, the route descends past a lake, crossing llama and alpaca pastures and following some pre-Columbian paving. Less than two hours later, you'll arrive in Pelechuco, at 3500m.

PELECHUCO

The lovely colonial village of Pelechuco nestles beneath the snowy peaks of the Cordillera Apolobamba. It's most often visited as a trailhead on the Curva to Pelechuco trek or as a staging point for the much longer and more challenging trek from Pelechuco down to Apolo in the northernmost reaches of the Yungas.

Places to Stay & Eat

Pelechuco has two alojamientos: *Alojamiento Rumillajta*, behind the church, and *Chujlla Wasi*, on the plaza, neither of which has electricity or running water. However, there's normally enough rainwater to keep the village hydrated. Both places charge around US$1.75 per person.

Meals are available from Señora Álvarez on the plaza, and staple supplies are sold at a couple of small tiendas.

Getting There & Away

Three buses leave La Paz for Pelechuco (15 to 24 hours, US$5.50) on Wednesday, beginning at 6 am; they stop en route at the market in Huancasaya, on the international border, before continuing to Ulla Ulla and Pelechuco. From Pelechuco, the buses head back to La Paz at 4 am on Friday morning and on Saturday afternoon. The Friday bus normally halts at the market in Chejepampa, near Suches. At both of these international markets you can purchase good-value alpaca wool products and change US dollars cash, bolivianos and soles.

If you're hiking into Pelechuco and aren't being met by a 4WD, it's worth hiking west along the road for two hours. Just beyond Antaquilla, you'll find luscious open-air bathing in the thermally heated adobe brick swimming pool. It's worth camping here because there's no place to stay or eat anyway before Escoma, five hours away, and you won't want to miss the views through the ANMI-Apolobamba. From Escoma it's another five hours back to La Paz.

A 4WD and driver cost around US$350 one way to or from La Paz – and must be arranged *in* La Paz! If you are going this route, try to approach or leave Pelechuco as early as possible, so you can enjoy the incredible mountain views to the west and over the 5000m pass, as well as on the scenic drive along Lago Cololo.

Cordillera Quimsa Cruz

The Cordillera Quimsa Cruz, an as-yet-undiscovered gem for mountaineers, was once described by the Spanish climbing magazine *Pyrenaica* as a 'South American Karakoram.' In 1999, near the summit of Santa Veracruz, the Spaniard Javier Sánchez discovered the remains of an 800-year-old ceremonial burial site with ancient artifacts and weavings.

The Quimsa Cruz is not a large range – it's only some 50km from end to end – and the peaks are lower than in other Bolivian ranges. The highest peak, Jacha Cuno Collo, rises to 5800m, and the other glaciated peaks range from 4500m to 5300m. Granite peaks, glaciers and lovely lakeside camping make the Quimsa Cruz arguably the most

scenically spectacular of Bolivia's four main cordilleras. It lies to the southeast of Illimani, separated from the Cordillera Real by the Río La Paz, and geologically speaking, it's actually a southern outlier of that range.

The Quimsa Cruz lies at the northern end of Bolivia's tin belt, and tin reserves have been exploited here since the late 1800s. However, with the replacement of tin by plastics and aluminum, the current market price of tin doesn't make it lucrative to extract it from such remote sites. The few miners who've stayed on and continue to work some of the mines here either take their chances with cooperatives or are employed as caretakers for mining companies who don't want to abandon their holdings and are presumably hoping for better days. In any case, all the major mining areas in the region – which includes every valley along the western face of the Quimsa Cruz – remain populated, and most of the remaining mining activity is divided between Mina Caracoles and Viloco.

Activities
The Quimsa Cruz offers some of the finest adventure climbing in all of Bolivia, and in every valley, mining roads provide access to the impressively glaciated peaks. Although all of the nevados of the Quimsa Cruz have now been climbed, there are still plenty of unclimbed routes, and expeditions are unlikely to encounter other climbing groups.

Trekking is also possible throughout the range, which is covered by IGM mapping. The main route is the two- to three-day trek from Viloco to Mina Caracoles. Of interest along this route is the renowned site of a 1971 airplane crash, which was already stripped by local miners before rescue teams could arrive at the scene two days later!

Staples are available in both Viloco and Quimé, but it's still best to carry everything you'll need – food, fuel and other supplies – from La Paz.

Getting There & Away
Road access is relatively easy owing to the number of mines in the area, and it's possible to drive within 30 minutes' walk of some

glaciers. Others, however, are up to a four-hour hike from the nearest road. The easiest access is provided by Flota Trans-Inquisivi, which leaves daily from La Paz's main bus terminal for the eastern side of the range (to Quimé, Inquisivi, Cajuata, Circuato, Suri, Mina Caracoles, and less often, to Yacopampa and Frutillani). Alternatively, take any bus toward Oruro and get off at the tranca at Khonani, about 70km short of Oruro. This is the turnoff for the main road into the Quimsa Cruz, and here you can wait for a truck or bus heading into the Cordillera.

Bus service is also available to the communities and mines on the western side of the range, as well as to Quimé on the eastern slope. To Viloco, Araca or Cairoma, buses leave most days of the week, but the biggest challenge can be finding their office in El Alto, as it seems to shift around with some frequency; you'll just have to ask locally.

Those with a bit more ready cash can hire a 4WD and driver for the five- to seven-hour journey; any of the services used by mountaineers and trekkers can organize the trip.

Lake Titicaca

Surprisingly reminiscent of the Aegean Sea, Lake Titicaca is an incongruous splash of blue amid the parched dreariness of the Altiplano, with clear sapphire-blue waters. Set in the rolling, scrub-covered hills in the heart of the Altiplano northwest of La Paz, it straddles the Peru-Bolivia border like a bridge between the two countries (Bolivians

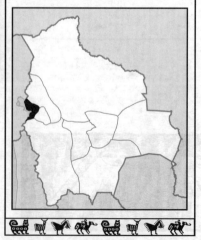

rather crudely but proudly like to say that they have the 'titty' and Peru has the *caca*!). At its present level of 3820m, it's one of the world's highest major lakes, but ignore claims that it's the world's highest navigable lake, as both Peru and Chile have higher bodies of water that can be navigated by small craft. Long rumored to be 'bottomless,' Lake Titicaca has now been determined to have a depth of up to 457m.

With a surface area of over 9000 sq km, Lake Titicaca is South America's second largest lake, after Venezuela's Lake Maracaibo. It's a remnant of the ancient inland sea known as Lago Ballivián, which covered much of the Altiplano before geological faults and evaporation brought about a drop in the water level. Its average dimensions are 230km long and 97km wide, but during the flooding of 1986, the water level rose several meters and inundated an additional 1000 sq km.

History

When you first glimpse the gemlike waters of Lake Titicaca, beneath the looming backdrop of the Cordillera Real in the clear Altiplano light, you'll see why early peoples connected it with mystical events. The pre-Inca peoples of the Altiplano believed that both the sun itself and their bearded, white leader/deity, Viracocha, had risen out of its mysterious depths, while the Incas believed it was the birthplace of their civilization.

When the Spanish arrived in the mid-16th century, legends of treasure began to surface, including the tale that certain Incas, in desperation, had flung their gold into the lake to prevent the Spanish carting it off. Because of the obvious fluctuation in the water level, other rumors alleged that entire ruined cities existed beneath the surface.

Although evidence of submerged cities is inconclusive, archaeologists have turned up interesting finds around Isla Koa, north of Isla del Sol. These include 22 large stone boxes containing a variety of artifacts: a

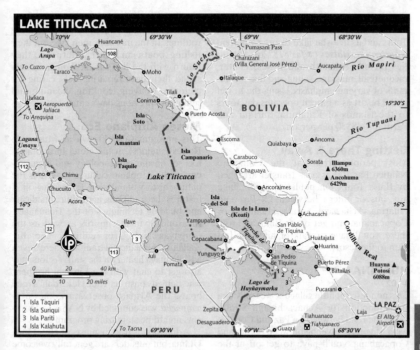

LAKE TITICACA

Map labels:
70°W, 69°30'W, 69°W, 68°30'W
Huancané
Lago Arapa
To Cuzco, Taraco, Moho, 108
Pumasani Pass
Charazani (Villa General José Pérez)
Italaque, Aucapata, Río Mapiri
Tilali
Juliaca, Aeropuerto Juliaca, Conima, Puerto Acosta, BOLIVIA, 15°30'S
To Arequipa
Isla Soto
Laguna Umayu, Isla Amantani, Escoma, Quiabaya, Ancoma, Río Tupuani
112, Puno, Chimu, Isla Taquile, Isla Campanario, Carabuco, Sorata, Illampu ▲ 6360m, ▲ Ancohuma 6429m
Chucuito, Lake Titicaca, Chaguaya
16°S, Acora, Ancoraimes, 16°S
Isla del Sol
Ilave, 32, Yampupata, Isla de la Luna (Koati), Achacachi, Cordillera Real
3, Copacabana, San Pablo de Tiquina, Chúa, Huatajata, Huarina
113, Juli, Yunguyo, San Pedro de Tiquina, Puerto Pérez, Batallas, Huayna ▲ Potosí 6088m
0 20 40 km, Pomata, 1 2 4, 3, Pucarani
0 10 20 miles, PERU, Lago de Huaynaymarka
Zepita, LA PAZ, El Alto Airport
1 Isla Taquiri
2 Isla Suriqui
3 Isla Pariti
4 Isla Kalahuta
Desaguadero, 69°30'W, Tiahuanaco, Laja, Guaqui, Tiahuanaco, 68°30'W
To Tacna, 69°W

silver llama, some shell figurines and several types of incense burners. They haven't, however, revealed much evidence of an underwater city.

Water-level changes from year to year are not uncommon, and previous fluctuations may have inundated other ruins and artifacts. In the floods of 1985-86, highways, docks, fields, and streets disappeared beneath the rising waters, adobe homes turned to mud and collapsed, and 200,000 people were displaced. It took several years for the Río Desaguadero, the lake's only outlet, to drain off the flood waters.

Organized Tours

You can choose from several guided lake excursions that begin in La Paz and include a stop in Copacabana, usually around lunchtime, and there's a choice of hydrofoils, catamarans, launches and several types of land transportation (including tourist coaches and minibuses). Given limited time (and in the case of the boat tours, unlimited funds), this is a quick way to 'do' Titicaca.

The most popular companies are Balsa Tours, with motor excursions around the lake (see Puerto Pérez, later in this chapter); Crillon Tours, an upmarket agency with a hydrofoil service and a posh lodge on Isla del Sol; and Transturin, which runs cruises in covered catamarans. The largest Transturin catamaran accommodates 150 passengers and charges US$129 per person for a day of cruising, stopping at Copacabana, Isla del Sol and Isla de la Luna. See Organized Tours in the Getting Around chapter for contact information on these and other tour companies.

PUERTO PÉREZ
☎ 02

Puerto Pérez, only 67km from La Paz, was the port established in the 1800s by English entrepreneurs as a home for the Lake Titicaca steamship service. Today, it's the site of a future 'eco-friendly' housing development for the wealthy and the home port of Balsa Tours and its five-star lake resort, *Complejo Náutico Las Balsas* (☎/fax 813226). Amenities include a health and fitness center, racquetball, massage, sauna and five restaurants of varying emphasis. Using the hostel at the resort as a base, it operates day tours to the islands of Kalahuta, Suriqui and Pariti for US$30 per person.

Getting There & Away

Most people arrive at the Complejo Náutico Las Balsas on a transfer arranged by Balsa Tours. On public transport, take any bus or micro between La Paz and Huarina, Achacachi, Sorata, Huatajata or Copacabana, and get off at Batallas. From there, you'll have to walk or hitch the last 7km to the resort.

HUARINA
☎ 02

This nondescript little village serves only as a road junction for Achacachi and Sorata along the road between La Paz and Copacabana. If you're traveling between Sorata and Copacabana, you'll have to get off at the tranca here and wait for the next bus going in your direction. Fortunately, the officers are typically friendly and will often try to help travelers find transport to their destinations.

HUATAJATA
☎ 02

The tiny community of Huatajata lies midway between Copacabana and La Paz beside Lago Huyñaymarka, the southern extension of Lake Titicaca. Huatajata, which is rapidly giving itself over to tourism, is mostly just a jumping-off point for trips to the Islas Huyñaymarkas and tourist cruises on Lake Titicaca. Crillon Tours (see Organized Tours in the Getting Around chapter) bases its hydrofoil services in Huatajata, and has also installed the five-star Hotel Inca Utama.

Life around this part of the lake remains much as it was when the Incas were capturing the imaginations – and the lands – of the Aymará inhabitants with dazzling tales of

their origins. The tourist scene aside, daily life in Huatajata is dominated by age-old routines. In the morning, men take out their fishing boats, and each afternoon, they return with the day's haul. Women mostly spend their days repairing nets, caring for children, weaving, cooking, cleaning and selling the previous day's catch.

Museo Altiplano Eco

This museum (also known as Museo de Raíces Andinos), at the Hotel Inca Utama, focuses on the anthropology and archaeology of the Altiplano cultures as well as the natural history of the Lake Titicaca region. It features the traditions, agriculture, medicine and building techniques of the Tiahuanaco, Inca and Spanish empires as well as the Chipayas and Uros cultures and the Kallahuayas medicinal tradition; there's even a Kallahuaya healer on the staff. Visitors may also get to chat with the Limachi brothers, who helped construct Thor Heyerdahl's reed boats. The Aymará observatory, known as *alajpacha*, was equipped by NASA and presents nighttime stargazing programs.

Admission is free to guests of Hotel Inca Utama, but outsiders are generally welcome if they first have a meal at the restaurant.

Museo Paulino Esteban

Paulino Esteban's small museum contains paraphernalia about *Ra II* and the other Heyerdahl expeditions that employed watercraft of ancient design, such as the *Ra I*, *Tigris* and the *Kon Tiki*, as well as the *Nazca* project balloon gondola. Museum displays also include the various types of totora reed boats used on the lake, and outside the owner's home sits a large example that was in use only a few years ago.

Organized Tours

The Catari brothers (☎ 0811-5058) at the Inti Karka restaurant run informative day visits to Suriqui, Pariti and Kalahuta for US$45 for groups of up to five people. See Islas Huyñaymarka, later in this chapter, for more information.

From its base at Huatajata, Crillon Tours operates hydrofoil cruises on Lake Titicaca for US$160 per person. The standard tour entails a bus trip from La Paz to Huatajata and a visit to the Museo Altiplano Eco before hitting the water. The cruise stops at the Estrecho de Tiquina (Straits of Tiquina), then continues to Copacabana before calling in at Isla de la Luna. It then proceeds to Isla del Sol for a quick stop at Pilko Kaina and lunch at Yumani before cruising back to Huatajata. From there, passengers are bused back to La Paz. The company also offers two-day tours around Lake Titicaca (US$264) and one-day transfers (US$183) by bus and hydrofoil between Peru and Bolivia. See Organized Tours in the Getting Around chapter for contact information.

Alternatively, you can do a catamaran tour with Transturin, which is based at Chúa. A two-day roundtrip from La Paz to Copacabana, Isla del Sol and Isla de la Luna, including bus transport from La Paz to Chúa, an overnight at the Hotel Titicaca and the lake cruise, costs US$175 per person. See Organized Tours in the Getting Around chapter for contact information.

Special Events
In late spring or early summer, depending on the year, the small lakeside community of Compi, midway between Huatajata and the Estrecho de Tiquina, stages a folk festival with dancing, feasting and – oddly enough – bicycle racing.

Places to Stay
The well-situated **Hostal Inti Karka** (☎ 0811-5058), run by the Catari brothers, has been recently renovated and offers basic rooms for US$3/3.50 per person with shared/private bath (but rarely does the advertised hot water make an appearance). It sits right on the shore and enjoys magnificent views of the lake, especially at sunset. It also has a small museum about reed boats and Thor Heyerdahl's expeditions. Look for a three-story white house on the waterfront, or ask directions at the Restaurant Inti Karka, on the main road, which is run by the same folks. This is also the place to find information on the Catari brothers' excursions to the Islas Huyñaymarka.

A decent alternative is the friendly but rather run-down **Hostal Lago Azul**, which charges about US$4.50/5.50 for singles/doubles.

Crillon Tours' perpetually expanding five-star **Inca Utama** (☎ 350363; fax 391039) resort provides a posh alternative for tour groups to Lake Titicaca and is featured prominently in the agency's Lake Titicaca hydrofoil cruise programs. Amenities include conference rooms, a natural health spa, and a floating restaurant/bar, **La Choza Nautica**, with fabulous lake views. Single/double rooms cost US$80/100 and must be either booked through Crillón Tours in La Paz or taken on a drop-in basis when room is available. The attached museum (see Museo Altiplano Eco, earlier in this section) describes lake ecology, natural healing and Aymará religious traditions.

Midway between Huatajata and Huarina, nearer La Paz, is the similarly upmarket **Hotel Titicaca**; book through Transturin (☎ 310545; fax 310647; sales@turismo-bolivia.com) in La Paz. Amenities include an indoor heated pool, sauna and racquetball courts. The website, which appears to be perpetually under construction, is www.turismo-bolivia.com.

Places to Eat
The **Inti Karka** on the main road sells inexpensive meals, and the specialty is – you guessed it – trout. It also prepares chicken and typical Bolivian dishes. Beyond that, there is a slew of tourist-oriented eateries along the shore, all serving trout and other standard fare, and there's not much to distinguish one from another: **Las Playas**, **La Kantuta**, **La Casa Verde**, **Inti Raymi**, **Lago Azul**, **Ollantay** and **Panamericano**. You may want to avoid the overpriced **Kala-Uta**, beside the gasoline station, which charges US$2 for a cup of coffee and US$20 for trout! The hotel Inca Utama adds to the choices with its upmarket **Jaipuru** dining room and its floating restaurant/bar **La Choza Nautica**. On weekends, the **Bolivia Yacht Club** is open to nonmembers for lunch.

At nearby Chúa is the beautiful colonial-style **La Posada del Inca** restaurant, which is open for lunch on weekends and holidays (and whenever it's booked by tour groups).

Getting There & Away

Lakeside communities between Puerto Pérez and Achacachi, including Huarina, Huatajata (1½ hours, US$1) and Chúa, are served by micros, which leave roughly every half hour between 4 am and 5 pm from the corner of Calles Manuel Bustillos and Kollasuyo in the La Paz cemetery district.

To return to La Paz, flag down any bus heading east along the main highway. The last one passes through Huatajata no later than 6 pm.

ISLAS DE HUYÑAYMARKA

The three most frequented islands in Lago de Huyñaymarka – Kalahuta, Pariti and Suriqui – are easily visited in a few hours. Tourism has become an island mainstay on these islands, but unfortunately, once-proud Kalahuta and Suriqui – and to a lesser extent, Pariti – have been sadly corrupted by outside influences. Mindless tourists poke cameras in people's faces while whining locals (mostly children) chase them around begging for money and gifts. Everyone winds up in a bad mood and the whole scene becomes unpleasant for all concerned. Please try to behave sensitively; ask permission before taking photos and refuse requests for money or gifts!

It's also possible to camp overnight, especially on the more sparsely populated islands, particularly Pariti. Those who dare to camp on Kalahuta will have the island to themselves since Kalahuta inhabitants are reluctant to venture out at night for fear of encountering spirits. As less superstitious campers will probably draw some measure of criticism from the locals, camping there is not a good idea.

Isla Kalahuta

When lake levels are low, the island of Kalahuta ('stone houses' in Aymará) becomes a peninsula. Its shallow shores are lined with beds of *totora* reed, the versatile building material for which Titicaca is famous. By day, fisherfolk ply the island's main bay in their wooden boats, and just a few years ago, you'd also have seen the totora reed boats, and men paddling around to gather the reeds to build them. Wood, however, has won out, and the typical totora reed boats are no longer used.

During Inca times, the island served as a cemetery, and it is still dotted with stone *chullpas* (funerary towers) several meters high. Legends abound about the horrible fate that will befall anyone who desecrates the cemetery, and locals have long refused to live in the area surrounding the island's only village, Queguaya, which is now almost utterly abandoned.

Isla Pariti

Like Kalahuta, much of Pariti is surrounded by marshes of totora reed. This small island provides a view into the tranquil lifestyle of its friendly inhabitants. The Indians there trade cheese, fish and woolen goods in Huatajata for items from the Yungas and La Paz. Their sailing boats, which are used for fishing, are beautiful to watch as they slice through the Titicaca waters in search of a bountiful catch.

Isla Suriqui

Suriqui, the best known of the Huyñaymarka islands, is world renowned for the totora reed boats that were, until just a few years ago, constructed there and used by many islanders in everyday life. The construction process was relatively simple. Green reeds were gathered from the lake shallows and left to dry in the sun. Once free of moisture, they were gathered into four fat bundles and lashed together with strong grass. Often a sail of reeds was added. These bloated little canoes didn't last long as far as watercraft go; after six months of use, they became waterlogged and began to rot and sink. In order to increase their life span, the canoes were often stored some distance away from the water.

In the early 1970s Dr Thor Heyerdahl, the unconventional Norwegian explorer and scientist, solicited the help of the Isla Suriqui shipbuilders, the Limachi brothers and Paulino Esteban, to design and construct his vessel the *Ra II*. Dr Heyerdahl wanted to test his theory that early contact and migration occurred between the ancient peoples of North Africa and the Americas. He planned to demonstrate the feasibility of traveling great distances using the boats of the period. Four Aymará shipbuilders accompanied him on the expedition from Morocco to Barbados.

Suriqui's former museum has now moved to Huatajata and has been replaced by an *artesanía* shop.

Isla Incas

Legend has it that this tiny, uninhabited island near Suriqui was part of an Inca network of underground passageways, apocryphally reputed to link many parts of the Inca empire with the capital at Cuzco.

Getting There & Away

The most experienced guides are the Catari brothers from the Hostal Inti Karka (see Places to Stay in Huatajata, earlier in this chapter), who will take up to five people to Kalahuta, Pariti and Suriqui for about US$45, or just to Suriqui for US$25. Sailing trips are also available for as little as US$20 per day. Thor Heyerdahl's balsa builder, Paulino Esteban, also conducts island tours, which may be booked through Servitur (☎ 340060; fax 391373) in La Paz.

On any of these trips, you'll get informative commentary (in Spanish) on the legends, customs, people, history and natural features of the lake. You're allowed as much time as you'd like on each island, and if you'd like to camp on one of the islands, you can arrange to be picked up the following day.

Relatively posh organized cruises to the islands by covered catamaran or hydrofoil are available through Balsa Tours, Transturin and Crillon Tours (see Organized Tours in the Getting Around chapter); most La Paz travel agencies also organize half-day and full-day tours to the islands from La Paz starting at around US$45 per person (with a minimum of two people).

Those who aren't pressed for time may want to speak with Aymará fisherfolk in Huatajata, who may agree to take a day off to informally shuttle visitors around the islands for a pre-negotiated price.

TIQUINA

The narrow Estrecho de Tiquina separates the main body of Lake Titicaca from the smaller Lago de Huyñaymarka, and flanking the western and eastern shores, respectively, lie the twin villages of San Pedro and San Pablo de Tiquina. A bridge across the strait is now in the planning stages, but it will surely be years before anything happens, and vehicles are still shuttled across the straits on *balsas* (rafts) for US$4, while passengers travel across in small launches (10 minutes, US$0.20). Bus travelers should carry onto the launch with them any bags that aren't in the hold of the bus.

To serve the traffic that bottlenecks here, a growing number of small restaurants and food stalls are springing up on both sides. Note that foreigners traveling in either direction must present their passports for inspection at San Pedro, which is home to Bolivia's largest naval base.

COPACABANA
☎ 0862

The bright town of Copacabana on the southern shore of Lake Titicaca was established around a splendid bay between two hills. As a stopover along the Tiquina route between La Paz and Cuzco, it served as a site of religious pilgrimage for centuries, beginning with the Incas.

Copacabana is still well known for its fiestas, which bring this ordinarily sleepy place to life with pilgrims and visitors from all over Bolivia. At other times, it's visited mainly as a pleasant stopover between La Paz and Puno (Peru), and also serves as a convenient base for visits to Isla del Sol and Isla de la Luna.

From February to November, the climate is mostly pleasant and sunny, but there's often a cool wind off the lake, and nights at this 3800m altitude can be bitterly cold.

COPACABANA

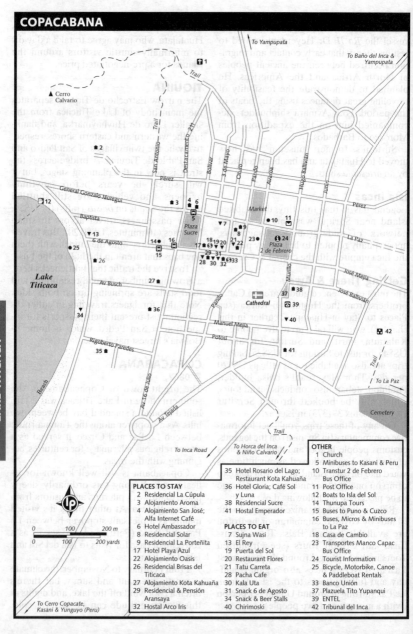

To Yampupata
To Baño del Inca & Yampupata

▲ Cerro Calvario

Lake Titicaca

Market

Plaza Sucre

Plaza 2 de Febrero

Cathedral

To Inca Road

To Horca del Inca & Niño Calvario

To Cerro Copacate, Kasani & Yunguyo (Peru)

To La Paz

Cemetery

0   100   200 m
0   100   200 yards

PLACES TO STAY
2 Residencial La Cúpula
3 Alojamiento Aroma
4 Alojamiento San José; Alfa Internet Café
6 Hotel Ambassador
8 Residencial Solar
9 Residencial La Porteñita
17 Hotel Playa Azul
22 Alojamiento Oasis
26 Residencial Brisas del Titicaca
27 Alojamiento Kota Kahuaña
29 Residencial & Pensión Aransaya
32 Hostal Arco Iris

35 Hotel Rosario del Lago; Restaurant Kota Kahuaña
36 Hotel Gloria; Café Sol y Luna
38 Residencial Sucre
41 Hostal Emperador

PLACES TO EAT
7 Sujna Wasi
13 El Rey
19 Puerta del Sol
20 Restaurant Flores
21 Tatu Carreta
28 Pacha Cafe
30 Kala Uta
31 Snack 6 de Agosto
34 Snack & Beer Stalls
40 Chirimoski

OTHER
1 Church
5 Minibuses to Kasani & Peru
10 Transtur 2 de Febrero Bus Office
11 Post Office
12 Boats to Isla del Sol
14 Thunupa Tours
15 Buses to Puno & Cuzco
16 Buses, Micros & Minibuses to La Paz
23 Transportes Manco Capac Bus Office
24 Tourist Information
25 Bicycle, Motorbike, Canoe & Paddleboat Rentals
33 Banco Unión
37 Plazuela Tito Yupanqui
39 ENTEL
42 Tribunal del Inca

Most of the rainfall occurs in midsummer (December and January).

History

After the fall and disappearance of the Tiahuanaco culture, the Kollas, or Aymará, rose to become the dominant population group in the Titicaca region. Their most prominent deities included the sun and moon (who were considered husband and wife), the earth mother Pachamama, and the ambient spirits known as *achachilas* and *apus*. Among the idols erected on the shores of the Manco Capac peninsula was *Kota Kahuaña* or *Copacahuana* (which sounds exotic but means simply 'lake view' in Aymará), an image with the head of a human and the body of a fish. It stood at the site now known as Asiento del Inca.

Once the Aymará had been subsumed into the Inca empire, Emperor Tupac Yupanqui founded the settlement of Copacabana as a wayside rest for pilgrims visiting the *huaca* (shrine). This site of human sacrifice (gulp!) was at the rock known as *Titicaca* (Rock of the Puma), at the northern end of Isla del Sol.

Before the arrival of the Spanish Dominican and Augustinian priests in the mid-16th century, the Incas had divided local inhabitants into two distinct groups. Those faithful to the empire were known as Haransaya and were assigned positions of power. Those who resisted, the Hurinsaya, were relegated to manual labor. This went entirely against the grain of the community-oriented Aymará culture, and the floods and crop failures that befell them in the 1570s were attributed to this social aberration.

This resulted in the rejection of the Inca religion and the partial adoption of Christianity and establishment of the Santuario de Copacabana, which developed into a syncretic mishmash of both traditional and Christian premises. As its patron saint, the populace elected La Santísima Virgen de Candelaria, and established a congregation in her honor. Noting the lack of an image for the altar, Francisco Tito Yupanqui, a direct descendant of the Inca emperor, fashioned an image of clay and placed it in the church.

However, the rude effort was deemed unsuitable to represent the honored patron of the village and was removed.

The sculptor, who was humiliated but not defeated, journeyed to Potosí to study arts and find the perfect model for the image he wanted to create. In June 1582, he was feeling suitably inspired and began carving a wooden image that took eight months to complete. On February 2, 1583, La Virgen Morena del Lago (The Dark Virgin of the Lake) was installed on the adobe altar at Copacabana, and shortly thereafter the miracles began. The number of early healings was reportedly 'innumerable,' and Copacabana quickly developed into a pilgrimage site.

In 1605, the Augustinian priesthood advised the community to construct a cathedral commensurate with the power of the image, and architect Francisco Jiménez de Sigueza was commissioned to design it. The altar was completed in 1614, but work on the building continued for 200 years. It wasn't until April 15, 1805, that the *mudéjar* (Moorish-style) cathedral was consecrated; construction wasn't completed until 1820. On August 10, 1925, Francisco Tito Yupanqui's image was canonized by the Vatican.

Information

Tourist Offices Copacabana has a little tourist information office in the middle of Plaza 2 de Febrero, but it appears never to be open.

Money Attached to the Hotel Playa Azul is a casa de cambio that is open Monday to Friday during business hours and on Saturday until noon; it changes both cash and traveler's checks for a whopping 4% commission. Up the same block, the Banco Union changes traveler's checks for a 5% commission and does Visa cash advances. It's open daily except Monday (on Sunday until noon only). Numerous small tourist shops also change US cash and traveler's checks, but again, the commission rates are excessive.

Those heading for Peru can buy *soles* at most artesanía shops, but you'll normally find better rates in Yunguyo, just beyond the Peruvian border.

Post & Communications The post office, on Plaza 2 de Febrero, is open Wednesday to Sunday, but you may have to hunt up the attendant. The modern-looking ENTEL office, on Plazuela Tito Yupanqui, is open daily. Internet and email access is available for US$3.50 per hour at the friendly Alfa Internet, in the same building as the Restaurant Colonial. This place also features a café, video rentals and pool tables. A less reliable service is available for US$4.25 per hour at the Café Sol y Luna in the Hotel Gloria.

Film With its constant stream of tourists and pilgrims, Copacabana is a good place to buy film. The vendors in front of the cathedral sell 36-exposure Kodak, Fuji or Agfa print film for around US$2.50 per roll, and 36-exposure Fujichrome Sensia 100 or 200 for US$6.

Dangers & Annoyances Police and *tranca* (highway police post) officials sometimes extract a US$0.20 entry 'tax' from arriving tourists and pilgrims, ostensibly for the upkeep of the sanctuary and the Virgin, but the church claims that they receive none of it. While the amount may seem like a pittance, please do your part to eliminate corruption and insist on a receipt for anything you pay. In addition, several travelers entering from Peru have reported spontaneous 'fines' for a variety of bogus 'infractions,' including taking photos without a permit and carrying 'illegal' US dollars.

Especially during festivals, be wary of light-fingered revelers; as usual, foreign tourists are prime targets. Also, stand well back during fireworks displays; when it comes to explosive fun, crowd safety takes a rather low priority.

The thin air and characteristically brilliant sunshine in this area combine to admit scorching levels of ultraviolet radiation. To minimize the risk, wear a hat, especially when you're out on the water, and use a reliable sunscreen. In addition, hikers in the hills should watch out for an insidious variety of thorn bush that will shred your skin on contact.

Cathedral
Built between 1605 and 1820, the sparkling white Moorish-style cathedral, with its mudéjar domes and colorful *azulejos* (blue Portuguese-style ceramic tiles), dominates the town. The cathedral's beautiful courtyard is usually ablaze with the colors of wild and cultivated flowers.

Virgen de Candelaria The cathedral is a repository for both European and local religious art, including the Virgen de Candelaria. The black statue was carved in the 1580s by the Indian artist Francisco Yupanqui, grandson of Inca Tupac Yupanqui (see History earlier in this section). It's encased in glass above the altar upstairs in the cathedral; follow the signs to the Camarín de la Virgen. The statue is never moved from the cathedral, as superstition suggests that its disturbance would precipitate a devastating flood of Lake Titicaca. The *camarín* (niche in which the statue is displayed) is open daily from 11 am (on weekends from 8 am) to noon and 2 to 6 pm; admission is US$0.60.

Museo de la Catedral The cathedral museum contains some interesting articles. Don't miss the ostrich vases or the hundreds of paper cranes donated by a Japanese woman hedging her bets with the Virgin in the hope of bearing an intelligent child. It's open Sunday only from 8:45 am to noon; admission is US$0.60.

Copacabana Beach
Okay, it can't hold a candle to the better-known beach of the same name in Rio de Janeiro (which was named for this one!), but on the weekends, the festive atmosphere of Bolivia's only public beach is a magnet for families from La Paz and elsewhere. Along the shore, you can sit in the sun, eat trout and drink beer in the many little beach stalls and restaurants, or rent bicycles, tricycles, small motorbikes, canoes and paddleboats. There's even a little carousel charging US$0.25.

Courtyard of the Copacabana cathedral

RICHARD I'ANSON

LAKE TITICACA

Cerro Calvario

Copacabana is set between two hills that offer bird's-eye views over both the town and the lake. The summit of Cerro Calvario can be reached in half an hour and is well worth the climb, especially in the late afternoon, to watch the sun setting over the lake. The trail to the summit begins near the church at the end of Calle Destacamento 211 and climbs upward past the 14 Stations of the Cross.

Niño Calvario & Horca del Inca

The small but prominent hill east of town is called Niño Calvario (Little Calvary), also known as Seroka and by its original name, Kesanani. Its weirdly rugged rock formations and oddly arranged boulders merit a couple of hours' exploration. From the end of Calle Murillo, a trail leads uphill to the Horca del Inca (Inca Gallows), an odd trilithic gate perched on the hillside. This pre-Inca observatory, which was built by the Chiripa culture for stringing up disobedient Incas but never used, is surrounded by pierced rocks that permit the sun's rays to pass through onto the lintel at the solstices.

There's now a legitimate US$1.80 entry fee to the hill, which is collected at the base. Foreigners approaching the site may also find themselves besieged by aspiring young guides; if you refuse their services, they may well tag along anyway and demand to be paid. Please help them get over this annoying behavior by ignoring them.

The higher hill behind Niño Calvario, Cerro Sancollani, is flanked by Inca-era *asientos* (seats), agricultural terraces and numerous unrestored and little-known ruins. To get there, follow Calle Murillo to its end, where it becomes a cobbled road. After 50m, a crumbling stone route (which might once have served as an irrigation aqueduct) leads off to the left about 1m above the road level. The easiest access to the summit of Cerro Sancollani is from the saddle between it and Niño Calvario.

Farther along, 4km down the road toward Kasani, lies Cerro Copacate, which features pre-Inca ruins and pictographs. The best known is the *Escudo de la Cultura Chiripa*, which is a unique icon attributed to the pre-Inca Chiripa culture.

Tribunal del Inca (Intikala)

North of the cemetery on the southeastern outskirts of town is a field of artificially sculpted boulders known as the Tribunal del Inca or Intikala. Its original purpose is unknown, but there are about seven carved stones with asientos, basins and *hornecinos* (niches), which probably once contained idols. During the rainy season, the place hops with thousands of tiny frogs.

Baño del Inca & Kusillata

A 2km walk along the Titicaca shoreline from the end of Calles Junín or Hugo Ballivián leads to a colonial manor building known as Kusillata, where there's a small archaeological display. Admission costs US$0.60 – if you can find someone to let you in; weekends are normally the best. The pre-Columbian tunnel beside the manor was originally used to access the subterranean water supply. The carved-stone water tank and tap are known as the Baño del Inca (Inca Bath).

Organized Tours

A large and growing number of tour agencies can organize tours around Copacabana's environs. They change names frequently, they all offer roughly the same things, and you'll find them on every street corner, so there's little use in running down a long list. The most popular tour is the half- or full-day trip to Isla del Sol; see the listing later in this chapter for details.

Special Events

Copacabana hosts several major annual fiestas. From February 2 to 5, the Fiesta de la Virgen de Candelaria honors the Dark Virgin of the Lake. Although the feast day is celebrated to varying degrees around Bolivia, Copacabana stages an especially big bash, and pilgrims and dancers come from Peru and around Bolivia. Traditional Aymará dances are performed, and there's much music, drinking and feasting. On the

third day, celebrations culminate with the gathering of 100 bulls in a stone corral along the Yampupata road, and the braver (and drunker) of the town's citizens jump into the arena and try to avoid attack.

On Good Friday the town fills with *peregrinos* (pilgrims) – a few of whom make the 158km journey from La Paz on foot – to do penance at the Stations of the Cross on Cerro Calvario. Beginning at dusk from the cathedral, pilgrims join a solemn candlelit procession through town, led by a statue of Christ in a glass coffin and a replica of the Virgen de Candelaria, the patron saint of Copacabana and all Bolivia. Once on the summit, they light incense and purchase miniatures representing material possessions in the hope that the Virgin will bless them with the real thing during the year of their pilgrimage. A local priest relates the significance of the holiday through a microphone, a military band plays dirges and city hall's audio system broadcasts *Ave Maria* for all to hear.

Copacabana stages its biggest bash during the week of Bolivian Independence Day (the first week in August). The most animated of the town's annual festivities, it's characterized by pilgrimages, round-the-clock music, parades, brass bands, fireworks and staggeringly high alcohol consumption. The town also celebrates the La Paz departmental anniversary on July 15.

Places to Stay

For a town of its size, Copacabana is well endowed with hotels, residenciales and alojamientos, and it's the least expensive town in Bolivia for accommodations. During fiestas everything fills up and prices increase up to threefold, but at other times, you'll have no trouble finding a good choice of inexpensive places to stay.

Despite its proximity to the lake, Copacabana's water and electric utilities are unpredictable. Many accommodations – even some budget places – commendably go to extreme efforts to fill water tanks in the morning (the supply is normally switched off at 11 am), so showers are available to guests at all hours.

Places to Stay – Budget

Camping Although the slopes around Copacabana are generally steep and rocky, there are several excellent campsites. The summits of both Niño Calvario and Cerro Sancollani have smooth, grassy saddle areas suitable for tent camping and also provide magnificent views of the lake, the surrounding farms and villages, and the Andean Cordillera. You'll find another pleasant campsite at the high point along the Inca road toward Kasani (the Peruvian border), about 1km from the end of Calle Murillo.

Hotels The budget travelers' choice is currently the **Hostal Emperador** (☎ 2083; Murillo 235). This upbeat and colorfully speckled place charges US$2 per person in rooms with shared baths and hot showers all day. It also has laundry services, cooking facilities, luggage storage, a travelers' book exchange, tourist information and a sunny mezzanine ideal for lounging. In the morning, you can even order breakfast in bed!

At the quite comfortable **Residencial Aransaya** (☎ 2229; 6 de Agosto 121), single rooms with shared baths cost US$3.50 per person, and the sunny patio is especially inviting. On the same street, the increasingly popular **Hostal Arco Iris** (☎ 2247; 6 de Agosto s/n) charges the same US$2 per person for comfortable rooms with shared baths; there's also an attached dining room.

The oddly designed but friendly **Alojamiento Aroma** (☎ 2004), west of the center, may seem a construction zone dump from the ground floor, but the cozy top-floor doubles cost only US$2 per person and open onto a sunny patio with tables and a superb lake view. The very clean **Alojamiento Oasis** (☎ 2037), on Calle Pando, is dominated by a multicolored pastel paint job. Rooms, some with carpeting, cost US$1.20 per person on weekdays and US$2 on Saturday night. Hot water in the communal showers is available at all hours, but it can get very noisy, especially when family members switch on the TV. Request room 14 if it's available.

Nearer the lake is the basic and friendly **Alojamiento Kota Kahuaña**, which charges

Cha'lla

The word *cha'lla* is used for any ritual blessing, toasting or offering to the powers that be, whether Inca, Aymará or Christian. On weekend mornings in front of the cathedral in Copacabana, cars, trucks and buses belonging to pilgrims, visitors and even flota companies are decked out in garlands of real or plastic flowers, colored ribbons, model reed boats, flags and even stuffed ducks. Petitions for protection are made to the Virgin, and a ritual offering of alcohol is poured over the vehicles' tires and hoods, thereby consecrating them for the journey home. The vehicle cha'lla is especially popular with pilgrims visiting Copacabana between Good Friday and Easter. On one of my visits, one La Paz flota had brought a newly purchased fleet of buses to Copacabana for the spiritual baptism to prepare them for the Bolivian highways.

US$2 per person for rooms with shared baths, and US$1.50 for dormitory accommodations. There's hot water all day, guests have access to kitchen facilities and some upstairs rooms have a lake view.

If you don't mind tiny rooms, the friendly **Residencial Solar** (☎ 2014), on Calle Oruro, is a good choice. The spacious rooftop patio has lake views and full exposure to the sun. Singles/doubles with baths cost US$5/8; without baths, they're US$4/6.50.

The **Alojamiento San José** (☎ 2066) has hot water from 7 to 11 am and enjoys a sunny terrace overlooking the chronically hectic bus parking area. Beds cost US$2 per person. Almost next door, the slightly aloof

Hotel Ambassador (☎ 2216; *Calle Jaúrequi s/n*) has comfortable rooms with bath and television for US$7/8.50. This is the acting youth hostel, and HI members receive a 10% discount. Okay, it's not that friendly, but the facilities are a step up from the cheaper places that dominate the town, and space heaters are available upon request.

The friendly *Residencial La Porteñita* (☎ 2006; *Gonzalo Jaúrequi s/n*), with its clean rooms, leafy patio and lovely trees, charges US$2.50 per person (US$3.50 with a private bath).

Residencial Sucre (☎ 2080), on Calle Murillo, seems more like a mid-range hotel than a budget place, and has been recommended for its friendliness, washing facilities and good-value accommodations. Rooms cost US$4 per person (US$7 with private baths). Color TV costs an additional US$2 per person.

Right on the beach, the *Residencial Brisas del Titicaca* offers an excellent value, with very amenable rooms. Many rooms with private baths, which cost US$7 per person, have private lake-view terraces. Rooms with shared baths, which cost US$5 per person, also enjoy good watery views.

Places to Stay – Mid-Range
Gleaming white domes mark the much-lauded *La Cúpula* (☎/fax 2029; *Michel Pérez 1-3*), owned and lovingly run by Amanda and Martin Strätker (Amanda is of Egyptian background, hence the obvious Middle Eastern theme). No two rooms are alike, so rates vary greatly; singles/doubles with shared baths start at US$8/12, and with private baths, US$20/24. The honeymoon suite with a double bed and private bath is US$32. All guests have access to the video room and kitchen and laundry facilities, and the attached vegetarian restaurant has now become a favorite. The hotel sits on the slopes of Cerro Calvario, overlooking the lake, and the grounds include shady spots with hammocks for relaxing and reading on your own time (note the unusual sculptures; everything sits on the back of a turtle, of course!).

Lots of organized tour groups wind up at *Hotel Playa Azul* (☎/fax 2227; *6 de Agosto s/n*), but it's certainly nothing special. Single/double rooms with private baths cost US$14/20 including breakfast.

A nicer alternative with a good lake view is the three-star colonial-style *Hotel Rosario del Lago* (☎ 2141; *fax 2140; turisbus@ caoba.entelnet.bo*), on Rigoberto Paredes at Costañera, which is run by the same operation as the Hostal Rosario in La Paz. In the high season, charming singles/doubles with solar hot water – many with lake views – cost US$39/53, with a buffet continental breakfast. Family rooms accommodating two adults and two children are US$73. Low season rates are about 10% lower.

The large and imposing *Hotel Gloria* (☎ 2002), near the shore, affords a lovely view of the lake and surrounding mountains, and on weekends it springs to life. Clean single/double rooms with baths and lake views (some even have sundecks) cost US$21/40 including breakfast, and hot water is available from 6:15 to 10 am. Without the view, you'll pay US$14 per person.

Places to Eat
As usual, the bargain basement is the food hall in the town market, where numerous small operations compete fiercely for your business. You can eat a generous meal of trout or beef for a pittance, while a contingent of the town's canine population patiently awaits handouts. If you're up to an insulin shock in the morning, treat yourself to a breakfast of hot *api morado* and syrupy *buñuelos*.

The local specialty is *trucha criolla* (salmon trout) from Lake Titicaca, which may be the world's largest and most delicious trout. The fish were introduced in 1939 by foreign pisciculturists in order to increase protein content in the local diet. For years the trout were also canned and exported, but that ended when fish stocks became severely depleted. Although dozens of tourist-oriented places serve trout for around US$4 to US$5, the best seem to be the Kota Kahuaña at the Hotel Rosario del Lago, the Kala Uta, La Cúpula and the Sujna Wasi.

The excellent *Sujna Wasi* (☎ 2091), with its delightful courtyard tables and rustic

Woman and alpaca, Isla del Sol

Isla del Sol

Farming on the shores of Lake Titicaca

Dressed up for the *cha'lla*

Copacabana

Hotel de Sal, Salar de Uyuni

Tupiza rock formations

Lagunas Verde and Blanca

'The new order,' expired railway car

Cacti, Isla de los Pescadores

Main street, Atocha

interior, offers a varied menu including many Bolivian, vegetarian and international specialties for breakfast, lunch and dinner. The name means 'your friend's home,' and that's the ambience aimed for. Allow US$5 to US$6 per person and enough time to savor the meal and appreciate the lovely wooden tables, simple ceramic dishes and tasteful Andean décor. You may also want to try the bizarre *vino de coca* (coca leaf wine), which is made only here.

Similarly, don't miss the equally appealing and original *Restaurant Kala Uta*, which serves imaginative breakfasts for US$1 to US$2; try the bizarre Poder Andino (Andean Power), which features quinoa pancakes topped with jam, bananas, yogurt, almonds, raisins and coconut, accompanied by an Andean grain drink, fruit juice and coffee for just US$2! Set vegetarian lunches or dinners cost US$1.80, and creative salads are US$2 to US$2.50. Again the Andean version is most unusual: potatoes, oca, sweet potato, quinoa, toasted haba beans, tomatoes and peanut sauce. They also do trout, pasta and pizza.

The third great option is the *vegetarian restaurant* upstairs in La Cúpula (see Places to Stay), where the glassy surroundings admit lots of that powerful Altiplano light and maximize the fabulous view of the lake, spreading out below. The menu isn't extensive, but everything they serve – breakfasts, salads, fish and veggie dishes – is an exceptional value. Plan on spending no more than US$5 for a memorable meal.

The *Kota Kahuaña* at the Hotel Rosario del Lago also offers exceptional fare, including a wonderful salad bar and a range of imaginatively prepared main courses. Plan on US$10 per person for a fine meal with wine and a lake view.

Otherwise, there's little gastronomic originality in Copacabana, and most dishes are served up with greasy rice, fried potatoes and lettuce. Nearly every place in town now serves breakfast in its many incarnations, including continental, American and English. Among the decent places that are accessible to slim budgets is the *Pensión Aransaya*; plan on about US$5 for a meal of

trout, trimmings and a tall, cold beer. At *Snack 6 de Agosto*, the service may be crusty, but the food is well prepared, and the patio seating area can be heavenly on a typically sunny day. The milanesa napolitana is especially recommended, as are the breakfasts, chicken dishes, pique a lo macho, pejerrey, and the specialty, suckling pig.

The snazzy exterior of *Puerta del Sol* unfortunately belies its comatose service and mediocre food, but several readers have objected to that assessment, so go and check it out for yourself. The similar and better *Restaurant Flores*, next door, has also been frequently recommended by readers. It's a great place to spend a mellow afternoon drinking a Paceña over your journal or letter writing. And, of course, they serve trout.

On the beach, *El Rey* and other restaurants serve up pizza, lasagna and Bolivian specialties, and a row of informal beachfront stalls sells snacks and drinks. These are especially pleasant on weekends, when you can sip a cold beer and observe quintessential Bolivian beach life. A popular spot for light meals and especially excellent pizza is the cozy *Pacha Café*, which also has a bar and occasional live entertainment.

Cafés & Pubs The atmospheric *Café Sol y Luna*, in the Hotel Gloria, serves coffee and light lunches from 11 am to 2 pm daily except Tuesday and Sunday; from 6 pm nightly (at least ostensibly) until late, they serve snacks and drinks. They also have a book exchange.

Argentine expats have also made a splash in Copacabana, with a pair of restaurants and bars catering to foreign travelers. The always relaxed *Chirimoski*, on Calle Murillo, plays great music, has a book exchange, and serves up pizza, pasta, snacks and drinks in a most informal setting (just *try* to pass between the bar and eating area after you've had a few beers!). On weekends, they sometimes sizzle up a friendly and filling barbecue for around US$3 per person. *Tatu Carreta*, on Oruro at 6 de Agosto, specializes in hamburgers, soup, juices, alcoholic drinks and Argentine cuisine (read: meat!), and also plays good classic rock music. They also occasionally stage live bands.

Shopping

Local specialties include handmade miniatures of totora reed boats, enormous peanuts, unusual varieties of Andean potatoes, and *pasankalla* (puffed choclo with caramel). This last item is a South American version of popcorn that, if crispy, can be fairly palatable. You'll also find dozens of shops selling lovely llama and alpaca-wool sweaters (jumpers) for excellent prices; a superb alpaca piece will cost as little as US$10. Vehicle adornments used in the cha'lla, miniatures and religious paraphernalia are sold in stalls in front of the cathedral, and votive miniatures are available en masse atop Cerro Calvario.

Getting There & Away

The impressive journey between La Paz and Copacabana follows a scenic route across the Altiplano and along the shoreline to the Estrecho de Tiquina (Straits of Tiquina). Vehicles are ferried by barge across these straits, between San Pablo and San Pedro, while passengers ride in launches (US$0.20, payable at the dock ticket offices). Even bus passengers must pay for the ferry.

Bus Two major bus companies run between La Paz and Copacabana. Both Transportes Manco Capac (☎ 02-350033) and Transtur 2 de Febrero (☎ 02-377181) have four to six daily connections to La Paz (US$2, 3½ hours), with extra departures on Sunday. Their booking offices are on Plaza 2 de Febrero, but all buses arrive at and depart near Plaza Sucre.

To reach Puno (Peru), either book a direct minibus through a tour agency (2½ hours, US$2) or catch a public minibus from Plaza Sucre to the border at Kasani (15 minutes, US$0.40), about 10km away. After crossing the border, you'll find frequent onward transport to Yunguyo (five minutes, US$0.60) and Puno (2½ hours, US$2), but be warned that the buses get quite crowded and you may not have a seat. If you're headed straight to Cuzco, check out any of the five or six Copacabana travel agencies offering tickets on the daily buses (they also offer efficient bus journeys to Arequipa,

Lima and other Peruvian destinations). The least expensive seems to be Thunupa Tours (☎ 784130; Calle Oruro 555), which consistently charges just US$10 for the 12-hour trip (most others charge anywhere from a negotiable US$12 to US$16). All require a two-hour layover in Puno, which will give you time to change money.

Coming from Puno, buses to Copacabana (2½ hours, US$2) depart from the Avenida Ejército side of the Mercado Laykakota between 8 and 9 am, and tour buses, such as those run by Colectur (Calle Tacna 221, in Puno) are also a convenient option; they'll even wait while you exchange money at the border. Bolivian visas are available from the consulate at Calle Arequipa 120 in Puno. For further information on travel to and around the Peruvian portion of Lake Titicaca – and beyond – see Lonely Planet's *Peru*.

Minibus Tourist micros and minibuses between La Paz and Puno provide the best sightseeing opportunities along the dramatic road between Tiquina, Copacabana and Peru. When buying a ticket from a minibus or travel agency, you can arrange to break the journey in Copacabana, then continue or return to La Paz or Puno. Although there are plenty of minibuses, they fill up quickly (especially on weekends), so book tickets in advance through a tour company (see Organized Tours, earlier in this section) if you want to be sure of a seat. The fare between Copacabana and either La Paz or Puno is around US$4. In Copacabana, minibuses leave when full from along Avenida 16 de Julio and from Gonzalo Jaúregui west of Destacamento 211.

For those heading into Peru, several Puno-based flotas travel daily between Puno and Copacabana (three to four hours, US$5), and Cruz del Sur continues on to La Paz. Be sure the drivers stop and wait while you complete border formalities. Alternatively, take a public minibus to Kasani (15 minutes, US$0.40), on the Peruvian border, where you can pass through customs and immigration formalities, then connect with onward transport to Yunguyo and Puno. The full trip to Puno costs around US$2.50

and takes three to four hours, depending on the whims of the Peruvian and Bolivian customs and immigration offices.

Note that Peruvian time is one hour behind Bolivian time.

Boat The days of haggling over transport to Isla del Sol are effectively over. Now you just go down to the beach in the morning and buy a US$2 ticket from one of the two cooperative offices. For more information, see Getting There & Away in Isla del Sol, later in this chapter.

Getting Around
On the beach, you can rent bicycles (US$1.50 per hour) and motorbikes (US$10 per hour).

COPACABANA TO YAMPUPATA TREK
A particularly enjoyable way of reaching Isla del Sol is to trek along the lakeshore to the village of Yampupata, which lies just a short rowboat ride from the ruins of Pilko Kaina on Isla del Sol. If you're arriving from La Paz, this four- to five-hour walk will help accustom your lungs to the altitude, and the glorious scenery along the way presents a suitable prologue to a couple of days' trekking around Isla del Sol.

For a longer trek, you can also opt to walk the pre-Hispanic route from Cruce Paquipujio, near the Estrecho de Tiquina. This route passes through the village of Chisi, where there's a **Templete Semisubterráneo** (sunken temple) that dates back to the pre-Tiahuanaco Chavín culture. It then continues through San Francisco, Chachacoyas, Kollasuyos, Santa Ana and the lovely cobblestoned village of Sampaya, on the hilltop about 5km from Yampupata. This route joins up with the Copacabana to Yampupata trek at Titicachi.

The Route
From Copacabana, strike out northeast along the road running across the flat plain. After about 40 minutes, the road turns sharply left and climbs gently onto a ledge overlooking the lake. About one to 1½

hours from Copacabana, you'll pass the isolated Hinchaca fish hatchery and reforestation project on your left. Beyond the hatchery, cross the stream on your left and follow the obvious Inca road up the steep hill. Just above the stream, you'll pass what is variously called the Gruta de Lourdes or Gruta de Fátima, a cave that for locals evokes images of its French or Portuguese namesake, respectively. This stretch includes some fine stone paving and makes a considerable shortcut, rejoining the main road at the crest of the hill.

From here, the road passes through more populated areas. At the fork just below the crest, bear left and descend to the shore and into the village of Titicachi, where there's a shop selling overpriced soft drinks and staple items.

In and around Titicachi are several sites of interest, among them the Tiahuanacota Inca cemetery, some pre-Inca walls and, on the offshore islet of Jiskha Huata, the Museo de Aves Acuáticos (Museum of Aquatic Birds). This small display of Lake Titicaca birdlife is reached only by boat. While you're in the area, watch in the reeds for the real things: the black ducklike bird known as *cho'k'a*; the gray-colored, blue-beaked water bird *pan'a*; and a small dark-brown bird with tiny eggs, the *solojita*, among others.

At the next village, Sicuani, José Quispe Mamani and his wife, Margarita Arias, and daughter, Rosemeri, run the ***Hostal Yampu*** (the name is Aymará for 'reed boat'). You can't miss it – just look for the bright rose-colored house. Basic accommodations with bucket showers cost US$1 per person, and meals are about US$1 each. Hikers can pop in for a beer or soft drink, and you can take a spin around the bay in a totora reed boat for US$1.80 per person. José is quite an amenable character and asserts that his prices are 'economical and within reach of all travelers.'

Four to five hours from Copacabana, you'll reach Yampupata, a collection of adobe houses on the lakeshore, where you can camp on the beach or hire a rowboat to take you across the Estrecho de Yampupata

COPACABANA TO YAMPUPATA TREK

1 Boat Landing
2 Hostal Yampu
3 Museo de Aves Acuáticos
4 Gruta de Lourdes
5 Hinchaca Fish Hatchery
   & Reforestation Project
6 Kusillata; Baño del Inca

Isla del Sol   Isla Chelleca
                  Lighthouse

To Isla de la
Luna (1 km)

Estrecho de Yampupata

Cerro
Pukhara
4014m
Yampupata

Lake Titicaca

Sampaya

Sicuani
2

Titicachi

Isla Jiskha
Huata

Cerro
Huara Huara
4092m

Santa
Ana

Lake Titicaca

Inca Road Shortcut 5

Hinchaca

Cerro
Jankho Khaua
4342m

To Tiquina
(25 km)

Chani

To Tiquina
(20 km)

Hueco

Marka Kosco

6

0   1   2 km
0   .5   1 mile

COPACABANA

To Peruvian border (9 km)
& Yunguyo (11 km)

to Pilko Kaina or the Escalera del Inca (see Isla del Sol, later in this chapter) for around US$3 for two people. If you opt for the Escalera del Inca, make sure that's where you're dropped off; some boat owners may well try to drop you at Pilko Kaina, anyway. Also, resist attempts to add extra charges, such as invented 'landing fees.'

Getting There & Away

For those who don't want to walk, the easiest ways to travel between Yampupata and Copacabana are by camión or on the daily minibus. The camiones travel infre-

quently and adhere to no particular schedule, while the minibuses run to and from Copacabana (30 minutes, US$0.80) one to three times daily; on most days, there's a bus from Copacabana at around 10 am and from Yampupata at 10:30 or 11 am.

ISLA DEL SOL

Isla del Sol (Island of the Sun) was known to early inhabitants as Titi Khar'ka, the 'rock of the puma,' from which Lake Titicaca takes its name. This island has been identified as the birthplace of several revered entities, including the sun itself.

There the bearded white leader/deity Viracocha and the first Incas, Manco Capac and his sister/wife Mama Ocllo, mystically appeared under direct orders of the sun. In fact, most modern-day Aymará and Quechua peoples of Peru and Bolivia accept these legends as their creation story.

The 5000 people of Isla del Sol are distributed between the main settlements of Cha'llapampa, near the island's northern end; Cha'lla, which backs up a lovely sandy beach on the central east coast; and Yumani, which straddles the ridge above the Escalera del Inca.

Exploring the Island

With a host of ancient ruins, tiny traditional villages, beautiful walking routes and a distinctly Aegean look, Isla del Sol merits a couple of days. Visitors can wander through the ruins at the island's northern and southern ends; explore its dry slopes, covered with sweet smelling *koa* (incense) brush; and hike over the ancient *pampas* (terraces), which are still cultivated by island families.

There are no vehicles on Isla del Sol, so visitors are limited to hiking or traveling by boat. The main ports are at Pilko Kaina, the Escalera del Inca and Cha'llapampa. There's also a small port at Japapi on the island's southwest coast.

The networks of walking tracks make exploration easy, but the altitude may take a toll. You can do a walking circuit of the island sights in a long day, but you'd be happier devoting a day each to the northern and southern ends. Hikers would be wise to carry a lunch and ample water, and to remember that the sun was born here and is still going strong; a good sunscreen is essential, particularly on the water.

Almost invariably, visitors who arrive on whirlwind tours will leave wishing they had more time to come to grips with this magical place. While the full-day tour does provide a decent introduction to the island (the half-day tour is strictly for the been-there-done-that crowd), most travelers will want to allow at least a night or two on the island. The most scenic place to stay is

A Bolivian Atlantis?

At low tide in Lake Titicaca, an innocuous-looking column of rock peeps just a few centimeters above the surface of Lake Titicaca, north of Isla del Sol. Most locals dismiss it as a natural stone column, similar to many others along the lake shoreline. In 1992, several stone boxes containing artifacts (including several made of pure gold) were discovered at the underwater site known as Marka Pampa (commonly dubbed 'La Ciudad Submergida'). In August 2000, further excavations near the site revealed a massive stone temple, winding pathways and a surrounding wall, all about eight meters underwater. Although it remains unclear who was responsible for the structures, it has been postulated that they are of Inca origin. Investigations are ongoing.

Yumani, high on the ridge, where a growing number of guesthouses are creating an emerging travelers' scene. There's also a basic hostal in Cha'llapampa, and in Cha'lla, Juan Mamani runs a pleasant guesthouse on the wide and lovely beach. It's also possible to camp on several secluded beaches around the island's wild northern and western shores.

Southern End

Pilko Kaina Near the southern tip of the island is the prominent ruins complex of Pilko Kaina, which sits well camouflaged against a steep terraced slope. The best-known site is the two-level Palacio del Inca, which is thought to have been constructed by Inca Tupac Yupanqui. The rectangular windows and doors taper upward from their sill and thresholds to narrower lintels that cover them on top. The arched roof vault was once covered with flagstone shingles and then reinforced with a layer of mud and straw.

Foreigners pay US$1 per person to visit the ruins complex; this ticket is also valid for entry to the Museo Étnico-Aymará, between

LAKE TITICACA

Cha'lla and Yumani (see Cha'lla, later in this section).

Escalera del Inca & Fuente del Inca

About an hour's walk north of Pilko Kaina you'll reach the Escalera del Inca/Fuente del Inca complex. Here, incongruous streams of fresh water gush from a natural spring and pour down three artificial stone channels alongside a beautifully constructed Inca-era staircase; they have inspired a lovely terraced and cultivated water garden on either side. Early Spaniards believed it was a Fountain of Youth, and for the Incas, the three streams represented their national motto: *Ama sua, Ama llulla, Ama khella*, meaning 'Don't steal, don't lie and don't be lazy.'

Today, the fountain provides a bountiful source of water for Yumani people, who come with their donkeys to fetch water and carry it up the steep trail to their homes on the ridge.

Yumani In Yumani, near the ridge, you'll see the small Iglesia de San Antonio, which serves the southern half of the island. Here you'll find three guesthouses and fabulous views over the water to Isla de la Luna. You can also climb up onto the ridge for a view down to the deep sapphire-colored Bahía Kona on the western shore. From the crest, you'll find routes leading downhill to the village of Japapi and north along the ridge to Cha'llapampa and the Chincana complex at the island's northern end.

About midway up the hill between the Fuente del Inca and the ridge, a short side track leads north to the Transturin agency's private Ethno Eco Complex, an underground archaeological and cultural museum with a medicinal herb garden, a corral with llamas and a typical Aymará house. It's open to Transturin clients only.

Kakayo-Queña Ridge With extra time, you can make your way over the isthmus and up onto the Kakayo-Queña Ridge, which is the island's southwestern extremity. This prominent feature slopes more gently on the east than it does in the west.

The serene walk along the ridge to the lighthouse on the southern end and back takes at least a half day from Yumani.

Northern End

There are two major routes between the northern and southern ends of Isla del Sol. The lower route winds scenically through fields, hamlets and villages, and around the bays and headlands above the eastern coast. The more dramatic route begins on the ridge in Yumani and heads north, roughly following the uninhabited ridge to the Chincana complex. The views down to both coasts of the island are nothing short of spectacular, and you'll encounter few people. About half an hour from Yumani, you'll reach a four-way trail junction: The track to the left leads to the shore at Bahía Kona, the one to the right descends to Bahía Kea, and straight ahead, it continues along the ridge to the Chincana ruins complex.

Cha'llapampa Most boat tours visiting the northern ruins land at Cha'llapampa, which straddles a slender isthmus. The wall dividing the village from the Co Kollabaya peninsula was designed to keep people out of the planted area; in the growing season, children aren't allowed onto the peninsula, lest they trample the precious crops.

The main attraction is the well-presented museum of artifacts excavated in 1992 from Marka Pampa, an archaeological site under 8m of water, at the center of a triangle formed by the islands of Chullo, Koa and Pallalla. It's fancifully referred to by locals as *la ciudad submergida*, 'the sunken city,' in reference to a legend that a city and temple existed between the islands of Koa and Pallalla in an age when the lake level was lower than it is today.

This small museum displays a boggling variety of interesting stuff: ancient spoons, blades, anthropomorphic figurines, stone tools, shells, animal bones, pot shards, Tiahuanaco-era artifacts, pots found in chullpas, vases, pitchers, bowls, skull parts, a jaguar statue, puma-shaped ceramic koa censers, and cups resembling Monty Python's Holy Grail. Most interesting,

ISLA DEL SOL & ISLA DE LA LUNA

Isla Pallalla

Isla Koa   ⊠ 1

Isla Chullo

Isla Kenata

Lake Titicaca

Isla de la Luna (Koati)

25 ⊠

▲ 3925m

Settlement ●

Same scale as main map

Bahía   Bahía   Isla Lavasani
Sabacera   Machamachani

Cerro   Cha'llapampa
Tikani ▲   Co
3936m   Kollabaya
Isla Jochihuata   ⊠ 3
              ⊠ 2 ▲ 4⊠ ⊠ 5   Punta Huayran Khala
              Santiago   ⊠ 8
              Pampa   ▲ 7
                     ▲ 6   Bahía
                              Cha'lla
Bahía Kona
del Norte   Bahía   Punta Huajra Khala
                              Kea
                                   Bahía
                                   Kea
                            ▲ 9   Cerro
                              Isla del Sol   Khea
                                              Kkollu
                                   Cha'lla   3990m
                            ▲⊠ 10   ⊠ 11 Bahía Pukhara
                     Cerro   ▲ Cerro   ⊞ 12
                     Chequesani Santa   To Isla de la Luna
                     4076m   Bárbara   (see inset map)
                                 4032m   Cerro
                                          Palla
                                          Khasa
                                          ▲ 4065m
                              Bahía   ⊠ 15 16 18
                              Kona   13⊠ 17 ⊠ 21
                                        ▲ 14 19 20 ⊠
                                        YUMANI 22 ⊠ 23
                            Japapi   ▲ 4024m
                                              ⊠ 24 Isla Chelleca
                              ⚜ Lighthouse   Lighthouse

                                              Yampupata

PLACES TO STAY
7 Hostal San Francisco
9 Posada del Inca
   (Alojamiento Juan Mamani)
15 Hostal Templo del Sol
16 Hostal Hijos del Sol
17 Hostal Casa Blanca
19 Hostal Mirador del Inca;
   Hostal Inti Marka
20 Hostal Imperio del Sol
22 Hostal Inti Wayra;
   Restaurant Incaico

OTHER
1 Marka Pampa
2 Chincana Ruins
   (Palacio del Inca or El Laberinto)
3 Titicaca Rock (Rock of the Puma)
4 Templo del Inca (Templo del Sol)
5 Piedra Sagrada; Snack Bar
6 Snack Bar
8 Wall
10 Ruins
11 Museo Étnico-Aymará
12 Soccer Field
13 Ruins
14 Ruins
18 La Posada del Inca (Crillon Tours)
21 Ethno-Eco Complex (Transturin Tours)
23 Escalera del Inca (Inca Stairway);
   Fuente del Inca (Inca Springs)
24 Pilko Kaina Ruins
25 Acllahuasi Ruins

LAKE TITICACA

however, are the Marka Pampa stone boxes and their contents: a medallion, a cup, a puma and a woman, all made of gold. The boxes were so expertly carved and capped that their contents remained dry until their relatively recent discovery.

For foreigners, admission is US$1; keep your ticket, because it's also good for entry to the Chincana ruins (and the Chincana ruins ticket is good here). It's normally open only in the mornings when there are tour groups about; in the afternoon, try asking around for Señor Hiriberto Ticoma, who has the key and may or may not be willing to open it up

for you (and once you're in, don't let anyone charge you extra to use the toilet).

Piedra Sagrada & Templo del Inca From Cha'llapampa, the Chincana route parallels the beach, climbing gently along an ancient route to the isthmus at Santiago Pampa (Kasapata).

Immediately east of the trail, an odd artificially carved boulder stands upright in a small field. This is known as the **Piedra Sagrada** (Sacred Stone). There are theories that it was used as an execution block for those convicted of wrongdoing or as a *huaca*, a rainmaking stone, but no one is entirely certain of its purpose. Today, its main function seems to be dragging flagging tourists off their feet and onto the picnic bench for cold beers and sandwiches, which are served up by an enterprising local.

Over the track, just southwest of the Piedra Sagrada, are the ancient walls of the complex known as the **Templo del Inca**, also called the Templo del Sol. Although little remains of this temple built for an unknown purpose, it contains the only Bolivian examples of expert Inca stonework comparable to the renowned walls found in Cuzco.

Chincana Ruins & Titi Khar'ka The island's most spectacular ruins complex, **Chincana,** lies near the northern tip of Isla del Sol. Its main feature is the **Palacio del Inca**, also known as El Laberinto (Labyrinth) or by its Aymará name, Incanotapa. This maze of stone walls and tiny doorways overlooks a lovely white beach lapped by deep blue waters.

Backing up the ruins, about 150m southeast, is the **Mesa Ceremónica** (Ceremonial Table), which appears to be a conveniently placed picnic spot – and indeed, it's often used as such. It's thought to have been the site of human and animal sacrifice. Behind (east of) the table stretches the large rock known as Titicaca – or more accurately, **Titi Khar'ka**, the Rock of the Puma – which is featured in the Inca creation legend. It's likely that the name derives from its shape, which, when viewed from the southeast, resembles a crouching puma.

Three natural features on the rock's western face also figure in legend. Near the northern end is one dubbed the Cara de Viracocha (Face of Viracocha – or is it the face of a puma?), which takes some imagination to distinguish. At the southern end are four distinctive elongated niches. The two on the right are locally called the Refugio del Sol (Refuge of the Sun) and those on the left, the Refugio de la Luna (Refuge of the Moon). According to tradition, it was here during the Chamaj Pacha, or 'times of flood and darkness,' that the sun made its first appearance, and later Manco Capac and Mama Ocllo appeared and founded the Inca Empire.

In the surface stone immediately south of the rock, you'll pass the Huellas del Sol

The Palacio del Inca labyrinth winds through the Chincana ruins.

(Footprints of the Sun). These natural markings resemble footprints and have inspired the notion that they were made by the sun after its birth on Titicaca Rock.

Admission to Chincana is US$1 per person for foreigners; a ticket from the museum in Cha'llapampa also covers entry to Chincana and vice versa.

Most north-end tours begin at the boat landing in Cha'llapampa and follow the prominent Inca route past the Piedra Sagrada and Templo del Sol to Chincana. Another access route is along the ridge from Yumani. When you reach a point directly above Cha'llapampa, leave the main trail and continue straight ahead along a jumble of light tracks for 2km, picking your route through the maze of goat tracks over shrub-covered slopes (mostly below the ridge) and around bizarre rock outcrops.

Cha'lla The agreeable village of Cha'lla, the site of the island's secondary school, stretches along a magnificent sandy beach that appears to be taken straight out of a holiday brochure for the Greek islands. It's a great place to soak up the sun and watch people playing soccer and families strolling. Literally 1m off the sand is the popular snack bar and Posada del Inca guesthouse, run by the friendly Juan Mamani.

In the pastoral valley over the low pass between Cha'lla and Yumani lies the Museo Étnico-Aymará, with exhibits that reveal the history and lifestyle of the hardy Aymará people who inhabit the Altiplano region. Admission is US$1; this ticket is also good for the Pilko Kaina ruins at the southern tip of the island.

Organized Tours

Numerous Copacabana tour agencies offer informal tours to Isla del Sol (US$2 per person half day, US$5 full day). The launches leave from the beach around 8 or 8:30 am and stop at the Escalera del Inca to drop off passengers before continuing north to Cha'llapampa. There, they allow time to hike up to the Chincana ruins, then return to the Escalera del Inca and Pilko Kaina. Some full-day tours also buzz over to Isla de

la Luna for a quick look around before returning to Copacabana, but these cost an additional US$2 or US$3.

Those who wish to hike can get off at Cha'llapampa in the morning and walk to the Escalera del Inca, rejoining the tour in the afternoon. Alternatively, you can opt to stay overnight or longer on the island, which is highly recommended – a day just isn't enough here – then find your own way back to Copacabana (see Boat under Getting There & Away, later in this section).

The company Turisbus, at the Hotel Rosario del Lago, offers guided half-day trips to the southern end of the island, including a ride on a reed boat at Sicuani and admission to the ruins and museum, for US$19. For US$35, they do a full-day tour that also takes in the northern end of Isla del Sol. See the hotel's listing in Copacabana for the agency's contact information.

Places to Stay

You can camp just about anywhere on the island, but it's best to set up away from villages, avoiding cultivated land. There are plenty of deserted beaches, and the wild and practically uninhabited western slopes of the island are especially appealing and secluded.

Cha'llapampa The best accommodations in Cha'llapampa are at the flowery *Hostal San Francisco*, run by friendly Señor Francisco Ramos. A night in the two four-bed sleeping huts costs US$2, and meals are available; note that you'll need a flashlight to climb to the outhouse at night. To reach the hostal from the landing site, follow the beach road to your left and look for the violet-colored house.

Cha'lla Right on the beach at Cha'lla is the simple and friendly *Posada del Inca* (also called *Alojamiento Juan Mamani* and not to be confused with Crillon Tours' upmarket La Posada del Inca, in Yumani). Juan is an excellent source of information on island ruins and hiking routes, and the colorful garden and outdoor tables tempt nonguests to stop for snacks and conversation. For beds, blankets and use of a stove, you'll pay

US$1.20 upstairs and US$1.80 downstairs per person. Note, however, that this place may be closed for part of the year, especially during the November to January low season.

Yumani Just below the ridge in Yumani village, above the Fuente del Inca, lies a growing number of hostal options. The beautiful and amicable *Hostal Inti Wayra* affords great views from every room, but those upstairs are larger and more open. You'll also have a fabulous rooftop vista over the water to Isla de la Luna, and coincidentally, the full moon rises behind the island. Rooms with communal facilities cost US$2 per person; American breakfasts are US$1, and other meals (including vegetarian options), US$1.80 each.

A real favorite – and with good reason – is the upbeat *Hostal Templo del Sol*, which sits right on the ridge and enjoys unsurpassed views down both sides of the island, including a rather haunting vista of the Kakayo-Queña ridge from the typically sunny patio area. The ambience here creates a real backpackers' scene, and many people who arrive for two days wind up staying a week. Meals, staples and cooking facilities are available, and beds cost US$2 per person.

The modern-looking *Hostal Casa Blanca* has a double and a five-bed dorm room for US$2 per person. Meals are available on request, but the outdoor facilities are straight out of the Middle Ages. The *Hostal Imperio del Sol*, run by Gualberto Mamani, has seven rooms and space for 18, and charges US$1.50 per person. Other budget options, all charging US$2 per person, include the *Hostal Hijos del Sol* and the *Hostal Inti Marka*.

The only upmarket choice is the rather stuffy *La Posada del Inca*, run by Crillon Tours (☎ 02-337533). It occupies a closed compound (open only to Crillon clients) near the church in Yumani and caters to tourists requiring more luxury than is offered by other local places. Rustic single/double rooms with solar power cost US$49/57, including breakfast and dinner.

The small village bakery sells fresh bread in the morning.

Places to Eat

Yumani has the small, friendly and recommended *Restaurant Incaico*, which serves excellent breakfasts, soup, pejerrey and trout. Otherwise, you're limited to the hostales for meals. The Posada del Inca in Cha'lla, where you'll get trout for as little as US$3, and the Templo del Sol and Inti Wayra in Yumani are generally the best. They prepare breakfasts and dinners for about US$2 each, but you normally need to book eight to 12 hours in advance.

Cooked snacks, such as potatoes, eggs and the like, are sometimes available near the Escalera del Inca in lower Yumani, and you'll find burgers, sandwiches and other light meals beside the Piedra Sagrada on the northern end of the island. A new snack bar is also planned along the ridge walk between Yumani and the Chincana ruins.

The lake water is generally clean, especially along the western shore, but it's still wise to boil or purify it before drinking.

Getting There & Away

Boat From the beach in Copacabana, numerous boat owners and tour companies provide launch transport to Isla del Sol. The set return fare between Copacabana and Isla del Sol is US$2 per person, and in theory, the return portion is valid for two or three days, but in practice, it'll be difficult to link up with your original boat for the trip back. For a one-way ticket, you'll pay US$1 to reach the island, but the normal charge is US$2 or US$3 for the return to Copacabana. In addition to the tour boats, community boats leave several times daily from Cha'llapampa and the Escalera del Inca.

Tickets may be purchased at the ticket kiosks on the beach or at agencies in Copacabana (see Organized Tours in Copacabana). Boats to the northern end of the island land at Cha'llapampa, while those going to the southern end land at either Pilko Kaina or the Escalera del Inca; many also make a circuit of all three landing sites.

Walking Although there have been lots of miracles at Lake Titicaca, you can't really walk to Isla del Sol. It is possible, however, to walk from Copacabana to the village of Yampupata on the mainland, just a short distance by rowboat from the island's southern tip. See Copacabana to Yampupata Trek, earlier in this chapter.

ISLA DE LA LUNA

Legend has it that the Island of the Moon, or Koati, was the place where Viracocha commanded the moon to rise into the sky. This peaceful little island is surrounded by clear aquamarine water, and a walk up to the summit eucalyptus grove, where shepherds graze their flocks, is rewarded by a spectacular vista of Cerro Illampu and the entire snow-covered Cordillera Real.

The ruins of an Inca nunnery for the Vírgenes del Sol (Virgins of the Sun), also known as Acllahuasi or Iñak Uyu, occupies an amphitheater-like valley on the northeastern shore. It's constructed of well-worked stone set in adobe mortar. Foreigners pay US$1 admission to the temple.

Places to Stay It's possible to camp anywhere on the small island away from the settlement, but expect a bit of attention.

Getting There & Away After dropping tourists at Cha'llapampa on Isla del Sol, some tours continue on to Isla de la Luna. Alternatively, you can charter a launch from Yampupata or the Escalera del Inca for around US$8 to US$10 roundtrip (for up to about 12 people).

NORTHEASTERN SHORE

If you're heading northwest from Huatajata toward the Peru-Bolivia border area at Puerto Acosta, you may be delayed by a couple of sites of minor interest.

About 90km north of La Paz, along the road to Sorata, is the large and aloof market town of Achacachi, where you'll find a couple of shabby alojamientos. The church in Ancoraimes, about 20km north of Achacachi, features a lovely ornamental screen above the altar. In the colonial township of Carabuco is a colorful Sunday market, and from Escoma (165km northwest of La Paz) a road strikes off the Cordillera Apolobamba (see the Cordilleras & Yungas chapter).

Just offshore near Puerto Acosta are a couple of submerged stone piers and breakwaters that may date from pre-Inca times. In 1980, however, diver and underwater researcher Carlos Ponce suggested that they may have been constructed as recently as 1900. There's little solid evidence for either notion.

Getting There & Away

Inexpensive micros run occasionally from the cemetery district in La Paz to Puerto Acosta, near the Peruvian border. Beyond there, you'll probably have to rely on the camiones, which run more or less daily from Puerto Acosta to Moho, on the Peruvian side, which has a small alojamiento and several daily buses to the larger town of Huancané. Sunday is market day in Puerto Acosta, so Saturday might be the best day to look for camiones coming from La Paz. There's also an infrequent micro (perhaps three times weekly) between Tilali, near the border in Peru (it's a four-hour walk from Puerto Acosta), and the larger town of Huancané, in Peru. If you don't catch up with the camión or the micro, it's a 15-hour walk from Puerto Acosta to Moho!

Note that to enter Peru by this little-known route, you'll have to check out of Bolivia at the migración in Puerto Acosta. In a hamlet on the Peruvian side of the border, the irritable police will check your documents and tell you to head straight for Puno, where migración will stamp you into Peru.

GUAQUI & DESAGUADERO

Three hours by bus from La Paz, Guaqui sits beside, and partially beneath, Lago Huyñaymarka, the southern extension of Lake Titicaca. It lies only 20 minutes by micro beyond Tiahuanaco, and about half an hour from the Peruvian frontier at Desaguadero.

This tranquil little Altiplano town has a truly beautiful church with a silver altar and some colonial artwork inside. Soporific little Guaqui sees most of its excitement during the riotous Fiesta de Santiago in the final week of July.

Evidence of the 1986 flooding, which left half the town in ruins, is still apparent. There's no longer a train service from La Paz, and the famous Guaqui-Puno lake steamer was discontinued when the lake port disappeared beneath rising flood waters.

Places to Stay & Eat

The *Residencial Guaqui*, near the port, provides really the only accommodations in town. It was damaged in the flooding but has since undergone repairs. Rooms, which aren't terribly secure, cost US$2 per person. There's a pleasant courtyard and the friendly attached restaurant is a good option. There's also a basic eatery on the main plaza.

The Peruvian side of Desaguadero has plenty of small and inexpensive places to stay. If you're stuck on the Bolivian side after the border closes, try the recom-

mended *Hotel Bolivia*, with a restaurant and clean singles/doubles for US$7/10.

Getting There & Away

Most of the Tiahuanaco buses from La Paz continue to Guaqui. The first micros from Guaqui back to Tiahuanaco and La Paz leave at 5:30 am, and there's something at least every hour until about 4 or 5 pm. They depart from the main avenue in the lower part of town.

The direct buses from La Paz to Des-aguadero (3½ hours, US$2.20), the destination for most people passing through Guaqui, leave from the Transportes Ingavi office in La Paz's Cemetery District.

From Guaqui, minibuses also run to Des-aguadero (30 minutes, US$0.50), where you can cross the border on foot, complete the normally quirky immigration formalities, and then catch a connecting bus on to Yunguyo (where you can cut back into Bolivia at Copacabana) or Puno. The border closes at 7 pm.

Southern Altiplano

Stretching southward from La Paz to the Chilean and Argentine frontiers and beyond is a harsh, sparsely populated wilderness of scrubby windswept basins, lonely peaks and glaring, almost lifeless salt

Highlights

- Feel small at the foot of Parque Nacional Sajama's hulking Nevado Sajama volcano
- Follow in the footsteps of Butch Cassidy and the Sundance Kid in the hills and cactus-spiked canyons and *quebradas*, and travel on horseback through the spectacular Wild West landscapes around Tupiza
- Experience the unearthly geology of Bolivia's remote southwest highlands with their brine-splashed landscape of steaming volcanoes, hot springs and flamingo-filled lakes
- See the enormous spikes of Comanche's 12m *Puya raimondii* erupt into flower for the first and only time in its 60 to 100-year life cycle
- Join in Oruro's wild annual La Diablada carnival celebration or scale nearby Rumi Campana with local rock climbers

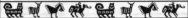

deserts. This is the archetypal Altiplano, a Tibet-like land of lonely mirages, indeterminable distances and an overwhelming sense of solitude. Though the air retains little warmth, the land and sky meet in waves of shimmering reflected heat and the horizon disappears. Stark mountains seem to hover somewhere beyond reality, and the nights are just as haunting, with black skies and icy stars. The moment the sun sets – or even passes behind a cloud – you'll realize this air has teeth.

During the Cretaceous period some 100 million years ago, the vast Altiplano plateau was a deep intermontane valley. Erosion in those mountains filled the valley with a 15,000m-deep deposit of sediment to create the base for the present-day Altiplano. With such porous alluvial soil, the basin's fertility might seem predictable, but the presence of salts, lack of adequate moisture and a rocky surface character make agriculture a challenging venture.

The relatively few inhabitants of the Southern Altiplano are among the world's hardiest souls. Many live at the ragged edge of human endurance, contending with wind, drought, bitter cold and high altitudes with few modern conveniences to make the harsh conditions more bearable. The *campesino* miners, farmers and herders of the Altiplano labor throughout their lives to wrest an existence from this land, and deserve a great deal of respect for their accomplishments.

Even given the opportunity of relative prosperity in the developing lowlands, few Aymará people have chosen to leave their ancestral homes. This is the same hardy culture that managed to resist efforts by the Inca to assimilate it, body and soul, into the empire. The Aymará rejected the Quechua language and the Inca culture, and was the only conquered tribe to get away with it. Fiercely proud and stubborn, they may well seem as harsh and cold as the land they inhabit; this attitude is spawned by a deep

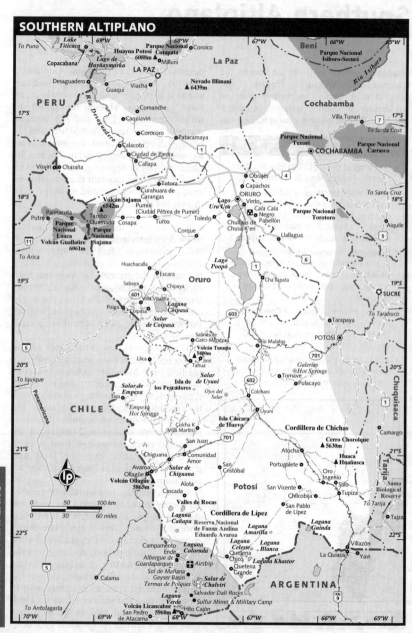

suspicion of foreigners who venture in with what seems to be a lot of money and no visible means of support. People who work hard at a meager survival just don't fathom someone trotting around the globe rather than attending to work or religious and family responsibilities at home (some of your relatives may feel the same way). However, with patience and diplomacy, the icy barrier can sometimes be broken and you'll catch a glimpse of a world and lifestyle that's harsh beyond imagining.

The sheltered and spectacular red rock country around the peaceful town of Tupiza represents a gentler side of southwestern Bolivia, and over the years its population has swelled with *mineros despedidos* (laid-off miners), victims of privatization and labor strife in the mines of Oruro and Potosí.

Economically, this mineral-rich region produces a large portion of Bolivia's non-illicit exports. Oruro and Llallagua are centers of tin production, and an enormous tin smelter operates at Vinto, near Oruro. Remote and antiquated mining operations, which dip into rich concentrations of antimony, bismuth, silver, lead, zinc, copper, salt, sulfur, magnesium and other buried treasures, are scattered throughout southern Potosí department.

Climatically, the best months to visit are August, September and October, after the worst of the winter chills and before the summer rains. From May to early July, nighttime temperatures combined with a good stiff wind can bring the windchill temperature down to just -40°C. Summers are warmer, but for an arid area, there's quite a lot of rainfall between November and March. At any time of year, you'll need protection against sun, wind and cold.

ORURO
☎ 052

Oruro, the Southern Altiplano's only city, lies north of the salty lakes Uru Uru and Poopó and 3½ hours by bus south of La Paz. It sits at the intersection of the railway lines between Cochabamba and La Paz to Chile or Argentina, crowded against a colorful range of mineral-rich low hills at an altitude of 3702m. The city's approximately 160,000 inhabitants, 90% of whom are of pure Indian heritage, refer to themselves as *quirquinchos* (armadillos), after the carapaces used in their *charangos*.

Visitors are rarely indifferent to Oruro; they either love it or hate it. Although it's one of Bolivia's most culturally colorful cities – indeed, it calls itself the 'Folkloric Capital of Bolivia' – there are few tourist attractions, and you'll need time for the place to grow on you. The crusty exterior of some *orureños* is balanced by the warm hospitality of others, and especially if you manage to attend the uncharacteristically riotous La Diablada, the wild annual Carnaval celebration, you won't regret a visit.

History
Settled in 1601 and founded in 1606, Oruro owes its existence to the 10-sq-km range of hills rising 350m above the city. Chock-full of copper, silver and tin, these hills form the city's economic backbone. Early mining activities focused almost exclusively on silver extraction, but when production declined in the early 1800s, indigenous workers moved on in search of more lucrative prospects, and the community was more or less abandoned. Oruro's importance as a mining town was revived during the late 19th and early 20th centuries, with the increasing world market for tin and copper.

By the 1920s, Bolivia's thriving tin-mining industry rested in the hands of three powerful capitalists. The most renowned was Simon I Patiño, an Indian from the Cochabamba valley who arguably became the world's wealthiest man. In 1897, Patiño purchased La Salvadora mine near the village of Uncia, east of Oruro, which eventually became the world's most productive source of tin. Patiño's success snowballed and by 1924, he had taken ownership of the rich mines at nearby Llallagua, thereby gaining control of about 50% of the nation's tin output.

Once secure in his wealth, Patiño migrated to Britain, where he started buying up European and North American smelters and tin interests. As a consequence, Bolivia found itself exporting both

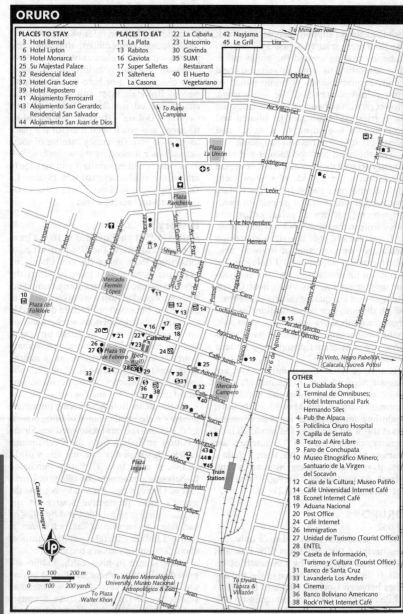

ORURO

PLACES TO STAY
3   Hotel Bernal
6   Hotel Lipton
15 Hotel Monarca
25 Su Majestad Palace
32 Residencial Ideal
37 Hotel Gran Sucre
39 Hotel Repostero
41 Alojamiento Ferrocarril
43 Alojamiento San Gerardo;
    Residencial San Salvador
44 Alojamiento San Juan de Dios

PLACES TO EAT
11 La Plata
13 Rabitos
16 Gaviota
17 Super Salteñas
21 Salteñería
    La Casona
22 La Cabaña
23 Unicornio
30 Govinda
35 SUM
    Restaurant
40 El Huerto
    Vegetariano
42 Nayjama
45 Le Grill

OTHER
1   La Diablada Shops
2   Terminal de Omnibuses;
    Hotel International Park
    Hernando Siles
4   Pub the Alpaca
5   Policlínica Oruro Hospital
7   Capilla de Serrato
8   Teatro al Aire Libre
9   Faro de Conchupata
10 Museo Etnográfico Minero;
    Santuario de la Virgen
    del Socavón
12 Casa de la Cultura; Museo Patiño
14 Café Universidad Internet Café
18 Econet Internet Café
19 Aduana Nacional
20 Post Office
24 Café Internet
26 Immigration
27 Unidad de Turismo (Tourist Office)
28 ENTEL
29 Caseta de Información,
    Turismo y Cultura (Tourist Office)
31 Banco de Santa Cruz
33 Lavandería Los Andes
34 Cinema
36 Banco Boliviano Americano
38 Rock'n'Net Internet Café

its tin and its profits. Public outcry launched a series of labor uprisings and set the stage for nationalization of the mines by Victor Paz Estenssoro in 1952 and the subsequent creation of the government-run Corporación Minera de Bolivia, COMIBOL. The two other 'tin barons,' Carlos Victor Aramayo of Tupiza and Mauricio Hothschild, of European Jewish extraction, kept their centers of operations in Bolivia, but the 1952 revolution didn't give them any breaks. Both men were also stripped of their wealth, and Aramayo fled to Europe in order to escape the ill will of his compatriots.

Over the years, government inefficiency and corruption ran Bolivia's mining interests into the ground, causing the industry and its profits to collapse. The resulting turmoil – accompanied by low world tin prices, stiff competition from abroad and turbulent labor unrest, left the already fluctuating population of Oruro in a state of uncertainty. The subsequent push for *capitalización* (fiscalization, a variation on privatization) brought about the dissolution of COMIBOL and the transfer of mining interests to the private sector.

Orientation
The best city map is probably the *Guía Turística de Oruro*, which is sold at the tourist offices for US$1; a less useful regional map, *Mapa Rutero Turístico Oruro*, costs the same and includes details about sites of interest outside the city.

Information
Tourist Offices The helpful Caseta de Información, Turismo y Cultura tourist office (☎ 57881), in a fishbowl kiosk in front of the ENTEL office, is open weekdays 8 am to noon and 2 to 6 pm (weekends also for two weeks before Carnaval). Several useful booklets are occasionally available here, including a nice little city guide, *Oruro en sus Manos*, and the museum periodical *Museo y Cultura*. During the same hours, the more bureaucratic Unidad de Turismo (☎/fax 50144) dispenses information on Plaza 10 de Febrero.

A great little booklet to look for is *Oruro – Destino Turístico*, by Juan Carlos Vargas; it's sometimes sold at the tourist office, or you can buy it directly from the author (see Organized Tours, later in this section). The recommended *Carnaval de Oruro* provides detailed information (in Spanish) on the dances and musical styles featured in La Diablada; it also contains a rundown of visitor attractions around Oruro department.

Immigration (☎ 50274) is on the main square, Plaza 10 de Febrero.

Money You can change cash at any shop displaying 'Compro Dólares' signs, and street moneychangers mill around the corner of 6 de Octubre and Aldana, near Plaza Ingavi. Banco Boliviano Americano and Banco de Santa Cruz, both on Bolívar, change cash and traveler's checks (for a 4% commission).

Post & Communications The post office lies just off Plaza 10 de Febrero. Parcels must first be inspected by the Aduana Nacional on Velasco Galvarro between Ayacucho and Junín. The ENTEL office, one of the nicest modern buildings in Oruro, is west of the corner of Soria Galvarro and Bolívar.

Oruro is now proudly online; try Café Internet in Edificio Oruro on 6 de Octubre, Rock'n'Net on Bolívar close to 6 de Octubre, Café Universidad on 6 de Octubre near Cochabamba, and Econet on Ayacucho, also near 6 de Octubre. All charge from US$1 to US$1.60 per hour.

Laundry Laundry service is available at Lavandería Los Andes, near the corner of Sucre and Presidente Montes.

Medical Services Oruro's best hospital is Policlínica Oruro (☎ 75082), on Rodríguez at the northern end of the central area.

Dangers & Annoyances Pickpocketing, bag-slashing and con artists are potential problems, especially at the Mercado Campero and around the train station.

Mines

Most of the old mines in the hills behind Oruro have now been closed and are dangerous to enter. Among them is Mina San José, high on the mountain behind the city, which claims to have operated for over 450 years. If you wish to hike around the colorful tailings heaps, take a yellow micro 'D,' marked 'San José,' which leaves from the northwest corner of Plaza 10 de Febrero near the tourist office.

The main mining operation in Oruro now is the gold mine, Inti Raymi. Prospective visitors will need to muster a group, and arrange for a guide and obtain permission from EMISA (☎ 50856 or 51713), Bolívar 1221.

Churches

The cathedral, just east of the main plaza, has fine stained glass above the altar. The adjacent tower was constructed as part of Iglesia de la Compañía de Jesús (the Jesuit order) before Oruro was founded. When the Jesuits were expelled, however, it was designated as the Cathedral of the Oruro Bishopric. In 1994, its original baroque entrance was moved and reconstructed at the Santuario de la Virgen del Socavón.

The Santuario de la Virgen del Socavón, on Cerro Pie de Gallo (Cock's Foot Hill), presents a grand city view. It was here that 16th-century miners began worshipping the Virgen de Candelaria, the patron saint of miners. In 1781, a church was constructed here in her honor and given the name Virgen del Socavón, or Virgin of the Grotto. The present church, which is a 19th-century reconstruction, figures prominently in La Diablada as the site where good ultimately defeats evil (see 'A Devil of a Good Time' later in this section).

For the energetic, there's also a good view from Capilla de Serrato, a steep climb from the end of Calle Washington.

Faro de Conchupata

On November 17, 1851, at the Faro de Conchupata, Bolivia's red, gold and green flag was first raised: red for the courage of the Bolivian army, gold for the country's mineral wealth and green for its agricultural wealth. The spot is now marked by a balcony and column topped by an enormous glass globe. It is illuminated at night and provides a fine vista over the town. Beside it is Teatro al Aire Libre, the open air theater. To get there, climb to the top of Avenida Presidente Montes.

Museo Patiño (Casa de la Cultura)

The university-administered Museo Patiño, in the Casa de la Cultura on Soria Galvarro, is a former residence of tin baron Simon I Patiño. Exhibits include his furniture and personal effects, and an ornate stairway. Visiting exhibitions are featured in the downstairs lobby. It's open weekdays 8:30 am to noon and 3:30 to 6 pm. Admission for foreigners is US$1.40.

Museo Etnográfico Minero

The Mining Museum, adjacent to Santuario de la Virgen del Socavón, is housed in an actual mine tunnel. It reveals various aspects and methods of Bolivian mining: tunnels, 'mailboxes,' tailing dumps, chimneys, El Tío (the devilish character who owns the minerals) etc. It's open daily 9 am to noon and 3 to 6 pm. Admission is US$1.20.

Museo Nacional Antropológico Eduardo López Rivas

This museum, at the south end of town, has been newly remodeled and upgraded with local contributions and the help of the German government. It's named for a mid-20th-century scholar who wrote extensively about Andean cultures and their archaeological and ethnographic heritage.

The museum's focus is on the Oruro area, and displays include artifacts and information on the early Chipayas and Uros tribes. It's open weekdays from 9 am to noon and 2 to 6 pm, and weekends 10 am to noon and 3 to 6 pm. Admission is US$0.75. Take an orange micro 'C,' marked 'Sud,' from the northwest corner of Plaza 10 de Febrero or opposite the train station, and get off just beyond the tin-foundry compound.

A Devil of a Good Time

La Diablada (Dance of the Devils) has become the most renowned and largest annual celebration held in Bolivia. In the broad sense, these Carnaval festivities can be described as reenactments of the triumph of good over evil, but the festival is so interlaced with threads of both Christian and indigenous myths, fables, deities and traditions that it would be inaccurate to oversimplify it in that way.

The origins of a similar festival may be traced back to 12th-century Cataluña, now in Spain, although orureños maintain that it commemorates an event that occurred during the early days of their own fair city. Legend has it that one night a thief called Chiruchiru was seriously wounded by a traveler he'd attempted to rob. Taking pity on the wrongdoer, the Virgin of Candelaria gently helped him reach his home near the mine at the base of Cerro Pie del Gallo and succored him until he died shortly after. When the miners found him there, over his head hung an image of the Virgin. Today, the mine is known as the Socavón de la Virgen (Grotto of the Virgin). This legend has been combined with the ancient Uros tale of Huari and the struggle of Michael the Archangel against the seven deadly sins into the spectacle that is presented during the Oruro Carnaval.

The design and creation of Diablada costumes has become an art form in Oruro, and several Diablada clubs consisting of members from all levels of Oruro society are sponsored by local businesses. Groups number anywhere from 40 to 300 dancing participants. Costumes, which may cost several hundred dollars each, are owned by individual dancers, and rehearsals of their diabolical dances begin on the first Sunday in November, several months in advance of Carnaval.

Festivities begin the first Saturday before Ash Wednesday with a glorious *entrada*, or opening parade, led by the brightly costumed Michael the Archangel character. Behind him, dancing and marching, come the famous devils and a host of bears and condors. The chief devil, Lucifer, wears the most extravagant costume, complete with a velvet cape and an ornate mask. Faithfully at his side are two other devils, including Supay, the Andean god of evil that inhabits the hills and mineshafts.

The procession is followed by vehicles adorned with jewels, coins and silverware (in commemoration of the *achura* rites in which the Inca offered their treasures to Inti – the sun – in the festival of Inti Raymi), and the miners offer the year's highest-quality mineral to El Tío, the devilish character who is owner of all underground minerals and precious metals.

Behind them follow the Inca and a host of conquistadores, including Francisco Pizarro and Diego de Almagro. When the Archangel and the fierce-looking devilish dancers arrive at the soccer stadium, a series of dances relates the ultimate battle between good and evil. When it becomes apparent that good has triumphed, the dancers retire to the Santuario de la Virgen del Socavón, and a Mass is held in honor of the Virgen del Socavón, who pronounces that good has prevailed.

For three days following the entrada, other dance groups perform at locations throughout the city. Each group has its specific costume and performs its own dance. For a brief rundown of the dances, refer to Dance, in the Arts section of the Facts About the Country chapter.

Museo Mineralógico

This museum, on the university campus south of the city center, has a wonderful collection of more than 5000 minerals, precious stones, fossils and crystals from around the world. It's open weekdays 9 am to noon and 2 to 5 pm and admission for foreigners is US$1.20. If the door is locked, visit the Departamento de Minas at the university and ask to be allowed in. From the patio outside there's a nice view of Lago Uru Uru, several kilometers away.

Access to the university is on green micro 'A,' blue micro 'F' or red minibus 102 (all marked 'Sud' or 'Ciudad Universitaria') from the YPFB gasoline station opposite the train station.

Zoo

Oruro's depressingly unkempt zoo lies near the children's playground opposite the Museo Antropológico. Its most interesting feature is the large aviary, where you'll have close-up views of Andean condors, but interest pales when you realize such large and stately birds would prefer to be soaring over remote Andean crags. It's open daily 10 am to noon and 3 to 6 pm and costs US$0.20. From the main plaza, take the orange micro 'C,' green micro 'A,' green minibuses 2, 4 or 7, or red minibuses 101, 102 or 105.

Activities

Rock climbers will enjoy the area known as Rumi Campana (Bell Rock), named after an unusual acoustic phenomenon. It lies about 2km northwest of town. (On the way, note the brilliantly colored mine tailings heaped around the hills.) On weekends, you can practice your skills with the friendly and enthusiastic local climbing club, Club de Montañismo Halcones. There's some excellent rock and a range of routes with protection already in place. Try your hand at the challenging overhanging route *Mujer Amante*, or the wonderful '7'-rated route known as *Sueño*.

Organized Tours

To travel into the wildest reaches of western Oruro department, where there's a wealth of cultural and natural interest – wildlife, volcanoes, hot springs, colorful lakes and lagoons and isolated communities – contact the private guide Juan Carlos Vargas (☎ 40333 or 40666), who can arrange adventurous custom trips.

Places to Stay

Accommodations are booked out during La Diablada, so make your reservation early or contact the tourist office about accommodations in local homes. Note that prices climb considerably during the festivities; during Carnaval, a basic US$3 room in a budget *alojamiento* will cost US$15 or more, and rates for rooms normally costing US$10 or more may increase by up to sixfold.

Budget Oruro's many alojamientos all charge US$3.50/4.50 for singles/doubles, but in most cases, foreigners are welcomed reluctantly. *Alojamiento Ferrocarril (☎ 74079; Velasco Galvarro 6278)* has been described as being 'like a prison, but without the showers.' A little better is *Alojamiento San Juan de Dios (☎ 77083; Velasco Galvarro 1846)*, while *Alojamiento San Gerardo* is just acceptable. Slightly nicer, but far from ideal, is *Residencial Ideal (☎ 77863; Bolívar 386)*, which charges US$3.50/4.50. *Residencial San Salvador (☎ 76771)*, near Alojamiento San Gerardo, has recently been improved and now charges US$7 for a double with bath.

The main advantage of *Hotel Lipton (☎ 76583; 6 de Agosto 625)* is its proximity to the bus terminal. Rooms with double beds, private bath and TV cost US$7.50 per person. A better value is the well-run *Hotel Bernal (☎ 79468; Brasil 701)*, opposite the bus terminal. It's actually a solid mid-range hotel, complete with a dining room. Acceptably clean singles and doubles with bath cost just US$7.50 per person.

A great-value option is the friendly *Pub the Alpaca (☎ 75715; La Paz 690)*, which has 10 beds and charges just US$3 per person. See Places to Eat for more information.

Mid-Range The comfortable *Hotel International Park (☎ 76227; fax 75187)*, on Calle

Rajka Bakovic literally on top of the bus terminal, provides convenient digs for travelers who have no interest in seeing more of Oruro than necessary. Singles/doubles with private bath, hot shower, heating, TV and use of the garage cost US$25/40.

The three-star *Hotel Monarca* (☎ 53400), on Avenida del Ejército at 6 de Agosto, charges US$18 for well-appointed single or double rooms with bath, and *Su Majestad Palace* (☎ 55132), on Adolfo Mier at Potosí, charges US$25.

At the relaxed *Hotel Repostero* (☎ 50505; Sucre 370), carpeted rooms with private bath, hot shower and TV cost US$13.50/20. With a youth hostel card, you're eligible for a 10% discount. More upmarket is the refurbished *Hotel Gran Sucre* (☎ 76320 or 76800; fax 54110; Sucre 510). Rooms located in the old section, without bath, cost just US$6/8.50. In the plush new section, rooms with bath are US$21/35, or US$12 for a single without bath. There's a great restaurant with unusual décor, including stained-glass and Carnaval paintings, and a running Charlie Chaplin theme in other parts of the building.

Places to Eat

Most places don't open up until 11 am or later, so *Mercado Campero* is your only option for an early breakfast. Excellent *salteñas* are found at *Salteñería La Casona* (☎ 52057), on Presidente Montes just off the main plaza, and *Super Salteñas* (☎ 55782; Soria Galvarro 5865). Both these places serve sandwiches at lunchtime and pizza in the evening.

Market food stalls in both *Mercado Campero* and *Mercado Fermín López* feature noodles, *falso conejo* (a rubbery meat-based concoction), mutton soup, beef and *thimpu de cordero*, which is boiled potatoes, oca, rice and carrots over mutton, smothered with hot *llajhua* (a tomato-based sauce).

For bargain lunch specials, check out the small eateries around the train station or at *Rabitos* on Ayacucho; *SUM* (☎ 55442) on Bolívar at Soria Galvarro; *Gaviota* (Junín 676), which has especially good-value almuerzos and cenas; and the reasonable and

recommended *Le Grill* on Aldana. *Unicornio*, on La Plata at Adolfo Mier, is good for snacks and lunches, and it's even open Sunday afternoon.

Nayjama (☎ 77699), on Pagador at Aldana, has good lunches and typical Bolivian dishes for less than US$4. Marginal vegetarian dishes are available from around US$1.50 at *El Huerto Vegetariano*, on Bolívar, and the Hare Krishna restaurant *Govinda* (6 de Octubre 6089).

For typical Bolivian dishes in a pleasant setting, try *La Cabaña* (Junín 609) or *La Plata*, on the street of the same name. La Plata specializes in *charque kan*, thimpu and *chairo* served in traditional ceramic bowls.

If you're after something totally unexpected, check out Finnish-, Swedish- and Bolivian-run *Pub the Alpaca* (☎ 75715; wcamargo@urano.uto.edu.bo; La Paz 690), near Plaza Ranchería. It's a lot like an English pub, and the owners Eva, Sinikka and Willy speak a range of European languages: English, French, Spanish, Swedish, German, Finnish and Russian (they'd love to have a flag of your home country to display on the wall!). It opens at 7 pm and they only serve dinner (except during Carnaval, when they also cook up breakfast specials). However, it's also a cozy place to linger over a few drinks, and they offer accommodations (see Places to Stay). If the door is locked, just ring the bell.

Entertainment

The best drinking spot is *Pub the Alpaca* (see Places to Eat). The cinema on Plaza 10 de Febrero is housed in the opulent baroque-style colonial-era concert hall. Films are screened nightly.

Shopping

The design, creation and production of Diablada costumes and masks has become an art and a small industry. On Avenida La Paz, between León and Villarroel, are small shops where artisans sell embroidered wall hangings, devil masks, costumes and other devilish things for US$2 to more than US$200.

Llama and alpaca wool bags and clothing are sold at artesanía shops in the center and

SOUTHERN ALTIPLANO

at the bus terminal, while less expensive articles are found around the northeast corner of Mercado Campero. Hawkers sell *zampoñas*, *charangos* and some other indigenous musical instruments near the train station. Tucked in the Mercado Fermín López is an impressive Mercado de Hechicería, while natural healers peddle their wares along Junín between Velasco Galvarro and 6 de Agosto.

Getting There & Away

Bus All long-distance buses use the Terminal de Omnibuses Hernando Siles, northeast of the center. While you're waiting for your bus, it's worth strolling out for a look at the rainbow-colored mural on Avenida 6 de Agosto, which welcomes visitors to Oruro.

Numerous companies run buses to La Paz (3½ hours, US$2) every half hour or so. About midway into the trip, watch for a shallow lake about 100m west of the highway that teems with flamingos.

There are also several daily buses to Cochabamba (six hours, US$3), Potosí (12 hours, US$6.50), Sucre (16 hours, US$7) and Santa Cruz (18 to 20 hours, US$10). Daily services connect Oruro with Uyuni (9 hours, US$4.20) along a very rough road that may be impassable after rains. To Llallagua (two hours, US$1.50), three flotas make the run at least once daily.

There are also at least five daily services to Arica, Chile (nine hours, US$15), via Patacamaya, Tambo Quemado and Chungará (Parque Nacional Lauca). Daily except Saturday, several flotas leave at night for the considerably rougher trip to Iquique, Chile (20 hours, US$18), which runs via the Pisiga border crossing.

Train Thanks to its mines, Oruro is a railroad center and has one of the most organized train stations in Bolivia. When the government was running the show, timetables were little more than some office slug's fantasy, but since FCA (☎ 74605 or 74679) took over, they're now followed surprisingly closely!

From Oruro, you can travel to Uyuni, where the railroad splits; one line goes to Tupiza and Villazón (on the Argentine border) and the other to Ollagüe and Calama, in Chile. However, the eastbound lines to Cochabamba, Potosí and Sucre have all suffered the disappearing-railroad blues. There are two standards of rail service from Oruro. The *Expreso del Sur* offers reclining seats, heaters, videos, ambient music, a dining car, and a choice of *salón*, *premier* and *ejecutivo* classes. To Villazón (11¼ hours, US$12/18.50/23.50), via Uyuni (6¼ hours, US$5.50/8/10) and Tupiza (11 hours, US$10.50/16.50/21), it leaves on Friday at 10:10 am and returns on Saturday from Villazón, leaving at 3:30pm. On Monday, it travels only as far as Tupiza, with a return trip on Tuesday, leaving Tupiza at 7 am. The *Wara Wara del Sur*, which carries only basic salón-class coaches, runs on Sunday and Wednesday at 7pm to Uyuni (seven hours, US$4.50), Tupiza (13 hours, US$7.50) and Villazón (16¾ hours, US$9.50).

Note that the Monday train from Uyuni to Avaroa and on to Calama, Chile, no longer departs from Oruro.

Getting Around

Oruro city micros (US$0.15) and minibuses (US$0.20) connect the city center with outlying areas. Their routes are designated by their letters, colors and signs (and in the case of minibuses, numbers). It's a fairly confusing system, because two micros with the same letter and different colors will follow entirely different routes, and unless the signs are clear, you'll probably have to ask locals for advice. Note that micros and minibuses are small and crowded, so if possible, avoid carrying luggage aboard.

Taxis around the center, including to and from the transportation terminals, cost a non-negotiable US$0.40 (B$2.50) per person. Alternatively, for a radio taxi (US$1), phone ☎ 76222 or 73399.

AROUND ORURO
Complejo Metalúrgico Vinto

The US$12 million Vinto tin smelter was constructed in the early 1970s during the presidency of General Hugo Banzer Suárez. By the time it was put into operation, the

Bolivian tin industry was already experiencing a steady decline, but it still processes up to 20,000 tons of ore annually.

Vinto lies 8km east of Oruro and may be visited on weekdays 9 am to noon, but it's wise to phone in advance (☎ 78078 or 78091) for permission to tour the operation. To get there, take micro 'D' marked 'Vinto ENAF' from the northwest corner of Plaza 10 de Febrero.

Capachos & Obrajes

The hot springs of Capachos and Obrajes lie 10 and 25km north of Oruro along the Cochabamba road, respectively. Both resorts have covered hot pools and individual baths, but Obrajes is the nicer of the two. Minibuses and micros (marked 'Obrajes' or 'Capachos') cost US$1 and leave when full from the corner of Calle Caro and Avenida 6 de Agosto. Admission to either place is US$2.

Calacala

The archaeological site at Calacala lies about 20km east of Oruro, along the road to Negro Pabellón. It consists of rock paintings and engravings in a rock shelter at the base of a hulking monolith. A llama theme is most prominent, but there is also a puma and some roughly human figures painted in white and earth tones. As yet, no definitive theory of their origin has been formulated, but some investigators suggest an Inca-era camelid cult (see 'Andean Camelids,' later in this chapter).

On Saturday and Sunday, micros run from Oruro to Calacala; at other times, you'll have to take a taxi, which costs US$10 roundtrip. Once in the village, you must track down the park guard, who will unlock the gate to the site and act as a guide. The paintings are about a 40-minute walk from the village, toward the old brewery.

On September 14, Calacala hosts a pilgrimage and fiesta in honor of Señor de las Lagunas (Lord of the Lakes).

Lago Uru Uru (Lago del Milagro)

Lago Uru Uru, a large shallow lake just south of town, offers good fishing for pejerrey, and you'll also see flamingos in the shallow water. There's a small restaurant and a cabaña at the shore where you may rent rowboats for fishing or exploring the lake. To reach the shore, take micro 'A' marked 'Sud' to its terminus at the university. From there, it's a 3km walk along the highway to the lake.

Three kilometers around the western shore of the lake from Puente Español, 7km southwest of Oruro, lie the Chullpas de Chusa K'eri. This ancient necropolis dates back at least 2000 years. Transport runs occasionally from Plaza Walter Khon to Puente Español; you'll have to walk the last 3km.

Cha'llapata & Lago de Poopó

About 75km south of Oruro is the large but shallow Lago de Poopó, which covers 2530 sq km but has an average depth of only 6m. This oversized puddle attracts flamingos and a host of other waders, making it an appealing spot for ornithologists and bird-watchers.

To visit some lesser-known chullpas, seek out the local indigenous leader Juvenal Pérez in Cha'llapata, which lies 110km south of Oruro and 12km east of the lakeshore. The spartan *Alojamiento Victoria* charges US$2.50 per person, and you can eat at *Pensión Potosí* for about the same price, including a beer. They can also arrange bicycle hire to the lake for US$2 per day. You can walk the 12km, but prepare for cold, windy conditions as well as a high UV factor. Overcrowded buses leave from near Mercado Campero in Oruro (three hours, US$1) a couple of times daily; southbound trains also make a brief stop.

Curahuara de Carangas

Curahuara de Carangas, at the foot of the Jank'l Khollo (Beautiful Little Heaven) mountains, was the site of the final battle between indigenous Paka Jakhes (Eagle Men) and conquering forces of Tupac Inca Yupanqui. After a diligent fight, the defenders were eventually defeated at the terraced hill fortress of Pukara Monterani (where several warriors are still buried), and the Inca leader declared his victory by thrusting a golden rod into the summit of the hill. The Quechua for 'golden rod' is *kori wara*, hence the Hispanicized name, Curahuara.

The village's lovely adobe-and-thatch church has rather hopefully been dubbed 'the Sistine chapel of the Altiplano.' While that's rather overblown, the charming little structure does contain a wealth of lovely naive 16th-century frescoes depicting typical mestizo-style themes – birds, flowers and other natural features – as well as Biblical scenes. Along the route eastward toward Totora lies the Yaraque archaeological site, with several stone ruins, numerous rock paintings and an Inca-era chullpa constructed in fine stonework comparable to that of Cuzco.

The signposted turnoff lies 100km west of Patacamaya and is accessible on any bus between Oruro and Arica, Chile. Get off at the turnoff and walk 5km south to the village, which has a small unnamed *alojamiento*. The area also offers some fabulous rock-climbing; for organized expeditions, contact Camel Expeditions in La Paz (see the list under Organized Tours in the Getting Around chapter).

Ciudad Pétrea de Pumiri

This bizarre complex of stone caves and eroded rock formations 185km southwest of Oruro was named the Stone City of Pumiri because it resembles a prehistoric village. It lies about 20km west of the village of Turco (where there's an alojamiento and restaurant), near the Thica Utha Cameloid Research Station. Getting there is quite an adventure. A weekly bus connects Oruro with Turco, while camiones and buses going all the way to Pumiri leave from the Plaza Walter Khon.

COMANCHE AREA

The area around Comanche, south of La Paz and northwest of Oruro, boasts several interesting natural history sites, and as yet lies well off the trodden track.

Reserva Natural de Comanche

This area, administered as a loosely defined national park, has been set aside to protect the incredible yucca-like *Puya raimondii*, which is actually a relative of the pineapple. These gigantic plants, which grow in the hills west of the village, reach heights of 12m, and their enormous spikes erupt into greenish flowers only after the plant has reached 60 to 100 years of age. Once they've flowered, they begin to self-destruct, slowly decomposing into a heap of blackened material. The best time to see one in flower is in the early summer, from November to December. The main site can be visited in a day trip from La Paz.

Also of interest are the 18th-century churches in the nearby villages of Callapa and Caquiaviri and the several chullpas along the route.

Corocoro

Corocoro, just east of the Río Desaguadero near the La Paz-Arica railroad line, is another Southern Altiplano mining town. The Corocoro mines produce nearly all of Bolivia's copper, and Corocoro is one of two major sources of native copper in the world today, the other being Michigan's Upper Peninsula on the US shore of Lake Superior. Since the copper is found in nugget form and not in ore, which must be smelted, the early native peoples of the Altiplano used it long before anyone knew what to do with ore copper. The Museo de Metales Preciosos Pre-Columbinos in La Paz displays some examples of their work.

Ciudad de Piedra

East of the village of Calacoto (not to be confused with the La Paz suburb of the same name) lies the forest of natural sandstone formations known as the Ciudad de Piedra. These pinnacles were formed by wind and rain erosion and are good for day hikes.

There are no formal accommodations in the area, but you can always find private accommodations in villages or camp in the hills. Caquiaviri has a small restaurant, but otherwise, you'll have to rely on stalls and small shops.

Getting There & Away

Micros from La Paz to Comanche (two hours, US$1), Callapa, Caquiaviri, Corocoro and Calacoto (3½ hours, US$1.50) leave in the early morning from Avenida Franco Valle 105 in the Zona 12 de Octubre, El Alto. To Calacoto and Ciudad de Piedra, they also leave from the Villa Adela crossroads, along the Viacha road, between 7:30 and 8 am. In Viacha, they leave from behind the market.

LLALLAGUA
☎ 058

First owned by the Chilean Llallagua Company, the town of Llallagua was bought out in 1924 by tin baron Simon Patiño once he'd gained the capital from his successful operation in nearby Uncia. The area's most famous mine, Siglo XX, grew into Bolivia's most productive. It remains the largest tin mine in the country, with 800km of underground passages.

History

With the nationalization of mining interests in 1952, control of Llallagua passed into the hands of COMIBOL (Corporación Minera de Bolivia). It was then operated by the federal government until the mid-1980s, when Victor Paz Estenssoro (the same president who had initiated the 1952 mining reform!) decided during his third non-consecutive term of office to return the project to private, miner-owned cooperatives.

Strikes, layoffs and the drop in tin prices have turned Llallagua into a near ghost town and often, promised severance pay hasn't materialized and many destitute, out-of-work miners have emigrated in search of better diggings. Given all this, plus the confusion from transition-related strife, catering for curious tourists is the least of the miners' concerns. Having said that, most of the cooperative miners are friendly, earnest and hardworking people. They passionately try to keep abreast of the politics that so profoundly affect their lives, and are normally happy to engage willing listeners in a discussion of their favorite topic.

Once you're through the security gate, there's no problem visiting. Mining methods are the same as they were centuries ago,

and the proud cooperative miners are normally happy to tell you about their work on the tailings dumps and in the rivers. The book by Domitila Barrios de Chungara, *Si Me Permite Hablar* (Let Me Speak), is a good description of living and working at Siglo XX.

Special Events

The fiesta of the Virgen de la Asunción, on August 14th and 15th, is celebrated with processions and drunken tinku fighting.

Places to Stay & Eat

From outside, the friendly *Hotel Llallagua* looks pretty basic, but inside, it's amazingly clean, airy and accommodating. They charge US$2 per person and the restaurant cooks up decent meals. Slightly more upmarket is *Hotel Bustillo*.

Getting There & Away

Llallagua lies 95km by road southeast of Oruro, and several flotas do the run at least once daily (two hours, US$2.20). There are also buses between Llallagua and Potosí and a direct bus to and from La Paz.

PARQUE NACIONAL SAJAMA

The recently expanded Parque Nacional Sajama occupies approximately 80,000 hectares abutting the Chilean border. It was created on November 5, 1945, for the protection of the hulking Nevado Sajama volcano and the wildlife that inhabits this northern extension of the Atacama desert. Unfortunately, depredation has already eliminated pumas, *huemules* (Andean deer), viscachas and guanacos; and only limited numbers of vicuñas, condors, flamingos, rheas and armadillos survive.

The world's highest forest covers the foothills flanking the impressive Nevado Sajama (or Volcán Sajama), which at 6542m is generally considered Bolivia's highest peak. The forest consists of dwarf queñua trees, a species unique to the Altiplano, but unless you're into checking off superlatives, it's nothing to get steamed up about. The 'trees' have the size and appearance of creosote bushes.

PARQUES NACIONALES SAJAMA & LAUCA (CHILE)

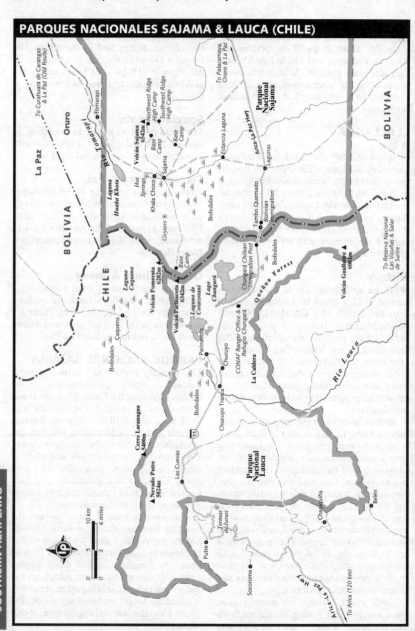

Orientation & Information

The best map of the park, the glossy *Nevado Sajama 1:50,000* that's published by Walter Guzmán Córdova, can be found in La Paz bookstores; try Librería Olimpia.

The US$2 admission is payable at the park headquarters in Sajama village. It applies to all foreigners, including those just visiting the village. The office will help climbing expeditions organize mules and porters. Señor Telmo Nina, in Sajama village, keeps a log of routes up the mountain; climbers will also want to check out Yossi Brain's *Bolivia – Climbing Guide* (Mountaineers, 1999), which describes several routes up the mountain.

Artesanía produced here – mostly articles of pastel-dyed alpaca wool – are sold in the shop of former Sajama resident Peter Brunnhart, on Calle Sagárnaga in La Paz; he may be another source of information on the mountain.

Nevado Sajama

This volcano is unquestionably the centerpiece of all it surveys. It's attracting increasing numbers of mountaineers who'd like to try their abilities (and luck) on its glaciers and wildly eroded slopes. There are no trails per se, so park hiking is strictly of the backcountry variety. On all hikes, remember to carry an ample supply of water.

Although it's a relatively straightforward climb, Sajama's altitude and ice conditions make the peak more challenging than it initially appears. Many of the glaciers are receding, turning much of the route into a sloppy and crevasse-ridden mess. If you're looking for an organized expedition, quite a few La Paz agencies offer organized climbs of Sajama. For suggestions, see Activities in the Facts for the Visitor chapter, or Organized Tours in the Getting Around chapter.

The easiest access to the mountain is from the village of Sajama, about 25km north of the Tambo Quemado-Patacamaya road. Experienced climbers can commence their assault on the mountain from the north, south (from Lagunas) or west (from Sajama); allow two or three days to reach the summit and prepare for extremely cold and windy conditions. When the wind really

picks up, dust and sand add to the discomfort. Carry lots of water, though once on the snow cap, there will be plenty in the form of ice and snow.

Hot Springs & Geysers

For a good warm soak, there are some lovely 43°C hot springs 5km northwest of Sajama village. The springs are relatively easy to find, and locals can point you in the right direction. About 1½ hours on foot due west of Sajama is a geyser field with some nice spouting hot springs. Given the temperature and the obvious risk, don't approach too closely.

Places to Stay & Eat

Camping is fine just about anywhere in this sparsely populated region, so a tent and a good cold-weather sleeping bag are highly recommended. Otherwise, see Señor Telmo in Sajama village, who keeps a list of families offering *private lodging* in their homes; it's organized on a rotation basis and costs about US$1 to US$1.50 per person. Most homes are very modest, so you'll still need a warm sleeping bag and many layers of clothing for the typically cold, windy nights. Alternatively, there's *Alojamiento El Dorado*, which costs US$2 per person plus US$1.20 for meals. The owner has a 4WD and for US$10, he'll take up to four people to the hot springs, then drop you along the paved road to catch the bus.

Only basic staples are sold in the village, so bring your hiking and climbing food from elsewhere.

Getting There & Away

All buses between La Paz and Arica (Chile) pass through Sajama National Park, but you may well be expected to pay the entire Arica-La Paz fare.

Once you've come this far, a visit to Chile's spectacular Parque Nacional Lauca (see later in this chapter) is highly recommended. For onward travel to La Paz or into Chile, go to the tarred road and flag down a bus or camión; most of the traffic passes after midday, but buses are normally full and passengers aren't permitted to sit in the aisle. The border crossing between

SOUTHERN ALTIPLANO

Tambo Quemado in Bolivia and Chungará in Chile is straightforward.

PARQUE NACIONAL LAUCA (CHILE)

Across the frontier from Sajama is Chile's poodle-shaped Parque Nacional Lauca – 138,000 hectares of marvelously intact Andean ecosystems. It was declared a national park in 1970 to protect its profusion of wildlife: flamingos, coots, Andean gulls, Andean geese, condors, vicuñas, guanacos, llamas, alpacas, rheas, viscachas, Andean foxes, armadillos, Andean deer and even pumas, as well as unusual vegetation such as the bizarre shaggy-barked *queñua* trees

---

Andean Camelids

Unlike the Old World, the Western Hemisphere had few grazing mammals after the Pleistocene era, when mammoths, horses and other large herbivores disappeared for reasons that appear to be linked to hunting pressure by the earliest human inhabitants of the plains and pampas of North and South America. For millennia, the Andean people relied on the New World camelids – the wild guanaco and vicuña and the domesticated llama and alpaca – for food and fiber.

Guanaco (*Lama guanicoe*) and vicuña (*Vicugna vicugna*) are relatively rare today but are the likely ancestors of the domesticated llama (*L. glama*) and alpaca (*L. pacos*). In fact, they were among very few potential New World domestic animals – contrast them with the Old World cattle, horses, sheep, goats, donkeys and pigs that have filled so many vacant niches in the Americas. Of the major domesticated animals from across the Atlantic, only the humped camel has failed to achieve an important role here. While the New World camels have lost ground to sheep and cattle in some areas, they are not likely to disappear.

Llama

The guanaco ranges from the central Andes to Tierra del Fuego at elevations from sea level up to 4000m or higher. In these regions, early native hunters ate its meat and dressed in its skin. In the central Andes, where the human population is small but widely dispersed and domestic livestock numerous, guanaco numbers are small. However, on the plains of Argentine Patagonia and in reserves such as southern Chile's Parque Nacional Torres del Paine, herds of rust-colored guanaco are still a common sight. Bolivia's only guanaco population, which amounts to just a few animals, shelters in the highland plains of the Reserva Nacional de Fauna Andina Eduardo Avaroa, in the extreme southwestern corner of the country.

By contrast, the vicuña occupies a much smaller area, well above 4000m on the puna and Altiplano from southern central Peru to northwestern Argentina. Although not as numerous as the guanaco, it played a critical role in the cultural life of pre-Columbian Peru, which assured its survival. Its very fine golden wool was the exclusive property of the Inca emperors, and the Spanish chronicler Bernabé Cobo wrote that the ruler's clothing 'was made of the finest wool and the best cloth that was woven in his whole kingdom…most of it was made of vicuña wool, which is almost as fine as silk.'

Guanaco

(Polylepis tarapana) and the rock-hard moss known as *llareta (Azorella compacta)*. Adjacent to the park, but more difficult to access, are Reserva Nacional Las Vicuñas and Monumento Natural Salar de Surire. Once part of the park, they now consitute separate units, but are still managed by CONAF (Chile's national-park service).

Lago Chungará

Near the Bolivian border beneath the volcanoes Pomerata and Parinacota, known collectively as Las Payachatas (both higher than 6000m), is the lovely alpine Lago Chungará. At 4517m, it's one of the world's highest bodies of water and was formed when a lava flow from Volcán Parinacota

Andean Camelids

Strict Inca authority protected the vicuña, but the Spanish invasion destroyed that authority, and over the past 500 years, the species has been under pressure from hunting. By the middle of this century, poaching reduced vicuña numbers from two million to perhaps 10,000 and caused its inclusion in Appendix I of the Endangered Species List. Conservation programs such as those in Chile's Parque Nacional Lauca and Bolivia's Parque Nacional Apolobamba have achieved so impressive a recovery that economic exploitation of the species may soon benefit the puna communities in that country. In Lauca and surrounding areas, vicuña numbers grew from barely 1000 in the early 1970s to more than 27,000 two decades later.

The communities of the puna and Altiplano – mostly Aymará – still depend on llamas and alpacas for their livelihood. The two species appear very similar but they differ in several important respects. The taller, rangier and hardier llama has relatively coarse wool that is used for blankets, ropes and other household goods. It also works as a pack animal, but thanks to the introduction of camión traffic on the Altiplano, llama trains are becoming increasingly rare in Bolivia; the last major trade route served by llama train is the salt trail from the Salar de Uyuni to Tarija.

Alpaca

Vicuñas

Llamas can survive and even flourish on relatively poor, dry pastures, whereas the smaller, more delicate alpacas aren't pack animals and require well-watered grasslands to produce their much finer wool, which has a higher commercial value than that of llamas. Both llama and alpaca meat are consumed by Andean households and are sold in urban markets all over Bolivia.

In recent years, the meager earnings from the sale of wool and meat haven't been sufficient to stem the flow of population from the countryside into such urban poverty traps as El Alto, near La Paz. However, the commercialization of vicuña wool might help do so, if international agreement permits it. According to a recent study by CONAF (the Chilean national-park commission), production and sale of vicuña cloth could bring a price of nearly US$290 per square meter; if local people were involved, it would also serve to diversify local economies and help keep people on the land.

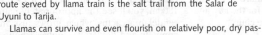

dammed a snowmelt stream. Visitors may walk at will, but will have to reckon with the high altitude and swampy ground, as well as frequently fierce climatic conditions. Snow is possible at any time of year.

Because of Arica's insatiable appetite for hydroelectricity and the Azapa valley's thirst, the Chilean electric company has built an intricate system of pumps and canals that may compromise the ecological integrity of Lago Chungará. Because the lake is so shallow, any lowering of its level would drastically reduce its surface area and affect feeding and nesting sites used by wading birds, including flamingos and giant coots.

Parinacota

The lovely pre-Columbian stone village of Parinacota sits along the Arica-Potosí silver route at an elevation of 4400m. In the background stretches the Laguna de Cotacotani and its surrounding *bofedales* (shallow marshes dotted with tussocks of vegetation and used as pasture for llamas and alpacas). CONAF operates a visitors center, museum and high-altitude genetic research station at the eastern end of the village.

The imposing whitewashed stone church was originally built in the 1600s but was reconstructed in 1789. The surreal 17th-century frescoes on the interior walls, the work of artists from the Cuzco school, recall Hieronymus Bosch's *The Last Judgment*. Note also the depiction of soldiers bearing Christ to the cross as Spaniards. Ask the caretaker Cipriano Morales for the key, and leave a small donation to the church.

Organized Tours

Regional tours from Putre, just outside the park, are conducted by the American-run Birding Alto Andino (fax 56-222735; Baquedano 299). Day trips cost around US$150 for two people.

Places to Stay & Eat

On Lago Chungará, CONAF runs *Refugio Chungará*, which has a warm stove and eight beds for US$10 each. At *Camping Chungará*, which has picnic tables and a wall to shelter it from the wind, sites cost US$7. At Parinacota village, CONAF operates the basic *Refugio Parinacota*. Beds are US$10, but you'll need your own sleeping bag. Campsites here cost US$7. Hot-water availability depends upon the arrival of gas canisters from Arica.

At Chucuyo (the Parinacota turnoff), *Restaurant Matilde* serves alpaca steaks and other simple meals for around US$1.50, and owners Matilde and Máximo Morales rent out two rooms in their home for US$2 per person. You'll also find two other passable restaurants serving inexpensive set meals and selling locally produced alpaca *chompas*, gloves, hats and scarves.

Putre is at a much lower elevation, so those with transport will probably find it more comfortable than places in the park. Here, *Restaurant Oasis* serves good plain meals and offers beds for US$4. *Residencial La Paloma* has hot showers and good beds for US$7. There's also CONAF's *Refugio Putre*, which costs US$10 per person. *Hostería Las Vicuñas* (☎ 224997) caters mainly to the local gold mine personnel, but has single/double tourist rooms for US$53/75, including meals.

Getting There & Away

The entire route from Arica to La Paz is now tarred. After leaving Arica, it follows the lovely oasis-like Lluta valley and climbs into the Atacama hills, past ancient petroglyphs and the interesting adobe church and cemetery at Poconchile. Between 1300 and 1800m, you'll see the appropriately named candelabra cactus, which grows just 5mm annually and flowers for only 24 hours. It virtually never rains in the Atacama, so the cactus must take its moisture from the fog.

Bear in mind that the trip from Arica to Lauca involves a climb from sea level to nearly 5000m, and there's a high risk of altitude sickness or at least light-headedness.

Independent access to Lauca isn't inordinately difficult. From Arica, several flotas leave the main bus terminal in the morning and pass Chungará (three hours, US$10), in Lauca National Park, en route to La Paz (nine hours, US$20 to US$24). Numerous

Arica tour operators also run guided day tours to Lauca for around US$50, but owing to the rapid elevation gain, participants are especially subject to altitude sickness.

TAMBO QUEMADO

The name of this Bolivian customs and immigration post east of Lago Chungará means 'burned inn.' It now has a simple restaurant and on Friday, it holds a colorful international market.

Southwestern Bolivia

The southwestern corner of Bolivia is the most remote highland area of the country. With few roads or inhabitants, unpredictable weather conditions, only a few scattered settlements and unreliable transport, travel into and around the region becomes an exercise in patience and creativity. Its boundaries are more or less demarcated by the railway lines between Uyuni and the Chile and Argentine frontiers and by the minor ranges known as Cordillera de López and Cordillera de Chichas. Nearly treeless, the country and villages south of the Salar de Uyuni are occupied only by a few miners, military personnel and some very hardy Aymará.

For adventurous travelers, this is paradise. Transport is scarce and expensive and amenities few, but visitors are rewarded with a firsthand view of a seemingly unearthly geology. The featureless salt deserts are some of the world's flattest terrain, and around these salares, bleached brine deposits provide an occasional white splash amid the prevailing browns. In the far southwest, the surreal landscape is punctuated by steaming, towering volcanoes; dozens of hot pools and springs; and flamingo-filled lakes stained by minerals and algae into a palette of rainbow hues.

History

The prehistoric lakes Minchín and Tauca, which once covered most of this highland plateau, evaporated some 10,000 years ago, leaving behind a parched landscape of brackish puddles and salt deserts. Humans haven't left much of a mark on the region; sometime in the mid-15th century, the reigning Inca Pachacuti sent his son Tupac Inca Yupanqui southward to conquer all the lands he encountered. He was apparently clever with public relations because the southwestern extremes of Bolivia and deserts of northern Chile were taken bloodlessly. Yupanqui and his fellow conquerors marched on across the wastelands to the northern bank of Chile's Río Maule, where a fierce band of Araucanian Indians inspired them to stake out the southern boundary of the Inca empire and turn back toward Cuzco.

Owing to the harsh conditions, the Inca never effectively colonized this desert area, and it's still sparsely populated. Beyond the towns of Uyuni, Tupiza and Villazón, most of the people cluster around mining camps, health and military outposts and geothermal projects.

Independent Travel

The remoteness of this area and the difficulties of individual travel cannot be overstressed. Those traveling in their own 4WD vehicles will need survival supplies, spares, extra gasoline and a good measure of resourcefulness. If you're relying on lifts in camiones or 4WDs, flexibility and self-sufficiency are the key, as days can pass without a sign of activity. Self-motivated explorers must come equipped with a tent, flashlight (torch), compass, warm sleeping bag, fuel, reliable stove, sunglasses, sunscreen, water and maps. It's also a good idea to carry twice as much food as you expect you'll need, as well as clothing for subzero temperatures. Soroche can also be a problem (see Health in the Facts for the Visitor chapter), especially for hikers.

The best time to travel in this region is from July to early October, when the days are dry and cool but not as cold as in early winter. From October to March, rainfall causes 4WD tracks to deteriorate badly and the salares to fill with water. Snow may fall at almost any time during the summer months (January to May, which is ironically known locally as *invierno boliviano*, the Bolivian winter).

Puestos sanitarios (health posts) are dotted around for the benefit of local miners, military personnel and campesinos, but their medical supplies and expertise are basic and shouldn't be counted on. Friendly locals and miners will normally do what they can to provide a place to crash and even share their limited food, but it's unfair to rely on them. You may want to bring small amounts of coffee, fruit, magazines, coca etc – anything that isn't locally available – to offer as gifts to helpful officials and workers.

Organized Tours

The easiest way to explore the region is with an organized tour. The most economical are those leaving from Uyuni, and a variety of itineraries is available (see Organized Tours in Uyuni). Further discussion of the main sites of interest is found under Salar de Uyuni, Salar de Coipasa and Los López & the Southwest Circuit, all later in this chapter.

UYUNI
☎ 0693

In politically correct terms, Uyuni is 'climatically challenged.' Mention its name to a Bolivian and the first response you're likely to hear is *harto frío*, 'extreme cold,' and one tourist brochure simply describes it as *frígido*. To compound things, buildings are generally drafty, indoor heating is all but unknown and the icy winds can bite through any number of clothing layers. Although the warmer summer brings some relief – and warm, sunny days certainly aren't unknown – this uninspiring desert community does receive more than its share of chills.

Nevertheless, Uyuni's isolated position and otherworldly outlook elicit an affectionate respect from both Bolivians and foreign travelers. In fact, it has been generously nicknamed *La Hija Predilecta de Bolivia* (Bolivia's Favorite Daughter). This stems not from any aesthetic merits, but from its pampering of Bolivian troops returning

from the Guerra del Pacífico, the war in which Bolivia lost its seacoast to Chile.

Uyuni was founded in 1889 by Bolivian president Aniceto Arce. Most of its current 11,000 residents are employed in three major enterprises: government (military and police personnel, and city officials), mining (mostly salt extraction from the Salar de Uyuni) and increasingly, tourism.

Information

Tourist Offices The Dirección Regional de Turismo (☎ 2679) is of little use, but you will find reliable tourist information from Señor Tito Ponce López (☎ 2259; fax 2098), at the restaurant Pizza's Palace.

The rangers for the Reserva Nacional de Fauna Andina Eduardo Avaroa (☎ 2225), with a well-organized main office at Bolívar and Potosí, and another planned for the clock tower, can provide lots of information on the Southwest Circuit. They also sell a map and pamphlet of the reserve (US$1) and a color field guide to Altiplano birds entitled *Aves de la Reserva Nacional de Fauna Andina Eduardo Avaroa* (US$6). It's open weekdays 9 am to 12:30 pm and 2 to 7 pm.

Immigration If you're traveling on to Chile from Uyuni, you must pick up a Bolivian exit stamp at the immigration office in Uyuni. Technically, you must leave Bolivia within three days of getting the stamp. Although this isn't always enforced, it's still best not to pick up the stamp until you've arranged transport to the border.

Money Despite Uyuni's tourism boom, the bank doesn't change money, but tour agencies and tourist restaurants are normally happy to change US dollars cash for a minimal commission, as is the Hostal Marith. Most tour agencies will also change traveler's checks, but at a 3% to 5% commission and only when they need foreign exchange.

Post & Communications The post office lies in a desolate part of town and the ENTEL office is a bit nearer, behind the clock tower.

Internet access and photocopies are available from Servinet@Uyuni, in a hectic glass box in the middle of Calle Bolívar. It's open 10 am until around 8pm daily and charges US$3 per hour. A more relaxed option is Café Internet in the Galería Urkupiña (yes, Uyuni now has a shopping arcade!). It charges US$3.50 per hour and is open daily 9 am to noon and 12:30 pm to early evening.

Cementerio de Trenes

Uyuni's only real tourist attraction is the 'train cemetery,' a large collection of historic steam locomotives and rail cars that are decaying in the yards about 1km southwest of the station along Avenida Ferroviaria (the route might well be called the *cementerio de basura*, the 'garbage cemetery'). There have long been plans to eventually turn them into a railway museum, but that seems a pipe dream, and they'll most likely just keep on rusting.

Salar & Southwest Circuit Tours

On my first visit to Uyuni in 1986, the town was utterly devoid of tourism and a trip into Bolivia's wild Southwest involved paying US$500 or more for a private 4WD and driver. Now the town has become a standard stop along the Gringo Trail, and a rapidly growing number of Uyuni tour agencies (25 at last count) arrange excursions around the Salar de Uyuni and the Southwest Circuit – and beyond.

The growing visitor numbers and increasing competition mean that tour prices are steadily declining. This may seem like a good thing, but in fact, it also means that the operators are likely to cut corners at every opportunity. As a result, most of them send substandard vehicles, poorly trained guides and the barest of food rations.

While some agencies are clearly better than others, there have been serious complaints about every single agency in Uyuni, and some of the situations reported have been life-threatening. Colque Tours (☎/fax 2199; Potosí 54), Toñito Tours (☎/fax 2094; Ferroviaria s/n) and Tunupa Tours (Ferroviara s/n) seem to be the most recommended. The second string includes AS

Dead trains look alive at Uyuni's train cemetery.

SANDRA BAO

SOUTHERN ALTIPLANO

(☎ 2772; Jeguivar 1751), Esmeralda (☎ 2130; Potosí 157), Pucara (☎ 2678; Potosí s/n) and Juliet (☎ 2687; Arce 27), but once again, there have been serious and well-founded complaints about all of these. (Sometimes, it's irrelevant which one you choose, however; if one agency's tour isn't filled, they transfer their clients to another agency to make up a full complement of passengers.) Note that it doesn't normally help to book your tour in La Paz, Potosí or elsewhere. Unless you go through a reputable upmarket agency – such as Crillon Tours, Balsa Tours or Hidalgo Tours in La Paz or Potosí (see Organized Tours in the Getting Around chapter or under Potosí in the Central Highlands chapter) – you'll pay a higher rate than you would in Uyuni and may well be shunted onto a tour run by any one of the local agencies.

Most local Uyuni agency tours include transport, a driver/guide and food, and some also provide bare-bones lodging (on the standard four-day tour, this is normally at San Juan and Laguna Colorada). While the food in question may be decent, there probably won't be enough of it, and it may consist of little more than four-day-old bread and boiled potatoes. As for the 'lodging,' it may well amount to a space on the earthen floor of an adobe hut; ask in advance about the standards and whether accommodations will cost extra.

Having said all that, your main concern should be the vehicle, which will be your lifeline in this wild region. Unfortunately, most vehicles used on these tours are ill maintained, and the companies will run them until they grind to a halt. If this happens in the middle of the Salar de Uyuni or halfway to Laguna Verde, you have a problem. Ascertain that the vehicle can withstand the harsh conditions and that there's sufficient oil and gasoline for the journey (beyond Uyuni, there's no reliable supply). Also carry enough food and water

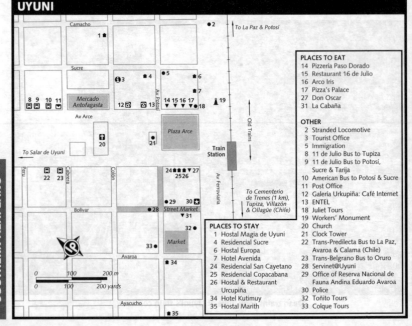

UYUNI

PLACES TO EAT
14 Pizzería Paso Dorado
15 Restaurant 16 de Julio
16 Arco Iris
17 Pizza's Palace
27 Don Oscar
31 La Cabaña

OTHER
2   Stranded Locomotive
3   Tourist Office
5   Immigration
8   11 de Julio Bus to Tupiza
9   11 de Julio Bus to Potosí,
    Sucre & Tarija
10 American Bus to Potosí & Sucre
11 Post Office
12 Galería Urkupiña: Café Internet
13 ENTEL
18 Juliet Tours
19 Workers' Monument
20 Church
21 Clock Tower
22 Trans-Predilecta Bus to La Paz,
    Avaroa & Calama (Chile)
23 Trans-Belgrano Bus to Oruro
28 Servinet@Uyuni
29 Office of Reserva Nacional de
    Fauna Andina Eduardo Avaroa
30 Police
32 Toñito Tours
33 Colque Tours

PLACES TO STAY
1   Hostal Magia de Uyuni
4   Residencial Sucre
6   Hostal Europa
7   Hotel Avenida
24 Residencial San Cayetano
25 Residencial Copacabana
26 Hostal & Restaurant
    Urcupiña
34 Hotel Kutimuy
35 Hostal Marith

To La Paz & Potosí
To Salar de Uyuni
Train Station
Old Trains
To Cementerio de Trenes (1 km), Tupiza, Villazón & Ollagüe (Chile)
Mercado Antofagasta
Av Arce
Plaza Arce
Street Market
Market
Av Ferroviaria
Camacho
Sucre
Bolivar
Avaroa
Ayacucho

0   100   200 m
0   100   200 yards

for several days beyond the projected length of your trip.

Organized Tours The main streets of Uyuni are lined with budget tour agencies, so you'll have little trouble finding one going your way, but the ease of organizing an expedition will depend largely on the season. From July to September, you'll rarely wait more than a day or two to find a full complement of tour participants. At other times the wait may be longer, but there's still sufficient off-season tourism to ensure that you'll eventually find something.

In the high season (July to early September), the popular four-day circuit around the Salar de Uyuni, Laguna Colorada, Sol de Mañana, Laguna Verde and points in between costs up to US$120 per person; during slower periods – say, from October to March – you'll pay as little as US$70 (plus US$15/20 for each additional day in the low/high season). With more time, you can add Laguna Celeste, a lake blue as a swimming pool, one day's drive northeast of Laguna Verde. For one/two days, this option will add US$15/20 to US$20/40 to your total tour price.

Colque Tours is the main operator offering three-day crossings between Uyuni and San Pedro de Atacama, Chile, via Salar de Uyuni, San Juan, Laguna Colorada, Laguna Verde and intermediate sites of interest. The price is around US$70/90 per person in low/high season with food, plus a modest amount for accommodations at San Juan and Laguna Colorada. Other companies offer the option to continue to San Pedro de Atacama with a Chilean operator for their regular tour price plus US$10. Travelers clear Bolivian immigration in Uyuni and are stamped into Chile near San Pedro de Atacama. (Note that there have been reports of drivers earning extra cash by transporting illicit substances across the border; before you leave Uyuni, make absolutely sure that isn't the case on your tour!)

Day trips to the Salar de Uyuni, stopping at Colchani, the Salt Hotels and Isla de los Pescadores, start at US$20/30 in low/high season. Alternatively, you can opt for a four-day Salar tour that includes Llica, Jiriri, surrounding archaeological sites and a climb up the 5432m Volcán Tunupa (across Salar de Uyuni); this costs around US$60/90 per person. For descriptions of these destinations, see Salar de Uyuni and Los Lípez & the Southwest Circuit sections, later in this chapter. Note that Uyuni agencies don't accept credit cards; that may well change in the near future, but for now, you'll need enough cash to cover your tour.

Most companies run covered 4WD vehicles holding up to six or seven people (uncomfortably), and you can either make up your own tour group or let the agency make up your group. For the invariably basic accommodations in private homes, alojamientos and *campamentos*, you'll need a warm sleeping bag. If you have any sort of appetite, it's best to supplement the food provided with items purchased in Uyuni. If you don't have a warm sleeping bag (which should be considered an essential for any traveler to Bolivia), make absolutely certain that the agency will provide one for you; you may have to bug them repeatedly, but no one should make these trips without one.

Previous editions of this book advised travelers to withhold 50% of the payment until they returned from their tour satisfied. Unfortunately, standards on some of these tours are below what even hard-bitten travelers expect (as noted earlier, there are horror stories aplenty), and quite a few were unsatisfied. Rather than improve operations, most agencies simply began requiring full payment in advance. Now you'll only get away with paying half in advance if a group is desperate for participants. Therefore, the importance of choosing a reputable operator cannot be overstressed; things still may not run according to plan, but there's less chance of a desert disaster.

For an excellent alternative – which involves doing the circuit from Tupiza and winding up in Uyuni – see Organized Tours in Tupiza, later in this chapter.

Special Events
Uyuni's big annual festival falls on July 11 and marks the town's founding. Celebrations

entail torch parades, speeches, dancing, music and, naturally, lots of drinking.

Places to Stay

Uyuni's recent tourism boom has meant that hotels fill up quickly, but it has also made for new hotels arriving on the scene. In any case, a booking may offer some peace of mind, especially if you're chugging in on the rails at 2 am!

The sparkling *Hostal Magia de Uyuni* (☎ 2541), on Colón, is arranged around a tidy courtyard and offers the best single/ double accommodations in the town for US$15/20 with bath and a continental breakfast. This is the venue for most upmarket tour groups. Also recommended is the friendly and comfortable *Hotel Kutimuy* (☎ 2199; kutimuy@yahoo.com), at Avaroa and Potosí, which is affiliated with Colque Tours. Rooms without bath cost US$3.50/7 and with bath, US$7.50/13.50. Laundry service is available.

The old standby is *Hotel Avenida* (☎ 2078), on Avenida Ferroviaria near the train station, run by the irascible Don Jesús Rosas Zúniga. Rooms without bath cost US$3.50/7; with private bath, they're US$7/13.50. Hot showers are available 7 am to 7 pm. The office locks up at midnight unless there's still space available.

Backpackers like to congregate at *Hostal Europa* (☎ 2126; fax 2122), Avenida Ferroviaria at Sucre, with various size rooms for US$4/7 with shared bath. Another travelers' favorite is *Hostal Marith* (☎ 2174; Potosí 61), which is clean, simple and cheap and has hot water all day. For US$2.50 per person, you'll get a room with shared bath; with private bath, it's US$5. Breakfast is served, but it costs extra.

Alternatively, the marginal *Residencial Sucre* (☎ 2047), at Sucre and Potosí, charges US$2.50 per person with shared bath, and if you're really desperate, there is a trio of cheap places on Plaza Arce: the unappealing *Residencial San Cayetano*, the barely adequate *Residencial Copacabana* (no shower or sink), and the greatly improved *Hostal Urcupiña*, which now has a restaurant (a pizzería of course) and is considerably cleaner and friendlier than the other two. The first two charge US$2 per person and the Urcupiña charges US$2.50.

In an emergency, you can crash out in the *sala de espera* at the railway station; it's free and with all the bodies in there, it can also be good and warm.

Places to Eat

Economical meals are prepared at the market comedor and food stalls. For a dose of local culture, look for charque kan (mashed hominy with strips of dried llama meat), an Uyuni specialty. Good snacks of potato cakes and hamburgers are sold at small stands in the middle of Calle Avaroa, as is fresh bread.

The boom of tourist-oriented restaurants in Uyuni means that visitors now have lots of choice, but most of those options involve pizza (Uyuni folks surely must get the impression that pizza is the national dish of every other country in the world – come to think of it, that isn't far from the truth!). Along Avenida Arce, you'll find the recommended *Pizza's Palace*, which does decent pizza as well as Bolivian dishes, burgers and snacks. It also serves great breakfasts.

Habitually recommended is nearby *Arco Iris*, which also specializes in pizza – as well as a host of other things – and has now become the nighttime hangout in Uyuni. There's a decent bar serving up cold beer and although service is slow, it's the place to see and be seen. It's also a good spot to look for people to make up a tour group.

Farther down the same street is the ever-popular *Restaurant 16 de Julio*, which has now risen to two stories. It opens at 7 am and offers a mean choice of breakfasts: the Continental (US$2), Americano (US$3), Ejecutivo with steak and french fries (US$3.50), Tortuguita with pancakes (US$2) or Vegetariano with muesli, yogurt and fruit salad (US$2). Later in the day, you'll get (you guessed it) pizza, Bolivian specialties and international cuisine featuring warming, high-carbohydrate fare. They also change money.

The next option down is nearby *Pizzería Paso Dorado*, which of course does pizza, as well as burgers and a variety of milanesa in-carnations, but you'll have to wait awhile.

Both **Don Oscar**, on the other side of the street, and **La Cabaña**, on the next block, serve less tourist-oriented fare; the former also does breakfast.

Getting There & Away

Bus Passengers traveling from Uyuni must pay a US$0.20 *derecho del terminal*, despite Uyuni not having a terminal (on my last visit, only foreigners were being charged). Buses leave from along upper Avenida Arce, northwest of the central area. There's a choice of services to most destinations, so ask around to get the best price.

Several flotas have morning and evening buses going to Potosí (five to seven hours, US$3.50), where you'll find connections to Sucre (11 hours, US$6.75) and Tarija (17 hours, US$13.50). On Wednesday and Sunday when the roads are passable, Flota 11 de Julio follows the rather excruciating but incredibly scenic route to Tupiza (10 to 12 hours, US$5). Similarly, the evening services to Oruro (nine to 10 hours, US$4.20) and La Paz (14 hours, US$6.20) run only when the roads are passable. There's also an international service to Calama, Chile (12 to 15 hours, US$12), via the Avaroa border crossing. An alternative route to Chile is on an organized tour, which will leave you in San Pedro de Atacama; see Organized Tours earlier in this section.

Train After years of ludicrous inefficiency – trains habitually ran 12 hours late – rail services to and from Uyuni now run roughly on time. That isn't due as much to the town's large and sparkling railway station as to the drastic cutback in the number of routes and services that occurred when the lines were privatized.

The *Expreso del Sur* leaves Uyuni for Oruro (6¼ hours, US$5.50/8/10 in salón/premier/ejecutivo class) Tuesday 12:20 pm and Saturday 6:50 pm, and the *Wara Wara del Sur* (seven hours, US$4.50 in salón) leaves 1:35 am Monday and Thursday.

To Tupiza (4¾ hours, US$5/8/10) and Villazón (eight hours, US$7/12/15), the *Expreso*

del Sur departs Monday 5:20 pm and Friday 4:30 pm (on Monday, it goes only as far as Tupiza). The *Wara Wara del Sur* goes to Tupiza (5½ hours, US$3.50) and Villazón (nine hours, US$5.50) Sunday and Wednesday 2:35 am.

Trains to the Bolivian-Chilean border at Avaroa (12 hours, US$6.50), with connections to Calama, Chile (22 to 28 hours, US$15), leave Monday 5 am. However, you'd have to be a real rail buff to suffer through this journey, which is perpetually cold and can take up to 28 hours (see 'By Rail to Chile' in this section).

SALAR DE UYUNI

The 12,106-sq-km Salar de Uyuni, Bolivia's largest salt pan, covers nearly all of Daniel Campos province. The Salar de Uyuni is now a center of salt extraction and processing, particularly around the settlement of Colchani, 20km up the railroad track from Uyuni. The estimated annual capacity of the Colchani operation is 19,700 tons, 18,000 tons of which is for human consumption while the rest is for livestock.

When the surface is dry, the salar becomes a blinding white expanse of the greatest nothing imaginable, but when there's a little water, the surface perfectly reflects the clouds and the blue Altiplano sky and the horizon disappears. When you're driving across the surface at such times, the effect is positively eerie, and it's hard to believe that you're not actually flying through the clouds.

History

In recent geological history, this part of the Altiplano was covered entirely by water. Around the ancient lakeshore, two distinctive terraces are visible, indicating the succession of two lakes; below the lower one are fossils of coral in limestone. From 40,000 to 25,000 years ago, Lago Minchín, whose highest level reached 3760m, occupied much of southwestern Bolivia. When it evaporated, the area lay dry for 14,000 years before the appearance of short-lived Lago Tauca, which lasted for only about 1000 years and rose to 3720m. When it

By Rail to Chile

The rail route between Bolivia and Chile passes through some spectacular landscapes, and if you're prepared for the uncomfortable conditions, the journey is highly worthwhile. Temperatures in the coaches may well fall below zero at night, so a sleeping bag or woolen blanket and plenty of warm clothing are essential. There's no dining car, so bring food as well. Any sort of fruit, meat or cheese will be confiscated at the border (you'll get a receipt), so eat it up before reaching customs at Ollagüe.

Between Uyuni and the border, the line crosses vast saltpans, deserts and rugged mountains and volcanoes. Flamingos, guanacos, vicuñas and wild burros are common, and thanks to a startling mirage effect, so is a host of other things. *Remolinos* (dust devils or willy-willys) whirl across the stark landscape beneath towering snowcapped volcanoes. One type of vegetation that flourishes is *llareta* (also spelled 'yareta'), a combustible salt-tolerant moss that oozes a turpentine-like jelly and is used by the locals as stove fuel. It appears soft and spongy from a distance but is actually rock hard. Llareta grows very slowly; a large clump may be several hundred years old. The plant is now an officially protected species in Chile and in the Reserva Nacional de Fauna Andina Eduardo Avaroa (REA).

Before the trip, you'll need to pass by the Migración office in Uyuni and pick up your Bolivian exit stamp. The Chilean immigration procedures at Avaroa/Ollagüe, a windy, dusty and unprotected outpost in a broad pass through the Andes, can be trying. You must line up for your entrance stamp, and then they may want to do a luggage search. All this takes place outside at nearly 5000m altitude, and it can be a miserable exercise in endurance.

The border crossing will probably also involve a wait for the arrival of the Bolivian or Chilean engine (which may arrive up to 12 hours late) to pull you to either Uyuni or Calama. The excruciatingly slow Chilean engine, especially when it's headed uphill from Calama to the border, appears to be the incarnation of *The Little Engine That Could*, but even if 'it thinks it can,' it does so with little conviction. Note also that the Chilean coaches are in surprisingly worse repair than their Bolivian counterparts. The Chilean service is run by British-owned Ferrocarril Antofagasta-Bolivia, which loses money on the line but is required by an 1888 mineral transport treaty to keep the passenger service running indefinitely. Perhaps that explains why the windows are broken and the coaches lack light and heating, why they have wooden benches instead of seats, why the loose boards allow cold winds to whistle through and why the toilets are located outside, exposed to the elements!

From Calama to the coast, there's still a railway, but no rail service, so you'll have a two- to three-hour bus trip to Antofagasta. It's sometimes possible to buy Chilean pesos in Uyuni or Ollagüe, but you'd probably have better luck at a casa de cambio in La Paz.

---

dried up, it left two large puddles, Lagos Poopó and Uru Uru, and two major salt concentrations, the Salares de Uyuni and Coipasa.

This part of the Altiplano is drained internally, with no outlet to the sea; the salt deposits are the result of the minerals leeched from the mountains and deposited at the lowest available point.

Colchani

There remain at least 10 billion tons of salt in the Salar de Uyuni, and around Colchani, campesinos hack it out with picks and shovels and pile it into small conical mounds that characterize the salar landscape in this area. In Colchani itself, several salt treatment plants iodize the salt according to WHO recommendations and bag it up for distribution to other parts of Bolivia.

Most of the salt is sold to refiners and hauled off by rail, but some is exchanged with local villages for wool, meat and grease. In the winter months, a rapidly decreasing number of people load the salt blocks onto llama caravans and transport them along the salt trail to Tarija, nearly 300km away, where it's traded for honey, chilies, maize, wood, coca leaves and other products that are otherwise unavailable on the Altiplano. This trade has been going on at least since 1612,

when it was described in the Aymará orthography published in that year.

A few kilometers southwest of Colchani is the extraordinary Cooperative Rosario workshop, also called *Bloques de Sal* (Salt Blocks). Here, blocks of salt are cut from the salar and made into furniture and lively works of art. You may see anything from souvenir carvings of vicuñas, condors and frogs to blocky lawn chairs and decorative model houses and churches. The operation employs 60 workers and has become a solid attraction on Salar de Uyuni tourist circuits.

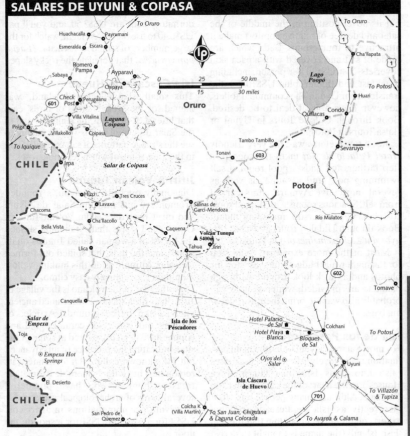

SALARES DE UYUNI & COIPASA

SOUTHERN ALTIPLANO

Ojos del Salar

In some areas of the salar, cold underground water rises to the surface and bubbles up through the salt layer, creating unusual-looking eruptions on the salt. Some of these are quite large, and when there's water on the salar, they create dangerous hazards for vehicles driving across the salar. One distinctive example west of Colchani is visited on most dry-season tours.

Hoteles de Sal (Salt Hotels)

Apart from its straw roof, the unusual *Hotel Playa Blanca* (☎ 2772; fax 2121) 20km west of Colchani, is constructed entirely of salt blocks. The exterior isn't much to look at, but its novel position in the middle of the salar and degree of relative comfort make it attractive to tour groups. Beds, which are made of salt and covered with alpaca skin coverlets, cost US$20 per person, including breakfast and dinner, plus US$10 for the transfer from Uyuni. The communal toilets, however, leave a great deal to be desired. Book through Colque Tours in Uyuni or Balsa Tours in Potosí.

Just a few meters away, the very friendly *Hotel Palacio de Sal* takes the concept a step farther, and adds a pool room, a salt swimming pool and a sauna, as well as several impressive Aymará altars carved from salt. Spacious rooms with domed roofs cost US$30 per person, including meals. Book through Hidalgo Tours (☎ 062-25186; uyusalht@ceibo.entelnet.bo) in Potosí.

Most of the more expensive tours stop for the night while budget tours just stop for photos and a quick look around. Although blankets are provided, winter visitors will probably also want to bring their own sleeping bags.

Isla de los Pescadores

For most Salar de Uyuni tours, the main destination is the lovely Isla de los Pescadores (also known as Isla Inca Huasi, 'Inca Houses'), in the heart of the salar 80km from Colchani. Although many people refer to it incorrectly as Isla de Pescado, reliable experts on the subject maintain that the real 'Fish Island' (the name is thought to derive from its shape, which resembles a fish when reflected in the Salar) actually lies about 25km to the northwest of here.

The Isla de los Pescadores is a hilly outpost in the middle of the salar, covered in *Trichoreus* cactus and surrounded by a flat, white sea of hexagonal salt tiles. It was once a remarkably lonely, otherworldly place. However, a tourist complex has now appeared and around midday, lunching tour groups trip over each other while following a tangle of walking tracks to reach the caves at the summit.

The friendly owner of this complex is currently creating a definitive map of the Salar de Uyuni. Camping costs US$2 per person, dormitory beds are US$3.50, and you'll pay US$0.40 to use the loo. At night, watch for the large numbers of stranded viscachas (*Lagidium viscaccia*) that populate the rocky slopes.

Isla Cáscara de Huevo

This small island, 'eggshell island,' was named for the broken shells of birds' eggs that litter it. It lies near the southern end of the Salar de Uyuni and is visited mainly to see the strange patterns of salt crystallization in the area, some of which resemble roses.

Jiriri & Volcán Tunupa

Diagonally opposite Colchani, a rounded promontory juts into the Salar de Uyuni and on it rises the 5400m Volcán Tunupa. One legend states that Atahualpa slashed the breast of a woman called Tunupa on its slopes, and the milk that spilled out formed the salar. Altitude aside, this hulking yellow mountain is a relatively easy climb.

At the foot of the volcano is the village of Jiriri, in an area specked with ruined ancient villages and burial grounds. Articles of clothing and artifacts in ceramic, gold and copper have been discovered at some of the sites, indicating the presence of an advanced but little-known culture. Unfortunately, its remoteness has left it vulnerable to amateur treasure hunters who have plundered several items of archaeological value.

Private accommodations in Jiriri cost US$2 for a bed and US$1 for a spot on the floor.

Llica

Directly across the Salar from Colchani is the village of Llica, the unlikely site of a teachers college. *Señor Ángel Quispe* on the plaza offers beds for around US$1.50, and there's also the basic *Alojamiento Municipal* charging US$2.50 per person. For meals, the pensiones *Inca Wasi*, *Bolívar* and *El Viajero* serve soup for US$0.20 and full meals for US$1. Micros leave Uyuni for Llica more or less daily at noon (four hours, US$3).

Getting There & Away

From the rail line between Uyuni and Oruro, you'll glimpse the salar during the stop at Colchani, but to fully appreciate the place, you need to get out onto the salt. The easiest access is with an organized tour (see Uyuni) but for those who prefer an independent approach, camiones leave for Colchani and Llica from Avenida Ferroviaria in Uyuni. You'll have the most luck between 7 and 9 am. Some salt workers living in Uyuni commute daily to Colchani in private vehicles or on motorcycles, and for a small fee you may be able to hitch along. Alternatively, you can walk between Uyuni and Colchani, but you need a good long day for the trip.

Getting Around

Camiones from Uyuni make the trip to Llica in a couple of hours and sometimes continue farther into the southwest region, carrying supplies to sulfur mines and other camps. This is an adventurous way to go, but come well prepared with food, water and camping gear.

For salar trips in your own vehicle, carry a compass, food, water, extra fuel, tools, spare parts and a means of warming up. Drivers have become lost on the white expanse, and have been known to drive in circles until the vehicle ran out of gas, which would not be a pleasant situation. Also, be sure to keep to the existing vehicle tracks on the salar; it's not only safer, but prevents damage to this amazing natural feature.

SALAR DE COIPASA

The more remote Salar de Coipasa, the great salt desert northwest of the Salar de Uyuni, lies at an altitude of 3786m and has an extent of 2218 sq km. It was part of the same system of prehistoric lakes as the Salar de Uyuni – a system that covered the area over 10,000 years ago. The road to the Salar de Coipasa is extremely poor and vehicles are subject to bogging in deep sand and mud, so access is by 4WD only. The salt-mining village of Coipasa, which (not surprisingly) is constructed mainly of salt, occupies an island in the middle of the salar.

Chipaya

Immediately north of the Salar de Coipasa, on the Río Sabaya delta, live the Chipaya Indians, who occupy two desert villages (Chipaya and Ayparavi) of unique circular mud huts known as *khuyas* or *putucus*. They survive in their harsh environment practicing communal agriculture and herding. Chipayas are best recognized by their earth-colored clothing and the women's unique hairstyle, which is plaited African-style into 60 small braids. These are in turn joined into two large braids and decorated with a *laurake* (barrette) at each temple.

Some researchers believe the Chipaya were the first inhabitants of the Altiplano, and may in fact be a remnant of the lost Tiahuanaco civilization. Much of this is based on the fact that their language, which is vastly different from both Quechua and Aymará, closely resembles Urus. Other researchers note similarities to Mayan, Arawak, Arabic and North African tribal languages.

Chipaya tradition maintains that the people descend from the builders of the chullpas scattered around Lake Titicaca. Their religion, which is nature-based, deifies phallic images, stones, rivers, mountains, animal carcasses and Chipaya ancestors, among other things. The rather phallic village church tower is worshipped as a demon – one of 40 named demons, who represent hate, ire, vengeance, gluttony, and other deadly sins. These are believed to inhabit the whitewashed sod cones that exist within a 15km radius of the village, where they're appeased with magic amulets, llama fetuses and mummified animals to prevent their evil from invading the village. The people also revere the Volcán Sajama and the Río Lauca, which provide fertile soil and fresh water, as honored entities.

The reverent commemoration of dead ancestors culminates on November 2, All Saints' Day, when bodies are disinterred from the chullpas. They're feted with a feast, copious drink and coca leaves, and informed about recent village events and the needs of the living. Those who were chiefs, healers and other luminaries are carried to the church where they're honored with animal sacrifices (oddly, a similar practice is salient in the indigenous religion of Madagascar).

Visiting Chipaya In general, tourists aren't especially welcome, but culturally sensitive visitors can still develop a rapport with the people. If you don't go to gawk or simply 'bag' photos, your chances of acceptance are much better. Traditionally, the Chipayas have been rather superstitious about cameras. Although some individuals are now willing to model for a fee, in the interest of avoiding confrontation, visitors should probably abstain from photographing people here.

Visitor 'hospitality' in Chipaya has been known to cost up to US$50 per person, and attempts at bargaining normally only aggravate matters and create ill will. The price decreases only if you're someone the locals want to have around, so put your best foot forward.

Accommodations are available at the school, with permission from the village administration, for around US$3 per person. For food, you're limited to the small village shop, and toilet facilities are limited to four open holes just outside the village, corresponding to the four compass directions.

Getting There & Away From Uyuni, Coipasa and Chipaya may be reached from Llica, across the Salar de Coipasa, or from Oruro via Toledo, Corque and Huachacalla. On most days, micros from Uyuni to Llica (four hours, US$3) leave at 11 am or noon. From Llica, you can wait for a camión or hire a motorcycle taxi to Pisiga for US$20; there

you'll find Iquique-Oruro buses headed for Sabaya (where you'll find an alojamiento and basic meals), Huachacalla and Oruro.

From Oruro, camiones leave from the Plaza Walter Khon once or twice a week (especially on Wednesday), while buses, which go only as far as Huachacalla (175km from Oruro and 21km from Chipaya) leave several times weekly, also from Plaza Walter Khon. Alternatively, you can reach Sabaya or Huachacalla on any bus between Oruro and Iquique. In addition, a growing number of tour companies organize visits to the village. Camiones that fetch the salt from Coipasa village also travel frequently to and from Oruro (20 hours, US$2).

LOS LÍPEZ & THE SOUTHWEST CIRCUIT

The southwestern 'toe' of Bolivia is comprised of the provinces of Nor Lípez, Sud Lípez and Baldiviezo, which collectively make up the region known as Los Lípez. Much of it is nominally protected in the Reserva Nacional de Fauna Andina Eduardo Avaroa (REA), which was created in 1973 and expanded to its present size in 1981. Its current emphasis is on preserving the vicuña and the llareta plant, both of which are threatened in Bolivia, as well as other unique species. Admission to the reserve costs US$5.

This high, wide and lonesome desert country represents one of the world's harshest wilderness regions and a final refuge for some of South America's hardiest wildlife. As a hotbed of volcanic and geothermal activity, the landscape literally boils with minerals. When you see the resulting spectrum of wild unearthly colors in the mountains and lakes, you'll suspect that Pachamama occasionally takes a walk on the wild side.

Salar de Uyuni to Laguna Colorada

The normal tour route from Uyuni is via Colchani, 20km to the northwest, then 80km west across the salar to Isla de los Pescadores (see Salar de Uyuni, earlier in this chapter). After a stop to explore the island, the route turns south and 45km later, reaches the edge of the salar, where there's a small house where you can buy soft drinks and biscuits.

After another 22km you reach the village of Colcha K (pronounced **col**-cha-**kah**), also known as Villa Martín, where you'll pass through a military checkpoint. In the village, there's a pleasant adobe church and rudimentary accommodations in a private home and shop 100m up the cobbled street.

About 15km farther along is the quinoa-growing village of San Juan, with a lovely adobe church, a cemetery and several burial chullpas in the vicinity. Budget accommodations are provided in private homes, basic alojamientos and the clean and well-appointed ***Posada Don Victor*** (which has gas-heated showers augmented by solar power). All charge around US$3 per person. Upmarket tours stay at the lovely British-run ***Magia de San Juan***, which charges US$15/20 for singles/doubles with bath and breakfast; here profits are shared with the community.

At this point, the route turns west and starts across the borax-producing Salar de Chiguana, where the landscape opens up and snowcapped Ollagüe, an active volcano straddling the Chilean border, appears in the distance. There's a rough road leading to a field of steaming fumaroles and sulfur lakes at the 5000m level near the summit, and it's possible to catch a ride up with miners working at the sulfur camps.

Before the Chiguana military camp, a side trip leads to the oddly named Comunidad Amor, 20km away, which subsists not on love, but on quinoa, and holds several interesting burial chullpas.

At Chiguana, across the Uyuni-Calama railway line, your passport will be scrutinized by gawking soldiers. The route then turns south and climbs into high and increasingly wild terrain, past the Lagunas Cañapa, Hedionda, Chiarkhota, Honda and Ramaditas. These mineral-rich lakes are filled with Andean, Chilean and James flamingos, and several are backed by hills resembling spilled chocolate sundaes. After approximately 170km of rough bumping through marvelous landscapes, the road winds down a hillside to Laguna Colorada.

Frozen Flamingos

Three species of flamingo breed in the bleak high country of southwestern Bolivia, and once you've seen these pink posers strutting through icy mineral lagoons at 5000m elevation, you'll abandon time-worn associations between flamingos, coconut palms and the hot, steamy tropics.

Flamingos have a complicated and sophisticated system for filtering the foodstuffs from highly alkaline brackish lakes. They filter algae and diatoms from the water by sucking in and vigorously expelling water from the bill several times per second. The minute particles are caught on fine hairlike protrusions that line the inside of the mandibles. The suction is created by the thick fleshy tongue, which rests in a groove in the lower mandible and pumps back and forth like a piston.

The Chilean flamingo (*Phoenicopterus chilensis*) reaches heights of just over one meter and has a black-tipped white bill, dirty blue legs, red knees and salmon-colored plumage. The James flamingo (*Phoenicoparrus jamesi*) is the smallest of the three species and has dark-red legs and a yellow-and-black bill. It's locally known as *jututu*. The Andean flamingo (*Phoenicoparrus andinus*) is the largest of the three and has pink plumage, yellow legs and a yellow-and-black bill.

Árbol de Piedra

This 'stone tree' – and it really does look like a tree – is made of wind-eroded igneous rock and rises from the bleak expanse of the Desierto Siloli (Siloli Desert), 18km north of Laguna Colorada. Tour groups like to stage climbing competitions here, but few people can make it to the top.

Laguna Colorada

Fiery red Laguna Colorada, 151km south of Chiguana, sits at 4278m, covers approximately 60 sq km and reaches a depth of just 80cm. The rich red coloration is derived from algae and plankton that thrive in the mineral-rich water, and the shoreline is fringed with brilliant white deposits of sodium, magnesium, borax and gypsum. The lake sediments are also rich in diatoms, tiny microfossils used in the production of fertilizer, paint, toothpaste and plastics, and as a filtering agent for oil, pharmaceuticals, aviation fuel, beer and wine. More apparent are the flamingos that breed here, and all three South American species are present (see 'Frozen Flamingos,' earlier).

On the western shore is the Campamento ENDE electric power station. This is a standard overnight stop on most tours. For accommodations, the bottom end is the *refugio* of Señor Eustaquio Bernal, where there's now a basic dining room and visitors pay US$3 in six-bed dormitories; those relegated to the adobe floor pay half price. Some visitors report also being charged to pitch a tent at the base of the hills, ostensibly because they were within view of the refugio.

Upmarket tours stay at **Hospedaría Hidalgo Laguna Colorada**, run by Hidalgo Tours. Alternatively, the REA runs **Albergue de los Guardaparques**, the rangers' hostel, which charges US$3.50 for a comfortable cot with a mattress in a six-bed dormitory. However, no food is available.

The clear air is bitterly cold and winter nighttime temperatures can drop below -20°C. Just as well; if it ever rose much above freezing, the stench would probably make the place unbearable. Instead, the air is perfumed with llareta smoke, which seems ironic given the proximity to potentially limitless solar, geothermal and wind power.

Sol de Mañana

Apart from tour groups, most vehicles along the tracks around Laguna Colorada will be supplying or servicing mining and military camps or the developing geothermal project 50km south at Sol de Mañana. The main interest here is the 4850m-high geyser basin with bubbling mud pots, hellish fumaroles and the thick and nauseating aroma of sulfur fumes. Approach the site cautiously; any damp or cracked earth is potentially dangerous and cave-ins do occur, sometimes causing serious burns.

Termas de Polques & Salar de Chalviri

At the foot of Cerro Polques lie the Termas de Polques, a small 28° to 30°C hot pool. Although they're not bathtub temperature by any means, they're suitable for bathing (avoid polluting them with soap!) and the mineral-rich waters are thought to relieve the symptoms of arthritis and rheumatism. To the east, the adjacent Salar de Chalviri and its many small lakes support populations of flamingos and ducks. In the middle of the Salar, a mining operation extracts borax.

Laguna Verde

Laguna Verde, a stunning blue-green lake at nearly 4400m, is tucked into the southwestern corner of Bolivian territory, 52km south of Sol de Mañana. The incredible green color comes from high concentrations of lead, sulfur, arsenic and calcium carbonates. In this exposed position, an icy wind blows almost incessantly, whipping the water into a brilliant green-and-white froth. This surface agitation combined with the high mineral content means that the temperature must drop well below freezing before ice can form. (I've seen it still liquid at -20°C!)

Behind the lake rises the cone of 5960m Volcán Licancabur, whose summit is said to have once sheltered an ancient Inca crypt. It's believed that on this and other prominent peaks, young Inca men were marched to the summit, exposed to the cruel elements and allowed to freeze to death as a sacrifice to commemorate critical events in the empire. Some tours include an ascent of Licancabur, and although it presents no technical difficulties, the wind, temperature, altitude and ball-bearing volcanic pumice underfoot may prove too much for most people.

There are two approaches to Laguna Verde. Where the route splits about 20km south of Sol de Mañana, the slightly shorter right fork winds along a relatively level route and around a range of caramel-colored hills to Laguna Verde. The more scenic left fork climbs up and over a 5000m pass, then up a stark hillside resembling a freshly raked Zen garden dotted with the enormous Rocas de Dalí, which appear to have been meticulously placed by the surrealist master Salvador Dalí himself.

Down the far slope are two sulfur mines, a military camp, a meteorological post and a refugio where overnight guests pay US$2 per person for a mattress on the floor and running water. Behind the complex, there's a hot spring in a creek where you can have a welcome bath.

To Chile Colque Tours in Uyuni offers a cross-border tour between Uyuni and San Pedro de Atacama, and other agencies are following its lead (see Uyuni earlier in this chapter) by arrangement with Chilean operators. Buses to San Pedro de Atacama meet tour groups at Laguna Verde at around 10 am. It's wise check out of Bolivia at immigration in Uyuni; the exit stamp allows three days to leave the country, and the Hito Cajón border post near Laguna Verde is staffed only sporadically. This is an increasingly popular way to travel between Bolivia and Chile.

Independent travelers should carry extra food, water and warm gear. Laguna Verde to Hito Cajón is a bitterly cold and windy walk at a 5000m elevation. You'd be very lucky to find a lift there, but fortunately, it's only about a 10km walk to the road, where you can hope for a camión running between one of the Chilean mining camps and San Pedro de Atacama, 35km away. Once in San Pedro, remember to check in with Chilean immigration.

Laguna Celeste
Laguna Celeste, which translates as either 'blue lake' or – more romantically – 'heaven lake,' is still very much a peripheral trip for

most Uyuni agencies, but it is gaining popularity with travelers who have the time. A local legend suggests the presence of a submerged ruin, possibly a chullpa, in the lake.

Behind the lake, a road winds its way up the 6020m Volcán Uturuncu to the Uturuncu sulfur mine, which lies in a 5900m pass between the mountain's twin cones. That means it's about 220m higher than the road over the Khardung La in Ladakh, India, making it the highest motorable road in the world.

Other Lakes
In the vast eastern reaches of Sud Lípez are numerous other fascinating mineral-rich lakes that are informally named for their odd coloration and have so far escaped much attention. Various milky-looking lakes are known as Laguna Blanca, sulfur-colored lakes are Laguna Amarilla and wine-colored ones are known as Laguna Guinda. Some of these may eventually find their way onto the circuit.

Quetena Chico
About 120km northeast of Laguna Verde and 30km southwest of Laguna Celeste is the squalid settlement of Quetena Chico, which subsists at the most basic of levels on the extraction of alluvial gold. The procedure takes place in a 1000-hectare concession around the place called Orckoya, 5km from Quetena Chico, which is overseen by the Cumbre de la Frontera cooperative. To isolate the gold, prospectors dig holes about 1m deep along the banks of the Río Quetena and manually wash it through sluices, where the gold is separated from gravel. Each prospector can hope to come up with between 15 and 30g of gold per month, which is scant reward for the amount of work involved – and the living standards reflect this disheartening fact.

Tomás Laka
The site called Tomás Laka, 2km from Quetena Chico, is conjectured to have been an ancient fort. Still visible are ruined walls, several incomplete chullpas and a stone

hollow that is thought to have been used as a mortar for pulverizing grain.

It lies in an area of bizarrely eroded rock formations that bear some equally unusual rock paintings. Subjects include the standard pumas and serpents, but there's also a line-up of bizarre-looking 'bugs' – a sort of cross between giant ants and space creatures – wearing World Cup referee uniforms.

Valles de Rocas & San Cristóbal

The route back to Uyuni turns northeast a few kilometers north of Laguna Colorada and winds through more high, lonesome country and several valleys of bizarre eroded rock formations known as Valles de Rocas. Gas is available sporadically at the village of Alota, from which it's a trying six-hour jostle back to Uyuni.

If you can still cope with sightseeing at this stage, a short side trip will take you to the village of San Cristóbal, in a little valley northeast of Alota. Here you'll find a lovely 350-year-old church constructed on an age-old Pachamama ritual site. The walls bear a series of paintings from the life of Christ, and the altar is made of pure silver and backed up by a beautifully preserved 17th-century organ. The site is so revered that the *llaves sagradas* (sacred keys) to the church may only be touched by 'pure spirits,' and at sowing time, there's a tradition of writing the names of one's vices on rocks from the fields and symbolically depositing them in the church.

PULACAYO

At the semi-ghost town of Pulacayo, 22km northeast of Uyuni, brilliantly colored rocks rise beside the road and a mineral-rich stream reveals streaks of blue, yellow, red and green. The Pulacayo mines north of the village, which yielded mainly silver, were first opened in the late 17th century (the grave of the company founder A Mariano Ramírez can still be seen), but they closed in 1832 on account of the Independence war. In 1873, however, the mining Compañía Huanchaca de Bolivia (CHB) took over operations and resumed silver extraction. At the time of its

final closure in 1959, it employed 20,000 miners, but today, just 800 people remain.

The little-known Museo de Minas, the mining museum, is a worthwhile attempt at reviving Pulacayo from the dead. Here you can explore nearly 2km of mine tunnels (the mine's entire extent is just under 6km) with local guides for US$2 per person. Also worthwhile is the mill that spins llama wool into cloth and Huanchaca, 15km from Pulacayo, where you'll see the colonial cemetery and the ruins of silver smelters from the same period.

Pulacayo is also home to several decaying steam locomotives that were originally imported to transport ore. They include Bolivia's first steam engine, *El Chiripa*, which dates from 1890, and others with such names as *El Burro*, *El Torito* and *Mauricio Hothschild*. There's also the ore train that was robbed by legendary bandits Butch Cassidy and the Sundance Kid, including the wooden railcar that bears the bullet holes from the attack.

Another interesting site is the historic 1878 home of Aniceto Arce, which features lovely marble fireplaces, pianos, old telephones and period furniture imported from Britain. Foreigners may have to pay a US$5 entry/photography fee.

Befitting its more active past, Pulacayo has two basic but surprisingly pleasant hotels. *Hotel El Rancho* charges US$2 per person and *El Rancho II* is US$1.80. Meals are available.

Getting There & Away

All transport between Uyuni and Potosí passes through Pulacayo. From Uyuni, you can also take a guided tour organized by the Proyecto Turístico Pulacayo (☎ 0694-3459). The US$5 charge for the tour includes transport to Pulacayo, a sandwich lunch and a folder describing village history.

TOMAVE

The centerpiece of Tomave is its unusual 1530 church, which took 100 years to build and is laid out in the form of a Latin cross. The pipe organ, which is probably the original one, dates from the 16th century. The ceiling windows are made of marble, as is the beautiful baptismal font. Some of the paintings on the walls were painted by the Cuzco school, and there are at least three by the Bolivian master Pérez de Holguín.

At the village of Asientos, 4km north of Tomave, is the ruin of another home of Aniceto Arce. The small village church houses a very impressive antique Bible. With a guide, visitors can enter the abandoned gold and silver mine that spawned and once sustained Asientos. The intact chimney on the hillside also merits a look.

Getting There & Away

Camiones leave for Tomave from in front of the police station in Uyuni Wednesday at 10 am, and return the following day at the same time. With a group, several Uyuni travel agencies offer day tours to Tomave. Try Agencia Tunupa.

UYUNI TO TUPIZA

The very rough road south of Uyuni initially heads out across the high desert. Immediately north of the market village of Cerdas, where vendors sell a range of snacks, lie several impressive fields of sand dunes. After it drops dramatically off the Altiplano, it descends into an otherworldly riverbed filled with bizarrely colorful, unusual and mineral-rich geology.

Just north of the active mining town of Atocha, which retains an Old West feel and doesn't appear to have progressed past the early 20th century, you'll pass a picturesque miners' cemetery spread across the hillside. In the center of Atocha, don't miss the Cessna that is impaled on a post in a small square along the main street.

Beyond Atocha, the road enters increasingly scenic country, with excellent views of the stunning cone of 5630m Cerro Cholorque. For the next four hours, the road twists through seriously mountainous country, past Huaca Huañusca (see Around Tupiza), Butch and Sundance country, then plummets into the fertile valley of the Río Tupiza, flanked by cactus and brilliant red rock.

TUPIZA
☎ 0694

In the background looms the Tupizan range, very red, or better, a ruddy sepia; and very distinct, resembling a landscape painted by an artist with the animated brilliance of Delacroix or by an Impressionist like Renoir…In the tranquil translucent air, flows the breath of smiling grace…

– Carlos Medinaceli, Bolivian writer

Tupiza, embedded in some of Bolivia's most spectacular countryside, is a real gem. The capital of Sud Chichas, a province of Potosí department, Tupiza is among Bolivia's most literate and educated cities. It's also a comparatively young city – half of its 20,000 inhabitants are under the age of 20, and its growth rate is one of the country's highest.

The city lies at 2950m in the valley of the Río Tupiza, surrounded by the rugged Cordillera de Chichas. The climate is mild year-round, with most of the rain falling between November and March. From June to August, days are hot, dry and clear, but nighttime temperatures can drop to below freezing.

Economically, the town depends on agriculture and the mining of antimony, lead, silver, bismuth, and some tin. A YPFB (Yacimientos Petrolíferos Fiscales Bolivianos) refinery 5km south of town provides employment, and the country's only antimony smelter operates sporadically along a dry tributary of the Río Tupiza. Although tourists have recently begun trickling into Tupiza, the Chichas area is still well off the rutted track.

The charm of Tupiza lies in the surrounding countryside – an amazing landscape of rainbow-colored rocks, hills, mountains and canyons. If it conjures up visions of the Old West, that's only appropriate, because Tupiza lies in the heart of Butch Cassidy and the Sundance Kid country. After robbing an Aramayo payroll at Huaca Huañusca, about 50km north of town, the pair reputedly met their untimely demise in the mining village of San Vicente (see later in this chapter).

TUPIZA

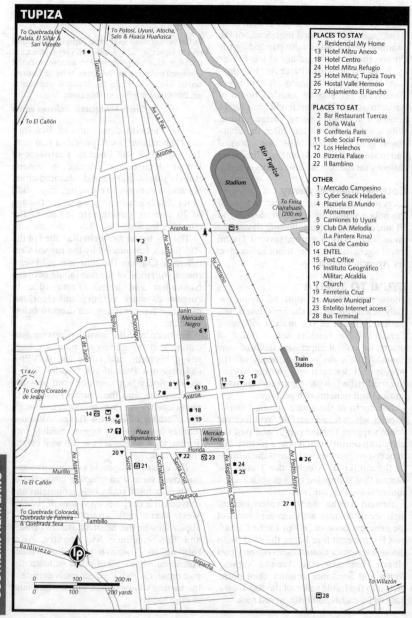

History

The tribe that originally inhabited the valley and surrounding mountains called themselves Chichas and left archaeological evidence of their existence. Despite this, little is known of their culture or language, and it's assumed they were ethnically separate from the tribes in neighboring areas of southern Bolivia and northern Argentina. Unfortunately, anything unique about them was destroyed between 1471 and 1488 when the Inca, under the leadership of Tupac Inca Yupanqui, annexed the region into the Inca empire. The Chichas were used by the Inca as a military nucleus from which to gather forces and organize armies to conquer the Humahuaca, Diaguitas and Calchaquíes tribes of northern Argentina.

Once the Inca empire had fallen to the Spanish, the entire southern half of the Viceroyalty of Alto Peru was awarded to Diego de Almagro by decree of King Carlos V of Spain. When Almagro and company arrived in the Tupiza valley on a familiarization expedition in October 1535, the Chichas culture had been entirely subsumed by that of the Inca. Almagro stayed briefly in the valley and then moved southward toward Chile, bent on exploring the remainder of his newly acquired spoils.

Officially, Tupiza was founded on June 4, 1574, by Captain Luis de Fuentes (who also founded Tarija), but this date is pure conjecture. The origin of the name is similarly hazy. The current spelling was derived from the Chichas word *Tope'sa* or *Tucpicsa*, but no one is sure what it meant. It has been suggested that it probably referred to 'red rock,' since that seems to be the area's predominant feature, but that's just a guess.

In the tumultuous Campesino Rebellion of 1781, the peasants' champion Luis de la Vega mobilized the local militia, proclaimed himself governor of Chichas, López, Cinti and Porco and encouraged resistance against Spanish authorities. The rebellion was squashed before it really got under way, but the mob was successful in executing the Spanish *corregidor* (chief magistrate) of Tupiza and leveling his estate. At the same time, 4000 Indian troops led by Pedro de la Cruz Condori, who had been charged with organizing and carrying out terrorist acts against the government, were intercepted by Spanish forces before reaching their destination.

On November 7, 1810, the first victory in Alto Peru's struggle for independence from Spain was won at the Battle of Suipacha, which took place just east of the Tupiza valley. At the end of the war, on December 9, 1824, the deciding battle took place at Tumusla in the northern Chichas.

From Tupiza's founding through the War of Independence, its Spanish population grew steadily, lured by the favorable climate and suitable agricultural and grazing lands. Later, the discovery of minerals in the Cordilleras de Chichas and López attracted even more settlers, and with them came indigenous people to do the manual labor. In 1840, Argentine revolutionaries fleeing the dictator Juan Manuel Rosas escaped to Tupiza and were incorporated into the community. More recently, campesinos have drifted in from the countryside, and many out-of-work miners and their families have already settled. The favorable climatic and economic conditions also attract migrants from other parts of Bolivia.

Information

There's no tourist office in Tupiza, but the friendly folks at the Hotel Mitru or the Hostal Valle Hermoso can answer most of your questions.

Money You'll see lots of 'Compro Dólares' signs in shops that are happy to change US dollars cash. The Casa de Cambio on Avaroa isn't especially reliable, but may be worth a try. To change traveler's checks, try the Hotel Mitru or Hostal Valle Hermoso, which charge a 5% commission, or Ferretería Cruz, which charges up to 7%.

Post & Communications The post and ENTEL offices lie west of the main plaza. Tupiza now has Internet and email options. The friendly Cyber Snack Heladería (gperez@cedro.pts.entelnet.bo) is open from 8 am to 10 pm every day and charges

US$2.50 per hour. Faster computers but less personal Internet connections are available for the same price at the Entelito, in a drinks distributor on Florida. Internet and email service is also available at the Hotel Mitru (hotel guests receive a discount) and Hostal Valle Hermoso for US$2.50 per hour.

Laundry The Hotel Mitru offers laundry services for US$1 per kilogram for their guests and US$1.50 for nonguests.

Finca Chajrahuasi

Across the river, mostly overgrown with weeds, is the abandoned farmstead of tin baron Carlos Victor Aramayo. Aramayo, who had maintained his business in Bolivia using Bolivian labor, was heaped into the same category as the absentee Simon Patiño, and when his mines were nationalized in 1952, the estate was confiscated and Aramayo fled to Europe to escape the backlash. Finca Chajrahuasi now serves as a rough soccer field, but it was apparently once quite a comfy residence.

Museo Municipal

Tupiza's municipal museum houses a mix of historical and cultural artifacts, including an antique cart, historical photos, archaeological relics, old weapons and historic farming implements. It's open Monday to Friday 6 to 8 pm and entry is free. To visit, pick up a key from the Jefatura, in the alcaldía.

Cerro Corazón de Jesús

The short trail to the summit of Cerro Corazón de Jesús, flanked by Stations of the Cross, is a pleasant morning or evening walk when the low sun brings out the fiery reds of the surrounding countryside. The hill, which is crowned by a statue of Christ, affords a good overall view of the town.

Markets

Mercado de Ferias takes place on Monday, Thursday, and Saturday mornings along Avenida Regimiento Chichas. Mercado Negro, where you'll encounter a mishmash of consumer goods, occupies the block between Regimiento Chichas, Santa Cruz, Junín and Avaroa. It's open daily.

Organized Tours

Tupiza Tours (☎/fax 3001; tpztours@ cedro.pts.entelnet.bo), at Hotel Mitru, runs good-value day trips exploring Tupiza's wild quebradas; stops include El Angosto, Entre Ríos, Quebrada Seca, a great lunch at Titihoyo, and then Valle de los Machos, the Quebrada de Palmira, El Cañón, Quebrada de Palala and El Sillar. With two/four people, this full-day trip costs US$21.50/37.50.

Tupiza Tours also runs wonderful two-day tours in the footsteps of Butch Cassidy and the Sundance Kid. On the first day, you'll head through the Wild West scenery north of Tupiza, past the pleasant village of Salo, to Huaca Huañusca. After visiting an ancient *apacheta* (stone mound), there's a 5km walk past the surprisingly idyllic site where the bandits staged their last robbery. On the second day, the tour passes the Quebrada de Palala, El Sillar and some wild puna country to reach the bleak mining village of San Vicente, where Butch and Sundance's careers abruptly ended in 1908. Here you'll see the house where the bandits holed up and the cemetery where they were buried after the final shoot-out. For groups of up to six people, the first day costs US$120, and the second day, US$180 (for the entire group).

In addition, Tupiza Tours offers unique Southwest Circuit tours, which begin in Tupiza and pass through the little-seen wild lands of Sud Lípez to connect with the main tourist route at Laguna Verde. These tours, which cost US$120 per person, wind up at Uyuni and offer a scenic alternative for reaching Uyuni from Tupiza.

Activities

A favorite activity in Tupiza is to hop on horseback and ride around the stunning Wild West landscapes, perhaps entertaining illusions of galloping through a shoot-'em-up Western. Tupiza Tours (see Organized Tours) offers three-, five- and seven-hour circuits through the red-rock quebradas south of town for US$3 per hour, including lunch. For those who really want to sample the cowboy life, they also offer long-distance horse tours of two to four days, including tents and campfire cooking, for US$24 per day. The two-day circuit covers Salo and Palala or the quebradas south of town, including a lead-mining ghost town. On the three- and four-day circuits, you can visit a rural weaving community, soak in hot springs and camp at the idyllic Huaca Huañusca site where Butch and Sundance committed their last crime. Hostal Valle Hermoso has also recently begun offering horseback riding for US$3 per hour.

Tupiza Tours and Valle Hermoso both rent bicycles for around US$3.50 per day.

Places to Stay

The friendly, bright and airy **Hotel Mitru** (*☎/fax 3001*) and the affiliated **Hotel Mitru Anexo** (*☎ 3002*) are both excellent choices. In the main hotel, single/double rooms with bath cost US$7/12. For a room without bath, you'll pay US$3.50 per person in either location. The lovely and flowery **Refugio** attached to the Hotel Mitru also offers comfortable rooms for US$3.50 per person, including use of the kitchen. In the garden, you can eat or write your letters and post cards at chunky tables made from slices of enormous tree trunks. They also offer a book exchange, money exchange, laundry service and fax and Internet access.

Another decent spot is the friendly **Hostal Valle Hermoso** (*☎ 2370; Pedro Arraya 478*), which charges US$2 per person; seven-minute showers cost an additional US$0.75 and a continental breakfast is US$1 (an American one is US$2). They also have a book exchange, sauna (US$2 per session) and laundry service, and they are now organizing tours and horseback riding in the Tupiza hinterlands (if you go, please write and let us know how it went). You may want to see their website, www.bolivia.freehosting.net, which was kindly created for them by a satisfied (and apparently enthusiastic) Dutch guest.

The comfortable **Hotel Centro** (*☎ 2705*), on Avenida Santa Cruz, charges US$3 per person for a room with private bath. It's clean, but don't put too much faith in their claims about having hot water. A popular, good-value option is the cozy-sounding **Residencial My Home** (*☎ 2947; Avaroa 288*), charging US$2.50 per person (US$4 with bath). A cheaper alternative is **Alojamiento El Rancho**, where you'll pay US$1.20 for a very basic room without water.

Places to Eat

In the afternoon, stalls outside the train station serve filling meals of rice, salad, potatoes and a main dish for US$1. The inexpensive market foods are especially good for breakfast. For a real morning treat, head for Mercado Negro after around 8:30 am, when the renowned Doña Wala starts serving up her fabulous charque-filled tamales for US$0.20 (go early because she always sells out). Her stall is just outside the market, to the right of the entrance.

You'll find Tupiza's best salteñas at friendly **Il Bambino**, which also offers excellent-value almuerzos for US$1.20. In the afternoon, you can snack on empanadas, pasteles and other savories. It's open all day every day except weekend evenings.

The friendly Internet café **Cyber Snack Heladería**, run by Gualberto and Laura, serves up sandwiches, tea, coffee and ice cream 8 am to 10 pm daily. You can also try their specialty drink, *ratapía*, which is homemade singani with white wine. Broiled and rotisserie chicken are the specialties at **Confitería Paris**, on Avenida Santa Cruz near Avaroa. **Bar Restaurant Tuercas** does inexpensive almuerzos, but it's often haunted by irritating drunks.

The Hotel Mitru Anexo's **Los Helechos**, the only restaurant that keeps reliable hours, sets the scene with a cactus skeleton done up in colored Christmas lights. The Continental and American breakfasts are especially inviting, served with quince jam and real coffee. Later in the day, they do good burgers, milanesa, chicken, and a host of international dishes. As a novelty, try one of their cocktails involving such tipples as sake, tequila, vodka, rum and of course, singani.

SOUTHERN ALTIPLANO

Also recommended is **Sede Social Ferroviaria**, the railway workers' club, which serves good-value parrillada and other meat-based Bolivian dishes. For pizza, you can make an attempt to eat at *Pizzería Palace*, which is open only sporadic hours.

Entertainment

Karaoke has arrived in Tupiza. For a novelty evening, check out bizarre **Club DA Melodía**, also known as La Pantera Rosa, which does drinks and offers a slew of Spanish-language pop hits. The only English-language offerings are old Beatles tunes.

At both Hotel Mitru and Hostal Valle Hermoso, you can watch the video *Butch Cassidy & the Sundance Kid* any evening you like.

Getting There & Away

Bus Tupiza now has a bus terminal, where several flotas leave morning and evening for Potosí (eight hours, US$4.50), Tarija (eight hours, US$4) and Villazón (two hours, US$2). On Monday and Thursday, Flota 11 de Julio and Flota La Predilecta leave for Uyuni at noon (10 to 12 hours, US$5).

Camión Thanks to mining activities on the Altiplano west of town, there's a relatively good network of crisscrossing roads. There's no public transport, but you can hitch lifts with the camiones that service the mines, foundries, geological camps and health posts scattered between Tupiza and the Chilean and Argentine frontiers. Camiones to Uyuni leave in the early morning from Calle Charcas, east of Plazuela El Mundo, a traffic circle identified by an enormous globe.

Train The ticket window has no set opening hours, so ask for local advice regarding when to line up. The *Expreso del Sur* leaves for Oruro (11 hours, US$10.50/16.50/21 in salón/premier/ejecutivo classes), via Uyuni (4¾ hours, US$5/8/10), at 7 am Tuesday and 6:30 pm Saturday, and for Villazón (three hours, US$2.50/4/5) at 9:25 pm Friday. The *Wara Wara del Sur* runs to Uyuni (5½ hours, US$3.50) and Oruro (13 hours, US$7.50)

Monday and Thursday 7 pm and to Villazón (three hours, US$2) Sunday and Wednesday 8:40 am.

AROUND TUPIZA

Much of Tupiza's appeal lies in the surrounding landscape. Hiking opportunities abound and even within 5km of town, the mazes of ridges, quebradas and canyons provide a good sampling of what the country has to offer. Occasionally, the Instituto Geográfico Militar (IGM) office on the plaza sells topographic sheets of the area. Otherwise, you can pick them up in La Paz, but even without a map it would be difficult to get lost.

Hikers should carry at least 3L of water per day in this dry desert climate. It's wise to wear shoes that can withstand assault by prickly desert vegetation, and to carry a compass or GPS if you're venturing away from the tracks. Flash flooding is also a danger, especially in the summer months; avoid camping in the quebradas, especially if it looks like rain.

Quebrada de Palala

Just northwest of Tupiza is the broad wash known as the Quebrada de Palala, which is lined with some very impressive red conglomerate formations known as *fins*. During the rainy season, it becomes a tributary of the Río Tupiza, but in the winter months, it serves as a highway into the backcountry and part of the salt route from the Salar de Uyuni to Tarija. Beyond the dramatic red rocks, the wash rises very gently into hills colored greenish blue and violet by lead and other mineral deposits.

To get started, head north on Avenida La Paz from Plazuela El Mundo to the campesino market; 2km ahead, along the railroad line, you'll see the mouth of the quebrada. Along the way, look for the two little vicuñas that reside in the children's playground, near the edge of town. About 5km farther along, the route passes some obvious fin formations and continues up the broad quebrada into increasingly lonely country, past stands of cactus and scrub brush.

AROUND TUPIZA

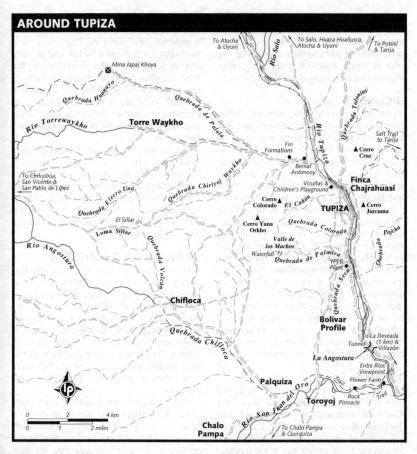

El Sillar

About 2.5km past the first large fin formations in the Quebrada de Palala, the road turns sharply left and begins to climb up the steeper and narrower Quebrada Chiriyoj Waykho. After another 10km of winding and ascending, you'll reach El Sillar (The Saddle), where the road straddles a narrow ridge between two peaks and two valleys. Throughout this area, rugged amphitheaters have been gouged out of the mountainsides and eroded into spires that resemble China's Shilin Stone Forest.

The distance from Tupiza to El Sillar is 16km; if you follow this road for another 3½ hours (95km), you'll reach San Vicente, of Butch and Sundance fame (see 'The Last Days of Butch Cassidy & the Sundance Kid,' later in this chapter). This entire route is part of a centuries-old trade route, and from May to early July, you'll see trains of llamas, alpacas and donkeys carrying blocks of salt mined in the Salar de Uyuni to trade in Tarija, a total distance of nearly 300km.

In Tupiza, you can arrange a taxi for up to five people to El Sillar or other sites in the area for US$4 per hour, which isn't bad, especially with a group – and because you're paying by the hour, the drivers will accommodate as many photo stops as you like. The folks at Tupiza Tours (☎ 3001) can arrange day tours or recommend specific drivers.

El Cañón

El Cañón, a lovely walk west of Tupiza through a narrow twisting canyon past dramatic fin formations, makes a great half-day stroll from town. It gently ascends for 2.5km along a sandy riverbed, to end at a waterfall. There are several good campsites along the route, but any rainfall will raise the risk of flash flooding in this constricted watercourse.

From town, the route begins along Calle Chuquisaca, heading west past the military barracks and cemetery (the route is obvious from the summit of Cerro Corazón de Jesús). The road then narrows to a sandy track paralleling the mountains. Here you'll have good views of some spectacular fin formations and steep cactus-filled ravines, backed by red hills. Bear left here and follow the narrowing quebrada into the hills. Along this route, two stone and chicken-wire fences block the way, but they're not too difficult to climb.

Quebrada Seca

Near the YPFB plant south of town, a road turns southwest into Quebrada Seca (Dry Wash). Unfortunately, the lower reaches of Quebrada Seca serve as a rubbish tip, but if you continue up the wash, the trash thins out and the route passes into some spectacular red-rock country. At the intersection, the right fork climbs the hill toward the village of Palquiza and the left fork crosses the Río San Juan del Oro, eventually losing itself in the side canyons opening into the main channel. This is a particularly beautiful route, and it's a good place to see condors.

During the dry season, hikers can turn left just before the Río San Rafael bridge (10km south of Tupiza) and follow the river's northern bank to Entre Ríos. If you wade the Río Tupiza at this point, you can return to town via the road coming from Villazón.

Quebrada de Palmira

Between Tupiza and Quebrada Seca lies the wonderful Quebrada de Palmira, a normally dry wash flanked by tall and precarious fin formations. The right fork of the wash is rather comically known as Valle de los Machos (Valley of Males) or the less genteel Valle de los Penes (Valley of Penises). The names stem from the crowds of exceptionally phallic pedestal formations that line it.

At the head of the main fork of the quebrada, you can ascend along a trickle of calcium-rich fresh water, up over boulders and through rock grottoes, into a hidden world beneath steep canyon walls. About 300m up the canyon you'll find several excellent campsites with some water available most of the year.

La Angostura & Entre Ríos

Eight kilometers south of town, the Río Tupiza narrows to squeeze through La Angostura (The Narrows), a tight opening in the rock. Here the Villazón road is conducted past it through a rock tunnel, with views through to the churning waters below.

As you approach La Angostura from Tupiza, watch along the ridge west of the river for the formation known as Bolívar, a rock outcrop resembling a profile of the liberator.

There's a nice view across the confluence of the Ríos Tupiza and San Juan del Oro from the lay-by at Entre Ríos, 10km south of Tupiza. Here you can ford the Río Tupiza on foot, pass some very nice flower farms, cross the railway bridge across the Río San Juan del Oro and follow it upstream for 1km to an unusual rock pinnacle.

La Deseada

The name La Deseada means 'The Desired.' This shady little spot beside the Río Tupiza, 12km south of town, has a broad flat area for camping near the river bank and is a favorite picnic site for Tupiza people. To get there, cross the Calle Beni bridge from Tupiza and look for a ride at the tranca on the Villazón road.

Huaca Huañusca

On November 4, 1908, Butch Cassidy and the Sundance Kid pulled off the last robbery of their careers when they politely and peacefully relieved Carlos Peró of the Aramayo company payroll, which amounted to US$90,000, at the foot of a hill called Huaca Huañusca. The name, which means 'dead cow,' was apparently applied because of the hill's resemblance to a fallen bovine.

From an obvious pass on the ridge, a walking track descends the steep slopes to the west for about 2km to the river, where there's a small meadow, a tiny cave (called a *cuevilla* in the description provided by the victim of the robbery) and some rugged rock outcrops where the bandits probably holed up awaiting the payroll to pass.

Of special interest along the route from Tupiza is the village of Salo, where a local woman produces the world's best cheese and onion empanadas – coming from Tupiza, it's the first house on the right; also delicious is the local *asado de chivo* (charbroiled goat). Along the way, you can marvel at red spires, pinnacles (the most prominent is known as La Poronga, a crude Argentine expression denoting a feature of male anatomy), canyons, tall cactus and tiny adobe villages. Note the incongruous telephone boxes in these settlements; thanks to ENTEL's experimental rural communications program, they provide direct dialing services to anywhere in the world!

SAN VICENTE

Kid, the next time I say let's go someplace like Bolivia, let's go someplace *like* Bolivia!

– Paul Newman in the film
Butch Cassidy & the Sundance Kid

This one-mule village, at 4800m above sea level, wouldn't even rate a mention were it not the legendary spot where the outlaws Robert LeRoy Parker and Harry Alonzo Longabaugh – better known as Butch Cassidy and the Sundance Kid – met their untimely demise. The mine in San Vicente is now closed and the place has declined into little more

than a ghost town, with a population of just 40. Most of those remaining are military people, mine security guards and their families.

San Vicente has become a bit of a pilgrimage site for Butch and Sundance fans, as well as for travelers taken with the lure of the Old West. That still amounts to only a trickle of visitors, however, and San Vicente continues to lack any semblance of tourist infrastructure. You can still see the adobe house where the bandits holed up and eventually died, the cemetery where they were buried and the sign welcoming visitors to the town: 'Here death's Butch Kasidy Sundance the Kid.' Someone knows we foreigners are interested in the place but probably doesn't have a clue why!

Places to Stay & Eat

The hotel and adjoining El Rancho restaurant are now closed, so overnight stays will invariably involve camping at this high, cold altitude. Bread is available at the village **bakery**, identifiable by morning lines, and you'll find grocery staples – canned milk, sardines, biscuits, soft drinks and beer – in the tiny unmarked **tienda** uphill from the main street. Occasionally, a **kiosk** on the plaza dishes up plates of llama fricassee.

Getting There & Away

There's no regular public transport to remote San Vicente from Tupiza, but a bus does leave for the world's largest working antimony mine at Chilcobija on Monday, Thursday and Saturday from in front of the Colegio Antofagasta on Calle Santa Cruz. From there, it's a good 60km by road on to San Vicente; it's walkable, but you'll need good cold-weather gear.

Very occasionally, a camión leaves for San Vicente early on Thursday morning from just over the railway line from Plazuela El Mundo in Tupiza, but it's mainly dependent on the current economic situation in San Vicente (which hasn't been too good of late). The route runs via El Sillar and the northward turning at the village of Nazarenito; this is also part of the salt route from the Salar de Uyuni.

The Last Days of Butch Cassidy & the Sundance Kid

Butch

The Kid

Butch and Sundance came to southern Bolivia in August 1908 and took up residence with the Briton AG Francis, who was transporting a gold dredge on the Río San Juan del Oro. While casing banks to finance their retirement, the outlaws learned of an even sweeter target: a poorly guarded US$480,000 (at the time, that was B$80,000) mine-company payroll to be hauled by mule from Tupiza to Quechisla.

On November 3, 1908, manager Carlos Peró picked up a packet of cash from Aramayo, Francke & Compañía in Tupiza and headed north with his 10-year-old son and a servant, but they were discreetly tailed by Butch and Sundance. Peró's party overnighted in Salo, then set off again at dawn. As the trio ascended the hill called Huaca Huañusca, the bandits watched from above with binoculars. In a rugged spot on the far side of the hill, they relieved Peró of a handsome mule and the remittance, which turned out to be a mere US$90,000 (B$15,000) – the prized payroll had been slated for shipment the following week.

Dispirited, Butch and Sundance returned to AG Francis' headquarters at Tomahuaico. The following day, Francis guided them to Estarca, where the three of them spent the night. On the morning of November 6, the bandits bade farewell to Francis and headed west to San Vicente.

Meanwhile, Peró had sounded the alarm, and posses were scouring southern Bolivia. A four-man contingent from Uyuni reached San Vicente that afternoon. Butch and Sundance arrived at dusk, rented a room from Bonifacio Casasola, and sent him to fetch supper. The posse came to investigate and had scarcely entered the courtyard when Butch shot and killed a soldier. During the brief gunfight that ensued, Sundance was badly wounded. Realizing that escape was impossible, Butch ended Sundance's misery with a shot between the eyes, then fired a bullet into his own temple.

At the inquest, Carlos Peró identified the corpses as those of the men who had robbed him. Although buried as *desconocidos* (unknowns) in the cemetery, the outlaws fit descriptions of Butch and Sundance, and a mountain of circumstantial evidence points to their having met their doom in San Vicente. For example, Santiago Lowe, Butch's well-known alias, was recently found among the hotel guest list published in the Tupiza newspaper just a few days before the Aramayo holdup, which confirms eyewitness accounts that he was there. Nonetheless, rumors of their return to the USA have made their fate one of the great mysteries of the American West.

In 1991, when a team led by forensic anthropologist Clyde Snow attempted to settle the question by excavating the bandits' grave, no one in the village had any knowledge of its location, except one elderly – and as it turned out, imaginative – gentleman, who led them to a specific tombstone. The grave's sole occupant turned out to be a German miner named Gustav Zimmer (who might well have been the legendary German – clearly a Darwin Award candidate – who blew himself up while trying to defrost dynamite on the stove).

– Anne Meadows & Daniel Buck, USA

(Anne Meadows is the author of *Digging up Butch & Sundance*, Bison Books, University of Nebraska Press, 1996); website http://ourworld.compuserve.com/homepages/danne

The easiest way to go is with Tupiza Tours, which takes four hours each way; see Organized Tours under Tupiza, earlier in this chapter. Although Tupiza taxi drivers may be willing to take you to San Vicente, the road is now so poor that nothing less than a high-clearance 4WD can get through.

VILLAZÓN
☎ 0696

Villazón, the most popular border crossing between Bolivia and Argentina, is a dusty, haphazard settlement that contrasts sharply with relatively tidy La Quiaca, Argentina, just over the border. In addition to being a point of entry, Villazón is a warehousing and marketing center for contraband (food products, electronic goods and alcohol) being smuggled into Bolivia on the backs of peasants, who form a human cargo train across the frontier. This is known as the *comercio de hormigos* (ant trade). Much of Argentina's Jujuy province is populated by Bolivian expats, and migration into Argentina continues, lending Villazón the nickname the 'Tijuana of Bolivia.'

From October to April, there's a one-hour time difference between Bolivia and Argentina (noon in Villazón is 1 pm in La Quiaca). From May to September, the Argentine province of Jujuy, where La Quiaca is located, operates on Bolivian time (only a bit more efficiently).

Information
Consulates The helpful Argentine Consulate, upstairs in the Galería Ojeda, is open Monday to Friday 10 am to noon and 2 to 5 pm.

Money To change US dollars cash or Argentine pesos into bolivianos, you'll get reasonable rates from the tour agencies and casas de cambio along Avenida República Argentina. Not all places offer the same rates, so shop around. If dollars are in demand, Casa de Cambio Trebol will change traveler's checks, but at a poor rate with 5% commission.

Post & Communications There are post and telephone offices on both sides of the border, but the Bolivian services are generally cheaper.

Dangers & Annoyances You'll need to be more on your guard in Villazón than other parts of Bolivia. I've encountered several 'fake police' scams there, and on my most recent trip, a bus station baggage handler attempted to disappear with my pack into a warehouse across the street. Readers also report some problems, mainly pickpockets, sneak thieves and the usual scams. Counterfeit US dollar bills (notes) are also making appearances.

Places to Stay
The nicest spot in town is ***Hostal Plaza*** (☎ 535; Plaza 6 de Agosto 138), which charges US$4.20 per person (US$8.50 with bath) and cable TV. It has a dining room as well.

Villazón also has a couple of economical hotels and alojamientos. An excellent choice is the clean and friendly ***Residencial Martínez*** (☎ 562), near the bus terminal. Singles/doubles without bath cost US$4/6. The hot showers are a real plus, and operate without an electric attachment. A travelers' favorite is the clean and cozy ***Residencial El Cortijo*** (☎ 209; 20 de Mayo 338), two blocks from the bus terminal. Rooms with shared bath cost US$4/7.

As for the ***Grand Palace Hotel*** (☎ 333; 25 de Mayo 52), don't be taken in by the name – or the advertising for the *pista de patinaje* (skating rink), which appears to be used only as a disco. It's not that bad at US$3 per person without bath, but service is indifferent and the atmosphere less than friendly.

Another cheap option is ***Alojamiento Quillacollo*** (☎ 399), on Avenida República Argentina. It's a real dump but costs only US$2 per person.

Places to Eat
For meals, there isn't much choice. The first option would be the dining room at the Hotel Plaza, followed distantly by ***Charke Kan Restaurant***, opposite the bus terminal, which is good but rather grimy. The owners are keen on music, and a bizarre round

VILLAZÓN & LA QUIACA

PLACES TO STAY
1 Residencial El Cortijo
6 Grand Palace Hotel
7 Residencial Martínez
10 Hostal Plaza
10 Alojamiento Quillacollo
19 Hotel Frontera
20 Hotel Crystal
24 Hotel de Turismo

PLACES TO EAT
5 Charke Kan Restaurant
9 Snack El Pechegón
16 La Tabita
17 Parrillada El Buen Gusto
18 Rosita
23 Club Atlético Argentino

OTHER
2 ENTEL
3 Post Office
4 Church
11 Argentine Consulate
12 Casa de Cambio Trebol
13 Bolivian Customs & Immigration
14 Argentine Customs & Immigration
15 Gas Station; ACA Representative
21 Bus Terminal
22 Cooperativa Telefónica
26 Banco de la Nación Argentina
27 Post Office
28 Bolivian Consulate

To Train Station (150 m), Tupiza, Uyuni & Oruro

Cochabamba

Market

Av República Argentina

Villazón Bus Terminal

Plaza

Tupiza

Choroloje

VILLAZÓN

BOLIVIA

Río Villazón

ARGENTINA

Av Internacional

LA QUIACA

Entre Ríos

Exodo Jujeño

Av España

Av Bolivar

Balcarce

República de Arabe Siria

Av Sarmiento

Av San Martín

9 de Julio

Belgrano

25 de Mayo

Sánchez de Bustamante

Rivadavia

Güemes

12 de Octubre

Salta

C Pellegrini

Market

Av Hipólito Yrigoyen

La Quiaca Train Station

Plaza

To Yavi

To Jujuy

To Jujuy

San Juan

Catamarca

La Madrid

Av Santiago del Estero

0   100   200 m
0   100   200 yards

record player hums in the background. Quick chicken and Bolivian staples are offered at **Snack El Pechegón**. In the market food stalls, which make up in price what they lack in variety, you'll find delicious *licuados* and fruit juices – incongruous treats in this climate. Alternatively, pop over to La Quiaca for meals (see La Quiaca, later in this chapter).

Getting There & Away

Bus All northbound buses depart from the central terminal; passengers pay US$0.20 to use the terminal. Tickets and reservations for Argentine buses are sold at the offices opposite the main terminal entrance, or in La Quiaca. All buses to Argentina leave from the main terminal in La Quiaca.

Flotas leave for Tupiza in the morning and afternoon (two hours, US$2). It's a beautiful trip, so go in the morning (the first bus is at 6:45 am) for maximum daylight viewing. There are also at least five daily buses to Potosí via Tupiza (10 hours, US$8), with connections to Sucre, Cochabamba and La Paz.

There are several nightly buses to Tarija, which leave daily between 7 and 8 pm (eight hours, US$3); it's too bad they travel at night, because the canyon country scenery – and the treacherous road – is exceptionally dramatic. From Tarija, Flota Trans Yacuiba continues along the equally beautiful route to Villamontes (20 hours, US$10) and Yacuiba (22 hours, US$10).

Train The *Expreso del Sur* leaves for Oruro (11¼ hours, US$12/18.50/23.50 in salón/premier/ejecutivo classes), via Tupiza (three hours, US$2.50/4/5) and Uyuni (eight hours, US$7/12/15), on Saturday at 3:30 pm. The *Wara Wara del Sur* heads for Tupiza (three hours, US$2), Uyuni (nine hours, US$5.50) and Oruro (16¾ hours, US$9.50) on Monday and Thursday at 3:30 pm. There's no longer onward rail service into Argentina.

Crossing into Argentina Villazón has an Argentine consulate and La Quiaca has a Bolivian consulate. For quick trips over the border, just walk straight across the bridge;

you don't have to go through immigration unless you're staying more than a couple of hours. Crossing the border is usually no problem, but avoid the contrabandistas' procession; otherwise it may take you hours to get through. Bolivian immigration is open 7 am to 7 pm and doesn't close for lunch. If the Argentine official is working alone, the post closes for lunch between noon and 2 pm.

Entering Argentina, both drivers and bus passengers can count on an exhaustive customs search about 20km south of the border. The entry/exit tax occasionally charged by Bolivian immigration officers is strictly unofficial.

LA QUIACA (ARGENTINA)
☎ (54) 0388

Villazón's twin town of La Quiaca lies at an altitude of 3442m, just across the Río Villazón in northern Argentina. The contrast between the two sides is striking; La Quiaca is a neatly groomed town with tree-lined avenues, surfaced streets, pleasant restaurants and well-stocked shops.

Information

There's no tourist office, but you'll find Argentine maps at the Automóvil Club Argentino (ACA), near the corner of RN9 and Sánchez de Bustamante.

Consulates The Bolivian consulate, at the corner of San Juan and Árabe Siria, is open weekdays 8:30 to 11 am and 2 to 5 pm. On Saturday, it opens 9 am to noon. It charges a hefty US$15 for visas.

Money On the Argentine side, US dollars are legal tender, and dollars and Argentine pesos are exchanged at a par. However, dollar bills with even the slightest flaw aren't accepted anywhere. Note that the province of Jujuy issues its own peso banknotes, which resemble Monopoly money and may be used only within the province.

Post & Communications Correo Argentino is at San Juan and Sarmiento, and the Cooperativa Telefónica is at Avenida

España and 25 de Mayo. The post is generally more reliable in Argentina than in Bolivia, and collect (reverse-charge) phone calls are accepted to limited areas.

Iglesia de San Francisco

If you're continuing into Argentina, a visit to Yavi, 15km east of La Quiaca, is recommended. Here you'll find the tiny Iglesia de San Francisco, built in 1680, which has an ornately gilded interior and translucent onyx windows. It's open Tuesday from 9 am to noon and 3 to 6 pm, and on Saturday from 9 am to noon. Find the caretaker, who can open the door and show you around.

From the bus terminal, the Flota El Quiaqueño serves Yavi, Abra Pampa and other nearby communities. Alternatively, there's a camioneta to Yavi every half hour or so from the Mercado Municipal on Avenida Hipólito Yrigoyen.

Places to Stay

The mid-range *Hotel Crystal* (☎ 452255; Sarmiento 543) charges US$17/28 for a single/double with bath and heat. Triples/quadruples cost US$38/46. Rooms without bath cost US$7 per person. Request the one that shares a wall with the bakery; it's almost as good as having a heater! The best value is the clean *Hotel de Turismo* (☎ 542243; fax 452201), on Árabe Siria at San Martín, where rates are US$25/35 with bath, breakfast and TV. They do have radiators, but they fire them up only in July. *Hotel Frontera*, on Belgrano, costs US$8 per person with shared bath. There's no heating, but you can get an electric shower.

Places to Eat

The food is generally better here than in Villazón, and it's worth tripping across the border for a meal, but as you'd expect in Argentina, menus are heavily weighted in favor of carnivores. The Hotel de Turismo has a warm dining room with a stone fireplace. An immense steak with french fries goes for US$5. The unassuming *Confitería La Frontera*, at Hotel Frontera, serves nice *tortillas españolas* and luscious *tallarines al pesto*, with real pesto sauce, for US$4. Four-course set-menu almuerzos cost a very reasonable US$3.50. Service can be a bit surly at times, but the food is sure to make up for it.

El Buen Gusto, a parillada on Avenida España between 9 de Julio and Belgrano, has decent food but an agonizingly slow kitchen. *La Tabita*, on España at Belgrano, is also a parillada. *Rosita*, on 9 de Julio between Balcarce and Árabe Siria, has simple inexpensive meals and fine takeout empandas. Also worth a look is *Club Atlético Argentino*, at the corner of Balcarce and 25 de Mayo.

Getting There & Away

Buses depart from the Terminal de Omnibuses at the corner of España and Belgrano, and most long-distance services offer heat, air-conditioning, video and onboard facilities. Several flotas leave almost hourly for Humahuaca and San Salvador de Jujuy (nine hours, US$14). The trip passes through some stunningly colorful, cactus-studded landscapes. From Jujuy, you'll find frequent connections to Salta, Cafayate, Rosario and Córdoba and Buenos Aires. Additionally, Andesmar offers daily connections to Santiago (Chile) and destinations all over Argentina, including Bariloche and Santa Cruz de Patagonia.

Central Highlands

Dominating the Bolivian interior, the Central Highlands remain home to an array of wonders and terrors sure to amaze, startle or shock travelers. Visitors to the region have the opportunity to reach back through the eons and touch traces of long-disappeared beasts, to marvel at the faded splendor of unimaginable riches, to recoil from still-horrifying labor conditions, and to experience local traditions that remain steadfastly free from commercialization and its accompanying dilution. These features, in addition to a proud colonial heritage and some of Bolivia's most beautiful and starkly surreal landscapes, render the region ideal for independent exploration.

Perhaps nowhere is the versatile character of the Central Highlands as evident as in the attitude of its people. Aware of their cities' storied histories and secure in their belief that theirs is one of the most beautiful and enchanting homes on earth, the inhabitants of the region live with a quiet dignity that reflects both their pride in a glorious past and their anticipation of a bright future.

Highlights

- Shop for just about anything imaginable at Cochabamba's vast, nerve-shattering, crowded and colorful La Cancha market

- Relax beside a waterfall in Parque Nacional Torotoro, bathe in idyllic swimming holes, and view fossilized dinosaur footprints

- Soak up Sucre's colonial charms

- Walk the brilliantly colored green-and-violet hillsides of the Cráter de Maragua and beyond into the Cordillera de los Frailes, and seek out the beautiful and colorful Jalq'a and Candelaria weavings

- Discover the Potosí's grand colonial architectural heritage, which dates from the time when this, the world's highest city, was larger than London or Shanghai

- Witness the appalling conditions inside the Potosí Cooperative Mines

- Tour the historical treasures held behind meter-thick walls in the icy interior of the restored colonial mint, Casa Real de la Moneda – but whatever the weather, put on your thermal underwear first

Cochabamba

☎ 04

Cochabamba, a progressive and active city, has a growing population of over 400,000 and a vitality that is visibly absent from the more traditional higher-altitude cities. The saying *'Las golondrinas nunca migran de Cochabamba'* ('The swallows never migrate from Cochabamba') aptly describes what *cochabambinos* believe is the world's most comfortable climate, with warm, dry, sunny days and cool nights. Despite its recent *crise económico* (economic crisis), Cochabamba maintains a positive and optimistic outlook for the future; perhaps that's a product of its idyllic climate and industrious populace.

The city's name is derived by joining the Quechua words *khocha* and *pampa*, meaning 'swampy plain.' Cochabamba lies

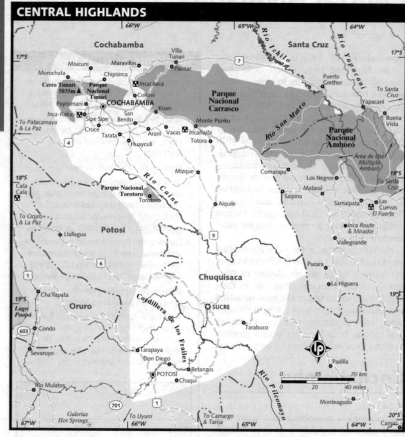

CENTRAL HIGHLANDS

in a fertile green bowl, 25km long by 10km wide, set in a landscape of fields and low hills. To the northwest rises 5035m Cerro Tunari, the highest peak in central Bolivia. The area's rich soil yields abundant crops of maize, barley, wheat, alfalfa, and orchard and citrus fruits.

Apart from the climate, however, there's little for tourists. Once you've seen the museums and done some shopping, it's time to head for the hinterlands. At some point, try to sample *chicha cochabambina*, an alcoholic maize brew typical of the region.

History

Cochabamba was founded in January 1574 by Sebastián Barba de Padilla. It was originally named Villa de Oropeza in honor of the Count and Countess of Oropeza, parents of Viceroy Francisco de Toledo, who chartered and promoted its settlement.

During the height of Potosí's silver boom, the Cochabamba Valley developed into the primary source of food for the miners in agriculturally unproductive Potosí. Thanks to its maize and wheat production, Cochabamba came to be the 'breadbasket of

Bolivia.' When Potosí declined in importance during the early 18th century, so did Cochabamba, and grain production in the Chuquisaca (Sucre) area, much closer to Potosí, was sufficient to supply the decreasing demand.

By the mid-19th century, however, the economic crisis stabilized, and the city again assumed its position as the nation's granary. Elite landowners in the valley grew wealthy and began investing in highland mining ventures in western Bolivia. Before long, the Altiplano mines were attracting international capital, and the focus of Bolivian mining shifted from Potosí to southwestern Bolivia. As a result, Cochabamba thrived and its European/mestizo population gained a reputation for affluence and prosperity.

Orientation

Cochabamba's central business district lies roughly between the Río Rocha in the north and Colina San Sebastián and Laguna Alalay in the southwest and southeast, respectively.

The largest market areas are on or south of Avenida Aroma, sandwiched between Colina San Sebastián and Laguna Alalay. The long-distance bus terminal and most of the intravalley bus terminals are also in this vicinity.

Cochabamba addresses are measured from Plaza 14 de Septiembre and are preceded by 'N' *(norte)*, 'S' *(sud)*, 'E' *(este)* or 'O' *(oeste* – to avoid alphanumeric confusion, a 'W' is sometimes used instead). Obviously, these stand for 'north,' 'south,' 'east' and 'west,' respectively.

Maps The tourist office sells very nice city maps for US$1.50. See the Instituto Geográfico Militar (☎ 255563 or 227965; 16 de Julio S-0237) for topo sheets from around the Cochabamba department.

Information

Tourist Offices The tourist office (☎ 223364), which occupies a glass kiosk beside ENTEL, dispenses visitor information on weekdays from 8:30 am to 6:30 pm and on Saturday from 8:30 am to noon. Good maps of the city cost US$2.

Chicha Cochabambina

Chicha quiero, chicha busco,
Por chicha mis paseos.
Señora, deme un vasito
Para cumplir mis deseos.

This longing old Bolivian verse cries, 'I want chicha, I search for chicha, for chicha are my wanderings. Lady, give me a glass to satisfy my longing.'

To most Bolivians, Cochabamba is known for one of two things: Romantics will dreamily remark on its luscious climate, whereas hardcore imbibers, such as the author of the above poem, will identify Cochabamba with its luscious chicha cochabambina. Both images of the city are well founded.

Throughout the valley and around much of southern Cochabamba department, you'll see white cloth or plastic flags flying on long poles, indicating that chicha is available. Traveling outside the town, you'll realize just how popular it is – and, at 2570m elevation, it does pack a good punch!

Information on Parques Nacionales Torotoro, Isiboro-Sécure and Carrasco can be found at the Servicio Nacional de Áreas Protegidas, or SENAP (☎ 235660; fax 259173; Julián María López 1194, Calle Calama extension, Casilla 4633).

Consulates Consular representatives in Cochabamba include:

Argentina Calle Federico Blanco O-929 (☎ 229347); open weekdays 8:30 am to 1 pm.

Brazil Edificio Los Tiempos II, 9th floor (☎ 255860); open weekdays 8:30 to 11:30 am and 2:30 to 5:30 pm.

Chile Avenida de las Heroínas at Lanza E-620 (☎ 253095); open weekdays 8:30 am to 1 pm.

Germany Edificio Promontora, 6th floor (☎ 254024); open weekdays 10 am to noon.

Peru Avenida Pando 1325, Recoleta (☎ 240296); open weekdays 8 am to noon and 2 to 6 pm.

USA Torres Sofer, Bloque A, Oficina 601 (☎ 256714); open weekdays 9 am to noon.

CENTRAL HIGHLANDS

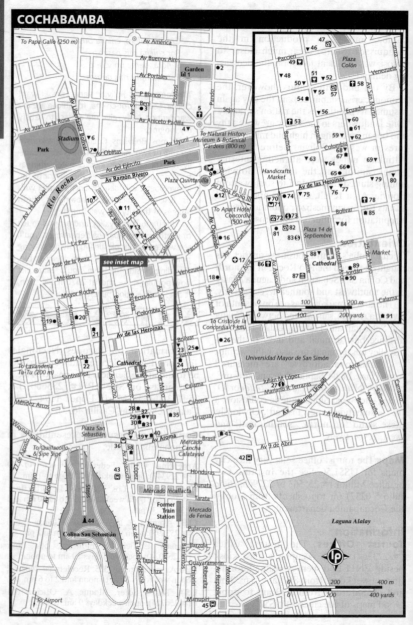

COCHABAMBA

COCHABAMBA

PLACES TO STAY
11 Pensión La Suiza
20 Hostal Jardín
21 Hostal Colonial
22 Hostal Central
24 Residencial Familiar
28 Alojamiento Cochabamba;
   Alojamiento Roma
29 Mary Hotel
30 Alojamiento Escobar
31 Residencial Escobar
35 Hostal Jordán II
38 Hostal Elisa
40 Hotel Americano; Rodizio Grill
   Americano
41 Hostal Jordán
54 Gran Hotel Ambassador
61 Residencial Familiar Anexo
67 Hotel Boston
85 Caesar's Plaza
89 City Hotel
91 Hostal Florida

PLACES TO EAT
4 La Estancia
6 Churrasquería Tunari
10 McDonald's
13 Savarín
14 El Paseo
15 Sucre Manta; Top Chop
23 Café Express Bolívar
33 El Caminante
34 Marvi
37 Churrasquería Hawaii
39 Palmar Restaurante Familiar
46 Govinda
48 El Palacio del Silpancho

50 La Cantonata
52 Pancho's
55 Café Bistro El Carajillo
56 Metrópolis
59 La Salsa Café
60 Eli's Pizza Express
62 Rondevu
63 Metrópolis Club
64 Café Frances
68 Confitería Bambi
69 Tea Room Zürich
70 Porkie's
75 Unicornio
76 Cristal
77 Heladería Dumbo
79 Confitería Cecy
80 Snack Uno
84 Restaurant Lose
88 Burger Plaza

OTHER
1 Simón I Patiño Cultural
   Center
2 IC Norte
3 Discoteca Lujos
5 Iglesia de la Recoleta
7 AeroSur
8 Brazilian Consulate
9 Nostalgias
12 Galería Torres Sofer: Rodizio
   Búfalo; US Consulate; Los
   Amigos del Libro
16 Caminante Equipo de
   Camping
18 Lavandería Tu-Tu
17 Hospital Viedma
19 Viajes Fremen

25 Instituto Cultural Boliviano-
   Alemán
26 Instituto Geográfico Nacional
   (IGM)
27 Servicio Nacional de Áreas
   Protegidas
32 Laboratorio Chagas
36 Micros to Quillacollo,
   Payrumani, Sipe Sipe
42 Micros & Buses to Chapare
43 Bus Terminal; Snack Terminal
44 Heroínas de la Coronilla
   Monument
45 Micros & Camiones to Tarata,
   Cliza, Arani, Punata, Aiquile,
   Mizque & Torotoro
47 Infonet Internet Netcafé Club
49 Viking Pub
51 Aladin's Pub
53 Convento de Santa Teresa
57 Ciberland I-Café
58 El Hospicio
65 Los Amigos del Libro
66 Casa de la Cultura
71 Post Office
72 ENTEL
73 Tourist Information
74 LAB Office
78 Iglesia & Convento de San
   Francisco
81 Los Amigos del Libro
82 Internet Alta Velocidad;
   Danielíssimo
83 Exprint-Bol
86 Iglesia de Santo Domingo
87 Archaeological Museum
90 Immigration

Immigration The Immigration office (☎ 225553), on Esteban Arce at Jordán, is the place to get visa and length-of-stay extensions.

Money The best places to change cash or traveler's checks are Exprint-Bol (☎ 254413; Plaza 14 de Septiembre O-0252) and American (☎ 222307; General Achá E-0162). Moneychangers gather around the ENTEL office and along Avenida de las Heroínas. Their rates are competitive, but they only accept US cash.

Visa cash advances are available at major banks and at Enlace machines around the city.

Post & Communications The post and ENTEL offices are both in the large complex on Avenida Ayacucho between General Achá and Avenida de las Heroínas. Postal service from Cochabamba is reliable and the facilities are among the country's finest. Downstairs from the main lobby is an express post office. ENTEL is open daily from 6:30 am to 10 pm. There's also one at the airport, but with more limited open hours.

A growing number of Internet cafés offer Internet and email access. One of the most popular is Internet Alta Velocidad, in the shopping arcade opposite the tourist office kiosk. They charge just US$1 per hour. The Ciberland I-Café, on 25 de Mayo at Mayor

Rocha, charges just a bit more. The Infonet Internet Netcafé Club, in the Edificio Colón mezzanine, is on Ballivián at México; it's open on weekends and holidays but closes for lunch. For their guests, most upmarket hotels, as well as the Hostal Elisa, offer Internet and email services.

Bookstores Los Amigos del Libro has several small outlets: at Avenida de las Heroínas E-0311 (☎ 254114; fax 0411-5128), at Calle General Achá E-110 (☎ 253878), in the Galería Torres Sofer (☎ 256471), and at the Aeropuerto Jorge Wilstermann. They sell a good range of English-, French- and German-language paperbacks (in fact, better than at their La Paz outlets), as well as reference books and souvenir publications. Among the *artesanía* stalls behind the post office are vendors selling Spanish-language literature and other books for reasonable and negotiable prices.

Film & Photography Slide film is sold at Foto Broadway (Colombia 283) and in the Korean-owned shops around the plaza. For camera repairs, you're better off going to La Paz, but in an emergency, try Maxell on the main plaza.

Cultural Centers Alliance Française (Santivañez O-187) and the Instituto Cultural Boliviano-Alemán (Sucre E-0693), at Antezana, sponsor cultural activities and have reading rooms with current newspapers and books in French and German, respectively. The reading room of the Centro Boliviano-Americano (☎ 221288; 25 de Mayo N-0567) is open weekdays from 9 am to noon and 3 to 9:30 pm. Its library, which is open until 7 pm, is limited to American literature.

Laundry Lavandería Tu-Tu (☎ 014-44718) has three outlets around town: on Ecuador at Oquendo, at Avenida Bolívar 1419 and at the corner of Heroínas and Abaroa. In one hour, they'll wash 5kg of clothing for just US$2. Most hotels also offer laundry services.

Medical Services Medical treatment is available at the Hospital Viedma, east of the center. If you might have been bitten by a vinchuca beetle, which carries Chagas' disease, take a test at the Laboratorio Chagas (☎ 222325 or 017-34672), on Calle Cabrera. The Chagas Institute at the Universidad San Simón also does testing and distributes information about the beetle and the disease.

Emergency The tourist police are available on ☎ 221793, 014-42953 and 019-62088. For police or an ambulance, phone ☎ 110; the fire brigade number is ☎ 119.

Dangers & Annoyances Readers have warned of impromptu passport checks and fines from fake police around the Colina San Sebastián; if you're stopped, ask to see some identification. If they continue to hassle you, insist that the matter be settled at the police station. Chances are the typically bogus 'officer' will retreat and look for an easier target.

In Cochabamba's rural hinterlands, be especially wary of vinchuca beetles, which live in thatched roofing and carry Chagas' disease (see Health in the Facts for the Visitor chapter, and Medical Services, earlier in this chapter).

Camping Equipment You'll find camping equipment at Berkman Sports Camping, Caza y Pesca (☎/fax 118466; San Martín S-0582) and Caminante Equipo de Camping, on Avenida Oquendo near Paccieri.

Churches

Cochabamba's churches are rarely open during the hours posted at the tourist office; you'll have the most luck in the early morning or late afternoon, on Saturday afternoon and on Sunday.

Cathedral The cathedral on the arcaded Plaza 14 de Septiembre was built in neoclassical style in 1571, making it the oldest religious structure in the valley. With a myriad of architecturally diverse additions over the years, the composition doesn't hang together well at all, but the frescoes and paintings inside are worth a look.

Iglesia & Convento de San Francisco Constructed in 1581, the Iglesia de San Francisco on Calle 25 de Mayo and Avenida Libertador Bolívar is Cochabamba's second-oldest church. Major revisions and renovation occurred in 1782 and 1925, however, and little of the original structure remains. The attached convent and cloister were added in the 1600s. In appreciation of the pleasant Cochabamba climate, the cloister was constructed of wood rather than the stone that was customary at the time. The pulpit displays fine examples of mestizo design. It opens at 9 am, when an obligatory guided tour is conducted.

Convento de Santa Teresa If you can look past the kitsch halo of lights over the altar, the interior of the Convento de Santa Teresa on Calle Baptista and Plaza Granado is quite impressive. It is actually a combination of two churches, one built on top of the other. Work on the first church was begun in 1753 by Jesuits. In theory, Santa Teresa is open from 7:30 to 8 am.

El Hospicio El Hospicio, on Plaza Colón, combines Baroque, Byzantine and neoclassical architectural styles. It was begun in 1875 and is the valley's most recent major church.

Iglesia de Santo Domingo The rococo-style Iglesia de Santo Domingo, on the corner of Calle Santiváñez and Avenida Ayacucho, was founded in 1612, but construction wasn't begun until 1778. When its chief promoter, Francisco Claros García, died in 1795, construction was still underway. The intriguing main doorway is flanked by two anthropomorphic columns.

Iglesia de la Recoleta The Iglesia de la Recoleta, north of the river, is a Baroque structure started in 1654. The attraction is a wooden carving entitled *Cristo de la Recoleta* that was hewn from a single piece of wood by Diego Ortiz de Guzmán.

Colina San Sebastián
This hill, just south of Avenida Aroma, towers over the airport and is a pleasant place to relax, read or watch the planes. There's also a nice view over the city. From San Sebastián a trail leads along a ridge to another hill, La Coronilla, with a monument dedicated to the women, children and senior citizens who courageously defended the city from the Spanish forces of José Manuel Goyeneche in 1812.

Museo Arqueológico
The Archaeological Museum, on Jordán between Ayacucho and Nataniel Aguirre, is one of Bolivia's finest. Exhibits include thousands of artifacts, dating from as early as 15,000 BC and as late as the colonial period.

Admission is US$1, and the excellent guided tour, conducted in English, French or Spanish, takes about 1½ hours. The museum is open Monday to Friday from 9 am to noon and 3 to 7 pm, and on Saturday from 9 am to 1 pm. Admission costs US$1.20.

Museo de la Historia Natural
The Natural History Museum and Botanical Gardens, once well displayed in the Casa de la Cultura, has been transferred to its current outpost in the botanical gardens. The insect collection, with thousands of beetles, bugs and butterflies, is impressive. Unfortunately, it's now crammed into an uncomfortably small room, making it difficult to appreciate. The museum also contains some colorful mineral specimens and a pathetic collection of moth-eaten stuffed animals.

The even less interesting **Martín Cárdenas Botanical Gardens** are little more than a four-hectare swath of dry grass studded with sickly shrubs and eucalyptus trees (they also include 6 hectares of wild bushland in the Serranía de San Pedro). For those who have nothing else to do, it's open from 6 am to 6 pm. Take Micro H from Avenida San Martín to Avenida Ramón Rivero at the end of Aniceto Arce.

Casa de la Cultura
The city archives, reading room and art exhibits are on the 3rd floor of the Casa de la Cultura (☎ 248030), on Avenida de las Heroínas at Calle 25 de Mayo. It's open

Monday to Friday from 9 am to noon and 2 to 6 pm, and admission is free. Ask the curator to show you the fascinating discoveries from Omereque, a pre-Inca burial site near Aiquile, southeast of Cochabamba. The faces bear an uncanny resemblance to the 'grays' – the alien types reported in UFO encounters around the world!

Simón I Patiño Cultural Center (Palacio de Portales)

The Palacio de Portales (☎ 243137; Potosí 1450), in the barrio of Queru Queru, provides evidence of the extravagance of tin baron Simón Patiño. Construction of this opulent home began in 1915 and the design, by French architect Eugene Bliault, was finalized in 1925. The building was completed two years later. Except perhaps for the brick, everything was imported: The fireplaces were constructed of flawless Carrera marble, the furniture and woodwork were carved in wood imported from France, and the walls were covered with silk brocade –

EDWARD AM SNIJDERS

Palacio de Portales

one intricate 'painting' is actually a woven silk tapestry. The gardens and exterior, which were inspired by the palace at Versailles, also reflect inconceivable affluence. In spite of all this extravagance, the house was never occupied, and today it is used as a teaching center, a hall for visiting exhibitions and an arts complex.

The building is open Monday to Friday from 5 to 6 pm and on Saturday from 11 am to noon. Foreigners pay US$1.50 for guided tours. The attached art museum is open Monday to Saturday from 2:30 to 6:30 pm, Saturday from 9 am to noon and Sunday from 10 am to noon. Take micro G from the corner of Avenida de las Heroínas and Calle San Martín.

Markets

Cochabamba is the biggest market town in Bolivia, and several formerly separate markets around San Antonio, south of the center, have now coalesced into one enormous market, known simply as 'La Cancha.' This is one of the best-stocked and most crowded and nerve-shattering places in the entire country.

The inordinate bustle is mostly a result of the 'New Economic Policy,' which has been promoting privatization of public services and cuts in public spending since 1985. It has resulted in massive unemployment and forced thousands of people to earn a living as street vendors or market stall holders. Around the markets, you'll find just about anything imaginable, and a wander through is both worthwhile and totally exhausting.

The largest and most accessible area is Mercado Cancha Calatayud, which sprawls across a wide area in Avenida Aroma and south toward the former railway station. Here is your best opportunity to see local dress, which differs strikingly from that of the Altiplano. The Cancha Francisco Rivas, Mercado Incallacta and Mercado de Ferias sprawl around the old railway station, and other minor markets are scattered around the city. The artesanía is concentrated near the junction of Tarata and Calle Esteban Arce, near the southwestern end of the market area. Here you'll find two alleys filled with friendly and reasonably priced stalls; one alley specializes in cloth and ornaments, the other has musical instruments.

Cristo de la Concordia
An immense Cristo de la Concordia (Christ of Concordance) stands on the Cerro de San Pedro behind Cochabamba. It's a few centimeters higher than the famous Cristo Redentor on Rio de Janeiro's Corcovado, which stands 33m high, or one meter for each year of Christ's life. Cochabambinos justify the one-upmanship by claiming that Christ actually lived '33 años y un poquito (33 years and a bit…).'

The return walk takes about two hours from the city center and half an hour (and 1250 uphill steps) on the new footpath from the base of the mountain, but beware of vicious dogs. Most people, however, opt for the *teleférico* (cable car), which costs US$0.50. On Sunday, for US$0.20 you can climb right to the top of the statue for a great overview of the city.

The closest public transportation access is on Micro LL, which leaves from the corner of Heroínas and 25 de Mayo. Taxis charge US$5 roundtrip, including a half-hour wait while you look around.

Laguna Alalay
The once rather fetid Laguna Alalay, south of the center, has now been made quite pleasant with walking and biking tracks and nice little shoreside restaurants that attract families on sunny weekend afternoons. The surrounding marshes have also been designated a wildlife refuge and attract lots of water birds.

Language Courses
Cochabamba is a popular place to hole up for a few weeks of Spanish or Quechua lessons. One option is the Instituto Cultural Boliviano Alemán, or ICBA (☎ 228431; fax 228890; Sucre 693), at Antezana, which charges US$6 per hour for Spanish lessons. However, they also take a hefty 'application fee.'

A recommended choice is the Escuela Runawasi (☎/fax 248923; runawasi@bo.net; Avenida Blanco, Barrio Juan XXIII, Casilla

4034); the program involves linguistic and cultural immersion and includes a trip to directors Joaquin & Janine Hinojosa's hideout in the Chapare rain forest!

For Quechua lessons, try the Academía Regional de Quechua Cochabamba, opposite the Iglesia Santa Clara at 25 de Mayo between Heroínas and Colombia; see the tourist office for details.

Plenty of private teachers also offer instruction. Most charge around US$5 per hour, but not all are experienced. You may have to try several before finding one that brings out the best of your abilities. Private teachers include Gloria or Miriam Ramírez (☎ 248963), Señor Reginaldo Rojo (☎ 242322), Gladys Espinoza (☎ 282414), Daniel Cotani (☎ 246820), Elizabeth Siles (☎ 232279), Ana Maria Franco (☎ 247365; idiomalanguage@hotmail.com), Claudia Villagra (☎ 248685), Jaime Claros (☎ 241241), Marycruz Almanza Bedoya (☎ 227923 or 287201), Blanca de La Rosa Villarreal (☎ 244298; Casilla 2707) and Silvia Torossi (☎ 271959). Many of these folks also teach Aymará or Quechua. Alternatively, seek recommendations at the Centro Boliviano-Americano (☎ 221288; 25 de Mayo N-365).

Organized Tours
A recommended agency is Viajes Fremen (☎ 259392; fax 0411-7790; fremencb@ pino.cbb.entelnet.bo; Tumusla 245, Casilla 1040), which organizes adventurous but comfortable excursions around Cochabamba and the Amazon Basin. They're not budget tours, but if you have a group, the per-person costs drop to quite reasonable levels. Tours are run to Chapare, Torotoro, the indigenous market at Pongo, Incallajta, Parque Nacional Tunari and several Cochabamba Valley villages. Other specialties include the Amazon area; see Villa Tunari and Trinidad in the Amazon Basin chapter, or check out the website www.andes-amazonia.com.

Special Events
A major annual event is the Heroínas de la Coronilla on May 27, a solemn commemoration in honor of the women

and children who defended the city in the battle of 1812. The fiesta of Santa Veracruz Tatala is celebrated annually on May 2, when farmers gather at a chapel 7km down the Sucre road to pray for fertility of the soil during the coming season. Their petitions are accompanied by folk music, dancing and lots of merrymaking.

See the Quillacollo section for information on the valley's biggest fiesta, the Virgen de Urcupiña.

Places to Stay

Budget The basic – and mostly rather shabby – alojamientos strung out along nerve-wracking Avenida Aroma make up Cochabamba's rock-bottom-end lodgings. For a bed and little else, you'll pay around US$2.

The cheapest decent accommodations are at friendly **Alojamiento Cochabamba** (☎ 225067; Nataniel Aguirre S-591). It's basically a flophouse but has become popular with budget travelers. Rooms with shared baths cost US$2.50 per person, and hot water is available only in the morning. **Alojamiento Roma** (☎ 258592), next door, also charges US$2.50 per person; there's also a triple room for US$6.

Near the Avenida Aroma action (and noise) are **Residencial Escobar** (☎ 229275; Uruguay E-0213), which charges US$3.50 per person with common bath, and **Alojamiento Escobar** (☎ 225812; Nataniel Aguirre S-0749), at US$3 per person.

A very nice (but far from perfect) and inexpensive spot is the **Hostal Elisa** (☎ 254406 or 554026; fax 235102; helisa@ comteco.entelnet.bo; Agustín López 834, Casilla 2649), near Avenida Aroma. Despite the sketchy location, just inside the door it's a different world, with a grassy courtyard and clean, sunny garden tables. Single/double rooms cost US$4.20/9; with a private bath, you'll pay US$10/15. Cable TV is available in the TV/video lounge, continental breakfasts are US$2 (American ones are US$3), and Internet and email access cost US$1.20 per hour.

Another excellent choice is **Hostal Florida** (☎ /fax 257911; floridah@elsitio.com; 25 de Mayo S-0583), which has a quiet patio

and lawn furniture on the main floor and a sun deck upstairs. It's in a nice location between the center and the bus terminal, and it's a good place to meet other travelers. There's hot water until 1 pm, and the friendly owner cooks up a mean breakfast for her guests. Continental breakfasts are US$1; you can opt for an American breakfast or pancakes for US$2. Rooms cost US$5 per person (US$7.50 with bath).

Residencial Familiar (☎ 227988; Sucre E-554) and **Residencial Familiar Anexo** (☎ 227986; 25 de Mayo N-0234) are popular with both Bolivian and foreign travelers. Just to reassure yourself that you won't be in questionable company, one posted regulation reads, 'Persons who register alone are not to be visited by persons of the opposite sex and particularly not by persons of doubtful morality or animals of any species.' Rooms, arranged around a central courtyard, cost US$4.50 per person with shared baths and US$8.50/14 with private baths. Note that the door locks aren't always secure.

The friendly, clean and secure **Hostal Colonial** (☎/fax 21791) is a travelers' favorite. Rooms with private baths cost US$7/12, and family rooms are US$23.50; ask for a room upstairs overlooking the leafy courtyard gardens. Breakfast costs an additional US$2.50.

Another good deal is **Hostal Central** (☎ 223622; fax 249397), on Calle General Achá, which charges US$7 per person for a room with private bath, TV and a continental breakfast. The quiet rooms are set well back from the street.

Mid-Range At the lower end of the middle price range is the four-star **Hostal Jardín** (☎ 247844; fax 522716; vemnet@mail. infonetcbba.com.bo; Hamiraya N-248, Casilla 4458). Singles/doubles with private baths cost US$12.50/17.50, and with shared baths, US$8.50/14. All rates include breakfast, and cable TV is an extra US$2. In the same league are **Hostal Jordán** (☎ 228069; Antezana S-0671) and **Hostal Jordán II** (☎ 225010; fax 224021; 25 de Mayo 651). All rooms have private baths, color TV and phones, and there's also a pool and solarium. Rooms cost US$12/18.50 with continental breakfast. The one on Antezana is the Hostelling International hostel for Cochabamba, so HI members get a 10% discount.

The reasonable mid-range *Hotel Boston* (☎ 224421; fax 257037; 25 de Mayo N-0167, Casilla 458) has rooms for US$22/32, including breakfast and private bath. The clean but rather noisy *City Hotel* (☎ 222993; Jordán E-341) charges US$12.50/19 for a room without bath. Rooms with shared baths on the upper floors are US$22/32.

A new mid-range choice within easy reach of the bus terminal is *Mary Hotel* (☎ 252487; fax 251746; Nataniel Aguirre S-601). Carpeted rooms with private baths, cable TV, telephones and continental breakfast cost US$20/30. Internet access is available in the lobby.

Units with kitchens are available at *Apart Hotel Concordia* (☎ 221518; fax 227980; hotelconcordia@hotmail.com; Aniceto Arce 690), at Juan de la Cruz Torres in Casilla 3314. Apartments cost US$15/18 and three-/four-person family units are US$28/38. Each unit has a bath, kitchenette and phone, and guests have access to the pool, laundry and Internet services.

Top End A prominent upmarket hotel is the four-star *Caesar's Plaza* (☎ 250045; fax 250324; cph@pino.cbb.entelnet.bo; 25 de Mayo S-210, Casilla 5447). Singles/doubles with heating, air-con, TV, phone and *frigobar* (minibar/fridge) start at US$50/60 and suites are US$70/80, including a buffet breakfast and access to the sauna and massage parlor. The front desk changes US cash for a reasonable rate.

The large four-star *Gran Hotel Ambassador* (☎ 259001; toll-free ☎ 0800-8282; fax 257855; ambassrv@comteco.entelnet.bo; España N-0349, Casilla 264) has rooms for US$40/50 with bath, TV, phone and breakfast included. Suites cost US$60/70.

The friendly three-star *Hotel Americano* (☎ 250552; fax 250484; americana@mail.infonetcbba.com.bo; Esteban Arce S-788, Casilla 4939) is a highly recommended upmarket option. The rooms are all bright and

clean with TV and private baths, and are a good value at US$25/35. Internet access is planned.

Places to Eat

One of the joys of a visit to Cochabamba is its wide choice of quality restaurants. You can easily spend a few days munching your way around the city, and some of the best places aren't necessarily expensive.

Breakfast Most of the popular heladerías – *Bambi*, *Dumbo*, *Cecy*, *Unicornio*, *Cristal* etc – open in the morning and serve up juice, eggs, toast, pancakes, chocolate, coffee, *salteñas* and other breakfast options. Near the corner of Calle General Achá and Avenida Villazón, street vendors sell delicious *papas rellenas* (potatoes filled with meat or cheese).

Snacks A good, friendly choice for snacks is the inexpensive *Danielíssimo*, in the shopping arcade opposite the tourist office kiosk. It's excellent for coffee, sweet treats, *empanadas*, salteñas, ice cream and cakes.

Avenida de las Heroínas is fast food row. *Confitería Cecy* is good for light lunches of burgers, chips, chicken, pizza and other snacks. The friendly owner speaks English, having spent many years in the USA, and although he has North American fast food culture down to an art, he also produces delicious award-winning salteñas, which are available mid-morning. Other similar places include the bizarrely decorated *Unicornio* and *Cristal*. *Heladería Dumbo* (☎ 253748; Avenida de las Heroínas E-345), with its landmark flying elephant, and *Confitería Bambi* (☎ 224005), on 25 de Mayo at Colombia, may infringe Disney copyright, but both serve good light meals and ice cream.

A step up, the popular *Café Frances* (☎ 017-32551; España 140) produces excellent coffee, tea, cakes, quiche and both sweet and savory crêpes. Alternatively, take the Swiss option and try the coffee, doughnuts and éclairs at *Tea Room Zürich* (San Martín 143), open daily except Tuesday from 9:30 to 11:30 am and 2 to 7:30 pm.

Café Express Bolívar, on Calle Bolívar, offers superb espresso and cappuccino. Around Calle España, near Ecuador and Major Rocha, you'll find lots of trendy little cafés and confiterías.

You'll also find decent sandwiches, cappuccino, espresso, tea and breakfast options at *Snack Terminal*, in the main bus terminal; it's an especially welcome option for overnight travelers arriving by bus in the wee hours of the morning.

At the little burger stand *Porkie's*, at the corner of Heroínas and Ayacucho, you can get delicious 'porkies' cheeseburgers for US$0.80, but note that the chili sauce provided is probably more potent than you expect. Porkies are also sold at other stands around the town.

Lunches & Dinners You'll find economical *almuerzos* at dozens of little mom & pop restaurants, where a cold beer is inexpensive and US$1.50 will get you at least three courses. Two nice family-run places are *Marvi*, on Avenida Cabrera, and *Palmar Restaurante Familiar*, on Avenida Aroma, where you'll get a meal of salad, soup, a main course and dessert for less than US$1.50; the latter also does *pacumutus* (think large quantities of beef!). At dinner, you'll pay a bit more for hearty helpings of 'comida típica Boliviana.'

El Caminante (*Esteban Arce S-0628*) serves inexpensive lunches, including some international options, in a pleasant open courtyard. For an interesting local alternative, check out *El Palacio del Silpancho*, on Baptista at Mayor Rocha, which dishes up the eponymous flattened schnitzel with egg, fried potatoes, rice and spicy onion salad.

Cochabamba is now the proud new home of the two fast food icons, *McDonald's* (☎ *523030*), on Avenida Ballivián (the Prado), and *Burger King* (☎ *591727*), at the recently renovated airport terminal. Bolivian-style burgers are found at the inexpensive *Burger Plaza*, in Plaza 14 de Septiembre. A relatively classy place for chicken & french fries is *Papa Gallo* (*241341; Adela Zamudio O-236*), at América, north of the river.

Moving up in price, there's a string of sidewalk cafés along Avenida Ballivián, which will carry you straight to southern California. Most serve European, Bolivian and North American fare and offer great almuerzos for around US$2. One of the most highly recommended is *Savarín* (☎ *257051; Ballivián 0626*), north of Plaza Colón. *Comida criolla* – traditional Bolivian cooking – is the specialty at *Sucre Manta*, which does à la carte dishes and almuerzos for as little as US$1.20. The basic but quality *Pensión La Suiza* (☎ *245485; Ballivián 820*) serves good cheap almuerzos, sandwiches and even that Altiplano specialty, *charque kan*. Also recommended is *El Paseo* (☎ *259295; Ballivián 540*), which serves both Bolivian and international cuisine.

Nearer the center is the appealing steak-oriented *Rodizio Grill Americano*, beside the Hotel Americano, which serves three meals daily, including outstanding almuerzos for US$2.50. It's a real carnivore's delight, but they do compensate with a great soup and salad bar. Just down Avenida Aroma is the inexpensive *Churrasquería Hawaii*, which also specializes in steak and is popular with locals. The renowned *La Estancia* (☎ *249262; Avenida Ballivián*) sizzles up steaks as well as grilled chicken and fish. Locals love *Churrasquería Tunari*, opposite the stadium, where pacumutus cost just US$2.50. Farther afield is the Brazilian-oriented *Rodizio Búfalo* (☎ *251597; Torres Sofer, Oquendo N-0654*), which offers a dinner buffet for US$6, including excellent grilled steaks. A nice outdoor churrasquería is *El Grillo* (☎ *218932; Laguna Alalay, Circuito Bolivia*), which features lunch and dinner grills and live music and dancing on weekends.

What may be Bolivia's finest Mexican food – tacos, enchiladas, burritos, quesadillas, nachos and other treats – is served up at the colorful *La Salsa Café* (*25 de Mayo N-217*). It also offers a variety of international fast food and Bolivian specialties. Big main courses cost less than US$4.50, and the music isn't bad, either. Another choice is the recommended *Pancho's*, on Mayor Rocha, which looks Mexican but is more a case of Bolivian with a few Mexican options.

A good choice for an inexpensive lunch or dinner is the Korean-run, Chinese-oriented *Restaurant Lose (Plaza 14 de Septiembre 0209)*, which dishes up abundant noodles, sweet-and-sour and vegetable dishes, pasta, and inexpensive Bolivian almuerzos. It's an excellent value, but don't be in too much of a hurry.

Cochabamba's best vegetarian food is served at *Govinda (México 3-0303)*, at España, which does lunch specials and dinners; and *Snack Uno*, on Heroínas at San Martín, where you'll get almuerzos for US$1.50 and also pizza and pasta dishes.

Pizza fans will enjoy the *Rondevu* (☎ 253937), on 25 de Mayo at Colombia. It does all sorts of pizzas, including unusual Bolivian combinations. Deliveries are available Monday to Saturday from 10 am to midnight and Sunday from 6 pm to midnight. Not quite as good but still popular is *Eli's Pizza Express (25 de Mayo N-0254)*, with its Marilyn Monroe-and-James Dean décor. Just a block away, concealed behind rose-colored stucco, is another Italian incarnation – and one of the city's finest restaurants – *La Cantonata*, on España at Mayor Rocha. You can't beat this place for a decadent splash-out. Sip fine Chilean wine before a roaring fireplace. (The menu, as the staff points out, is based on that of the *Porto Bello* in Houston, Texas.) It's closed on Monday.

Diagonally across the street is the aloof *Café Bistro El Carajillo (España N-0386)*. Foreigners are just tolerated, but it is a lively place for a drink, Spanish-style tapas, wholemeal bread sandwiches and other trendy bar snacks, as well as beer and light pub meals. The music reflects a strong taste for reggae and jazz.

Top eating, drinking and socializing spots for NGOs and volunteer organizations are *Metrópolis (España N-0299)* and *Metrópolis Club*, on Calle Colombia. Specialties include soup, salad, pasta, sweet or savory German-style pancakes and occasionally even ceviche or goulash. For afters, don't miss the fresh fruit salad with cream or ice cream. Pizza by the slice costs US$0.60 and draft beer costs US$1.60.

Markets & Self-Catering The enormous *main market area* stretches northward from the Mercado de Ferias, near the former railway station, to Cancha Calatayud, along Avenida Aroma between San Martín and Lanza. The most central market is on Calle 25 de Mayo between Calles Sucre and Jordán. For lunch or dinner, markets cook up inexpensive but tasty meals. They're also the cheapest places to find coffee – albeit rather insipid – and a roll for breakfast. Since the mild Cochabamba Valley is known for its fruit production, there's also a nice selection of orchard and citrus produce. If you're up for something more traditional, try the local breakfast specialty, *arroz con leche*.

If you prefer more processing and packaging, heaven is represented by the enormous and trendy North American-style supermarket *IC Norte*, on Avenida Pando. A good place to find fine Bolivian and imported wine is *Chávez e Hijos* (☎ 225444; *Calama 0477*).

Entertainment

For information about what's on, phone or see the newspaper entertainment listings; note that by law, all nightspots must close no later than 2:30 am. On Calle España, there's more drinking than eating at *Aladin's Pub* and the *Viking Pub*, both of which feature loud music. On Avenida Ballivián, try *Top Chop*, which is a sort of Bolivian beer barn. Popular dancing spots include *Nostalgias* (☎ 255955), on Plaza Quintanilla beside Los Piempos, and *Discoteca Lujos*, both of which operate nightly Wednesday to Sunday, with a matinee on Sunday afternoon.

High up on the hillside is a bar called *Loco's*, in a two-story corner house with red curtains; to find it, follow the right arm of Cristo de la Concordia – he's pointing right at it (what a recommendation!). Expats also like *La Pimienta Verde*, on Avenida Ballivián. Recommended nightclubs include *D'mons* (☎ 285745; *Tarija 1535*); *Cain* (☎ 281270), on J Freire between López y Césped; *Alcatraz*, on Avenida Ballivián; and *Arlequín* (☎ 244802), on Uyuni at Pasaje M Saracho.

Cochabamba also has eight *cinemas*, and good films quite often sneak in; watch the newspapers for listings.

Shopping

Locally produced woolens are available at three main outlets: Fotrama (☎ 325222; 16 de Julio 1405); the more expensive Asarti, on Paccieri at 25 de Mayo; and Casa Fisher (☎ 249846; Ramón Rivero E-0204), on the Plaza Cala Cala (the circle near the entrance to Parque Nacional Tunari). Fotrama (☎ 240567; fax 244693; Avenida Circunvalación 01412) also has a bargain factory outlet up the hill from Plaza Cala Cala. Cheaper alpaca and llama wool *chompas* (sweaters) are found in the markets. For inexpensive souvenirs and trinkets, ramble among the artesanía stalls behind the main post office.

Getting There & Away

Air Cochabamba's Jorge Wilstermann Airport is served by LAB (☎ 250760 or 0800-3001) and AeroSur (☎ 228385 or 0800-3030) from La Paz, Sucre, Santa Cruz and Tarija (LAB only), and on TAM from La Paz and Santa Cruz. The flight between La Paz and Cochabamba must be one of the world's most incredible; coming from La Paz, sit on the left side of the plane for an incredible – and disconcertingly close-up – view of the peak of Illimani, and a few minutes later, a bird's-eye overview of the dramatic Cordillera Quimsa Cruz.

On Monday, Wednesday and Saturday at 2:30 pm, TAM Mercosur (☎ 251066; Calle Ayacucho 250, US$154) connects Cochbbamba with Asunción, Buenos Aires and São Paulo.

Bus Cochabamba's central bus terminal (☎ 155) is on Avenida Ayacucho just south of Avenida Aroma, and charges a US$0.50 terminal fee.

Most buses to La Paz (seven hours, US$3.50) – there are at least 20 daily – leave between 7 and 9 pm, but some also leave in the morning. About 20 companies have daily services to Oruro between 7 am and 10 pm (four hours, US$2). Jumbo Bus Ballivián has a Friday-morning service to Vallegrande (11 hours, US$7) at 8:30 pm. Most Santa Cruz buses (11 hours, US$3.50) leave from 4 to 6 pm, but there are also lots of morning departures. Santa Cruz buses

now follow the Chapare route rather than the more scenic route over Siberia Pass. Flotas América and Unidos go to Trinidad (24 to 30 hours, US$14) via Santa Cruz, at 8:30 am and 7:30 pm.

Five to 10 buses leave daily for Sucre between 4:30 and 6:30 pm (11 hours, US$5). Some then continue on to Potosí (15 hours, US$8). Micros and Villa Tunari (five hours, US$2) and Puerto Villarroel (seven hours, US$3), in the Chapare region, leave between 6 and 10:30 am near the corner of 9 de Abril and Oquendo.

Flechabus offers international services to Buenos Aires, Argentina (72 hours, US$120), with connections to Porto Alegre, Brazil, and Montevideo, Uruguay. Departures are at 5:30 am and 8:30 pm.

Trufis and micros to eastern Cochabamba Valley villages leave from the corner of Avenida República and 6 de Agosto. To the western part of the valley, they leave from the corner of Avenidas Ayacucho and Aroma. Micros to Torotoro leave on Thursday and Sunday at 6 to 6:30 am from near the corner of Avenida República and 6 de Agosto.

Camión Camiones to Sucre and Santa Cruz leave from Avenida de la Independencia, 1.5km south of the former railway station; you'll pay roughly half the bus fare. In the dry season, several weekly camiones leave for Torotoro at around 5 am from near the Mercado de Ferias.

Getting Around

To/From the Airport The Jorge Wilstermann Airport is accessible on Micro B from the main plaza. Taxis to or from the center cost from US$3 to US$4.50.

Bus Lettered micros and trufis (both US$0.25 per ride) run to all corners of the city but don't display their destinations, making them rather difficult for the uninitiated to use. Fortunately, Cochabambinos are normally happy to help.

Taxi The taxi fare to anywhere south or east of the river, or north or west of Laguna Alalay, is US$0.40 (B$2.50) per person.

Beyond those limits, it doubles. For a radio taxi, phone EBA (☎ 255511) or Ciudad Jardín (☎ 241111).

Around Cochabamba

PARQUE NACIONAL TUNARI

The Parque Nacional Tunari was created in 1962 to protect the forested slopes above Cochabamba, as well as the wild summit of Cerro Tunari. However, in the section directly north of town, regulations aren't enforced and the park's fringes have now been invaded by urban development.

Cochabamba Area

A good dirt road zigzags its way from the park gate (open until 4 pm) up the steep mountain face. If you're on foot, you'll find it more interesting to turn left 100m up the track and walk up a stony avenue of eucalyptus toward some farm buildings. In less than 1km, you'll reach a pleasantly cool and shady woodland. In less than 1km, you'll reach a pleasantly cool and shady woodland. From here, several shortcut routes lead up the hill, but all eventually rejoin the road. After 3km from the gate, you'll reach a picnic site with barbecues and a children's playground with slides, firefighters' poles, swings, mini-golf and other amusements.

Immediately beyond the playground you'll see the sign for a *sendero ecológico* (nature trail). Don't expect too much in the way of *ecología* – there is one sign announcing a type of cactus – but it's a well-made path that gains altitude rapidly, winding into thickening mature woodland. Already the views are tremendous, with Cochabamba spread out below, and in the opposite direction, Cerro Tunari and other hills in the Cordillera. At the middle elevations, you'll be in temperate forest with small waterfalls, wildflowers, ferns and mosses, and a variety of colorful butterflies and moths. With an early start and plenty of water, you should be able to make it up to some of the nearer peaks on a long day hike.

At 4000m, 25km from Cochabamba, are the two small trout lakes known as the Lagunas de Huarahuara. In a day, you can hike from here to the summit of La Pirámide, northwest of the lakes, for views down the other side of the cordillera. The area offers a choice of wild camping sites.

Coming from town, take micro F2 or trufi 35 from Avenida San Martín, which will drop you three minutes from the park entrance, which is a big wooden archway with a fire-risk indicator. You may have to show identification and sign into the park. From the gate, turn right, then turn left after 100m; the road then zigzags up to the playground and the lakes.

Cerro Tunari Area

Snow-dusted Cerro Tunari, at 5035m, is the highest peak in central Bolivia. Its flanks lie 25km west of Cochabamba, along the road to Independencia. This spectacular area offers excellent camping and hiking, but access is admittedly less than straightforward. For climbs, pick up the IGM map *Cordillera de Tunari*, sheet 6342III at a scale of 1:50,000, which costs US$5.

The first step is to catch a micro to Quillacollo, 13km from Cochabamba (see Cochabamba Valley), then walk or take a trufi from Plaza Bolívar to Cruce Liriuni, about 5km from Quillacollo. From there, it's a complicated four- to five-hour ascent to the summit, including some sections requiring technical equipment. Experienced climbers can manage the roundtrip in a long day, but the stiff, high-altitude ascent will be more pleasant if you allow two days and camp overnight. A guide will be very useful to find the best route.

An easier route ascends from Estancia Chaqueri or Tawa Cruz, which lies 12km beyond Cruce Liriuni at 4200m. Micros and camiones toward Morochata leave on Monday, Thursday and Saturday at 7 am from three blocks off the main plaza in Quillacollo; they return to Cochabamba in the afternoon on Tuesday, Friday and Sunday. The relatively easy path, which takes around five hours, ascends the north face of the peak.

AROUND COCHABAMBA

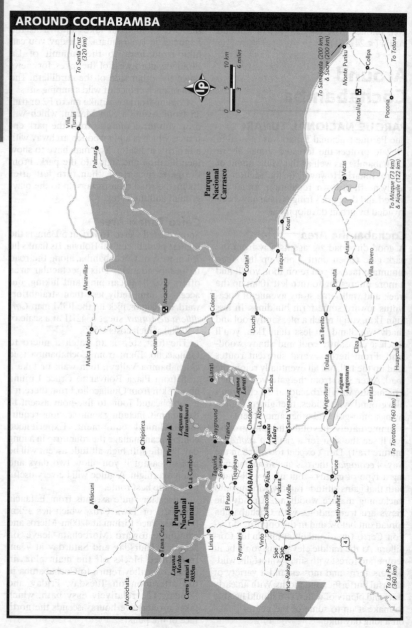

To Santa Cruz (320 km)

To Totora

To Colpa

Monte Punku

Incallajta

Pocona

Villa Tunari

Palmar

Parque Nacional Carrasco

To Samaipata (200 km) & Sucre (200 km)

Vacas

To Mizque (73 km) & Aiquile (122 km)

Maravillas

Incachaca

Koari

Tiraque

Arani

Villa Rivero

Maica Monte

Corani

Colomi

Cotani

Punata

Ucuchi

Huayculi

Maica Monte

San Benito

Cliza

Tarata

Chipisirca

Ikariti

Laguna Larati

Sacaba

Tolata

Angostura

Laguna Angostura

El Pirámide

Laguna de Huanchuara

Playground

Taquiña Brewery

Trança

La Abra

Chacacollo

Santa Veracruz

Cruce

To Torotoro (160 km)

La Cumbre

El Paso

Tiquipaya

Laguna Alalay

Misicuni

Parque Nacional Tunari

Cerro Tunari 5035m

Laguna Macho

Liriuni

Tawa Cruz

Payrumani

Vinto

Sipe Sipe

Inca-Rakay

Quillacollo

Alba

Pukara

Molle Molle

Santiváñez

COCHABAMBA

Morochata

To La Paz (360 km)

4

0   5   10 km
0   3   6 miles

There's also a two- to four-day route that ascends 2500 vertical meters from the village of Payrumani (see Cochabamba Valley). There's plenty of running water in all but the driest times (late winter), but it needs to be purified, as there's a village at 4200m.

Another option is Viajes Fremen (see Organized Tours in Cochabamba). It leads all-inclusive two-day excursions from Cochabamba, using the northern route. With two people, you'll pay US$161 per person, while groups of three to five pay US$118 per person.

The only accommodations are at Liriuni (see Cochabamba Valley) or the village school at Cruce Liriuni.

COCHABAMBA VALLEY
Quillacollo
Besides Cochabamba itself, Quillacollo is the largest and most commercially important community in the Cochabamba Valley. Its name is derived from *khella-collu*, meaning 'ash hill.' Apart from the Feria Dominical (Sunday market) and the pre-Inca burial mound discovered beneath Plaza Bolívar, the main attraction is the church, which houses the shrine of the Virgen de Urkupiña. The niche lies to the right of the altar in a little side chapel, which is full of candles and commemorative plaques thanking the Virgin for blessings received. Elsewhere in the well-kept church, note the interesting religious statues. Be prepared for the squad of women who pin pilgrims' badges on visitors' clothing and then ask for money.

Sunday visitors to the market may want to sample *garapiña*, Quillacollo's answer to the dessert drink. This deceptively strong combination is a blend of chicha, cinnamon, coconut and *ayrampo*, a local mystery ingredient that colors the drink red. In Cochabamba, you can try garapiña at the El Caminante restaurant, on Calle Esteban Arce near Cabrera.

Special Events If you're in the area around August 15 to 18, try to catch the Fiesta de la Virgen de Urkupiña, which is the biggest annual celebration in Cochabamba department. Folkloric musicians and dancers come from around Bolivia to perform, and the chicha flows for three days.

The celebration commemorates repeated visitations of the Virgin Mary and child to a shepherd girl at the foot of the hill known as Calvario. The visits were later witnessed by the girl's parents and a crowd of villagers when the shepherdess shouted *'Orkopiña'* ('there on the hill') as the Virgin was seen ascending toward heaven. At the summit of the hill, the townspeople discovered a stone image of the Virgin, which was carried to the village church and thereafter known as the Virgen de Urkupiña.

Places to Stay & Eat At Estancia Marquina, 4km north of Quillacollo on the Liriuni road, is *Eco-Hostal Planeta de Luz* (☎ *261234; fax 291031; pachamam@ ngweb.com; Casilla 318, Cochabamba)*. It was conceived by the Movimiento Pachamama Universal as part of an experiment in eco-tourism, but in truth, it's more a bizarre experiment in Gaudi-esque architecture and pretentious New Age dogma: vegetarian food, a solar sauna, solar lighting, music therapy, meditation, chanting, tai chi, natural health remedies, catchy signs reading 'te invito a ser libre' ('I invite you to be free') and 'disfruto luego existo' ('I enjoy therefore I am'), a 'clinic of happiness' and even a resident guru called Chamalu, who apparently cuddles trees to encourage them to dance. It might be fun, but you'll get more spirituality watching daily life at the market in Cochabamba! On the practical side, the pool and showers are 'naturally heated' (read: cold). Cabañas cost US$15 per person plus US$5 for meals, and day admission is US$10.

La Posada de los Cisnes, in the same area, is another resort with a swimming pool, which is open for day use for US$2 per person. The main attraction is their US$4 beef parrillada, which is grilled up on weekends. Cabañas are available on weekends only and cost US$15 per person, including use of the pool and sauna.

Getting There & Away Micros and trufis to Quillacollo (1/2 hour, US$0.25) leave from the corner of Avenidas Ayacucho and Aroma in Cochabamba. In Quillacollo, the trufi stop is on Plaza Bolívar.

Sipe Sipe

The quiet and friendly village of Sipe Sipe, 27km southwest of Cochabamba, is the base for visiting Inca-Rakay, the most easily accessible of the Cochabamba area ruins. If you're in Sipe Sipe on a Sunday between February and May, try to sample the local specialty, a sweet grape liquor known as *guarapo*.

Places to Stay Near Sipe Sipe is *La Cabaña* (☎/fax 81038) resort, which features good food and a mineral hot spring and pool. Transfers are available from Cochabamba. Rooms with private bath cost US$25 per person, including full board.

Getting There & Away On Wednesday and Saturday, micros run directly to Sipe Sipe from the corner of Avenidas Ayacucho and Aroma in Cochabamba. On other days, take a micro from the same spot to Plaza Bolívar in Quillacollo and then a trufi or a micro to Sipe Sipe.

Inca-Rakay

The ruins of Inca-Rakay, in the Serranía de Tarhuani, are mostly crumbling stone walls these days, and you'll need some imagination to conjure up their former glory. It has been postulated that Inca-Rakay served as an Inca administrative outpost, to oversee agricultural colonies in the fertile Cochabamba Valley. That seems unlikely, however, given its lofty position and difficulty of access.

The site includes the remains of several hefty buildings and a large open plaza overlooking the Cochabamba Valley. One odd rock outcrop resembles the head of a condor, with a natural passageway inside leading to the top. Just off the plaza area is a cave that may be explored with a flashlight. Legend has it that this cave is the remnant of another of those apocryphal Inca tunnels – this one linking Inca-Rakay with faraway Cuzco.

On a smog-free day, the plaza affords a spectacular overview of the valley. It also makes an excellent campsite, and a night

spent amid these secluded and unattended ruins is quite the haunting experience. However, no water is available.

You may want to look at the Spanish-language book *Inkallajta & Inkaraqay*, by Jesús Lara, which is occasionally available from Los Amigos del Libro in Cochabamba for US$5. It contains good maps of the site and theories about its origins and purposes.

About once weekly, camiones travel to Li'pichi from Sipe Sipe and pass within several hundred meters of Inca-Rakay. If you stay on the road, it's a relatively easy 12km uphill climb that will take about four hours. You'll eventually come across a sign on the roadside pointing toward the ruins, which are hidden from view amid rocky outcrops and a clump of molle trees (which resemble willows); from the road, it's five minutes downhill to the ruins.

Otherwise, it's a 5km, two-hour cross-country walk up a steep hill. If you've arrived in Cochabamba from the lowlands, allow a couple of days to acclimatize before tackling this hike. From the main plaza in Sipe Sipe, follow the road past the secondary school. From there the road narrows into a path and crosses a small ditch. Across the ditch, turn right onto the wider road. From several hundred meters up the road from town, follow a water pipeline uphill to the first major ridge; there'll be a large ravine on your left. From there, bear to the right, following the ridge until you see a smaller ravine to the right. At this point, you'll be able to see Inca-Rakay atop a reddish hill in the distance, but from so far away it won't be obvious what you're looking at.

Cross the small ravine and follow it until you can see two adobe houses on the other side. In front you'll see a little hill with some minor ruins at the top. Climb the hill, cross the large flat area, and then climb up two more false ridges until you see Inca-Rakay.

Getting There & Away Inca-Rakay is accessed on foot from Sipe Sipe. If you're not staying overnight, get an early start out of

Cochabamba; the trip takes the better part of a day and you'll need time to explore the ruins.

Taquiña Brewery

In the hills along the road to Tiquipaya, 10km northwest of Cochabamba, is the source of that refreshing brew, Taquiña. On weekends, you can have a meal at the restaurant, which boasts a delicious view across the valley. Recommended menu specialties include trout, lamb, duck and *lechón* (suckling pig) – washed down, of course, with the star tipple, and followed by a specialty ice cream concoction. You can take trufi 101 from Aroma and Ayacucho in Cochabamba; taxis cost US$2.

Tiquipaya

The village of Tiquipaya, 40 minutes from Cochabamba, is known for its cultivation of flowers and strawberries, and its array of unusual festivals. In late April or early May, there's an annual Chicha Festival; the second week in September sees the Trout Festival; around September 24 is the Flower Festival; and in the first week of November there's the Festival de la Wallunk'a, which features colorfully dressed traditional women from around Cochabamba department.

Places to Stay The mid-range *Hostal Tolavi* has chalet-style cabañas constructed of perfumed wood, which occupy a gardenlike setting among the trees. These cost US$80 for up to five people, including use of the pool. German-style meals, including a buffet breakfast, are US$4. It lies three blocks from the trufi stop in Tiquipaya.

Getting There & Away Micros leave half-hourly from the corner of Avenidas Ladislao Cabrera and San Martín in Cochabamba.

Liriuni

At Liriuni, 7km northwest of Quillacollo on the Cerro Tunari route, you may want to stop at the Termas de Liriuni (Liriuni Hot Springs) for a good, relaxing soak. Here

you'll find the natural health resort *Janajpacha* (☎/fax 221793; Casilla 318, Cochabamba), which specializes in alternative medicine. Accommodations in the double cabañas cost US$9 per person, including meals. Trufis run from Quillacollo on Sunday.

Payrumani

If you haven't already had your fill of Simón Patiño's legacy in Oruro and Cochabamba, you can visit Payrumani and tour the home actually occupied by the tin baron. This enormous white mansion, which could have inspired the television home of the Beverly Hillbillies, was named for his wife. Albina was presumably as fussy as her husband when it came to the finer things in life, and the elegant French décor of the main house and the Carrera-marble mausoleum seem typical of royalty – mineral or otherwise – anywhere in the world. In 1964, the estate was donated to the nonprofit Salesian Congregation by the Simón I Patiño University Memorial fund, which still represents the tin baron's heirs.

Villa Albina is open weekdays from 3 to 4 pm; admission is free.

Getting There & Away To reach Payrumani, take trufi 211Z or Micro 7 or 38 from Avenida Aroma in Cochabamba or from Plaza Bolívar in Quillacollo and get off at Villa Albina. It's only 22km from Cochabamba, but getting there may take a couple of hours.

Vinto

Vinto, not to be confused with the tin smelter of the same name near Oruro, is best known for two annual celebrations. On March 19, it celebrates the Fiesta de San José (St Joseph, the patron saint of carpenters). The Fiesta de la Virgen del Carmen is celebrated on July 16 with folkloric groups, Masses, parades and military bands.

The easiest access is by trufi 211Z from the corner of Avenidas Ayacucho and Aroma in Cochabamba. Micros run on Wednesday and Saturday from the same corner, but on other days, you have to change in Quillacollo.

La Angostura

The village of La Angostura, near the large reservoir of the same name, lies on the route to Tarata and is known mainly as a place to eat fish. Of the several informal restaurants, the best is away from the highway, over the bridge near the railway. Here you'll pay US$3.50 for excellent fish dishes with enough pejerrey, rice, salad and potato to fill up two people. From near the corner of Barrientos and 6 de Agosto in Cochabamba, take any micro (US$0.25) toward Tarata or Cliza and get off at the Angostura bridge.

En route, 18km east of the city, is Lago del Edén Angostura, a small park and restaurant that is popular with families on weekends. An overnight at *Cabañas del Edén* costs US$15 per person. A 3km walk west of the park is an open-air restaurant, *Las Carmelitas*, where on weekends Señora Carmen López serves up delicious cheese, egg, olive and onion *pukacapas*, baked on the spot in a large beehive oven. At US$0.40 each, they're a real bargain.

Punata

The small market town of Punata, 48km east of Cochabamba, is known for the finest chicha in all Bolivia. If you can't make it to the source, you can sample Punata chicha in Cochabamba from a small shop on the northern side of Avenida Aroma between Calles 25 de Mayo and Esteban Arce. Tuesday is market day in Punata. It is accessed by micros that depart every half hour from the corner of Avenida República (the southern extension of Antezana) and Pulacayo, at Plaza Villa Bella in Cochabamba.

Tarata & Huayculi

Tarata, 30km southeast of Cochabamba, lives in infamy as the birthplace of the mad president General Mariano Melgarejo, who held office from 1866 to 1871. Its name is derived from the abundant tara trees, whose fruit is used in curing leather.

Tarata's enormous neoclassical church, the Iglesia de San Pedro, was constructed in 1788 and restored between 1983 and 1985; several of the interior panels include mestizo-style details, carved in cedar. The 1792 Franciscan Convent of San José, which contains lovely colonial furniture and an 8000-volume library, was founded as a missionary training school. It now contains the ashes of San Severino, the patron saint of Tarata, whose feast day is celebrated in grand style on November 30.

The village also has several other historic buildings: the government palace of President Melgarejo, which was constructed in 1872, and the homes of President Melgarejo, General Don Esteban Arce and General René Barrientos.

Huayculi, 7km from Tarata, is a village of potters and glaziers. The air is thick with the scent of eucalyptus branches and leaves being burned in cylindrical firing kilns. The local style and technique are passed down from generation to generation and remain unique in Bolivia.

Micros leave Cochabamba hourly from Avenida República and 6 de Agosto. There are no micros to Huayculi, but taxis from Cochabamba cost around US$4.

Cliza

The Sunday market in Cliza is a good alternative to the utter Sunday shutdown in Cochabamba, and it's a good place to sample squab, which is a local specialty. Micros make the 25-minute trip to Cliza from Avenida República and 6 de Agosto in Cochabamba.

Arani & Villa Rivero

Arani, 53km east of Cochabamba, stages a Thursday market. To look for the locally produced woolens for which the region is famous, see the Fotrama co-op, beside the church. Arani is also known for *pan de Arani*, a bread concocted from a blend of grains to yield a distinct flavor. Also look at the intricately carved wooden altars in the church, which once served as the seat of the Santa Cruz Bishopric. On August 26, the town celebrates the Festividad de la Virgen de la Bella, which dates from colonial times.

At Villa Rivero, 6km south of Arani, both men and women weave magnificent carpets in zoomorphic patterns and high relief. Bear in mind that purchasing weavings and carpets directly from the source rather than from a shop decreases the price and increases the artisan's percentage of the sale. A 2m by 2m carpet, which requires 15kg of wool and at least 15 days of spinning and weaving, will start at around US$40.

For lunch, stop by the friendly pensión *Doña Alicia*, at the corner of the plaza.

Micros to Arani leave from the corner of Avenida República and 6 de Agosto in Cochabamba. Taxis from Arani to Villa Rivero cost US$3, and from Punata, micros are US$0.20.

INCALLAJTA

The nearest thing Bolivia has to Peru's Machu Picchu is the remote and little-visited site of Incallajta (meaning 'land of the Inca'), which lies 132km east of Cochabamba on a flat mountain spur above the Río Machaj-marka. This was the easternmost outpost of the Inca empire and after Tiahuanaco, it's the country's most significant archaeological site. The most prominent feature is the immense stone fortification that sprawls across alluvial terraces above the river, but at least 50 other structures are also scattered around the site.

Incallajta was probably founded by Inca Emperor Tupac Yupanqui, the commander who had previously marched into present-day Chile to demarcate the southern limits of the Inca empire. It's estimated that Incallajta was constructed sometime in the 1460s as a measure of protection against attack by the Chiriguanos to the southeast. In 1525, the last year of Emperor Huayna Capac's rule, the outpost was abandoned. This may have been due to a Chiriguano attack, but was more likely the result of increasing Spanish pressure and the unraveling of the empire, which fell seven years later.

The ruins were made known to the world in 1914 by Swedish zoologist and ethnologist Ernest Nordenskiold, who spent a week at the ruins, measuring and mapping them. However, they were largely ignored – except by ruthless treasure hunters – for the next 50 years, until the University of San Simón in Cochabamba launched its investigations. The road in was built in 1977, and the site became a national monument in 1988. The archaeological museum in Cochabamba is now working to restore the ruins and translate Nordenskiold's writings on Bolivia into Spanish.

For more information, look for a copy of Jesús Lara's now rare book *Inkallajta & Inkaraqay*. Although based on original research carried out in the 1920s, it was published in 1967. You'll need to read Spanish, but the site map is also useful.

Organized Tours

Cochabamba agencies run tours to Incallajta when they have a group large enough to make it worthwhile. The best is probably Viajes Fremen, which runs day tours for US$110/70 per person in groups of two/four people. For two-day tours, the price jumps to US$171/128. Fridays are the best for joining a pre-organized tour.

Places to Stay & Eat

Without your own transportation, visiting Incallajta will prove inconvenient at best. Additionally, if you can't arrange lodging in private homes, you'll probably have to camp for two or three nights, so be sure to take plenty of water, food, warm clothing and camping gear. Camping and basic shelters are available for about US$1 per person at the *Centro de Investigaciones*.

Getting There & Away

From Cochabamba, take the daily micro toward Totora, which leaves from the corner of Avenida República and 6 de Agosto, and get off at Inca Cruce. From there, it's a 14km walk (or an unlikely hitch) to Collpa. At the Koari turnoff, opposite a church on the left side of the road, turn west and follow the largely uphill route for 10km. After crossing the Río Machajmarka, you'll enter the Incallajta archaeological park.

TOTORA

Totora, 140km east of Cochabamba, huddles in a valley at the foot of Cerro Sutuchira, and was once the loveliest colonial village in the department. Unfortunately, on May 22, 1998, it was destroyed by an earthquake that measured 6.7 on the Richter scale. Many of the governmental and international funds that were designated to rebuild Totora and similarly devastated Aiquile were diverted into the black hole of unethical officialdom, and the towns still lie largely in ruin.

The colonial-style Gran Hotel Totora collapsed in the earthquake, and there's now just a small *alojamiento* charging US$3.50 for basic single or double rooms.

Micros leave for Totora daily from the corner of Avenida República and 6 de Agosto in Cochabamba. Totora lies on the main route between Cochabamba and Sucre, but few travelers ever see it because most buses run at night.

AIQUILE

Dusty little Aiquile, which was decimated by the same 1998 earthquake that destroyed Totora, is known for some of Bolivia's finest charangos. In late November, it holds the Feria del Charango featuring this unusual instrument. Local services extend to post and ENTEL offices and a medical clinic. Market day is Sunday.

Places to Stay & Eat

Accommodations are available at the basic *Hotel Los Escudos* and the pleasant *Hostal Campero*, the latter of which charges US$2 per person and serves meals. It's in an old colonial building surrounding a nice courtyard, and the personable owner likes to chat with guests. Both places offer simple meals.

Getting There & Away

Aiquile lies on the main route between Cochabamba and Sucre, but most buses pass in the wee hours of the night when this already soporific little place is soundly asleep. Micros to Aiquile run on Monday, Wednesday and Friday at 3 pm from the corner of Avenida República and 6 de Agosto in Cochabamba.

It's about a 60-minute drive between Aiquile and Mizque. You can readily thumb a ride on passing camiones, but be prepared for a real dust bath.

MIZQUE
☎ 0411

The pretty colonial town of Mizque, which is smaller and even dustier than Aiquile, enjoys a lovely pastoral setting on the Río Mizque. Founded as the Villa de Salinas del Río Pisuerga in 1549, it soon came to be known as the Ciudad de las 500 Quitasoles (City of 500 Parasols), after the shields used by the locals against the brilliant sun.

Mizque makes a great escape from the cities and main tourist sights, and the few visitors who see the area are impressed by the beauty of the Mizque and Tucuna Valleys, as well as the variety of bird species in the area. Along the Tucuna Valley, you may even see the flocks of endangered scarlet macaws, which squawk and frolic in the early morning.

The lovely Iglesia Matríz, which was slightly damaged in the 1998 earthquake, once served as the seat of the Santa Cruz bishopric (until the seat was shifted to Arani in 1767). There's also a small museum of artifacts unearthed from the 45 archaeological sites around Mizque. Volunteers are currently establishing horseback trips to several of these sites, and they should be available by the time you read this.

From September 8 to 14, Mizque holds the Fiesta del Señor de Burgos.

Places to Stay & Eat

The *Hospedaje Graciela* is probably the nicest place in town, with private baths and decks. Rooms cost US$4.50 per person and breakfast/lunch/dinner cost US$0.40/1/1. There's no phone, but they can be reached through the ENTEL office (☎ 115055). The clean *Residencial Mizque* (☎ 5071), set amid nice gardens, charges US$4.50 for rooms with shared baths. For the same price, you can also stay at the simple *Residencial Señor de Burgos*.

Mizque also has four little pensiones that serve Bolivian dishes, including almuerzos for around US$1. They're all within a block of the plaza. Alternatively, you can eat at the street stalls beside the church.

Getting There & Away

To Mizque, a daily micro leaves Cochabamba at noon from the same corner; from Mizque, it leaves at 3 pm.

PARQUE NACIONAL TOROTORO

Parque Nacional Torotoro, created in 1988, is now administered by the Asociación Conservacionista de Torotoro, which has an office in the village. Most of the treasures of this absolute jewel – caves, ruins, rock paintings, waterfalls and fossilized dinosaur tracks – are difficult or uncomfortable to reach without private transportation, but that only adds to the appeal. Further information is available at the Servicio Nacional de Áreas Protegidas in Cochabamba (see Information under Cochabamba, earlier in this chapter).

The village of Torotoro, founded during the colonial era, sits on a small plain between the sharp Serranías de Huayllas and Cóndor Khaka.

Dinosaur Tracks

Most visitors to Torotoro come for the paleontology. The village, which sits in a wide section of a 20km-long valley at a 2600m elevation, is flanked by enormous inclined mudstone rock formations, bearing biped and quadruped dinosaur tracks from the Cretaceous period. As the road flattens out beside the stream northwest of Torotoro, it actually crosses the path of a group of three-toed tracks, each measuring about 25cm long.

A short distance from the village, just beyond the Río Torotoro crossing, the area's largest tracks march up from just above the waterline. They were made by an enormous quadruped dinosaur, and they measure 35cm wide, 50cm long and 20cm deep – at a stride of nearly 2m!

Several hundred meters farther upstream from the crossing, a group of small three-toed tracks climbs out of the water and under a layer of rocks. More tracks can be found 5km upstream, and dinosaur bone fragments have been found in layers of red earth.

All the tracks in the Torotoro area were made in soft mud, which then solidified into

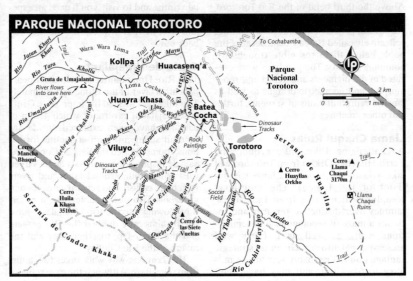

PARQUE NACIONAL TOROTORO

mudstone. They were later lifted and tilted by tectonic forces. For that reason, nearly all the tracks appear to lead uphill. The exception is the set known as the Carreras Pampa site, along the route to Umajalanta Cave. These tracks, which were made by three-toed biped dinosaurs, run in several different directions, suggesting a dancelike frolic.

Sea Fossils
In a small side gully, an hour's walk west of Torotoro, on the Cerro de las Siete Vueltas (so called because the trail twists seven times before reaching the peak), is a major deposit of sea fossils. At the base of the ravine, you may see petrified shark teeth, while higher up, the limestone and sedimentary layers are set with fossils of ancient trilobites, echinoderms, gastropods, arthropods, cephalopods and brachiopods. The site is thought to date back about 350 million years. Another major sea-fossil site lies in the Quebrada Thajo Khasa, southeast of Torotoro.

Batea Cocha Rock Paintings
Above the third bend of the Río Torotoro, about 1.5km downstream from the village, are several panels of ancient rock paintings collectively called Batea Cocha because the pools below them resemble troughs for pounding laundry. The paintings were executed in red pigments and depict anthropomorphic and geometric designs as well as fanciful representations of serpents, turtles and other creatures.

Llama Chaqui Ruins
A challenging 19km hike around the Cerro Huayllas Orkho from Torotoro will take you to the ruins of Llama Chaqui (Foot of the Llama). The multilevel complex, which dates from Inca times, rambles over distinctive terraces and includes a maze of rectangular and semicircular walls, as well as a fairly well preserved watchtower. Given its strategic vantage point, it probably served as a military fortification, and may have been somehow related to Incallajta, farther north. A guide is probably essential, as it's very difficult to find on your own.

El Vergel
Thanks to the perennial water, the lovely 100m-deep canyon known as El Vergel (or Huacasenq'a – 'cow's nostrils' in Quechua) is filled with incongruous moss, vines and other tropical vegetation. At the bottom, a crystal-clear river tumbles down through cascades and waterfalls, forming idyllic pools perfect for swimming. To get there, follow the main road out of town to the first big bend, where a 4WD track takes off straight ahead. This track will eventually turn into a footpath and lead to a set of steps down into the canyon. Despite what some locals may tell you, it's not necessary to hire a guide.

Cavernas de Chillijusk'o
These undeveloped caverns – the Quechua name means 'little eye of the needle' – lie just 500m from the village. Unlike the more amenable Gruta de Umajalanta, they're comprised of a maze of galleries and labyrinths, and to visit, you'll need an experienced guide, several backup light sources and a cord that will show you the way back out.

Gruta de Umajalanta
The Río Umajalanta, which disappears beneath a layer of limestone approximately 22m thick, has formed the impressive Gruta de Umajalanta cavern, of which 4.5km of passages have been explored. Inside are fanciful stalagmite and stalactite formations; rooms dubbed the Sala de Conciertos, Sala de Inspiraciones, and Sala de La Virgen y El Niño; underground lakes and rivers with blind catfish; and several cascades and waterfalls. Two of the subterranean waterways flowing into the Río Umajalanta have been whimsically dubbed the Río Singani and the Río 7-Up; together, they exit the cavern as the Río Chuflay!

The 7km one-way walk takes two hours from the village. Although the cave remains undeveloped, there are plans to install pathways, artificial lighting and stairs. To see it in a natural state, find a torch, then go to the village administration to pay the US$2 fee and pick up the entrance key to the cave. Although local guides know little about the cave itself, they can show you the safest route through.

Organized Tours
Viajes Fremen organizes three-day Torotoro tours that take in most of the major sites. They use air transportation in the rainy season and a 4WD vehicle between April and October. For a three day all-inclusive 4WD tour, groups of four pay US$267 per person, while two people pay US$356 each; by plane, groups of two/four pay US$573/288 per person. For contact details, see Organized Tours in Cochabamba.

Special Events
On July 25, Torotoro stages the Fiesta del Tata Santiago, which features sheep sacrifices as well as tinku fights (see 'Tinku – the Art of Ritual Mayhem,' later in this chapter). This may be an interesting time to visit – and a good time to look for transportation – but it's not the best for visiting the natural attractions.

Places to Stay & Eat
Torotoro isn't exactly prepared for mass tourism, but facilities are improving. Señor Saúl Foronda's *Alojamiento Trinidad* charges US$1.50 per person. Alternatively, there's Señor Romero's *Alojamiento Charcas*, where you'll pay US$2. Visitors may also lodge with private families. Both are near the ENTEL office (☎ 113927).

If you want to camp, locals will expect you to pay; it's important to set a mutually agreeable price (US$1 per group per night would be generous) and pay only the family in control of the land. Be sure to keep your tent closed to avoid contact with vinchuca beetles.

For meals, you're limited to the Thursday and Sunday markets or *Pensión Las Delicias*, which is open most of the time. There

are also several small tiendas selling staple supplies.

Getting There & Away
Air The Free Swedish Mission of Cochabamba flies into Torotoro from time to time and may have space for passengers. If you charter the plane, the flight costs US$120 for up to five passengers. Inquiries may be directed to Captain Arvidsson (☎ 227042) in Cochabamba.

Bus By road, Parque Nacional Torotoro lies 198km southeast of Cochabamba, in Potosí department. Micros (six hours, US$3.50) depart on Thursday and Sunday at about 6 or 6:30 am from the corner of Avenida República and 6 de Agosto in Cochabamba. They return on Friday and Monday at 7 am from near the plaza in Torotoro. During school holidays it's often completely booked by student groups.

Camión During the dry season, there are a couple of weekly camiones between Cochabamba and Torotoro (nine hours, US$2.50), departing at 5 am from the Mercado de Ferias in Cochabamba. Alternatively, you can avoid the bone-chilling early-morning departure by taking a micro to Cliza and picking up the camión as it passes between 6:30 and 9 am. The route traverses several climatic zones, so bring a range of clothing.

Car & Motorcycle Fortunately, there's now a bridge across the Río Caine, but you'll be happiest with a good motorbike or a 4WD to do this trip on your own. You can rent a Toyota Landcruiser in Cochabamba from International Rent-A-Car (see the Getting Around chapter) for US$40 per day plus US$0.45 per kilometer. Follow the highway toward Sucre for 31km, turn right and continue 7km to the village of Cliza. There's no gasoline available beyond Cliza, so make sure you have enough for the return trip to Torotoro – about 400km. Follow the Oruro road 10km beyond Cliza and turn left onto the Torotoro road.

CENTRAL HIGHLANDS

INCACHACA & THE CHAPARE ROAD

In the highlands, 93km northeast along the Santa Cruz road from Cochabamba, you'll pass the 1500-hectare Corani reservoir, which was created in 1966 to provide water for the city. On its shores is a popular weekend resort complex favored by cochabambinos. Also look for the bizarre Casa de los Brujos (House of the Warlocks), an exceptional but now-dilapidated dwelling constructed by a local eccentric.

Farther down the valley, half an hour on foot from kilometer 84, is the semi-abandoned settlement of Incachaca (Inca bridge), which enjoys a Yungas-like micro-climate that covers the slopes with lush tropical forest. Here, the Río Alisu Mayu crashes down through convoluted rock formations, and a hanging bridge – the Puente del Inca – crosses a 60m deep gorge. An unusual sight is the Ventana del Diablo (Devil's Window), where a water-fall issues from the rock. Early in the morning, you may see the hooded moun-tain toucan, the Andean guan and other birds.

Organized Tours

Viajes Fremen in Cochabamba organizes day excursions to Corani and the Ventana del Diablo for US$64/56 per person in a group of two/four people.

Getting There & Away

From Cochabamba, Incachaca is accessi-ble by micros going to Villa Tunari or buses to Santa Cruz. The former leave every half hour from the corner of Oquendo and 9 de Abril. From kilometer 84, walk about 100m down the road, where you'll find an unpaved road leading up the mountain. Follow it for about 30 minutes (or take a shortcut along the power lines) until you reach the site. Allow several hours to look around the small lake, bridge, old hydroelectric plant and the Ventana del Diablo. For the last two sites, visitors must report to the caretaker's office.

CHAPARE

For details on the Chapare region of north-ern Cochabamba department, see the Amazon Basin chapter.

Sucre

☎ 064

Any Bolivian who knows Sucre will tell you it's their nation's most beautiful city. As a result, its inhabitants have reverently be-stowed upon it romantic-sounding nick-names: 'The Athens of America,' 'The City of Four Names,' 'The Cradle of Liberty' and 'The White City of the Americas.' At an al-titude of 2790m, it enjoys a mild and com-fortable climate nearly as appealing as that of Cochabamba.

Set in a valley surrounded by low moun-tains, Sucre is a small, pleasant city of 100,000 people, and it boasts numerous churches, museums and ancient mansions. Like the Netherlands, Libya and South Africa, Bolivia divides its bureaucracy between multiple capitals. Although La Paz has usurped most of the governmental power, the Supreme Court still convenes in Sucre and with some sort of twisted pride, sureños maintain that their city remains the real heart of Bolivian government.

Today, Sucre struggles to retain the flavor of its colonial heritage. All buildings within the central core of the city must be either whitewashed or painted white. The city remains a center of learning, and both Sucre and its university enjoy reputations as focal points of liberal and progressive thought within the country.

History

Throughout its history, Sucre has served as the administrative, legal, religious, cultural and educational center of the easternmost Spanish territories, and in the 17th century it came to be known as the Athens of America.

Prior to Spanish domination, the town of Charcas, where Sucre now stands, was the in-digenous capital of the valley of Choque-Chaca. It served as the residence of local

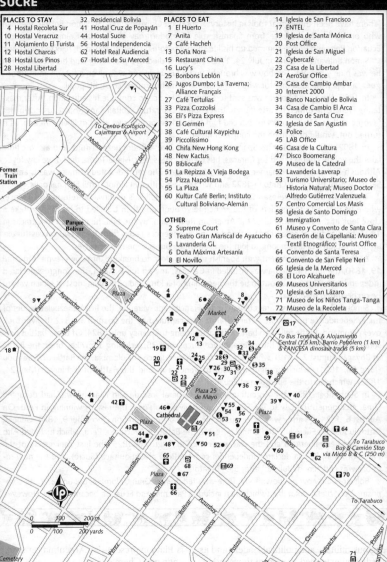

SUCRE

PLACES TO STAY
4 Hostal Recoleta Sur
10 Hostal Veracruz
11 Alojamiento El Turista
12 Hostal Charcas
18 Hostal Los Pinos
28 Hostal Libertad
32 Residencial Bolivia
41 Hostal Cruz de Popayán
44 Hostal Sucre
56 Hostal Independencia
62 Hotel Real Audiencia
67 Hostal de Su Merced

PLACES TO EAT
1 El Huerto
7 Anita
9 Café Hacheh
13 Doña Nora
15 Restaurant China
19 Lucy's
25 Bonbons Leblón
26 Jugos Dumbo; La Taverna;
   Alliance Français
27 Café Tertulias
35 Pizza Cozzolisi
36 Eli's Pizza Express
37 El Germén
38 Café Cultural Kaypichu
39 Piccolíssimo
40 Chifa New Hong Kong
48 New Kactus
50 Bibliocafé
51 La Repizza & Vieja Bodega
54 Pizza Napolitana
55 La Plaza
60 Kultur Café Berlin; Instituto
   Cultural Boliviano-Alemán

OTHER
2 Supreme Court
3 Teatro Gran Mariscal de Ayacucho
5 Lavandería GL
6 Doña Máxima Artesanía
8 El Novillo
14 Iglesia de San Francisco
17 ENTEL
19 Iglesia de Santa Mónica
20 Post Office
21 Iglesia de San Miguel
22 Cybercafé
23 Casa de la Libertad
24 AeroSur Office
29 Casa de Cambio Ambar
30 Internet 2000
31 Banco Nacional de Bolivia
34 Casa de Cambio El Arca
35 Banco de Santa Cruz
42 Iglesia de San Agustín
43 Police
45 LAB Office
46 Casa de la Cultura
47 Disco Boomerang
49 Museo de la Catedral
52 Lavandería Laverap
53 Turismo Universitario; Museo de
   Historia Natural; Museo Doctor
   Alfredo Gutiérrez Valenzuela
57 Centro Comercial Los Masis
58 Iglesia de Santo Domingo
59 Immigration
61 Museo y Convento de Santa Clara
63 Caserón de la Capellanía: Museo
   Textil Etnográfico; Tourist Office
64 Convento de Santa Teresa
65 Convento de San Felipe Neri
66 Iglesia de la Merced
68 El Loro Alcahuete
69 Museos Universitarios
70 Iglesia de San Lázaro
71 Museo de los Niños Tanga-Tanga
72 Museo de la Recoleta

El Libertador

'There have been three great fools in history: Jesus, Don Quixote and I.' So Simón Bolívar, the man who brought independence from Spanish rule to modern-day Venezuela, Colombia, Panama, Ecuador, Peru and Bolivia summed up his life shortly before he died abandoned, rejected and poor.

Simón Bolívar was born on July 24, 1783. His father died five years later, and his mother when he was nine years old. The boy was brought up by his uncle and was given a tutor, Simón Rodriguez, an open-minded mentor who had a strong formative influence on his pupil.

In 1799, the young Bolívar was sent to Spain and France to continue his education. After mastering French, he turned his attention to that country's literature. Voltaire and Rousseau became his favorite authors. Their works introduced him to the new, progressive ideas of liberalism and, as it turned out, would determine the course of his life.

In 1802, Bolívar married his Spanish bride, María Teresa Rodríguez del Toro, and a short time later the young couple sailed for Caracas, but eight months later, María Teresa died of yellow fever. Although Bolívar never remarried, he had many lovers. The most devoted of these was Manuela Sáenz, whom he met in Quito in 1822 and who stayed with him almost until his final days.

The death of María Teresa marked a drastic shift in Bolívar's destiny. He returned to France, where he met with the leaders of the French Revolution and then traveled to the USA to take a close look at the new order after the American Revolution. By the time he returned to Caracas in 1807, he was full of revolutionary theories and experiences taken from these two successful examples. It didn't take him long to join the clandestine pro-independence circles.

At the time, disillusionment with Spanish rule was close to breaking into open revolt. On April 19, 1810, the Junta Suprema was installed in Caracas, and on July 5, 1811, the Congress declared independence. This turned out to be the beginning of a long and bitter war, most of which was to be orchestrated by Bolívar.

Simón Bolívar's military career began under Francisco de Miranda, the first Venezuelan leader of the independence movement. After Miranda was captured by the Spanish in 1812, Bolívar took over command. Battle followed battle with astonishing frequency until 1824. Of those battles personally directed by Bolívar, the independence forces won 35, including a few key ones: the Battle of Boyacá (August 7, 1819), which secured the independence of Colombia; the Battle of Carabobo (June 24, 1821), which brought freedom to Venezuela; and the Battle of Pichincha (May 24, 1822), which led to the liberation of Ecuador.

In September 1822, the Argentine liberator General José de San Martín, who had occupied Lima, abandoned the city to the Spanish, and Bolívar took over the task of winning in Peru. On August 6, 1824, his army was victorious at the Battle of Junín, and on December 9, 1824, General Antonio José de Sucre inflicted a final defeat at the Battle of Ayacucho. Peru, which included Alto Perú, had been liberated and the war was over. On August 6, 1825, the first anniversary of the Battle of Junín, Bolivia declared independence from Peru at Chuquisaca (Sucre), and the new republic was christened 'Bolivia,' after the liberator.

Bolívar could now get down to his long-awaited dream: Gran Colombia, the unified state comprising Venezuela, Colombia (which then included Panama) and Ecuador, became reality. However,

religious, military and political leaders, and its jurisdiction extended to several thousand inhabitants. When the Spanish arrived, the entire area from Southern Peru to the Río de la Plata in present-day Argentina came to be known as Charcas.

In the early 1530s, Francisco Pizarro, the conquistador who felled the Inca empire,

El Libertador

the task of setting the newborn state on its feet proved even more difficult than winning battles. 'I fear peace more than war,' Bolívar wrote in a letter, aware of the difficulties ahead.

The main problem was the great racial and regional differences in Gran Colombia, which Bolívar, as president, was unable to hold together, even with strong central rule. The new state began to collapse from the moment of its birth. However, the president insisted upon holding the union together, although it was rapidly slipping from his hands. The impassioned speeches for which he was widely known could no longer sway the growing opposition, and his glory and charisma faded.

In August 1828, he took drastic action: He ousted his vice president Santander and assumed dictatorship, maintaining that 'Our America can only be ruled through a well managed, shrewd despotism.' His popularity waned further, as did his circle of friends and supporters, and a short time later, he miraculously escaped an assassination attempt in Bogotá. Disillusioned and in poor health, he resigned from the presidency in early 1830 and planned to leave for Europe, just in time for the formal disintegration of Gran Colombia.

Venezuela broke away in 1830, approved a new congress and banned Bolívar from his homeland. A month later, Antonio José de Sucre, Bolívar's closest friend, was assassinated in southern Colombia. These two news items reached Bolívar just as he was about to board a ship for France. Depressed and ill, he accepted the invitation of a Spaniard, Joaquín de Mier, to stay in his home in Santa Marta, Colombia.

Bolívar died on December 17, 1830 of pulmonary tuberculosis. A priest, a doctor and a few officers were by his bed, but none of these were his close friends. Joaquín de Mier donated one of his shirts to dress the body, as there had been none among Bolívar's humble belongings. So died perhaps the most important figure in the history of the South American continent.

It took the Venezuelan nation 12 years to acknowledge its debt to the man to whom it owed its freedom. In 1842, Bolívar's remains were brought from Santa Marta to Venezuela and deposited in the cathedral in Caracas. In 1876, they were solemnly transferred to the Pantheon in Caracas, where they now rest.

Today, Bolívar is once again a hero – his reputation polished and inflated to almost superhuman dimensions. His cult is particularly strong in Venezuela, but he's also widely venerated in the other nations he freed. His statue graces nearly every central city plaza and at least one street in every town bears his name.

El Libertador – as he was called at the beginning of his liberation campaigns and is also called today – was undoubtedly a man of extraordinary gifts. An idealist with a poetic mind and visionary ideas, his goal was not only to topple Spanish rule, but also to create a unified America. This, of course, proved an impossible ideal, yet the military conquest of some five million square kilometers remains a phenomenal accomplishment. This inspired amateur with no formal training in war strategy won battles in a manner that still confounds the experts.

One of the final remarks in Bolívar's diary reads, 'My name now belongs to history. It will do me justice.' And history has duly done so.

sent his brother Gonzalo to the Charcas region to oversee Indian mining activities and interests that might prove to be valuable to the Spanish realm. Uninterested in the Altiplano, he concentrated on the highlands east of the main Andean Cordilleras. As a direct result, in 1538 the city of La Plata was founded by Pedro de Anzures,

Marques de Campo Redondo, as the Spanish capital of the Charcas. As his Indian predecessors had done, he chose the warm, fertile and well-watered valley of Choque-Chaca for its site.

During the early 16th century, the Viceroyalty of Lima governed all Spanish territories in central and eastern South America. In 1559, King Phillip II created the Audiencia (Royal Court) of Charcas, with its headquarters in the city of La Plata, to administer the eastern territories. The Audiencia was unique in the New World in that it held both judicial authority and executive powers. The judge of the Audiencia also served as the chief executive officer. Governmental subdivisions within the district came under the jurisdiction of royal officers known as *corregidores*.

Until 1776, the Audiencia presided over Paraguay, southeastern Peru, northern Chile and Argentina, and most of Bolivia. When Portuguese interests in Brazil threatened the easternmost Spanish-dominated regions, a new Viceroyalty, also named La Plata, was established in order to govern and ensure tight control. The city of La Plata thereby lost jurisdiction over all but the former Choque-Chaca, one of the four provinces of Alto Peru, which comprised leftover territories between the Viceroyalties of Lima and La Plata. The city's name was changed to Chuquisaca (the Spanish corruption of Choque-Chaca), presumably to avoid confusion between the city and the new Viceroyalty.

The city had received an archbishopric in 1609, according it theological autonomy. That, along with the establishment of the University of San Xavier in 1622 and the 1681 opening of a law school, Academía Carolina, fostered continued growth and development of liberal and revolutionary ideas and set the stage for 'the first cry of Independence in the Americas' on May 25, 1809. The mini-revolution set off the alarm throughout Spanish America and, like ninepins, the northwestern South American republics were liberated by the armies of the military genius Simón Bolívar.

After the definitive liberation of Peru at the battles of Junín and Ayacucho on August 6 and December 9, 1824, Alto Peru, historically tied to the Lima government, was technically free of Spanish rule. In practice, however, it had carried on closer relations with the La Plata government in Buenos Aires and disputes arose about what to do with the territory.

On February 9, 1825, Bolívar's second-in-command, General Antonio José de Sucre, drafted and delivered a declaration that stated in part:

> The…Viceroyalty of Buenos Aires to which these provinces pertained at the time of the revolution of America lacks a general government which represents completely, legally, and legitimately the authority of all the provinces.…Their political future must therefore result from the deliberation of the provinces themselves and from an agreement between the congress of Perú and that…in the Río de la Plata.

Bolívar, unhappy with this unauthorized act of sovereignty, rejected the idea, but Sucre stood his ground, convinced that there was sufficient separatist sentiment in Alto Peru to back him up. As he expected, the people of the region refused to wait for a decision from the new congress to be installed in Lima the following year and rejected subsequent invitations to join the Buenos Aires government.

On August 6, the first anniversary of the Battle of Junín, independence was declared in the Casa de la Libertad at Chuquisaca and the new republic was christened 'Bolivia' after its liberator. On August 11, the city's name was changed for the final time to Sucre, in honor of the general who promoted the independence movement.

Difficult years followed in the Republic of Bolivia, and at one stage the Great Liberator became disenchanted with his namesake republic. After a particularly tumultuous period of political shuffling, he uttered, 'Hapless Bolivia has had four different leaders in less than two weeks! Only the kingdom of Hell could offer so appalling a picture discrediting humanity!'

Orientation

Laid out in an easily negotiated grid pattern, Sucre is small and compact. There isn't really a good city map available, but a decent photocopy is available for US$1 from the main tourist office, and most hotels distribute maps on the back of their advertising. You can pick up topo sheets of Chuquisaca department from the Instituto Geográfico Militar (☎ 55514; Aniceto Arce 172).

Information

Tourist Offices The Dirección Departamental de Turismo office (☎ 55983; Caserón de la Capellanía) isn't terribly helpful, but the staff can usually answer specific questions. It's open weekdays from 8 am to noon and 2 to 6 pm. The more useful Turismo Universitario (☎ 23763; Nicolás Ortiz 182) dispenses good information and provides student guides for city sightseeing. Clients pay only transportation expenses and an optional tip. It's open weekdays from 8 am to 12:30 pm and 2:30 to 6:30 pm.

Immigration Migración (☎ 32770), on Calle Calvo, is generally a no-fuss place to extend visas and lengths of stay.

Money Casa de Cambio Ambar (San Alberto 7) and Casa de Cambio El Arca (España 134) both change traveler's checks, but the latter normally offers better rates. Street moneychangers operate along Avenida Hernando Siles, behind the market. Quite a few businesses display 'Compro Dólares' signs, but they only change cash. The Banco Nacional de Bolivia changes traveler's checks at an outrageous 4% commission. Visa cash advances are available without ado at the casas de cambio and at the Banco de Santa Cruz, on the corner of San Alberto and España. You'll find Enlace machines on the plaza and on Calle San Alberto.

Post & Communications The post office is on the corner of Estudiantes and Junín, and the smart-looking ENTEL office on the corner of España and Urcullo opens at 8 am.

Email and Internet access is available at a growing number of places. Internet 2000, on Ravelo, is small but convenient to the budget hotels; the Cybercafé (☎ 44306; Estudiantes 33 & 79) is open until 9 pm every night (and sometimes later); and El Loro Alcahuete (☎ 61333; Nicolás Ortiz 118) entices cyber-heads with a café serving tacos and beer. All of these charge US$2.50 to US$3.50 per hour.

Cultural Centers The Instituto Cultural Boliviano Alemán (☎ 52091; Avaroa 326), at Kultur Café Berlin, has a selection of German-language books and newspapers as well as a café and news from the German community. Better known as ICBA, it also offers Spanish lessons (see Language Courses later in this chapter).

Alliance Française (☎ 53599; Avenida Aniceto Arce 35) keeps a supply of French-language reading material and newspapers and shows foreign films several times weekly (see the notice board at the northern corner of the plaza). It also operates the restaurant La Taverna.

The Centro Boliviano-Americano (☎ 51982; Calvo 437) brings Yankee culture to Sucre with its Rainbow Room Café and plenty of North American reading material.

Laundry Lavandería GL (☎ 21243; Loa 407) and Lavandería Laverap (☎ 42598; Bolívar 617) wash, dry and iron laundry in 90 minutes for US$2.50 per kilogram. They're open every day (in the morning only on Sunday and holidays) and will even deliver to your hotel. Hostal Charcas (☎ 41892; Ravelo 62) also has a laundry, which charges US$1 per kilogram and can handle washing, drying and ironing in three hours.

Medical Services If you need medical assistance, you may want to see Dr Gaston Delgadillo (☎ 51692; Colón 33, Casilla 78), who speaks Spanish, English, French and German.

Dangers & Annoyances Sucre is one of Bolivia's safest towns, but occasionally, visitors are harassed by bogus police. If you do have a problem, report it to the tourist police (☎ 25983) or the *radio patrulla* (☎ 110).

Museums

Museo & Convento de Santa Clara The museum of religion art in the Convento de Santa Clara (☎ 52295; Calvo 212), founded in 1639, contains several works by Bolivian master Melchor Pérez de Holguín and his Italian instructor, Bernardo de Bitti. In 1985 it was robbed, and several paintings and gold ornaments disappeared. One canvas, however, was apparently deemed too large to carry off, so the thieves sliced a big chunk out of the middle and left the rest hanging – and it's still hanging just that way. Guides may also demonstrate the still-functional pipe organ, which was fabricated in 1664.

The museum is open Monday to Saturday from 9 to noon and 3 to 6 pm. If it's closed, knock on the door on Calle Abaroa. Admission is US$0.75.

Museo de la Catedral The recently renovated Museo de la Catedral, beside the Capilla de la Virgen de Guadalupe, holds what is probably Bolivia's best collection of religious relics. Half of these were donated by one archbishop. Along with paintings and carvings, there are some priceless gold and silver religious articles set with rubies, emeralds and other precious stones. It's open Monday to Friday from 10 am to noon and 3 to 5 pm, and on Saturday from 10 am to noon. Admission is US$1.50.

Museos Universitarios The three university museums (☎ 53285; Bolívar 698) make a worthwhile visit. When all is well in Sucre academia, they're open weekdays from 8 am to 8 pm, on Saturday from 9 am to noon and 3 to 6 pm, and on Sunday from 9 am to noon. Admission is US$2.50, and photography permits cost an additional US$2.50 (in the dim light, you'll need at least 200 ASA film). The affiliated Museo de Historia Natural and the historical furniture museum, Museo Doctor Alfredo Gutiérrez Valenzuela (☎ 53828; Plaza 25 de Mayo 23), both on the plaza, are open

weekdays from 8:30 am to noon and 2 to 6 pm; admission to either costs US$0.50.

The Museo de Charcas was founded in 1939 and occupies a home with 21 large rooms. It houses Bolivia's best-known works of art, including some by Holguín, Padilla, Gamarra and Villavicencio. You'll also see ornate furniture that was handcrafted by Indians of the Jesuit missions.

The Museo Antropológico, founded in 1943, contains separate exhibits dealing with folklore, archaeology and ethnography. Highlights include mummies, skulls, and artifacts from the eastern jungles of Bolivia. There are also the usual collections of pottery, tools and textiles.

The Museo de Arte Moderna features excellent examples of modern Bolivian painting and sculpture, as well as pieces from around Latin America. Don't miss the handcrafted charangos by Bolivian artist and musician Mauro Núñez, and the section devoted to native art.

Museo Textil Etnográfico (ASUR) Highly worthwhile is Fundación Antropólogos del Surandino's (ASUR's) Museo Textil Etnográfico (☎ 53841; fax 61294; asur@ mara.scr.entelnet.bo; San Alberto 413, Casilla 662), in the 17th-century Caserón de la Capellanía. The museum conducts art workshops and displays permanent and itinerant art exhibitions. These feature lovely local ceramics and beautiful and practical weavings, known as *axsus*, from both the Candelaria (Tarabuco) and Jalq'a (Potolo) traditions, among others, all tastefully displayed in appropriate light and background colors.

In the contiguous shop, the Proyecto Textil ASUR markets locally produced ceramics and weavings and ensures that a good share of the profits goes to the artisans. However, it's more interesting (and cheaper) to visit the weaving villages and buy directly from the artisans.

The foundation is open Monday to Friday from 8:30 am to noon and 2:30 to 6 pm, and Saturday from 9:30 am to noon (in July and August until 6 pm). There's one major sticking point: Although this is a private nonprofit concern and it's not supported by taxes, foreigners pay US$2 admission, which is double the local rate. Scheduled cultural events are posted on the notice board at the northern corner of the plaza.

Museo de la Recoleta La Recoleta (☎ 51987), in Plaza Pedro Anzures, was established by the Franciscan Order in 1601 and overlooks the city of Sucre from the top of Calle Polanco. It has served not only as a convent and museum but also as a barracks and prison. In one of the stairwells is a plaque marking the spot where, in 1828, President D Pedro Blanco was assassinated. Outside are courtyard gardens brimming with color and the renowned Cedro Milenario – the ancient cedar – a huge tree that was once even larger than its current size. It is the only remnant of the cedars that were once abundant around Sucre.

The museum is worthwhile for its anonymous paintings and sculptures from the 16th to 20th centuries, including numerous interpretations of St Francis of Assisi.

The highlight is the church choir and its magnificent wooden carvings dating back to the 1870s, each one intricately unique. They represent the Franciscan, Jesuit and Japanese martyrs who were crucified in 1595 in Nagasaki, Japan.

La Recoleta is open from 9 to 11 am and 3 to 5 pm. Admission, including a guided tour, costs US$1. Check out the price list for religious services on the notice board at the entrance!

Museo de los Niños Tanga-Tanga Just downhill from La Recoleta is the Museo de los Niños Tanga-Tanga (☎ 40299; wawas@mara.scr.entelnet.bo; Pasaje Iturricha 281, Casilla 826), the children's museum, started by a US volunteer. The attached café is a great place to have coffee and cake or drink a beer while gazing out across the best view in town. Their motto is 'We always have change,' which has to be worth something, and proceeds from the café go toward the development of the museum and its children's cultural programs.

The Virgin of Guadalupe

Churches
Cathedral The cathedral (☎ 52257; Plaza 25 de Mayo) was begun in 1551 and completed 15 years later, but major sections were added between 1580 and 1650. Of interest is the bell tower, a Sucre landmark, and the statues of the 12 Apostles and four patron saints of Sucre. The tower clock was ordered from London in 1650 and installed in 1772. Unfortunately, the present interior is rather overburdened with kitsch.

Around the corner is the Capilla de la Virgen de Guadalupe, which was completed in 1625. Encased in the altar is the Virgen de Guadalupe de la Extremadura, named after a similar image in Spain. She was originally painted by Fray Diego de Ocaña in 1601. The work was subsequently coated with highlights of gold and silver and adorned in robes encrusted with diamonds, amethysts, pearls, rubies and emeralds donated by some wealthy colonial parishioners. The jewels alone are said to be worth millions of dollars, and one can only wonder why the priceless Virgin's head is ringed with cheap incandescent Christmas bulbs!

The chapel and cathedral are open daily between 7 and 8 am. The Museo de la Catedral is described earlier in this section.

San Francisco The Iglesia de San Francisco (☎ 51853; Ravelo 1) was established in 1538 by Francisco de Aroca soon after the founding of La Plata. It began as a makeshift structure; the current church wasn't completed until 1581. In 1809, when the struggle for Bolivian independence got under way, a law passed by Mariscal Sucre transferred San Francisco's religious community to La Paz and turned the building over to the army, to be used as a military garrison, market and customs hall. In 1838, the top floor collapsed, but it was rebuilt and later used as military accommodations. It wasn't re-consecrated until 1925.

Architecturally, the most interesting feature of San Francisco is its *mudéjar* ceiling. In the belfry is the Campana de la Libertad, Bolivia's Liberty Bell, which called patriots to revolution in 1825. The church is open daily from 7 to 9 am and 4 to 7 pm, and during Mass on weekends.

Convento de San Felipe Neri For evidence of why Sucre was nicknamed the White City of the Americas, visit the bell tower and tiled rooftop of the Convento de San Felipe Neri (Nicolás Ortiz 165).

In the days when the building served as a monastery, asceticism didn't prevent the monks coming to meditate over the view; you can still see the stone seats on the roof terraces. The church was originally constructed of stone but was later covered with a layer of stucco. Gardens of poinsettias and roses are in the courtyard, and a nice painting of the Last Supper hangs in the stairwell.

In the catacombs are tunnels where priests and nuns once met clandestinely and where, during times of political unrest, guerrillas hid and circulated around the city. The building now functions as a parochial school.

The church and roof are open Monday to Friday from 4:30 to 6 pm. Visitors must first check in with the university tourist information office and procure a guide (no charge). Admission is US$1, payable at the convent entrance.

Santa Mónica The mestizo-style Iglesia de Santa Mónica, on Arenales at Junín, was begun in 1574 and was originally intended to serve as the Monasterio de las Religiosas Mónicas for the Ermitañas de San Agustín. However, the order ran into serious financial difficulties in the early 1590s, eventually resulting in its closure and conversion into a Jesuit school.

The interior is adorned with mestizo-tradition carvings of seashells, animals and human figures; the ceiling features impressive woodwork; and the courtyard is one of the city's finest, with lawns and a variety of semitropical plants. It now serves as a civic auditorium and is open only during special events held there.

San Miguel Built between 1612 and 1621, the Iglesia de San Miguel (☎ 51026; Arenales 10) reflects mudéjar influences, mainly in the arched galleries around the courtyard and Doric columns supporting the choir. Originally a Jesuit church, it was rededicated when the order was expelled from Bolivia. Highlights include the painted ceiling, the silver altar and several period paintings and sculptures. The interior is open Monday to Friday from 11:30 am to noon and during Mass on weekends; the dress code excludes short sleeves, short skirts and shorts.

La Merced Although it appears ordinary from the exterior, the Iglesia de la Merced (☎ 51338), on Azurduy at Pérez 1 and diagonally opposite San Felipe Neri, contains the most beautiful interior of any church in Sucre and possibly in Bolivia. Because the order of La Merced left Sucre for Cuzco in 1826, taking its records with it, the founding date of the church is uncertain, but it is believed to be sometime in the early 1550s. The building was completed no later than the early 1580s.

The Baroque-style altar and carved mestizo pulpit are decorated with filigree and gold inlay. Several paintings by the esteemed artist Melchor Pérez de Holguín – notably *El Nacimiento de Jesús*, *El Nacimiento de María* and a self-portrait of the artist rising from the depths of Purgatory – are on display, as are sculptures by other artists.

Owing to clerical shortages, La Merced has been decommissioned. It's meant to be open Monday to Friday from 10 to 11:30 am and 3 to 5:30 pm, but this is rarely the case, and prospective visitors may have to rap on the door and hope for the best.

Santo Domingo The Baroque-style Iglesia de Santo Domingo (☎ 51483; Bolívar 13), at Calvo, was constructed in the mid-16th century by the Dominican Order. During the war for Bolivian independence, the Spanish crown forced the church to liquidate its gold and silver in order to pay for the war effort. After the war, it was transformed into the official residence of the governor, and was also used as a post office. The building is now part of the University's Junín College. It contains a superb wooden carving of Christ.

San Lázaro The 1544 Iglesia de San Lázaro, on Calvo at Padilla, was the first church in the historic Audiencia de Charcas. The original building was constructed of simple adobe brick and covered with a thatched roof, but it has been thoroughly reworked. Items of note include the original silverwork on the altar and several paintings attributed to Zurbarán, of the Polanco school. It's open for Mass daily at 7 am.

Convento de Santa Teresa The brilliant white Convento de Santa Teresa (☎ 51986; San Alberto 42) belongs to an order of cloistered nuns. From 10 am to noon, they sell candied oranges, apples, figs and limes that they've prepared. Don't miss strolling down the lovely Callejón de Santa Teresa, a lantern-lit alleyway that was once partially paved with human bones laid out in the shape of a cross. This gruesome motif was intended to remind passersby of the inevitability of death. In the 1960s, it was repaved with its current cobbles.

Casa de la Libertad

For a dose of Bolivian history, visit the Casa de la Libertad, the house on the main plaza

where the Bolivian declaration of independence was signed on August 6, 1825. The building has been designated a national memorial in commemoration of this and other historical events. A replica of the actual document (the original is in the Sucre branch of the Banco Nacional!) and numerous other mementos of the era are on display.

The first score of Bolivian congresses were held in the Salon, originally a Jesuit chapel. Doctoral candidates were also examined here. Behind the pulpit hang portraits of Simón Bolívar, Hugo Ballivián and Antonio José de Sucre. General Bolívar said that this portrait, by Peruvian artist José Gil de Castro, was the most lifelike representation ever done of him.

The museum also includes portraits of presidents, military decorations, war- and independence-related art and relics, and old governmental documents. The most memorable is a huge wooden bust of Bolívar carved by artist and musician Mauro Núñez. Note the magnificent gilded loft in the Aula de Independencia.

It's open Monday to Friday from 8:30 am to noon and 2:30 to 6 pm, and on Saturday from 9:30 to 11:30 am. Admission costs US$2, photography costs an additional US$2 and video permits are US$3.50.

Cemetery

The enthusiasm surrounding Sucre's cemetery seems disproportionate to what's there. Locals make a point of reminding visitors not to miss it. 'See it,' they urge, 'it's wonderful.' Such assessments may be a tad excessive. There are some arches carved from poplar trees, as well as unkempt gardens and the mausoleums of wealthy colonial families, but it's a mystery why it should inspire such local fervor. To enliven the experience, you may want to hire one of the enthusiastic child guides who offer their services for US$0.50. You can walk there from the center, or take a taxi or Micro A.

FANCESA Dinosaur Tracks

It seems that 60 million years ago, the site of Sucre's FANCESA cement quarry served as a sort of Grumman's Chinese Theatre for large and scaly types. When the grounds were being cleared, plant employees uncovered a nearly vertical mudstone face bearing hundreds of tracks – some of which measure up to 80cm in diameter – from tyrannosauri rex, iguanadons and other dinosaurs. There are also petrified remains of prehistoric algae and fish.

You'll get within a dusty 2km walk from FANCESA on Micro A from the center. The site, 5km north of town, is officially open to the public only on Saturday, but those who turn up at other times probably won't be turned away unless the gate guard is in a bad mood. The plant will appoint an employee to act as a guide, who will expect a tip (and will probably remind you several times of that fact), but you'll have to insist that they actually provide some information and resist requests for outrageous amounts of cash. Currently, US$1.50 is the standard tip per group for a 10 to 15-minute look around.

La Glorieta

After an extended tour of Europe, the wealthy entrepreneur Don Francisco Argandoña decided to build a home on the outskirts of Sucre that reflected the various architectural traditions he'd encountered overseas. He commissioned the architect Antonio Camponovo to design a castle that incorporated a hodgepodge of European styles, and the result was the imposing La Glorieta, which is difficult to discuss without passing judgement. Now a classic example of faded grandeur, it serves as the Lyceo Militar (military high school).

To get there, take a taxi, Micro I or Micro 4 from the corner of Ravelo and Aniceto Arce and get off 7km south of town on the Potosí road. It's open Monday to Friday from 9 am to noon and 2 to 6 pm, and on Saturday from 9 am to noon. Admission costs US$1.20, including a guide, but because this is a military installation, visitors must leave their passports or cédulas de identificación at the entrance.

Language Courses

Although Cochabamba has long been the city of choice for Spanish and Quechua language instruction, prospective students are now discovering that Sucre is lovelier and also has a healthy climate and youthful atmosphere. A lot of people wind up at the Instituto Cultural Boliviano Alemán (☎ 52091; Avaroa 326), but they currently charge a gratuitous application/admission fee of US$90, and there are plenty of private teachers who provide more personable and equally professional service. Highly recommended teachers include Doña Sofía Sauma (☎ 51687; sadra@mara.scr.entelnet.bo) and Margot Macías Machicado (☎ 53567; mamaci@latinmail.com; Olañeta 345). Both charge US$5 per hour and include plenty of practice while visiting sites of interest around the city. The former is currently setting up the Instituto Charcas, in affiliation with the Hostal de Su Merced.

Organized Tours

Most Sucre tour companies run Sunday excursions to Tarabuco and also offer jaunts into the Cordillera de los Frailes. For independent treks into the wild Cordillera de los Frailes or Cordillera de los Sombreros, or an incredible 10-day trek from Sucre to Torotoro, hire the local trekking enthusiasts, Lucho & Dely Loredo (see Guides under Cordillera de los Frailes, later in this chapter), who will provide an unforgettable experience.

Some other options for tours of Sucre and its surroundings include Altamira Tours (☎/fax 53525; mobile ☎ 017-600008; altamira@ sucre.bo.net), on Aniceto Arce at San Alberto; Eclipse Travel (☎/fax 43960 or 52091; gmielke@mara.scr.entelnet.bo; Avaroa 326, Casilla 648); Gumer's Tours (☎ 61575; fax 41876; Junín 442); Turismo Sucre (☎ 52936; mobile ☎ 011-32858; fax 60349; Bustillos 117); SurAndes (☎/fax 56232; Nicolás Ortíz 6); and Tarco Tours (☎ 61688; fax 40938; tarco@ mara.scr.entelnet.bo; Plaza 25 de Mayo, Multicentro Céspedes).

Groups of two people or more pay roughly the following rates: Cerro Churuquella (US$28, with trekking), Cerro Sica-Sica (US$28, with trekking), Supay Huasi (US$28), Incamachay (US$28, with trekking), Yotala-Cachimayu (US$28, with trekking), Potolo (US$46/64 for one/two days, with trekking), Quila Quila (US$28), Maragua (US$35 per day or US$135 for a five-day trek), Chaunaca & Chataquila (US$61 for two days) and Humaca (US$64, two days trekking).

An unusual option is offered by Joy Ride Bolivia (☎ 25544; mobile ☎ 019-73146; fax 60141; gertmans@yahoo.com; Calle Emilio Mendizabal 229), which runs motorcycle and ATV tours around Sucre and to Potosí, Uyuni and the Southwest Circuit. For trips on a Honda XR400 motorcycle, you'll pay US$100 to US$120 per person per day; for a Honda Foreman ES ATV, the price is US$120. Costs include gas, insurance, guide, food and lodging. Protective gear costs an additional US$15 per day.

Special Events

On the evening of September 8, local campesinos celebrate the Fiesta de la Virgen de Guadalupe with songs and poetry recitations. The following day, they dress in colorful costumes and parade around the main plaza carrying religious images and silver arches.

The Fiesta de la Empanada, which occurs several times a year in the Casa de la Libertad, draws chefs and bakers from around the area who compete for prizes with their original salteña and empanada recipes. The festival includes folkloric music, dancing, costumes and tables where artisans sell their handicrafts and weavings. The tourist office can provide specific dates.

Places to Stay

Budget Because Sucre is growing more popular with well-heeled visitors, lots of budget accommodations options are converting into more upmarket establishments. Most of the places that charge in bolivianos rather than US currency are clustered around the market and along Calles Ravelo and San Alberto.

The friendly *Alojamiento El Turista* (☎ 53172; Ravelo 118) is musty and mediocre, but at US$2.50/4 for a single/double, it's a good value for strict budgets. Try to get a room on the top floor; one even has a private bath. In the middle of nowhere, opposite the

bus terminal, is the misnamed *Alojamiento Central* (☎ 53935), with rooms with shared baths for US$4/6. It's ten minutes from town on Micro A.

The friendly *Hostal Charcas* (☎ 53972; fax 55764; hostalcharcas@latinmail.com; Ravelo 62) is a real winner and represents one of Sucre's best values. Showers combine solar and electric heat, so hot water is available around the clock. Sparkling clean rooms cost US$9/15 with private baths and US$6.50/10 with shared baths. Breakfast is available, and the attendants are helpful and can provide reliable tourist information.

In the same neighborhood, *Hostal Veracruz* (☎ 51560), on Calle Ravelo, is a newly renovated and good-value choice, with a variety of rooms. Without a private bath, you'll pay US$4 per person; with private baths, rooms are US$12/17. Breakfast is available but costs extra.

Residencial Bolivia (☎ 54346; fax 53388; San Alberto 42) charges US$8.50/14.50 for a room with bath and US$5/9.50 without. All rates include an unmemorable breakfast, but it's friendly and centrally located.

If you prefer a country retreat, check out the very friendly *Kantu Ñucchu*, at the village of Ñucchu, 21km south of Sucre along the Potosí road. Double rooms with a kitchen and private bath cost US$12, including meals; if you prefer to cook on your own, you'll pay just US$5! The surroundings are excellent for hiking into the wild hills and valleys. To get there, take a bus or camión from the cemetery or the El Tejar gas station in Sucre. For information, contact Augusto Marion at San Alberto 237 in Sucre.

Another out-of-town choice is *Centro Ecológico Cajamarca* (☎ 40606; office at Nicolás Ortiz 198), which can be reached by taking the Potolo road 3.5km from La Punilla, then traveling north along a side road for 4km. Cabins with solar lighting, private baths and use of kitchen facilities cost US$5/7, and camping is US$0.50 per person. Horseback riding is available for US$1 per hour. To get there, take a camión toward Chataquila, get off at the turn and walk the final 4km to the complex.

Mid-Range & Top End The three-star *Hostal Sucre* (☎ 51411; fax 61928; tursucre@ mara.scr.entelnet.bo; Bustillos 113) is one of Sucre's nicest places to stay. It has a lovely antique dining room and a sunny, flowery courtyard where you can kick back and read or catch up on letters. For singles/doubles with private baths, breakfast and cable TV, you'll pay US$19/25; a continental breakfast costs an additional US$1.60 while an American one goes for US$2.50. For the same price, there's *Hostal Recoleta Sur* (☎ 54789; fax 069-12077; hostrecs@mara.scr.entelnet.bo), on Ravelo at Loa, which offers similar amenities as well as email and Internet access.

One of a new crop of spiffy mid-range places is *Hostal Independencia* (☎ 42256; fax 61369; jacosta@mara.scr.entelnet.bo), which features 19th-century architecture and a conference salon that emulates a colonial-era hall of government. Carpeted rooms with private baths, breakfast and cable TV cost US$25/36. The rooms are arranged around a very pleasant courtyard, creating a strong colonial atmosphere. A similar place is the very lovely and recommended *Hostal de Su Merced* (☎ 42706; fax 069-12078; sumerced@mara.scr.entelnet.bo; Azurduy 16). Here, rooms cost US$27/40 (ask for room 7), plus US$2 for a continental breakfast (US$3 for an American one). For a look at its charming architecture, see the website www.boliviaweb.com/companies/ sumerced.

Hostal Libertad (☎ 53101; fax 60128; Aniceto Arce 99), a block from the plaza, offers TV, telephones, piped music, private baths and frigobars (minibar/fridge). Rooms cost US$17/20. The spacious suite with huge wraparound windows and lots of light costs US$25, but it suffers from traffic noise.

The three-star *Hostal Cruz de Popayán* (☎ 55156; Loa 881) has a reputation for its charm and comfort, and is reminiscent of a Spanish *parador* or a Portuguese pousada. It's a pretty good value at US$20/25 for bright rooms with private baths. Breakfast in the courtyard is a real treat.

For a quiet retreat, there's *Hostal Los Pinos* (☎ 54403; Colón 502), which sits at the outer edge of town. This squeaky-clean place features cozy rooms and a beautiful courtyard and garden. Rooms with private baths and a good breakfast cost US$17/21.

Sucre's poshest digs, *Hotel Real Audiencia* (☎/fax 60823; Potosí 142), charges US$50/80 for single/double rooms with private baths, TV, telephones and breakfast included.

Places to Eat

Sucre has a pleasant variety of quality restaurants and is a good place to spend time lolling around coffee shops and observing the youthful Bolivian university life.

The market provides some highlights. Don't miss the fruit salads and juices, which are among the best in the country. You'll have to search for the correct stalls; they're tucked in an obscure corner of the ground floor. Try *jugo de tumbo* (juice of unripe yellow passion fruit) or any combination of melon, guava, pomelo, strawberry, papaya, banana, orange, lime etc. The vendors and their blenders always come up with something indescribably delicious. Upstairs in the market, you'll find good, filling meals in unusually sanitary conditions (for a market, anyway) for US$0.50 to US$0.75. For breakfast, you can enjoy a *pastel* (pastry) or a salteña and a glass of *api* for as little as US$0.30. Good salteñerías include *Anita* and *Lucy's*.

Jugos Dumbo, near the plaza, opens early to serve salteñas, coffee, tea, juice and *licuados*. For a friendly, good-value breakfast, see *Doña Nora*, who serves up bread, coffee, juice and two eggs for US$1.50. Later in the day, she cooks up excellent burgers with all the trimmings for less than US$1.

Café Tertulias (☎ 20390; Plaza 25 de Mayo 59), popular with writers, artists and journalists, is slightly pricey with US$5 main courses, but the food is good and the bar cozy. The nearby *Pizza Napolitana* plays good British and US music and does well as a hangout for the university crowd, with ice cream and pizzas leading the menu selections. Drinks and coffee are on the expensive side, but a pizza large enough to fill two people costs only US$4.

Also excellent for pizza – as well as pasta, chicken, steak and even ribs – is the *New Kactus* (☎ *52788; Dalence 39*). It serves a wicked steak with baked potato for around US$5 and features a pool table, large-screen TV, bar, disco and other trendy amenities. A host of chicken-and-french-fries shops line up along Hernando Siles between Tarapaca and Junín.

The rather pretentious but very popular *La Repizza* (☎ *51506; Nicolás Ortíz 78*) does stone-baked meat or vegetarian pizzas, milanesas, pacumutus and pasta dishes, including vegetarian lasagna. The four-course almuerzos cost only US$1.50 and are a favorite with university students. The rustic *Vieja Bodega*, nearby, offers five-course almuerzos for just US$2. The ubiquitous *Eli's Pizza Express* (*España 126*) has also made its appearance in Sucre, as has *Pizza Cozzolisi*, on España at San Alberto.

At the long-running *La Plaza* (alas, no slot machines), the mostly meat-based meals are filling and adequate, and the outdoor balconies are a great place to drink beer on a lethargic Sunday afternoon. An expensive but very good Chinese place is *Chifa New Hong Kong* (☎ *41776; San Alberto 242*). *Restaurant China* offers Chinese and Bolivian cuisine in a good, clean environment. Almuerzos cost US$1, and for dinner you can choose from a range of Chinese options, as well as fish or schnitzel, for US$1 to US$2.

For upmarket Italian food, including lasagna, ravioli, cannelloni etc, there's *Piccolíssimo* (☎ *53247; San Alberto 237*). It's about as elegant as Sucre gets, but its attempts at creating a highbrow atmosphere joyfully fail. Plan on US$5 to US$7 per person, or more if you splurge on a bottle of Chilean wine. Afterwards, enjoy a cup of espresso or cappuccino – so good one could wax poetic! It's open nightly except Sunday. Mexican choices are limited to the intermittent tacos at the cybercafé *El Loro Alcahuete* (☎ *61333; Nicolás Ortíz 118*) and the highly recommended offerings at *El Huerto* (☎ *51538; Ladislao Cabrera 86*).

The excellent Alliance Française restaurant, *La Taverna*, serves a mean ratatouille for US$1.50, as well as coq au vin, quiche Lorraine and other continental favorites. The menu reflects a laudable trilingual harmony: 'con eggs ou sin eggs.' And then there are the sinful desserts…

The best vegetarian option is undoubtedly the ultra-popular *Café Cultural Kaypichu* (☎ *43954; San Alberto 168*), run by a pair of very upbeat Bolivians. For breakfast, they offer muesli, granola, yogurt and fresh fruit; lunch is a set vegetarian almuerzo and dinners feature á la carte vegetarian options, from pizza and pasta to soups and salads. Here you can also buy Artecampo's natural-material greeting cards and lampshades produced by rural women in Santa Cruz department. It's open Tuesday to Sunday from 7:30 am to 2 pm and 5 to 9 pm.

Sucre is growing increasingly popular with German and Swiss expatriates, resulting in a trio of fine Teutonic options. A nice one is *Bibliocafé* (*Nicolás Ortiz 50*), with a dark but cozy atmosphere, good music and stacks of *Geo* and *Der Spiegel* magazines on the shelves. The pasta dishes (US$3.50) – including the multinational Thai pasta – are recommended, as are the sandwiches (US$1), Greek salads (US$2), and sweet and savory crêpes (US$2.20). It's open only in the evening (closed Mondays) and often gets crowded, so go early.

The coffee shop and restaurant *Kultur Café Berlin* (*Avaroa 326*) is open for lunch from 12:30 to 3 pm. Don't miss the *papas rellenas* (spicy filled potatoes), which cost just US$0.50. The third German option is the bright and airy *El Germén*, on San Alberto, which does excellent vegetarian dishes – tofu curry, veggie lasagna and pizza – and German-style gateaux and pastries. Vegetarian almuerzos cost just US$1.50, and there's also a book exchange with titles in both English and German. It's open daily from 3:30 to 8 pm.

A student hangout with a Bolivian twist is *Café Hacheh* (*Pastor Sainz 233*). It's open from 11 am to midnight, and the décor may well remind you of a low-key art gallery. Specialties include sandwiches, coffee and fruit juice.

Thanks to Sucre's status as Bolivia's chocolate capital, there's plenty of scope for a sweet fix. For the best offerings from Cadbury, Breick, Hershey's, Mars, Nestlé and other companies, a good choice is **Bonbons Leblón**, which is on Arenales at Aniceto Arce.

Entertainment

Some of the bars and restaurants on and around the plaza have live music and peña nights. For discos and karaoke, look around Calle España, just up from the plaza. On Friday nights, **El Novillo** (☎ 60150; Aniceto Arce 230) serves meals and holds a folk music peña. From Thursday to Sunday, **Disco Boomerang** (☎ 52783; Dalence 39) serves pizza, pasta and other meals for around US$4, depending on the evening. Admission is free until 11 pm and US$3.50 thereafter. When you don't want to dance, check out the dart board or billiards table.

The **Centro Cultural los Masis** (☎ 53403; Bolívar 561) sponsors concerts and other cultural events, and has a small museum of local musical instruments. It also offers Quechua classes. It's open weekdays from 10 am to noon and 3:30 to 9 pm.

The **Teatro al Aire Libre**, southeast of the center, is a wonderful outdoor venue for musical and other performances. On Plaza Pizarro, there's an opulent old opera house, the **Teatro Gran Mariscal de Ayacucho**. Cultural events are announced on the notice board on the northwest corner of the plaza. Café Tertulias (see Places to Eat) serves as a venue for cultural programs and music and theater productions. The tourist office and the Casa de la Cultura (☎ 5083) both distribute a monthly calendar of events.

Shopping

A good place to look for local weavings is the ASUR Proyecto Textil, in the Caserón de la Capellanía (see Museo Textil Etnográfico, earlier in this chapter). Prices are steep by Bolivian standards, but the quality of the items justifies them and the artisans generally receive a fair

percentage. Plan on US$100 to US$200 for a high-quality Jalq'a or Candelaria weaving, and more for an exceptional one. Alternatively, opt for the *oferta del mes*, the 'monthly sale item'; with luck, you may find a fabulous piece for as little as US$50. Alternatively, check out the little shop next door, which sells very nice weavings and other traditional items for considerably less.

If you prefer to buy genuine Candelaria and Jalq'a weavings that have not been produced expressly for tourists, visit the jam-packed cubbyhole of Doña Máxima (Centro Comercial Guadalupe, Calle Junín 411). With hard bargaining, you'll find excellent deals on less decorative and more utilitarian pieces. If Doña Máxima isn't in the shop, ask around and someone will hunt her up.

Some of Bolivia's best charango makers are based around Sucre, and several shops sell local pieces. Learning to play one is another matter, but if you already play the guitar, you should be able to coax out some pleasant sounds; some artisans may even throw in a lesson or two. Try the shops at Calle Junín 1190 and Destacamento 59, but in the interest of endangered armadillos everywhere, please avoid armadillo-shell charangos.

Getting There & Away

Air LAB (☎ 54445) and AeroSur (☎ 62141) both have flights to and from La Paz, Cochabamba (LAB only), Santa Cruz, Tarija (LAB only), Camiri and other towns. Note that when it's raining or cloudy, Sucre's mountain-girded airport resists the best efforts of even the expert LAB pilots, so in inclement weather, don't traipse out to the airport until the airline has confirmed that the flight is operating.

Bus The bus terminal is unfortunately not within walking distance of the center, but is readily accessed by Micro A, which may be crowded with luggage. Unless you're headed for Potosí, it's wise to book long-distance buses a day in advance, in order to reserve a good seat if nothing else. Long-distance bus fares are usually lowered if you request a discount when buying the ticket.

Numerous daily buses run to Cochabamba (10 hours, US$4), all of which leave around 6 or 7 pm; many of these continue on to Santa Cruz (15 to 20 hours, US$6.75). Some buses follow the scenic direct route via Samaipata rather than going through Cochabamba.

Lots of flotas also have morning and evening departures for La Paz (16 hours, US$6.50) via Oruro (12 hours, US$6.20). Numerous companies leave for Potosí (3½ hours, US$2.50) several times daily from 6 am to 6 pm. Alternatively, you can take a taxi to Potosí, which costs US$5 per person with four people and is much faster than the bus. You'll find daily connections to Uyuni (10 to 12 hours, US$8.50), but they normally entail changing buses at Potosí.

Whenever the road is passable, Flota Chaqueño does the beautiful-but-rough trip to Camiri (US$13.50; 18 hours) at least twice weekly.

Charter buses to the Sunday market in Tarabuco (US$2.80 roundtrip) may be booked through any Sucre hotel or guest house. From Sucre, they leave at 7 am, and from Tarabuco, between 1 and 3 pm. Alternatively, take a micro from along Avenida de las Américas between 6:30 and 9:30 am on Sunday (2½ hours, US$1). Buses and camiones returning to Sucre wait at the top of the main plaza in Tarabuco.

Camión Camiones for Punilla, Chataquila, Potolo, Ravelo, and points north and west leave in the morning from Calle Canelas in the northern suburbs; to get there, take Micro D or Trufi 5 from the corner of Hernando Siles and Junín. There are usually two or three services daily to each destination, departing between 10 and 11 am. Camiones to Tarabuco, Candelaria, Padilla, and points south and east leave from the stop on Avenida de las Américas. Micros and camiones to Potosí leave when full from the railway tracks at Avenida Ostria Gutiérrez.

Train Unfortunately, Sucre's charming train station is no longer used, though there has been talk of implementing a tourist rail service between Sucre and Potosí. Don't hold your breath.

Getting Around
To/From the Airport The airport, 9km northwest of town, is accessed by Micro F (US$0.20) from Avenida Hernando Siles or by taxi for a negotiable US$3 to US$4.

Bus Lots of micros ply the city streets, and all seem to congregate at or near the market between runs; they're usually crowded, but fortunately, Sucre is a town of short distances. The most useful routes are those that climb the steep Avenida Grau hill to the Recoleta, and Micro A, which serves the main bus terminal. The standard fare for any route is US$0.20. Micros to the colonial village of Yotala leave from the cemetery and also cost US$0.20.

Taxi Taxis between any two points around the center, including the bus terminal, cost US$0.60 for up to three people.

Around Sucre

TARABUCO
☎ 0691
The village of Tarabuco, a dusty 65km southeast of Sucre, lies at an elevation of 3200m and enjoys a mild climate, just a bit cooler than Sucre's. Most *tarabuqueños* are involved in agriculture or textiles, and the colorful handmade clothing and weavings produced there are some of the most renowned in Bolivia.

On March 12, 1816, Tarabuco was the site of the Battle of Jumbati, in which the villagers defended themselves under the leadership of a woman, Doña Juana Azurduy de Padilla, and liberated the town from Spanish forces.

Mercado Campesino
Although most visitors will miss the annual Phujllay celebrations, you will want to catch

Tarabuco's colorful Sunday market, which features generally high-quality artesanía: charangos, pullovers, coca pouches, ponchos and weavings that feature geometric and zoomorphic designs. The colorful wares laid out in stalls around the plaza and on side streets lend a festive and lighthearted atmosphere, while strolling, charango-playing campesinos model their local dress. The men wear distinctive *monteras* (also known as *morriones*), which are leather hats patterned after those worn by the conquistadores. You may also want to seek out the snake-oil vendors in the central market, who proffer the universal curative powers of leftover bits of snakes and other (by this time) anonymous reptiles.

This scene draws both independent and organized tourists. Even well-bargained prices tend to be high, and sales tactics are somewhat less than passive, so you'll have to appreciate skill and quality, even when it's being shoved up your nose. If it's all too overwhelming, you may want to visit other weaving villages in the area, such as Candelaria, southeast of Tarabuco, or Ravelo and Potolo, northwest of Sucre.

Special Events

In commemoration of the Battle of Jumbati, the village stages Phujllay ('amusement' or 'play' in Quechua) on the second weekend of March, when over 60 surrounding communities turn up in local costume. The celebration begins with a Quechua Mass and procession followed by the Pukhara ceremony, a Bolivian version of Thanksgiving. Folkloric dancers and musicians perform throughout the two-day weekend fiesta. It's one of Bolivia's largest festivals and is worth attending.

The smaller local celebration of La Virgen de Rosario takes place in October and it features bullfights, Masses and parades.

Places to Stay & Eat

During Phujllay, accommodations fill up quickly, so you may want to hedge your bets and carry camping gear. The ephemeral *Alojamiento Florida* (☎ 2233), half a block north of the plaza, charges US$3 per person for a shabby room and dirty communal facilities. The attached restaurant isn't too bad. A nicer option is *El Alojamiento* on the plaza, which is run by a friendly local woman who also charges US$3 per person.

Meals of chorizo, curry, charque kan and soup are available from street stalls during market hours. The plaza also has a couple of basic restaurants.

Getting There & Away

All the Sucre travel agencies offer guided Sunday excursions to Tarabuco (around US$15 per person), but you might as well take the charter buses, which cost US$2.80 roundtrip and pick up clients at their hotels and guest houses around 7 am. From Tarabuco, they leave for the return trip anytime between 1 and 3 pm.

Alternatively, camiones, micros and minibuses (2½ hours, US$1) leave when full from Avenida de las Américas on Sunday between 6:30 and 9:30 am. Either walk from the center or take Micros B or C. Camiones returning to Sucre park at the top of the main plaza in Tarabuco, leaving anytime from 11 am to 3:30 pm.

CORDILLERA DE LOS FRAILES

The Cordillera de los Frailes, the imposing serrated ridge in Sucre's backdrop, creates a formidable barrier between the departments of Chuquisaca and Potosí. The best way to see this region is on foot, but trekking on your own isn't recommended and a local guide will be indispensable when it comes to route-finding or communicating with the Quechua-speaking campesinos. A guide will also help to avoid misunderstandings, minimize your impact and help you get a better feeling for local culture.

Orientation

There are numerous walking routes through the Cordillera de los Frailes, some of which are marked on the 1:50,000 topo sheets *Sucre*, sheet 6536-IV, and *Estancia Chaunaca*, sheet 6537-III.

A recommended six-day circuit begins at Chataquila, on the ridge above Punilla,

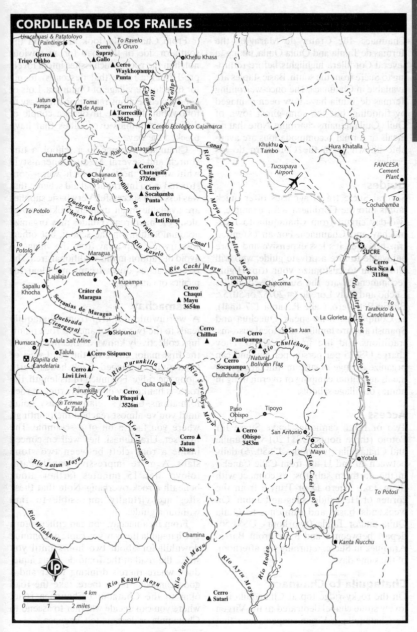

CORDILLERA DE LOS FRAILES

Uracahuasi & Patataloyo Paintings
Cerro Triqo Orkho
To Ravelo & Oruro
Cerro Supray Gallo
Khellu Khasa
Cerro Waykhopampa Punta
Jatun Pampa
Toma de Agua
Cerro Torrecilla 3842m
Río Cajamarca
Río Kollpa
Punilla
Centro Ecológico Cajamarca
Chaunaca
Inca Road
Chataquila
Canal
Río Quilaqui Mayu
Khukhu Tambo
Hura Khatalla
FANCESA Cement Plant
Cerro Chataquila 3726m
Chaunaca Baja
Cordillera de los Frailes
Cerro Socabamba Punta
Tucsupaya Airport
To Cochabamba
Quebrada Charco Khea
To Potolo
Cerro Inti Rumi
Canal
Río Talina Mayu
To Potolo
Maragua
Río Ravelo
Río Cachi Mayu
SUCRE
Cerro Sica Sica 3118m
Lajalaja
Cemetery
Irupampa
Tomapampa
Charcoma
Cráter de Maragua
Sapallu Khocha
Serranías de Maragua
Cerro Chaqui Mayu 3654m
La Glorieta
Río Quirpinchaca
Río Yotala
To Tarabuco & Candelaria
Quebrada Cienegayaj
Humaca
Talula Salt Mine
Sisipuncu
Cerro Chillhui
Cerro Pantipampa
San Juan
Río Chullchuta
Talula
Capilla de Candelaria
Cerro Sisipuncu
Cerro Liwi Liwi
Río Purunkilla
Cerro Socapampa
Natural Bolivian Flag
Chullchuta
Purunkilla
Cerro Tela Phaqui 3526m
Quila Quila
Río Saychayu Mayu
Termas de Talula
Río Pilcomayo
Paso Obispo
Tipoyo
Cerro Jatun Khasa
Cerro Obispo 3453m
San Antonio
Cachi Mayu
Río Cachi Mayu
Yotala
Río Jatun Mayu
To Potosí
Río Wilakkota
Chamina
Kanta Ñucchu
Río Kaqui Mayu
Río Panti Mayu
Río Ayta Mayu
Río Rodeo
Cerro Satari

0   2   4 km
0   1   2 miles

25km northwest of Sucre. It begins with a side trip to Incamachay, then loops through Chaunaca, the Cráter de Maragua, the Termas de Talula and Quila Quila, taking in several Cordillera highlights before returning to Sucre from the south. Basic staples are available in Chaunaca. The once-welcoming Termas de Talula have now been damaged by flooding, but the semi-ghost town of Quila Quila remains charming. Note that no meals or formal accommodations are available anywhere in the Cordillera de los Frailes.

Guides

Several Sucre travel agencies offer quick jaunts into the Cordillera – for example, a two-day circuit from Chataquila to Incamachay and Chaunaca. For an extended trip, however, it's less expensive and more enjoyable to hire a private guide, who will allow you to customize your trip. Highly recommended are the Sucre-based guides Lucho and Dely Loredo (☎ 20752 or 50752; Barrio Petrolero, Calle Panamá 127 final), at Comparapa, who speak Quechua and Spanish and are familiar with local customs, traditions and life in the campo. They charge US$25 per person per day and can organize a range of custom itineraries, with meals and either camping or overnighting in homes or village schools.

Access

Two or three camiones leave Sucre for Potolo (three hours, US$1.20) via Punilla and Chataquila (two hours, US$0.75) daily between 10 and 11 am from Calle Canelas in the northern suburbs; to connect with them, take Micro D or Trufi 5 from the corner of Hernando Siles and Junín. On weekends, buses and camiones to Quila Quila and/or Talula (two hours, US$1.50) depart between 6 and 8 am from Barrio Aranjuez in Sucre, returning the afternoon of the same day.

Chataquila to Chaunaca

On the rocky ridge top at Chataquila is a lovely stone chapel dedicated to the Virgen de Chataquila, a Virgin-shaped stone that has been dressed in a gown and placed on the altar.

From Chataquila, look around on the southern side of the road for an obvious notch in the rock, which issues into a lovely pre-Hispanic route that descends steeply for 6km to the village of Chaunaca. Lots of good paved sections remain and it's easy to follow, but the route involves a couple of difficult scrambles over slides that have blocked the way.

Chaunaca is home to a school, a tiny church and several Mediterranean-style whitewashed houses, which were constructed in an international aid scheme that was less than successful. Very basic supplies are available in an unlikely-looking hovel along the main road. Guides may organize accommodations in the school, but otherwise try to camp away from the village to avoid disruption in this traditional area. The river beaches downstream are ideal for picnics or camping.

Incamachay

A worthwhile day trip from Chataquila leads to the two sets of ancient rock paintings collectively known as Incamachay. At the first major curve on the road west of Chataquila, a rugged track heads north along the ridge. For much of its length, the route is flanked by impossibly rugged rock formations, but it's relatively easy going until you've almost reached the paintings, where you face a bit of a scramble. The first set, Uracahuasi, lies well ensconced inside a rock cleft between two stone slabs. A more impressive panel, Patatoloyo, lies 15 minutes farther along beneath a rock overhang. Note that these sites are virtually impossible to find without a guide.

From Incamachay, you can either return to Chataquila the way you came or continue downhill for about two hours until you strike the road at the Tomo de Agua aqueduct, where there's drinking water and a good campsite. From there, take the road 6km to the Chataquila-Chaunaca road, where you can decide whether to ascend to Chataquila or descend to Chaunaca.

Chaunaca to the Cráter de Maragua

Follow the road south from Chaunaca (not the one that continues toward Potolo) for about 7km, passing brilliantly colored green-and-violet hillsides into the Cráter de Maragua. This unearthly natural formation, sometimes called the Umbligo de Chuquisaca or 'navel of Chuquisaca,' features surreal settlements scattered across a red-and-violet crater floor, and bizarre slopes that culminate in the gracefully symmetrical pale green arches of the Serranías de Maragua. It's one of the most bizarre places in all Bolivia.

Maragua to Talula

You can leave the Cráter de Maragua either toward the south through Irupampa and Sisipunku to Purinquilla, or west to Sapallu Khocha or Lajalaja. The latter route will take you over some challenging up-and-down terrain studded with brilliant mica deposits to Hacienda Humaca, past some isolated dinosaur tracks, and to a lovely ghost oasis between high peaks, with mud ruins, palm trees and the saline Río Khoya Mayu. From Humaca, access to the Termas de Talula, 5km away, requires two fords of the Río Pilcomayo; it's best to cross in the morning when the water level is at its lowest.

Those who head directly south from Maragua can reach the Talula by turning west at Purunkilla and sauntering 4km down the road. No river fords are required.

The Talula hot springs issue into three pools that have temperatures up to 45°C. Camping is possible anywhere in the vicinity, but unfortunately, the bath house was severely damaged during recent floods and it may or may not reopen as a public spa.

From Talula, it's 500m to the constricted passage that conducts the Río Pilcomayo between the steep walls of the Punkurani gorge. When the river is low, you can cross over to the Potosí shore and see the many rock-painting sites above the opposite bank.

Talula to Sucre

From Talula, the route back to Sucre begins by following the road (which was constructed to serve less than a dozen vehicles

per week!) back up to Purunkilla. From there, it's 5km of well-kept farmland to Quila Quila (spelled Quilla Quilla on the topo sheet). This crumbling and bizarrely beautiful ghost village is now being revived by Sucre people exchanging city life for an agricultural lifestyle. There's little of interest here, but the enormous church does occupy an imposing position beneath the dramatic peak of 3526m Cerro Tela Phaqui. Soft drinks are sold at one home on the plaza, but no other supplies are available. The only vehicular traffic passes on weekends, when day-trippers travel between Sucre and Talula.

Continuing back toward Sucre, the road climbs through a barren but colorful landscape of red hills and maguey to the pass at the foot of 3453m Cerro Obispo. Here, you can turn off along the 12km track through Tipoyo and Hacienda Cachi Mayu to the colonial village of Yotala, which lies about 16km south of Sucre on the main road. Alternatively, continue another 4km down the road past the well-watered flower-growing village of Chullchuta, over the shoulder of Cerro Pantipampa. About 2.5km farther along, look across the quebrada at the bands of red, yellow and green in the hillside, which form a natural Bolivian flag.

From the crest, the road drops steeply to Hacienda San Juan on the Río Cachi Mayu, where sand is extracted to make cement, then climbs to the plateau for the final – and rather tedious – 11km into Sucre.

Potolo

The village of Potolo is the origin of some of Bolivia's finest Jalq'a tradition weavings, particularly the renowned red-and-black (or magenta-and-black) animal-patterned pieces sold throughout the Andes and esteemed by experts worldwide.

Supay Huasi

Among the most interesting rock paintings in the Cordillera de los Frailes are those at Supay Huasi, the 'house of the devil.' These unusual zoomorphic and anthropomorphic images in ochre, white and yellow include a white long-tailed animal, which could be a monkey; a humpbacked llama that bears a remarkable resemblance to a camel; a 12cm two-headed creature, which may represent a pair of amorous canines; an ochre-colored 40cm man wearing a sunlike headdress; and several faded geometric figures and designs.

The paintings are about a 2½ hour walk upstream from the point where the Río Mama Huasi crosses the Ravelo road, north of Punilla. However, they're almost impossible to find without a local guide.

Potosí

☎ 062

I am rich Potosí,
The treasure of the world…
And the envy of kings.

The renown of Potosí – its history and splendor as well as its tragedy and horror – is inextricably tied to silver. The above legend from the city's first coat of arms wasn't far off the mark, but any city with a mountain of silver in its backyard is certain to attract attention. The city was founded in 1545, following the discovery of ore in silver-rich Cerro Rico, and the Potosí veins quickly proved the world's most prolific – and lucrative.

Despite its setting at an altitude of 4090m (it's the world's highest city), Potosí blossomed, and toward the end of the 18th century, it grew into the largest and wealthiest city in Latin America. Silver from Potosí underwrote the Spanish economy – and its monarchs' extravagance – for over two centuries. Now, anything incredibly lucrative is said to 'vale un Potosí' ('be worth a Potosí'). In fact, in the 1600s, this mountain of wealth bestowed its name upon the city of San Luis Potosí in central Mexico, but those diggings, however productive, never did live up to those of its Bolivian namesake.

Visitors to modern Potosí will find remnants of a grand colonial city – ornate churches, monuments, and colonial architecture – in a most unlikely setting. This is truly a Bolivian highlight, and not to be missed.

History

No one is certain how much silver has been extracted from Cerro Rico (the 'rich hill' in Potosí's backdrop) over its four centuries of productivity, but a popular boast was that the Spanish could have constructed a silver bridge to Spain and still had some left to carry across on it. The Spanish monarchs, who personally received 20% of the booty, were certainly worth more than a few pesetas.

Although the tale of Potosí's origins probably takes a few liberties with the facts, it's as good a story as any. It begins in 1544 when a Peruvian Indian, Diego Huallpa, was tending his llamas. When he noticed that two of the beasts were missing, he set forth to search for them. By nightfall, however, he still hadn't found them and the cold grew fierce, so Diego stopped to build a fire at the foot of the mountain known in Quechua as 'Potojsi' (meaning 'thunder' or 'explosion' in Quechua, although it might also have stemmed from *potoj*, 'the springs'). The fire grew so hot that the very earth beneath it started to melt, and shiny liquid oozed from the ground.

Diego immediately realized he'd run across one of the commodities for which the Spanish conquerors had an insatiable appetite. Perhaps he also remembered the Inca legend associated with the mountain, which recounted that Inca Huayna Capac had been instructed by a booming voice not to dig in the hill of Potojsi, but to leave the metal alone, because it was intended for others.

At this point, accounts of the legend diverge. One version maintains that Diego Huallpa kept his discovery secret, lest he upset the mountain *apus* (spirits). Others relate that his instincts got the best of him, and that he informed a friend, Huanca, of the discovery, and together they formulated a plan to extract the silver themselves. According to the account, the vein proved extremely productive, but a dispute between the partners escalated into a quarrel about the division of profits and Huanca, now weary of the whole mess, told the Spaniards about the mine.

Whatever the case, the Spanish eventually learned of the enormous wealth buried in the mountain of Potojsi and determined that it warranted immediate attention. On April 1 (according to some sources, April 10), 1545, the Villa Imperial de Carlos V was founded at the foot of Cerro Rico and large-scale excavation began. In the time it takes to say 'Get down there and dig,' thousands of Indian slaves had been pressed into service and the first of the silver was headed for Spain.

The work was dangerous, however, and so many Indians died of accidents and silicosis pneumonia that the Spanish imported literally millions of African slaves to augment the labor forces. In order to increase productivity, in 1572 the Viceroy Toledo instituted the Ley de la Mita, which required all Indian and black slaves over the age of 18 to work in shifts of 12 hours. They would remain underground without seeing light of day for four months at a time, eating, sleeping and working in the mines. When they emerged from a 'shift,' their eyes were covered to prevent damage in the bright sunlight.

Naturally, these miners, who came to be known as *mitayos*, didn't last long. Heavy losses were also incurred among those who worked in the *ingenios* (smelting mills), as the silver smelting process involved mercury. In all, it has been estimated that over the three centuries of the colonial period – 1545 to 1825 – as many as eight million Africans and Indians died from the appalling conditions in the Potosí mines.

Inside the mines, silver was smelted in small ovens known as *huayrachinas*, which were fueled with wood and the spiky grass *paja brava*. The silver was then transported by llama train to Arica (Chile), along the Camino de Plata, or to Callao (now Lima, Peru) on the Pacific coast. From there, it was carried by ship to Spain, providing spoils for English, Dutch and French pirates along the way.

In 1672, a mint was established to coin the silver, reservoirs were constructed to provide water for the growing population, and exotic European consumer goods found their way up the llama trails from Arica and Callao. Amid the mania, more than 80 churches were constructed, and Potosí's population grew to nearly 200,000, making it the largest city in Latin America and one of the largest in the world. One politician of the period put it succinctly: 'Potosí was raised in the pandemonium of greed at the foot of riches discovered by accident.'

As with most boom towns, Potosí's glory was not to last. During the early 19th-century independence struggles in Alto Perú, Potosí was naturally coveted by both sides. The city's many churches were looted, its wealth was removed to Europe or other parts of the Spanish realm and the population dropped to less than 10,000.

At the same time, Cerro Rico, the seemingly inexhaustible mountain of silver, began to play out, and by the time of Bolivian independence in 1825, the mines were already in decline. The mid-19th century drop in silver prices dealt a blow from which Potosí has never completely recovered.

In the present century, only the demand for tin has rescued Potosí from obscurity and brought a slow but steady recovery. Tin has now taken over as Bolivia's major metallic export, and *potosinos* are now mining previously discarded tailings for lead, zinc, copper and tin. Silver extraction continues only on a small scale, but reminders of the grand colonial city are still evident in the narrow streets, formal balconied mansions and ornate churches.

The mining reforms of 1952 brought the Pailaviri mine under government control, and mining conditions improved immensely. Most of the Cerro Rico operations, however, are now in the control of miner-owned cooperatives. The government mine has closed, having been plagued by strikes, protests and general dissatisfaction, while the cooperatives continue operating under conditions that have changed shamefully little from the colonial period.

In 1987, UNESCO named Potosí a World Heritage Site in recognition of its rich and tragic history and its wealth of colonial architecture.

POTOSÍ

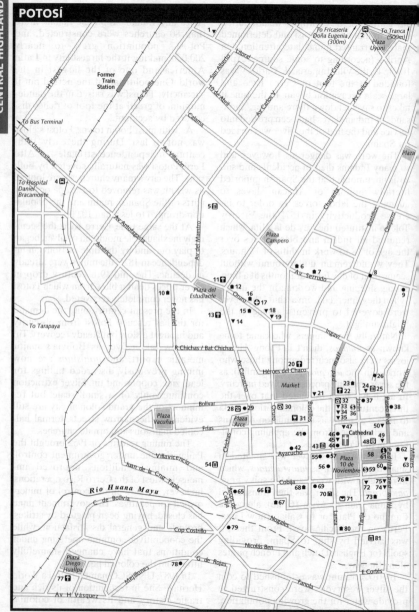

To Fricasería
Doña Eugenia
(300m)

To Tranca
(500m)

Plaza
Uyuni

1

2

Former
Train
Station

To Bus Terminal

To Hospital
Daniel
Bracamonte

To Tarapaya

H Players

Av Sevilla

San Alberto

Litoral

10 de Abril

Calama

Santa Cruz

San Carlos V

Av Carlos V

Av Cívica

Plaza

Av Universitaria

Av Villazón

Chayanta

Bustillos

Quijarro

Av del Maestro

Av Antofagasta

América

F Camacho

4

5

Plaza
Campero

Av Serrudo

6 7

8

9

11

Plaza del
Estudiante

10

Oruro

12

16
17

18
19

15

13

14

Ingavi

Sucre

Chacon

R Chichas / Bat Chichas

20

Héroes del Chaco

Av Camacho

Market

21

26

23

22

24 25

37

38

Bolívar

28 29

Oruro

30

Bustillos

Paseo Bld

Plaza
Vacuñas

Frías

Plaza
Arce

31

32
33
34
35

36

47

50

41

Villavicencio

54

42

Ayacucho

43
44

45
46

Cathedral

48

49

Padilla (red mat).

58

61

62

63

55
56

57

Plaza
10 de
Noviembre

59 60

Río Huana Mayu

Juan de la Cruz Tapia

65

66

Cobija

68

69
70

75
72 74

73

76

C. de Bolivia

Arco de Cobija

67

Nogales

71

Tarija

80

Cop Costrillo

79

81

Nicolás Ben

Plaza
Diego
Huallpa

78

G. de Rojas

Mejillones

Fanola

E Cortés

77

Av H Vásquez

POTOSÍ

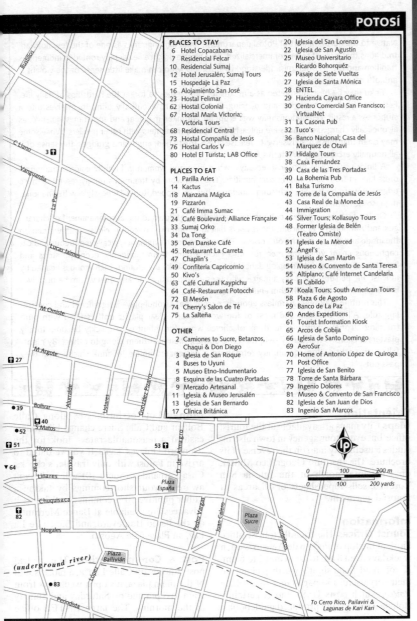

PLACES TO STAY
6 Hotel Copacabana
7 Residencial Felcar
10 Residencial Sumaj
12 Hotel Jerusalén; Sumaj Tours
15 Hospedaje La Paz
16 Alojamiento San José
23 Hostal Felimar
62 Hostal Colonial
67 Hostal María Victoria;
 Victoria Tours
68 Residencial Central
73 Hostal Compañía de Jesús
76 Hostal Carlos V
80 Hotel El Turista; LAB Office

PLACES TO EAT
1 Parilla Aries
14 Kactus
18 Manzana Mágica
19 Pizzarón
21 Café Imma Sumac
24 Café Boulevard; Alliance Française
33 Sumaj Orko
34 Da Tong
35 Den Danske Café
45 Restaurant La Carreta
47 Chaplin's
49 Confitería Capricornio
50 Kivo's
63 Café Cultural Kaypichu
64 Café-Restaurant Potocchi
72 El Mesón
74 Cherry's Salon de Té
75 La Salteña

OTHER
2 Camiones to Sucre, Betanzos,
 Chaqui & Don Diego
3 Iglesia de San Roque
4 Buses to Uyuni
5 Museo Etno-Indumentario
8 Esquina de las Cuatro Portadas
9 Mercado Artesanal
11 Iglesia & Museo Jerusalén
13 Iglesia de San Bernardo
17 Clínica Británica

20 Iglesia del San Lorenzo
22 Iglesia de San Agustín
25 Museo Universitario
 Ricardo Bohorquéz
26 Pasaje de Siete Vueltas
27 Iglesia de Santa Mónica
28 ENTEL
29 Hacienda Cayara Office
30 Centro Comercial San Francisco;
 VirtualNet
31 La Casona Pub
32 Tuco's
36 Banco Nacional; Casa del
 Marquez de Otavi
37 Hidalgo Tours
38 Casa Fernández
39 Casa de las Tres Portadas
40 La Bohemia Pub
41 Balsa Turismo
42 Torre de la Compañía de Jesús
43 Casa Real de la Moneda
44 Immigration
46 Silver Tours; Kollasuyo Tours
48 Former Iglesia de Belén
 (Teatro Omiste)
51 Iglesia de la Merced
52 Ángel's
53 Iglesia de San Martin
54 Museo & Convento de Santa Teresa
55 Altiplano; Café Internet Candelaria
56 El Cabildo
57 Koala Tours; South American Tours
58 Plaza 6 de Agosto
59 Banco de La Paz
60 Andes Expeditions
61 Tourist Information Kiosk
65 Arcos de Cobija
66 Iglesia de Santo Domingo
69 AeroSur
70 Home of Antonio López de Quiroga
71 Post Office
77 Iglesia de San Benito
78 Torre de Santa Bárbara
79 Ingenio Dolores
81 Museo & Convento de San Francisco
82 Iglesia de San Juan de Dios
83 Ingenio San Marcos

Tinku – The Art of Ritual Mayhem

Native to the northern part of Potosí department, tinku fighting ranks as one of the few Bolivian traditions that has yet to be commercialized. This bizarre practice lies deeply rooted in indigenous tradition and is thus often misunderstood by outsiders, who can make little sense of the violent and often grisly spectacle.

Tinku may be best interpreted as a means for campesinos to forget the hardships of daily life. Festivities begin with singing and dancing, but participants eventually drink themselves into a stupor. As a result, celebrations may well erupt into drunken mayhem and sometimes violence, as alcoholically charged emotions are unleashed in hostile encounters with other revelers. While some may claim that these brawls serve to release stress, frustration, anger and grudges, the sense of it all normally escapes any Western spectators.

A tinku usually last two or three days, when men and women in brightly colored traditional dress hike in from surrounding communities. The hats worn by the men strongly resemble those originally worn by the Spanish conquistadores, but are topped Robin-Hood-style with one long, fluorescent feather.

On the first evening, the communities parade through town to the accompaniment of charangos and zampoñas. Perodically, the revelers halt and form two concentric circles, with women on the inside and the men in the outer circle. The women begin singing a typically repetitious and cacophonous chant while the men run in a circle around them. Suddenly, everyone stops and launches into a powerful stomping dance that seems to shake the ground. Each group is headed by at least one person – normally a man – who uses a whip to urge on any man whom he perceives isn't keeping up with the rhythm and the pace.

This routine may seem harmless enough, except that alcohol plays a significant and controlling role. All of the men and most of the women carry clear plastic bottles filled with puro (rubbing alcohol), which is the drink of choice when the intent is to quickly become totally plastered. Dancers frequently swig from the bottles, then pass them along to others. By nightfall, each participating community retreats to a designated house to drink chicha until they pass out.

Orientation

Maps City maps are available at the tourist office, but every tour agency in town also includes a useful city map on the reverse of its brochure. The Instituto Geográfico Militar, on Chayanta, north of the Iglesia San Lorenzo, sells topo sheets of all areas of Potosí department.

Information

Tourist Offices The friendly tourist office kiosk at the top of Plaza 6 de Agosto is open weekdays from 8 am to noon and 2 to 6 pm. If you read Spanish, it's worth picking up their very useful 130-page *Guía Turística de Potosí*, which costs US$5 and is certainly Bolivia's best locally produced guidebook.

Money Lots of businesses along Calle Bolívar and Calle Sucre change US dollars cash at a reasonable rate – look for the 'Compro Dólares' signs. If you've dared to arrive in Potosí with only traveler's checks, Casa Fernández (Sucre 10) will make you aware of your shortcomings by taking a rather punitive 10% commission. Visa cash advances are available at Banco Mercantil, on the Paseo Boulevard, and Banco de La Paz, on Plaza 6 de Agosto.

Post & Communications The central post office is on Calle Lanza, a block south of the main plaza; it's open weekdays from 9 am to 8 pm and on Saturday and Sunday in the morning. The large ENTEL office

Tinku – The Art of Ritual Mayhem

This excessive imbibing inevitably results in social disorder, and by the second day, the seriously drunk participants tend to grow increasingly aggressive. As they roam the streets, they encounter people from other communities with whom they may have some quarrel – either real or imagined. Common complaints include anything from land disputes and extramarital affairs to the supposed theft of farm animals, and may well result in a challenge to fight.

The situation rapidly progresses past yelling and cursing to pushing and shoving before it turns into a rather mystical – almost choreographed – warfare. Seemingly rhythmically, men strike each other's heads and upper bodies with extended arms (in fact, this has been immortalized in the tinku dance, which is frequently performed during carnaval entradas – especially in highly traditional Oruro). To augment the hand-to-hand combat, the fighters may also throw rocks at their opponents, occasionally resulting in serious injury or death. Any fatalities, however, are resignedly considered a blood offering to Pachamama in lieu of a llama sacrifice for the same purpose.

The best known and arguably most violent tinku takes place in Macha during the first week of May, while the villages of Ocurí and Toracarí, among others, also host tinkus. Note that the village of Torotoro, which attracts visitors to its wonderful national park, no longer holds a tinku.

As you'd imagine, few foreigners aspire to witness this private and often violent tradition, and many people who have attended insist they'd never do it again. For the terminally curious, however, Koala Tours and Altiplano Tours in Potosí conduct culturally sensitive – and patently less-than-comfortable – visits to several main tinku festivities. Note however that if you do go, it will be at your own risk. Keep a safe distance from the participants and always remain on the side of the street to avoid being trapped in the crowd. When walking around the village, maintain a low profile, speak in soft tones and ignore any taunting cries of 'gringo.' Also, bear in mind that these traditional people most definitely do not want hordes of foreign tourists gawking at them and snapping photos; avoid photographing individuals without expressed permission and do not dance or parade with the groups unless you receive a clear invitation to do so.

Most importantly, keep in mind that some violence can be expected during a tinku, especially on the final day. If you can't keep Western sensitivities at bay, it's best to stay away.

---

occupies the corner of Frías and Camacho; it offers high-speed email and Internet access for US$2.50 per hour.

The nicest Internet café is the friendly Tuco's (☎ 25489), on the third floor at the corner of Junín and Bolívar, which is open from 7 am to 11 pm and charges US$1.50 per hour. The adjoining café serves breakfast, soda, juice and beer. Other choices include VirtualNet, in the incongruously modern Centro Comercial San Francisco on Oruro at Bolívar, and Café Internet Candelaria on Ayacucho, which is open daily except Sunday.

Film & Photography You'll find Fuji and Agfa slide film at Casa Fernández (Sucre 10).

Laundry As usual, hotels can organize laundry services for their guests. Failing that, try either outlet of Limpieza La Veloz, one at Camacho 258 and the other on Quijarro at Matos, both of which charge US$1.50 per kilogram.

Medical Services & Emergencies If you need a doctor, see the Clínica Británica (☎ 25888; Oruro 221) or the Hospital Daniel Bracamonte (☎ 23900). If you're harassed by bogus police, contact the radio patrulla (☎ 110) or the tourist police (☎ 25288).

Casa Real de la Moneda

The Royal Mint, on Calle Ayacucho, is the city's star attraction and one of South

SANDRA BAO

Detail of doors at Casa Real de la Moneda

America's finest and most interesting museums. The first mint in Potosí was constructed on the present site of the Casa de Justicia in 1572 under orders of the Viceroy Toledo. The present building, which occupies an entire block near the cathedral, was built between 1753 and 1773 to control the minting of colonial coins right where the metal was mined. These coins, which bore the mint mark 'P,' were known as *potosís*.

The exceptionally impressive building has been carefully restored. Its massive walls are more than a meter thick and it has not only functioned as a mint, but also done spells as a prison, a fortress and, during the Chaco War, as the headquarters of the Bolivian Army.

From the entrance, visitors are ushered into a courtyard where they're greeted by a stone fountain and a mask of Bacchus, hung there in 1865 by Frenchman Eugenio Martin Moulon for reasons known only to him. In fact, this aberration looks more like an escapee from a children's fun fair, but it has become a town icon and in fact, the Roman god of wine now figures prominently as the de facto patron saint of Potosí!

The museum houses a host of historical treasures. Among them are the first locomotive used in Bolivia and a beautiful salon brimming with religious paintings (lots of blood). In the basement are a couple of still-functional hand-powered minting devices that were in use until 1869, when the minting machines were imported from Philadelphia. The obligatory tours are conducted on weekdays from 9 am to noon and 2 to 5:30 pm and on Saturday from 9 am to noon and 2 to 4 pm (note that it's often closed for cleaning on Monday). Foreigners pay US$1.80 and photography permits cost an extra US$2. Whatever the outside temperature, wear thermal underwear and several layers of clothing, as the vast dungeonlike spaces in this building never feel the warmth of day!

Museo Universitario

The Museo Universitario Ricardo Bohorquéz (Bolívar 54) displays a diverse but rather haphazard and mostly unlabeled collection of paintings, pottery, antiques, stuffed birds etc. It's open weekdays from 9 am to noon and 2 to 6 pm. The US$1 admission helps support the university.

Calle Quijarro

North of the Iglesia de San Agustín, Calle Quijarro narrows as it winds between a wealth of colonial buildings, many with doorways graced by old family crests. It's thought that the bends in Calle Quijarro were an intentional attempt to inhibit the cold winds that would otherwise whistle through and chill everything in their path. (This concept is carried to extremes on the Pasaje de Siete Vueltas – 'the passage of seven turns' – which is an extension of Calle Ingavi, east of Junín.) During colonial times, Calle Quijarro was the street of potters, but it's now known for its hat makers. One shop worth visiting is that of Don Antonio Villa Chavarría (Quijarro 41). The intersection of Calles Quijarro and Modesto Omiste, farther north, has been dubbed the Esquina de las Cuatro Portadas because of its four decorative colonial doorways.

Museo & Convento de San Francisco

The Convento de San Francisco, on Tarija at Nogales, was founded in 1547 by Fray Gaspar de Valverde, making it the oldest monastery in Bolivia. Owing to its inadequate size, it was demolished in 1707 and reconstructed over the following 19 years. A gold-covered altar from this building is now housed in the Casa Real de la Moneda. The statue of Christ that graces the present altar features hair that is said to grow miraculously, and for some reason the stone cupolas have been painted to resemble brickwork.

The museum has examples of typical religious art, including various paintings from the Escuela Potosina Indígena (Indigenous Potosí School), such as *The Erection of the Cross*, by Melchor Pérez de Holguín, various mid-19th century works by Juan de la Cruz Tapia, and 25 scenes from the life of St Francis of Assisi. Another notable painting is a portrait of Antonio López de Quiroga, a wealthy 17th-century philanthropist who donated generously to the Church.

The museum is open Monday to Saturday from 10 am to noon and 2:30 to 4:30 pm. Foreigners pay US$1.50. The highlight comes at the end, when you're ushered up the tower and onto the roof for a grand vista over Potosí. Photography permits cost an extra US$2 for still cameras and US$3 for videocameras.

Museo & Convento de Santa Teresa

The oddly orange-colored Carmelite Convento de Santa Teresa, on Ayacucho at Santa Teresa, was founded in 1685 by Mother Josepha de Jesús y María and a band of Carmelite nuns from the city of La Plata (now Sucre). The construction, which reflects heavy mestizo influence, was completed seven years later, in 1692.

A visit to Santa Teresa may provide an unsettling vision into a hidden facet of the colonial Church. At the entrance you can still see the 17th-century wooden turnstile that sheltered the cloistered nuns from the outside world. Visitors to the convent may still hear them conducting prayers and songs from their self-imposed seclusion. The display of religious art is more interesting than most. It includes works of Bolivia's most renowned artist, Melchor Pérez de Holguín, as well as a collection of morbid disciplinary and penitential paraphernalia (fortunately no longer in use), a skeleton in the old dining room ('ashes to ashes, dust to dust') and – as one correspondent put it – 'evidence of lots of flagellation.'

The museum is open Monday to Saturday from 8:30 am to noon and 2:30 to 6 pm and Sunday from 9 am to noon and 3 to 6 pm. Admission and a one-hour guided tour cost US$2, and photography permits cost US$2 for cameras, US$3 for videos. Visitors can purchase *quesitos*, the marzipan sweets that have become a Potosí specialty.

Museo Etno-Indumentario

This little museum (☎ 23258; Serrudo 152) features the weaving styles and costumes from each of the 16 provinces of Potosí department. It's open Monday to Friday from

CENTRAL HIGHLANDS

9 am to noon and 2:30 to 6 pm, and Saturday from 9 am to noon.

Churches

Such was the wealth of colonial Potosí that over 80 churches were constructed in the city, and it's worth visiting the roof of the aforementioned Convento de San Francisco for a striking view over the urban forest of towers and spires.

Cathedral Construction of Potosí's cathedral, which lies on Plaza 10 de Noviembre, was initiated in 1564, officially founded in 1572 and finally completed around 1600. The original building lasted into the early 19th century, when it mostly collapsed. During the reconstruction from 1808 to 1838, the original structure gained some neoclassical Greek and Spanish additions, courtesy of architect Fray Manuel Sanahuja.

The interior décor represents some of the finest in Potosí and merits a look around. Note the bases of the interior columns, which still bear colonial-era tiles; the mid-17th century works of sculptor Gaspar de la Cueva titled *Señor de las Ánimas* and *Cristo de la Columna*; and the mausoleum, which holds the remains of colonial notables. Half-hour tours (US$1) are conducted Monday to Friday from 9:30 to 10 am and 3 to 5:30 pm, and Saturday from 9:30 to 10 am.

San Bernardo This immense former church and convent on Plaza del Estudiante displays impressive Baroque architecture and an elaborate ornamented portal. The original structure dates back to 1590, but it was completely renovated in the late 1720s, and through the 19th century it was used as Potosí's parochial cemetery. It now houses an art restoration workshop for university students, and is open during normal office hours. The church immediately behind it is now occupied by a cinema.

Belén The former Iglesia de Belén, near the main plaza, with its three-tier Baroque façade, was constructed in 1735 as a church and later served as a hospital. It is now occupied by Teatro Omiste.

Torre de la Compañía de Jesús The ornate and beautiful bell tower, on what remains of the former Jesuit church on Calle Ayacucho, was completed in 1707 after the collapse of the original church (which had been completed in 1590). Both the tower and the doorway are adorned with examples of Baroque mestizo ornamentation.

San Benito The Iglesia de San Benito, on Plaza Diego Huallpa, is laid out in the form of a Latin cross and features Byzantine domes and a distinctive mestizo doorway. In fact, from a distance, it resembles the traditional Christmas card rendition of the city of Bethlehem! The structure was begun in 1711 and completed in 16 years, which must have been a colonial construction record.

San Martín The rather ordinary-looking Iglesia de San Martín, on Calle Hoyos, was built in the 1600s and is today run by the French Redemptionist Fathers. Inside is a veritable art museum, with at least 30 paintings beneath the choir area depicting the Virgin Mary and the 12 Apostles. The Virgin on the altarpiece wears clothing woven from silver threads. However, San Martín lies outside the center and is often closed owing to the risk of theft, so phone (☎ 23682) before traipsing out there. Try on weekdays after 3:30 pm.

San Lorenzo The ornate Baroque mestizo portal of San Lorenzo de Carangas, on Calle Héroes del Chaco, is probably one of the most photographed subjects in Bolivia. It was carved in stone by master Indian artisans in the 16th century, but the main structure wasn't completed until the bell towers were added in 1744. Inside are two Holguín paintings and handcrafted silver work on the altar. The church was renovated in 1987. It's open Monday to Saturday from 10 am to noon.

San Agustín San Agustín, with its elegant Renaissance doorway, is known for its eerie underground crypts and catacombs. To visit them, pick up a guide and the key at the tourist office (US$1 per person) or organize a spooky nighttime visit with a tour agency.

Jerusalén The Iglesia Jerusalén, on Camacho at Maestro, with its golden ornamentation and several paintings by Holguín, was constructed in the 17th century as a sanctuary in honor of the Virgen de Candelaria. It now houses a museum of Viceroyalty-era art, including paintings, murals and sculptures. It's open Monday from 9 am to noon and 3 to 6 pm, Tuesday to Friday from 4 to 8 pm and Saturdays from 8 am to noon. Admission costs US$1, including a guided tour.

Other Churches Other churches of note include **San Juan de Dios**, which has stood since the 1600s despite its adobe construction. **La Merced**, on Calle Hoyos, is also lovely, with its carved pulpit and a beautiful 18th-century silver arch over the altarpiece. It was constructed between 1555 and 1687. The recently renovated **Santo Domingo**, on Oruro at Cobija, contains an ornate portal, an unusual paneled ceiling, and one of the eight original panels from the life of Santa Rosa de Lima, by Juan Díaz and Juan Francisco de la Puente, among other colonial paintings and sculptures. You can visit on Sunday prior to the Mass. All that remains of **Santa Bárbara**, on Calle Dolores, constructed from 1548 to 1552, is its lovely rose-colored adobe tower.

Historic Buildings

The architecture of Potosí is unique in Bolivia and merits a stroll around the narrow streets to take in the ornate doorways and façades, as well as the covered wooden balconies that overhang the streets and provide an almost Alpine sense of coziness to the city's bleak surroundings.

Architecturally worthy homes and monuments include El Cabildo (the old town hall) on Plaza 10 de Noviembre, the home of 17th-century miner Antonio López de Quiroga on Calle Lanza, the Casa de las Tres Portadas (Bolívar 1052), the Palacio de Cristal (Sucre 148-156) and the Arcos de Cobija (Arches of Cobija) on the street of the same name. These arches honor not the present-day Pando capital, but the Pacific port of Cobija that now

belongs to Chile. Just downhill from the first arch is the Ingenio Dolores, which bears a 1787 inscription.

On Calle Junín, between Matos and Bolívar, is an especially lovely and elaborate *portón mestizo*, a mestizo-style doorway that's flanked by twisted columns. It once graced the home of the Marquez de Otavi, but now ushers patrons into the Banco Nacional.

Los Ingenios de la Ribera de Veracruz

On the banks *(la ribera)* of the Río Huana Maya, in the upper Potosí barrios of Cantumarca and San Antonio, are some fine ruined examples of the ingenios. These were formerly used to extract silver from the ore hauled out of Cerro Rico. There were originally 82 ingenios along 15km of the stream. Some remaining ones date back to the 1570s and were in use until the mid-1800s.

Each ingenio consists of a floor penetrated by shallow wells, called *buitrones*, where the ore was mixed with mercury and salt. The ore was then ground by millstones that were powered by water impounded in the 32 artificial Lagunas de Kari Kari, southeast of the city.

Ingenio San Marcos The renovated Ingenio San Marcos, on La Paz at Betanzos, houses a fine restaurant (see Places to Eat), museum and artesanía shop and has now become a solid Potosí attraction. Constructed in the 18th century, it belonged to the Condesa (Countess) de la Casa Real de la Moneda (the royal mint). Most of the original construction remains, but the highlight is the impressive and still-functional wooden water wheel, which measures 5m in diameter; it once processed about 120kg of silver per month and was later used in tin smelting. In the restaurant and museum are displayed all sorts of colonial mining equipment and paraphernalia.

Many tours to the cooperative mines stop here en route to Cerro Rico. The museum is open Monday to Saturday from 2:30 to 6:30 pm. The Calcha weaving exhibit and artesanía opens from 11 am to 3:30 pm and 6 to 7:30 pm to catch the lunch and dinner crowds.

Ingenio Dolores The Ingenio Dolores, on Calle Mejillones, actually still operates – or rather, the modern version does. Inside, however, remain the ruins of the colonial-era mill. It's open during business hours.

Pailaviri

The former government mine, Pailaviri, which is headquartered in Cerro Rico's most imposing structure, was the first mine in Potosí and has operated continuously since 1545. It descends through 17 levels to a depth of 480m, where temperatures soar above a stifling 50°C, and it's laced with more than 5000 interconnected shafts. It was originally worked for silver, but as with the cooperatives, it now produces mainly tin.

Pailaviri was run by the government until the early 1990s, and conditions until then contrasted sharply with those of the cooperatives. Salaried miners were provided with electric lamps, jackhammers and elevators, and enjoyed some measure of safety standards and favorable medical and pension plans. When it was taken over by the private Empresa Minera Sumaj Orcko in the early 1990s as part of the government capitalization program, miners were awarded severance pay of US$1000 for each year spent underground.

The sale of Pailaviri and other mines illustrates the tragedy of mining in Bolivia. Given diminishing ore-metal ratios, limited investment capital, labor unrest and high-level corruption, the cost of implementing humane mining conditions may render operations noncompetitive and result in mass unemployment.

On occasion, Andes Expeditions conducts tours of Pailaviri (see Organized Tours, later in this chapter).

Cooperative Mines

A visit to the cooperative mines will almost surely be one of the most memorable experiences you'll have in Bolivia, providing an opportunity to witness working conditions that should have gone out with the Middle Ages. You may be left stunned, incredulous and/or ill (see 'A Job from Hell').

Quite a few young Potosí men offer guided tours through the mines, and each tour agency has its own pool of guides. Some guides are well known and well tested, but you may also want to try our new and enthusiastic guides.

Mine visits aren't easy, and the low ceilings and steep, muddy passageways are best visited in your worst clothes. Temperatures can reach 45°C, and the altitude can be extremely taxing. You'll be exposed to noxious chemicals and gases including silica dust (the cause of silicosis), arsenic gas, acetylene vapors and other trapped mine gases, as well as asbestos deposits and the byproducts of acetylene combustion and the detonation of explosives. Anyone with doubts or medical problems should avoid these tours. The plus side is that you can speak with the friendly miners, who will share their insights and opinions about their difficult lot. Surprisingly, most of them are miners by choice, carrying on family traditions by working there.

Mine tours begin with a visit to the market, where miners stock up on acetylene rocks, dynamite, cigarettes and other essentials. In the past, gifts weren't expected, but with the growing number of tourists through the mines, you'd be very unpopular if you didn't supply a handful of coca leaves and a few cigarettes – luxuries for which the miners' meager earnings are scarcely sufficient. Photography is permitted, but you'll need a flash.

Mine tours run in the morning or afternoon and last from three to five hours. The city permits agencies to charge up to US$8.50 per person, but lower rates are available during periods of low demand. This price includes a guide, transportation from town and equipment: jackets, helmets, boots and lamps (these days they're normally battery-powered rather than acetylene). Wear sturdy clothing and carry water and a handkerchief/headscarf to filter some of the

The Job from Hell

In the cooperative mines on Cerro Rico, all work is done with primitive tools, and underground temperatures vary from below freezing – the altitude is over 4200m – to a stifling 45°C on the fourth and fifth levels. Miners, exposed to all sorts of noxious chemicals and gases, normally die of silicosis pneumonia within 10 to 15 years of entering the mines.

Contrary to popular rumor, women are admitted to many cooperative mines – only a few miners hang on to the tradition that women underground invite bad luck, and in many cases, the taboo applies only to miners' wives, whose presence in the mines would invite jealousy from Pachamama. In any case, lots of local women are consigned to picking through the tailings, gleaning small amounts of minerals that may have been missed. These women are known as *pailiris*, Quechua for 'those who select.'

Since cooperative mines are owned by the miners themselves, they must produce to make their meager living. All work is done by hand with explosives and tools they must purchase themselves, including the acetylene lamps used to detect pockets of deadly carbon monoxide gas.

Miners prepare for their workday by socializing and chewing coca for several hours, beginning work at about 10 am. They work until lunch at 2 pm, when they rest and chew more coca. For those who don't spend the night working, the day usually ends at 7 pm. On the weekend, each miner sells his week's production to the buyer for as high a price as he can negotiate.

When miners first enter the mine, they offer a propitiation at the shrine of the miners' god Tata Kaj'chu, whom they hope will afford them protection in the harsh underground world. Deeper in the mine, visitors will undoubtedly see a small, devilish figure occupying a small niche somewhere along the passageways. As most of the miners believe in a god in heaven, they deduce that there must also be a devil beneath the earth in a place where it's hot and uncomfortable. Since hell (according to the traditional description of the place) must not be far from the environment in which they work, they reason that the devil himself must own the minerals they're dynamiting and digging out of the earth. In order to appease this character, whom they call Tío (Uncle) or Supay – never Diablo – they set up a little ceramic figurine in a place of honor.

On Friday nights a *cha'lla* is offered to invoke his goodwill and protection. A little alcohol is poured on the ground before the statue, lighted cigarettes are placed in his mouth and coca leaves are laid out within easy reach. Then, as in most Bolivian celebrations, the miners smoke, chew coca and proceed to drink themselves unconscious. While this is all taken very seriously, it also provides a bit of diversion from an extremely difficult existence. It's interesting that offerings to Jesus Christ are only made at the point where the miners can first see the outside daylight.

In most cooperative operations, there is a minimal medical plan in case of accident or silicosis (which is inevitable after seven to 10 years working underground) and a pension of about US$14.50 a month for those so incapacitated. Once a miner has lost 50% of his lung capacity to silicosis, he may retire, if he so wishes. In case of death, a miner's widow and children collect this pension.

noxious substances you'll encounter underground. For tour agency suggestions, see the following Organized Tours discussion.

Organized Tours In addition to the cooperative mine tours described earlier, there are lots of guided tours offered and lots of agencies offering them. Apart from the ultra-popular visits to the cooperative mines, popular options include Tarapaya (US$8.50), the ingenios (US$10), and trekking and camping trips around the Lagunas de Kari Kari (US$25 per day). All quoted prices are average. Most agencies are professional, but it's still wise to seek recommendations from other travelers. Unless you're booking an upmarket tour or are short of time, Southwestern Circuit tours (around US$100 from Potosí) are generally more inexpensively arranged in Uyuni (see the Southern Altiplano chapter). Agencies include:

Altiplano Tours Calle Ayacucho 19, Casilla 204 (☎/fax 25353). This company does all the standard tours.

Andes Expeditions Plaza Alonso de Ibañez 3 (☎ 25175 or 24304; fax 25175; exp.sal@cedro.pts.entelnet.bo). Raúl Braulio Mamani organizes tours through several cooperative mines: Rosario, Pailaviari, Santa Elena, Candelaria and Santa Rita, and guarantees at least one dynamite detonation.

Balsa Turismo Calle Bustillos 1062 (☎/fax 26270). In addition to the standard tours, this company runs the Hotel Playa Blanca on the Salar de Uyuni and does trips around the Southwest Circuit.

Hidalgo Tours Bolívar at Junín, Casilla 314 (☎ 25186; fax 061-227077; uyusalht@ceibo.entelnet.bo). This agency, which runs the Hotel Palacio de Sal on the Salar de Uyuni and the Hospedaría Hidalgo at Laguna Colorada, is one of your best options for upmarket tours of the Salar de Uyuni and the Southwest Circuit, including San Pablo de Lípez, Tupiza, Laguna Celeste and Monte Uturuncu (the world's highest road). With a group of five people, you'll pay US$586 per person. For this, you'll get the most luxurious accommodations available on this route. It also offers the standard Potosí tours – but with as little pain as possible.

Koala Tours Ayacucho 5, Casilla 33 (☎ 24708; fax 22092; wgarnica@hotmail.com). With its blunt motto, 'Not for wimps or wussies,' Koala Tours is run by Eduardo and Wilber Garnica and Juan Mamani. In addition to the standard mine tours, which are very good, they offer culturally sensitive three-day excursions to local fiestas that feature tinku fighting (January 6 at Ocuri, May 3 in Macha, July 25 in Maragua and September in Tiquipaya, among others) for US$50. Food and accommodations are very basic, so unless you're prepared to live as the locals do, try another option! Interestingly, the company name is derived from the cuddly Aussie marsupial that chews eucalyptus all day the way the miners chew coca (donations of koala-related Australiana would be most welcome for display in the office).

Kollasuyo Tours Quijarro 12 (☎ 28921) This company does all the standard tours.

Potosí Tours Plaza Alonzo de Ibañez 16 (☎ 25786). This company offers all the standards: the cooperative mines, the ingenios, city tours, the Lagunas de Kari Kari, Tarapaya, Chaqui and the Southwestern Circuit.

Silver Tours Edificio Cámara de Minería, Quijarro 12 (☎/fax 23600). This agency offers all the standard tours around Potosí.

South American Tours Ayacucho 11 (☎/fax 28919; mobile ☎ 018-21153; sud_american@hotmail.com). This agency visits the mine San Miguel la Poderosa and also does the standard tours.

Sumaj Tours Oruro 143 (☎ 24633; fax 22600). This friendly agency organizes mine tours.

Victoria Tours Bustillos 1196-A/Chuquisaca 148 (☎/fax 22144). This agency runs mine tours, as well as city tours and tours to Tarapaya, colonial estates and the Lagunas de Kari Kari.

Special Events
Fiesta del Espíritu Potosí's most unusual event, the Fiesta del Espíritu takes place on the last three Saturdays of June and the first Saturday of August. It's dedicated to the honor of Pachamama, the earth mother, whom the miners regard as the mother of all Bolivians.

Campesinos bring their finest llamas to the base of Cerro Rico to sell to the miners for sacrifice. The entire ritual is conducted according to a meticulous schedule. At 10 am, one miner from each mine purchases a llama and their families gather for the celebrations. At 11 am, everyone moves to the entrances of their respective mines. The miners chew coca and drink alcohol from 11 to 11:45 am. Then, at precisely 11:45 am, they prepare the llama for Pachamama by tying its feet and offering it coca and alcohol. At high noon, the llama meets its maker. As its throat is slit, the miners petition Pachamama for luck, protection and an abundance of minerals. The llama's blood is caught in glasses and splashed around the mouth of the mine in order to ensure Pachamama's attention, cooperation and blessing.

For the following three hours, the men chew coca and drink while the women prepare a llama parrillada. The meat is served traditionally with potatoes baked along with habas and oca in a small adobe oven. When the oven reaches the optimum temperature, it is smashed in on the food, which is baked beneath the hot shards. The stomach, feet and head of the llama are buried in a three-meter hole as a further offering to Pachamama, and then the music and dancing begin. In the evening, truckloads of semi-conscious celebrants are escorted home in transportation provided by the honored miner who secured the llama for his respective mine.

Fiesta de San Bartolomé (Chu'tillos)

This rollicking celebration, best known as Chu'tillos, takes place on the final weekend of August or the first weekend of September and is marked by processions, student exhibitions, traditional costumes and folk dancing by people from all over the country. In recent years, it has even extended overseas and featured musical groups and dance troupes from as far away as China and the USA. Given all the practicing during the week leading up to the festival, you'd be forgiven for assuming it actually started a week early.

Exaltación de la Santa Vera Cruz

This festival, which falls on September 14, honors Santo Cristo de la Vera Cruz. Activities occur around the church of San Lorenzo and the railway station. Silver cutlery features prominently, as do parades,

dueling brass bands, dancing, costumed children and, of course, lots of alcohol.

Places to Stay

Few budget hotels have heating, so you may want to hedge your bets by bringing a sleeping bag. Unless your hotel has water tanks or goes through an arduous daily water-collection ritual, water is available only in the morning. Some cheapie places charge an extra US$0.50 for hot showers.

Budget The cheap and nasty bottom of the barrel is represented by *Alojamiento San José* (☎ 22632; Oruro 173) and *Hospedaje La Paz* (☎ 22632; Oruro 262), both of which charge US$2.50 per person.

Much better is the friendly and good-value *Residencial Felcar* (☎ 24966; Serrudo 345), which offers clean, simple rooms, good hot showers and a sunny and flowery patio. Single/double rooms cost US$4.50/6.50, and a full breakfast costs US$0.80. The large and less-personable *Hotel Copacabana* (☎ 22712; Serrudo 319), which somehow continues to hang in there, charges the same rates.

A perpetually popular place is *Residencial Sumaj* (☎ 23336; F Gumiel 12), where small, dark rooms with shared baths cost US$5/8, plus US$1 for a basic breakfast. Cooking is permitted and there's a garage for vehicles and a TV lounge where you can catch up on popular culture. Internet access costs US$2 per hour and laundry is US$1.50 per kilogram. Note that guests may face a fair bit of hassle from would-be guides and thieves posing as would-be guides. This is the youth hostel in Potosí.

Another budget favorite is *Hostal Carlos V* (☎ 25121; Linares 42). This cozy old colonial building has a pleasant covered patio, but the 'hot' showers barely rate as tepid. Rooms cost US$5 per person. The adequate *Residencial Central* (☎ 22207), on Bustillos at Cobija, in a quiet old part of town, has a traditional potosino overhanging balcony. Chilly rooms with piles of blankets cost US$4.50/7. Hot water is available with an hour's notice. The drafty but pleasant *Hotel El Turista* (☎ 22492; fax 22517; Lanza 19) offers sporadically excellent hot showers, friendly tourist information and superb views from the top floor. Rooms cost US$8.50/15.

The pleasant but rather overpriced **Hostal María Victoria** (☎ 22132; *Chuquisaca 148*) occupies an old colonial home on a quiet colonial passageway. The rooms surround a classic courtyard, and guests have access to a bright, sunny terrace. Dorm beds are US$3.50, rooms with shared baths cost US$6/8.50, and with private baths, they're US$10 for one or two people. A continental breakfast costs US$1.20 while an American one goes for US$1.80, and Internet access is US$1.80 per hour. Beware attempting to do your laundry here, however, as they may try to 'fine' you about US$100 for the infraction!

Mid-Range For sparkling clean rooms, firm mattresses, lots of blankets and a very friendly atmosphere (courtesy of the Alurralde-Pérez family), stay at **Hostal Compañía de Jesús** (☎/fax 23173; *Chuquisaca 445*), which occupies an old Carmelite monastery. Singles/doubles cost US$6/11; with private baths, they're US$8.50/15. Room 18 is especially nice.

The recommended **Hotel Jerusalén** (☎ 26095 or 24633; fax 22600; *hoteljer@cedro.pts.entelnet.bo; Oruro 143*) has a friendly, helpful staff, nice balconies and a mellow atmosphere. Rooms with private baths cost US$8.50/13.50 in the summer months and US$13.50/20 in the winter high season. All rates include a buffet breakfast.

The pleasant and centrally located **Hostal Felimar** (☎/fax 24357; *Junín 14*) charges US$6.50 per person for rooms without bath and US$10/17 for those with bath. Rates include breakfast. The place is solar powered, and some upstairs rooms have balconies and a fine view over the colonial street.

Another choice is the four-star **Hostal Colonial** (☎ 24265; fax 27146; *Hoyos 8, Casilla 332*), which occupies a well-kept colonial building near the main plaza. Rooms with private baths and central heating cost US$33/43.

Places to Eat

Stalls in the *market comedor* serve inexpensive breakfasts of bread, pastries and coffee. For great salteñas, check out **La Salteña** (☎ 26938; *Padilla 6*) or **Café Imma Sumac** (☎ 22160; *Bustillos 987*). In the morning, street vendors sell meatless salteñas potosinas near Iglesia de San Lorenzo for US$0.20. Meat empanadas are sold around the market until early afternoon, and in the evening, street vendors sell cornmeal *humintas*. To sample real Potosino cuisine, check out **Fricasería Doña Eugenia** (☎ 62247), at the end of Santa Cruz, where it intersects Hermanos Ortega. Here you can sample such things as chicharrón, chacchu, ckocko, fricasé and the unique K'ala-phurka – a Potosino variation on llajhua that is cooked on a hot flat stone.

In the morning, **Café Internet Candelaria**, on Calle Ayacucho, serves full breakfasts and coffee specialties. Later, they move on to pizza (US$1 per slice), burgers (US$0.50 to US$0.75) and healthy lunch specials. **Restaurant La Carreta**, near the cathedral, serves pizzas, burgers and US$2 almuerzos, including vegetarian choices.

Sumaj Orko (☎ 23703; *Quijarro 46*) does filling almuerzos of salad, soup, a meat dish and dessert for just US$1.50. In the evening, à la carte options include *trucha al limón* (lemon trout) and *picante de perdíz* (spicy partridge). Down the street, you'll find Chinese meals at **Da Tong**, which charges US$2 for almuerzos with a pot of jasmine tea and a beer. A huge plate of fried rice with chicken curry big enough for two people costs US$2.20.

As Potosí gains popularity with travelers, a growing crop of trendy places is springing up around town. A good place for almuerzos is small and smart **Kactus**, on Avenida Camacho. If you're hankering after pizza, good choices are **Kivo's** (☎ 28404), on Pasaje Boulevard, and **Pizzarón** (*Oruro 257*); the latter is open only in the evening. Relatively sophisticated French cuisine is offered at **Café Boulevard**, on Calle Bolívar at the Alliance Française.

The by-the-book vegetarian choice is the very small **Manzana Mágica** (Oruro 239), open Monday to Saturday from 8 am to 10 pm. The breakfasts are excellent and feature muesli, juices, eggs and brown bread for US$1.50; the almost excessively healthy almuerzos are just US$1.80 and à la carte dinners average around US$2. However, it's very cramped, especially at lunch. If you're not by the door, don't bother eating quickly, because once you're in, you won't get out until everyone is finished.

As in Sucre, Potosí's friendly **Café Cultural Kaypichu** (☎ 22467; Millares 24) starts the day with a healthy vegetarian breakfast, and serves a wonderful set vegetarian lunch from noon to 2 pm (except on Sunday) and à la carte dinners from 5 to 9 pm. It's open daily except Monday. Opposite, **Café-Restaurant Potocchi** (☎ 22759; Millares 13) serves inexpensive lunches in a pleasant space. On Wednesday and Friday evenings, it hosts a folk peña.

The friendly **Chaplin's**, on Calle Matos, serves breakfasts from 7:30 to 10 am and healthy dinners from 4:30 pm, featuring burgers and vegetarian food – vegetable noodle soup, pumpkin soup, spicy lentils, potatoes, rice dishes, fruit and so on. Monday and Tuesday, they do noodle specialties, and on Friday and Saturday, the Mexican señora prepares excellent tacos (they're very popular, so go early). Meals cost US$2 to US$2.50.

In addition to vegetarian food, **Den Danske Café**, on Quijarro at Matos, serves muesli, french toast and pancake breakfasts, lasagna, spaghetti, cannelloni, burgers, salads, sandwiches. Occasionally, it hosts live music performances in the evening. Believe it or not, they also offer weaving lessons.

For good-value spaghetti, pizza, burgers, apple strudel, chocolate cake, lemon meringue pie (pai de limón) and other decadent cakes and pastries, or just a hot drink (sadly, they haven't yet discovered filter coffee), try the popular **Cherry's Salon de Té** (☎ 25367; Padilla 8). It's open all afternoon and makes a nice but very slow pit stop while you're out exploring the town. A faster snack option is **Confitería Capricornio**, which serves tasty breakfasts, fast food, soup, pizza, spaghetti, coffee and fruit juices daily from 7 am to 10 pm.

When you've had enough vegetables and are ready for a grilled steak, chateaubriand, filet mignon etc, see **Parilla Aries** (☎ 29275; M Ascencio Torrico 222), which is popular with locals. The set almuerzo costs just US$1.50. For elegant dining – inasmuch as Potosí has such a thing – you can't beat **El Mesón** (☎ 23087), on Tarija at Linares. It's generally regarded as the nicest international restaurant in Potosí, but for a very good meal, you won't pay much more than US$5.

Another good choice is the atmospheric **San Marcos** (☎ 22781), on La Paz at Betanzos, inside the Ingenio San Marcos. It's open from 8 am to midnight every day. Set almuerzos (US$3) are served from noon to 2:30 pm, and in the evening they do a range of well-prepared soups (US$2.50), salads (US$2) and main courses: ceviche (US$2), shellfish (US$2.50), and fish, beef, chicken and llama (US$5). Reservations are highly recommended, especially if you have a group.

Entertainment

La Bohemia Pub (☎ 24348), on Matos at La Paz, serves drinks and light pub meals from 7 pm nightly. Another pleasant drinking den is the atmospheric **La Casona Pub** (☎ 22954; Tomás Frías 41), tucked in the historic 1775 home of the royal envoy sent to administer the Casa Real de la Moneda. On Friday, they stage live music performances.

On Wednesday and Friday, the Café-Restaurant Potocchi (see Places to Eat) holds traditional folk music peñas (US$1.50 admission). For karaoke and disco dancing, try the locally popular **Ángel's** (☎ 27840; Matos 90).

Potosí has two cinemas, the Imperial (☎ 26133; Padilla 31) and the Universitario (Bolívar 893).

Shopping

Naturally, favored Potosí souvenirs will include silver and tin articles available in stands near the market entrance on Calle Oruro; many of them were produced in the village of Caiza, south of Potosí. Here, small dangly earrings cost about US$2 per set, larger ones go as high as US$5, hoop earrings are US$0.80 to US$1.50, and spoons and platters start between US$1.20 and US$1.50. A recommended place is Arte Nativo (☎ 23544; Sucre 32), which sells indigenous handiwork and thereby improves the economic condition of rural women. Other possibilities include La Palomita (Serrudo 148), El Candelabro de Plata, in Edificio C&C on Calle Bolívar, and Artesanía Andina (Sucre 92).

If your wallet is becoming a burden, see the Mercado Artesanal, on Omiste at Sucre, or the artesanía shop in the Ingenio San Marcos, which caters specifically to tourists. The smaller shops along Sucre north of Bolívar Cheaper are cheaper.

Getting There & Away

Air Potosí boasts the world's highest commercial airport, Aeropuerto Capitán Rojas. In the early 1990s, the runway was extended to 4000m to accommodate larger planes. Aerosur attempted it for a while, but their five putative weekly connections with La Paz were invariably canceled for one reason or another. In any case, it's not that inconvenient to fly into Sucre and travel to Potosí by bus.

Bus All routes into Potosí are quite scenic, and arriving by day will always present a dramatic introduction to the city. The bus terminal (☎ 43361) lies about half an hour on foot downhill from the center, but micros and minibuses (US$0.20) run every minute or two.

Numerous flotas offer daily service to La Paz (10 hours, US$5 to US$7) via Oruro (seven hours, US$3.50); you can also opt for a *bus cama* (10 hours, US$10) with comfortable reclining seats that theoretically accommodate a sound sleep en route.

Buses leave for Tupiza (8 hours, US$4.50) and Villazón (11 hours, US$8.50) daily in the morning and evening. Buses to Tarija (12 hours, US$6) run at least three times daily, and there are numerous daily services to Cochabamba (12 to 15 hours, US$6 to US$8). Several flotas also have daily services to Santa Cruz (at least 16 hours, US$12), but it's a long, arduous trip.

Quite a few flotas leave for Sucre (3½ hours, US$2.50) several times daily from 7 am to around 6 pm. Alternatively, if you have four people, you can take a taxi to Sucre for US$5 per person; phone Taxi Expreso Potosí-Sucre (☎ 28919 or 24192). Alternatively, head for the tranca about 500m north of Plaza Uyuni, where micros leave for Sucre (five hours, US$1.50) all day when full. En route between Sucre and Potosí, watch for the picturesque Puente Sucre with its castle-like buttresses just 1km from the new bridge at the Río Pilcomayo crossing.

Buses to Uyuni (five to seven hours, US$3.50 to US$5) depart between 9:30 am and noon from just below the rail line, higher up on Avenida Antofagasta. The route to Uyuni is quite spectacular, passing through some mysterious-looking valleys and canyons with unusual vegetation and rock formations. At Ticatica, which is backed by a stunning violet mountain amid classic badlands, you'll pass a prominent geothermal site with interesting travertine deposits.

Camión Camiones to Uyuni leave from roughly the same place as the bus, but even after a 'departure,' they may well cruise around for several hours attempting to cram in enough people to ensure a miserable trip for everyone. Unless you're a real glutton for punishment – and have lots of warm clothing – forget it and just take the bus.

Getting Around

Bus Micros and minibuses provide transportation between the center and the Cerro Rico mines, as well as the bus terminal, for US$0.20 per ride.

Taxi Taxis around the center and to the bus terminal cost US$0.50. The main stands are on the northern side of Plaza 10 de Noviembre.

Around Potosí

LAGUNAS DE KARI KARI

The artificial lakes of Kari Kari were constructed in the late 16th and early 17th centuries by 20,000 Indian slaves to provide water for the city and hydropower to run the city's 82 ingenios. In 1626, the retaining wall of Laguna San Ildefonso broke and caused an enormous flood that destroyed operations along La Ribera de los Ingenios and killed 2000 people. Of the 32 original lagunas, only 25 remain and all have been abandoned – except by waterfowl, which appreciate the incongruous surface water in this otherwise stark region.

Hiking

The easiest way to visit the lakes of Kari Kari is with a Potosí tour agency (see Organized Tours under Potosí, earlier in this chapter). If you prefer to strike out on your own, carry food, water and warm clothing. In a long day, you can have a good look around the lagunas and the fringes of the Cordillera de Kari Kari, but it may also be rewarding to camp overnight in the mountains.

Access is fairly easy. Take a micro (Pailaviri or Calvario) heading toward Cerro Rico and get off at the Tupiza turnoff. Follow that road until the pavement ends at a tranca, then head southeast along a stream. Any of the numerous uphill tracks will lead onto an open plain, where you should bear left and climb past a llama pasture and onto a ridge where you'll have a superb view of the Lagunas San Sebastián. At this point, you're about 4km southeast of the Potosí center. Continue along this ridge until you cross a track, which will lead you through a hamlet and along the Río Masoni into the mountains.

Alternatively, cross the Masoni valley and scramble up the ridge on the other side and climb to the summit of Cerro Masoni for an excellent view of Lagunas San Ildefonso and San Pedro. Descending along the same ridge will lead you back to Potosí.

SANDRA BAO

View of Cerro Rico from Potosí

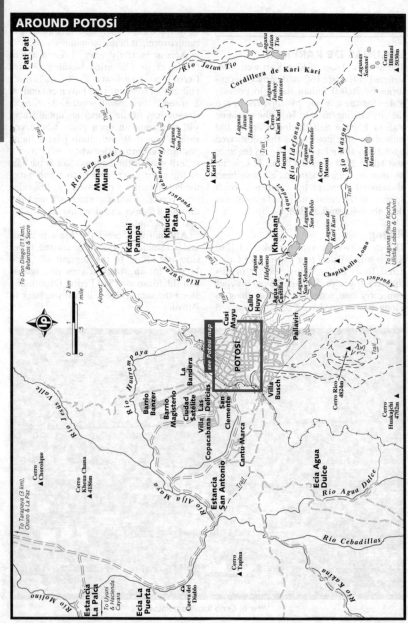

AROUND POTOSÍ

Alternatively, descend to Laguna San Ildefonso, then follow the track around its northern shore and continue up the valley or strike off eastward into the hills. The higher you go, the more spectacular the views become. The area is riddled with open mine entrances, mining detritus and remains of mining equipment.

Those prepared for an overnight stay can travel even farther into the mountains, since there are no difficult summits in the area. As long as you can catch sight of Cerro Rico, the route back to Potosí will be obvious. Remember, however – as if you could forget – that the altitude hereabouts ranges from 4400 to 5000m. The Cordillera de Kari Kari is included on the IGM topo sheet *Potosí (East) – sheet 6435*, available from IGM in Potosí or La Paz.

HACIENDA CAYARA

For a peaceful retreat or some comfortable hill walking, visit Hacienda Cayara, which lies 25km down the valley northwest of Potosí at an elevation of 3550m. Set amid lovely hills, this beautiful working farm produces vegetables and milk for the city. It dates back to colonial times, when it was owned by the Viceroy of Toledo. In the name of King Felipe II, its title was later handed to Don Juan de Tendones and was thence transferred to the Marquez de Otavi, whose coat of arms the ranch still bears. In 1901, it was purchased by the English Aitken family, who still owns it. They converted it into a hostel in 1992. 'Cayara' is the Aymará name for the *Puya raimondii* plant, which flowers after 100 years, then decomposes.

The hostel is like a museum: an opulent colonial mansion furnished with original paintings and period furniture. Guests have use of the fireplace and extensive library, which includes works dating from the 17th century.

Rooms with private baths cost US$25 per person, including breakfast. Other meals are available for US$7 each. For bookings, go to the office 10m up the street from ENTEL in Potosí, in the back of the glass-fronted shop selling cakes and cheese.

Alternatively, phone Señora Luisa Serrano (☎/fax 26380), in Potosí.

Getting There & Away

Transportation can be arranged in Potosí at the time of booking the hostel, but it would actually be cheaper to go by taxi, especially if you're in a group; have the driver take the left fork to La Palca instead of heading through the canyon toward Tarapaya.

BETANZOS

Set in a landscape of rugged, rocky mountains, the traditional town of Betanzos lies about an hour from Potosí along the Sucre road. On Sunday, when the market is in full swing, campesinos wearing local dress bring their weavings, ceramics and crops from the countryside to sell. The surrounding hills are full of ancient rock paintings; the beautiful sites of Lajas-Mayu and Inca Cueva lie only about 5km from Betanzos.

On April 4 and 5, Betanzos celebrates the Fiesta de la Papa (Potato Festival), which features up to 200 varieties of potatoes. Although it isn't well known, it does attract major Andean dance and musical groups from all over Bolivia.

If you want to crash in town, the best option is the *Residencial Bolívar*, which charges US$2.50 per person, but it's pretty grubby and lacks water.

Camiones and micros leave for Betanzos from Plaza Uyuni in Potosí early in the morning, with extra departures on Sunday. All Sucre buses also pass Betanzos, but make sure they drop you in the village, which lies 1km off the main road.

TARAPAYA

Belief in the curative powers of Tarapaya, the most frequently visited hot-springs area around Potosí, dates back to Inca times. It even served as the holiday destination for Inca Huayna Capac, who would come all the way from Cuzco (now in Peru) to bathe.

Ojo del Inca

The most interesting sight is the 30°C Ojo del Inca, a perfectly round, green lake in a

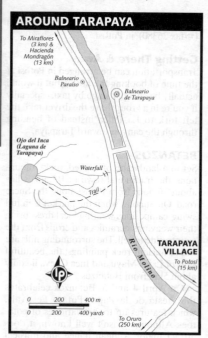

AROUND TARAPAYA

To Miraflores
(3 km) &
Hacienda
Mondragón
(13 km)

Balneario
Paraíso

Balneario
de Tarapaya

Ojo del Inca
(Laguna de
Tarapaya)

Waterfall

Trail

Río Mojina

TARAPAYA
VILLAGE

To Potosí
(15 km)

0   200   400 m
0   200   400 yards

To Oruro
(250 km)

low volcanic crater, 100m in diameter. Along the river below the crater are several *balnearios* (resorts) with medicinal thermal pools utilizing water from the lake.

Locals claim that in the morning it's safe to bathe in the Ojo del Inca, but that *remolinos* (whirlpools) may develop early in the afternoon and cause drownings. There have indeed been bizarre fatalities and disappearances here, and it would be wise to err on the side of caution and avoid swimming at any time.

To reach Ojo del Inca, cross the bridge 400m before the Balneario de Tarapaya, turn left and walk about 200m. Just past the waterfall on the right, a washed-out road leads uphill about 400m to the lake.

Places to Stay

The *Balneario Paraíso* has a hostel for overnight guests and there's also lodging

at *Balneario de Tarapaya*. Campers will find a number of level and secluded sites near the river, but all water should be purified.

Getting There & Away

Roughly half-hourly from 7 am to 7 pm, camiones leave for Tarapaya (1/2 hour, US$0.50) from Plaza Chuquimia in Potosí. Taxis charge US$7 for up to four people. The last micro back to Potosí leaves Tarapaya at around 6 pm.

Ask the driver to let you off at the bridge where the gravel road turns off. The Balneario de Tarapaya is 400m from the bridge along the paved road. Balneario Paraíso is over the bridge and 400m down the road to the right. Miraflores lies 3km beyond Paraíso.

CHAQUI

Another major hot spring bubbles away 3km uphill from the village of Chaqui, 45km by road southeast of Potosí. The countryside around nearby Puna and Belen is particularly interesting, but transportation may be a problem. On Sunday, potosinos come with loads of sugar, flour, rice and bread to exchange in the markets for potatoes, cheese and local farm products. The climate is considerably more agreeable than in Potosí, and superior quality handicrafts, such as weavings and blankets, are sold in small villages.

Places to Stay

The *Hotel Termas de Chaqui* has rooms for US$3 per person, including use of the hot pools. Nonguests may use the pools and sauna for US$1 per person. Chaqui village also has a couple of *alojamientos*, but they're 3km downhill from the resort.

Getting There & Away

Chaqui is reached by micro or camión from Plaza Uyuni in Potosí (two hours, US$0.50); the first one leaves at around 8 am. Alternatively, arrange transportation through Hotel Termas de Chaqui; inquire at the Potosí office (☎ 22158; Chuquisaca

587). Getting there is one thing, but returning to Potosí can be more difficult, as some drivers won't leave until there's sufficient interest (or until you're prepared to pay to hire the whole truck or micro).

DON DIEGO

The hot springs at Don Diego are along the Sucre road and can be reached by micro or camión from Plaza Uyuni, or on a Sucre bus. The resort has a hostel costing US$2 per person, with use of the baths.

South Central Bolivia & the Chaco

Drier and more desolate than the country farther north, the isolated highlands of Tarija department are home to a people who have historically identified and traded more with Argentina than with the rest of Bolivia. In fact, the department bills itself as the Andalucia of Bolivia, in reference to its dry, eroded badlands, neatly groomed vineyards and orchards, and white-stucco and

red-tile architecture, all of which are reminiscent of the Iberian Peninsula. Here the people call themselves *chapacos* and speak with the lilting dialect of European Spanish. The river flowing past the departmental capital is even called the Guadalquivir!

In the far eastern regions of Tarija and Chuquisaca departments, the highlands roll down into the petroleum-rich scrublands and red earth of the Gran Chaco. Villamontes, a small place on the Santa Cruz-Yacuiba railway line, claims the distinction of being literally the country's hottest spot.

Down in the southernmost 'toe' of Bolivia, oil-bearing veins and lush sugarcane-producing valleys bring prosperity to the town of Bermejo, on the Argentine border.

Highlights

- Spot the dogs with flowery collars at Tarija's Fiesta de San Roque and listen to some of Tarija department's bizarre musical instruments
- Find a prehistoric mammal on a fossil hunt in the Tarija badlands
- Make the rugged journey between Bolivia and Filadelfia (Paraguay) along the rough-and-ready Chaco Road
- Hike the fabulous Inca Trail in the Sama Biological Reserve
- Look for endangered Chaco wildlife in the Tariquía, Aguargue and Corvalán Reserve.

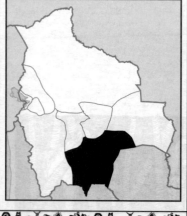

South Central Bolivia

In spite of Tarija's grand illusions of spiritual kinship with Andalucia, more urbanized Bolivians regard south central Bolivia as a half-civilized backwater, and tasteless jokes are told in La Paz with 'Chapaco' forming the standard butt of the humor. In rebuttal, the regionalistic southerners are quick to point out that in 1810, the year that followed Chuquisaca department's 'first cry of independence in the Americas,' part of Tarija department declared independence from Spain and operated briefly under a sovereign government with its capital at Tarija.

TARIJA
☎ 066

With a population of 90,000, Tarija lies at an elevation of 1924m. The valley climate resembles the eternal spring of Cochabamba, although winter nights may be slightly cooler. As in most of Bolivia, the dry season lasts from April to November.

Tarija's distinctly Mediterranean flavor is evident in its climate, architecture and

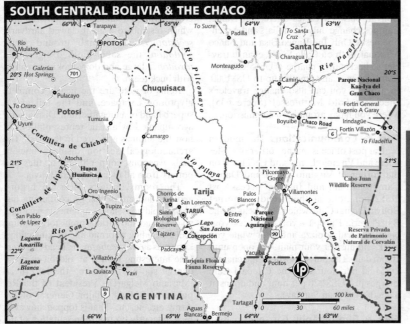

SOUTH CENTRAL BOLIVIA & THE CHACO

SOUTH CENTRAL BOLIVIA

PARAGUAY

vegetation. Its inhabitants are proud to be accused of considering themselves more Spanish or Argentine than Bolivian; many *tarijeños* – they prefer the term 'chapacos' – are descended from Argentine gauchos. Around the main plaza grow stately date palms, and the surrounding landscape has been wildly eroded by wind and water into badlands reminiscent of the Spanish meseta.

History

Tarija was founded on July 4, 1574, as La Villa de San Bernardo de Tarixa by Don Luis de Fuentes y Vargas under the orders of Viceroy Don Francisco de Toledo. In 1810, Tarija and the surrounding area declared independence from Spanish rule. Although the breakaways weren't taken very seriously by the Spanish, the situation did erupt into armed warfare on April 15, 1817. At the Batalla de la Tablada, the Chapacos won a major victory over the Spanish forces; Tarija's departmental holiday is now celebrated on April 15.

In the early nineteenth century, Tarija actively supported Bolivia's struggle for independence, and although Argentina was keen to annex the agriculturally favorable area, Tarija opted to join the Bolivian Republic when it was established in 1825.

Information

Tourist Offices The Oficina Departamental de Turismo (☎ 31000; fax 42593) in Plaza Luis de Fuentes y Vargas, distributes basic town maps and is reasonably helpful with queries regarding sites both within the city and out of town. It's open weekdays 7:30 am to noon and 3 to 6:30 pm.

Note that between 1 and 4 pm, Tarija becomes a virtual ghost town; if you don't conduct all your business in the morning, you'll wait until late afternoon.

Immigration To extend visas or lengths of stay, see Migración (☎ 43450) on Bolívar at Ballivián.

Money The casas de cambio on Calle Bolívar, between Calles Sucre and Daniel Campos, change only US dollars and Argentine pesos. Only the Banco Bisa and Banco Nacional, both on Calle Sucre, change traveler's checks; they charge a US$5 commission to change any amount up to US$1000. In a pinch, you can also change traveler's checks at Foto Methfessel (Sucre 635), where you'll pay around 5% commission.

Post & Communications The modern central post office is on the corner of Calles Sucre and Virginio Lema, and ENTEL is on the corner of Virginio Lema and Daniel Campos. Email and Internet access cost US$2 per hour at the friendly Internet Bolivia Digital Café, which also includes the Bar/Pizzería Europa – you can check your email and enjoy pizza and beer while you work and answer your mail! It's open until 10 pm daily. The SurNet Cyber Café charges US$1.80 per hour and the Citeco I-Café charges just US$1.20 per hour and opens at 8 am daily (10 am Sunday).

Film & Photography For some reason, Tarija is packed with film and photo shops. A recommended one is the very traditional-looking Foto Methfessel (☎ 42062), Sucre 635, which sells Fuji print and slide film.

Medical Services The Hospital San Juan de Dios (☎ 45555) can treat basic medical problems and emergencies; for an ambulance dial ☎ 118. The police can be reached at either ☎ 42222 or the radio *patrulla* number (☎ 110).

Museo de Arqueología y Paleontología

The Archaeology & Paleontology Museum, operated by the university, is on the corner of General Bernardo Trigo and Virginio Lema, one block from the main plaza. It provides a convenient overview of the prehistoric creatures and the early peoples that once inhabited the Tarija area.

Downstairs, you'll see the well-preserved remains of several animals: *megatherium*, a giant ground sloth; *mastodon*; *glyptodon*, a

giant prehistoric armadillo; *macrauchenia*, a cross between a llama and a tapir; *lestodon*, which resembled a giant-clawed aardvark; *scelidotherium*, a small ground sloth; *smilodon*, the saber-toothed tiger; and *toxodon*, a large and dozy-looking creature with buck teeth.

Items of note are the nearly complete glyptodon carapace, and the tail and a superb hand of a megatherium. Displays are accompanied by artistic representations of how the animals appeared in the flesh. The archaeological section displays ancient tools, weapons, copper items, textiles and pottery from all over southern Bolivia.

The rooms upstairs focus on history, geology and anthropology, containing displays of old household implements, weapons, an old piano and various prehistoric hunting tools, including a formidable-looking cudgel known as a *rompecabezas*, or 'head-breaker.' One interesting item is an old bit of presidential stationery bearing the letterhead 'Mariano Melgarejo, President of the Republic of Bolivia, Major General of the Army, etc, etc, etc.' That is topped, however, by a hideously bizarre representation of the Antichrist made from nuts, seeds, grass, wool hair, shells, flowers, wood and lichen.

The museum is open weekdays 8 am to noon and 3 to 6 pm; on weekends, it opens at 9 am. Admission is free but donations are gratefully accepted.

Churches

The **cathedral** at the end of La Madrid, a block from the main plaza, contains the remains of prominent Chapacos, including Tarija's founder, Luis de Fuentes y Vargas. It was constructed in 1611 and expanded and embellished in 1925. By Bolivian standards, the interior is fairly ordinary.

The **Basílica de San Francisco**, on Daniel Campos at La Madrid, was founded in 1606 and is now a national monument. The 16th-century convent library and archives, which may conjure up images from *The Name of the Rose*, may be used only by researchers with permission from the Franciscan order. The general reference library in the Ecclesiastical Documentation Center contains all

TARIJA

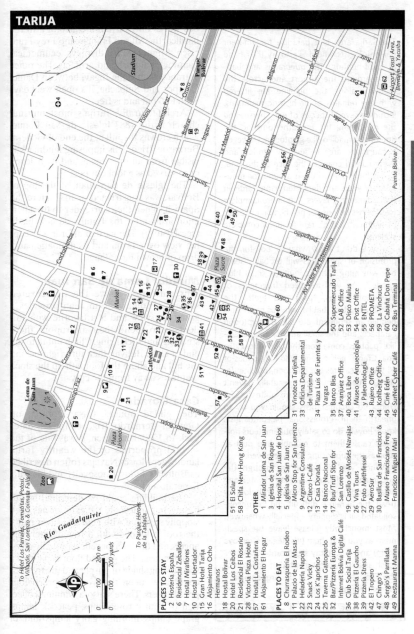

PLACES TO STAY

2 Hostería España
6 Residencial Zeballos
7 Hostal Miraflores
10 Hostal Libertador
15 Gran Hotel Tarija
16 Alojamiento Ocho
   Hermanos
18 Hostal Bolívar
20 Hotel Los Ceibos
21 Residencial El Rosario
28 Victoria Plaza Hotel
57 Hostal La Costañera
61 Alojamiento El Hogar

PLACES TO EAT

8 Churrasquería El Rodeo
11 Palacio de las Masas
22 Heladería Napolí
23 Snack Vicky
24 Los K'aprichos
25 Taverna Gattopardo
32 Bar/Pizzería Europa &
   Internet Bolivia Digital Café
36 Club Social Tarija
38 Pizzería El Gaucho
39 Pizzería Stress
42 El Tropero
47 Chingo's
48 Sergio's Parrillada
49 Restaurant Manna

51 El Solar
58 Chifa New Hong Kong

OTHER

1 Mirador Loma de San Juan
3 Iglesia de San Roque
4 Hospital San Juan de Dios
5 Iglesia de San Juan;
   Micro Stop for San Lorenzo
9 Argentine Consulate
12 Citeco I-Café
13 Casa Dorada
14 Banco Nacional
17 Bus/Trufi Stop for
   San Lorenzo
19 Castillo de Moisés Navajas
26 Viva Tours
27 Foto Methfessel
29 AeroSur
30 Basílica de San Francisco &
   Museo Franciscano Frey
   Francisco Miguel Marí

31 Vinoteca Tarijeña
33 Oficina Departamental
   de Turismo
34 Plaza Luis de Fuentes y
   Vargas
35 Banco Bisa
37 Aranjuez Office
40 Boca Libre
41 Museo de Arqueología
   y Paleontología
43 Rujero Office
44 Kohlberg Office
45 Ciné Edén
46 SurNet Cyber Café

50 Supermercado Tarija
52 LAB Office
53 Disco Malius
54 Post Office
55 ENTEL
56 PROMETA
59 La Vinchuca
60 Cabaña Don Pepe
62 Bus Terminal

Fragments of the Past

The Tarija area is a paradise for amateur paleontologists who'd like to try their hand at fossil-hunting. The *quebradas* and badlands around the airport and across the highway along the pipeline are littered with the remains of prehistoric mammals, including several species of early horses and the mastodon, the megatherium and the 3m-long, armadillo-like glyptodon. However, because the area is severely eroded and every rainfall changes the face of the land, bones have been sloshed around for thousands of years and deposited haphazardly in the sedimentary layers. The more complete fossil bones lie loose or perched on pedestals of sediment, but it's rare to find a complete skeleton.

If you don't know what to look for, the profusion of specimens will probably seem overwhelming. The ubiquitous small blue 'stones' are well-fossilized fragments of mastodon bones, tusks and teeth; the crumbly rosettes that lie in heaps or are embedded in sediment are bits of glyptodon carapace; and the small and rounded chalk-like 'pebbles' come from the hide of megatheria. Crania, pelvic bones and long bones of all these creatures are common, but the dry climate means that they generally haven't been well petrified and are quite fragile. Under no circumstances should you try to unearth them. Professional paleontologists know how to do so safely, but amateurs normally cause them to crumble into dust as soon as the supporting soil is removed.

When you're wandering through the quebradas and badlands, carry water and wear good hiking footwear with lots of tread; the terrain is difficult and the unconsolidated silt is slippery, especially when wet. Most importantly, please leave the specimens as you find them (it's illegal to remove them) and report any significant discoveries (such as a fully intact glyptodon skeleton or the like!) to the Museo de Arqueología y Paleontología in town.

sorts of reference works, including numerous works on Bolivian archaeology. In the basilica, the Museo Franciscano Frey Francisco Miguel Mari displays ecumenical painting, sculpture and artifacts. The office entrance is on Calle Ingavi between Daniel Campos and Suipacha; it's open weekdays 8 am to 6 pm and is free.

Architecturally, Tarija's most unusual church is the 1887 **Iglesia de San Roque**, which crowns the hill at the end of General Bernardo Trigo. This imposing landmark is visible from all over town, and its balcony once served as a lookout post.

The **Iglesia de San Juan**, at the top of Bolívar, was constructed in 1632. Here the Spanish signed their surrender to the liberation army after the Batalla de la Tablada (see History). The garden affords a sweeping view over Tarija and its dramatic backdrop of brown mountains.

Mirador Loma de San Juan

This park area above the tree-covered slopes of Loma de San Juan provides a grand city view and is a favorite with students, who spend their afternoons there studying and socializing. Climb uphill to the end of Calle Bolívar, then turn right behind the hill and climb the footpath up the slope that faces away from the city.

Casa Dorada

The 'gilded house,' Casa Dorada, on General Bernardo Trigo at Ingavi, dates back to 1930. Back then, it was one of the several properties of the wealthy Tarija landowner Moisés Navajas (often described as Bolivia's Teddy Roosevelt) and his wife, Esperanza Morales.

The building could be described as imposing, but amusingly, the exterior has been sloppily splashed with gold and silver paint, the roof is topped with a row of liberating angels, and the interior reflects equally questionable taste. The ground floor is painted a scintillating shade of purple and the frescoes could have been the work of precocious preschoolers. There's also a winning collection of lamps: rose lamps, peacock lamps, grape lamps, morning glory lamps and, of course, crystal chandeliers that sprout light bulbs. Perhaps the most worthwhile relic is the *funola*, an early type of player piano that produced music by forcing air through a strip of perforated paper.

The building now belongs to the university and houses the Casa de la Cultura. It's open Monday to Friday 8 am to noon and 2:30 to 6 pm. For brief guided tours, foreigners pay US$1.

Castillo de Moisés Navajas
The Castillo de Moisés Navajas, another of Moisés Navajas' homes, is an oddly prominent and deteriorating mansion on Bolívar between Junín and O'Connor. It is currently inhabited, but the exterior is plainly visible from the sidewalk.

Zoo
The zoo lies on the western outskirts of town at the end of Domingo Paz, about 15 minutes' walk from the city center. The animals are mostly in poor condition, and it's unkempt and depressing. The surrounding park is more pleasant, with a nice children's playground. Admission is US$0.20.

Parque Héroes de la Tablada
Across the Río Guadalquivir, 4km by road from Tarija, is the historic battlefield of La Tablada, where José Eustaquio 'Moto' Méndez and his forces defeated the Spanish royal armies in 1817. It's now a pleasant park and national monument to the fallen Bolivian soldiers who took part in the battle. Take Micro C from the center.

Wineries
The Tarija region is known for its wines, some of which are palatable and others of which produce a spontaneous reaction of the facial muscles. The first grapevines were brought by 17th-century missionaries who recognized the region's climate and soils as similar to those they'd known in wine-growing regions of Iberia. The region now produces well over two million liters annually, and the wines improve all the time.

To visit the wineries and sample their products, inquire at their town offices:

Rujero/La Concepción (☎ 45040), on La Madrid at Suipacha, is the best and has shops at Ingavi E-311 and at O'Connor N-642; Kohlberg, 15 de Abril O-275; Aranjuez (☎ 45651), 15 de Abril O-241; and Casa Real (☎ 45498), 15 de Abril E-0259. The offices of Kohlberg, Aranjuez and Casa Real have small shops where they sell wine at factory prices. Besides the wine, all the wineries produce *singani*, a distilled grape spirit.

Only the Aranjuez cellars (☎ 42552), Los Sauces 1976, are near town; Kohlberg and Casa Real are in Santana, 17km from Tarija, and Rujero is near Concepción, about 30km away. Travelers without transportation may approach them politely and see if the in-town offices may be able to organize lifts with the staff. Alternatively, both Viva Tours and VTB Tours (see below) offer wine-tasting day tours.

A great place in town to purchase local wine for good prices is La Vinoteca Tarijeña (☎ 35494; fax 47233; vinoteca@tarijanet .com) in Plaza Luis de Fuentes y Varga. The friendly staff is well versed in local vintages and is happy to answer your questions. They'll also provide a brochure with a map showing all the region's major vineyards and cellars.

Organized Tours
For city tours, wine tours and adventurous trips around Tarija's hinterlands – including Tarija department's four new National Reserves – you can't beat Viva Tours (☎/fax 38324; vivatour@cosett.com.bo), Sucre 0615. VTB Tours (☎ 43372; fax 44341; patyvica@olivo.tja.entelnet.bo), Ingavi O-0784, also runs tours to most sites of interest around the city and the region.

Special Events
Carnaval Tarija's Carnaval is one of the most animated in Bolivia and is well worth attending. To launch the festivities, two Thursdays before Carnaval, Tarija celebrates first the Fiesta de Compadres, and then, the following Thursday, the unique Fiesta de Co-madres. The latter, which is Tarija's largest pre-Carnaval festival, was probably inspired by the wives of Spanish colonial authorities

Music & Dance, Chapaco-Style

Not only is Tarija Bolivia's land of wine, it's also rich in music and song, as evidenced by its musical and dance traditions, which are unique in the country.

The traditional dance *La Rueda* is featured at all Tarijeño festivities, as are the *chunchos*. These men have vowed to the Virgin Mary to perform their gyrating Bolivian version of British Morris dancing every year for 10 to 50 years. Their colorful costumes are assembled from half-length silk shirts, scarves, veils and stockings, clown shoes, gaudy silk hearts decorated with shells, and polychrome feather top hats adorned with assorted bangles. The lively, rhythmic music is accompanied by the clicks of their small metal castanets.

Woodwinds unique to the Tarija area are the *erke*, the *caña* and the *camacheña*. The erke, also known as the *phututu*, is made from a cow's horn and is played exclusively between New Year's and Carnaval. From San Roque to the end of the year, the camacheña, a type of flute, is featured. The caña, a 3m-long cane pole with a cow's horn on the end, is similar in appearance and tone to an alphorn. It's played throughout the year in Tarija. The stringed *violín chapaco*, a variation on the European violin, originated in Tarija and is the favored instrument between Easter and San Roque. Among percussion instruments, Tarija loves the *caja*, a tambourine-like drum played with one hand. Instruments popular elsewhere in Bolivia, such as *charangos*, guitars and flutes, also feature prominently in Tarijeño merrymaking.

and soldiers, who saw to it that strict social customs and morals were followed in this sophisticated community. This festival, which originated in Pola de Siero, Asturias, Spain, was eventually adopted by the indigenous population and is now celebrated by the entire community with music, dancing and special basket tableaux constructed of bread known as *bollus preñaus*, flowers, fruits, tubers, small cakes and other gifts, which are passed between female friends and relatives.

Throughout the Carnaval season, the festivities are dedicated to good fun and the streets fill with joyful dancing, original Chapaco music and colorfully costumed country folk who come to town for the event. There's a Grand Ball in the main plaza after the celebration and the entire town turns out for dancing and performances by folkloric groups, bands and orchestras. Water balloons figure prominently in the festivities.

On the Sunday after Carnaval, the barrio near the cemetery enacts a bizarre 'funeral' in which the devil is burned and buried in preparation for Lent. Paid mourners lend the ritual a very morose air – but they're actually lamenting that they must remain free of vice for the 40 days until Easter!

Rodeo Chapaco In keeping with its gaucho heritage, Tarija stages a rodeo in Parque La Tablada from April 15 to 21. It includes all the standard cowboy events and prizes for the overall winner. Take Micro C from the center.

Fiesta de San Roque Tarija's well-known Fiesta de San Roque, the patron saint of the city, falls on August 16, when canines parade through the street in festive dress (San Roque is the patron saint of dogs). The main celebration, however, doesn't begin until the first Sunday of September and then continues for eight days; it features traditional musical performances and a chuncho procession. During the procession, participants wearing costumes highlighted with bright feathers, ribbons, glittering sequins and other small, festive objects masquerade as members of a Chaco tribe that has been recently converted to Christianity.

Fiesta de las Flores This annual religious celebration, dedicated to the Virgen de Rosario, begins on the second Sunday in October. It begins with a procession of the faithful led by an image of the Virgen de

Rosario, which sets off from the Iglesia de San Juan. Along the route, spectators shower participants with flower petals. The highlight of the day is a colorful fair and bazaar in which the faithful spend lavishly for the benefit of the Church.

Places to Stay – Budget

When it isn't raining, the best campsites are hidden amid the quebradas and fossil areas near the airport. Less secluded is the inviting far bank of the Río Guadalquivir, which is accessible via the bridge near the intersection of 15 de Abril and Avenida Victor Paz Estenssoro.

Alojamiento El Hogar (☎ *43964*), on Victor Paz Estenssoro at La Paz, opposite the bus terminal, is dirt cheap at US$2.50 per person with a shared bath, but it offers comfortable accommodations and a friendly, family-run atmosphere. It's a good 20-minute walk from the center.

The central and recommended *Alojamiento Ocho Hermanos* (☎ *42111; Sucre N-782*), with a nice flowery courtyard and a sunny terrace, offers tidy singles/doubles with shared bath for US$5/8.50. Laundry service is available, as at most Tarija accommodation options.

Residencial Zeballos (☎ *42068; Sucre N-0966*) has bright, comfortable rooms with shared baths for US$5/8.50 and rooms with private baths and TV for US$10/15. It's friendly enough, but the obstreperous TV does tend to make its presence known.

Next door is *Hostal Miraflores* (☎ *43355; fax 30391; Sucre 920*), in a restored colonial-style building. Rooms with baths cost US$6.20/10.50; with bath and cable TV, US$11/17. Note, however, that some rooms occupy a dark warren at the back. Visa cards are accepted.

The *Residencial El Rosario* (☎ *43942*), on Ingavi at Ramón Rojas, is a favorite haunt of volunteer workers. It doesn't have the warmest atmosphere, but it's comfortable and a good value at US$5 per person (US$8.50 with bath). It's advantages include the TV room and the reliable gas hot showers rather than the usual electrical attachment.

Hostal Bolívar (☎ *42741; Bolívar 256*), features hot showers, a TV room and a sunny courtyard. Rooms with baths range from US$7.50/11 to US$15/20, depending on the amenities. Only the least expensive rooms lack TV.

Hostería España (☎ *43304; Corrado 546*), is a good all-around choice, with a nice flowery patio. Rooms with shared baths cost US$5/9 and with bath US$8/14. Note, however, that even the private baths aren't attached to the rooms and require a jaunt across the patio.

Places to Stay – Mid-Range

A passable lower-mid-range choice is the central and welcoming *Hostal Libertador* (☎ *44231; Bolívar O-649*). Singles/doubles with private baths, telephones and TV cost US$14/22; breakfast runs an additional US$1.50.

If being central is your main objective, try *Victoria Plaza Hotel* (☎ *42600; fax 42700*), on La Madrid at Sucre, which charges US$30/50 for rooms with baths, TV, phones and *frigobars*. Just a block away is the similar *Gran Hotel Tarija* (☎ *42684; fax 44777; Sucre 770*), which charges US$31/51 for comfortable air-conditioned rooms just a block from the plaza.

The pleasantly posh *Hostal La Costañera* (☎ *42851; fax 32640; costanera@ olivo.tja.entelnet.bo; Saracho 594*) provides most amenities: heat, air-con, phone, cable TV and private parking. The good-value rooms cost US$32/47, including a continental breakfast, and lower rates may be negotiated in the low season or for longer stays. They also have a website at www.hostal-costanera.com.

Hotel Los Ceibos (☎ *34430; fax 42461*), on Victor Paz Estenssoro at La Madrid, offers the same amenities as Hostal La Costañera and charges US$35/50. All rooms have balconies overlooking the pool. Rooms with double beds are US$45 and suites (two normal rooms combined) cost US$90.

Places to Stay – Top End

The five-star *Hotel Los Parrales* (☎ *48444; fax 30415; parraleshotel@mail.com; Urbanización Carmen de Aranjuez, Casilla 23*), in a nice setting 3.5km from the center, is the pinnacle of Tarija's accommodation choices. Single/double rooms cost US$95/115, plus US$8 per person for an American breakfast. Amenities include a swimming pool and all the other trappings of a business-class resort hotel, as well as a lovely open-air dining area overlooking the campo. Hotel transfers from the center cost US$10 for up to three people, but taxis are just US$1.

Places to Eat

Northeast of the market, on the corner of Calles Sucre and Domingo Paz, street vendors sell local pastries and snacks unavailable in other parts of Bolivia, including delicious crêpe-like *panqueques*. In the back of the market, there's a section selling breakfast, and lots of stalls in the produce area sell fresh juices and *licuados*. Other meals are served upstairs.

The *Palacio de las Masas*, on Calle Campero, bakes up a range of breads, cakes and pastries that includes French-style baguettes, chocolate cake, *cuñapes* (cassava and cheese rolls) and both chocolate and meringue confections. Tarija's best self-serve venue is the *Supermercado Tarija*, on 15 de Abril at Delgadillo.

Snack Vicky, on La Madrid, serves snack meals and almuerzos for about US$1, and is OK for a quick bite. An excellent spot for ice cream is *Heladería Napoli*, on General Campero at Ingavi, with memorable Italian gelato for a good price.

The still-great Swiss- and Czech-run *Taverna Gattopardo* (☎ 30656; La Madrid 318), which is probably Tarija's most popular restaurant, provides a cozy, friendly atmosphere. You can start the day with an excellent espresso or cappuccino; for lunch you can enjoy well-prepared salads, soups and pasta dishes for US$1, burgers for US$2 to US$2.50, *ceviche* for US$2.50 or large pizzas for US$4.50 to US$7. More substantial meals range from chicken, filets or fish for US$4.50 to fondue bourguignonne for US$7.50. It also does excellent desserts. There's a stone-lined alcove at the back with straw on the floor and a nice social bar. When the weather's good, you can sit

outside and enjoy a beer while you observe plaza life.

Los K'aprichos (☎ 47365), next door, attempts to emulate Gattopardo's ambience and its success. Although it's pretty good and is also popular with afternoon imbibers, it doesn't quite measure up to its neighbor. Inside the Internet café, also on the main plaza, is the friendly *Bar/Pizzería Europa*, which serves pizzas as well as drinks, including Bolivian wine. On the other side of the plaza, you'll find the more conservative *Club Social Tarija* (☎ 42108), serving inexpensive almuerzos on weekdays.

A bit farther down Calle 15 de Abril is the recommended *Restaurant Manna*, which does excellent down-to-earth almuerzos for US$1.80, including soup, a salad bar, a main dish and dessert. A la carte options include pasta, meat dishes and sandwiches.

For lunch, the popular *El Solar* vegetarian restaurant, on Campero at Virginia Lema, is superb – if a bit freaky – and proudly caters to Tarija's New Age fringe. (In the affiliated office next door, you can indulge in the wonders of chromotherapy, aromatherapy, geotherapy, natural baths, psychic readings, group yoga sessions etc.) The restaurant experiments with such nontraditional practices as serving the dessert before the meal, and you're not even in Southern California! Four-course macrobiotic lunches are served from noon to 2 pm for US$1.50, and it's a real cow's delight: You can guzzle green alfalfa juice and graze on avocado salad, oat soup, bulgur wheat, cream of mango puree and straw tea. Go early to beat the herd.

Plaza Sucre is Tarija's new youth hangout. At *Chingo's* (☎ 44864), in Plaza Sucre, you'll find hefty Argentine beef *parrillada* with all the standard trimmings – rice, salad and potatoes – for about US$4. It also serves burgers, pizza, chicken & french fries and other things fried. Just around the corner are the side-by-side *Pizzería El Gaucho* and *Pizzería Stress* – you can choose between riding the range or languishing in angst!

With Argentina so close, it's not surprising that steaks are popular. Some options for hungry carnivores are the sparkling

Churrasquería El Rodeo, on Oruro at O'Connor; the rustic *El Tropero*, on Calle Virginio Lema; and *Sergio's Parrillada*, in Plaza Sucre, which is lively in the evenings. Although they all have salad bars, the only available main course is steak. Dinner at any of these runs about US$5 per person, without drinks.

For Chinese food, your best choice is *Chifa New Hong Kong* (☎ 37076), on Calle Sucre. The extensive menu features all the usual Chinese choices, which are well done and available as take-out for a discounted price.

Entertainment

Near the southern end of Daniel Campos, *La Vinchuca (Daniel Campos 147)* is a bar and 'cultural center' popular with expats and foreign NGO people. It presents traditional music and dancing, drumming sessions, art exhibitions, discussions, poetry readings, theater and art films. Something happens most nights Tuesday to Saturday, 7:30 pm to 2 am. Drinks and snacks are served.

The classic old *Cine Edén* screens double features of recent films for US$2, and on Friday and Saturday, you can catch live music and local karaoke at *Boca Libre*. Housed in the weird green-glass building near the southern end of Calle Sucre is *Disco Malius*, which caters to Tarija's 17-to-25 crowd.

On Fridays, the *Hotel Los Parrales* holds a peña at 9 pm. *Cabaña Don Pepe (☎ 42426; Daniel Campos 236)* also holds peñas on weekends and has a disco and karaoke venue. Additionally, there are several karaoke places around Plaza Sucre.

Shopping

The best handcrafted souvenirs typical of Tarija would naturally be its unique musical instruments. Granted, it would be difficult to carry a caña around in your pack, but smaller instruments may be mailed home.

For the best selection of Chapaco and Bolivian music, go to Disco Foto Rodríguez, on Sucre at La Madrid. Some suggestions include the tape *Tarija y su Música* by various

artists, and anything by the groups Los Trobadores Chapacos and Los Sapos Cantores de Tarija (the 'singing toads of Tarija').

Getting There & Away

Air The Oriel Lea Plaza Airport lies 3km east of town along Avenida Victor Paz Estenssoro. Lloyd Aéreo Boliviano (LAB; ☎ 42282; General Trigo 329) connects Tarija with La Paz (US$98), Cochabamba (US$69) and Santa Cruz (US$75) several times weekly. TAM has more or less weekly connections to La Paz (US$76), Sucre (US$32) and Cochabamba (US$60). Although AeroSur has a booking office in Tarija, the airline no longer flies to or from the city.

Bus The bus terminal (☎ 36508) is a 20-minute walk from the city center, east along Avenida Victor Paz Estenssoro. Several *flotas* run buses to Potosí (14 hours, US$10), with connections to Uyuni (20 hours, US$13), Oruro (21 hours, US$15), Cochabamba (26 hours, US$18.50) and Sucre (18 hours, US$11); most leave daily in the afternoon. Buses to Tupiza (10 hours, US$5) and Villazón (12 hours, US$5) depart daily in the evening. It's a pity there are no daytime services, because the spectacular route passes through some incredible 'Wild West' mountain and canyon landscapes. About the best you can hope for is a full moon.

To Yacuiba (12 hours, US$7), buses leave daily between 6 and 7 pm; this is also a lovely journey. If you manage to pass during the day, have a look at Palos Blancos' rustic church, a tumbledown whitewashed mud building set in a lovely red and green landscape.

There are also daily services to Camiri (19 hours, US$12), with connections to Santa Cruz (24 hours, US$17) on Monday, Thursday and Saturday, and numerous buses head daily for Bermejo (six hours, US$7).

Daily, you can also travel directly to most Argentine cities, including Buenos Aires (32 hours, US$98), as well as Santiago, Chile (34 hours, US$115).

Camión To go to Yacuiba or Villamontes, the best place to wait for a camión is at the *tranca* east of town. Although it's an uncomfortable ride, you'll pass through some fabulous scenery, especially the stretch between Entre Ríos and Palos Blancos, and through the Cañón del Pilcomayo (Pilcomayo Gorge) near Villamontes.

For other destinations, take a taxi to the appropriate tranca and wait for a vehicle going your way. Use the north tranca for Villazón and Potosí and the southeast tranca for Yacuiba and Bermejo.

Getting Around

To/From the Airport Taxis from the airport to the center cost around US$2, but if you walk past the airport gate (about 100m from the terminal), you'll pay just US$0.80. Otherwise, cross the main road and take a passing micro or trufi (US$0.30).

Bus City micros and trufis cost US$0.25 per ride; routes are clearly marked on the front windows of the vehicles.

Taxi Although you can walk just about anywhere in Tarija (even to the airport!), taxis cost US$0.60/0.90 per person for day/night trips around the center, including the bus terminal. For a radio taxi, phone Moto Méndez (☎ 44480), Tarija (☎ 44378) or 4 de Julio (☎ 42829).

AROUND TARIJA
San Jacinto

The 1700-hectare San Jacinto reservoir, 7km southwest of town, provides landlocked Tarija with watery recreation. There's a tourist complex with little cabañas serving *dorado* (a delicious local fish), a canoe rental and nice walks along the shore and surrounding ridges. It's very popular with chapacos on Sunday afternoons. Micro H and the trufi Línea San Jacinto (10 minutes, US$0.20) leave every 20 minutes from the Palacio de la Justicia, at the corner of Ingavi and Daniel Campos in Tarija.

San Lorenzo

San Lorenzo, 15km from Tarija, is a lovely colonial village with cobbled streets, carved balconies, a 1709 church and a flowery plaza with palm trees. It's best known, however, as the home of one José Eustaquio 'Moto' Méndez, the hero of the Batalla de la Tablada, whose home now houses the **Museo Moto Méndez**. Displays consist mainly of his personal belongings, which he bequeathed to the people of Tarija. As in so many such museums, they've been left exactly as they were when he died. The museum is open Monday to Saturday 9 am to 12:30 pm and 3 to 5 pm and Sunday 10 am to noon. Admission is free.

After seeing the museum, head 2km north to the **Capilla de Lajas**, a delicate chapel of exquisite proportions and fine colonial architecture. It was once the Méndez family chapel and remains in private hands. Just to the north is the former home of Jaime Paz Zamora, with an adjacent billboard paying homage to the ex-president.

Special Events The popular Fiesta de San Lorenzo takes place on August 10 and features Chapaco musical instruments and dancing.

Getting There & Away San Lorenzo lies 15km north of Tarija along the Tupiza road. Micros and trufis (½ hour, US$0.40) leave from Plaza Guemes (the Capilla de San Juan) in Tarija approximately every 20 minutes during the day. Along the route, you'll pass through the Parque Nacional las Barrancas, which was created in the 1960s to foster tree-planting and thereby control erosion in the crumbling fossil-rich badlands. (To hike in the park, take Micro A and get off at any of the park gates.)

El Valle de la Concepción

El Valle de la Concepción, or simply 'El Valle,' as locals affectionately refer to it, is the heart of Bolivian wine and singani production. The town itself still bears lots of picturesque colonial elements and the plaza sports some lovely flowering ceibo trees, which are endemic to the Chaco region. To visit the valley wineries, see the Tarija office of the Bodegas y Viñedos de la Concepción (☎ 45040), on La Madrid at Suipacha. The Fiesta de la Uva (Grape Festival) is held in

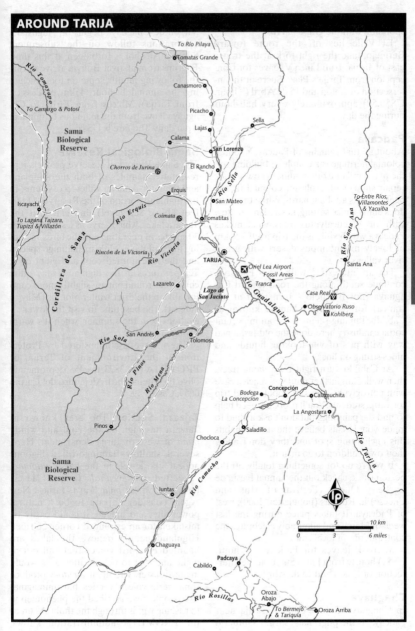

AROUND TARIJA

To Río Pilaya

Río Tomayapo

To Camargo & Potosí

Sama Biological Reserve

Tomatas Grande

Canasmoro

Picacho

Sella

Lajas

Calama

San Lorenzo

Chorros de Jurina

El Rancho

Iscayachi

To Laguna Tajzara, Tupiza & Villazón

Cordillera de Sama

Río Erquis

Erquis

Coimata

San Mateo

Río Sella

To Entre Ríos, Villamontes & Yacuiba

Rincón de la Victoria

Río Victoria

Tomatitas

Santa Ana

Río Santa Ana

TARIJA

Oriel Lea Airport

Fossil Areas

Lazareto

Lago de San Jacinto

Tranca

Río Guadalquivir

Casa Real

Observatorio Ruso

Kohlberg

San Andrés

Río Sola

Tolomosa

Río Pinos

Río Mena

Concepción

Bodega La Concepción

Calamuchita

La Angostura

Pinos

Choclaca

Saladillo

Río Tarija

Sama Biological Reserve

Juntas

Río Camacho

Chaguaya

Cabildo

Padcaya

Oroza Abajo

Río Rosillas

To Bermejo & Tariquía

Oroza Arriba

0   5   10 km

0   3   6 miles

the valley for three days in March, corresponding with the grape harvest.

El Valle lies off the route toward Bermejo; take the right fork at the tranca east of Tarija. Trufi Linea V leaves for Concepción from Tarija's Plaza Sucre at the intersection of Colón and 15 de Abril (½ hour, US$0.50) approximately every half-hour during the day.

Padcaya

About all that remains of Padcaya's touted colonial heritage is a couple of buildings on the plaza and one other edifice (now a truck repair shop) with a plaster colonial façade peeling to its adobe innards. While the town does enjoy a nice setting, nestled in a hollow with lots of eucalyptus trees, what makes Padcaya worthwhile is the trip itself – 50km of lovely mountainous desert with green river valleys.

For an interesting walk from Padcaya, continue south along the road toward Chaguaya (not Bermejo – turn right at the tranca) for 3km to a hamlet known as Cabildo. Tanning seems to be an important cottage industry here, done the old-fashioned way with pits of vile-looking liquids and hides strung on lines.

At Cabildo, turn right on a llama track, then walk 5km farther until you reach a cave with petroglyphs. This is a popular field trip for Tarija students. You'll probably need help to find the paintings, but don't ask a child to guide you: Locals believe the devil inhabits this enchanting spot and they don't allow their own children to go near it.

If you're up for something totally off the beaten track, check out the annual Fiesta de Leche y Queso (Festival of Milk and Cheese) in Rosillas (population 1000), west of Padcaya. It takes place during the last week of March and admirably celebrates the contributions of local cows.

Micro P leaves for Padcaya (½ hour, US$1) hourly from Plaza Sucre, at the intersection of Colón and 15 de Abril.

Chaguaya

In Chaguaya, 51km south of Tarija near Padcaya, is the pilgrimage shrine Santuario de la Virgen de Chaguaya. The Fiesta de la Virgen de Chaguaya begins on August 15; celebrations follow on the subsequent Sunday. Alcohol is forbidden at this time. Pilgrims from all over Bolivia arrive during the following month, some on foot (including the annual 12-hour, 45km procession from Tarija). Micros from Tarija to Chaguaya leave from the main bus terminal at 4 pm daily. The fare is US$1.

Sama Biological Reserve

The Sama Biological Reserve protects representative samples of both the Altiplano and the inter-Andean valley ecosystems. In the highland portion of the Reserve (11,000 feet above sea level) one can visit the Tajzara lakes, which serve as a stop for over 30 species of migrating aquatic birds, including three of the world's six flamingo species and the rare horned coot and giant coot. Temperatures in the highlands stay quite chilly year-round but are slightly more comfortable in the drier winter months (May to August). The best time to visit the lower elevations is in the summer, when it's warm enough to swim.

The reserve is administered by Protection of the Environment of Tarija, or PROMETA (☎ 33873; fax 45865; prometa@ olivo.tja.entelnet.bo), Alejandro del Carpio 0659, Casilla 59.

Tajzara Section The area known as Tajzara lies high on the cold and windy *puna* of western Tarija department. Here, several shallow flamingo-filled lagoons appear like jewels in the harsh *altiplano*, vegetated only by *thola* (a small desert bush) and spiky *paja brava*. Tarija's New Agers consider Tajzara to be a natural power site, and indeed, it could easily be mistaken for an estranged corner of Tibet. Highland people believe the lakes are haunted by spirit voices that call out at night, and that to be out after dark would invite disaster. The night air *does* produce some eerie voicelike cries, but unimaginative people have ascribed the phenomenon to rushing winds through the thola. As far as the PROMETA administration knows, there's no truth to the rumor that aliens frequent Tajzara…but who can be sure?

Along the eastern shores of the lagoons, the wind has heaped up large *arenales* (sand dunes). An interesting climb takes you to the symmetrical peak of Muyuloma, which rises about 1000m above the plain. The summit affords views across the lagoons and beyond to the endless expanses of the southern altiplano. The return climb takes the better part of a day.

From the Tajzara Vistors Center, hikers can spend a very enjoyable six to eight hours on the wonderful Inca Trail as it descends 2000m to the valley below. With luck, hikers may see vicuñas, condors, the rare Andean deer, and the mysterious petroglyphs of unknown origin. Arrive the night before you intend to hike. Accommodations are available at the visitors center, where beds and use of the hot showers and communal kitchen cost US$13 for those over 25 years of age and US$10 for folks from 14 to 25. Bring all your food from elsewhere.

Inter-Andean Valleys During the summertime, there are several places in the valley to go swimming in the rivers, including Tomatitas, Coimata and Chorros de Jurina.

Tomatitas, with its natural swimming holes, it's three lovely rivers (the Sella, Guadalquivir and Erquis) and happy little eateries is popular with day-trippers from Tarija. The best swimming is immediately below the footbridge, where there's also a park with a campground and barbecue sites. From here, you can walk or hitch the 5km to Coimata. Coming from Tarija, turn left off the main San Lorenzo road. After less than 1km, you'll pass a cemetery on the left, which is full of flowers and brightly colored crosses. Just beyond it, bear right toward Coimata. Once there, turn left at the soccer field and continue to the end of the road. Here you'll find a small cascade and swimming hole that makes a great escape, as lots of *tarijeño* families can attest. There's also a choice of little restaurants serving *misquinchitos* and *doraditos* (fried local fish with white corn), as well as *cangrejitos* (small freshwater crabs). From this point, you can follow a walking track 40 minutes upstream to the base of the two-tiered Coimata Falls, which has a total drop of about 60m.

Another swimming hole and waterfall are found at Rincón de la Victoria, about 6.5km from Tomatitas in a green plantation-like setting. Instead of bearing right beyond the colorful cemetery, as you would for Coimata, follow the route to the left. From the fork, it's about 5km to Rincón de la Victoria. Note that the hiking track that ascends to the falls is quite steep and potentially slippery.

The twin 40m waterfalls at Chorros de Jurina also make an agreeable destination for a day trip from Tarija. Set in a beautiful but unusual landscape, one waterfall cascades over white stone while the other pours over black stone. In late winter, however, they may diminish to a mere trickle or even be dry.

The route from Tarija to Jurina passes through some impressive rural landscapes. From near the flowery plaza in San Lorenzo, follow the Jurina road, which turns off beside the Casa de Moto Méndez. After 6km, you'll pass a school on the left side. Turn left 200m beyond the school and follow that road another 2.5km to the waterfalls. From the end of the road, it's a five-minute walk to the base of either waterfall. The one on the left is accessed by following the river upstream; for the other, follow the track that leads from behind a small house.

Getting There & Away From Tarija, Viva Tours organizes trips to several areas of Sama (see Organized Tours under Tarija). However, it is possible to reach Tajzara by local transportation. From Tarija, take a bus toward Villazón and ask the driver to point out the Tajzara Visitors Center, which is a 20-minute walk from the road. Otherwise, you can get off at Pasajes, 7km from the visitors center. PROMETA provides return transportation from Tarija for around US$15 per person.

Micros A and B to Tomatitas leave every few minutes from the western end of Avenida Domingo Paz in Tarija, and on weekends occasional trufis go all the way to Coimata. A taxi from Tomatitas to Coimata costs about US$2.50 with up to four people; all the way from Tarija to Coimata costs around US$5. Trufis San Lorenzo leave for Jurina from near the Iglesia de San Juan in Tarija around 8:30 am and 2:45 and 5 pm. Get off near the school and then walk the rest of the way. Hitching is feasible only on weekends.

Reserva Nacional de Flora y Fauna Tariquía

Created in 1989, this lovely and little-known 247,000-hectare reserve protects a large portion of the dense cloud-forest ecosystem on the eastern slopes of Tarija department's mountains. Ranging in altitude from 400m to 1500m, the reserve features such rare animals as the spectacled bear, jaguar, tapir, collared peccary and Andean fox, as well as hundreds of bird species. Beginning in 2001, visitors may be charged an entry fee.

The only way to see this largely wild reserve is on foot, but hiking can be challenging and is most comfortably done with a guide and pack animal. The best time to visit Tariquía is during the dry winter months (May-September), since river crossings become treacherous during the rainy season. In winter, the climate is generally mild and sometimes even quite warm, especially at the lower altitudes.

PROMETA (see Sama Biological Reserve, earlier in this chapter) operates seven camps in Tariquía, including the Tariquía Community Center in the heart of the reserve. From the road, it's a two-day hike to the center and requires camping gear, but allow six days to fully explore the area on foot.

Transportation to the reserve may be organized by PROMETA, which does day trips and in August leads a guided hike. Alternatively, you can go with Viva Tours in Tarija.

BERMEJO
☎ 0696

Bermejo, Bolivia's southernmost town, is a hot, muggy and dusty community 170km south of Tarija on the banks of the Río Bermejo, at the southwest end of Bolivia's oil-bearing geologic formation. Most of its 15,000 people earn their living from the YPFB (petroleum) plant or from the refinery that processes locally grown sugarcane. The international bridge, 5km upriver from the town, provides a highway link with Aguas Blancas on the Argentine side.

Thanks to its border location, Bermejo has plenty of casas de cambio that change cash. Bolivia is one hour behind Argentine time. Both the Bolivian and Argentine posts are open the same hours: 7 am to 4 pm *mas o menos* in Bolivia and a more reliable 8 am to 5 pm in Argentina. The *chalanas* (ferries) over the river charge US$0.20 per person and leave when full, which is every few minutes. Be sure to pick up an exit stamp before crossing.

Email and Internet access is available at the Café Internet Cotabe, which is on Arce at Ameller.

Places to Stay & Eat

There's a surprising choice of accommodations in little Bermejo. *Hotel Paris* (☎ /fax 61562), on Tarija at La Paz, is pretty nice, as is *Hotel San Diego* (☎ 61333; Cochabamba 118). The clean *La Casona del Turista* (☎ 61198; carello@cotabe.com; Barranqueras 147) has rooms with private baths and hot water for US$6 per person. There are no accommodations in Aguas Blancas.

Don Javier on the plaza serves standard Bolivian favorites for equally standard prices. Nothing is outstanding – just *lomo*, chicken, soup and rice. There is, however, a good *heladería* on the plaza.

Getting There & Away

The bus terminal is about eight blocks southeast of the main plaza. Between Bermejo and Tarija (six hours, US$7), buses run just about every hour. From Aguas Blancas, Argentine buses to Orán (one hour, US$2) depart hourly from the terminal opposite the immigration office. From Orán, you can connect to Salta, Jujuy, Tucumán, Tartagal (the connection to Pocitos and Yacuiba) and Asunción (Paraguay).

The Chaco

The Chaco, an immense flat expanse of thorn scrub parceled into vast estancias, takes in most of southeastern Bolivia and western Paraguay, and spills into bits of neighboring Argentina. The human population of this expansive region is limited to a handful of widely dispersed ranchers, isolated Indian groups, resourceful Mennonite colonists and troops at police and military posts.

What the Chaco lacks in up-and-down scenery, it makes up for with its colorful variety of flora and fauna. Butterflies and birds are abundant here, and it's one of the dwindling South American strongholds of larger mammals such as the tapir, jaguar and peccary (locally called *javeli*).

The thorny scrub that characterizes the Chaco's unusual flora is enlivened by brilliant flowering trees and bushes, including the yellow *carnival* bush; the yellow-and-white *huevo*; the pink or white thorny bottle tree, locally known as the *toboroche* or *palo borracho* (drunken branch); and the red-flowering *quebracho* (*quebra acho*, or ('break-axe' tree). Beautiful quebracho wood, which is too heavy to float, is one of the Chaco's main exports. There are also numerous species of cactus.

History

Before the 1932-35 Chaco War, most of Paraguay northeast of the Paraguay and Pilcomayo Rivers – encompassing about 240,680 sq km – and the 168,765-sq-km chunk of Argentina north of the Río Bermejo lay within Bolivian territory.

The dispute between Bolivia and Paraguay that led to the Chaco War had its roots in Paraguay's formal 1842 declaration of independence, which omitted official demarcation of Paraguay's boundary with Bolivia. In 1878, the Hayes Arbitration designated the Río Pilcomayo as the boundary between Paraguay and Argentina, which was duly accepted. The empty land to the north, however, became a matter of conflict between Paraguay and Bolivia. Subsequent attempts at arbitration failed and Bolivia began pressing for a settlement.

After losing the War of the Pacific in 1884, Bolivia more than ever needed the Chaco as an outlet to the Atlantic via the Río Paraguay. Hoping that physical possession would be interpreted as official sovereignty, the Bolivian army set up a fort at Piquirenda on the Pilcomayo.

Arbitration attempts failed because Bolivia refused to relinquish rights to Fuerte Vanguardia, its only port on the Río Paraguay. Paraguay was unwilling to concede and, in 1928, the Paraguayan military seized the fort. Although the situation heated up, both sides maintained a conciliatory attitude, hoping that a military solution would not be necessary.

While negotiations were underway in Washington (the USA never could stay out of a good conflict), unauthorized action on the part of the Bolivian military erupted into full-scale warfare. While casualties on both sides were heavy, the highland Bolivians, unaccustomed to the subtropical terrain, fared miserably. No decisive victory was reached, but the 1938 peace negotiations awarded most of the disputed territory to Paraguay. Bolivia retained only the town of Villamontes, where, in 1934, it saw its most successful campaign of the war (see Villamontes, later in this chapter).

YACUIBA
☎ 0682

Straddling the transition zone between the Chaco and the Argentine Pampa, Yacuiba is the easternmost border crossing on the Bolivian-Argentine frontier. It's the terminus for both the railway from Santa Cruz and the 10,000-barrels-a-day YPFB oil pipeline from Camiri. The railway line was constructed with Argentine capital according to the terms of a February 10, 1941, treaty, in which Bolivia agreed to export surplus petroleum to Argentina in exchange for a 580km rail approach to the Buenos Aires-Pocitos line terminus. Although construction began immediately, it wasn't completed until the 1960s.

As a typical border town, Yacuiba has lots of shoddy commercial goods for sale and many shoppers scrambling to buy stuff nobody really wants or needs. The town and the surrounding area are really of little interest, but you could be stranded here overnight, awaiting a train or a bus out.

Information

Yacuiba's main north-south street is flanked by several casas de cambio, but none of them change traveler's checks. If you're changing

cash, calculate the amount you're to receive before leaving the exchange window and watch for counterfeit US dollar bills.

Thanks to heavy cross-border traffic, pocket picking and petty theft are on the increase, especially in crowded shopping areas.

Places to Stay & Eat

The number of hotels, bars and restaurants in Yacuiba is completely disproportionate to

The Chaco Road

One of South America's great journeys stretches across the vast Gran Chaco between Filadelfia in Paraguay and Boyuibe (or Santa Cruz) in Bolivia. Now that several bus lines have taken up the Santa Cruz-Asunción challenge, the route has lost some of its romanticism, but most of the old uncertainties remain, and you can be assured that it's still an exciting haul through raw, wild and thorny country. Between Filadelfia and La Patria, the road is good gravel, but from there it's little more than deep, parallel sand ruts. You can choose between buses, camiones and private 4WD vehicles, but however you go, expect lots of jolts, bounces and repeated immigration, customs, police and military checkpoints before you can settle back and relax at journey's end. If you're passing through the Asunción bus terminal before or after the trip, have your passport handy at all times, as the police like to 'fine' foreigners US$100 for being 'undocumented.'

However you look at it, this trip is still an adventure through one of the South America's wildest regions. Two friends and I recently traveled the Chaco Road in the bed of a camión carrying a load of uncured cowhide, which oozed rancid fat and saturated the 40°C heat with an aromatic bovine perfume. On one 5km stretch immediately south of Fortín General Eugenio A Garay, the crew and passengers spent 12 hours digging sand, cutting trees and laying branches to make the road passable. At the end of the day, the always jolly Bolivian crew rewarded the exhausted passengers – the three of us, a German backpacker and a Colombian Hare Krishna devotee – with a delicious meal around a cowboy-style campfire.

The bugs were as bad as rumored, but the big surprise is the butterfly population. When they're in season, the poor mosquitoes and flies don't stand a chance because there is simply no room for them in the air. At least the butterflies only sit on your toes and lick your sweat!

In the bus, they wouldn't open the toilet for fear of cholera, so when nature called, passengers headed into the bush with warnings from the drivers about pumas, jaguars and lurking vipers. At the Bolivian border post, our bus stopped to give the guards a few supplies – not a bribe but rather an act of mercy. Then it began to drizzle – drizzle, mind you, not gush down – and the road quickly turned to mud. Now I understood why we were carrying tree trunks in the aisle of the bus. Off we got – not the women, children or bus owners (who were monitoring the expedition) – and stuck the trunks under the wheels. The bus heaved, jerked, spun and got lodged in a ditch. Three hours later we had pushed the bus onto slightly drier ground and were off again.

The Chaco Road may be as adventurous as the above traveler describes, but it's also fraught with bureaucracy. Travelers by camión or private vehicle from Bolivia to Paraguay can pick up exit stamps from the military post at Boyuibe (along the railway south of the village) and from the its size. Passable budget accommodations include the **Residencial Aguaragüe**, which charges US$3/3.75 for a single/double with shared bath. Other cheap digs include **Alojamiento Ferrocarril** and **Residencial San Martín**, which charge around US$2.50 per person.

A good deal is **Hotel Valentín** (☎ 2317), opposite the railway station, with an attached bar/restaurant. Rooms with shared baths are US$5/8, and those with private baths are US$16.

The next-best alternative is the older **Hotel Monumental** (☎ 2088; Comercio 1270). In the newer section, rooms cost US$10/15, but in the older annex, you'll pay considerably less. The **Hotel Paris** (☎ 2182; fax 3059) has rooms with bath and air-con for US$17/21.

For a taste of Argentina north of the border – that means huge slabs of meat – try

The Chaco Road

immigration/police post on the highway 1km farther out. At the Bolivian border post at Fortín Villazón, your passport will be checked and you may receive another exit stamp. The Paraguayan border post is at Irindágüe, 5km farther along, but you pick up Paraguayan entry stamps at the military post, Fortín General Eugenio A Garay, 15km into Paraguay. Between there and Mariscal Estigarribia there are a couple more checks, one at a remote police post and another at La Patria. At Mariscal Estigarribia, travelers coming from Bolivia may be subjected to a military inspection.

Traveling from Paraguay to Bolivia you'll have all the same checks, and you must also check in at both the immigration/police post and the military post in Boyuibe. Those stopping in Camiri must also visit immigration there, but you won't actually receive your passport length-of-stay stamps until you reach immigration in Santa Cruz, which you must do within 72 hours of entering the country.

Crossing the Chaco

In winter, several bus companies tackle the Chaco Road between Santa Cruz and Filadelfia (Paraguay), then continue on to Asunción, in Paraguay (see Getting There & Away in Santa Cruz). During the wet season, however, the rough, sandy road becomes impassable quicksand and slimy mud. If you're coming from Filadelfia, you'll have to reserve a seat via Asunción and meet the bus at Cruce de los Pioneros by taking the connecting bus from Filadelfia. The full trip takes a minimum of 40 hours and costs US$72/65 between Santa Cruz and Asunción/Filadelfia. It's probably not wise to book a return ticket – few people who've done it would ever consider returning by the same route!

Overland travelers from Bolivia to Paraguay should allow a few days to wait for a camión in either Boyuibe or Filadelfia. In the dry season, camiones leave for Mariscal Estigarribia and Filadelfia more or less weekly, but there's no set schedule, so allow several days to find transportation. It may help to go to Boyuibe, Bolivia's launch point into the Chaco, and ask around for transportation or wait at the immigration/police post 2km south of town. Coming from Paraguay, trucks run roughly every few days whenever the road is dry and passable. In Filadelfia, drivers park at the vacant lot 1½ enormous blocks east of the Esso station. Prospective travelers need only make arrangements with the drivers. Alternatively, you can wait at the military checkpoint at the southern entrance to Mariscal Estigarribia. Passengers in either direction can expect to pay US$10 to US$15 per person for the two- to three-day trip.

Those with a hardy 4WD vehicle can attempt this trip independently, but serious preparations are necessary. A supply of fuel, water, food, spare parts, tires and so on is essential. There are no spares or fuel available until well into Paraguay, road conditions change with each rainfall and traffic is intermittent at best. If you break down, it may be days before someone passes by.

any of the several parrilladas around Yacuiba. Typical Bolivian meals and decent breakfasts are available at the unfortunately named *Swin*, which was probably intended to be 'Swing.' There are also numerous snack restaurants peppered all over the shopping district.

Getting There & Away
Air TAM (☎ 3853) flies Saturday between Santa Cruz and Yacuiba (US$59), with connections to Tarija (US$59).

Bus There are morning and evening departures to Tarija (12 hours, US$7) and numerous flotas leave every evening for Santa Cruz (15 hours, US$11) via Villamontes and Camiri. Believe it or not, there's also a daily departure to La Paz, via Potosí and Oruro, which would truly be an exercise in endurance.

Shared taxis go to immigration at Pocitos (US$1 per person), 5km away. After crossing the border on foot, you can connect with Argentine bus services. To Tartagal, they leave every two hours or so. At the TVO Expreso Café in Yacuiba, you can pick up tickets from the Argentine company Veloz del Norte to Salta, Jujuy, Tucumán, Buenos Aires and Santiago del Estero. The bus terminal is in Pocitos.

Train The railway station (☎ 2308) ticket window opens in the morning on the day of departure, but line up early. Trains to Santa Cruz (12 hours, US$14/16 in 2nd/1st class) leave on Tuesday, Thursday and Saturday at 5 pm. There's no longer a *bracha* (sleeper) service on this run.

POCITOS
Tiny Pocitos straddles the Bolivia-Argentina border 5km south of Yacuiba. From the Argentine side, buses depart roughly every two hours to Tartagal and Embarcación, where you can make connections to Salta, Jujuy, Orán and Buenos Aires. Bear in mind that Bolivian time is one hour behind Argentine time. The Argentine bus terminals are just a couple of minutes' walk from immigration.

Shared taxis for the 5km trip between Yacuiba and the immigration post at Pocitos cost around US$1 per person, regardless of the number of passengers. There's no consulate for either country.

VILLAMONTES
☎ 0684
Villamontes, Bolivia's main outpost in the true Chaco, prides itself on being the hottest place in the country – which doesn't seem amiss when the mercury rises above the 40°C mark and a hot, dry wind coats everything with a thick layer of red dust. As with the rest of the Chaco, it's famous for its wildlife, particularly small buzzing varieties like flies and mosquitoes.

History
During Inca times, tribes of Guaraní Indians immigrated to western Chaco from present-day Paraguay, and their descendants now comprise most of the town's indigenous population.

Villamontes remained a small, lonely outpost until it emerged as a strategic Bolivian army stronghold during the Chaco War. The Paraguayans considered Villamontes their key to undisputed victory over the Bolivian resistance. In 1934, in the Battle of Villamontes, the Bolivian army enjoyed its most significant victory of the war under the command of General Bernardino Bilbao Rioja and Major Germán Busch. The momentum gained in that battle allowed them to recapture portions of the eastern Chaco and some of the Santa Cruz department oil fields previously lost to Paraguay.

In the Villamontes market, look for baskets and furniture made from natural Chaco materials by the indigenous Guaraní people. Also note that in August, Villamontes holds a fishing festival that focuses on the Río Pilcomayo.

Cañón del Pilcomayo
At El Chorro Grande waterfall, in the beautiful Cañón del Pilcomayo, fish are prevented from swimming farther upstream and *surubí*, *sábalo* and dorado are abundant and easily caught. This makes the area a

favorite with anglers from all over the country. The prized dorado is particularly interesting because it has an odd hinge at the front of its jawbone that allows the mouth to open wide horizontally.

There are great views from the restaurants along the Tarija road seven to 10km west of town. There you can sample local fish dishes for about US$2.50.

To reach the gorge, take any Tarija-bound bus or gasoline truck, or go by taxi to the tranca and hitch or walk from there (as usual, weekends are the best time to hitchhike). Where the road forks, bear right and continue another 2km or so to the mouth of the gorge.

Places to Stay & Eat
Residencial Raldes (☎ 2086), near the railway line two blocks east of the main plaza, isn't that clean, but the grounds are nice and flowery. Rooms costs US$4 per person. A nicer place in the center is the *Gran Hotel Avenida* (☎ 2297; fax 2412), which charges US$14/17 for singles/doubles with private baths, cable TV and breakfast. At the appealing *Hotel El Rancho* (☎ 2049; fax 2579), opposite the railway station, 2km north of town, bungalows with baths and TV cost a reasonable US$10 per person. Cheaper accommodations are available in the older section, and it also has a very nice restaurant.

There are a couple of good restaurants on the plaza, one of which serves Chinese food.

Getting There & Away
TAM (☎ 2135) flies Saturday from Santa Cruz to Yacuiba via Villamontes (US$50), then returns in the afternoon, via Tarija.

Buses run several times daily between Villamontes, Yacuiba, Tarija (most will pass through Yacuiba) and Santa Cruz. Camiones going to Tarija, Yacuiba, Boyuibe, Palos Blancos, Camiri and Santa Cruz line up along the strip marked 'Parada de Camiones,' near the northern end of the market. To hitchhike toward Yacuiba, take a taxi to the southern tranca, 5km south of town, and hitch from there.

Villamontes lies two hours by rail north of Yacuiba and 10 hours south of Santa Cruz. Taxis to the railway station, 2km north of town, charge US$0.50 per person.

PARQUE NACIONAL AGUARAGÜE
The new, long and narrow Aguaragüe National Park takes in much of the Serranía de Aguaragüe, which divides the vast Gran Chaco and the highlands of Tarija department. The region is also well known as having Bolivia's hottest climate, with summer temperatures as high as 46°C. Although it currently lacks specific visitor facilities, the Cañón del Pilcomayo is readily accessible from Villamontes (see earlier in this chapter). The Guaraní name of the park means 'the lair of the jaguar,' and the range protects not only this rare cat, but also the fox, tapir, anteater, lynx, assorted parrots and numerous plant species. Viva Tours in Tarija

conducts guided visits and hikes (see Organized Tours in Tarija).

BOYUIBE
Diminutive Boyuibe, which serves mainly as a transit point, sits on the fringes of the Chaco along the railway line three hours north of Villamontes and seven hours south of Santa Cruz. Roads lead north to Camiri and Santa Cruz, south to Villamontes and Yacuiba, and east into Paraguay.

Places to Stay & Eat
Boyuibe's two lodgings, *Hotel Rosedal* and *Hotel Guadalquivir*, are both on the main street through town. Both charge around US$4 per person but provide little more than

a place to crash. For meals, your best option is *Pensión Boyuibe*, also on the main street.

Getting There & Away

Buses, colectivos and camiones from Boyuibe to Camiri, Villamontes and Yacuiba wait in front of the Tránsito office on the main street. The trip to Camiri takes only an hour on the newly asphalted road; the bus fare is US$1.50. All trains between Santa Cruz and Yacuiba stop in Boyuibe (see Getting There & Away in Santa Cruz and Yacuiba).

RESERVA PRIVADA DE PATRIMONIO NATURAL DE CORVALÁN

This small reserve on the Paraguayan border protects an ideal slice of the Gran Chaco, the second most diverse ecosystem in South America, after that of the Amazon Basin. In addition to the jaguar, puma, tapir, giant anteater and armadillo, it's also home to the ñandu (rhea), iguana, alligator and all the classic Chaco vegetation. The only access route is the poor road from Villamontes, which takes about four hours with a good vehicle. Accommodations are limited to a simple park rangers' camp, and visitors should be self-sufficient in food, water and other supplies. Currently, the only commercial access is with Viva Tours in Tarija (see Organized Tours under Tarija).

CAMIRI
☎ 0952

Situated at the edge of the Chaco with a favorable climate, Camiri has grown phenomenally in recent years owing to lucrative employment opportunities with the national oil company, YPFB (known affectionately as 'Yacimientos'). Camiri is a center for the production of petroleum and natural gas and bills itself as the Capital Petrolífero de Bolivia (Oil Capital of Bolivia).

In 1955, two pipelines were constructed to carry natural gas and petroleum to Yacuiba on the Argentine frontier. The following year, a US$1.5 million natural gas reinjection plant was built by YPFB atop Cerro Sararenda to recover liquid petroleum gas by injecting natural gas into oil-bearing formations. Another plant to process this liquid petroleum gas was built and began functioning in 1968, and a refrigeration and dehydration plant to recover liquid petroleum was put into operation at nearby Taquiparenda in 1983. Decreased production closed it, however, after only three years of operation. Camiri has since experienced ups and downs in the industry, but it remains the center of Bolivia's fossil fuel production.

Note that foreigners staying overnight must register with the police upon arrival; for this privilege, you get a permit titled 'autorización de alojamiento.' If they try to charge you for the document, refuse to pay unless you get an official receipt.

Information

Immigration Visitors arriving from Paraguay must register with immigration, on Avenida 1 de Mayo, downhill from Calle Tarija.

Money Librería Ramirez will change cash and up to US$100 in traveler's checks. Hotel Ortuño changes US dollars at a relatively good rate and will sometimes also change traveler's checks.

Post & Communications The friendly post office, on Avenida Mariscal Santa Cruz, is a relic from the days when most people had a lot more time than they do now.

Things to See & Do

Camiri may not be well endowed with attractions, but it is proud of its **YPFB plant**. There's no formal tour, but if you turn up at 8 am and appear to be interested in oil, you may get a look around. Even if you're not into oil, an item not to miss is the **Petrolero (Oil Worker) monument** in the middle of Avenida Petrolero, which is inscribed with the slightly excessive *Himno al Petrolero* (Hymn to the Oil Worker).

There are also a couple of nice **walks**. One will take you up to the statue of St Francis of Assisi on the hill behind the market for a super view over the town and the surrounding hills. Another pleasant walk is down Avenida Mariscal Sucre to the Río Parapeti. On the bank, turn south and walk several hundred meters downstream, where you'll find a clean sandy beach and a good, deep swimming hole.

Places to Stay

The immaculate **Residencial Premier** (☎ 2204), on Calle Santa Cruz, charges US$4 per person for a room with a private bath and hot water whenever both water and electricity are available. Rooms with shared baths cost US$3. Try for one of the light and airy upstairs rooms, which open onto a leafy patio. Another decent choice is the friendly **Residencial Las Mellizas** (☎ 2614; Capitán Manchego 300). Clean rooms with baths cost US$4.50 per person.

The **Residencial Marietta** (☎ 2254; Petrolero 15) is slightly more expensive at US$4 per person (US$5 with bath). It's owned by the Italian consul Federico Forfori and his wife, Ana – hence, this place doubles as the Italian consulate. It also houses the AeroSur office.

Camiri's most upscale digs, the friendly **Hotel JR** (☎ 2200; Sánchez 247), may sometimes accommodate visiting oil barons, but prices are quite reasonable at US$13.50/23 for singles/doubles with bath, phone, heat, air-con and TV. Peripherals include an à la carte restaurant, a bright sitting area and good views of the surrounding hills.

Places to Eat

By Bolivian standards, Camiri has a limited choice of restaurants. The one favored by visiting businesspeople is the **Gambrinus Grill** (Mariscal Santa Cruz 149), which has an international menu.

On the rare occasions when it's open, **La Estancia**, on Comercio at Busch, does almuerzos for US$1.50 and à la carte evening meals, but it's nothing special. The Chinese-oriented **Chifa Hong Kong**, on the plaza, also appears to be closed most evenings. For some greasy lubrication, **El Palacio del Pollo**, near the plaza, and **El Pollo Ejecutivo** (yes, the Executive Chicken), opposite the LAB office, serve chicken and french fries. In the morning, street vendors on the corner of Avenida Bolívar and Calle Comercio, near the market, sell coffee, tea, chocolate, bread and delicious licuados. Inside, you'll find some good deals on basic meals.

Getting There & Away

The airport lies just outside town on the Sucre road. AeroSur has flights from Santa Cruz to Camiri (US$59) Monday to Friday at 6:30 am, returning at 7:55 am the same day.

There's no central terminal, but most flotas leave from the corner of Bolívar and Cochabamba. After 5 pm, numerous flotas have nightly services to Santa Cruz; buses coming from Yacuiba via Villamontes normally pass in the middle of the night. When the road is passable, Flota El Chaqueño leaves for Sucre daily in the morning. The road to Boyuibe (one hour, US$1.50) passes through some beautiful hilly Chaco scrub; micros leave from Bolívar, four blocks uphill from the main market.

Camiones to Santa Cruz and Sucre park along Calle Comercio near the market and leave when full.

Santa Cruz & Around

Traveling through the Santa Cruz area is like taking a walk through time. From bustling Santa Cruz, you can visit pre-Inca ruins and the relatively undisturbed Parque Nacional Amboró, home to several species of endangered wildlife.

Santa Cruz

☎ 03

Since 1950, Santa Cruz has mushroomed from a backwater cattle-producing town to its present position as Bolivia's second city and a hub of transportation and trade. With over one million inhabitants, it's a metropolis on the fringe of a diminishing wilderness, sporting an incongruous amount of money as well as 12-bedroom homes, Toyota 4WDs, BMWs and other playthings not normally associated with Bolivia.

Santa Cruz' overall climate is tropical, but because it occupies the transition zone between the Amazon rain forest, the highlands and the dry Chaco plains, it enjoys more sun and less stifling temperatures than the humid, rainy Amazon Basin farther north and west. Winter rainfalls mean little more than 10-minute downpours, but a single summer deluge can last for days. Santa Cruz also experiences heavy winds that rarely subside, and at times during winter, chilly winds called *surazos* blow in from Patagonia and the Argentine *pampas*.

Happily, Santa Cruz' longstanding reputation as a drug-trafficking mecca is now being eclipsed by a boom in tropical agriculture. Large corporate plantations of sugar, rice, cotton, soybeans and other warm-weather crops now dominate the lowlands east of the city, which only a decade ago were covered with thick tropical forest. This economic and agricultural potential has attracted not only opportunists and optimistic settlers from the highlands, but also folks from many other walks of life: The region boasts rice-growing Japanese colonies as well as settlements of

Italians, Palestinians, Indian Sikhs and thousands of German-Canadian Mennonites fleeing governmental conflicts in Mexico and Belize. It has also been a haven for escaped Nazis (a rapidly diminishing group) and is now attracting throngs of Brazilian opportunists, foreign oil workers, agribusiness tycoons, drug traffickers, foreign researchers, missionaries and environmental activists.

Despite its phenomenal growth rate, however, Santa Cruz retains traces of its dusty past, evident in its wide streets, frontier

> ### Highlights
>
> - Watch the sloths hanging around in Santa Cruz's Plaza 24 de Septiembre
> - Pig out in this cosmopolitan city's range of excellent eateries
> - Acclimatize to the altitude in the laid-back village of Samaipata and explore the mysterious pre-Inca ruins of El Fuerte
> - Hike and search for the blue-horned curassow in Parque Nacional Amboró
> - Follow in the footsteps of El Ché from Vallegrande to La Higuera

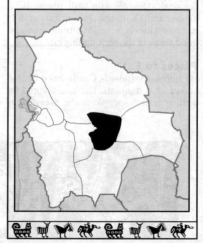

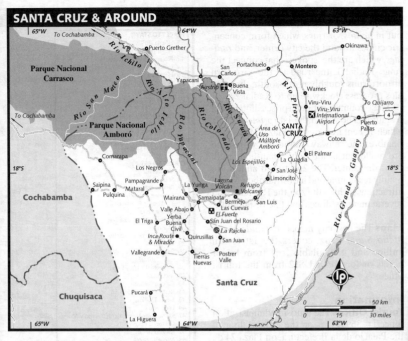

SANTA CRUZ & AROUND

architecture and a rapidly fading small-town atmosphere. The town may have an international airport with direct flights to Miami, but forest-dwelling sloths still hang in the trees of the main plaza. Few foreign visitors fail to notice that the streets shaded with colonnade-supported awnings recall the days of the North American Wild West, which leaves Santa Cruz looking like a bizarre cross between Miami and Tombstone!

As the country's richest city, this is where Bolivia's action is, and while some people love it, others find it far too expensive and North American for their tastes. If you're young and Bolivian, or a businessperson interested in cutting deals, you're likely to be numbered among the former. However, travelers in search of the 'real' Bolivia probably won't want to linger too long.

History
Santa Cruz de la Sierra was founded in 1561 by Ñuflo de Chavez, a Spaniard who hailed from what is now Paraguay. The town originally lay 220km east of its current location. However, around the end of the 16th century, it proved too vulnerable to attack from local tribes and was moved to its present position 50km east of the Cordillera Oriental foothills.

Santa Cruz was founded to supply the rest of the colony with products such as rice, cotton, sugar and fruit. Its prosperity lasted until the late 1800s, when transportation routes opened up between La Paz and the Peruvian coast and made imported goods cheaper than those hauled from Santa Cruz over mule trails.

In 1954 a highway linking Santa Cruz with other major centers was completed, and the city sprang back from the economic lull imposed by its remoteness. The completion of the railway line to Brazil in the mid-1950s opened trade routes to the east. Tropical agriculture prospered, and the city entered a flurry of growth that has continued to the present day.

Orientation

Roughly oval in shape, Santa Cruz is laid out in *anillos*, or rings, which form concentric circles around the city center, and *radiales*, which are the 'spokes' that connect the rings. Radial 1, the road to the Viru-Viru airport, runs roughly north-south; the radiales progress clockwise up to Radial 27.

Most commercial enterprises, hotels and restaurants lie within the 1st *(primer)* anillo, which is centered on the Plaza 24 de Septiembre. The railway station lies within the 3rd anillo but is still only a half-hour walk from the center. The 2nd to 7th anillos are mainly residential and industrial; their tourist attractions include the zoo, the Río Piray and several markets, discos and fine restaurants.

Maps The best city map, *City Guide Multiplano Santa Cruz*, covers the 1st to 4th anillos and is available free from larger hotels or for about US$2 from the tourist office.

Information

Tourist Offices The tourism administration office (☎ 369595) is on the ground floor of the Palacio de la Prefectura, on Plaza 24 de Septiembre. It's open weekdays from 8 am to 4 pm, but you'll need to speak Spanish to communicate. The less convenient head office (☎ 368900; fax 368901) is on Avenida Omar Chavez Ortiz, four blocks south of the bus terminal. On a grander geographical scope, there's an outside chance that you'll get some joy from the departmental tourism body (☎ 338393; fax 334632; ofcultursc@ scbbs-bo.com). However, English-language queries will more than likely be ignored.

For national park information, especially on Noel Kempff Mercado in the Amazon Basin, see Fundación Amigos de la Naturaleza, or FAN (☎ 337475; fax 329692; fan@ fan.rds.org.bo). It's behind the McDonald's near El Trompillo airport, south of the center.

A useful publication is the *Handbook of Santa Cruz*, published by the US consulate, which costs US$15 and details most tourism- and commerce-oriented businesses. It's sold in most bookstores.

SANTA CRUZ & AROUND

SANTA CRUZ

PLACES TO STAY
3 Hotel Lido
7 Hotel Tropical Inn
12 Alojamiento Santa Bárbara
14 Hotel Bibosi
15 Hotel Amazonas
22 Hotel Globetrotter
23 Hotel Felimar
32 Residencial Bolívar
37 Hotel Excelsior
38 Residencial Ballivián
42 Hotel Italia
54 Alojamiento Lemoine
57 Residencial 15 de Octubre
63 Residencial Grigotá

PLACES TO EAT
1 Yogen Fruz
6 Sabor Brasil
9 Rincón Brasileiro
10 Crêperie El Boliche
11 Tradiciones Peruanas
13 Guang Zhou
19 Pizzería Mama Rosa
20 Manolo
24 Kivón, Caribe & Dumbo
29 La Pascana
30 Bar Hawai
31 Café Babilonia
34 Restaurant Vida y Salud
35 McDonald's
40 Galeón Peruano
41 Restaurante 16 de Julio
43 Bar El Tapekuá
44 Leonardo's
47 Restaurante Vegetariano Cuerpo y Mente
48 California Burgers
52 México Lindo
53 Michelangelo's
56 La Bella Napoli
62 El Mandarín

OTHER
2 Alliance Française
4 Museo Etno-Folklórico
5 Micros to Cotoca & Puerto Pailas
8 Safari Camping, Caza y Pesca
16 Galería Casco Viejo
17 Banco de Santa Cruz
18 Post Office
21 Clapton's Blues Bar
25 Casa de la Cultura Raúl Otero Reiche; Tourist Information
26 Plaza 24 de Septiembre
27 Shopping Bolívar: Café Internet Milenium & Shamrock Irish Pub/Bar Irlandés
28 Casa de Cambio Alemán
33 Launderette
36 Cambatur
39 Centro Boliviano-Americano
45 Magri Turismo
46 El Rincón Salteño
49 ENTEL office
50 LAB Office
51 Iglesia 'Viva Jesús El Señor'
55 La Cueva del Ratón
58 Bus Terminal
59 Taxis to Yapacaní & Buena Vista
60 AeroSur Office
61 Museo de la Historia Natural
64 Expreso Samaipata Taxis
65 Tourist Office

University

Av Centenario

Comercia
Cañote

Av Landivar

To Río Piray,
Jardín Botánico

Av Saucedo S

Machiri

Mercado
La Ramada

Av Grigotá

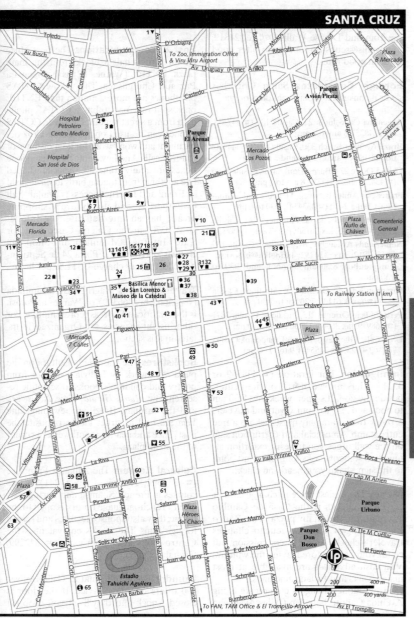

SANTA CRUZ & AROUND

Businesspeople in need of a good Spanish-English translation service should see Tom and Denise Wallis (☎/fax 524819; tom.wallis@scbbs-bo.com), who offer good value at good rates.

Foreign Consulates Santa Cruz has several consulates, open weekdays only:

Argentina Calle Junín 22, Casilla 187 (☎ 347133; fax 324825); 8 am to 2 pm

Brazil Avenida Busch 330, Casilla 191 (☎ 344400; fax 350488); 9 am to 1 pm and 3 to 6 pm

Chile 5 Oeste 224, Barrio Equipetrol, Casilla 2896 (☎ 434272; fax 434373); 8 am to 1 pm

France 3er Anillo between Alemana and Mutualista, Casilla 2430 (☎ 433434); 4:30 to 6 pm

Germany Avenida de las Américas 241, Casilla 2101 (☎ 324825; fax 367585); 8:30 am to noon

Netherlands Ayacucho 284, 2nd floor, Casilla 139 (☎ 347812; fax 334752; ludoalke@bibosi.scz .entelnet.bo); 8:30 am to noon and 2:30 to 6:30 pm

Paraguay Edificio Oriente 505, 5th floor, Casilla 1574 (☎/fax 366113); 7:30 am to 2:30 pm

Peru Edificio Oriente 213, 2nd floor, Casilla 3871 (☎ 368979; fax 368086); 8:30 am to 1:30 pm

USA Calle Güemes 6, Barrio Equipetrol, Casilla 76 (☎ 330725; fax 325544); 9 to 11:30 am

Immigration Immigration (☎ 438559 or 332136) has moved north of the center, beside the zoo. It's open weekdays 8:30 am to noon and 2:30 to 6 pm. Overland travelers arriving from Paraguay must pick up a free entry stamp. An official anti-corruption sign on the wall urges you to resist extortion attempts; if someone asks for money, just point to the sign, shake your head and cluck!

Money The easiest place to change cash or traveler's checks is the Casa de Cambio Alemán, on the main plaza. The Banco Económico on Calle Ayacucho changes traveler's checks for a 1% commission, but count your cash before leaving the window. Visa cash advances are available at most major banks and Enlace machines.

Street moneychangers congregate along Avenida Cañoto between Calles Ayacucho and Junín as well as near the bus terminal and occasionally around the main plaza.

Post & Communications The post office (Junín 146) is half a block from the main plaza. ENTEL (Warnes 82) is between La Paz and Chuquisaca. The yellow COTAS payphones are more common than ENTEL ones, so it may pay to buy a COTAS phone card from a street vendor. However, COTAS phones can be used only in Santa Cruz department and won't work for long-distance or toll-free calls. And hey, Santa Cruz telephone boxes are really something special, shaped like anything from toucan birds to *surubí* fish!

Email and Internet access is available all over the city, and nearly every shopping arcade has an Internet café. Try Infonet (☎ 370370) in the Galería Casco Viejo or Café Internet Milenium in Shopping Bolívar, on Bolívar at Plaza 24 de Septiembre. Most places charge US$1.80 per hour.

Travel Agencies Magri Turismo Limitada (☎ 345663; fax 366309), on Warnes at Potosí, is the American Express representative. For other useful agencies, see Organized Tours, later in this section.

Bookstores The Casa de la Cultura on the plaza sells work by Bolivian authors, from poetry and children's books to scientific research. The *Miami Herald*, *Time*, *Newsweek* and the brilliant Brazilian newsmagazine *Veja* are sold at street kiosks opposite the post office and near the southwestern corner of the main plaza.

Cultural Centers The Alliance Française (☎ 333392; Andrés Ibáñez 241) offers courses in French, Spanish and Portuguese. Their French-language library is open to the public; they also sponsor lectures and screen foreign films. The USA's equivalent is the Centro Boliviano-Americano (☎ 342299; Cochabamba 66).

Laundry The laundromat at Calle Bolívar 490 offers one-day service. If the door is closed, knock and they'll let you drop off clothes. Washing, drying and ironings cost just US$1 per kg.

Camping Equipment The Safari Camping, Caza y Pesca, on 21 de Mayo at Seoane, sells a range of camping gear.

Medical Services The Clínica Japonesa (☎ 462031), on the third anillo, east side, is recommended for inexpensive and professional medical treatment. Clínica Ángel Foianini (☎ 362211 or 326020; Irala 468) delivers quality care, but travelers have reported unnecessary tests and longer stays than necessary. An alternative is the Clínica Santa María (☎ 342001; Viedma 754).

The best pharmacy is the efficient and inexpensive Farmacia América (Libertad 333). Next door is the Policonsultorio Central, with the recommended Dr Ana María López, who trained in the USA and speaks English.

Emergency The police can be reached at ☎ 110, and the tourist police at ☎ 225016. Report fires to the fire brigade (☎ 119).

Dangers & Annoyances Although Santa Cruz continuously grows more relaxed, foreigners must still carry proof of identification at all times. If you're caught without documents, you'll be fined US$50 and waste several hours at a police station while paperwork is shuffled.

Beware of bogus immigration officials, particularly at the railway station, and carefully check the credentials of anyone who demands to see your passport or other identification. If you're suspicious, insist that they accompany you to the police station, where things can legitimately be sorted out.

Plaza 24 de Septiembre

Santa Cruz' very tropical main plaza provides a great place to relax for both visitors and locals. One reader wrote:

Here you can kick back and watch folks, have your shoes shined, be asked to buy everything under the sun (and a few things you'd never think of, like Teenage Mutant Ninja Turtle marionettes). You can also engage in the lazy traveler's favorite restful activity, sloth-watching. Keep your eyes peeled and you'll find a couple grooming or eating or just hanging around.

– Mary Ann Springer, USA

Basílica Menor de San Lorenzo & Museo de la Catedral

Although the original cathedral on Plaza 24 de Septiembre was founded in 1605, the present structure dates from 1845 and wasn't consecrated until 1915. The decorative woodwork on the ceiling and silver plating around the altar are worth a look.

The cathedral museum has a collection of religious icons and artifacts but very little typical religious art. Most interesting are the many gold and silver relics from the Jesuit Guarayos missions northeast of Santa Cruz. There's also a collection of religious vestments and medallions, as well as one of the world's smallest books, a thumbnail-sized volume containing the Lord's Prayer in several languages. The museum is open Tuesday and Thursday 8:30 am to noon and 2:30 to 6 pm. Admission is US$0.75.

Iglesia 'Viva Jesús El Señor'

One of the most incongruous buildings in Santa Cruz is the small church on the corner of Salvatierra and Izozog. Covered with colored bathroom tiles and topped with an onion dome, it might not seem out of place along the Silk Road in Central Asia. Emblazoned across the building are the words *Viva Jesús El Señor* (Long Live Christ the Lord). On one outer wall hangs a large copper crucifix and above, a tiled cross. It's clearly the product of someone's devout imagination and merits at least a good look as you pass by.

Parque El Arenal & Museo Etno-Folklórico

Locals relax around the lagoon at Parque El Arenal. On an island in the lagoon, a bas-relief mural by renowned Bolivian artist Lorgio Vaca depicts historic and modern-day aspects of Santa Cruz. Inside the building is the newish Museo Etno-Folklórico, which displays a small collection of traditional art and artifacts from several *camba* (lowland) cultures.

Casa de la Cultura Raúl Otero Reiche

The chaotic corridors of the Casa de la Cultura, on the plaza, contain a rather informal and haphazardly arranged museum of Bolivian art. Although the paintings are poorly lit, originality runs high and it's a breath of fresh air if you've overdosed on the blood and flagellation typical of most Bolivian art. Especially look for the works of Vaca and other contemporary Bolivian artists such as Herminio Pedraza and Tito Kurasotto. It's open weekdays 8:30 am to noon and 2:30 to 6 pm; admission is free.

Museo de la Historia Natural

The Natural History Museum, in the old Immigration building on Avenida Irala, gives you the lowdown on the flora, fauna and geology of eastern Bolivia. Exhibits include pickled frogs and the usual stuffed animals, fish and birds, as well as information on seeds, wood, fruit, gardening and other lowland pursuits. The bug collections include specimens large enough to inspire psychosis or keep you out of rain forests forever. It's open daily 9 am to noon and 3 to 6 pm. Admission is free but donations are gratefully accepted.

Zoo

The Santa Cruz zoo was once one of the few on the continent that was worth the time and admission charge, but indications are that it has been going downhill in recent years. Its collection is limited to South American birds, mammals and reptiles, and all appear to be humanely treated (although the llamas appear a mite overdressed for the climate). It features endangered and exotic species such as tapirs, pumas, jaguars and spectacled bears. Sloths, which are too slow and lazy to escape successfully, are not confined to cages and hang about in the trees, occasionally mustering enough energy for a slow crawl around the grounds.

The zoo is open daily 9 am to 7:30 pm; admission costs US$1. Take Micro 58 from Vallegrande, 76 or 77 from Calle Santa Bárbara or 8, 11 or 17 from El Arenal. Taxis for up to four people cost around US$1.50.

Río Piray

The Jardín Botánico (Botanical Garden) here was destroyed in a flood over a decade ago, and plans to renovate it were reduced to the creation of a park requiring less maintenance. The riverbanks are good for a picnic, especially on weekends, when local families make an outing of it and small stalls and teahouses sell basic meals and drinks. To get there, take Micro 6 or 9 from Avenida Cañoto, near the bus terminal, and get off at the western end of Avenida Roca y Coronado (Radial 20).

Activities

If you're looking for a bit of exercise, check out Urbari (☎ 522288; fax 522255; bolivia.resort@scbbs-bo.com; Barrio Urbari, Calle Igmiri 506), which has a pool, tennis courts, saunas, racquetball courts and a fitness gym.

Organized Tours

Numerous companies offer organized tours. One highly recommended agency is Cambatur (☎ 324770 or 349999; fax 349998; cynthia_otalora@hotmail.com; Sucre 8), on the plaza, which offers city tours (US$18); day trips to Samaipata (US$51); two-day trips through the Jesuit Missions Circuit with an overnight in San Javier (US$235); and custom trips to the national parks, Amboró and Noel Kempff Mercado.

Rosario Tours (☎ 269977; fax 369656; aventura@tucan.cnb.net; Arenales 193, Casilla 683) offers tours to sights all around Santa Cruz, including the Pantanal, the Jesuit missions, Parque Nacional Amboró, Los Espejillos, Samaipata and Dunas de Palmar. Uimpex Travel (☎ 220924; fax 220512; Laguna Las Garzas, Zona Sur, Casilla 3845) is an imaginative and long-established agency that does tours to the Bolivian Pantanal, the Jesuit missions and sites of interest around the city. Other recommended agencies that offer similar tours include Balas (☎ 333933;

fax 343102; turbalas@roble.scz.entelnet.bo;
Beni 218, Casilla 541); Gama Tours (☎ 340921;
fax 363828; gamatur@roble.scz.entelnet.bo;
Arenales 566, Casilla 5082); Totaitu (☎ 345452;
fax 344700; totaitu@em.daitec-bo.com; Irala
421, Casilla 1389); and Tuyuyú (☎/fax 364003;
Ñuflo de Chávez 45).

For two days in Parque Nacional Amboró,
most agencies will charge US$380/165 per
person with two/four people; for a four-day
fly-in tour to Noel Kempff Mercado, you'll
pay US$1494/962; seven-day camping trips
to Noel Kempff and the Jesuit Missions are
US$949/644; and four-day trips in the Boli-
vian Pantanal are US$625/520. You can
even arrange 21-day bird-watching trips
throughout the Bolivian Amazon for
US$2990/2360.

Special Events

If you're in Santa Cruz for Carnaval, you
can either head for the paintball-plagued
streets and join in the madness or pick up a
few supplies and hole up somewhere until it
passes. Alternatively, check out the Mau-
Mau in the auditorium on the corner of
Ibáñez and 21 de Mayo. It attracts over
10,000 people with its dancing, music shows
and coronation of the carnival queen.

Every year in mid- to late September,
Santa Cruz hosts an enormous two-week
fair where you can buy anything from a
toothbrush or clothing to a new house, a
combine harvester or a 20-ton truck. To accommodate it, a temporary village is constructed, including banks, an ice cream
parlor and an ENTEL office. It's worthwhile even if you're not shopping, especially
at night when it takes on a carnival atmosphere as Bolivians stroll, browse, listen to
music, eat, drink and have a good time.

Places to Stay

Budget There are several cheap places near
the bus terminal. On a crowded market
street is the friendly *Residencial Grigotá*
(☎ 541699; *Muchirí 15*), where fairly clean
rooms cost US$4.50 per person with shared
baths. A double with private bath costs
US$14.50. Nearby is *Residencial 15 de
Octubre* (☎ 342591; *Guaraní 33*). It's more

spartan than the Grigotá but charges the
same. The basic-looking *Alojamiento
Lemoine* (☎ 346670; *Lemoine 469*) is actually very clean, with decent singles/doubles
for US$4.50/7 with shared bath. Unfortu-
nately, there are no fans.

More central and appealing, *Alojamiento Santa Bárbara* (☎ 321817; *Santa
Bárbara 151*) is fairly friendly and offers
simple but comfortable accommodations
arranged around a sunny courtyard for
US$5/7. It's popular with young Bolivians
and is recommended by travelers.

A longtime backpackers' favorite is the
clean and bright *Residencial Bolívar*
(☎ 342500; *Sucre 131*). With good breakfasts,
inviting courtyard hammocks, wonderful
hot showers and a charming toucan (which
has the run of the place), it's a pretty good
choice at US$7.50/10. It may be wise to
agree in writing on the price for your room.
If the Bolívar is full, a fine alternative is
Residencial Ballivián (☎ 321960), which
has a lovely courtyard and decent rooms,
but has been going downhill of late. Rooms
cost US$5 per person without bath. If you
believe the rumors, Ché Guevara once
stayed here. According to one reader, 'It's
like staying at your grandmother's house.'

Mid-Range Santa Cruz has a growing
number of mid-range hotels, which are very
reasonably priced and cater mainly to business travelers.

The very central *Hotel Bibosi* (☎ 348548;
fax 348887; Junín 218, Casilla 2866) has a
cheery proprietor, clean, spacious rooms
and a great rooftop view. Singles/doubles
with fans, telephones, cable TV, private
baths and breakfast cost US$20/25. Next
door is *Hotel Amazonas* (☎ 334583; *Junín
214*), where rooms with fans, cable TV and
private baths cost US$15/20.

The amenable *Hotel Tropical Inn*
(☎ 346666; *fax 328154; España 351, Casilla
907*) has comfortable rooms with cable TV,
air-conditioning, private bath and phone for
US$30/36. When the weather's nice, you can
leave the city behind on the sunny terrace.

The centrally located *Hotel Italia*
(☎ 323119; *fax 361708; René Moreno 167*)

charges US$20/30 for decent rooms with private baths, phones, cable TV and continental breakfast. On the same street, the pretty nice **Hotel Excelsior** (☎ 340664; fax 325924; Rene Moreno 70) charges US$15/25. A bit more upmarket is **Hotel Felimar** (☎ 346677; fax 323232; tramitur@roble.scz .entelnet.bo; Ayacucho 445, Casilla 1219), with carpeted, air-conditioned rooms for US$35/45. Cable TV costs an additional US$2 per night.

Another good mid-range choice is **Hotel Globetrotter** (☎ /fax 372754; Sara 49, Casilla 4986), where the management appropriately speaks a globetrotting variety of languages: Swedish, German, French, English and Danish. Rooms cost US$22/25.

Top End Most of Santa Cruz' top-end hotels are well away from the center and are more like resorts than simple accommodations. A nice but relatively simple upmarket choice in the center is **Hotel Lido** (☎ 363555; fax 363322; 21 de Mayo 527, Casilla 2533), which straddles the middle and top price ranges. Comfortable singles/doubles that have private bathrooms, air-conditioning, color TV and access to laundry facilities, fax and Internet services cost US$55/65.

Several five-star resort hotels are sprouting on the Santa Cruz outskirts. **Hotel Los Tajibos** (☎ 421000; fax 426994; lostajib@ bibosi.scz.entelnet.bo), on Avenida San Martín in Barrio Equipetrol, has a nightclub, swimming pools, a health club, racquetball courts, a casino, a massage parlor, fountains and tropical gardens. Standard rooms start at US$155/175 and nonsmoking rooms are available; suites cost US$165/185. All rates include breakfast. For more, see their website at www.bolivianet.com/lostajibos.

In the same neighborhood is **Hotel Yotaú** (☎ 367799; fax 363342; yotau@ yotau.com.bo; Avenida San Martín 7, Barrio Equipetrol, Casilla 3377). This beautiful tropical-style high-rise has executive rooms from US$159/181; family rooms for up to six people cost US$300. Lunches and dinners are US$7 each. The website is www.yotau.com.bo.

Places to Eat

When it comes to culinary matters, cosmopolitan Santa Cruz won't disappoint; it has a staggering number of very nice restaurants and the food is generally good. The better places, however, can be quite expensive and most are found outside the center.

For a simple and inexpensive breakfast, try Mercados **La Ramada** and **Los Pozos**. The licuado de papaya or guineo con leche – puréed papaya or banana with milk, whipped in a blender and served cold – costs only US$0.40. It's hard to tear yourself away after only one glass! You'll also find meals during the day, but you may be put off by the heat around the cooking areas. Los Pozos is especially good for unusual tropical fruits; try some of the more exotic ones such as guaypurú and ambaiba. For a good variety of (not cheap) fixings to prepare meals yourself, try **Supermercado Santa Cruz**, on Cuéllar at 24 de Septiembre.

You'll find an exhaustive choice of roast chicken, churrasco, french fries and fried plantain along Avenida Cañoto (also known as Pollo Alley), where there are dozens of nearly identical barbecue restaurants, including the oddly named **Super Gordo** (Super Fat). A great, friendly little snack place is **Café Babilonia**, on Calle Sucre, which brews up excellent Turkish coffee and serves falafel, schwarma, burgers and hot dogs. For a great lunch in the sun or just a large afternoon beer, head for the palm-shaded terrace at the very popular **Victory Bar**, upstairs in the Galería Casco Viejo. On the terrace, you can enjoy salads, sandwiches, burgers, pasta and Bolivian specialties, as well as western breakfasts in the morning. You'll spend around US$4.50 for lunch, plus US$1.80 for a large beer.

Similar and just as popular with travelers is the **Café/Bar Irlandés** (☎ 338118; Shopping Bolívar, Plaza 24 de Septiembre). It's open for breakfast, lunch and dinner, and you'll find not only your favorite dishes from home, but also local specialties. The service and music are outstanding, and you can easily pass a pleasant afternoon nursing a beer or two while watching life on the plaza below.

Of course Santa Cruz also features the two big fast-food icons. The most convenient, **McDonald's** (☎ 361212; Ayacucyho 268), is just three blocks from the plaza, while the drive-thru outlet (☎ 341212) on El Trompillo at René Moreno attracts time-stressed locals. **Burger King** (☎ 437292), on Avenida San Martín at Calle 7 in Barrio Equipetrol, caters mainly to the suburban crowd. A more healthy version of fast food is available at the several **Subway** outlets, the best known of which is on the main floor at Viru-Viru Airport.

When it comes to over-the-top ice cream places, Santa Cruz outdoes itself. **Kivón** (☎ 331333; Ayacucho 267), with its bright green neon and huge, ostentatious waterfall attracts teenyboppers in droves. It's a bit expensive, but when you're young and in Santa Cruz, this is the place to see and be seen. The nearby **Dumbo** (☎ 367077; Ayacucho 247) and **Caribe** (☎ 362286; Ayacucho 239) are almost as extravagant. Frozen yogurt hasn't totally caught on yet, but you will find excellent choices – the usual flavors plus maracuya, papaya, chirimoya, grape, almond, tangerine and so on – at **Yogen Fruz** (☎ 1018440), on Monsignor Rivero at Cañada Strongest.

A cross between an ice cream joint and a pretty nice eatery is **Bar Hawai**; for US$3.50, you'll get an enormous steak, a salad and a bit of yucca and delicious *arroz con queso* (rice porridge). For other beef- or chicken-oriented specials – including shish kebabs – see the *pacumutu* menu. You can follow up a satisfying meal with an equally decadent ice cream confection. Another highly recommended heladería is the clean and shiny **Manolo** (24 de Septiembre 170), which serves not only ice cream, but also excellently cooked meals. **California Burgers** (☎ 334054; Independencia 481) serves coffee, burgers, tacos, burritos and sticky doughnuts.

The popular **La Pascana**, in Plaza 24 de Septiembre, dishes up huge *platos fuertes* (four-course meals) for US$4.50; try the *surubí à la thermidor* for US$5. Another plaza option, the popular **Pizzería Mama Rosa**, also in the plaza, does good pizzas,

chicken dishes, Mexican burgers, hot dogs and other meat dishes and fast foods. It's open daily from noon to midnight.

Inexpensive vegetarian almuerzos and dinners are served at **Restaurant Vegetariano Cuerpo y Mente** (☎ 371733; Pari 228), where you'll get healthy green meals for US$2.50 per kilogram. **Restaurant Vida y Salud**, on Calle Ayacucho near Vallegrande, serves vegetarian almuerzos for US$1.75.

Other lunch spots popular with locals include **Galeón Peruano** and **Restaurant 16 de Julio**, side by side on Calle Ingavi, near Calle España, which are always full and serve good food for very good prices. Dinners cost around US$3 and a four-course almuerzo costs under US$2.

The cozy Swiss/Bolivian-owned **Bar El Tapekuá** (☎ 345905), on Ballivián at La Paz, serves pub grub Wednesday to Saturday evenings. The musician owner appreciates good music, and Thursday to Saturday there are live performances for a US$1 cover charge. Phone in advance to find out what's on. A fine place to splurge is **Crêperie El Boliche** (☎ 339053; Arenales 135). You can choose from crêpe dishes, salads, ice cream confections, cakes and cocktails for about US$11 per person.

La Bella Napoli (☎ 325402; Independencía 635), in a rustic barn six blocks south of the plaza, serves fine pasta dishes – including ravioli, canelloni and lasagna – on chunky hardwood tables, but it's not cheap – small pizzas cost US$5.50 and main courses, US$7 – and it's a dark walk back to the center at night.

An alternative for excellent Italian cuisine is **Michelangelo's** (☎ 348403; Chuquisaca 502), housed in a romantically dark, wooden home, complete with fireplaces and marble floors. There must be something about Italian Renaissance artists (or perhaps Ninja Turtles), because there's also **Leonardo's** (☎ 338282; Warnes 366), where you can enjoy a cozy candlelit dinner of pasta or shellfish in a beautiful old converted mansion.

If you're craving Mexican food, try **México Lindo** (☎ 323056; Independencia 561), where tacos are a good value at US$1.80 each, enchiladas de mole are US$4 and admirable attempts at combinations cost around US$6 per person. Drink options include Mexico's own Corona beer or *grandes* (margaritas) for around US$2.50 each.

If you prefer more Tex with your Mex, try **Texas Rodeo Grill** (☎ 527215), on 26 de Febrero beside the obtrusive Hotel La Quinta. Here you'll get real nachos and salsa, quesadillas, chili and other favorites of the Texan oil workers. Lower key is **Texas Burger** (☎ 422138; *San Martín 918, Barrio Equipetrol*), which is great for grabbing a burger and watching the latest American football game. The food is genuine (the owner worked in Texas for years), the prices are fine and the fries are among the best in town.

Brazilian places are also the rage in Santa Cruz these days, mainly because the food is filling and is normally sold by the kilogram. One of the best is **Rincón Brasileiro** (☎ 331237; *Libertad 321*); another is **Sabor Brasil**, on Calle Seoane. Heading the other direction from Bolivia, you can try **Tradiciones Peruanas**, where you'll find ceviche, shellfish and other Peruvian specialties.

Santa Cruz' Japanese immigrants fill a wide-open niche in Bolivia. An unforgettable choice that serves sushi, sashimi, tempura and other Japanese specialties is **Yorimichi** (☎ 347717; *Avenida Busch 548*). Although pricey, this place gets lots of votes (including this writer's) for the best restaurant in Santa Cruz. Bookings are recommended. Plan on around US$10 per person, including a beer.

A decent Chinese choice is **El Mandarín** (☎ 348388; *Potosí 793*), at Irala. There's also the very low-key **Guang Zhou** on Calle Junín, a block west of the post office.

Entertainment

Santa Cruz has a disproportionate number of discos and karaoke bars, which reflects the city's young, liberal and cosmopolitan character. Most nightspots are outside the central area, so you'll need a taxi (US$1 to US$2). Cover charges start at about US$2; most places start selling drinks between 6 and 9 pm but don't warm up until 11 pm,

then continue until 3 or 4 am. One relatively central disco inside the first anillo is the tropically themed **El Loro en Su Salsa**, on Warnes at Cochabamba, which operates every night from 8 pm.

Popular travelers' bars in the center include **Victory**, in the Galería Casco Viejo, and **Bar Irlandés** (☎ 338118), in Shopping Bolívar. Another pleasant spot is **Bar El Tapekuá** (☎ 345905), on Ballivián at la Paz – see Places to Eat.

La Cueva del Ratón (☎ 326163; *La Riva 173*) is also relatively central and offers live music most weekends. You might expect it to be an intimate venue, but it's actually a barnlike bar with big-screen music videos. Also nice is **Clapton's Blues Bar**, on Murillo at Arenales, which can be great fun but is open only Tuesday to Saturday. The cover charge is US$2.

Homesick Canadians can don their flannel shirts and Baffin boots and head out to the **Canadian Grill & Bar** (☎ 434757; *3er anillo interno 1212*), which features Molson, Grizzly, Moosehead and northern-style steaks (alas, no moose). It's open 4 pm Monday to Saturday.

Traditional *peñas* are scarce in modern Santa Cruz. However, an excellent choice is **El Rincón Salteño** (☎ 536335), in the second anillo on 26 de Enero at Charagua, which is indeed a corner of Salta, Argentina. Nowhere else in Santa Cruz will you hear such a variety of musical styles, from Argentine guitarists to Cuban village drummers and local singers and dancers in native costume. On Friday night, it cranks up at around 10 pm.

For the younger set, the bars bear such monikers as **Insomnio** (*Florida 517*), **Kamikaze**, on Calle Chuquisaca, and **Delirium Tremens** (*René Moreno 477*).

The city also has a number of cinemas, and the films are generally better and more recent than elsewhere in Bolivia. For schedules and venues, see the daily newspapers *El Deber* and *El Mundo*.

Shopping

There are artesanía shops scattered around town at which you can buy beautiful

Western-style clothing made of llama and alpaca wool. Mercado Los Pozos is good for inexpensive basketry, but if you're after genuine indigenous articles, the Altiplano is a better area to look in. Woodcarvings made from the tropical hardwoods *morado* and the more expensive *guayacán* are unique to the Santa Cruz area. You'll pay from US$20 for a nice piece. Relief carvings on *tari* nuts are also interesting and make nice portable souvenirs. Local Indians also make beautiful macramé *llicas* (root-fiber bags). Santa Cruz leatherwork is expert, but most items are unfortunately adorned with kitsch designs and slogans.

Perhaps the best place to find superb artesanía is Artecampo (☎ 341843; fax 521933; Salvatierra 407), which provides an outlet for the work of 1000 rural cruceña women and their families. The truly inspired and innovative pieces include leatherwork, hammocks, weavings, handmade paper greeting cards and lovely natural-material lampshades. You'll also find some examples for sale at the Casa de la Cultura in Plaza 24 de Septiembre.

For those who love Jesuit mission artwork, one can commission a wooden angel carving of the type seen in the mission churches. Commissions, which take about a month, cost around US$80 to US$100 and are really nice; they're hand carved and painted by Chiquitano Indians in the missions. Visit La Misión (☎ 328143; René Moreno 60).

Getting There & Away

Air Viru-Viru International Airport, 15km north of the center, handles domestic and international flights, while TAM and charter flights use El Trompillo Airport. Both LAB (☎ 344159; fax 344709), on Warnes at Chuquisaca, and AeroSur (☎ 364446; fax 362600), on Irala at Colón, have daily services to Cochabamba, La Paz, Sucre and Trinidad, as well as most other Bolivian cities. LAB offers the lower fares, but AeroSur, which charges 10% to 20% more, provides better service.

As usual, the best deals are available from Transportes Aéreos Militares, or TAM (☎ 531993), which connects Santa Cruz' El Trompillo airport with La Paz (US$62.50), Puerto Suárez (US$59), Guayaramerín (US$100), Riberalta (US$100), San Matías (US$65) and Yacuiba (US$58.50). Note that the Tuesday and Saturday flights to and from Puerto Suárez, which actually use the airport in Corumbá, Brazil, obviate a long rail trip and fill up quickly.

LAB offers direct international service from Santa Cruz to Manaus, São Paulo, Belo Horizonte, Rio de Janeiro, Caracas, Panama City and Miami; and via La Paz, to Lima, Arica, Iquique and Santiago. TAM Mercosur (☎ 371999) flies three times weekly to Asunción, with connections to Miami, Buenos Aires and several Brazilian cities. VARIG (☎ 349333; toll free ☎ 0800-8484; fax 341114; Edificio Nago, Celso Castedo 39) flies to Rio de Janeiro and São Paulo; American Airlines (☎ 341314; Beni 202) flies daily to Miami; and Aerolíneas Argentinas (☎ 339776), in Plaza 24 de Septiembre, flies daily to Buenos Aires.

Bus The long-distance bus terminal is on the corner of Avenidas Cañoto and Irala. Keep in mind that during the rainy season even this progressive city is often cut off by highway flooding. There are plenty of daily morning and evening services to Cochabamba (12 hours, US$8.50), from where you'll find easy connections to La Paz, Oruro, Sucre, Potosí and Tarija. Cosmos has a direct service to La Paz (15 to 20 hours, US$20).

Several companies offer daily services to Sucre (15 to 25 hours, US$13.50), where you'll find connections to Potosí. Most services to Camiri (six hours, US$4.50) and Yacuiba (15 hours, US$11) depart in the mid-afternoon. Buses to Comarapa and Vallegrande (seven hours, US$6) leave in the morning and afternoon.

To the Jesuit missions and all of Chiquitanía, Misiones del Oriente (☎ 467878) buses leave in the morning and afternoon. Buses run to San Ramón (2¾ hours, US$3.50), Asunción de Guarayos (5¾ hours, US$5), San Javier (four hours, US$5), Concepcion (seven hours, US$7), San Ignacio (10 hours, US$10), San Miguel

(12 hours, US$12) and San Rafael (13 hours, US$13.50). Several other companies do the same routes but may be less comfortable.

To Trinidad (12 hours, US$6.50) and beyond, a number of buses leave every evening. Although the road is theoretically open year-round, at least to Trinidad, the trip gets rough in the rainy season and is frequently canceled for weeks on end. To Riberalta (27 to 35 hours, US$29) and Guayaramerín (30 to 38 hours, US$30), you can leave on Tuesday, Thursday, Friday and Sunday when the road is passable (normally only in the dry season).

Several companies also offer international services. Daily services connect Santa Cruz with Buenos Aires, Argentina (36 hours, US$108). In the dry season, you can travel the Chaco Road to and from Asunción, Paraguay (36 hours to four days; US$60/100 one way/roundtrip). Choose between Paraguay Internacional, which leaves on Tuesday to Thursday, Saturday and Sunday; Flecha Bus, running on Thursday and Saturday; Transbolpar (☎ 363866 or 366800), on Tuesday, Thursday and Saturday; Yacyreta (☎ 349315), on Monday, Tuesday, Thursday and Saturday; and Transamérica, on Tuesday and Saturday. All these flotas leave from along Avenida Cañoto or near the corner of Izozog (sometimes spelled Isoso) and Monsignor Salvatierra, outside the main bus terminal. Don't expect much from any of these companies.

Smaller micros and trufis to Viru-Viru (the international airport), Montero (with connections to Buena Vista, Yapacaní and Okinawa), Cotoca, San Juan, Limoncito, La Angostura, Samaipata, Mairana, Comarapa, Siberia and other communities in Santa Cruz department also depart regularly from or near the main bus terminal. To Buena Vista and Yapacaní, they wait along Calle Izozog (Isoso). To Samaipata (three hours, US$4.50), trufis leave on the opposite side of Avenida Cañoto, about two blocks from the terminal. Alternatively, contact Expreso Samaipata (☎ 335067; Omar Chávez Ortíz 1147) at Soliz de Olguin, which charges US$17 for up to four passengers. A good

private driver is Martín Saleem (☎ 420066), who speaks English.

Camión Camiones to Cochabamba depart from Avenida Grigotá, near the third anillo, and some cargo traffic still uses the old road via Samaipata and Siberia. Alternatively, take Micro 17 to the tranca 12km west of town, where all traffic must stop. You'll pay from US$2 to US$4 for the 16-hour trip. Be prepared with warm clothing!

Train The new railway station, on Avenida Brasil just inside the third anillo, lies 10 minutes from the center on Micro 12 or 13; catch the micros on Avenida Cañoto near the bus terminal, or along Calle Sucre. The Red Oriental (eastern network) is comprised of two railway lines – one to Quijarro on the Brazilian border and the other to Yacuiba on the Argentine border – but is not connected with the Red Occidental between Oruro, Villazón and Chile.

Santa Cruz has a large, sparkling railway station. While things are constantly improving, there are still quirks involved with rail travel here. At the time of writing, rail tickets could only be purchased on the day of departure. Whatever anyone tells you about the ticket window at the station, it's unlikely to open before 8 am.

When demand is high, tickets can be hard to come by – especially to Quijarro – and carriages may be crowded with people and luggage, so arrive early to stake out a place. Especially on overnight trips, it's wise to chain and padlock your luggage to the racks.

To Brazil The rough-and-ready railway line between Santa Cruz and Quijarro, on the Brazilian border, conducts the affectionately named 'Death Train' like a bucking bronco past the soy plantations, lowland forest, scrubland and oddly shaped mountains to the steamy, sticky Pantanal on the Brazilian frontier. Highlights include the long bridge over the Río Grande, and westbound travelers will witness a special spectacle: As the train from the frontier chugs into the outskirts of Santa Cruz, Bolivian passengers will often jettison baskets, parcels and boxes of innocent Brazilian contraband (noodles, wine and the like) to be retrieved by friends waiting with vehicles alongside the tracks just prior to the customs inspections at the station.

Be sure to carry enough mosquito repellent to fend off the voracious bloodsuckers during long and unexplained stops in swampy, low-lying areas. A pleasant place to break the long journey is the lovely Jesuit mission town of San José de Chiquitos (see the Eastern Lowlands chapter), but getting an onward ticket may be problematic.

From Santa Cruz to Quijarro, the *Expreso del Oriente* (18 hours, US$20/25 in 2nd/1st class) leaves Monday, Wednesday and Friday at 1 pm; from Quijarro, it departs at 3 pm Tuesday, Thursday and Saturday. The poorly monikered *tren rápido* (18 hours, US$15/20 in 2nd/1st class) runs between Santa Cruz and Quijarro (very slowly) Tuesday and Sunday at around 3 pm eastbound and Monday and Thursday at 9:45 pm westbound; note however that the days of this service may be numbered. The *tren mixto* (20 hours, US$15/20/45 in 2nd/1st/bracha) leaves Santa Cruz on Mondays and Fridays at 7:15 pm and arrives in Quijarro at around 3 pm the next day. Information on the questionably comfortable bracha service is available from Bracha (☎ 467795; brachalevy@scbbs.com; Estación Ferroviaria local 11).

Freight trains run at any time; in theory you can simply hop into the passenger bodega and pay the 2nd-class fare of US$20 between Santa Cruz and Quijarro, although polite inquiries beforehand are normally appreciated.

Taxis from Quijarro to the Brazilian border (US$1 per person), 2km away, meet arriving trains. You can change dollars or bolivianos into *reais* (pronounced 'hey-ICE') on the Bolivian side, but the boliviano rate is poor. Note that there's no Brazilian consulate in Quijarro, so if you need a visa, pick it up in Santa Cruz. Officially, yellow fever certificates are required to enter Brazil from Bolivia.

To Argentina To Yacuiba (12 hours, US$15/16 in 2nd/1st class), trains leave at 5 pm on Monday, Wednesday and Friday, and from Yacuiba at 5 pm on Tuesday, Thursday and Saturday.

Getting Around

To/From the Airport Frequent minibuses leave Viru-Viru for the center (½ hour, US$0.75) when flights arrive. Minibuses to the airport leave every 20 minutes from the corner of Avenida Cañoto and La Riva, near the bus terminal. Taxis for up to four people cost US$6 to US$7.

In the past, this airport was notorious for drug-related activities, but the city is attempting to improve its image and it has been some time since problems have been reported.

Bus Santa Cruz' handy system of city micros connects the transportation terminals and all the anillos with the center. Micros 17 & 18 circulate around the first anillo. To reach Avenida San Martín in Barrio Equipetrol, take Micro 23 from anywhere on Vallegrande between Monsignor Salvatierra and Florida. The fare is US$0.30 per ride (US$0.10 for students). Micros and colectivos to small towns around Santa Cruz leave from the northern end of the bus terminal or, in the case of Cotoca, from the corner of Oruro and Suárez Arana.

Taxi Generally, Santa Cruz taxis are slightly more expensive than in highland Bolivia. The official rate is US$1 to anywhere in the first anillo for one person, plus US$0.20 for each additional person and about US$0.20 for each additional anillo. Therefore, from the center to Barrio Equipetrol should cost about US$1.20/1.40 for one/two people. If you have lots of luggage, however, drivers may try to extract up to 50% more.

You can hire private long-distance taxis to sites of interest around Santa Cruz from City Tours Santa Cruz (☎ 537332), within the third anillo, opposite Comercio Chiriguano). Sample fares for up to four people include the following: Cotoca (US$15), Samaipata (US$70), Vallegrande (US$160), Yapacaní (US$80), Los Espejillos (US$60) and Dunas de Palmar (US$30).

Around Santa Cruz

DUNAS DE PALMAR

These large sand dunes, 16km (about 45 minutes) south of Santa Cruz on the road to Palmasola, are popular on weekends. The largest is Loma Chivato. There's an artificial lake and freshwater lagoons where locals swim, picnic and ride motorcycles. There are plans to improve the road and build facilities at the site but, as yet, nothing has happened.

Getting There & Away

Take the micro marked 'Palmar' from the corner of Grigotá and Cañoto in Santa Cruz and get off at the turnoff for 'las lomas de arena.' From there it's an 8km walk along a track to the dunes, but if you go on Sunday, there's a good chance of catching a lift. Alternatively, you can organize a tour at almost any agency in town for US$45/30 per person with two/four people. There's also a local cruceño (☎ 525300, cellular ☎ 019-59983) who offers four-hour tours from the city for US$11/15 for two/four people, including admission to the dunes. Travelers who rent cars will be happiest with 4WD.

COTOCA
☎ 0388

In the mid-1700s, two woodsmen discovered a miraculous image in a tree trunk 20km east of Santa Cruz. In 1799, in honor of this image, an opulent church was constructed. Each year on December 8, the Virgin's discovery is celebrated in the Fiesta de la Virgen de Cotoca, which draws thousands of pilgrims from Bolivia and beyond. At this time, Santa Cruz residents who are grateful for responses to special petitions customarily walk to the shrine overnight from Santa Cruz.

Getting There & Away

Micros leave for Cotoca approximately every 10 minutes from the El Deber building, on the corner of Oruro and Suárez Arana in Santa Cruz. The trip takes 35 minutes.

PUERTO PAILAS

Puerto Pailas, 40 minutes along the railway line east of Santa Cruz, is the base of operations for a growing Sikh colony, which is building a temple amid agricultural and reforestation projects. This town could easily win an international competition for the volume of trash on the ground – the streets are literally paved with plastic bags – and it's truly a sight to behold.

Puerto Pailas lacks tourist infrastructure, but alojamiento accommodations are available for about US$2 per person. On Sunday, horse races begin at 5 pm.

Although there's little reason to go (unless you just want to see all the trash), Puerto Pailas is accessible by train from Santa Cruz or camión from Cotoca. Micros (US$0.50) leave Santa Cruz from the front of the El Deber building on the corner of Oruro and Suárez Arana.

MONTERO
☎ 092

The rapidly growing community of Montero, named for the Independence war hero General Marceliano Montero, sprawls across the flat agricultural lands north of Santa Cruz. Its immediate surroundings are planted with bananas, sugarcane and rice. Soybeans, sesame and peanuts, which are used to produce vegetable oils, are also cultivated. With a population of 60,000, it's one of the largest cities in the Bolivian lowlands.

Visitors to the town have several accommodations options. Among them are the aptly named **Alojamiento Central**, which appears to be clean and pleasant, as well as the recommended **Alojamiento Pinocho** (☎ 20305), with singles/doubles with air-con, TV and private bath for US$9/12.

Micros and trufis leave the Santa Cruz bus terminal for Montero (US$1) every 10 minutes, and transportation back to Santa Cruz lines up two blocks south of the plaza, on Calle Antofagasta. Micros to Puerto Banegas, Yapacaní, Buena Vista, Okinawa and other villages also leave from Calle Antofagasta, four blocks west of the less-than-appealing market.

OKINAWA
☎ 0923

Okinawa, the Japanese rice-growing colony northeast of Montero, makes an interesting excursion. This colony is comprised mainly of Japanese immigrants who arrived after WWII and received 50 hectares each from the government for opening up the then-inhospitable eastern lowlands. Farming equipment was provided by the US government. Unfortunately, recent competition from big agribusiness has meant a decline in smaller farms, and the colony is on the wane as settlers migrate in search of greener pastures.

The Okinawa turnoff, north of Montero, is marked by an enormous Japanese parasol. Near Okinawa is Puerto Banegas, on the Río Grande. When the water level is high, it may be possible to catch a boat from here to Trinidad, but it's not a well-established cargo route. Micros between Montero and either Okinawa or Puerto Banegas cost US$1.

YAPACANÍ
☎ 0933

At the bridge over the Río Yapacaní, 85km from Montero on the new Cochabamba road, sits a row of haphazardly built eating establishments serving *surubí* and other fresh fish. Sadly, they also cook up more exotic species like *jochi* (agouti) and *tatu* (armadillo). These places are often washed away by flooding in the rainy season and must be rebuilt each year, so they are best visited between April and October. The best place to stay in the horrendously ugly settlement is *Residencial Santa Cruz*, which charges US$5 per person.

BUENA VISTA
☎ 0932

The little village of Buena Vista, two hours northwest of Santa Cruz, makes an ideal staging point for trips into the forested lowland section of Parque Nacional Amboró. Lots of new accommodations options and restaurants are springing up here, and Buena Vista is well on its way to becoming a major stop along the Gringo Trail.

Information

For information on Parque Nacional Amboró, visit the park administration, about 1½ blocks south of the plaza. Here you can book park cabañas for US$2 per person per day and hire guides into the park for about US$5 per day. A two-day trip to Amboró's Macuñucu camp with *guardaparque* guides runs about US$30 with up to four people.

All of the hotels are able to provide reliable park information at their guests' request.

Iglesia de los Santos Desposorios

The Jesuit mission of Buena Vista was founded in 1694 as La Misión de los Desposorios de San José, the fifth mission in the Viceroyalty of Perú. The need for a church was recognized, and 29 years later, after a search for a high-standing location with sufficient water and potential cropland, the first building was finally constructed.

By late 1750, 700 Chiraguano people had been converted to Christianity. The Swiss Jesuit missionary and architect Padre Martin Schmid recognized the need for a new church, and in 1767, the current structure was completed. When the Jesuits were expelled from Bolivia later that year, the administration of the church passed to the Bishop of Santa Cruz. Although the building is now deteriorating, its lovely classic form merits a look.

Amboró Butterfly Farm

The conservation agency Fundación Amos is now developing a butterfly farm in the friendly nearby village of Potrerito. It will concentrate on breeding and selling butterfly pupae to live exhibits around the world. Here visitors will be able to see and photograph these beautifully colorful creatures.

To get there, take the main highway toward Cochabamba. After passing the large metal silos and the Amboró Eco-Resort on the right side and two white houses on the left, look for an unpaved left turn. After 2km, you'll reach Potrerito; the butterfly farm will be on a hillock, behind the brick school buildings. Before visiting, check with Mirian Chorioco or Seferino Orellana in Potrerito or the very helpful Ambrocio Vallejos in Buena Vista, to make sure the farm is operational. It's a one-hour walk from Buena Vista; taxis cost US$5 roundtrip, including waiting time.

Curichi

This region south of Buena Vista is now slated to become a municipally designated reserve. The lovely marshy wetland provides Buena Vista's water supply and also serves as a habitat and breeding site for both migratory and native birds. Future plans include an elevated boardwalk and viewing tower.

Río Surutú, Santa Bárbara & El Cairo

Río Surutú is a popular excursion for locals. There's a pleasant sandy beach ideal for picnics, swimming and camping during the dry season. From Buena Vista, it's an easy 3km walk to the river bend nearest town. The opposite bank is the boundary of Parque Nacional Amboró.

A good longer option is the six-hour circuit walk through the community of Santa Bárbara, through pleasant and partially forested tropical plantation country. From Buena Vista, follow the unpaved road to Santa Bárbara and ask for the Ucurutú track, which leads to a lovely river beach on the Río Ucurutú. After a picnic and a dip, you can return to Buena Vista via the Huaytú road.

An even better swimming hole is at El Cairo, which lies an hour's walk from town. To get there, pass Los Franceses and follow the unpaved road as it curves to the right. About 2km from town, take the left fork and cross over a bridge. After passing El Cairo, on your right, keep going until you reach the river.

Special Events

The local fiesta, Día de los Santos Desposorios, which features bullfights, food stalls and general merrymaking, starts on October 26. There's also a Rice Festival that takes place in early May, following the rice harvest.

Places to Stay

Basic accommodations are available at *Residencial Nadia* (☎ 2049; Mariano Saucedo Sevilla 186) for US$3.50 per person. The owner is a former park ranger and a good source of information on Amboró. Even nicer is *Las Palmas*, which charges US$5 per person with private bath. It's on the main highway, 10 minutes' walk from the plaza.

Thanks to the appeal of Amboró, there's now an upmarket resort, the rustic German-run *Amboró Eco-Resort* (☎ 2085; fax 2048; biancka@yupimail.com), surrounded by its own little tropical forest complete with walking paths. Cramped singles/doubles with an American breakfast cost US$80/90 and suites are US$140. Amenities include a swim-up bar in the pool, a sauna, a disco and sports options. In Santa Cruz, you can contact them at ☎ 422372/fax 421909.

One good-value option is *Cabañas Quimorí* (☎ 2081 or 016-45266), a simpler place just off the road toward Santa Bárbara. The individual cabins are spread over a large area with a great view over Amboró. On weekdays they charge US$10 per person, including breakfast, and on weekends, US$11. From Santa Cruz, you can book at ☎ 423414. *Hotel Sumuqué* (☎ /fax 2080), on Avenida José Steinbach, charges US$20 per cabin, without breakfast, and lacks the view.

Ornithologist Robin Clarke's *Hotel Flora & Fauna* (cellular ☎ 019-43706; Casilla 2097, Santa Cruz), better known as the 'Double-F,' 4km south of town on the Huaytú road, occupies a breezy ridge overlooking Parque Nacional Amboró. Double cabins with use of the shared kitchen and cooking implements cost US$30 on weekdays, US$40 on weekends, plus US$5 for each additional person. A full breakfast costs US$5 and full board is US$10. Hotel-style accommodations with a full breakfast are US$24 per person for the first night and US$18 for subsequent nights. Guided walks are available for US$5 for guests and US$10 for day visitors. Access is by car/motorbike taxi (US$1.40/1) from Buena Vista.

Places to Eat

For meals, the most recommended restaurant is the French-run *Los Franceses*, which serves up pan-fried steak, Provençal chicken, pork in white wine sauce, surubí in a special tomato and garlic sauce, and so on. All dishes are served with bread, salad, french fries and rice for US$3.50 to US$5, and vegetarian options are available on request. It's a highlight of Buena Vista.

Another excellent choice is *Las Tranqueras*, which serves beef and chicken as well as wild game – agouti, peccary and armadillo; in the interest of wildlife, you might want to avoid these and opt instead for the exotic rain forest juices (US$3.50 for a jug). The US$5 main dishes are accompanied by salads and a major starch blitz: chips, yucca, plantains and rice.

The Argentine-owned *Don José*, on the plaza, offers such recommended choices as pastas, typically Argentine beef concoctions and *majadito*, which is a beef, rice and tomato casserole.

An excellent local alternative is *Jasayé*, beneath a large *pahuichi* (thatched dwelling). Here you'll find beef, fish and chicken dishes for US$3.50 to US$5. For budget travelers, there's a good family-run place between the high school and the Hotel Sumuqué, serving burgers and daily specials for reasonable prices.

Shopping

The Jipijapa shop and Jipijapa Kiosk sell lampshades, handbags, boxes, panama hats etc made from *jipijapa*, the fronds of the cyclanthaceae fan palm tree *(Carludovica palmata)*. The recommended Artecampo shop also sells *jipijapa* products, among other local creations.

Getting There & Away

From Santa Cruz, shared taxis leave for Yapacaní from behind the long-distance bus terminal. Make it clear that you want to get off at Buena Vista, which costs US$15 for the whole taxi or US$3 per person. You can also take a slow micro to Montero and change to a micro that continues to Buena Vista. The bus stop is near the pharmacy. To return to Santa Cruz, either take the micro to Montero or wait for a shared taxi coming from Yapacaní, which will cruise around the plaza in search of passengers with its horn blaring.

Getting Around

Car- and moto-taxis wait at one corner of the plaza; there's also another taxi stand along the road to Santa Bárbara, which can take you to Cabañas Quimorí and Hotel Flora y Fauna.

PARQUE NACIONAL AMBORÓ & ÁREA DE USO MÚLTIPLE AMBORÓ

The 430,000-hectare Amboró National Park lies in a unique geographical position at the confluence of three distinct ecosystems: the Amazon Basin, the northern Chaco and the Andes. The park was originally created in 1973 as the Reserva de Vida Silvestre Germán Busch, with an area of just 180,000 hectares. In 1984, thanks to the efforts of British ornithologist Robin Clarke and Bolivian biologist Noel Kempff Mercado, it was given national-park status and in 1990 was expanded to 630,000 hectares. In late 1995, however, amid controversy surrounding campesino colonization inside park boundaries, it was pared down to its current size (see the 'The Struggle for Amboró').

The park's range of habitats means that both highland and lowland species are found here. All species native to Amazonia, except those of the Beni savannas, are

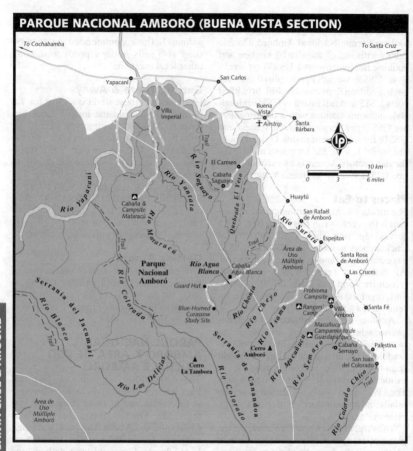

PARQUE NACIONAL AMBORÓ (BUENA VISTA SECTION)

represented, including the now almost-extinct spectacled bear. Jaguars, capybaras, river otters, agoutis, tapirs, deer, peccaries and various monkeys still exist in relatively large numbers, and over 700 species of birds have been identified. The unfortunately tasty *mutún (Mitu tuberosa)*, or razor-billed curassow, is still native to the area, and even rare quetzals have been spotted. The park is also one of the only remaining habitats of the rare and endangered blue-horned curassow *(Crax unicornis)*, also known as the unicorn bird.

Buena Vista Section

Access to the eastern part of the Área de Uso Múltiple Amboró requires crossing over the Río Surutú, either in a vehicle or on foot. Depending on the rainfall and weather, the river may be anywhere from knee- to waist-deep. For information on huts and campsites throughout the park, see Places to Stay, later in this section.

Río Macuñucu The Río Macuñucu route is the most popular into the Área de Uso Múltiple and begins at Las Cruces, 35km southeast of Buena Vista. It's a US$5 taxi ride from Buena Vista. From there, it's 7km to the Río Surutú, which you must drive or wade across. Just beyond the opposite bank you'll reach the village of Villa Amboró. Note that villagers may illegally try to charge an entrance fee to any tourist who passes their community en route to Macuñucu, whether or not the visitor intends to stay there. In fact, the only body authorized to charge a fee is the park administration, and they currently don't do so. If you're accosted, politely refuse to pay and just keep walking.

Here you'll pick up a track that continues several kilometers through the trees and homesteads and past a few cattle gates to the banks of the Río Macuñucu. The track continues upriver through thick forest for about two hours, then disappears into the river course. Continue upstream another hour or so, hopping over river stones past beautiful red rocks, cliffs and overhangs. Beyond a particularly narrow canyon, which confines hikers to the river, you'll reach a large rock overhang accommodating up to 10 campers. If you have a tent, the sandy river beaches also make pleasant campsites.

At this point, the upriver walk becomes increasingly difficult and entails negotiating some large and slippery river boulders and scrambling past obstructing landslides. Several hours of heavy slogging upstream from the cave is a nice waterfall and another potential campsite. The very daring can continue the increasingly treacherous boulder-hopping to more overhangs farther upstream. The terrain becomes increasingly rugged, so a guide is recommended for overnight or extended trips above the waterfall.

Río Isama & Cerro Amboró The Río Isama route turns off at the village of Espejitos, 28km from Buena Vista, and provides access to the base of 1300m Cerro Amboró, the bulbous peak for which the park is named. It's possible to climb to the summit, but it's a difficult trek and a guide is essential. An alternative way to reach the peak is

on the wonderful 18-day traverse from Samaipata to Buena Vista (see Organized Tours in Samaipata).

Upper Saguayo The objective of this route is the study site on the upper Río Saguayo, where researchers rediscovered the rare blue-horned curassow, once thought to be extinct. It's very rough going in places – in fact, it may well be overgrown by the time you read this – so prospective hikers need a guide and a good machete. Without a 4WD to take you to the end of the motorable track, the return trip requires about five days.

The hike begins at the mouth of the Río Chonta. To get there, take a taxi or micro from Buena Vista to Huaytú. Here, turn right (southwest) and walk 5km to the Río Surutú. In the dry season, you can ford the river by vehicle or on foot. From the opposite bank, it's 12km along the 4WD track to the end of the motorable track at the ranch belonging to Don Arnaldo Hurtado.

From the ranch, keep going a short distance along the track to the Agua Blanca cabaña, watching along the way for herons, toucans, parrots, kingfishers and other colorful birds. If the route to the study site proves impassable, this makes a pleasant base for a couple of days exploring.

Beyond the cabaña, the track crosses the 'red line,' the new boundary between the Área de Uso Múltiple and the Parque Nacional Amboró, and descends through thick forest to the Río Saguayo. On the bluff above the opposite bank is an abandoned guard hut and a viable campsite.

Alternatively, after an hour from Don Hurtado's ranch, watch for a dim path leading off to the right. If it isn't totally overgrown, it will also take you to the guard hut, passing first through mixed forest and overgrown fields. Just beyond a derelict house is a large area of *curichi* marsh, which is home to the *tojo*, or yellow-rumped cacique *(Cacicus cela)*, whose bizarre cry sounds remarkably like a manual cash register ringing up a purchase.

If you do get as far as the guard hut, look for a trail heading upstream. Under optimal

The Struggle for Amboró

The location of Parque Nacional Amboró is a mixed blessing; although it's conveniently accessible to visitors, it also lies practically within spitting distance of Santa Cruz, Bolivia's second-largest city, and squarely between the old and new Cochabamba-Santa Cruz highways. At a time when even the remote parks of the Amazon Basin are coming under threat, this puts Amboró in an especially vulnerable position.

The first human settlers in the area were Chiriguano and Yuracare Indians, who occupied the lowlands, while Altiplano peoples, such as the Aymará, probably settled parts of the highland areas. Although agriculture was introduced after the arrival of the Spanish in the late 16th century, the remote Amboró region remained untouched until the late 20th century, when unemployed opportunity seekers began migrating from the highlands in search of land.

When Parque Nacional Amboró was created in 1973, its charter included a clause forbidding settlement and resource exploitation. Unfortunately for naturalists and conservationists, hunters, loggers and campesino settlers continue to pour in – many of them displaced from the Chapare region by the US Drug Enforcement Agency – and the northeastern area is already settled, cultivated and hunted out. For poor farmers, cultivation practices have changed little since the 1500s, and slash-and-burn is still the prevailing method of agriculture.

Although NGOs have attempted to train committed guardaparques and educate people about the value of wilderness, more land is lost every year and the future of Parque Nacional Amboró is far from certain. In 1995, conflicts between colonists and authorities heated up, and as a result the park was informally redefined to include only land that lay 400m beyond the most remote cultivated field, effectively shrinking the protected area by about 200,000 hectares.

In July of the same year, campesinos pressing for official recognition of their rights to occupy the land prevented tourists and researchers from entering the park. The following October, with regional elections coming up, the government abandoned the struggle and issued an official decree reducing the park by over 200,000 hectares. The decommissioned area was then redesignated as the Área de Uso Múltiple Amboró, which effectively opened it up for agriculture, settlement, mineral exploration and timber extraction. The affected portion includes a band across the southern area from Comarapa to Samaipata, all of the eastern bit up to the headwaters of the Surutú tributaries, and parts of the far north.

conditions, it entails boulder-hopping and wading, but at last report, one critical section which detoured around a particularly deep river pool was overgrown and impassable, so this is probably as far as you'll go.

If the way has been cleared again, you can also explore distracting side trips up clear streams and observe an amazing variety of birdlife: tanagers, *orpendolas* (blackbirds), honeycreepers, hummingbirds, warblers, herons and a host of others. After about five hours, you'll reach the abandoned hut that served as the research base for the blue-horned curassow, but you'll need a great deal of luck to see one. This is also an ideal habitat for the colorful military macaw.

The downhill return to the road is the same way you came; on foot, this takes about two days from the research camp and one long day from the Agua Blanca cabaña.

Mataracú From near Yapacaní, on the main Cochabamba road, a 4WD track heads south across the Río Yapacaní into the northern reaches of the Área de Uso Múltiple Amboró and, after a rough 18km, rolls up to the Mataracú cabaña and campsite. This is the only Amboró cabaña accessible by motor vehicle. Naturally, it can also be reached on foot. Except in the driest part of the year, however, crossing the Río Yapacaní may be a problem.

Samaipata Area

Samaipata sits outside the southern boundary of the Área de Uso Múltiple Amboró and is the best access point for the Andean section of the former park. There's no real infrastructure, and public facilities and walking tracks are still in the planning stages.

Guides to the region are available in Samaipata. The road uphill from Samaipata ends at a small cabin, and from there it's a four-hour walk to a camping spot near the boundary between the primary forest, giant ferns and Andean cloud forest. From this point, you can continue an hour farther into the park.

If you can't find a guide, a recommended two-day walk is the 23km traverse between Samaipata and Mairana via the hamlet of La Yunga. Most of the route is depicted on the IGM 1:50,000 topo sheet *Mairana – 6839-IV*. Samaipata appears at the northern edge of *Samaipata – 6839-III*.

For more information, see Organized Tours in Samaipata, later in this chapter.

Mairana Area

From Mairana, it's 7km uphill along a walking track to the hamlet of La Yunga, where there's a guest hut. It's in a particularly lush region of the Área de Uso Múltiple Amboró, surrounded by some tree ferns and other cloud-forest vegetation. From La Yunga, a 16km forest traverse connects with the main road near Samaipata.

To enter the park here, visit the guard post at the south end of the soccer field in La Yunga. Access to Mairana is by micro or camión from Santa Cruz or Samaipata.

Comarapa Area

Northwest of Comarapa, 4km toward Cochabamba, is a little-used entrance to the Área de Uso Múltiple Amboró. After the road crosses a pass between a hill and a ridge with a telephone tower, look for the minor road turning off to the northeast (right) at the hamlet of Khara Huasi. This road leads uphill to verdant stands of cloud forest, which blanket the peaks.

Other worthwhile visits in this area include the 36-sided Pukhara de Tuquipaya, a set of pre-Inca ruins on the summit of Cerro Comanwara, 1.5km from Comarapa; and the colonial village of Pulquina Arriba, several kilometers east of Comarapa.

For a list of companies running guided excursions into the park, see Organized Tours in the Santa Cruz section.

Places to Stay

Inside the park, you'll find five wilderness cabañas that you can rent for US$2 per person per day. They're very basic, so you'll need your own sleeping bag. The most popular and accessible cabaña is the one on the Río Macuñucu. Others can be found on the lower Río Semayo, above the Río Mataracú, on the Río Agua Blanca, and on the lower Río Saguayo. For bookings and information, see the park administration office in Buena Vista.

The *Macuñucu Campamento de Guardaparques*, 4km upstream, has a sleeping loft for US$2 per day, including the use of rudimentary cooking facilities. The main camp activity is sitting beside the river and waiting for wildlife to wander past. Jaguar and puma tracks are frequently seen along the riverbank, but large cats are rarely observed.

At Villa Amboró, near the mouth of the Macuñucu, the controversial Santa Cruz aid agency Probioma (☎ 431332 or 432098; probioma@roblescz.entelnet.bo) has established a community campsite with clean showers, toilets and several hiking trails, including a two-hour route to a lovely 50m waterfall and a four-hour return hike to a marvelous viewpoint over Cerro Amboró. Local Spanish-speaking guides can provide information on the flora and fauna, and the community can organize meals and arrange horse transportation for visitors who might not want to walk. A two-day stay, including guides, horses, camping gear and meals costs US$31/33 per person with groups of two/four people. With your own food and camping equipment, you'll pay half price.

Getting There & Away

Every morning a micro heads south from Buena Vista, running beside the Río Surutú, which forms Amboró's eastern boundary (it passes through Huaytú, San Rafael de Amboró, Espejitos, Santa Rosa de Amboró, Santa Fé and Las Cruces). This boundary provides access to several rough routes and tracks that lead southwest into the interior, following tributaries of the Río Surutú: the Quebrada El Yeso and the Ríos Agua Blanca/Chonta/Cheyo, the Isama, Macuñucu, Semayo and Colorado Chico. Note that all access to the park along this road will require a crossing of the Río Surutú. In Buena Vista, you can hire a 4WD vehicle to reach Macuñucu Camp for around US$60.

SANTA CRUZ TO SAMAIPATA

Los Espejillos

Los Espejillos is a popular retreat west of Santa Cruz. Its name, which means 'the little mirrors,' is derived from the surrounding smooth black rock, polished by a small mountain river. The site, which features cascades and refreshing swimming holes, lies across the Río Piray about 18km north of the highway.

About 400m beyond the public site is *Hotel Espejillos* (☎ 330091; fax 334674), which has a clean private stretch of the river for bathing and a bar where you can enjoy a beer in the sun. Double rooms cost US$40 weekdays, US$50 weekends, and camping costs US$5 weekdays, US$6 weekends.

Catch any micro or trufi going toward Santiago del Torno, Limoncito, La Angostura or Samaipata, and get off just beyond the village of San José. From here, Los Espejillos is an 18km walk or hitch north along the 4WD track (which isn't passable by vehicle at all during the rainy season). Weekends are best for catching lifts from the turnoff.

Bermejo & Volcanes Region

Bermejo, about 85km southwest of Santa Cruz on the Samaipata road, is marked by a hulking slab of red rock known as Cueva de los Monos, which is flaking and chipping into nascent natural arches.

The intriguing crater lake, Laguna Volcán, lies 6km up the hill north of Bermejo. It was once a popular stopover for migrating ducks, but in the late 1980s it was purchased by a cruceño who cleared all the vegetation and thereby banished the wildlife as well. However, it still makes for a pleasant walk from the highway. A lovely walking track climbs from the lake to the crater rim; it begins at the point directly across the lake from the end of the road. Coming from Santa Cruz, take a micro or trufi toward Samaipata and get off 1km beyond Bermejo; the route is signposted 'Laguna Volcán 2.5km del Camino.'

More amazing is the bizarre nearby region known as Los Volcanes, which lies north of the main road and features an otherworldly landscape of tropical sugarloaf hills. In the dry season, Hans Riega operates *Refugio Volcanes*, where you'll pay US$50 per person per day for accommodations, meals, transportation from the main road and guided hikes through the impossible landscapes. This wonderfully wild and very lonely site lies 4km off the main road (that's one to 1½ hours on foot, or 45 minutes from the end of the easily motorable section of the side road into the complex). In addition to 10km of hiking trails through the tropical forests, you'll find paradisiacal waterholes where you can cool off; fascinating flora, including several unusual species of wild orchids; and also some of the Bolivia's most interesting bird-watching. *Camping* is also possible. Unfortunately, it isn't always open; for information contact Norah Ferrel Urquidi at Forest Tour (☎/fax 372042; forest@mail.zuper.net; Cuéllar 22, Casilla 6611) in Santa Cruz and hope for the best. It really is worthwhile!

Las Cuevas

Las Cuevas lies on the road toward Samaipata, 100km southwest of Santa Cruz and 20km east of Samaipata. If you walk upstream on a clear path away from the road, you'll reach two lovely waterfalls that spill into eminently swimmable lagoons bordered by sandy beaches. Admission to this little touch of paradise costs US$1 per person.

SAMAIPATA

☎ 0944

The village of Samaipata, at 1660m in the foothills of the Cordillera Oriental, is a popular weekend destination for cruceños and a great place to hole up for a couple of days. The Quechua name, meaning 'rest in the highlands,' could hardly be more appropriate. This quiet village has also attracted a few foreign settlers and both highland and lowland Bolivians, and a cosmopolitan society is developing. If you're coming from the lowlands, it's also a good place to begin altitude acclimatization by degrees. The main attractions are the pre-Inca ceremonial site of El Fuerte, 10km east of the village (see Around Samaipata later in this chapter), and the Parque Nacional Amboró, which is accessible from Samaipata.

Samaipata is one of the few places where the guerrilla band of Ché Guevara actually had a taste of revolutionary success. On 6 July 1967, about three months before their leader's death, the band rolled into town in a truck they'd stopped on the highway. In his journals, Ché recounts:

The men went in…to Samaipata, where they captured two soldiers and the chief of the post, Lieutenant Vacaflor. The sergeant was forced to give the password and a lightning action captured the post with its ten soldiers after a brief exchange of fire with a soldier who resisted. They succeeded in taking five Mausers and one ZB30 and drove away with the ten prisoners, leaving them naked 1km from Samaipata…. The action took place in front of the whole town and a group of travelers, so the news will spread like wildfire.

Information

Reliable tourist information is available at Bar Amboró (☎ 6220), at the restaurant La Chakana (☎ 6207) and from the recommended Don Gilberto (☎ 6050). The post office in Samaipata only delivers mail; they can't accept outgoing post (and if they did, it would probably never be heard from again).

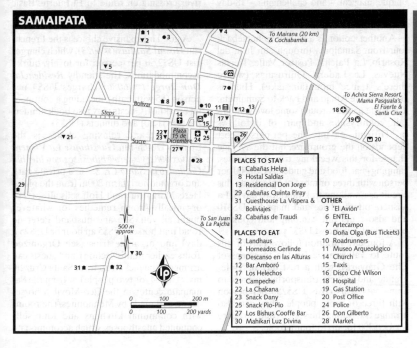

SAMAIPATA

To Mairana (20 km) & Cochabamba

To Achira Sierra Resort, Mama Pasquala's, El Fuerte & Santa Cruz

To San Juan & La Pajcha

To San Juan & La Pajcha

500 m approx

0   100   200 m
0   100   200 yards

PLACES TO STAY
1 Cabañas Helga
8 Hostal Saldías
13 Residencial Don Jorge
29 Cabañas Quinta Piray
31 Guesthouse La Víspera &
   Boliviajes
32 Cabañas de Traudi

PLACES TO EAT
2 Landhaus
4 Horneados Gerlinde
5 Descanso en las Alturas
12 Bar Amboró
17 Los Helechos
21 Campeche
22 La Chakana
23 Snack Dany
25 Snack Pio-Pio
27 Los Bishus Cooffe Bar
30 Mahikari Luz Divina

OTHER
3 'El Avión'
6 ENTEL
7 Artecampo
9 Doña Olga (Bus Tickets)
10 Roadrunners
11 Museo Arqueológico
14 Church
15 Taxis
16 Disco Ché Wilson
18 Hospital
19 Gas Station
20 Post Office
24 Police
26 Don Gilberto
28 Market

SANTA CRUZ & AROUND

Museo Arqueológico

Samaipata's small archaeological museum makes an interesting visit, but it offers little explanation of the El Fuerte site. It does have a few Tiahuanaco artifacts and some local pottery. It's open daily 9 am to noon and 2:30 to 6:30 pm. Admission is US$1.

Organized Tours

Boliviajes (☎/fax 6082; vispera@bibosi.scz .entelnet.bo), at the Guesthouse La Víspera, runs several exciting adventure tours into wonderfully remote places south of Samaipata. One is the alternative 'back route' trek to the El Fuerte ruins, which includes a six-hour walk and a refreshing dip in a mountain stream, as well as a guided tour of the ruins and vehicle transportation back to Samaipata. The cost per group of up to four or five people is US$75. One/two/three-day guided hikes into Amboró cost US$155/175/250 per person with two people and US$155/175/200 with a group of four. You can also organize a unique, magical – and challenging – 18-day crossing from Samaipata to Buena Vista; contact them for details!

Another option is a roundtrip horseback tour from Samaipata through San Juan del Rosario, La Pajcha, Postrer Valle, Tierras Nuevas, La Ladera, Quirusillas (where there's a nice mountain lake), Hierbas Buenas, Valle Abajo and back to Samaipata. The route passes through some lovely mountain countryside, and part of it follows pre-Hispanic paving. The per-person cost depends on the group size, but the average charge for this weeklong trip, with horses, camping gear, food and guides, is US$500 per person with three or more people. To do this circuit as a walking trek (about 10 days), La Víspera offers advice and maps for US$10 and also rents out camping and cooking equipment. Tents cost US$5 per day.

A four-day variation follows part of this route to Vallegrande (in the footsteps of Ché Guevara), with a rest day in Vallegrande and vehicle transportation back to Samaipata. This costs US$250 per person with three or more people. They can also arrange taxis along the scenic route to Sucre for US$300 for up to four people.

Independent hiking guides are available through the Austrian-run Roadrunners (☎ 6193), in Barrio La Glorieta II, which does informative tours to El Fuerte, waterfall visits and treks in the cloud forests. The local guide Don Gilberto (☎ 6050) also provides hikes and excursions into Amboró and along the Ché Guevara trail, as well as trips to local ruins and archaeological sites.

Places to Stay

Bolivia's leap into European-style camping begins at **Achira Sierra Resort** (☎ 522288; fax 522255; bolivia.resort@scbbs-bo.com; Igmiri 506, Barrio Urbari, Casilla 1020, Santa Cruz), at Km 112, 8km east of Samaipata. It has cabañas, campsites, baths, showers and washing sinks, as well as a social hall with a restaurant and games room. More basic camping is available at the secluded **Mama Pasquala's**, set in a beautiful valley around some great swimming holes. It lies 500m upstream from the river crossing en route to El Fuerte. Basic campsites cost US$4 per person; cabañas run $5 per person.

A good inexpensive choice is the French-run **Hostal Saldías** (☎ 6023), which charges just US$2.50 per person for lovely, quirky accommodations. The friendly **Residencial Don Jorge** (☎ 6086) charges US$4 per person ($5 with bath), including a continental breakfast. Guests may also book almuerzos (US$1.50) and dinners (US$3).

A quiet and relaxing choice is the friendly Dutch-run **Guesthouse La Víspera** (☎ /fax 6082; vispera@bibosi.scz.entelnet.bo; Casilla 3636, Santa Cruz), on a private park and organic herb farm 800m from the plaza. Here, Margarita van't Hoff sells all sorts of organically grown remedies for whatever might ail you. She and husband Peter de Raad rent horses (US$5 an hour or US$25 a day) and organize trips (see Organized Tours earlier in this section), and guests can arrange to be picked up from Santa Cruz by taxi (US$64 for two people) or from the Samaipata center in the Eco-Movil, a horse-drawn cart made by Mennonites. The rooms with communal kitchens and four self-contained guesthouses, which accommodate two to 12 people, are clean and warm and enjoy commanding views across the valley. Accommodations cost US$12 per person; backpackers carrying *Lonely Planet* pay US$7 per person. Camping is available on their lovely green lawns for US$4 in your own tent or US$5 in pre-erected tents, including use of the hot showers and kitchen facilities. Bring a flashlight, as there's no street lighting between the village and the guesthouse.

Across the road, you'll find the very amenable Austrian-run *Cabañas de Traudi* (☎ *6094; traudiar@bibosi.scz.entelnet.bo*). During the week, cabañas without baths cost US$5 per person; with baths, they're US$15/20 for two/three people; add about 20% on weekends. The swimming pool is open to the public for US$3.50 per person (half price for residents of Guesthouse La Víspera). *Cabañas Quinta Piray* (☎ /fax *6136; quinta-piray@cotas.com.bo; Casilla 2153, Santa Cruz*), is a complex of self-contained cabins that strongly resembles a development in US suburbia. Depending on the number of rooms and beds, cabañas range from US$20 to US$55 on weekdays and from US$25 to US$65 on weekends.

More upmarket is the tasteful *Cabañas Helga* (☎ *6033; landhaus@cotas.com.bo*), behind the Landhaus restaurant near the landmark *avión* (airplane). Each cabaña has cooking and bathroom facilities and accommodates up to seven people in three bedrooms, making it ideal for families. During the week, you'll pay US$25/45/60 for one/two/three bedrooms, and on weekends, US$45/90/100. Singles/doubles with baths cost US$10/15, including use of the swimming pool. Breakfast costs an additional US$2 and saunas are available for two to four people for US$20.

Places to Eat

You'll find great breakfasts, pizza and home-baked goodies at the friendly and interestingly decorated *Descanso en las Alturas*. If you're up for a European gourmet-style meal, try *Landhaus*, near the avión at the northern end of town. The food here is superb by anyone's standards; it's

open Thursday to Sunday for lunch and dinner. The door may be locked, but if you knock they'll open up. On weekends, you'll also find elegant cuisine at *Campeche* (☎ *6046*), which does salads, vegetarian fare and European-style meals with an excellent view.

Samaipata's best and friendliest eatery is the Dutch- and Hungarian-run 'Southern Cross,' *La Chakana* (☎ *6207; chakanabol@yahoo.com*), located on the plaza; the name means 'Southern Cross.' Here, Erik and Krisztina Velde serve up breakfasts, sandwiches, vegetarian meals, excellent pizza and European specialties, as well as a welcome dose of hospitality and good conversation. On Friday nights, they host a gathering of locals with music, drinking, dancing and socializing.

Los Bishus Cooffe Bar, on the Plaza, may not be able to spell but it does serve up reasonable Bolivian fare for good prices. Another decent option for international cuisine is *Los Helechos*, which is open Thursday to Monday for lunch and dinner.

For baked goods, cheese, yogurt, muesli, organic fruit, vegetables, meats and healthy snacks and remedies, see the very popular German-run *Horneados Gerlinde* (☎ *6175*). It's open from 8 am to early evening. Coffee, snacks and ice cream confections are the specialty at *Bar Amboró* (☎ *6220*) and *Snack Dany* (☎ *6063*), and quick fast food is available at *Snack Pio-Pio*.

On the hill, along the road toward Guesthouse La Víspera, the Japanese religious sect Mahikari grows and sells fresh vegetables. For US$1, you can be blessed with the 'energy' of the Mahikari Luz Divina (divine light).

Entertainment & Shopping

A slice of Santa Cruz teenage nightlife is transported to Samaipata each weekend and revived at the popular *Disco Ché Wilson*. Anyone over 21 will probably prefer the Saturday disco at the *Landhaus* (see Places to Eat), which cranks up as the restaurant winds down; dancing normally starts around 10 pm. Children may enjoy the playground area beside the avión.

You'll find locally produced ceramics at the Landhaus, and Artecampo has a recommended shop selling the work of women from around Santa Cruz department.

Getting There & Around

Four-passenger trufis leave Santa Cruz for Samaipata (three hours, US$4.50) when full, from the corner of Omar Chávez and Soliz de Hulguín, two blocks from the bus terminal. However, the spot changes frequently, so you may have to ask for directions. Alternatively, micros (three hours, US$2.50) leave at 4 pm from the Santa Cruz bus terminal.

From Samaipata to Santa Cruz, you can buy bus tickets at Snack Dany or from Doña Olga, a block north of the plaza. You'll find taxis (☎ 6133, 6016 and 6129) from the gasoline station and micros from the main plaza between 5 and 7 am and Sunday from noon to 5 pm. Alternatively, wait on the main road for trufis returning in the afternoon. Finding transportation west to Mairana, Comarapa, Siberia, Vallegrande or Cochabamba is a bit more difficult, but if you wait on the main highway, a micro or camión will eventually come along. For a private taxi, phone ☎ 6050.

Public taxis are available at ☎ 6133, 6016 or 6129.

AROUND SAMAIPATA

For information on access to Parque Nacional Amboró from Samaipata, see that section earlier in this chapter.

El Fuerte

Samaipata's main attraction is El Fuerte, which is most likely the remains of a pre-Inca ceremonial site. It occupies a hilltop about 10km from the village and affords a commanding view across the rugged transition zone between the Andes and low-lying areas farther east.

Early conquerors assumed the site had been used for defense, hence its Spanish name, 'the fort.' In 1832, French naturalist Alcides d'Orbigny visited the site and decided that the pools and parallel canals had been used for washing gold. In 1936, German anthropologist Leo Pucher

described it as an ancient temple to the serpent and the jaguar.

Recently, the place has gained a New Age following, and in one of his fits of extra-terrestrial fancy, Erich von Daniken visited El Fuerte and proclaimed that it was a takeoff and landing ramp for ancient spacecraft. (One can hardly blame him; take a look into the valley below and you'll see a large flying saucer that has landed – and remains – on the grounds of Achira Sierra Resort!)

In fact, no one knows the exact purpose of El Fuerte. The site has been radiocarbon dated at approximately 1500 BC. There are no standing buildings, but the remains of 500 dwellings have been discovered in the immediate vicinity and ongoing excavation reveals more every day. The main site, which is almost certainly of religious significance, is a 100m-long stone slab with a variety of sculpted features: seats, tables, a conference circle, troughs, tanks, conduits and *hornecinos* (niches), which are believed to have held idols. Zoomorphic designs on the slab include a raised relief of a puma and numerous serpents, which probably represented fertility. Most intriguing are the odd parallel grooves that appear to shoot off into the sky and inspired von Daniken's UFO launch-ramp hypothesis.

About 300m down an obscure track behind the main ruin is El Hueco, a sinister hole in the ground that appears all the more menacing by the concealing vegetation and sloping ground around it. It's almost certainly natural, but three theories have emerged about how it might have been used: that it served as a water storage cistern; that it functioned as an escape-proof prison; or that it was part of a subterranean communication system between the main ruin and its immediate surroundings. El Hueco has been partially explored, but the project was abandoned when excavators heard mysterious sounds emanating from the walls. Openings of suspected side passages are now blocked with earth.

El Fuerte is open daily 9 am to 5 pm. Admission for foreigners is US$2 (students

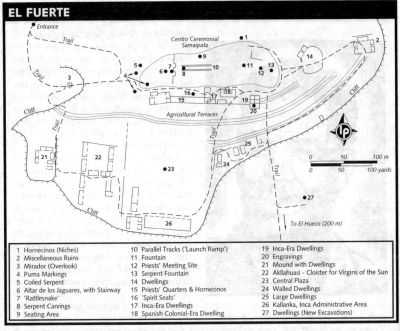

EL FUERTE

- Entrance
- Trail
- Centro Ceremonial Samaipata
- Cliff
- Trail
- Agricultural Terraces
- Trail
- Cliff
- To El Hueco (200 m)

0   50   100 m
0   50   100 yards

1	Hornecinos (Niches)	10	Parallel Tracks ('Launch Ramp')	19	Inca-Era Dwellings
2	Miscellaneous Ruins	11	Fountain	20	Engravings
3	Mirador (Overlook)	12	Priests' Meeting Site	21	Mound with Dwellings
4	Puma Markings	13	Serpent Fountain	22	Akllahuasi - Cloister for Virgins of the Sun
5	Coiled Serpent	14	Dwellings	23	Central Plaza
6	Altar de los Jaguares, with Stairway	15	Priests' Quarters & Hornecinos	24	Walled Dwellings
7	'Rattlesnake'	16	'Spirit Seats'	25	Large Dwellings
8	Serpent Carvings	17	Inca-Era Dwellings	26	Kallanka, Inca Administrative Area
9	Seating Area	18	Spanish Colonial-Era Dwelling	27	Dwellings (New Excavations)

US$1). On weekends, snacks and refreshments are served from trailers outside the entrance.

Getting There & Away Hitching from Samaipata is easiest on weekends – especially Sunday – but the 20km roundtrip walk also makes a rewarding day trip. Follow the main highway back toward Santa Cruz for 3.5km and turn right at the sign pointing uphill to 'Ruinas de El Fuerte.' From there, it's a scenic 5km to the summit. Watch for small condors, and in the morning and afternoon for the flocks of commuting parakeets that chatter overhead.

Taxis for the roundtrip, including a 1½-hour stop at the ruins, cost US$12 for up to four people.

La Pajcha
A series of three beautiful waterfalls on a turbid mountain river, La Pajcha has a sandy beach for swimming and some inviting campsites. It lies 42km (one to two hours by jeep) south of Samaipata, toward San Juan, then 7km on foot off the main road. The site is now privately owned and visitors are charged a small fee to visit and swim there. You'll occasionally find transportation from Samaipata, but unless you have guaranteed transportation back, take camping gear and plenty of food. Also see Organized Tours in Samaipata.

Pampagrande
An especially nice spot is Pampagrande, which is surrounded by a desertlike landscape of cactus and thorny scrubland. There are no hotels, but the Dominican friar Hermano Andres (☎ 0911-3155 in Pampagrande or 0944-6011 in Samaipata) operates a basic bunkhouse with cooking facilities. He also guides informal and highly worthwhile tours into the

Ché Guevara – 'The Most Complete Man'

Ernesto 'Ché' Guevara de la Serna was born on June 14, 1928, in Rosario, Argentina, to wealthy middle-class parents. He qualified as a doctor at the University of Buenos Aires, but his conscience was awakened at an early age. Idealistically, he decided that personal sacrifice and violent revolution were the only ways to create an equal society, and rejecting his comfortable life, he set off to travel penniless around Latin America.

His travels took him to Guatemala, where in 1954 he held a minor position in the Communist government of Jacobo Arbenz. It was around this time that he earned his nickname, Ché, after the Argentine habit of punctuating sentences with that word, meaning 'buddy.' After the CIA-aided overthrow of Arbenz the following year, he fled to Mexico, where he and his first wife, Peruvian socialist Hilda Gadea, met Fidel Castro. Guevara decided his calling was to bring about a worldwide socialist revolution, first by overthrowing the administration of Fulgencio Batista in Cuba, which was accomplished on January 2, 1959, after much struggle and bloodshed on both sides.

Through the late 1950s, Guevara worked as a doctor, military commander and adviser in Castro's revolutionary forces. In 1959, Castro appointed him president of the Banco Nacional de la Cuba, and in 1961 he became the Minister of Industry and was responsible for land redistribution and industrial nationalization. He persuaded Castro to ally Cuba with other Communist nations.

What happened then is rather mysterious. In 1965, the ever-zealous Guevara decided to take his Marxist message to Africa. Before he left, Castro required him to sign a resignation from his affiliation with the Cuban government. While Guevara was in the Congo, Castro made public Guevara's resignation, making it clear that his African activities were not sanctioned by the Cuban government.

When he returned to Cuba in 1965, feeling betrayed and disappointed with Castro's bureaucratization of the Marxist ideal, Ché turned back to Latin America. The following year, with a

---

surrounding hills and imparts his extensive knowledge of the local flora and fauna (especially birds and snakes). The only charge for these tours is a donation to the church and its many good causes, so if you've enjoyed yourself, please don't skimp. For meals there's only the small eatery near the market, three blocks north of the plaza.

Micros to Pampagrande leave from Santa Cruz late in the afternoon; they leave for the return journey at 7 am daily.

Archaeological Sites

The Samaipata region abounds in painted caves and semi-explored archaeological sites, including examples at Mairana, Pampagrande, Mataral, Saipina and others.

Ché Guevara – 'The Most Complete Man'

motley band of guerrillas, he set up a base at the farm Ñancahuazú, 250km southwest of Santa Cruz, in hopes of fomenting revolution. Marching through the rural lands of western Santa Cruz department, he attempted to convince the local campesinos that they were in fact oppressed, and to inspire them to social rebellion. Rather than being supported, however, he was either ignored or met only with suspicion, and not even the local Communist party would take up his cause, or even recognize it.

The rejection took its toll. On October 8, 1967, when he was captured near La Higuera by the CIA-trained troops of Bolivian military dictator René Barrientos Ortuño, Guevara wasn't the T-shirt icon of his sympathizers, but a pathetically emaciated figure, suffering at the age of 39 from chronic asthma, arthritis and malnutrition. He was taken to a schoolroom in La Higuera and, just after noon the next day, was executed by the Bolivian army.

Ché's body was flown to Vallegrande, where it was displayed until the following day in the hospital laundry room. Local women noted an uncanny resemblance to the Catholic Christ and took locks of his hair as mementos. His hands, which were cut off to prevent fingerprint identification, were smuggled to Cuba by a Bolivian journalist and remain there in an undisclosed location.

The same night, he was buried with his comrades in an unmarked grave to deny him a place of public homage. In 1995, General Vargas, one of the soldiers who carried out the burial, revealed that the grave was beneath the airstrip in Vallegrande. The Bolivian and Cuban governments called for exhumation, which resulted in the July 13, 1997, return of Ché's body to Cuba. He was officially reburied in Santa Clara de Cuba on October 17, 1997.

Ché's final speech, relayed from the Bolivian forests via the Tri-Continental Conference in Havana in April 1967, became a rallying cry around the world: 'Wherever death may surprise us, let it be welcome, provided that this, our battle cry, may have reached some receptive ear and another hand be extended to wield our weapons and other men be ready to intone the funeral dirge with the staccato singing of machine guns and new battle cries of war and victory. *Venceremos* (We shall overcome).'

According to philosopher Jean-Paul Sartre, Ché Guevara was 'the most complete man of our age.' Ché's international appeal, however, rests in his greatest quotation, which transcends any political ideology and taps into universal spirituality: 'I'm not a liberator – they do not exist. Only the people can achieve their own liberation.'

For more on Ché's extraordinary life – straight from the horse's mouth – look for *Bolivian Diary*, which was written during the final months of his life, or his myth-shattering book *The Motorcycle Diaries* (translated by Ann Wright, Verso, 1995), which presents a less politically correct side of this enduring legend. A recent attempt to follow his South American escapades by motorbike is chronicled in *Chasing Ché*, by Patrick Symmes.

SANTA CRUZ & AROUND

Access is extremely difficult, but if you're adequately motivated, it's simply a matter of speaking with locals or just exploring.

VALLEGRANDE
☎ 0942

Set in the Andean foothills at 2100m, Vallegrande enjoys a lovely temperate climate. Like most rural towns in Bolivia, life starts up at about 4:30 am, when the micros start arriving from the campo, delivering people to the markets.

After Ché Guevara was executed in La Higuera, south of Vallegrande, his body was brought to the now-dilapidated hospital laundry here, where graffiti lends its homage to this controversial figure. The revolutionary's body was clandestinely buried beneath the airstrip and stayed there until 1997, when the responsible official admitted to the cover-up (see 'Ché Guevara – "The Most Complete Man"'). Most visitors to the town are passing through on a Ché pilgrimage, but Vallegrande is also a nice spot to relax and walk in the hills.

Information

The *alcaldía* (☎ 2149; fax 2091) is keen to promote tourism in Vallegrande and is happy to answer queries. For cultural or historical information, see the Casa de la Cultura. For information on local rock paintings, fossils and archaeological sites, see Don Lalo Carrasco, president of the Grupo Yungauri; you'll find him at the Librería Acuarela.

Special Events

The daily market in the plaza begins about 5 am, but the weekly *feria* is on Sunday. Nearly every week, there's some sort of small festival at the sports ground featuring traditional music and dancing, and around February 23 the town celebrates its anniversary with various local sports and cultural events. Since the bodies of Ché Guevara and several of his men were recovered from the airport in 1997, the town has also celebrated an annual Ché Guevara festival, featuring folk art and cultural activities.

Places to Stay & Eat

Vallegrande has a growing number of places to stay, so you're unlikely to be without accommodations. The *Alojamiento Teresita* (☎ 2151; *Escalante/Mendoza 107*), *Hotel Copacabana* (☎ 2014; *Escalante/Mendoza 100*) and *Residencial Vallegrande* all charge US$4 to US$5 per person. *Hotel Sede Ganaderos* (☎ 2176; *Bolívar 115*) charges US$8 per person for rooms with private baths, including breakfast, and it's the best place in town to look for the latest tourist information.

Among the restaurant choices are the chicken joint *La Casita*, near the cathedral; *La Chujlla*, near the post office, which charges US$1.50 for an almuerzo; and *El*

Mirador, on El Pichacu near La Cruz, where you'll find trout, pork, steak and other carnivorous goodies for around US$3. The cheap pensión, *Los Chinos*, near the police station, serves almuerzos and cenas for about US$1.

Getting There & Away

From the terminal in Santa Cruz, buses leave for Vallegrande at around 9 am to 2 pm (seven hours, US$6). There may also be a later bus, but don't count on it. From Samaipata, an unreliable Vallegrande bus leaves at about 2 pm. If you're hitching, get off at Mataral, 55km north of Vallegrande, and wait there for something headed south. From Cochabamba (11 hours, US$7), buses leave several times weekly in the morning. Buses leave for Cochabamba from near the market in the late afternoon or evening on Monday, Friday and Sunday.

PUCARÁ & LA HIGUERA

To reach La Higuera, the site of Ché Guevara's final struggle and execution, you must first go to Vallegrande and catch a taxi (US$2) or camión (US$1) to Pucará. Camiones leave around 8 am – or when full – from a couple of blocks uphill from the market. For a taxi, ask around on Calle Pedro Montano, near the school.

On the plaza in Pucará, a grizzled campesino runs the local bar/tienda, and his daughter serves meals in a basic *comedor*. They're both very kind, and if you buy the man a couple of beers, he'll probably start talking about Ché or suggest people who rent horses to go to La Higuera. They also have a room to rent on the roof at the back of the house, with marvelous views over the mountains and the upper Río Grande. From Pucará, the trip to La Higuera requires seven or eight hours on foot, five hours on horseback or a fortuitous taxi ride or hitch (one hour, US$0.50). Along the route, signposts point out sites of historic interest that relate to Ché.

Approaching La Higuera, you can see the long *barranca* where Ché was captured. Apart from that, there's little to recall the incident but the schoolroom – now the local clinic – where Ché was kept before being executed. It's the yellow building just off the plaza, with a solar panel on the roof.

La Higuera has few amenities, but there is a small *bar/shop* where you can buy a beer and converse with locals about the historical events – and also about the devoted outsiders who turn up every October for the anniversary of the shootout. La Higuera has no formal accommodations, so you may wind up camping, but unless you're invited to do otherwise, select a secluded spot outside the village.

Eastern Lowlands

The vast, sparsely populated lowlands of the Bolivian Oriente take in all of crescent-shaped southeastern Bolivia. The region is bounded on the west by the foothills of the Cordillera Oriental, on the north by Llanos de Guarayos, and on the south and east by the international boundaries of Paraguay and Brazil.

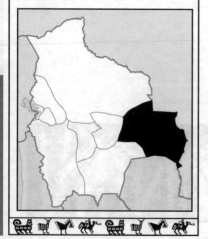

The land is generally flat, broken by long, low ridges and odd monolithic mountains. Much of the territory lies soaking under vast marshes such as the Bañados del Izozog (now part of the Parque Nacional Kaa-Iya del Gran Chaco) and the magnificent Pantanal on the Brazilian frontier. Mostly, however, it serves as a transition zone between the hostile, thorny Chaco scrubland in the south and the low, jungle-like forests and savannas of the Amazon Basin to the north.

The film *The Mission*, which was set in the South American Jesuit missions, awakened an interest in Jesuit work in the continent's interior regions. Perhaps the height of mission architecture is represented in the unique and well-preserved churches of southeastern Bolivia. The most interesting and accessible are those at Concepción, San Javier, San Miguel de Velasco, Santa Ana de Velasco, San Rafael de Velasco and San José de Chiquitos, all of which lie in the lowlands north and east of Santa Cruz.

Culturally and economically, the Oriente looks toward Brazil rather than La Paz, and the 'Death Train' between Santa Cruz and Quijarro on the Brazilian border is its lifeline; over this dilapidating link flows a stream of largely contraband commerce and undocumented imports.

History

In the days when eastern Bolivia was still unsurveyed and largely unorganized territory, the Jesuits established an autonomous religious state in Paraguay. From there they spread outwards, founding missions and venturing into wilderness previously unexplored by other Europeans. The northern reaches of this territory were inhabited by tribes of Indians- including the Chiquitanos, Chiriguanos, Moxos, and Guaraníes – whose descendants inhabit the area to the present day.

Each mission became an experiment in communal living for the Indians, who had

The Jesuits & the Transformation of Lowland Culture

Upon the arrival of the Jesuit missionaries, the native Chiquitano Indians, traditionally nomadic hunters and gatherers, were instructed in European agricultural techniques and animal husbandry and successfully integrated into a predominantly agricultural economy. The reverse also held true: The native inhabitants, with more than a millennium of nomadic existence behind them, showed the Europeans how to adapt to the demanding tropical environment. Unlike some of their contemporaries, the Jesuits were wise enough to heed the Indians' suggestions, and as a result the missions grew. Over the years a trade network was established between these communities and the Aymará and Quechua villages in the altiplano. Beeswax, cotton, honey, textiles and indigenous artwork were exchanged for imported goods and raw silver mined in the highlands.

The Indians also were exposed to and inculcated with Christianity. Although subtle at first, the cumulative effect was that the new religion eventually obliterated any trace of their original tenets. To this day, almost nothing is known of the beliefs and practices of these tribes prior to the arrival of the Jesuits.

In addition to economic and religious ventures, the Jesuits promoted cultural and educational expansion among the tribes, cautiously avoiding the too typical 'all or nothing' approach. The Jesuits sought to incorporate the best of both cultures, and to an astonishing extent succeeded. With Jesuit training, the Indians became accomplished artisans and produced outstanding work in cloth, silver and wood, even handcrafting the renowned harps and violins that still play a prominent role in traditional Paraguayan music. They also became formidable artists: At the height of this revolutionary cultural transition, the inhabitants of the missions were performing concerts, dances and plays that rivaled the best of Europe – and this in a wilderness completely cut off from the outside world. Each mission had its own complete orchestra, furnished with handcrafted instruments, in many cases qualitatively superior to their European counterparts. These communities even performed sophisticated Italian Renaissance madrigals and Baroque masques and operas – in the heart of the Bolivian wilderness!

For those interested in learning more about this fascinating culture, two books, both in Spanish, are highly recommended: *Misiones Jesuíticas*, by Jaime Cisneros, and the preeminent *Las Misiones Jesuíticas de Chiquitos*, edited by Pedro Querejazu.

survived by their wits in a nomadic environment from time immemorial. The Jesuits established what they considered an ideal community hierarchy. Each population unit, known as a *reducción*, was headed by two or three Jesuit priests. A self-directed military unit was attached to each of these reducciones, and for a time the Jesuit armies were the strongest and best trained on the continent. This makeshift military force shielded the area from both the Portuguese in Brazil and the Spanish to the west, creating what was in effect an autonomous theocracy.

Politically, the reducciones were under the nominal control of the *audiencia* of Chacras, and ecclesiastically under the bishop of Santa Cruz, although the relative isolation of the settlements meant that the Jesuits really controlled things. Internally, the settlements were jointly administered by two or three priests and a council of eight natives representing specific tribes (a rare example of Colonial-era power sharing) who met daily to monitor the progress of the community. A less altruistic motive for the Indians' cooperation was that those who elected to live in the missions (residence was voluntary, not enforced) could escape the harsh *encomienda* system or, worse still, outright slavery that awaited them elsewhere.

The mission settlements reached their apex under Father Martin Schmidt, an indefatigable Swiss priest who not only built the missions at San Javier, Concepción and San

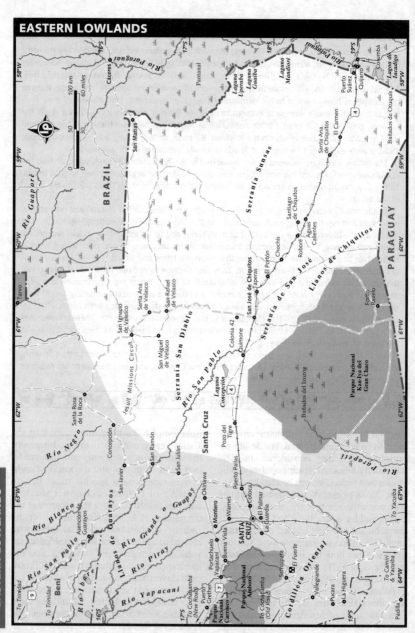

EASTERN LOWLANDS

Rafael, but also designed many of the altars, created the musical instruments, acted as the chief music master and composer for the reducciones, as well as publishing a Spanish-Chiquitano dictionary! Unfortunately, Schmidt was among those later expelled from the region and died in Europe in 1772.

Ironically, the growing strength of the Jesuits proved their eventual undoing. By the mid-1700s political strife in Europe had escalated into a power struggle between the Church and the governments of France, Spain and Portugal. When the Spanish in South America fully realized the extent of Jesuit influence and got wind of all the wealth being produced in the wilderness, they decided the Jesuits had usurped too much power from the State. Portuguese slave traders were encroaching westward as Spanish imperial troops marched eastward to fortify the vague eastern border of Alto Perú. Caught in the military-political crossfire, the lucrative Jesuit missions proved easy pickings for the Spanish. In 1767, swept up in a whirlwind of political babble and religious dogma, the missions were disbanded, and King Carlos III signed the Order of Expulsion, which evicted the Jesuits from the continent.

In the wake of the Jesuit departure, the carefully managed balance between the Europeans and local peoples shifted dramatically. The Spanish overlords, after realizing that their newly acquired lands were sources of neither unlimited mineral wealth nor slave labor for the mines of Potosí, essentially abandoned the settlements, allowing them to decline. Without the Jesuits' adeptness at benevolently integrating the two cultures, the Indians soon left, and the towns became little more than agricultural backwaters, their amazing churches standing as mute testimony to the incredible experiment that ended so abruptly.

During the period leading up to Bolivian independence in 1825, the eastern regions of the Spanish colonies were largely ignored. Possession of the hostile lowlands and the hazy boundaries between Alto Peru, the Viceroyalty of La Plata and Portuguese territory was of little concern. Although agricul-ture was thriving around Santa Cruz, the Spanish remained intent upon extracting every scrap of mineral wealth that could be squeezed from the rich and more hospitable highlands.

Jesuit Missions Circuit

The vast expanses of the Oriente, Bolivia's eastern lowlands, may at first glance appear to offer little to the traveler. But in fact, some of the country's richest cultural and historic accomplishments are found within a seven-town region known as Las Misiones Jesuíticas, the Jesuit Missions circuit.

The seven towns of San Javier, Concepción, San Ignacio de Velasco, Santa Ana, San Miguel, San Rafael, and San José de Chiquitos compose this circuit. The main attractions in most of these villages are, of course, the mission churches, whose incongruous architecture once represented a Christian voice in the wilderness. To travel through the entire circuit takes five or six days, but it's one of Bolivia's most rewarding excursions.

Hidden in obscurity for more than two centuries, the area was raised to international prominence by the 1986 film *The Mission*, which gave impetus to the growing interest in the unique synthesis of Jesuit and native Chiquitano Indian culture and society in the South American interior. Five years later, UNESCO declared the region a World Heritage site. Thanks largely to a painstaking 25 years of restoration work by the late architect Hans Roth and his team of German and Swiss experts, all but one of the magnificent, centuries-old mission churches of these towns have been restored to their original splendor.

The Jesuit circuit can be traversed either clockwise or counterclockwise: that is, going by bus from Santa Cruz to San José de Chiquitos, or by train to San José de Chiquitos and then between the missions by bus or by hitching.

Organized Tours

Among the several Santa Cruz agencies offering tours through the Jesuit Missions circuit are Selva (☎ 332725; Bolívar 262); Fremen (☎ 338535), on Cañoto at 21 de Mayo; and Rosario Tours (☎ 369656; Arenales 193).

SAN RAMÓN
☎ 0965

Although dusty San Ramón lacks a mission-era church, it's a significant crossroads between Santa Cruz, Trinidad, the missions and Brazil. It may be the site of a new gold mine, but anything taken out of the ground is quickly transported somewhere else.

Hotel Manguarí (☎ 6011), two blocks from the plaza on the Trinidad road, charges US$6 per person for basic facilities. For meals, wander the few meters to the recommended *Boliche de Arturo*.

Buses to Trinidad pass between 10 pm and midnight, as do those headed east to San Ignacio. The first bus leaves for Santa Cruz at 7 am, but camiones also run relatively frequently.

SAN JAVIER
☎ 0963

San Javier, the oldest mission on the circuit, was founded in 1691. Martin Schmidt arrived in 1730 and founded the region's first music school and workshop to produce violins, harps and harpsichords. He also designed the present church, which was constructed between 1749 and 1752. It sits on a forested ridge with a commanding view over the surrounding low hills. Restoration work moved along slowly on a meager budget, but the church was finally completed in 1992. The newly restored building appears pleasantly old.

San Javier is also proud of its cheese factory, which you can visit. In addition, there are some inviting hot springs that lie 14km northwest of town; you can reach them on a motorcycle taxi for US$7.50. A farther 6km along is a pool and waterfall, Los Tumbos de Suruquizo, which is suitable for swimming.

Currently, this pleasant little town is becoming a repository for holiday homes that belong to wealthy Cruceño families.

Places to Stay & Eat

Cabañas Totaitu (☎ 5063), easily the nicest accommodations in the missions, occupies a dairy farm 4km northwest of town. Cabañas for four/six/eight people cost US$75/95/110 on weekends, with a US$20 discount on weekdays. Camping is also available here. Amenities include a pool, golf and tennis. Hikers can do some lovely day walks, and there are horses and mountain bikes for rent to explore the area. The booking office (☎ 345452; fax 344700) is in the Centro Comercial Paititi, on Independencia at Paititi, in Santa Cruz.

In town itself, you can choose between *Ame-Tauna* ('welcome friend' in Guaraní), on the plaza, which charges US$6.50 per person for comfortably cool rooms and shared facilities, and *Alojamiento San Javier* (☎ 5038), which has simple rooms for US$4.80 per person. Offering the most amenities is the more upscale *Gran Hotel El Reposo del Guerrero* (☎ 5022) – yes, the 'warrior's rest.'

Restaurants include *El Turista*, frequented by mission-bound tour groups, as well as the more down-to-earth *La Pascana*, *El Snack* and the highly regarded *El Ganadero*.

Getting There & Away

All buses between Santa Cruz and San Ignacio pass through San Javier, 68km west of Concepción (one hour, US$1) and 229km from Santa Cruz (five hours, US$5).

CONCEPCIÓN
☎ 0964

Concepción lies 182km west of San Ignacio in an agricultural and cattle-ranching area. The main appeal is the friendliness and tranquility of the village. Possibly because it's the nerve center for all the mission restoration projects, the church, which was founded in 1709, has been excessively restored, and parts of it appear to have fallen prey to kitsch tendencies, with gaudy plastic and Disneylike

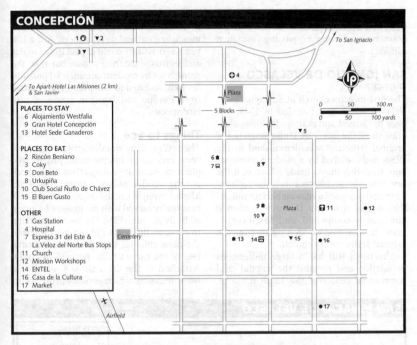

CONCEPCIÓN

PLACES TO STAY
6 Alojamiento Westfalia
9 Gran Hotel Concepción
13 Hotel Sede Ganaderos

PLACES TO EAT
2 Rincón Beniano
3 Coky
5 Don Beto
8 Urkupiña
10 Club Social Ñuflo de Chávez
15 El Buen Gusto

OTHER
1 Gas Station
4 Hospital
7 Expreso 31 del Este &
   La Veloz del Norte Bus Stops
11 Church
12 Mission Workshops
14 ENTEL
16 Casa de la Cultura
17 Market

To San Ignacio

To Apart-Hotel Las Misiones (2 km)
& San Javier

Plaza

5 Blocks

Plaza

Cemetery

Airfield

0   50   100 m
0   50   100 yards

décor. Despite the intimidating signs on the gate, it's interesting to visit the restoration workshops behind the mission, where most of its fine replicas and restored artworks were – and continue to be – crafted.

Places to Stay & Eat
Concepción's choice of budget accommodations includes *Alojamiento Westfalia* (not recommended unless you relish drunken noise at all hours) and *Residencial 6 de Agosto*, both of which charge around US$5 per person. The most upscale lodging is at the three-star *Gran Hotel Concepción* (☎ 3031), which charges US$23/31 for singles/doubles. It features a nice patio with an exotic garden and carved wooden pillars reminiscent of the Jesuit style. The *Hotel Sede Ganaderos* (☎ 3055) is a good value and recommended as well.

Concepción is also attempting to capitalize on the region's pleasant countryside ambience and historical heritage with the deluxe

Apart-Hotel Las Misiones (☎ 3021), just out of town. In Santa Cruz, book through Señora Carmen Flores de Ribero at Exprinter (☎ 03-335133; fax 03-324876).

Recommended restaurants include the *Coky*, the inexpensive *Urkupiña*, the *Rincón Beniano*, *Don Beto*, *El Buen Gusto* and *Club Social Ñuflo de Chávez*, which has bargain set meals, music on Friday nights and bats in the rafters. All are found in the central area.

Getting There & Away
All buses between Santa Cruz (four hours, US$6) and San Ignacio pass through Concepción, stopping on the main road about 1km from the town center (only buses destined for Concepción actually enter the center). Coming from Trinidad, take a Santa Cruz bus and get off at San Ramón, where you can pick up a bus to Concepción and points east. Micros leave for San Javier (one hour, US$1) and Santa Cruz (six hours,

EASTERN LOWLANDS

US$5) daily at 7 am and 2 and 6 pm. Otherwise, wait near the gasoline station and flag down whatever may be passing (usually a camión).

SAN IGNACIO DE VELASCO
☎ 0962

The first mission church at San Ignacio de Velasco, which was founded in 1748, was once the largest and perhaps the most elaborate of all the missions. Unfortunately, the original structure was demolished in the 1950s and replaced by a modern abomination. Realizing they'd made a hash of it the first time, the architects razed the replacement and designed a reasonable facsimile of the original structure. This new version is now nearly completed, and has incorporated the altar and wooden pillars from the original 18th-century church.

The town still has a large indigenous population and remains the 'capital' and commercial center of the Jesuit missions.

Along with San Javier, it is also falling prey to Brazilian-influenced agribusiness, commercialization and development. Just a few years ago, visitors could expect to see mules and burros wandering about, but now the scene is set by modern commercial pursuits, Jet Skis on Laguna Guapomó and hunters from Europe and Japan in search of rare bird species.

Things to See

The several large wooden crosses that have been erected at intersections just off the plaza create an appealing effect. Also check out the wooden pillars in front of the Casa Miguel Areijer on the plaza; one pillar is beautifully carved with the image of a group of Bolivian musicians. The owner intended to carve all the posts, but the city preferred the plain colonial style, and the municipal fate of the carved pillar remains in doubt. Attached to the Casa de la Cultura is a small museum, which is noteworthy for its

SAN IGNACIO DE VELASCO

Laguna Guapomó

To Concepción

Plaza

Santa Cruz
La Paz
Sucre
Cochabamba
Oruro
Potosí

24 de Septiembre
31 de Julio
Pasaje Central
6 de Agosto

To San Miguel
To Santa Ana

San Ignacio International Airport

PLACES TO EAT
5 Restaurant Acuario
11 Snack Marcelito
12 Pizzería Pauline
14 Parrillada Las Palmares
22 Hamburguesas Chachi

OTHER
1 Church
6 Casa Miguel Areijer
9 Post Office
10 Expreso San Ignacio
13 Flota Trans Jao/Trans Brasil
18 Police
19 Market
20 Flota Transical Velasco
21 Flota Trans Bolivia
   (Micros to San Miguel & San Rafael)
23 ENTEL
24 Veloz del Este Micro Stop
25 Town Gate Shrine
26 Camión Stop
27 Expreso 31 del Este
28 Kiosk

PLACES TO STAY
2 Casa Suiza
3 Hotel 31 de Julio
4 Hotel Palace
7 Plaza Hotel
8 Hotel Misión
15 Apart-Hotel San Ignacio
16 Hotel Guapomó
17 Hotel Oriental

0   100   200 m
0   100   200 yards

EASTERN LOWLANDS

collection of musty, centuries-old musical instruments.

Only 700m from the church – and visible from the plaza – is the imposing Laguna Guapomó reservoir, where you can swim or rent a boat and putter around.

Places to Stay

Because San Ignacio is the commercial heart of the missions district, there's a choice of accommodations. The nicest place in town is the *Apart-Hotel San Ignacio* (☎ 2157), which charges US$18 for a double with bath and breakfast. *Casa Suiza*, seven blocks west of the plaza, has rooms for US$10 per person, with meals. The proprietor, Señora Cristina, speaks German and Spanish and can organize horseback riding, fishing trips and visits to surrounding haciendas. She also has a wonderful library.

Hotel Palace (☎ 2063) and *Plaza Hotel* (☎ 2035), both on the plaza, charge US$6.60 per person. Other basic and inexpensive possibilities include *Alojamiento Guapomó* (☎ 2094); *Hotel Oriental* (☎ 2150), on Calle 24 de Septiembre; *Hotel 31 de Julio*; and *Hotel Misión*.

Places to Eat

On the plaza are *Restaurant Acuario*, which specializes in *asados griegos* (Greek barbecue – a variation on *parrillada*); *Pizzería Pauline*, serving acceptable pizza (served by a waiter straight from the cast of *La Cage aux Folles*); and *Snack Marcelito*, with more down-to-earth offerings. *Parrillada Las Palmares* serves up beef dishes and *Hamburguesas Chachi*, 2½ blocks south of the plaza, also does a range of snacks. You'll also find decent meals at the *market*, one block west and three blocks south of the plaza. Note that on Sunday everything is locked up tight except Snack Marcelito, which on the Sabbath dispenses only sinful ice cream!

Getting There & Away

Air From Santa Cruz, TAM (US$30) flies weekly on Wednesday morning. In theory, Lloyd Aéreo Boliviano (LAB) also services San Ignacio from Santa Cruz, departing Monday, Wednesday and Friday at 7:30 am, but the flights are frequently canceled at the last minute. The fare on any of these services ranges from US$30 to US$50. To check on departures, phone ☎ 181 in Santa Cruz. TransBrasil connects San Ignacio with Cáceres, in Brazil.

Bus Bus travelers to San Ignacio will want to cover their luggage to prevent it from arriving in a thick coating of red dust. Most buses and micros leave from near the market. At least 10 flotas offer transportation between Santa Cruz and San Ignacio (11 hours, US$8.40) via San Javier, Concepción and Santa Rosa de la Roca. Most are based near the bus terminal in Santa Cruz. Flotas Universal and Chiquitano (☎ 360320) and Trans-Bolivia compete with the more commodious Expreso Misiones del Oriente (☎ 03-467878; Avenida Virgen de Cotoca 235), which has departures for San Ignacio from Santa Cruz at 8 am and 8 pm daily. Note that the only rest stop is at Cotoca, 19km outside Santa Cruz, so deal with all your bodily necessities there. Some buses continue from San Ignacio to San Miguel (one hour, US$1).

Coming from Trinidad, take a Santa Cruz bus and get off at San Ramón (usually in the middle of the night); there you can hitch or wait for an eastbound bus to San Ignacio.

In the dry season, the Santa Cruz bus companies Veloz del Norte, Transical Velasco, Expreso 31 del Este and Trans-Brasil operate buses between the mission towns. Transical Velasco and Trans-Brasil also leave San Ignacio daily from early to mid-morning for San Matías, on the Brazilian border, where you'll find connections to the Brazilian towns of Cáceres and Cuiabá. The Flota Trans-Bolivia micro departs daily to San Miguel (1/2 hour, US$1.25), San Rafael (one hour, US$1.25) and Santa Ana around 8 am, passing through dusty but scenic campo and marshland that is slated to be included in a new national park, called Parque Nacional Lomerío.

EASTERN LOWLANDS

SAN MIGUEL DE VELASCO

The village of San Miguel de Velasco, lost in the scrub 38km from San Ignacio, seems to be permanently on siesta. Its church was founded in 1721 by the Jesuit fathers Francisco Hernán and Felipe Suárez and is, according to the late Hans Roth, the most accurately restored of all the Bolivian Jesuit missions. Its spiral pillars, carved wooden altar with a flying San Miguel, extravagant golden pulpit, religious artwork, toylike bell tower and elaborately painted façade are simply superb.

Although not designed by Martin Schmidt, the church does reflect his influence and is generally considered the most beautiful of Bolivia's Jesuit missions. During the restoration, which took place from 1978 to 1984, Hans Roth and his colleagues set up workshops and trained local artisans, probably much as the Jesuits did two centuries earlier. The restoration artisans remained and now work in cooperatives making furniture and carvings, such as small carved-cedar chests painted in pastels. Their pieces are also available in Santa Cruz.

The best time to photograph the church is in the morning light. The nightly mass at 7 pm will also provide a pleasant local perspective.

Places to Stay & Eat

The basic but acceptable *Alojamiento Pascana*, on the plaza, charges US$3 per person, and the attached restaurant serves simple meals and cold drinks. The *Alojamiento Pardo*, just off the plaza, charges the same, but you may have to chase up the owner to get a room. If you'd prefer to camp, speak with the nuns at the church, who can direct you to a suitable site.

Getting There & Away

The Flota Trans-Bolivia micro leaves daily at 8:30 am for San Ignacio, then returns and leaves at about 10 am for San Rafael. Next it travels back through San Miguel at around noon before returning to San Ignacio. It's also easy to get to San Ignacio with the camionetas that buzz around town honking for passengers in the early morning and after lunch.

SANTA ANA DE VELASCO

The mission at the tiny Chiquitano village of Santa Ana de Velasco, 24km north of San Rafael, was established in 1755. The church, with its earthen floor and palm-frond roof, is more rustic than the others and recalls the preliminary churches constructed by the Jesuit missionaries upon their arrival. In fact, the building itself is post-Jesuit, but the interior contains exquisite religious carvings and paintings.

Given its age, the original structure is in remarkable condition. Sadly, its ongoing 'renovation' is more utilitarian than preservationist and is limited to 'band-aid' repairs made as bits of the building collapse. So far, the work has been done by unskilled labor using cheap modern materials and shoddy techniques, but thanks to well-conceived plans by Roth and others, the church will eventually be professionally restored to its original state.

Getting There & Away

You shouldn't have problems finding transportation from either San Ignacio or San Rafael. Most days, micros run between San Ignacio and San Rafael via Santa Ana. Because most traffic now uses this route, hitching is also a possibility.

SAN RAFAEL DE VELASCO

San Rafael de Velasco lies 132km north of San José de Chiquitos. Founded in 1696, its church was constructed between 1740 and 1748 – the first of the mission churches to be completed in Bolivia. In the 1970s and 1980s, the building was restored by the same Swiss architects responsible for the restoration of the churches in Concepción and San José de Chiquitos.

The interior is particularly beautiful, and the original paintings and woodwork remain intact. The pulpit is covered with a layer of lustrous mica, the ceiling is made of reeds and the spiral pillars were carved from *cuchi* (ironwood or *Argania sideroxylon*) logs. San Rafael is the only mission church to retain the original style, with cane sheathing. Of perhaps the most interest are the lovely music-theme paintings in praise of God along the entrance wall, which include depictions of a harp, flute, bassoon, horn and maracas.

Places to Stay & Eat

At the corner of the main road and the street running south from the church is *Alojamiento San Rafael* (no sign). There's also *Alojamiento La Pascana*, on the plaza. Both are very basic and charge US$3.50 per person.

Getting There & Away

The best place to wait for rides south to San José de Chiquitos (five to six hours) or north to Santa Ana, San Miguel or San Ignacio is on the main road in front of Alojamiento San Rafael. In the morning, buses run in both directions. To reach Santa Ana, use the right fork north of town.

SAN JOSÉ DE CHIQUITOS
☎ 0972

One of the most accessible Jesuit missions, San José de Chiquitos was named for the Chiquitano Indians who were the original

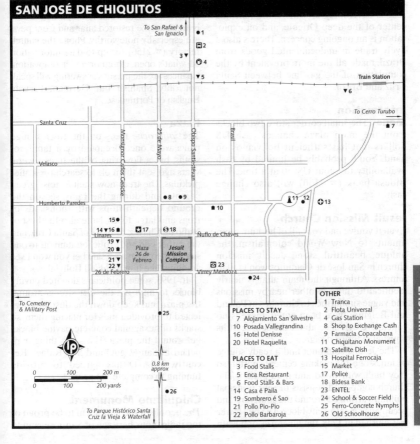

SAN JOSÉ DE CHIQUITOS

To San Rafael & San Ignacio

Santa Cruz

Velasco

Humberto Paredes

Linares

Montsenor Carlos Gericke

25 de Mayo

Obispo Santistevan

Brasil

Train Station

To Cerro Turubo

Nuflo de Cháves

Plaza 26 de Febrero

Jesuit Mission Complex

26 de Febrero

Virrey Mendoza

To Cemetery & Military Post

0.8 km approx

0   100   200 m
0   100   200 yards

To Parque Histórico Santa Cruz la Vieja & Waterfall

PLACES TO STAY
7   Alojamiento San Silvestre
10 Posada Vallegrandina
16 Hotel Denisse
20 Hotel Raquelita

PLACES TO EAT
3   Food Stalls
5   Enca Restaurant
6   Food Stalls & Bars
14 Casa é Paila
19 Sombrero é Sao
21 Pollo Pio-Pio
22 Pollo Barbaroja

OTHER
1   Tranca
2   Flota Universal
4   Gas Station
8   Shop to Exchange Cash
9   Farmacia Copacabana
11 Chiquitano Monument
12 Satellite Dish
13 Hospital Ferrocaja
15 Market
17 Police
18 Bidesa Bank
23 ENTEL
24 School & Soccer Field
25 Ferro-Concrete Nymphs
26 Old Schoolhouse

EASTERN LOWLANDS

inhabitants of the area. Just 4km to the west was the original location of Santa Cruz de la Sierra, but the city that is now Bolivia's second metropolis was moved to its present site soon after its founding in 1561. The Jesuits arrived sometime in the mid-1740s, and construction of the magnificent mission church that today dominates the town was begun around 1750.

San José de Chiquitos surprises its few visitors with the atmosphere and beauty of an Old West frontier town, complete with dusty streets straight out of *High Noon* and footpaths shaded by pillar-supported roofs. Flanked on the south by a low escarpment and on the north by flat, soggy forest, San José is developing into the cattle ranching center of the deep Oriente, and oil exploration is an ongoing concern. There's also a lively trade in undocumented goods from Brazil, made all the more prevalent by the completion of the gas line between Santa Cruz and Brazil.

Information

Money The small corner store two blocks from the main plaza changes cash US dollars if it has sufficient bolivianos on hand. You'll probably be limited by cash availability to about US$50 at a time. The Bidesa bank (☎ 2130) will also change cash.

Jesuit Mission Church

Even if you've had your fill of ho-hum monuments to New World colonialism, the unique, beautiful stone Jesuit mission church in San José de Chiquitos won't fail to impress. Although the main altar is nearly identical to those in other nearby missions and vague similarities to churches in Poland and Belgium have been noted, there is no conclusive evidence about the source of its unusual exterior design.

The Jesuits could not find a ready source of limestone for making cement mortar, so they built with wood and mud plaster. The church compound consists of four principal buildings arranged around the courtyard and occupying an entire city block. The bell tower was finished in 1748, the *funerario*, or 'Death

Chapel,' is dated 1752 and the *parroquio*, or living area, was completed in 1754. It is believed, however, that only the façades were completed before the Jesuits were expelled in 1767. All construction work was done by the Chiquitano Indians under Jesuit direction. The doors, some of the altar work and one magnificent bench seat were handcarved in wood by expert Chiquitano artisans.

Massive renovations and restorations have been underway for the past decade and are still incomplete (this is rather reminiscent of colonial days, when church construction often required an entire lifetime!), and the altar is currently a series of bare, empty niches. Nevertheless, what has been accomplished to date is amazing; the restored altar and front pews are especially noteworthy. Phone the church rectory (☎ 2156) for up-to-date information on what's open, closed or under renovation. Chances are the persons answering will speak not only Spanish but German, French, English or Portuguese.

Plaza

The *toboroche* trees on the town's huge plaza were once occupied by a family of sloths, but a flowering of the trees several years ago sent them off to search for leafier pickings. The trees now shelter noisy green parrots, and during the rainy season the ground beneath hops with thousands of frogs and large toads. Note also the bust of Ñuflo de Chavez, founder of Santa Cruz, and the rather odd and erotic fountain off to one side of the plaza; it's a safe bet you won't see anything like it in highland Bolivia!

In 1993, some politicians donated paving blocks to improve the dirt streets around the plaza and keep down the dust, but neglected to provide funds for placing them, so stacks of hexagonal concrete paving blocks lie around the plaza. The same thing happened in San Miguel and San Rafael. Recently, USAID has agreed to provide funding to complete the project.

Chiquitano Monument

The people of the area seem to be proud of the indigenous heritage of San José, and to

Musicians at Tarabuco's Phujllay celebration

Quechua woman, Cochabamba

Miners' strike, Potosí

Sucre, Bolivia's other capital city

Counting minutes at Bolivian immigration

Mission, San Miguel de Velasco

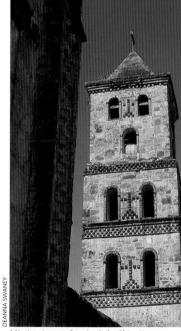

Mission tower, San José de Chiquitos

prove it they've erected a monument of an archetypal Chiquitano maiden with her obligatory water jar at the entrance to town. This also serves as a major meeting spot.

Santa Cruz la Vieja Walk

Just south of town, the road passes beneath an archway supported by bikini-clad ferro-concrete nymphs welcoming you to the old Santa Cruz highway (the route to the original Santa Cruz de la Sierra). These beauties were obviously designed by the same person responsible for the Chiquitano maiden and the plaza fountain. About 1km farther along, through dusty ranchland, you'll pass an abandoned schoolhouse from bygone days. After 3km or so, the road enters more jungle-like vegetation, which supports throngs of squawking green parrots.

Along this road, 4km south of town, is the Parque Histórico Santa Cruz la Vieja, on the site of the original Santa Cruz de la Sierra, but there's little to see other than an abandoned guard house. Over the road is a small park where locals go to cool off in a murky green swimming pool. Admission is US$2.20 per person, but the walk itself is more appealing than the pool. In the forest nearby is a waterfall, the source of San José's drinking water; it's a cool spot sheltered from the tropical heat, but swarms of biting insects may limit you to a fleeting visit. Carry insect repellent and wear good shoes and pants to protect your feet and legs from ferocious ants.

If you continue another 2km to 3km up the switchbacks onto the escarpment, you'll have a far-ranging view of San José and the surrounding plains. Farther along are some nice eroded landscapes and a series of lovely waterfalls known as the Cascadas del Suruquizo.

Cerro Turubo

Another possible day takes you to the forested summit of Cerro Turubo, the prominent peak that rises to the east of town. From the top, you'll have one of the finest views in the Eastern Lowlands.

Places to Stay

Alojamiento San Silvestre (☎ 2041), opposite the railway station, charges US$5 per person with breakfast. Double rooms have private baths. Guests may use the pool table, but beware of the stereo system that swallowed South America. The cheapest place is the very basic *Posada Vallegrandina*, which isn't recommended.

Despite its lackadaisical staff, the best place to stay is *Hotel Raquelita* (☎ 2037), on the plaza, which has a laundry service, fans and sparkling clean facilities. The rate schedule is rather complicated, but essentially it works out to about US$5 per person (US$7 with bath), depending on the time of your visit, the number of people in your party and whether or not they size you up as a tourist.

A block north is the more basic *Hotel Denisse* (☎ 2230), on Calle Ñuflo de Chavez, which charges US$4.20 per person.

If you prefer to camp, ask the priest at the mission church whether you can pitch a tent in the courtyard.

Places to Eat

There's a good, clean snack bar in *Hotel Raquelita* where you'll get breakfast for US$0.80, lunches for US$1.50, a mean *guineo con leche* and excellent homemade ice cream. It's also worth a look to see the unusual wall décor, especially the bizarre simian representation of the Uganda General Idi Amin with brightly painted toenails!

Sombrero é Sao (☎ 2033), next door, serves chicken and beef dishes with rice, french fries and salad. It's a great spot to sit outside and down a couple of cold brews. Another decent spot for an evening meal is the cheaper *Casa é Paila* (☎ 2174), around the corner, but it's rarely open. The small attached *artesanía* is open weekdays.

Pollo Pio-Pio, on the Virrey Mendoza side of the plaza, serves up chicken and french fries but is notorious for overcharging foreigners. A better choice is *Pollo Barbaroja*, a few meters farther along. Brazilian influences are in evidence at the *Enca Restaurant*, north of the railway line.

EASTERN LOWLANDS

Watch for the army of lads who emerge from plaza doorways selling *salteñas* in the morning and cheese bread in the afternoon from heaped trays, tellingly recycled from blue Santa Fe lard tins. There are also some informal restaurant stalls near the railway station and along the road toward San Ignacio, north of the railway line, which serve snacks and inexpensive lunch and dinner specials. On Monday, the Mennonites come into town from the colonies and sell homemade cheese, butter, bread and produce.

Getting There & Away

Bus There are currently no bus or micro services between San José de Chiquitos and Santa Cruz, although various government agencies continue to promise 'tourist-class' bus and rail services. At present, you must first reach San Ignacio and pick up transportation from there. On Monday, Wednesday and Friday at 10 am, micros leave for San José de Chiquitos from the market in San Ignacio; they return on Tuesday, Thursday and Saturday.

If you prefer to take your chances with a camión to San Rafael, Santa Ana or San Ignacio, wait at the tranca beyond the railway line 300m north of town. In the dry season, camiones go to San Ignacio with some regularity – there are usually at least a couple every day. Plan on about US$5 per person as far as San Ignacio.

Train The easiest way to travel between San José de Chiquitos and Santa Cruz or Quijarro, both roughly eight hours away, is on the infamous 'Death Train.' Most trains arrive and depart at night, which is a shame because the countryside here – especially to the east of San José de Chiquitos – is the most scenic stretch of the FVA's Red Oriental.

The eastbound *Expreso del Oriente* passes on Monday, Wednesday and Friday at 9 pm, and the westbound goes on Tuesday, Thursday and Saturday at 11 pm. The fare is US$12/10 for 1st/2nd class to either Santa Cruz or Quijarro. The *tren mixto* leaves Santa Cruz on Monday and

Friday at 7:15 pm and arrives in San José de Chiquitos at around 5 am; it leaves less than an hour later and arrives in Quijarro at around 3 pm the next day. The 1st/2nd-class services to Santa Cruz or Quijarro cost US$12/10. The ironically named *tren rápido* passes (very slowly) on Tuesday and Sunday at 9:50 pm eastbound and Monday and Thursday at 9:45 pm westbound, and costs US$11/8 to either end of the line; note however that the days of this service may be numbered.

Freight trains run at any time; in theory you can simply hop into the passenger *bodega* and pay the 2nd-class fare of US$10 to either Santa Cruz or Quijarro, although polite inquiries beforehand are appreciated. The *boletería* opens whenever the ticket seller rolls up and feels ready to work, which may be anytime between 6 am and 3 pm. Buying train tickets is a slow process, and you need to show a passport or *cédula de identidad* for each person traveling (to forestall ticket scalping). Intermediate stations such as San José de Chiquitos receive only a few ticket allotments, and they are sold only on the day of departure (or, in the case of departures in the wee hours, on the previous day).

COLONIA 42

Although not a tourist attraction, the Mennonite colony of Colonia 42, which is 42km north of San José de Chiquitos, makes for an interesting cultural side trip. The highly traditional Mennonites belong to a religious sect founded by Menno Simons, a 16th-century Dutch reformer, and speak a German dialect known as Platt-Deutsch, which is actually more of a German-Dutch hybrid.

Colonia 42 is only one of numerous Mennonite colonies in Bolivia, but it's one of the most conservative. Others are scattered around the Oriente, including Santa Cruz and farther north toward the Beni, and there are colonies throughout Paraguay, northern Argentina and southwestern Brazil.

Despite this colony's Canadian roots, few Bolivian Mennonites – locally known as *menonos* – speak English, and many don't even speak Spanish. They're easily recognized by their dress, as the men all wear hats and identical blue or green overalls, and the women, who are required to appear inconspicuous and unadorned, wear head coverings and plain monochrome knee-length dresses. The Mennonites live in simple farmhouses typical of the North American Midwest and travel about in horse-drawn carts. Most of the farm work is done by hand or by draft animals.

Visitors to the colony should respect the privacy of the colonists. Many prefer not to have their photos taken and a few, especially the women, wish to avoid contact with the outside world.

History

The Mennonites in Colonia 42 originally came from Saskatchewan, Canada, and they set out in search of a place where they could practice their religion, farm their land and live peaceful and self-sufficient lives without the influences of modern society. Originally, they came to rest in Belize, Central America, but hassles with the Belizean government in the mid-70s sent them off in search of a new home.

Recognizing the agricultural potential of the Bolivian Oriente, thousands of Mennonites came to the central regions of South America, including the wilderness north and east of Santa Cruz. They cleared vast tracts of forest and re-created a rustic cross between the north German plain and the North American Midwest in the heart of Bolivia. So far the Bolivian government has appreciated the role that the Mennonites have played in opening up previously uninhabited territory, but as more and more highland Bolivians look toward the Oriente for economic opportunities, their unique situation may become threatened.

Getting There & Away

San José de Chiquitos merchants trade here for milk, cheese, butter and poultry from Colonia 42 on a regular basis. Usually at least one camión does the run each day. If you'd like to ride along, wait at the tranca north of San José de Chiquitos before 9 am;

expect to pay between US$2 and US$3.50 per person for the return trip.

On Monday and Thursday, a local bus leaves San José de Chiquitos at 4am to pick up the Colonia 42 Mennonites and bring them into town for half a day of shopping. At 3 pm it leaves from Hotel Raquelita and returns to the colony, dropping the farmers back at their various homesteads before returning to San José de Chiquitos at around 8 pm. The one-way/roundtrip fare runs US$2.50/3.50.

Far Eastern Bolivia

Between Roboré and San José de Chiquitos the railway line passes through a bizarre and beautiful region of wilderness hills and monoliths. Farther east, along the Brazilian border, much of the landscape lies soaking beneath the wildlife-rich swamplands of the Pantanal, while the southern area of the region is dominated by the equally soggy Bañados del Izozog. This latter wetland area has recently been incorporated in the Parque Nacional Kaa-Iya del Gran Chaco, which is Latin America's largest national park.

ROBORÉ

☎ 0974

The town of Roboré, about four hours along the railway east of San José de Chiquitos, began in 1916 as a military outpost, and the military presence remains a bit overwhelming. You can probably imagine what happens when a lot of bored soldiers posted in the middle of nowhere encounter tourists in a town that rarely sees outsiders. The situation seems to have improved over the past few years, but it's still best not to appear conspicuous.

Things to See & Do

The cool and clean **Río Roboré**, which flows through town, offers some pleasant and refreshing swimming. You may want to move several hundred meters upstream from the bridge to avoid the curious eyes of local crowds. A pleasant day trip will take you to

El Balneario, a mountain stream with a waterfall and natural swimming hole. It's a two-hour walk each way from town, and you'll need a local guide to find it. There's another closer swimming hole that is accessible by taxi for US$1.50 roundtrip.

Culturally, the Jesuit mission at **Santiago de Chiquitos**, 20km from Roboré, is more interesting than San José de Chiquitos. It's set in the hills, and the cooler climate provides a welcome break from the tropical heat of the lowlands. The roundtrip taxi fare from Roboré is US$10 for up to four people. Camiones and military vehicles occasionally do the run from the east end of town for US$1 per person one way.

The 40 to 41°C thermal baths at **Aguas Calientes**, 31km east of Roboré, are popular with Bolivian visitors who believe in their curative powers. The Santa Cruz-Quijarro train stops in Aguas Calientes, and camiones leave from the eastern end of Roboré, charging US$1.10 per person. Taxis charge US$12 for up to four passengers. There are no accommodations, so the baths are best visited on a day trip.

Chochís, two stops along the railway toward San José de Chiquitos, has a lovely church.

Finally, if you're keen to see the best of the landscape between Roboré and San José de Chiquitos, the most convenient station is **El Portón**, which lies immediately west of the spectacular and oft-photographed rock pillar of the same name. There are no tourist facilities, so carry food and camping gear.

Places to Stay & Eat

Roboré's main accommodation option is *Hotel Pacheco* (☎ *2074*), on Calle 6 de Agosto, where doubles cost US$5, US$7 with private baths. The alternative is *Residencial San Martín* (☎ *2192*), on Avenida Ejército Nacional. For meals, apart from the hotels you can check out *Pollo de Oro*, near the railway station. In the evening, it livens up appreciably when the alcohol-assisted celebrants provide a bit of diversion to accompany the inevitable wait for the typical *tren atrasado* (late train)!

Getting There & Away

By train, Roboré lies about four hours west of Quijarro and the same distance (timewise) east of San José de Chiquitos. TAM (☎ 2035) flies from Santa Cruz to San Matías on Friday mornings, returning via Roboré.

PARQUE NACIONAL KAA-IYA DEL GRAN CHACO

In the late 1990s, the local Guaraní people, in conjunction with the Bolivian Ministerio de Desarrollo, the World Bank, the Swiss government, the Wildlife Conservation Society and the Armonía Foundation, succeeded in having their ecological treasure protected in the two million-hectare Parque Nacional Kaa-Iya del Gran Chaco, which is now Latin America's largest national park. The huge and enigmatic Bañados del Izozog wetland, in the heart of this vast wilderness, lies buried in a wild and relatively inaccessible expanse of territory between San José de Chiquitos and the Paraguayan border.

Of the total area, 800,000 hectares belong to the Guaraní people and 300,000 hectares to the neighboring Ayoreos. Currently, the only access into this fabulous region is by 4WD or on foot from El Tinto, on the railway line west of San José de Chiquitos, but expect organized tours from Santa Cruz to begin soon. This is a true wilderness and there are no facilities or services anywhere in the area, but if you enjoy places that recall the Brazilian Pantanal and have a way to get into the area, it's most emphatically worth a visit.

PUERTO SUÁREZ
☎ 0976

If it could only get its act together, Puerto Suárez, set in a watery wilderness with some of the densest wildlife populations on the continent, could be a legitimately profitable and attractive tourist center. Although it's improving, this hot, steamy backwater remains infamous as the place where São Paulo car thieves dump their spoils and 80% of the community is in some way involved in illicit dealings.

Places to Stay

At US$8 for a double, *Hotel Bamby* (☎ 2015), on Avenida 6 de Agosto, probably offers the best value. Alternatively, try the inexpensive *Hotel Sucre* (☎ 2069; *Bolívar 63*), *Frontera Verde* (☎ 2468; *fax 2469*), or *Residencial Puerto Suárez* (☎ 2750; *Bolívar 105*), among numerous others.

Getting There & Away

TAM (☎ 2205) has very popular Tuesday and Saturday morning flights from Santa Cruz to Puerto Suárez (US$59), returning the same afternoon. Call them for flight information in Puerto Suárez. These flights actually land in Corumbá, but passengers intending to cross into Brazil must first return to Bolivia to exit the country before checking into Brazil at the Polícia Federal in Corumbá.

Puerto Suárez is also on the railway line, 15km west of Quijarro.

QUIJARRO
☎ 0978

Quijarro, a muddy collection of shacks at the eastern terminus of the Death Train, sits on slightly higher and drier ground than Puerto Suárez and serves as the border crossing between Bolivia and Corumbá (Brazil). Visitors heading east will be treated to a wonderful preview of Corumbá: From muddy Quijarro, it appears on a hill in the distance, a dream city of sparkling white towers rising above the vast green expanses of the Pantanal. In Mutún, just south of Quijarro, what may be the richest deposits of iron manganese on the continent are currently being developed.

The Bolivian Pantanal

Hotel Santa Cruz in Quijarro organizes boat tours through the wetlands of the Bolivian Pantanal and provides an alternative to the well-visited Brazilian side. A comfortable three-day excursion, including transportation, food and accommodations (on the boat), costs about US$100 per person.

Places to Stay & Eat

The friendly *Hotel Santa Cruz* (☎ 2113), two blocks from the railway station, charges US$12/18 for clean, air-conditioned single/double rooms. The three-star *Hotel Oasis* (☎ 2159) offers pleasant rooms for the same rates. More basic accommodations are available for US$2.50 to US$3 per person at several alojamientos on the left as you exit the railway station; a recommended cheap one is the very spartan *Hotel Carmen*.

The five-star *El Pantanal Hotel Resort & Casino* (☎ 2020; *fax 2290*), sits in the beautiful Arroyo Concepción, 12km from Puerto Suárez and 7km from Corumbá, Brazil. With over 600 hectares of grounds, it sits atop a bluff overlooking the Río Paraguay and the Cidade Branca of Corumbá. All of its 75 rooms have private baths, TV, phones and air conditioning, and guests have access to the swimming pool, Jacuzzi, game rooms, tennis and volleyball courts, child care, indoor tropical gardens (the point of this is lost on many…) and several restaurants, including an Argentine *churrasquería*. Standard two-day, three-night packages, with meals and airport transfers, cost US$120/200, and three-day, four-night packages are US$194/298. The current program may attract Bolivian interest, but foreigners would probably expect more emphasis on the Pantanal and wildlife-viewing.

Lots of good inexpensive restaurants are lined up along the street perpendicular to the railway station entrance.

Getting There & Away

Train By rail, the trip between Quijarro and Santa Cruz takes anywhere from 16 to 23 hours, depending on which train you take. The *Expreso del Oriente* leaves Quijarro on Tuesday and Saturday at 2:15 pm and costs US$17/20.50 in 2nd/1st class. The tren rápido leaves Monday and Thursday at 1:45 pm and costs US$16.70/14.50. The slow and cumbersome tren mixto chugs out Tuesday and Saturday at 6:30 pm. You can buy only 2nd-class tickets, which cost US$12.50. You'll pay the same to ride in a bodega on a freight train.

You may have the same problems buying tickets in Quijarro as in Santa Cruz.

To Brazil When the train pulls into Quijarro, a line of taxis waits to take new arrivals

EASTERN LOWLANDS

to the border. The border post is just 2km from the station, so if you can't bargain the drivers down to something reasonable – say US$0.75 per person – it's a pretty easy walk to the border. Travelers report being charged up to US$10 for Bolivian exit stamps, but this is entirely unofficial; politely explain that you understand there is no official charge for the stamp, and appear prepared to wait until they get real.

Over the bridge, you pass through Brazilian customs. From there, city buses will take you into Corumbá. Brazilian entry stamps are given at the Polícia Federal, at the *rodoviária* (Portuguese for 'bus terminal,' pronounced 'haw-doo-VYAHR-ya'); it's open until 5 pm.

Technically, travelers arriving in Brazil from Bolivia need a yellow fever vaccination certificate. Officials don't always ask for one, but when they do, the rule is inflexibly enforced. In a pinch, a clinic in Corumbá provides the vaccine. You can change US dollars in cash or traveler's checks at the Banco do Brasil, two blocks from Praça Independência.

To reach the Bolivian border from Corumbá, catch a bus from Praça Independência, opposite the cathedral. If you're entering Bolivia, you can change Brazilian reis and US dollars at the frontier (you may have problems with US$100 notes – especially the new ones with the larger portraits

of Benjamin Franklin – which are normally suspected of being counterfeit).

SAN MATÍAS
☎ 0968

The border town of San Matías is the main Bolivian access point into the northern Brazilian Pantanal. Travelers between Cáceres and Bolivia must pick up Brazilian entry or exit stamps from the Polícia Federal office at Rua Antônio João 160 in Cáceres. On the Bolivian side, you'll have to hunt up the immigration officer; otherwise, pick up your entry or exit stamp in Santa Cruz.

For accommodations, you're limited to *Hotel San José*, which charges US$4 per person for basic, stifling rooms. The best restaurant, which serves a very limited menu, is *BB's* (it stands for Bolivia/Brazil – cute).

TAM (☎ 2256) does a return flight between Santa Cruz and San Matías (US$65) on Friday morning. In the dry season, a Trans-Bolivia bus leaves from Cáceres (Brazil) to Santa Cruz (30 hours, US$30), via San Matías (four hours, US$7) at 5 to 6 am daily. Coming from Brazil, get your exit stamp the night before; in San Matías, the bus will stop and wait while you visit immigration (US$1 by taxi from the bus terminal). It's possible to change dollars or reis to bolivianos at the Trans-Bolivia bus office.

Amazon Basin

Although it lies more than 1000km upstream from the great river itself, Bolivia's portion of the Amazon Basin better preserves the classic image many travelers associate with that river than the real thing itself. While Brazilian rain forests continue to suffer heavy depredation, the archetypal Amazon forests of northern Bolivia remain relatively intact. Although facing similar threats, they still offer a glimpse of the deep and mysterious Eden (they've also been called the Green Hell!) that beckons from the glossy pages of travel brochures.

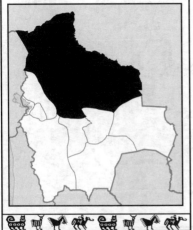

History

The Beni, Pando and surrounding areas have weathered continuous human immigration and boom-bust cycles. Only a few of the original forest-dwelling tribes remain, and even fewer continue their traditional subsistence hunting-and-gathering lifestyles. Indigenous peoples occupying the western regions of the Bolivian Amazon were conquered early on by the Inca.

Then came the Spanish, who wandered all over the Americas chasing rumors of a mystical city of unimaginable wealth, which they called El Dorado (The Gilded One). One such tale was of Paititi, an incredibly opulent land east of the Andean Cordillera near the source of the Río Paraguai. It was said to be governed by a particularly affluent king named El Gran Moxo. Though the would-be looters scoured the region for traces of the coveted booty, they found nothing but a few primitive and hostile tribes and muddy jungle villages. There was neither a single street paved with gold nor a single royal treasury brimming with precious gems and metals. In the mid-17th century, the Spanish turned elsewhere in their quest for El Dorado.

The Missionaries The Spanish may have found nothing in the Moxos region that interested them, but the Jesuits did, seeing an area that was rich in souls that were ripe for the plucking by the messengers of the Christian god. The first significant European penetration of these lowlands was staged by these hardy missionaries, whose first mission was founded at Loreto, in the Moxos region, in 1675.

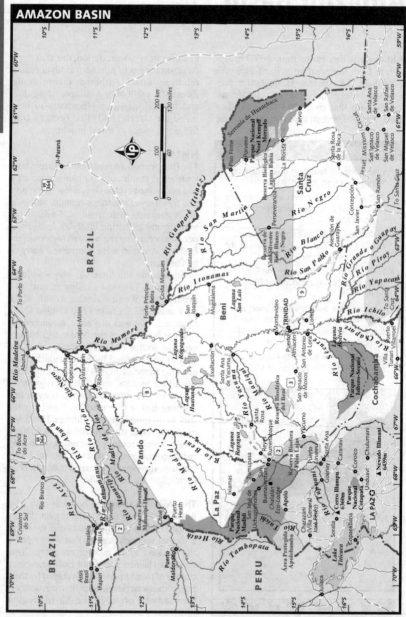

The Jesuits set up a society similar to the one they would establish in the Llanos de Chiquitos and Llanos de Guarayos during the following century. They imposed Christianity and taught the indigenous people European ways – metal and leatherwork, weaving, basketry, writing, reading, printing and so on. They recognized a natural expertise in woodcarving, which eventually produced the brilliant carvings now characteristic of the missions. They also imported herds of cattle and horses to some remote outposts, and, thanks to the prolific natural vegetation, the animals fared well. The descendants of these herds still thrive throughout most of the department.

From the locals, the Jesuits learned about agricultural methods in the tropical and often flooded lowlands. They, in turn, introduced unfamiliar crops, and the Beni today produces bananas, coffee, tobacco, cotton, cacao, peanuts and a host of other warm-weather crops.

After the expulsion of the Jesuits in 1767, the Franciscan and Dominican missionaries, as well as the opportunistic settlers who followed, brought slavery and disease. Other than that, the vast, steamy forests and plains of northern Bolivia saw little activity for 50 years.

The Rubber Boom The migration of the Suárez family from Santa Cruz to Trinidad in the late 19th century marked the beginning of serious economic exploitation of the region. While the senior Suárez was occupied with cattle ranching, young Nicolás Suárez set off to explore the inhospitable wilderness of Bolivia's northern hinterlands (at the time, this included a sizable portion of what is now western Brazil). He developed a substantial business dealing in quinine, derived from the bark of the *cinchona* tree.

When the rubber boom descended upon Amazonian Brazil, it was a simple matter for Suárez to arrange a system for transporting rubber around the Mamoré rapids into Brazil, and then down the Río Madeira to the Amazon and the Atlantic. Before the turn of the century, the Suárez family owned

Rubber trees fueled a 19th century boom.

about six million hectares of lowland real estate. However, a good proportion of these holdings lay in the remote Acre territory, which Bolivia lost to Brazil in 1903. Although a large percentage of the Suárez fortune was lost with the Acre, and Bolivia's rubber boom ground to a halt, the family was by no means devastated.

The Cocaine Trade Less than a century later, a member of the Suárez family came to control another booming industry. Coca, the leaf revered by the highland Indians for its ability to stave off the discomforts of altitude, thirst, hunger, discontent and stress, grows primarily in the Yungas mountains north of La Paz and in the Chapare region of northern Cochabamba department. The Yungas produce the more palatable leaves, while the Chapare crop tastes bitter. Although local Indians prefer the former for everyday consumption, the Chapare coca has an international market. Dried, soaked in kerosene and mashed into a pasty pulp, the leaves are treated with hydrochloric and sulfuric acid until they form a foul-smelling brown base. Further treatment with ether creates cocaine.

So profitable is the modern cocaine industry that as much as 60% of Bolivia's gross national product is derived from it, and the country has become synonymous with large-scale production of illicit substances. By the mid-1980s, US yuppiedom was consuming so much Bolivian cocaine that the US government decided something had to be done about it. Realizing that it would be unpopular to bomb the cocaine users among its own population, the USA pointed an accusing finger at Bolivia and threatened drastic Drug Enforcement Agency (DEA) action should the Bolivian government not cooperate with US military action aimed at curtailing the production of Bolivia's most lucrative export. When US President Ronald Reagan proposed some joint cleaning up of the remote reaches of the Beni and Chapare regions, Bolivian President Victor Paz Estenssoro agreed to go along with the plan.

The operation was prematurely leaked to the press, however, giving remote processing labs sufficient warning to clear out before the bombs arrived. Only minor damage was done, and the US government found itself in a rather embarrassing situation.

In 1987 the Bolivian army noisily raided the ranch of the elusive Roberto Suárez Gómez by helicopter, but failed to make any arrests. In Suárez's absence, the Bolivian government sentenced him to 12 years in prison, and in 1988, Bolivian soldiers, sent in quietly and under cover of night, managed to arrest the cocaine king while he slept.

Modern Bolivian Amazonia Despite all the attention focused on the environment and the drug issue, northern Bolivia is not all cocaine and rain forest. Cattle ranching continues on a large scale, especially in the savannas north and west of Trinidad.

The region's main highways are Amazon tributaries – the Mamoré, Ichilo, Beni, Madre de Dios and Guaporé, to name but a few – which elsewhere would be considered great rivers in their own right. Along these jungle waterways, riverboats, barges, buckets and bathtubs are the predominant methods of transportation for passengers, livestock, freight and vehicles.. Villages are still thin on the ground, and some remote tribes have had only minimal contact with modern civilization. All that is changing, however, with the recent spate of road construction, leading to an influx of highland settlers and a subsequent upsurge in logging and land clearance.

Chapare Region

The word 'Chapare' is synonymous both with coca and with DEA attempts to eradicate it, which have resulted in a few messy confrontations between campesinos, the DEA and the Bolivian government. The Bolivian media frequently expose cases of human-rights abuse and disregard for property. Although it isn't inherently unsafe to travel in the Chapare, violence may flare up at any time, especially in more remote areas. Currently, it's probably best not to stray too far off the Cochabamba-Santa Cruz highway.

VILLA TUNARI
☎ 0411

The spectacular route from Cochabamba to Villa Tunari passes between peaks and mountain lakes before dropping steeply into deep, steaming valleys and leveling out into remnants of tropical forest. Villa Tunari is mainly a tropical resort for cold-weary highlanders and a quiet spot to relax, hike and swim in cool rivers. In the wet season, there's a small waterfall on the Río Chapare behind the public toilets (don't worry – there's no connection between the two!).

A good independent walk will take you to the friendly village of Majo Pampa. Follow the route toward Hotel El Puente and turn right onto the walking track about 150m before the hotel. After crossing the Valería Stream, it's 8km to the village.

Orchideario

Villa Tunari's orchid center, lovingly tended by German botanists, is a beautiful garden that's home to over 70 species of tropical orchids. From the tranca at the Cochabamba

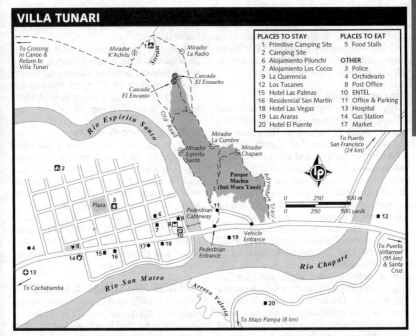

VILLA TUNARI

PLACES TO STAY		PLACES TO EAT
1	Primitive Camping Site	5 Food Stalls
2	Camping Site	
6	Alojamiento Pilunchi	**OTHER**
7	Alojamiento Los Cocos	3 Police
9	La Querencia	4 Orchideario
12	Los Tucanes	8 Post Office
15	Hotel Las Palmas	10 ENTEL
16	Residencial San Martín	11 Office & Parking
18	Hotel Las Vegas	13 Hospital
19	Las Araras	14 Gas Station
20	Hotel El Puente	17 Market

entrance to town, turn left; it's just off the road.

Parque Machía (Inti Wara Yassi)

A totally new concept in Bolivian conservation is being set forth by the 36-hectare Parque Machía (☎ 014-96991; fax 02-414270; ashoka@caoba.entelnet.bo; Casilla 9519, Villa Tunari, or Casilla 4034, Cochabamba) wildlife park, which rescues injured wild animals, abandoned tropical pets, former zoo inhabitants, old circus animals and other abused critters, and provides volunteers with a sense of satisfaction in exchange for their sweat. (The alternative name, Inti Wara Yassi, means 'sun, moon, stars' in Quechua, Aymará and Guaraní, respectively.) It's also a relaxing place to camp and wander through the forest, taking in the sights, sounds and tranquility.

Visitors pay US$2.50/5 to take photographs/videos. Volunteers must stay for a minimum of two weeks and can choose

between rustic camping and the hostel, both of which cost US$2.50 per person, including use of the hostel showers and access to cooking facilities (volunteers normally take turns cooking and share meals).

Organized Tours

Villa Tunari is a main focus for Viajes Fremen (☎ 04-259392; fax 04-117790; fremencb@pino.cbb.entelnet.bo; Tumusla 0245, Cochabamba), which arranges tours, accommodations, river trips and other activities at out-of-the-way sites (see Parque Nacional Carrasco, later in this chapter). Fremen's Chapare programs for two/three/four days cost US$188/261/341 per person with two people and US$156/215/271 per person with four people, including a guide, transportation, accommodations and meals.

Fremen also organizes adventure tours in Parque Nacional Isiboro-Sécure and cruises around Trinidad (see later in this chapter).

Special Events

In the first week of August, Villa Tunari hosts the Feria Regional del Pescado, in which a wide variety of lowland fish dishes are served up. Recipes feature *pacu, dorado, surubí* and other Amazonian species.

Places to Stay & Eat

Camping is possible at Parque Machía and also at the *camping site* in the sporting ground, north of the center. The cheap and simple *Alojamiento Los Cocos* charges US$4.50 per person, and the even simpler *Alojamiento Pilunchi*, just US$2.50. Other inexpensive choices include the friendly *Hotel Las Vegas*, which charges US$2.50 per person and also serves decent meals, and *La Querencia*, charging US$3 per person.

Viajes Fremen (see Organized Tours, earlier in this chapter) operates *Hotel El Puente* (☎ 43827), delightfully hidden in a remnant island of rain forest 4km from Villa Tunari, near the point where the Ríos San Mateo and Espíritu Santo join to form the Río Chapare. The highlight is a walk around Los Pozos, 14 idyllic natural swimming holes deep in the forest, where you're guaranteed to see blue morpho butterflies. It's a great place to mellow out and savor the slow tropical pace. Booked from Cochabamba, single/double cabañas cost US$27/38 and family rooms with one double bed and two twin beds are US$65. Meals cost US$3 for a full American breakfast, and US$4 each for lunch and dinner. To get there, catch a micro heading east from Villa Tunari; get off at the first turnoff after the second bridge, turn right and walk for 2km. Taxis from the center charge about US$4 for up to four people.

The five-star cabañas at *Los Tucanes* (☎ 4108), which cost US$35 per person, are the most luxurious option in Villa Tunari. The modern and recommended *Las Araras*, which charges US$18/28 for singles/doubles, is just over the first bridge east of the highway; meals cost a rather pricey US$5.

Hotel Las Palmas (☎ 4103) charges from US$35 for a double cabaña, including use of the swimming pool. It's not the best value for the money, but the attached restaurant serves well-prepared locally caught fish. At the friendly *Residencial San Martín* (☎ 4115), you'll pay US$15/25 for singles/doubles, with use of the pool.

Along the main road is a string of small *food stalls* selling inexpensive tropical fare. For a pleasant surprise, ask around for the little *restaurant* (☎ 4148) of Roxana Paz Siles, where you'll find well-prepared dishes featuring disinfected vegetables.

Getting There & Away

The bus and micro offices are sandwiched amid the line of food stalls along the main highway. From Cochabamba (five hours, US$2), micros leave in the morning from near the corner of 9 de Abril and Oquendo; some continue on to Puerto Villarroel (two hours, US$1). From Villa Tunari to Santa Cruz, several services operate in the early afternoon, but most Santa Cruz traffic departs in the evening. To Cochabamba, micros leave at 8:30 am.

PARQUE NACIONAL CARRASCO

Created in 1988, the 622,600-hectare Parque Nacional Carrasco takes in some of Bolivia's most readily accessible rain forest habitats. It skirts a large portion of the road between Cochabamba and Villa Tunari, and also includes a large lowland area of the Chapare region. Most rain forest mammal species are present, as well as an array of birds, reptiles, amphibians, fish and insects.

The easiest way to visit is with Viajes Fremen (see Organized Tours in Villa Tunari). Programs include the Cavernas del Repechón, also known as the Cuevas de los Pájaros Nocturnos (Caves of the Night Birds), where you'll see the rare nocturnal *guáchero (Steatornis caripensis)*, also known as the oilbird. Access is from the village of Paractito, just west of Villa Tunari. This four-hour excursion includes a short slog through the rain forest and a thrilling crossing of the Río San Mateo on a single cable. You can also take an excursion to Todos Santos, an abandoned Italian colony near Puerto Aurora that has been swallowed by the forest 55km from Villa Tunari. All that remains is a church tower and the ruins of the old hospital.

PUERTO VILLARROEL

The muddy tropical settlement of Puerto Villarroel, one of northern Bolivia's major river ports, lies two hours northeast of Villa Tunari. Although it's little more than a collection of tumbledown wooden hovels, a military installation, a YPFB (petroleum) plant and a loosely defined port area, it's both a vital transportation terminal and a gateway to the Amazon lowlands. For a quick look at the rain forests, it makes an easy two-day roundtrip from Cochabamba.

Bring lots of insect repellent and wear strong old shoes with lots of tread. Even in the dry season, the muddy streets of Puerto Villarroel will crawl up past your ankles and devour your footwear.

Viajes Fremen's three-day or longer Chapare Tours (see Organized Tours in Villa Tunari) visit Puerto Villarroel, including a cruise on the Río Ibabo and an overnight at their remote jungle camp.

Places to Stay & Eat

A good choice is **Amazonas Eco-Hotel** (☎ 017-32349; fax 04-235105; tombol@ hotmail.com), with 10 rooms costing from US$3.50/6.50 for singles/doubles with shared baths to US$8/13.50 with private baths. Meals are available.

Of Puerto Villarroel's other hotels, none will win any awards. At just US$2.50 per person, **Hotel Amazonas** is probably the best choice. The alternative, **Hotel Sucre**, charges the same, but it suffers from an excess of noise, thanks to the attached bar and disco. Fortunately, those who've arranged river transportation will normally be permitted to sleep on the boat.

Half a dozen restaurant shacks opposite the port captain's office serve up fish and chicken dishes. For good empanadas, snacks, hot drinks and juice, try the market on the main street.

Getting There & Away

Bus & Camión Micros from Cochabamba to Puerto Villarroel (seven hours, US$2.20) are marked 'Chapare' and leave from the corner of Avenidas 9 de Abril and Oquendo, near Laguna Alalay, in Cochabamba. The first one sets off at about 6:30 am, and subsequent buses depart when full. The first micro back to Cochabamba leaves at 7 am from the bus stop on the main street. Camiones leave from the same place at any hour of the day, especially when there are boats in port. Transportation between Cochabamba and Santa Cruz doesn't stop at Puerto Villarroel.

Boat Two types of local boats run between Puerto Villarroel and Trinidad. The small family-run cargo boats that putter up and down the Ríos Ichilo and Mamoré normally only travel by day and reach Trinidad in around six days. Larger commercial craft travel day and night and do the run in three or four days. The Capitanía del Puerto, Puesto Trans-Naval, CEPIMA, and Transportes Fluviales offices in Puerto Villarroel can provide sketchy departure information on cargo transporters. You shouldn't have more than a three- or four-day wait unless military exercises or labor strikes shut down cargo transportation.

The average fare to Trinidad on either type of boat is US$20 to US$25, including food (but it's still wise to carry emergency rations); you can buy a passage without food for a few dollars less. The quality of food varies from boat to boat, but overall the shipboard diet consists of fish, dried meat, *masaco* and fruit; in the interest of endangered turtles, avoid turtle eggs if they're offered. Few boats along the Ichilo have cabins, and most passengers sleep in hammocks (sold in Cochabamba markets) slung out in the main lounge.

PARQUE NACIONAL ISIBORO-SÉCURE

Created in 1965, this 1.2 million-hectare national park occupies a large triangle between the Ríos Isiboro and Sécure and the Serranías Sejerruma, Mosetenes and Yanakaka. It takes in mountains, rain forest and savanna and, in its remoter sections, is home to profuse wildlife. However, an obscure 1905 Department of Cochabamba resolution opening the region to settlers has resulted in much of it being overrun by outsiders with no way to halt the influx. As a result, the natural environment and the once-prevalent Indian population, which consisted of Yuracarés, Chimanes, Sirionós and Trinitarios, have been compromised.

As if that's not enough, the park also lies along cocaine-producing and drug-running routes, so independent visitors must exercise extreme caution. Thanks to DEA activity, locals may regard any foreigner as an *anti-cocalero* and hence fair game for abuse or violence in defense of their turf. Independent travelers would be wise to carry letters of recommendation from the coca growers' association.

There's also a dispute over whether Isiboro-Sécure belongs to Cochabamba department (Chapare) or whether it lies in the Beni. The suspected presence of oil – which is being explored by oil companies – makes the issue all the more relevant.

For more information, contact the park administrator Iván Dávalos L (☎ 04-235660) in Cochabamba or visit SENAP (see Information under Cochabamba in the Central Highlands chapter).

Organized Tours
Currently, the only truly safe way to visit the park is with Viajes Fremen (see Organized Tours in Villa Tunari). Their worthwhile seven-day boat trip from Trinidad to Laguna Bolivia, which is the park's best-known destination, includes stops at riverside settlements, rain forest walks, horseback riding, wildlife viewing and a canoe trip on the Río Ichoa. Tours cost US$551 on a comfortable fully equipped houseboat (with accommodation in beds or hammocks) and US$395 per person on five- to 20-passenger riverboats without facilities. Rates include accommodations in Trinidad before and after the trip as well as transfers, meals, transportation and a guide.

Getting There & Away
Owing to seasonal flooding, the park is inaccessible between November and March. If you wish to attempt an independent trip – which probably wouldn't be a very good idea – take a bus from the end of Avenida

Oquendo in Cochabamba to the village of Eterezama, which has an alojamiento. There, look for a camión to Isinuta, which also has alojamiento accommodations. In Isinuta, you must wait for yet another camión to the Trinitarios Moxos community of Santísima Trinidad (not to be confused with the city of Trinidad farther north). To continue north of there – through Aroma, Ycoya and Río Moleto and deeper into the park's forests and savannas – will probably involve traveling on foot.

Western Bolivian Amazon

The wildlife-rich bit of the Bolivian Amazon nearest La Paz makes an ideal introduction to the country's northern rain forests. Indeed, the lovely town of Rurrenabaque now sits solidly as a way station along the Gringo Trail, and the Parque Nacional Madidi is surely one of South America's finest wilderness gems.

RURRENABAQUE
☎ 0832
Rurrenabaque, a bustling little frontier settlement on the Río Beni, is the loveliest village in the Bolivian lowlands, and its changing moods can be magical. The sunsets are normally superb, and at night dense clouds of fog roll down the river and create beautiful effects, especially during the full moon.

The area's original people, the Tacana, were one of the few lowland tribes that resisted Christianity and Western-style civilization. It was they who were responsible for the name Beni, which means 'wind,' as well as the curious name of this town, which is commonly shortened to 'Rurre.' It's derived from 'Arroyo Inambaque,' the Hispanicized version of the Tacana name 'Suse-Inambaque,' the 'Ravine of Ducks.'

Information
Tourist information about the protected areas is available at the offices of Conservation International and Pilón Lajas, and town

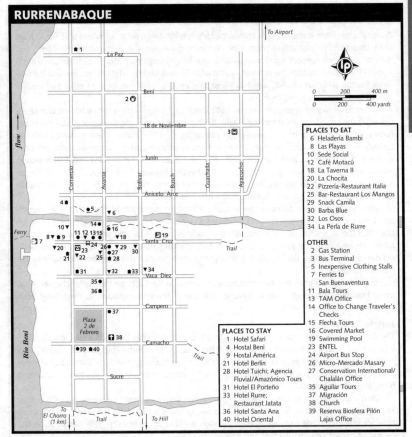

RURRENABAQUE

To Airport

flow

Ferry

Rio Beni

Plaza
2 de
Febrero

To
El Chorro
(1 km)   Trail   To Hill

0   200   400 m
0   200   400 yards

PLACES TO EAT
6 Heladería Bambi
8 Las Playas
10 Sede Social
12 Café Motacú
18 La Taverna II
20 La Chocita
22 Pizzería-Restaurant Italia
25 Bar-Restaurant Los Mangos
29 Snack Camila
30 Barba Blue
32 Los Osos
34 La Perla de Rurre

OTHER
2 Gas Station
3 Bus Terminal
5 Inexpensive Clothing Stalls
7 Ferries to
   San Buenaventura
11 Bala Tours
13 TAM Office
14 Office to Change Traveler's
   Checks
15 Flecha Tours
16 Covered Market
19 Swimming Pool
23 ENTEL
24 Airport Bus Stop
26 Micro-Mercado Masary
27 Conservation International/
   Chalalán Office
35 Aguilar Tours
37 Migración
38 Church
39 Reserva Biosfera Pilón
   Lajas Office

PLACES TO STAY
1 Hotel Safari
4 Hostal Beni
9 Hostal América
21 Hotel Berlin
28 Hotel Tuichi; Agencia
   Fluvial/Amazónico Tours
31 Hotel El Porteño
33 Hotel Rurre;
   Restaurant Jatata
36 Hotel Santa Ana
40 Hotel Oriental

information is found at most hotels. Useful background reading would be *Exploration Fawcett*, by the explorer Colonel Percy Harrison Fawcett, or *Back from Tuichi* (also published as *Heart of the Amazon*), about the 1981 rescue of Israeli Yossi Ghinsberg, who was lost in the rain forest on an ill-fated expedition. If you need reading material, go to Café Motacu (see Places to Eat), where there's a book exchange (US$5 per book or US$1 plus a book in exchange).

There's no bank, but you can change cash or traveler's checks at Hotel Tuichi or at the private office diagonally opposite the market.

You can phone any hotel or business in town by leaving a message at ENTEL (☎ 2205). Electricity services are sporadic at best, and in any case, the power shuts down between 10 pm and 7 am. There's still no Internet or email access, but numerous folks are working on the problem, so it's sure to arrive soon.

Things to See & Do

Most of Rurrenabaque's appeal is natural beauty, and it's worth spending a day or two here. Behind the town is a low but steep hill that affords a view across the seemingly

Take a Walk on the Wild Side

Rurrenabaque is the Kathmandu of Bolivia, and tourism has taken off to an extent that would have been unimaginable just a few years ago. The main draws are the surrounding rain forest and pampa, which still support Amazonian wildlife in relatively large numbers. Recent welcome additions to the options include the culturally sustainable Reserva de la Biosfera Pilón Lajas and the fabulous Parque Nacional Madidi, which is home to a mind-boggling number of plant and wildlife species and is surely a world treasure.

Numerous Rurrenabaque agencies run both jungle and pampas tours, and while no two agencies offer the same trips, most include hiking, fishing, relaxing and wildlife viewing. You can either form your own group or let the agencies put you on the next tour going. The trips, which aren't as touristy as they may sound, normally last from three to six days and include canoe transportation, guides and food; for the basic Pampas Tours, plan on US$20 to US$25 per day in the rainy season and US$25 to US$35 during the drier period between May and September; in general, Jungle Tours cost around US$5 per day less. In the interest of maintaining standards, it's wise to negotiate to pay half the price in advance and half when you return.

Note that to get the most out of these tours, at least a minimal knowledge of Spanish is requisite. Even more essential, however, is a strong insect repellent; without it, your misery will know no bounds, especially when you're faced with the insidious *marigui* sandfly, which inhabits the riverbanks. Please also advise your guides not to disturb animals – that is, not to capture caimans, anacondas or capybaras for the benefit of tourist photo opportunities. (Isn't it more interesting to just observe nature as it is?)

For guidelines on gear, see the What to Bring section in the Facts for the Visitor chapter. Also, avoid leaving anything of value in storage with any of the tour agencies, as there have been reports of items disappearing.

Jungle Tours

The Bolivian rain forest is full of more interesting and unusual things than you'd ever imagine. The local guides, most of whom have grown up in the area, are knowledgeable about the fauna, flora and forest lore; they can explain animals' habits and habitats and demonstrate the uses of some of the thousands of plant species, including the forest's natural remedies for colds, fever, cuts, insect bites, and other ailments.

Most trips begin by canoe upstream along the Río Beni as it winds between high, steep hills. Then you ascend the Río Tuichi, camping and taking shore walks along the way, with plenty of time for swimming and relaxing. Accommodation is either in agencies' private camps or on the river sand beneath a tarpaulin tent and a mosquito net.

endless Beni lowlands; it's accessed by climbing up the track from near the *colegio* (secondary school).

Another nice excursion is to El Chorro, an idyllic pool and waterfall 1km upstream. A track leads from the wet-sand beach to this favorite swimming and picnicking spot, which is accessible only by boat. On a rock roughly opposite El Chorro is an ancient serpent engraving that was intended as a warning to travelers; whenever the water reached serpent level, the Beni was considered unnavigable.

For US$1.80, you can cool off in the green-but-clean municipal pool.

Places to Stay

The backpacker scene is most in evidence at *Hotel Tuichi* (☎/fax 2372), on Calle Avaroa. Run by Tico and Eli Tudela, it features laundry service, cooking facilities, and hammocks and tables in a pleasant garden.

It's a good place to form tour groups if you're using Agencia Fluvial, but patrons of other agencies get a less enthusiastic reception. Single/double rooms cost US$3.50/5 without bath and US$4.50/8 with bath. On June 20, it celebrates the Día de los Turistas, which began as a joke and has escalated into an annual event; it's worth checking out.

An excellent choice, where you'll be privileged to hear the nightly frog chorus on the plaza, is the friendly and lovely *Hotel Oriental* (☎ *2401*). Here you'll pay US$3.50/6.50 for rooms with shared baths and US$6.50/10 with private baths. Breakfast and drinks are available, and in the stifling afternoon hours, you can lazily lie in the garden hammocks and snooze or read until the heat subsides.

The friendly and welcoming *Hotel Rurre* (☎ *2481*) is also recommended. Single or double rooms cost US$5 per person (US$7 with private bath). Laundry services are available for US$1.20 per kilogram. The basic *Hotel Santa Ana* (☎ *2399*), on Calle Avaroa, has a nice leafy courtyard with tables for enjoying the sun. Rooms with shared baths cost US$3.50/7, and with private baths, they're US$7/13.

The relaxing *Hotel El Porteño* (☎ *2558*), which features a huge and prolific carambola tree (the delicious juice is free to guests!), charges US$2.50 per person (US$5 with private bath). Garden hammocks are available for relaxing, and there's also a secure garage where travelers can leave their rented vehicles.

Hostal Beni (☎ *7408; fax 2407*) offers popular rooms with fans and shared baths for US$4.50/6.50. Add a TV and you'll pay US$5/8. With a private bath, it's US$8/12. With air conditioning, the charge becomes US$22/25.

The bottom of the barrel, *Hotel Berlin*, offers friendly but rather unkempt accommodations and cold showers for US$3 per person. Note the wall facing the thatched restaurant, graced with a mural of a German warship being tossed about the waves before a Río Beni shoreline! The similarly basic *Hostal América*, which charges the same, is worthwhile only if you can get a room on the top floor, which affords a superb view of the river and the hills.

Your most upmarket option is the quiet Korean-run *Hotel Safari* (☎/fax *2210*), on the riverbank, which offers simple but comfortable rooms well beyond the noisy central area of town. Economy rooms with private baths and fans cost US$20/30, and family-size rooms are US$50. In the restaurant, lunches cost US$2.50 and à la carte dinners are US$3 to US$5.

Places to Eat

An exploding number of eateries in Rurre reflects the corresponding eruption in tourist numbers. The good news is that everywhere in town you'll find freshly brewed Yungas coffee.

Several fish restaurants line up in wooden shelters along the riverfront: *La Chocita* and *Las Playas* fry up the catch of the day, and in addition to the Beni standard, masaco, you can try the excellent *pescado hecho en taquara*, which is fish baked in a special local pan, or *pescado en dunucuabi*, which is fish wrapped in a rain forest leaf and baked over a wood fire.

For breakfast, coffee or snacks – including cakes, juice, biscuits, brownies and vegetarian burgers – you can't beat the friendly and extremely popular *Café Motacú*, where you sit beneath the street-side awning and watch Rurre's comings and goings. It's especially useful for those awaiting the latest flight news from TAM, next door. It's open daily except Tuesday and Sunday from 8:30 am to noon and 5:30 to 8:30 pm.

The long-standing and atmospheric *Sede Social* serves drinks and set meals for US$1.20. Meat and chicken dishes are available on an à la carte basis, and if you arrive early enough, you can also enjoy well-prepared pasta and Mexican dishes for US$2.50 to US$3.50. *Heladería Bambi*, run by a German gold prospector, is recommended for toasted sandwiches, burgers, pasta, banana pancakes, ice cream, soda and beer, all of which go down well on a typically hot and sticky Rurre afternoon. The laid-back *Restaurant Jatata* at the Hotel Rurre serves up beef, chicken and fish dishes, as well as a US$4.75 buffet. For pizza, pasta and other excellent Italian choices, as well as wine and vegetarian options, there's the *Pizzería-Restaurant Italia*, which is affiliated with the famous one in Sorata.

The tree-shaded *Bar-Restaurant Los Mangos* does daily almuerzos and cenas. *La*

Dead Meat

I wanted to include a mention of the infamous 'meat planes' between La Paz, Rurrenabaque and other parts of the Beni Lowlands, but one reader said it all for me:

People heading into the Beni Lowlands may possibly find an alternative to flying with TAM. If you're on a shoestring budget, aren't too fussy and have a real Indiana Jones sense of adventure, you can take the flight with the carniceros (meat haulers) operating out of La Paz. They fly vintage cargo planes into the lowlands, weather permitting; these are stripped-down DC-3s, DC-4s and C-46s, which head for Rurrenabaque and other places to pick up freshly butchered meat and fly it back to La Paz unrefrigerated. If you don't mind sitting on the floor surrounded by the smell and all the blood – and can overlook the fact that they have the highest commercial aviation accident rate in the world – then this could be for you. Rates are based on your weight (just like the meat), and it's an option favored by Bolivian campesinos.

However, I don't recommend flying on anything smaller than a DC-3. I was fortunate enough not to be killed in the crash of a lighter plane, and suffered only a broken ankle, pulled tendons, cuts etc. DC-3's are built like tanks, so I think the survivability factor is a lot better.

– Brad Mackay, Canada

Perla de Rurre, which is often cited as the town's finest restaurant, specializes in fish and chicken dishes, but also does steak, milanesa, filet mignon and an excellent *pescado en dunucuabi*. *Los Osos* offers breakfasts, stroganoff, spaghetti, curry, fondue and vegetarian dishes, and *La Taverna II* happily does cholesterol-laden American and 'diplomatic' breakfasts, as well as pizzas, omelets and chicken dishes. The very friendly *Snack Camila* serves muesli breakfasts, juices, salads, pasta, burgers, vegetarian lasagna, burritos and chicken dishes in the shade. The nearby *Barba Blue*, where the menu is more of a dream-list than a reflection of reality, claims to do international breakfasts, Chinese dishes, tacos, burgers, pizzas, fish and a host of other unlikely options.

If you wish to pick up a few extra snacks for your wilderness tour, check out the friendly *Micro-Mercado Masary*, where you'll find a selection of groceries and alcohol.

Entertainment & Shopping

If you're looking for nightlife in Rurre, you're scraping the barrel. A pleasant place for an evening drink or two is the Sede Social, where the river slides by while the beer slides down, but the local place to be seen on weekend evenings is the bizarre black-lighted karaoke bar at the Hotel Safari.

As for local merchandise, Rurrenabaque is a good place to pick up hammocks, which sell for US$12/18 for singles/doubles. Finely woven mosquito nets start at about US$11. The Café Motacú also sells typical local handicrafts.

Getting There & Away

Apparently not realizing that tourists are the town's bread and butter, Rurrenabaque charges foreigners a rather unfriendly 'tourist tax' of US$1. That's in addition to both the bus terminal tax and the US$1 AASANA airport tax.

Air TAM (☎ 2398) flies between the La Paz military airport and Rurrenabaque (one hour, US$54), often via Apolo, twice on

Monday and once each on Wednesday and Saturday. On Friday, there's also a flight between Cochabamba and La Paz via Rurrenabaque. If you can't get a flight to Rurre, you might take a flight to Reyes, which is one hour from Rurre by minibus. Even when the windows are hopelessly scratched, these glorious flights afford superb views of 6000m peaks as they climb over the Cordillera Real, then pass over the Yungas, where the land dramatically drops away and opens onto the forested expanses of the Amazon Basin.

Despite its poor reputation, TAM offers as good a service as a government entity can provide, and if a flight is delayed owing to weather or mud on the runway in Rurre, it will run as soon as conditions permit. Note, however, that every TAM ticket is standby; reserving a seat from La Paz to Rurre does not guarantee a place on the return flight, so be sure to confirm your return booking as soon as you arrive in Rurre.

Bus The bus terminal lies a good walk from the center; allow at least 20 minutes. When the roads are dry, several flotas run daily between Rurrenabaque and La Paz (18 hours, US$10), via Yolosa (15 hours, US$10), for Coroico. There are also daily runs to Trinidad (eight hours, US$9) via Yucumo, San Borja and San Ignacio de Moxos. Dry-season services operate to Riberalta (17 to 40 hours, US$18) and Guayaramerín (19 to 42 hours, US$20). Minibuses to Reyes (one hour, US$1) leave when full from the corner of Comercio and Santa Cruz.

Boat Thanks to the Riberalta road, river-cargo transportation on the Beni between Riberalta and Rurrenabaque is now very limited, and there's no traffic at all during periods of low water. If you do find something, plan on four or five days at about US$10 per day, including meals, for the 1000km trip. Going upstream, the journey takes as many as 10 days.

Except at times of low water, motorized canoe transportation upriver to Guanay (10 hours, US$20) may be occasionally available. Taxi ferries to San Buenaventura, on the opposite shore of the Río Beni, depart from the riverbank when full and cost US$0.20.

Getting Around
The stifling TAM micros to the airport cost US$1 from the TAM office; if you choose to use the quicker and cooler moto-taxis (also US$1), you'll have to carry all your luggage. Moto-taxis around town cost US$0.40 per ride.

SAN BUENAVENTURA
On the La Paz department bank of the Río Beni, opposite Rurrenabaque, is the laid-back tropical town of San Buenaventura. Since residents mostly conduct their business across the river in Rurre, nothing much happens in San Buenaventura, and that's how they seem to like it. If you're looking for fine Beni leather wallets and bags, visit the well-known shop of leather artisan Manuel Pinto, but avoid purchasing anything made from wild rain-forest species.

The only accommodations are in the basic *Alojamiento Florida*, which charges US$2 per person. San Buenaventura can be accessed only by the ferry across the Río Beni from Rurrenabaque.

RESERVA DE LA BIOSFERA PILÓN LAJAS
A successful experiment in community-based tourism functions in the Reserva de la Biosfera Pilón Lajas, which takes in six traditional communities of Tacana, Chimane and Mosetén peoples, northwest of Rurrenabaque. Because lumbering was stopped in 1998, the ecosystem is relatively intact and the wildlife is quickly returning to the region.

For information or to arrange access, contact one of their offices: in Rurrenabaque; Mapajo-Asociación Indígena, on Calle Comercio near Santa Cruz; Reserva de la Biosfera Pilón Lajas (☎/fax 2524), on Calle Bolívar at Tarija, in Casilla 935-4; or in La Paz (☎/fax 02-227337), on Calle República Dominicana at Nicaragua, in Miraflores. All profits from the project go to finance community development projects.

ERIC WHEATER

A ride in a dugout canoe includes service with a smile.

Places to Stay

About 800m up the Río Quiquibey from the village of Asunción, rustic double cabañas are available to visitors. Package visits from Rurrenabaque are offered for groups of two to eight people and include rain forest hikes, canoe trips, swimming in the river, wildlife-viewing and relaxing, as well as cultural visits and interchange with indigenous communities. All-inclusive tours cost around US$35 per person per day, but may vary depending on group size. In addition, two camps farther upstream offer beds and dining areas for groups of four to eight people.

PARQUE NACIONAL MADIDI

The Río Madidi watershed contains one of the most intact ecosystems in South America. Most of it is protected by the 1.8 million-hectare Parque Nacional Madidi, which takes in a range of wildlife habitats, from the steaming lowland rain forests to 5500m Andean peaks. This wild, little-trodden utopia is home to a mind-boggling variety of Amazonian wildlife, including 44% of all New World

mammal species, 38% of tropical amphibian species, and more than 1100 bird species – that's over 10% of all avian species known to science.

The populated portions of the park along the Río Tuichi have been accorded a special UNESCO designation permitting indigenous inhabitants to utilize traditional forest resources, but the park has also been considered for oil exploration and as a site for a major hydroelectric scheme (see *National Geographic*, March 2000). In addition, illicit logging has affected several areas around the park perimeter, including parts of the Tuichi watershed and the vicinity of Ixiamas.

An excellent publication for visitors is *A Field Guide to Chalalán*, which costs US$4.50 at the Conservation International office in Rurrenabaque.

San José de Uchupiamonas

The lovely little traditional village of San José de Uchupiamonas, deep in the park, has worked with Conservation International to operate the eco-lodge at Laguna

Chalalán (see Places to Stay). However, the village itself also merits a visit, and both jungle walks and boat trips are available with local guides. Plan on negotiating US$12 per day for the guide, plus US$100 per day for a motorized canoe.

While organized tours to the village can be arranged from Chalalán, there are also a couple of more adventurous approaches. First, it's possible to hire a guide in Apolo and hike for four days down to the village, following the historic route taken by Colonel Percy Harrison Fawcett. To reach Rurrenabaque from here, you'll have to hire a canoe for the six-hour downstream trip.

Alternatively, take a ferry from Rurrenabaque to San Buenaventura; there, micros leave around midday for Ixiamas. Get off at the village of Tumupasa (which has an alojamiento half a block from the plaza). From here, it's a relatively easy 30km hike to San José de Uchupiamonas, but there are numerous river fords (throw in rocks or slap the water with a stick before crossing, to disperse the stingrays). You'll need to carry all your gear and supplies for the typically two-day trip. (Note that a road is now being constructed along this route, so its adventure possibilities are short-lived!)

Places to Stay
At the lovely and idyllic oxbow lake, Laguna Chalalán, sits the only formal visitor accommodation in the park. This simple but comfortable lodge, buried in the rain forest, provides the opportunity to amble through the deep forest and appreciate the incredible richness of life there. Although the flowers and vegetation are lovely, it is sounds more than sights that provide the magic here: the incredible dawn bird chorus, the evening frog symphony, the collective whine of zillions of insects, the roar of bucketing tropical rainstorms and, in the early morning, the thunderlike chorus of every howler monkey within a 100km radius!

The lodge operates thanks to the efforts of the community of San José de Uchupiamonas with assistance from Conservation International. For a stay in a simple but comfortable lodge made of natural materials,

you'll pay US$50 per person per day in groups of six or more and US$65 with two to five people, with seasonal variations. Rates include two nights in Rurre before and after the trip, transfers to and from the airport, three excellent meals per day at Chalalán, a local guide to lead you on wildlife and bird-watching hikes in the rain forest, canoe trips on the beautiful black waters of the lake, and nighttime excursions in search of colorful forest frogs. Incorporated into the price are local taxes and a community levy. In La Paz, book through América Tours (see Organized Tours in the Getting Around chapter). In Rurrenabaque, visit the Conservation International office and see what's available.

Getting There & Away
Most of the national park is effectively inaccessible, which is why it remains a treasure. Guests of Chalalán pay US$75 for roundtrip canoe transfers between Rurrenabaque and the lodge (five hours upstream and three downstream, plus a 2km hike each way through the rain forest).

REYES & SANTA ROSA
In the area of Reyes and Santa Rosa, you'll find lovely lagoons with myriad birds, alligators and other local wildlife. Reyes is only an hour from Rurrenabaque, and Santa Rosa, with its attractive Laguna Rogagua, is 1½ hours farther on. These places are popular destinations for Pampas Tours from Rurrenabaque (see earlier in this chapter).

In Reyes, a good place to stay is **Alojamiento Teresita**, with a beautiful garden, which charges US$2.50 per person. In Santa Rosa, recommended places include the very simple **Residencial Los Tamarindos** and **Hotel Oriental**, both of which charge US$2.50 to US$3.50 per person; for meals, try **Restaurante Triángulo**, where breakfast is under US$2 and other meals are around US$2.50.

If you can't get a TAM flight to Rurre, it's easy enough to fly to Reyes instead; minibuses and camionetas leave from the airport to Rurrenabaque (one hour, US$1) as soon as flights arrive. Micros between

Santa Rosa and Rurrenabaque (four hours, US$4.50) normally leave in the morning.

YUCUMO

The main thing to know about Yucumo, a frontier El Dorado for development-crazed settlers, is how to get there and away as quickly as possible. It lies at the intersection of the La Paz-Guayaramerín road and the Trinidad turnoff. The road between Rurrenabaque and Yucumo passes through a devastated environment of cattle ranches and logged-out forest. For those stuck here, a decent hike leads along the road south of town; after the bridge, turn left and follow the walking track to the colony of scarlet macaws.

If you're trapped for the night, you can stay at **Hotel Palmeras**, which charges around US$2.50 per person. **Hotel Tropical** charges US$6.50 per person (US$8.50 with private bath).

All buses and camiones traveling between Rurrenabaque and La Paz or Trinidad pass through Yucumo. Once in Yucumo, connect with the white camionetas, which will take you through the savanna to San Borja (one hour, US$2), where you'll find camiones and buses to the Reserva Biosférica del Beni, San Ignacio de Moxos and Trinidad.

SAN BORJA

☎ 0848

With a penchant for illicit dealings, San Borja takes on a dark cast, and travelers may sense unsettling vibes. However, it's dangerous only to those involved in the cocaine trade. There's not a lot to keep one occupied around San Borja, but the town's prosperity is revealed in the rather palatial homes that rise on the block behind the church.

A long day's walk along the relatively little-traveled road west of town will take you through an area of wetlands and small ponds frequented by numerous species of tropical birds. You may see rheas, jabirus and other storks, limpkins, spoonbills, hawks, caracaras and a host of other birds.

Places to Stay & Eat

At the top of the hotel heap is the friendly and clean **Hotel San Borja**, at the corner of

the plaza, which charges US$5 per person (US$7 with bath). Its courtyard restaurant is one of the best eateries in town, and there's ceaseless entertainment provided by the caged parrots and other birds, whose constant babble resembles the sound of a schoolyard at break time! Other good choices are **Hotel Manara** and **Hostal Jatata**, which provide decent accommodations for US$6.50 and US$10 per person, respectively. Meals are available, and the latter has a beautiful patio enhanced by hammocks and bird sounds.

Hotel Victoria, opposite Hotel Trópico, charges US$3 per person with private bath, but it's a bit of a dump. If you thought that was bad, check out **Residencial San Luis**, two blocks from the plaza, which charges US$3 per person for some of the scummiest rooms in Bolivia.

For eats, a block off the plaza is the unmemorable **La Pascana de Camba**, where it's lomo, lomo, lomo – as well as an assortment of lesser incarnations – all orchestrated by pounding rock music and slobbering drunks.

Shopping

The Proyecto Comunidad Galilea, 15km east of San Borja, sells hand-woven Panama hats and other items made of *jipijapa*.

Getting There & Away

TAM (☎ 3272) flies between La Paz and Santa Cruz, via Trinidad and San Borja, on Monday and Wednesday, and to and from La Paz on Saturday.

In the dry season, buses and camionetas leave several times daily from the new bus terminal to the Reserva Biosférica del Beni (one hour, US$2.50), San Ignacio de Moxos (five hours, US$4), Trinidad (eight to 12 hours, US$8) and Santa Cruz (20 to 24 hours, US$17). To La Paz (23 to 27 hours, US$20), you can travel several times weekly, and there are daily services to Rurrenabaque (five to eight hours, US$6).

If you're Trinidad-bound, remember that the Mamoré balsa crossing closes at 6 pm, and you need five to six hours to reach it from San Borja. There are no accommodations on either side of the crossing. Between San Borja and San Ignacio de Moxos, watch for wildlife and birds: herons, jabiru storks, cormorants, birds of prey, egrets and countless others. You may also spot capybaras and pink river dolphins at small river crossings.

RESERVA BIOSFÉRICA DEL BENI
☎ 0895

Created by Conservation International in 1982 as a loosely protected natural area, the 334,200-hectare Beni Biosphere Reserve was recognized by UNESCO in 1986 as a 'Man & the Biosphere Reserve.' The following year, it received official Bolivian congressional recognition through a debt trade agreement with the Bolivian government.

The abutting Reserva Forestal Chimane, a 1.15 million-hectare buffer zone and indigenous reserve, has also been set aside for sustainable subsistence use by the 1200 Chimane people living there. The combined areas are home to at least 500 tropical bird species as well as more than 100 mammal species, including monkeys, jaguars, deer, two species of peccary, river otters, foxes, anteaters and bats.

In 1990, the Chimane reserve was threatened when the government opened it up to logging interests. In response, 700 Chimanes and representatives of other tribes staged a 'March for Dignity and Territory' from Trinidad to La Paz to protest what would amount to the wholesale destruction of their land and its flora and fauna. Logging concessions were rezoned but not altogether revoked.

Owing to increasing human pressures, the already degraded western 20% of the reserve has been lopped off and sacrificed to settlement and exploitation in hopes that the remaining pristine areas can be more vigilantly protected.

Information
Admission to the reserve (☎ 3385) is US$5/3.50 for foreigners/Bolivians (free for those over 60 or under six years of age). Horse rentals are also available for US$7.50 per eight-hour day. Information is available by shortwave radio on 5850-USB at 9:30 am and noon and on 8550-USB at 3:30 and 6 pm.

Visiting the Reserve
The best time to visit is in June and July, when there's little rain and days are clear; bring warm clothing to protect yourself from

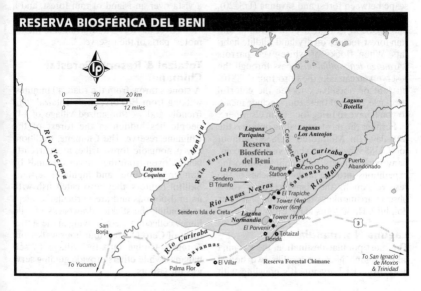

RESERVA BIOSFÉRICA DEL BENI

0   10   20 km
0   6   12 miles

Laguna Botella
Laguna Pariquina
Lagunas Los Anteojos
Reserva Biosférica del Beni
Sendero Cero Siete
Río Curiraba
Río Maniqui
Rain Forest
Laguna Coquina
La Pascana
Ranger Station
Cero Ocho
Puerto Abandonado
Savannas
Río Matos
Sendero El Triunfo
Río Aguas Negras
El Trapiche
Tower (4m)
Tower (6m)
Sendero Isla de Creta
Laguna Normandia
Tower (11m)
San Borja
El Porvenir
Totaizal
Florida
Río Curiraba
Savannas
Río Yacuma
To Yucumo
Palma Flor
El Villar
Reserva Forestal Chimane
To San Ignacio de Moxos & Trinidad

the occasional *surazo*. During the rainy season, days are hot, rainy, muggy and miserable with mosquitoes, so bring plenty of repellent. In August and September, the atmosphere becomes somber with the smoke from El Chaqueo.

The reserve headquarters, El Porvenir, lies in the savannas quite a distance from the true rain forest, so walks around the station will be of limited interest. The best way to see the reserve and observe its wildlife is to hire a guide for a hike through the savannas and the primary- and secondary-growth rain forests.

From El Porvenir, several tours are offered: a four-hour canoe trip to see the black caimans in Laguna Normandia (US$8); a four-hour savanna hike to see Laguna Normandia and several monkey-infested islands of rain forest (US$11); a two-day El Trapiche tour to the ruins of an old sugarcane mill, to fish in the river and observe rain forest birds and monkeys (US$20); and the two-day Las Torres tour, either on foot or horseback, to three wildlife-viewing towers where you can observe both savanna and rain forest ecosystems, and see the progression of the landscape between forest and savanna (US$20). The more challenging three-day La Pascana hike (US$40), through both savanna and rain forest, focuses on dry-land wildlife habitats. When flocks of white-eyed parrots (*Aratinga leucopthalmus*) pass through the reserve, you can take the Loro Tour (US$10) on foot or horseback to see the colorful spectacle. None of these tours include meals, so you'll have to bring food from elsewhere.

Perhaps the most interesting option is the four-day 'Tur Monitoreo' (US$80 without food, US$89 with), in which visitors accompany park rangers on wildlife-monitoring expeditions into the farthest reaches of the reserve. Among the many creatures you'll observe are monkeys, macaws and pink river dolphins. These tours leave every four days.

Laguna Normandia

The most popular destination, the savanna lake, Laguna Normandia, lies two hours' walk from El Porvenir. It's crawling with

rare black caimans (*caimanes negros*) – 400 at last count – which are descendants of specimens originally destined to become shoes and handbags. When the caiman breeder's leather business failed, the animals were left to fend for themselves, and the vast majority perished from neglect, crowding and hunger. The survivors were confiscated by Bolivian authorities and, with the aid of a US$20,000 grant from France, were airlifted into Laguna Normandia.

Fortunately, the caimans have little interest in humans, so it's safe to observe them at close range. There's a rowboat at the lake for public use – and close-up caiman viewing – but the shore is quite muddy, and launching it will involve slogging through slime. At the lake, an 11m viewing tower allows you to gain enough elevation for a wider perspective.

The Rain Forest

Beyond Laguna Normandia, you'll need to take a tour (see Visiting the Reserve). From the lake, it's a four-hour walk to the margin of the secondary-growth rain forest. A further four hours' walk through secondary forest takes you to the primary forest. Along the way, a 6m viewing tower provides a vista over an island of rain forest, and a 4m tower along the Río Curiraba provides views over the forest and savanna in the remotest parts of the reserve.

Totaizal & Reserva Forestal Chimane

A stone's throw from the road, 40 minutes' walking from El Porvenir, is Totaizal. This friendly and well-organized village of 140 people lies hidden in the forest of the Chimane reserve. The Chimane, traditionally a nomadic forest tribe, are currently being driven from their ancestral lands by lumber companies and highland settlers. Skillful hunters, they also catch fish with natural poisons and are particularly adept at avoiding the stickier drawbacks of wild honey collection. People living in the settlement of Cero Ocho, a four-hour walk from Totaizal, trudge into the village to sell bananas, while others provide guiding services for visitors.

Places to Stay & Eat

To promote visitation, there are now four nice airy rooms with three beds and four with two bunk beds each. Older rooms include two dormitories with five and six beds, respectively, and two three-bed rooms. Accommodations with simple meals in any of these rooms cost US$12 per person. Other services here include a bar, a researchers' workshop, a library, an interpretive center, as well as a small cultural and biological museum.

Getting There & Away

El Porvenir lies 200m off the highway one hour east of San Borja and is accessible on any bus or camioneta between Trinidad and San Borja or Rurrenabaque. Reserve personnel provide at least two daily camionetas (one hour, US$3.50) from San Borja.

SAN IGNACIO DE MOXOS
☎ 0482

This Moxos Indian village 89km west of Trinidad was founded as San Ignacio de Loyola by the Jesuits in 1689. In 1760 the village suffered pestilence and had to be shifted to its present location on higher and healthier ground.

Although the Jesuits were expelled from South America in 1767, Jesuit priests are now returning not only to work among the Moxos but also to strike an understanding among the Moxos, the dispossessed Chimane people and the newly arriving settlers and loggers.

Despite all the outside factions in the Beni, San Ignacio de Moxos remains a friendly and tranquil agricultural village with an ambience quite distinct from any other in Bolivia. The people speak an indigenous dialect known locally as Ignaciano, and their lifestyles, traditions and foods are unique in the country.

Things to See & Do

In the main plaza is a monument to Chirípieru, El Machetero Ignaciano, with his crown of feathers and formidable-looking hatchet. The relatively recent church on the plaza is filled with local art and Ignaciano religious murals.

At the museum in the Casa Belén, near the northwest corner of the plaza, you'll see elements of both the Ignaciano and Moxos cultures, including the *bajones*, or immense flutes introduced by the Jesuits.

At the large Laguna Isirere, north of town, you can go fishing and swimming, or just observe the profuse bird life. It's accessible on a 30-minute walk or by hitching from town. The greater area also boasts a number of obscure – and hard-to-reach – sights of interest: the Lomas de Museruna, several archaeological ruins, and the ruins of the missions San José and San Luis Gonzaga.

Special Events

Annually, July 31 is the first day of the huge Fiesta del Santo Patrono de Moxos, in honor of the sacred protector of the Moxos. As in most Bolivian fiestas, the celebration includes games, music, dancing and drinking. The festivities culminate at 2 pm on the final day of the fiesta, when wildly clad dancers led by El Machetero himself proceed from the church, accompanied by fiddles and woodwind instruments.

Places to Stay & Eat

The friendly *Residencial 31 de Julio*, a block off the plaza, charges US$2.50 per person for clean and basic accommodations (prices double during the Fiesta del Santo Patrono). *Residencial 22 de Abril*, on the plaza to the right of the church, is known for its good breakfasts. It charges US$2.50 per person, and hot water is occasionally available.

The outstanding *Residencial Don Joaquín*, at the corner of the plaza near the church, has a nice patio and charges US$3 per person (US$5 with bath). The cheery *Plaza Hotel* (☎ 2032), also on the plaza, charges US$2.50/5 for singles/doubles (US$5/10 with bath). The doubles are spacious, and all rooms have fans. Another similarly priced place is *Residencial Tamarindo*, on the main street. During the fiesta, visitors can also set up tents at established sites in the environs of town.

The recommended eating establishment here is the wonderfully friendly *Restaurant Don Chanta*, on the plaza; don't miss the

Ignaciano specialties: *chicha de camote* (sweet potato chicha) and the interesting *sopa de joco* (beet and pumpkin soup). Another good dining choice is **Restaurant Cherlis**, a block east of the southeast corner of the plaza.

Getting There & Away

From Trinidad, micros and camionetas (three hours, US$2.50) leave for San Ignacio when full from the terminals on Calle La Paz, and camiones leave in the morning from the east end of La Paz, near the river. There's good forest scenery all along the way, but prepare for delays at the Río Mamoré balsa crossing (US$6 per vehicle) between Puerto Barador and Puerto Ganadero. From March to October, it's two to three hours from Trinidad to San Ignacio, including the balsa crossing, but this route is impassable during the summer rainy season. Note that the balsa shuts down at 6 pm (it may stay open later at times of heavy traffic) and there are no accommodations on either side, so check the timing before setting out between San Ignacio and Trinidad.

Eastern Bolivian Amazon

Trinidad, which is the population center of the Bolivian Amazon, is still very much a frontier settlement, but it provides an access point for dozens of smaller communities, wild rivers and remote jungle reserves. The treasure of the region, however, is the spectacular Parque Nacional Noel Kempff Mercado, which has only recently become known to adventurers and wildlife enthusiasts.

TRINIDAD
☎ 046

The tropical city of Trinidad, at an altitude of 237m, looks somewhat like Santa Cruz did 20 years ago. It is now the Beni capital and the nerve center of the Bolivian Amazon. Although not Bolivia's most prepossessing city – the open sewers are a nauseating health

hazard – Trinidad has a growing population that has now passed 80,000.

Only 14° south of the equator, Trinidad has a humid tropical climate. The seasons are less pronounced than in other parts of Bolivia, and temperatures are uniformly hot year-round. Most of the rain falls during the summer in unrelenting downpours, and during wet times, the streets fill with mud and the air with the sound of croaking frogs. Although winter is drier than summer, it also sees a good measure of precipitation.

History

The city of La Santísima Trinidad (the Most Holy Trinity) was founded in 1686 by Padre Cipriano Barace as the second Jesuit mission in the flatlands of the southern Beni. It was originally constructed on the banks of the Río Mamoré 14km from its present location, but floods and pestilence along the riverbanks necessitated relocation. In 1769 it was moved to the Arroyo de San Juan, which now divides the city in two.

Orientation

Street names are a major confusion here, and have been changed several times over the past decade; in fact, no two maps seem to agree. Fortunately, the city isn't too big. Of note, Avenida Mariscal Santa Cruz is sometimes known as Avenida Pedro Ignacio Muiva, and Calle Junín is sometimes called Calle Pedro de la Rocha.

Information

The tourist office in Trinidad isn't worth even mentioning, but you may find some information on protected areas in the Beni at the SENAP office (☎ 20087 or 42138) on Bolívar at Ejército. At the Beni Hotel, you can buy the useful booklet *Beni Turístico*, produced by the Camara Hotelera, for US$4.50.

Money You'll find street moneychangers on Avenida 6 de Agosto between Calle Nicolás Suárez and Avenida 18 de Noviembre, but they only deal in US dollars cash. You can change traveler's checks for a 2% commission at the friendly and efficient

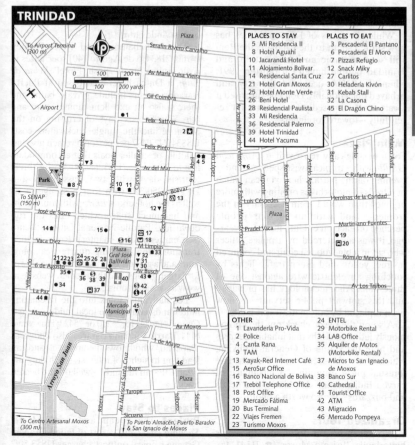

TRINIDAD

PLACES TO STAY
- 5 Mi Residencia II
- 8 Hotel Aguahí
- 10 Jacarandá Hotel
- 11 Alojamiento Bolívar
- 14 Residencial Santa Cruz
- 21 Hotel Gran Moxos
- 25 Hotel Monte Verde
- 26 Beni Hotel
- 28 Residencial Paulista
- 33 Mi Residencia
- 36 Residencial Palermo
- 39 Hotel Trinidad
- 44 Hotel Yacuma

PLACES TO EAT
- 3 Pescadería El Pantano
- 6 Pescadería El Moro
- 7 Pizzas Refugio
- 12 Snack Miky
- 27 Carlitos
- 30 Heladería Kivón
- 31 Kebab Stall
- 32 La Casona
- 45 El Dragón Chino

OTHER
- 1 Lavandería Pro-Vida
- 2 Police
- 4 Canta Rana
- 9 TAM
- 13 Kayak-Red Internet Café
- 15 AeroSur Office
- 16 Banco Nacional de Bolivia
- 17 Trebol Telephone Office
- 18 Post Office
- 19 Mercado Fátima
- 20 Bus Terminal
- 22 Viajes Fremen
- 23 Turismo Moxos
- 24 ENTEL
- 29 Motorbike Rental
- 34 LAB Office
- 35 Alquiler de Motos (Motorbike Rental)
- 37 Micros to San Ignacio de Moxos
- 38 Banco Sur
- 40 Cathedral
- 41 Tourist Office
- 42 ATM
- 43 Migración
- 46 Mercado Pompeya

Banco Sur, half a block from the plaza beneath the old Hotel Ganadero. There's a useful ATM that accepts international credit cards on the eastern side of Avenida Mariscal Santa Cruz, just south of the main plaza.

Post & Communications Service at the main post office, just off the plaza, moves at a suitably tropical pace. For telephone calls, see Trebol, at Cipriano Barace 23-A. Internet and email access are available at Kayak-Red Internet Café, in the shopping center near the corner of Simón Bolívar and Cochabamba, which charges US$2.50 per hour.

Laundry When your clothes can no longer cope with the sticky heat, drop in at the Lavandería Pro-Vida on Calle Felix Sattori.

Dangers & Annoyances Although mud is the biggest problem for pedestrians around Trinidad, the open sewers will make anyone retch – except perhaps the 3m boa constrictor I once found swimming in one of them! Be especially careful at night. Note also – especially if you're staying near the plaza – that a sort of town *reveille* sounds at about 6:15 am.

While the focus of DEA activities has now shifted south to the Chapare, the Beni still sees sporadic anti-drug action, and Trinidad people haven't forgotten 1991, when the DEA occupied the city and behaved objectionably. Don't be surprised if locals react bemusedly – or even a bit resentfully – toward foreigners.

Main Plaza

For a nostalgically retro visit to *American Graffiti* with a tropical twist, spend a Sunday evening on the plaza, where you can watch hundreds of motorbikes orbiting with more urgency than would seem necessary in the tropics – and with up to four people perched on each bike! Until just a few years ago, it was all refereed by a police officer who sat in a big wooden chair and conjured up red, yellow and green traffic lights by touching an electric wire against one of three nails. Alas, technology has prevailed and this stalwart public servant has now been replaced by automatic traffic lights.

Also on the plaza, check out the eponymously lethargic sloths that inhabit the trees and note the statue of General Ballivián, which bears the Beni coat of arms. The unusual plaza fountain – a mishmash of carved Indians, pink dolphins, puma heads and buzzards – is also worth a photo.

Organized Tours

Several agencies run tours into the city's hinterlands. Turismo Moxos (☎ 21141; fax 22189; turmoxos@sauce.ben.entelnet.bo; Avenida 6 de Agosto 114, Casilla 252) organizes three-day cruises on the Río Ibare (US$180), visits to Sirionó villages (US$98), four-day canoe safaris into the jungle (US$180) and one-day horseback trips into remote areas (US$50). The recommended Paraíso Travel (☎/fax 20692; paraiso@ sauce.ben.entelnt.bo; 6 de Agosto 138, Casilla 261) does four-day bird-watching safaris (US$530 per person with four people), jungle camping trips (US$90), day cruises on the Rio Mamoré (US$45/35 per person with two/four people), and

excursions to Laguna Suárez (US$22/15). See the website at www.ben.entelnet.bo/paraiso/index.htm.

The Cochabamba-based Viajes Fremen (☎/fax 21834; 6 de Agosto 140) specializes in river cruises on the posh 'Flotel' *Reina de Enin*, a Dutch hotel-boat based at Puerto Barador; cabins include private baths and there's also an excellent dining room and bar. Four/five/six days of cruising on the Mamoré and the jungle backwaters costs US$349/423/497 per person. Fremen also has a flotilla of smaller boats that accommodate five to 20 people (US$268/300/365 for three/four/six days with two passengers and US$190/250/320 with four passengers), as well as the houseboat *Ebrio*, with four berths and hammock space, which does the run down into Parque Nacional Isiboro-Sécure (see earlier in this chapter). Rates include transportation, sleeping quarters/camping, tours and a guide. Per-person prices are lower for larger groups. See the Fremen website at www.andes-amazonia.com.

For individual tours into the fascinating hinterlands, contact the local guide Ademar Campos (☎ 24110, 25210 or 25423; Huacaraje 6111, Barrio Cipriano Barace), also known as 'Papacho,' who knows the area well and can lead you to sights of interest – including the bizarre 'Paititi mounds' – well off the beaten track.

Places to Stay

Budget The cheap and seedy *Hotel Yacuma* (☎ 22249), a sort of faded Graham Greene tropical outpost, charges US$3.50/7 for basic, musty singles/doubles with shared baths and US$8.50/12 with private baths. Although meals are no longer served, the patio is a decent place to quietly pass a sultry afternoon.

A budget alternative is the central *Residencial Paulista* (☎ 20018 or 20118), which charges US$5 per person without bath and US$10/17 with bath. *Alojamiento Bolívar* (21726) charges just US$3.50 per person, and *Residencial Santa Cruz* (☎ 20711) wants US$6.50 per person with shared baths and US$17 for singles or doubles with private baths and fans. *Residencial Palermo*

(☎ 20472), two blocks off the plaza, charges US$3.50 per person with a fan but no private bath.

Mid-Range At *Beni Hotel* (☎ 22788 or 20522; fax 20262; benihotel@latinmail.com; Casilla 195), you'll get a decent single/double with a fan and a private bath for US$16/20. Try to avoid the ground floor, where the high water table seems to cause plumbing odors. The central *Hotel Monte Verde* (☎ 22750; fax 22044; 6 de Agosto 76) charges US$16/27 for rooms with private baths, cable TV and phones. Once you've checked in (especially if you're an obvious foreigner), be especially wary of scams to extract more money.

Hotel Trinidad (☎/fax 21380; Pedro de la Rocha 80) has rooms with private baths, air-conditioning, cable TV and breakfast for US$35/50. *Jacarandá Hotel* (☎ 22033; fax 23990; Simón Bolívar 229), with its distinctive – and rather interesting – architecture, is a very nice mid-range choice. Rooms with air-conditioning, cable TV and private baths cost US$35/50; children under 12 stay free of charge.

Excellent mid-range choices are the very friendly *Mi Residencia* (☎ 21535; fax 22464; Manuel Limpias 76), in the center, and its annex, *Mi Residencia II* (☎ 21543; fax 22464; Félix Pinto Saucedo 555), on a quiet but notoriously muddy street beside an appropriately named little shop, the Canta Rana (song of the frog). Each charges US$45/65.

Top End The conference center and current business travelers' choice is the centrally located four-star *Hotel Gran Moxos* (☎/fax 22240; 6 de Agosto 146), where singles/doubles with air-conditioning and cable TV cost US$50/75, including use of the gym, pool and sauna (which is fairly redundant in this climate!). Credit cards are accepted here.

The comfortable and very nice *Hotel Aguahí* (☎ 25569; fax 25570), on a quiet section of Bolívar at Santa Cruz, a few blocks from the center, has rooms with private baths, TV and breakfast for US$50/65. Amenities include air-conditioning and a beautiful swimming pool.

Places to Eat

If budget is a major concern, go to the *Mercado Municipal*. For a pittance, you can pick up tropical fruits or sample the local specialty, *arroz con queso* (rice with cheese), as well as shish kebabs, yucca, plantains and salad.

Since Trinidad is the heart of cattle country, it's a practical place to indulge in beef, and any of the major hotel dining rooms feature it on the menu. A popular and inexpensive place to enjoy parrillada is *Carlitos*, on the plaza, which sizzles up some of the best steaks you'll ever taste.

A very popular place for inexpensive snacks and ice cream in the evening is *Snack Miky*. Light meals, full breakfasts, ice cream, cakes, sweets, pastries, sandwiches, coffee and juice are served at *Heladería Kivón*, the local youth hangout on the plaza. It's open when everything else is closed, including mornings and Saturday afternoons. Next door there's an unassuming little *kebab stall* with no name or sign. Also on the plaza is *La Casona* pizzería, which serves pizza and nothing else. Another pizza option is the normally lively *Pizzas Refugio*, on Avenida Santa Cruz.

A friendly choice is the long-standing *El Dragón Chino*, on Calle Cipriano Barace, opposite the Mercado Municipal, which does Beijing/Bolivian fare. For excellent local fish specialties, try *Pescadería El Moro*, on Bolívar at Velasco, which is just a short hike from the center; unfortunately, in the evening it becomes a real drinking den. After dark, you may want to catch a taxi. In a quieter part of town is *Pescadería El Pantano*, appropriately on Avenida del Mar. For something less formal, head out to Puerto Barador in the afternoon, where makeshift restaurants serve up the catch of the day.

Entertainment & Shopping

Apart from the bars in the main hotels and restaurants, your entertainment options are limited to the lovely frog choruses, which resonate through the evening, and the several discos along Avenida Santa Cruz.

As for shopping, local Beni crafts, including weavings, woodworking and ceramics, are sold at the Centro Artesanal Moxos (☎ 22751), on Calle José Bopi in Casilla 48.

Getting There & Away

Air In addition to the US$1.80 AASANA tax, departing air travelers must pay US$1 to support senior citizens and finance public works.

TAM (☎ 22363) flies on Monday between Santa Cruz (US$100) and La Paz (US$100), via Trinidad; on Wednesday, they fly from Cochabamba to Santa Cruz, via Trinidad; and on Thursday, from Santa Cruz to Cochabamba, via Trinidad. On Thursday, you can fly to Riberalta (US$65), Guayaramerín (US$65) and Cobija (US$59).

Subject to seasonal fluctuations, LAB (☎ 20595) and AeroSur (☎ 20765) both fly to La Paz (US$67), Cochabamba (US$55), Santa Cruz (US$67), Riberalta (US$84), Guayaramerín (US$84) and Cobija (US$100), and offer weekly flights to San Joaquín (US$42), Magdalena (US$38) and San Ramón (US$38). Note that the inter-Beni flights are frequently suspended for long periods. AeroSur provides overpriced connections to Santa Cruz (US$80) and La Paz (US$110). The sporadic and not-too-reliable charter airline Servicios Aéreos Vargas España, or SAVE (☎ 22806 or 25063), flies between Trinidad, Santa Cruz, Guayaramerín, Riberalta, Cobija and San Borja.

See Air in the Getting Around chapter for information on LAB's Benipass, which allows you to visit four Amazon Basin towns for US$231.

Bus & Camioneta In the dry season (and at other times when the road is passable), several flotas depart nightly for Santa Cruz (11 to 12 hours, US$15) from the main terminal at the corner of Calles Pinto and Rómulo Mendoza. Several companies leave for San Borja, Rurrenabaque and La Paz daily between 9 and 10 am. Three

Down the Lazy River

River trips from Trinidad will carry you to the heart of Bolivia's greatest wilderness area, where you'll experience the mystique and solitude for which the Amazonian rain forests are renowned. For optimum enjoyment, go during the dry season, which lasts roughly from May to September.

Although the scenery along the northern rivers changes little, the diversity of plant and animal species along the shore picks up any slack in the pace of the journey. The longer your trip, the deeper you'll gaze into the forest darkness and the more closely you'll scan the riverbanks for signs of movement. Free of the pressures and demands of active travel, you'll have time to relax and savor the passing scene.

In general, the riverboat food is pretty good, but meals consist mainly of masaco, charque, rice, noodles, thin soup and bananas in every conceivable form. After a couple of days you'll probably start dreaming of pizza, so you may want to bring along some treats to supplement the daily fare. It's also wise to carry your own water or some form of water purification.

Be sure to discuss sleeping arrangements with the captain before setting out. Passengers must usually bring their own hammocks (available in Trinidad), but you may be allowed to sleep on deck or on the roof of the boat. You'll also need a sleeping bag or a blanket, especially in the winter, when jungle nights can be surprisingly chilly. If you're fortunate enough to be on a boat that travels through the night, a mosquito net isn't necessary, but on one that ties up at night, passengers without a mosquito net will find the experience from utterly miserable to unbearable.

times weekly, there are also services to Guayaramerín and Riberalta, with connections to Cobija.

Micros and camionetas run to San Ignacio de Moxos (three hours, US$2.50) when full from Calle La Paz, near Avenida 18 de Noviembre. Some continue to San Borja (eight hours, US$8 in the cab or US$7 in the back).

Boat Trinidad isn't actually on the bank of a navigable river; Puerto Barador lies on the Río Mamoré, 13km away, and Puerto Almacén is on the Ibare, 8km from town. Camionetas charge US$1 to Puerto Almacén and US$2 to Puerto Barador. (See Puertos Almacén & Barador under Around Trinidad.)

If you're looking for river transportation north along the Mamoré to Guayaramerín, or south along the Mamoré and Ichilo to Puerto Villarroel, inquire at the Distrito Naval (☎ 23000) – the navy sails comfortably to Puerto Villarroel three times monthly. If nothing turns up, head for Puerto Barador and check departure schedules with the Capitanía del Puerto or inquire around the riverboats themselves.

The Guayaramerín run takes a week or less (larger boats do it in three to four days) and costs about US$30, including food. To Puerto Villarroel, smaller boats take four to six days and cost US$20 to US$25, normally including meals.

Getting Around
To/From the Airport The airport is on the northwest edge of town, a half-hour walk from the center. Moto-taxis charge US$1, and you'd be surprised how much luggage they can accommodate with a bit of creativity. Car taxis should cost US$1.50 per person, though drivers will try to charge more. But hey, it's a nice 30-minute walk into town.

Motorcycle Moto-taxi drivers are normally happy to take the day off and rent out their vehicles, but you'll need a regular driving license from home. Plan on US$1.50 per hour or US$15 for a 24-hour day. The moto-taxis hang out around the southwest corner of the plaza. Alternatively, you can rent motorbikes at Alquiler de Motos for US$1.80 per hour, US$10 from 8 am to 6 pm, or US$17 for 24 hours.

Taxi Motorcycle taxis around town cost US$0.30 (B$1.50), while car taxis charge US$0.40 (B$2). A taxi to the airport or bus terminal costs US$1.

For taxis to outlying areas, phone Radio Taxi Progreso Beniano (☎ 22759). It's important to know the distances involved and to bargain well for a good rate, which should be about US$5 per hour for up to four people. Be sure to include any waiting time you'll need to visit the sights.

AROUND TRINIDAD
Loma Suárez
Although it's of little real interest, the little hillock Loma Suárez, 9km from Trinidad, is a local landmark and a good motorbike destination. This artificial mound on the banks of the Ibare was first known as Loma Mocovi. When it was purchased by the Suárez brothers, it was renamed Loma Ayacucho, but through common usage, it came to be known as Loma Suárez. There's a military post at the loma, and you'll have to pass a checkpoint to continue past it to Chuchini.

Transportation in this direction from Trinidad leaves from the gasoline station, a 15-minute walk from town beyond the Pompeya bridge. Continuing to Chuchini will probably involve a 5km walk from Loma Suárez.

Santuario Chuchini
In the Llanos de Moxos, between San Ignacio de Moxos and Loreto, the heavily forested landscape is crossed with more than 100km of canals and causeways and dotted with hundreds of *lomas* (artificial mounds), embankments and more fanciful prehistoric earthworks depicting people and animals. One anthropomorphic figure measures over 2km from head to toe – a rain forest variation on Peru's famed Nazca Lines. The original purpose of the earthworks was probably to permit cultivation in a seasonally flooded area, but inside the mounds were buried figurines, pottery, ceramic stamps, human remains and even tools made from stone imported into the region.

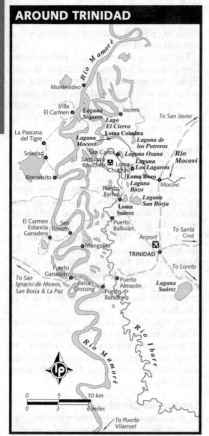

AROUND TRINIDAD

which is only one of many dotted throughout the surrounding forest. From the camp, you can take short walks in the rain forest to lagoons with profuse bird life, caimans and other larger animals.

The camp has shady, covered picnic sites, trees, children's swings and a variety of native plants, birds and animals. There's also an archaeological museum displaying articles excavated from the loma, including bizarre statues with distinctly Mongol queues and slanted eyes as well as a piece that appears to be a female figure wearing a bikini (it's actually thought to be an identification of and homage to specific body areas rather than an article of clothing!).

Chuchini may be a lovely place, but it's grossly overpriced for what's offered. Foreign visitors are now charged an unrealistic US$10 admission fee just to see the museum. For a day visit, including admission, a three-hour cruise and a meal, the price is US$50, and to stay overnight, it's US$100.

Places to Stay & Eat Bungalows, with meals included, are also overpriced at US$60 per person. If you're not staying, exotic dishes are available in the restaurant; the food is great, but again, it's pricey. If you prefer just a snack, try the tasty *chipilos* (fried green plantain chips). Further information is available from Lorena Hinojoso (☎ 21968; 25 de Noviembre 199, Trinidad).

Getting There & Away Hitching is best on Sunday, though you may have to walk the last 5km from Loma Suárez. It's also a good destination for those who've rented motorbikes.

Laguna Suárez

This large 1.5m-deep artificial lake, 5km from Trinidad, was originally known as Socoreno ('Lagoon of Animals'). Lying 5km from Trinidad, it was constructed by the Paititis. On Sunday, local families turn out to picnic, drink and eat lunch at the lakeside Restaurant-Bar Tapacaré, and children swim in the pool, canoe, and play soccer and volleyball.

According to archaeologists, the prehistoric structures of the Beni were constructed by the Paititi tribe 5500 years ago and provide evidence of much larger pre-Columbian populations than were previously suspected. It's likely that this ancient Beni civilization was the source of popular Spanish legends of the rain forest El Dorado known as Gran Paititi.

The Santuario Chuchini, 14km from Trinidad, is one of the few easily accessible Paititi sites. The name means 'the jaguar's lair' (*madriguera del tigre* in Spanish). This camp sits on an eight-hectare artificial loma,

Along Río Mamoré

Marilyn fan in Rurrenabaque

Parque Nacional Madidi

Making a fan, Parque Nacional Madidi

Life on Río Beni

Woman, Isla del Sol

Aymará woman weaving

Spinning alpaca wool into yarn

Reveler at Tarabuco's Phujllay festival

There's no public transportation, but it's easy enough to get there on foot or by moto-taxi. Follow the ring road toward Santa Cruz and turn right at a small, white police post. From there, it's 4km to the lake. Admission to the resort is US$0.30, and it costs US$1 to use the pool. Single/double kayak rental costs US$1.50/2 per hour and motorboats rent for US$7 per hour.

Puertos Almacén & Barador

Puerto Almacén, 8km from Trinidad, is best known for its lineup of rickety fish restaurants, which provide excellent lunch options. Otherwise, this now pointless little place is the proud home of a massive concrete bridge, and vehicles no longer have to be shunted across on balsas.

You may prefer to continue 4km farther to Puerto Barador, where you can observe pink river dolphins in small Mamoré tributaries or sample fresh fish at one of several pleasant portside restaurants. One of the best is *El Pantanal*, which serves excellent surubí for US$2.50. It's very popular with Bolivians, especially on Sunday.

Taxis from Trinidad to either port cost about US$10 each way, but camiones and camionetas leave frequently from Avenida Mariscal Santa Cruz, 1½ blocks south of Pompeya bridge in Trinidad. All transportation to San Ignacio de Moxos also passes both Puerto Almacén (US$0.80) and Puerto Barador (US$1.20). For information on boat travel from Puerto Barador, see Getting There & Away in Trinidad, earlier in this chapter.

The Farm

For a rain forest getaway, check out The Farm (lastfrontiers@yahoo.co.uk), a Bolivian- and European-run dairy farm 55km southeast of Trinidad, along the tarred Santa Cruz road. For guests, Sarah, Dieter and Celia provide campsites and the use of clean bucket showers and toilets for US$6 per person, including meals and soft drinks. Tents and hammocks are also available. For US$28, they conduct short horseback tours into the surrounding jungle and pampas. Other possibilities include hiking, village visits, piranha fishing, cattle drives, participation in the milking, and wildlife viewing.

In the dry season (June to October), six-day rain forest tours by boat into the Reserva de Vida Silvestre Ríos Blanco y Negro cost US$230 per person with four people. From October to June, you'll pay US$250 to US$280 per person, including airfare from Trinidad (boat access isn't possible in this season). Note that groups must form themselves. These trips feature Bolivian guides, interpreters, rain forest treks, canoe trips, wildlife viewing, fishing and exploration of the Ríos Blanco y Negro by dugout canoe.

To get to The Farm (you can just turn up – no bookings are necessary), take a taxi from Trinidad (US$10 for up to four people) and ask for 'la estancia,' opposite the El Diablo dairy, 2km beyond Casarabe along the Santa Cruz road. Alternatively, take a taxi from central Trinidad to the Parada Sintrabe (US$0.50 per person) and wait for a minibus to Casarabe (US$2). In a pinch, The Farm is also accessible on any bus between Trinidad and Santa Cruz, but note that the flotas may not accept short-haul passengers.

Loreto

Loreto, founded on June 28, 1675, was the first Jesuit mission in the Beni lowlands, but all that remains of the original church is a graceful façade. From October 4 to 7, 1959, its otherwise ordinary-looking image of Nuestra Señora de Loreto was seen to weep, as witnessed by the entire town, and Loreto has now become a pilgrimage destination. The pilgrimage takes place from March to October, the town founding is celebrated on June 28, and the religious festival of the Santuario de Loreto occurs on December 10.

Asención de Guarayos

This small Jesuit Indian settlement, with a very nice old church, lies on the Santa Cruz-Trinidad road, five to eight hours from Trinidad. The town is known for its *maricas*, little palm-leaf backpacks woven by the local women.

MAGDALENA
☎ 0886

One of the loveliest towns in Bolivian Amazonia is Magdalena, which lies 220km northeast of Trinidad in the heart of vast, low-lying forest and pampa beside the Río Itonamas. It was founded by the Jesuits in 1720 and was the northernmost of the Bolivian missions. Today, the atmosphere surpasses *tranquilo*, and most of the local vehicles are just horse- or ox-drawn carts.

The area is rich in birds and other wildlife and has yet to be discovered by tourism. About 7km and 30 minutes upstream is the inviting Laguna Baíqui, which is excellent for swimming, picnics and fishing, and is accessible by boat from town; expect to pay about US$1 per person. Another pleasant excursion will take you to Bella Vista, which is considered one of the most charming villages in the Beni – and one of its finest fishing venues – at the junction of the Ríos San Martín and Blanco. In the dry season, minibuses do the two-hour trip, passing en route through the rustic village of Orobayaya.

Magdalena's biggest festival, Santa María de Magdalena, takes place on July 22.

Places to Stay & Eat
The best accommodations are at the lovely Swiss-run *Hotel Internacional (☎ 2210; satellite phone 00874-761-866681; Switzerland fax 41-71-352-5472; info@hwz-inc .com)*, which promises to become an Amazonian standard, with a fine restaurant/bar and two swimming pools to help you cope with the tropical heat. Singles/doubles cost US$33/45 including breakfast; suites cost US$50/60. The friendly management is happy to provide assistance in organizing excursions through the surrounding areas. For more information, see their website at www.hwz-inc.com.

Budget choices include *Hotel Ganadero*, near the plaza, which offers rooms with shared baths for US$8 per person and one with a shower for US$10, and *Hotel San Carlos*, which charges US$8 per person (US$12 with private bath).

Getting There & Away
LAB has flights daily except Wednesday and Friday between Magdalena and assorted other places: Trinidad, Guayaramerín, San Joaquín and San Ramón. SAVE also flies with some regularity from Santa Cruz and Trinidad. The very poor road from Trinidad, passable only in the dry season, is served by hardy camiones and an occasional bus, but realistically, it should only be tackled with 4WD.

SANTA ANA DEL YACUMA
☎ 0484

Originally known as San Lorenzo, Santa Ana del Yacuma, northwest of Trinidad, was founded by the Jesuits in 1693. This low-lying town is surrounded by a dyke to prevent flooding during the diluvian rainy seasons.

Traditionally a cattle town, in the early 1990s it became a booming cocaine-processing and trafficking capital and one of the few towns to organize resistance to the DEA forces. In June 1991, an intensive DEA cleanup of Santa Ana netted 10 homes, 15 labs, 28 airplanes, assorted supplies and spare parts, and 110kg of cocaine base, but no one was arrested: Processors, traffickers and their Colombian accessories had all melted into the forest. Throughout this period, the Club Social on the plaza served as the unashamed headquarters for the *narcotraficante* movers and shakers. Now, however, much of this affluence has migrated, and the town has relaxed into relative obscurity.

Although it's accessible by boat or air from Trinidad, Santa Ana del Yacuma is scarcely worth a special trip. If you've somehow landed up here, check out the former palaces in the center and the extravagant and incongruous air terminal that graces the airstrip of this remote settlement.

PERSEVERANCIA & RESERVA DE VIDA SILVESTRE RÍOS BLANCO Y NEGRO
The 1.4 million-hectare Ríos Blanco y Negro Wildlife Reserve, created in 1990, occupies the heart of Bolivia's largest wilderness area

and contains vast tracts of undisturbed rain forest with myriad species of plants and animals. These include giant anteaters, peccaries, tapirs, jaguars, bush dogs, marmosets, river otters, capuchin monkeys, caimans, squirrel monkeys, deer and capybaras. The diverse bird life includes curassows, six varieties of macaw and over 300 other bird species.

The area's only settlement, the privately owned estancia of Perseverancia, lies 350km north of Santa Cruz. It started as a center of rubber production in the 1920s and continued until the last *seringueros* (rubber tappers) left in 1972. When the airstrip was completed, professional hunters went after river otters and large cats. By 1986, the estancia had again been abandoned, and it remained so until tourism – albeit scanty – began being promoted in 1989.

In the mid-1990s, Moira logging concerns began encroaching on the eastern portion of the reserve and USAID recommended that loggers clear a section of the forest rather than cut selective trees. They apparently considered it preferable to endure a total loss over a small area than partial loss of a large area.

Organized Tours

The best way to visit Ríos Blanco y Negro is with The Farm (see Around Trinidad, earlier in this chapter). In the dry season, adventurous camping tours along wild rivers start at US$230 per person with at least four people, including boat transportation, a guide and meals. If these trips are to remain magical, it's essential to limit access to small groups and to practice cultural and environmental sensitivity.

Rosario Tours (☎ 03-369977; fax 03-369656; aventura@tucan.cnb.net; Arenales 193, Casilla 683, Santa Cruz) sometimes offers excursions to the park, but the lodge is now closed. For the latest information, check with them or with other Santa Cruz travel agencies.

Getting There & Away

The privately owned estancia of Perseverancia is accessible only by a 1½-hour charter flight from El Trompillo airport in Santa Cruz. The return flights are included in tour packages.

There's also a 100km track between Asención de Guarayos and Perseverancia, but it's not passable by vehicle, even in the dry season. On foot, it would take at least five hot, sticky days each way.

PARQUE NACIONAL NOEL KEMPFF MERCADO

Remote Noel Kempff Mercado National Park lies in the northernmost reaches of Santa Cruz department, between the Serranía de Huanchaca (also called Caparúch or just Caparú) and the banks of the Ríos Verde and Guaporé (marked Río Iténez on some maps). Not only is it one of South America's most spectacular parks, but it also takes in a range of dwindling habitats, lending it world-class ecological significance. The park encompasses 1.5 million hectares of the most dramatic scenery in northern Bolivia – rivers, rain forests, waterfalls, plateaus and rugged 500m escarpments – as well as a broad spectrum of Amazonian flora and fauna (see 'Wildlife of Noel Kempff Mercado National Park').

History

Originally known as Parque Nacional Huanchaca, the fabulous park was created in 1979 to protect the Serranía de Huanchaca and its wildlife. Many of the people living around the fringes of the park are descended from workers who were brought in as rubber tappers in the 1940s. When synthetic rubber was developed, their jobs disappeared and they turned to hunting, agriculture, logging and the illegal pet trade.

Tragically, on September 5, 1986, distinguished Bolivian biologist Noel Kempff Mercado, who had originally lobbied for the creation of the park, was murdered by renegades at a remote park airstrip east of the Río Paucerna, along with pilot Juan Cochamanidis and environmental guide Franklin Parada. In 1988 the park's name was officially changed to Noel Kempff Mercado in honor of its de facto founder. In

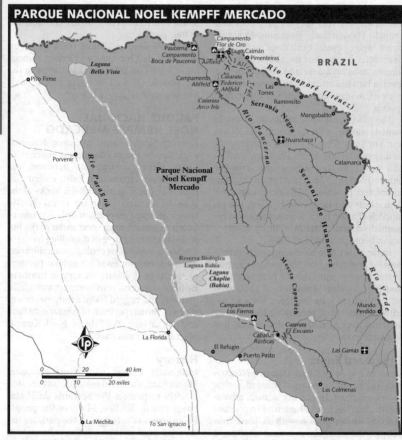

PARQUE NACIONAL NOEL KEMPFF MERCADO

May 1995, two Brazilians and a Colombian were convicted of the murders.

Information

Responsibility for park conservation and infrastructure is currently in the hands of the Fundación Amigos de la Naturaleza, or FAN (☎ 03-337475; fax 03-329692; fan@fan-bo.org; Casilla 2241, Santa Cruz), which operates with the assistance of The Nature Conservancy and other international organizations. For more information, see their website at www.scbbs-bo.com/fan. Every

prospective visitor to the park must first visit the Santa Cruz or San Ignacio FAN offices, in order to ensure that park personnel will be available to accompany them on their visit.

The park administration and the Noel Kempff Mercado Natural History Museum in Santa Cruz are currently organizing transportation and facilities for low-budget park visitors interested in backpacking, wilderness canoeing and mountain biking, in hopes of demonstrating to local people that conservation pays. Local guides can be hired for approximately US$15 per group per day. Fortunately, the local Chiquitano guides have grown up in the region and are very familiar with the natural history of the area. In addition to guiding, they'll help carry gear, set up camp and keep visitors out of danger.

In the small communities on the southern and western borders of the park, rustic lodging is available for US$5 to US$15.

When to Go There's no wrong season to visit the park. The wet season is great for river travel, especially if you want to boat up to the two big waterfalls. The wettest months are from December to March. The dry season is obviously better for vehicles, but in the late winter months, smoke from forest burning can obliterate the scenery, especially from mid-August to October. March to June is pleasant and not overly hot or rainy, and from October to December, the spring blooms add another fabulous dimension.

Dangers & Annoyances A major concern will be insects. During rainy periods, the mosquitoes are fierce and voracious and tiny *garapatilla* ticks can be especially annoying. In the wet season, be especially wary of the blood-sucking sandfly, which carries leishmaniasis (see the Health section in the Facts for the Visitor chapter). These flies are a real pest at some campsites, particularly in the high forest around the Huanchaca I laboratory ruins.

Between September and December there's a phenomenal bee hatch-out, when the bees seek out human campsites for salt. At such times, it's not unusual to have as many as 10,000 bees hanging around a single site, so if you're allergic, avoid the park during these months. The best way to avoid attracting such numbers is to change campsites daily.

Leafcutter ants may also become a problem, and although their six-inch-wide forest highways, choked with trains of leaf-bearing workers, can be fascinating to watch, they also seem to thrive on the ripstop nylon used in tents. In fact, they can destroy a tent in less than an hour – even

The Lost World

Although it's commonly assumed that Sir Arthur Conan Doyle's classic *The Lost World* was set among the *tepuis* (flat-topped mountains) of Amazonian Venezuela, it was actually inspired by the Bolivian plateaus and escarpments in the region of Parque Nacional Noel Kempff Mercado.

In his journals, British explorer Colonel Percy Harrison Fawcett, who was commissioned by the Bolivian government early this century to survey the boundary between Bolivia and Brazil, wrote the following:

> Above us towered the Ricardo Franco Hills, flat-topped and mysterious, their flanks scarred by deep *quebradas*. Time and the foot of man had not touched these summits. They stood like a lost world, forested to their tops, and the imagination could picture the last vestiges there of an age long vanished. Isolated from the battle with changing conditions, monsters from the dawn of man's existence might still roam those heights unchallenged, imprisoned and protected by unscaleable cliffs. So thought Conan Doyle when later in London I spoke of these hills and showed him photographs of them. He mentioned an idea for a novel on Central South America and asked for information. The fruit of it was his *Lost World* in 1912, appearing as a serial in the *Strand Magazine*, and subsequently in the form of a book that achieved widespread popularity.

while you're sleeping in it. Don't set up camp anywhere near an ant trail. If that isn't enough, termites have a taste for backpacks that have been left lying on the ground.

Fire is also a concern. The main natural fire season in the park is from July to November, and since the savanna doesn't burn every year, the amount of dead vegetation is substantial. Never cook or even camp in grassland habitat, no matter how flat and inviting, and never leave a cooking fire unattended, even in the forest.

Surface water in the park is delicious and safe to drink, but it's still wise to purify it. Note that surface water can be scarce between August and November.

La Florida

La Florida is essentially the only access point to the park interior, and will be the headquarters for budget travelers. The Museo Noel Kempff is now providing the community with canoes, bicycles, tents and backpacks to encourage La Florida residents to work as park guides. It's also financing low-budget hostels and eateries in the community.

In La Florida, visitors can now rent dugout canoes for US$10 per day to visit the black-water oxbow lakes and backwater channels of the Río Bajo Paraguá. Camping is currently permitted anywhere along the river, but it's likely that campsite restrictions will be implemented in the near future. Along the river, you're likely to see colonies of herons, cranes, river otters, howler monkeys, black caimanes, and dozens of bird species.

To travel beyond La Florida and into the park, you have three options. You can walk along the old logging road into the park, rent a mountain bike for US$10 per day, or rent a 4WD taxi for US$50 per day (this option is available from April to December). Sometimes you can hitch a ride with the park rangers to Campamento Los Fierros, 40km away inside the park, but this is likely to change as soon as the local taxi service takes hold. If you decide to hike, carry plenty of water and allow two days for this pleasant forest walk along a good logging road, which is open to vehicular traffic from April to December.

Campamento Los Fierros

Campamento Los Fierros lies in the high Amazonian forest about 2km from the ecological habitat known as 'seasonally inundated termite savanna.' This is an excellent staging point for jaunts around the southern end of the park, such as bicycle trips to Laguna Chaplin and the Catarata El Encanto, and hikes up onto the wild Huanchaca Plateau.

There's excellent bird-watching along the forested roads near Los Fierros, and a nearby creek for cooling off or watching fish-eating bats at night. A visit to the termite savanna early in the morning will frequently yield glimpses of maned Andean wolves, crab-eating foxes and even the odd jaguar (which may be a danger to small children).

Visitor facilities include an airstrip and three levels of accommodations (see Places to Eat later in this section).

Catarata El Encanto The objective of most visitors to Los Fierros is Catarata El Encanto, a spectacular 150m waterfall that spills off the Serranía de Huanchaca. It makes for an enchanting three-day hike from Los Fierros. With a mountain bike, it's a long and tiring day trip; with a vehicle, it can be done in a day with lots of time for stops along the way.

The excursion begins along the 4WD track that heads east from Los Fierros. Along the way, you'll pass through high Amazonian forest, seasonally inundated termite savanna (that is, plains dotted with termite mounds) and the threatened cerrado savanna.

Once you've crossed the savanna area, continue until you reach a fork in the road; take the left fork (there should be a sign, but don't count on it). This abandoned logging road passes through some attractive forest, and you're almost guaranteed to observe – or at least hear – spider monkeys in this area.

Eventually, you'll reach a brook with potable water. Here the logging road ends and you follow a trail running alongside the stream to the foot of the waterfall. It's a beautiful spot, so please don't disturb anything. Camping is allowed along the stream below the trailhead, but not along the trails to the waterfall. In the evening, ask your guide to take you to the natural salt licks, which attract tapirs, peccaries and other large mammals.

Serranía de Huanchaca (La Subida de las Peladas) This excursion begins the same as the trip to Catarata El Encanto, but while crossing the seasonally inundated termite savanna, you'll see a small track that turns left (northeast) off the road and leads through the cerrado and forest to the foot of the escarpment. From here, it's a 500m climb up a steep footpath that crosses three bald hills known as Las Peladas. On the way,

---

Wildlife of Noel Kempff Mercado National Park

Noel Kempff Mercado National Park is both spectacularly scenic and ecologically extraordinary because of the diversity of its habitat. It contains elements of five distinct ecosystems – broadleaf evergreen forest, dry forest, inundated forest, dry savanna and inundated savanna – each of which is composed of numerous distinct biological communities.

Recent studies put the number of mammal species at 130, birds at 630, reptiles at 75 and frogs at 63. In addition, researchers have collected more than 260 different species of fish from park rivers, and it's estimated that the park supports over 4000 plant species, including dozens of orchid varieties and some of the last remnants of cerrado vegetation in South America. This makes Noel Kempff Mercado one of the biologically richest parks in the world, surpassed only by parks in the Andean foothills (such as Manu in Peru or Alto Madidi in Bolivia), which have the advantage owing to their 3000m altitudinal ranges.

Patient and observant visitors are likely to see a rich variety of wildlife. If you're very lucky, you may even see a jaguar. Note, however, that full-time researchers only see them perhaps twice in a year. More predictably observed is the maned wolf, found mainly around Los Fierros. It's the most endangered species in the park – not to mention the most glamorous. Go out onto the termite savanna in the early morning and the odds are that you'll see one when they come to the road culverts to drink. You can sometimes hear them barking at night. The best time is June and July. Also relatively easy to see are the pampas deer. These are most readily observed on the track up onto the plateau from Los Fierros, or around Las Gamas.

In the rivers, you'll see alligators, caimans, pink river dolphins and perhaps even a rare river otter. Also around are peccaries, tapirs and spider monkeys, which are frequently observed around Lago Caimán and Catarata El Encanto, and along the plateau track from Los Fierros. Less common are howler monkeys, giant anteaters, bush dogs, short-eared dogs and giant armadillos, all of which are considered endangered or threatened species.

And don't forget your binoculars – Noel Kempff Mercado has more bird species than all of North America! Especially interesting are the very rare grassland species that are largely restricted to Brazil but are becoming threatened there by conversion of their cerrado habitat to cattle ranches and soybean farms. Species that will get birders' juices flowing include the rusty-necked piculet, Zimmer's tody tyrant, collared crescent-chest, ocellated crake, rufous-winged antshrike, rufous-sided pygmy tyrant, campo miner, yellow-billed blue finch, black and tawny seed-eater, and a host of others. For the nonenthusiast, there is easy bird-watching at Flor de Oro along the river. The guans and curassows are especially tame, as there hasn't been much hunting pressure in recent years.

– Timothy J Killeen, Bolivia

Tapir

you'll pass through dry forest on the lower slopes, and cerrado and bamboo groves on the upper slopes. Once at the top, you're ushered onto a spectacular grassy plain dotted with unusual rock outcrops that lend it the name *campo rupestre* (rocky landscape). There are also plenty of islands of gallery forest, where the park administration has established some excellent campsites.

From the escarpment on a clear day, you can see the Amazon forests, termite savannas, Laguna Chaplin and the gallery forests of the Río Paraguá. It's also a good vantage point to watch hawks and vultures riding the thermals and flocks of blue and yellow macaws migrating between their nesting sites in the highland palm groves and their feeding grounds in the forests below.

On the plateau, you can hike for two or three days north to a spectacular unnamed waterfall or south to the escarpment overlooking the Catarata El Encanto. Along the way, watch for the endangered *gama* (white-tailed deer), which has its last stronghold here. You'll also pass numerous crystalline ponds that make for refreshing swimming holes; at least one species of fish here is found nowhere else on earth, and although it may nip at your legs, it's not dangerous.

The park administration has now cut a 140km, seven-day hiking route across the plateau, but owing to environmental sensitivity and the possibility of contracting tropical ailments, they haven't yet determined to what degree it will be open to hiking groups and their guides.

Those with adequate financial resources can fly into one of two remote airstrips at the abandoned drug-processing laboratories Huanchaca I (now used as an overnight camp on FAN's extension tour) and Las Gamas. The former lies on the northern end of the plateau amid cerrado savanna dotted with islands of Amazonian forest. From there, it's a short day hike to the upper reaches of the Río Paucerna, which is a fast-running blackwater river. Strong swimmers will be OK, but drag yourself out before you reach the Arco Irís waterfall! Las

Gamas is a beautiful place at the southern end of the escarpment, and may soon have trail access from Los Fierros.

Piso Firme & Porvenir

Piso Firme is a pleasant little place with several alojamientos and restaurants as well as a small shop selling staples – rice, salt, sardines etc. The occasional barge service between Piso Firme and Pimenteiras takes 12 hours. Pimenteiras is only a short boat ride from Flor de Oro, making this an alternative to the expensive flight. Porvenir is just a tiny village with no lodging, but you'll usually find something to eat.

Flor de Oro

At Flor de Oro, FAN runs an upmarket tourist lodge for their package visitors. Around the camp, you'll find examples of periodically inundated termite savanna, degraded cerrado (gallery forest), oxbow lakes and riverine flooded forests, all of which afford superb bird-watching opportunities. More than 300 bird species have been recorded here, and sightings of pink river dolphins are almost guaranteed.

It's a four-hour hike along the trail from Flor de Oro to Lago Caimán, which is the trailhead for Allie's Trail to the Mirador de los Monos. Visitors wanting to see the big waterfalls must travel by boat up the Río Paucerna.

Lago Caimán Lago Caimán, 30 minutes by motorboat (or five hours on foot) upstream from Flor de Oro, is a superb spot for bird-watching and seeing caimans. Allie's Trail, named for the Peace Corps volunteer who constructed it in the early 1990s, begins at Lago Caimán and climbs up through dry forest to the Mirador de los Monos, with great scenery along the edges of the escarpment. It then wanders through dwarf evergreen forest and high forest until eventually passing the Catarata Arco Irís and winding up at the Catarata Federico Ahlfeld, where there's a small campamento (open only during periods of high water, from December to May).

Unfortunately, the trail hasn't been maintained beyond the Mirador de los Monos for several years now, and may be overgrown. If you want to attempt it, hire a guide with a big machete and allow at least five days for the hike.

Río Paucerna The two spectacular waterfalls Arco Irís and Federico Ahlfeld tumble down the Río Paucerna above the Campamento Boca de Paucerna ranger station (camping may be available here, but there are no facilities). From July to early December, the boat trip from Flor de Oro to Campamento Ahlfeld takes about five hours each way, depending on water levels. From the campamento, it's a short walk to the spectacular 35m waterfall, Catarata Ahlfeld, and its lovely swimming hole. The more adventurous can spend four hours hiking to the fabulous Catarata Arco Irís.

Monster fans will be interested in one local legend, which describes a four-meter sharklike fish called the Paraíba that supposedly inhabits the Río Paucerna. Its existence has apparently been confirmed by diving Brazilian *garimpeiros* (gold prospectors).

Organized Tours

FAN offers a variety of package tours to the park, including both wet- and dry-season options, as well as other tours that run at any time of the year. All include guides, accommodations, food and local transportation (but not flights from Santa Cruz – see Getting There & Away); on the longer tours, Bolivians pay about 10% less than foreigners. In the rainy season, a five-/seven-day package at Flor de Oro costs US$737/1170 per person with two people and US$570/914 with four people. In the dry season, a seven-day excursion to both Los Fierros and Flor de Oro costs US$1176/888 per person with two/four people. A ten-day bird-watching expedition costs US$2059/1508 with two/four people, and extensions to include the Serranía de Caparúch – the inspiration for Conan Doyle's *The Lost World* – cost an additional US$430/243 per person with two/four people.

Places to Stay

The *Campamento Los Fierros*, in the southwestern part of the park, lies 10km directly west of the escarpment. Visitors pay US$10 for dormitory accommodations, US$20 to stay in a cabaña, and US$5 per day to use the cooking facilities. Camping in your own tent is free. In addition, running water and showers are offered. There are also rustic *cabañas* available just below the Catarata El Encanto.

The more plush *Campamento Flor de Oro* is open to FAN's package visitors. At the *Flor de Oro Ecolodge*, you'll pay US$65 per person per day, including meals. To explore the river, you can hire four-person boats here for a rather steep US$35 per hour. The area also offers around 40km of walking tracks. The simple *Campamento Ahlfeld*, at the waterfall of the same name, is accessible by boat from Flor de Oro during periods of high water – normally from December to May.

Private lodging is available in La Florida, Piso Firme and Porvenir.

Getting There & Away

Air Several remote airstrips exist around the park; the main access fields are at La Florida, Los Fierros, Piso Firme and Flor de Oro. The easiest – and most expensive – way into the park is by chartered five-seater aerotaxi from Santa Cruz. FAN charges US$1374 and US$1259 for roundtrip flights for up to five passengers from Santa Cruz to Flor de Oro and Los Fierros respectively.

Bus & Camión Reaching the park by land transportation will require effort and perhaps some patience, but connections have recently improved significantly. However, without a rented 4WD vehicle, reaching the park independently will require a great deal of effort and a good measure of your own steam.

When the roads are very dry (normally from May to November), you can take the bus from Santa Cruz headed for Piso Firme (US$20) and get off at La Mechita, a wide spot in the road that is the turnoff to La

Florida, 55km away. It's operated by Trans-Bolivia (☎ 363866; Suárez Arana 332) and departs on Thursday at 7:30 pm. Be sure to book well in advance! If you're traveling this route, it's wise to speak with Susy at the FAN office in San Ignacio and see if she can arrange to have a 4WD taxi meet you in La Mechita at a prearranged time. Alternatively, you can try to hitch a ride with the park rangers or a passing logging truck. There are also plans to provide bicycle rental in La Mechita. If you decide to walk, attempt it only at night and be sure to carry plenty of water, as there's none available anywhere along the route.

At other times, take any bus from Santa Cruz to San Ignacio de Velasco (10 hours, US$8) – most companies leave between 6 and 8 pm. Once there, visit the FAN office and speak with Susy about your plans to visit the park; she'll generally be able to help you find a 4WD taxi service. This is 'jalopy transport,' and it normally comes complete with a garrulous driver-mechanic. Similar arrangements can be made in Concepción, where the taxi stand is just off the plaza. Costs are negotiable, but drivers tend to charge by the kilometer (and it's 250km to the park!); you can minimize costs by sharing transportation with four or five travelers.

Alternatively, you can take the Santa Cruz-San Ignacio bus to Santa Rosa de la Roca (nine hours, US$8), or take a micro there from San Ignacio. After you've secured a good supply of food and drink, go to the restaurant El Carretero, five minutes' walk from Santa Rosa de la Roca along the road toward San Ignacio, and look for a camión headed north toward La Mechita. (If you're unsuccessful – which will be rare- you can always stay overnight in Santa Rosa at either Alojamiento Bárbara, which charges US$3.50 per person, or Alojamiento La Chocita, where you'll pay US$4.50 per person.)

At La Mechita, you'll find a couple of alojamientos, but with luck, your camión may be passing the La Florida turnoff, 20km away, where it's possible to camp. From the turnoff, you'll probably have to walk the remaining 35km to La Florida. After 34km

from the turnoff, turn right and continue the last kilometer into the village. Here it's possible to camp. On the next day, register at the park rangers' office and embark on the 40km hike to Los Fierros.

A more radical alternative is the Brazilian connection to Lago Caimán and Flor de Oro. (Note that the nearest place to pick up a Brazilian visa is in Santa Cruz.) From Santa Cruz, take a bus to San Matías on the Brazilian border and then on to Cáceres, four hours into Brazil. From there, catch another bus to Vilhena in the southern part of Rondônia state. From there, daily buses leave for the village of Pimenteiras, which lies opposite the Lago Caimán and about 20 minutes by boat upstream from Flor de Oro.

Car & Motorcycle The easiest way to reach the park is with a rented 4WD vehicle from Santa Cruz. At US$100 per day, this probably blows most people's budgets, but sharing the costs among four or five people will make it relatively affordable. Try Localiza Rent-a-Car (☎ 03-372223; Independencia 365, Santa Cruz) or Barron's Rent-a-Car (☎ 03-338886; C de Mendoza 286, Santa Cruz).

From Santa Cruz, it takes at least 14 hours to reach Los Fierros, so most people take two days for the trip, spending the night in Concepción en route.

Boat From Piso Firme, there's an occasional barge service to Pimenteiras, Brazil (12 hours). From there, it's just a 30-minute boat ride to Flor de Oro.

There's also a fair amount of Brazilian cargo transportation along the Ríos Mamoré and Guaporé between Guajará-Mirim and Costa Marques, in the Brazilian state of Rondônia, and Vila Bela, in Mato Grosso. Although river transportation passes Paucerna, Las Torres and Mangabalito, access to the Bolivian shore is limited to small independent boat owners. As yet, there's no immigration officer in the park, so after your visit, you'll probably have to return to Brazil or head straight for immigration in Santa Cruz.

Getting Around

At Campamento Los Fierros, FAN rents mountain bikes and two-person dugout canoes for US$10 per day.

The Northern Frontier

While the once untouched rain forests of Bolivia's little-regulated northern frontier are rapidly being tamed by fire, chainsaws and grazing cattle, the region's wild spirit continues to attract dreamers, developers, opportunists and renegades from around the country. Visitors are still rare and facilities few here, but for adventurous travelers who do make the effort to reach the far north, memorable experiences are almost guaranteed.

GUAYARAMERÍN

☎ 0855

Guayaramerín, on the Río Mamoré opposite the Brazilian town of Guajará-Mirim, is a rail town where the railway never arrived. The line that would have connected the Río Beni town of Riberalta and the Brazilian city of Porto Velho was completed only as far as Guajará-Mirim and never reached Bolivian territory.

Historically, the area was a center of rubber production; in fact, Nicolás Suárez had his rubber-exporting headquarters at Cachuela Esperanza, 40km northwest of Guayaramerín. From there, he transported cargo overland past the Mamoré rapids to the Río Madeira and shipped it downstream to the Amazon, the Atlantic and on to markets in Europe and North America (see 'Memories of Mad María,' later in this chapter).

A typically friendly Amazon town of 14,000 people, Guayaramerín serves as a river port and a back door between Bolivia and Brazil. It's actually the northern terminus for river transportation along the Río Mamoré, thanks to the same rapids that plagued the rubber boomers and rendered the river unnavigable just a few kilometers to the north.

Of late, Guayaramerín has sprung to life with a thriving commercial trade. Although it retains its frontier atmosphere, the town is growing quickly – a constant stream of motorcycles buzzes around the streets, and the shops are overflowing with electronic and bootlegged goods from China and Taiwan.

Information

Tourist Offices There's a tourist office (of sorts) at the port. There's no tourist literature, but the staff will happily help with general information.

Consulates The relatively efficient Brazilian consulate, a block east of the plaza, is open weekdays from 9 am to 1 pm. Visas, which are issued in two days, cost US$45 for US citizens, US$35 for Australians and US$40 for Canadians; most other travelers who need visas tend to pay US$40 to US$50.

Money US dollars cash and traveler's checks may be exchanged at the Hotel San Carlos for a decent rate or at Amazonas Tours for a poorer rate. Alternatively, moneychangers hang around the port area and change cash dollars, Brazilian reais and bolivianos.

Organized Tours

Amazonas Tours (☎/fax 4000; Federico Román 680, Casilla 222) does five-hour city tours of Guayaramerín and Guajará-Mirim (US$35), as well as La Ruta de la Goma (The Rubber Trail) Tour to Cachuela Esperanza (US$80). You can also arrange one-day cruises on the Río Yata (US$80) or fishing trips to Rosario del Yata (US$150), and four-day tours that include hiking and fishing at the Lago Santa Cruz and a cruise along the Río Guaporé to Brazil's Forte Principe da Beira (US$350). For multiday trips, camping equipment is available for an additional US$7.

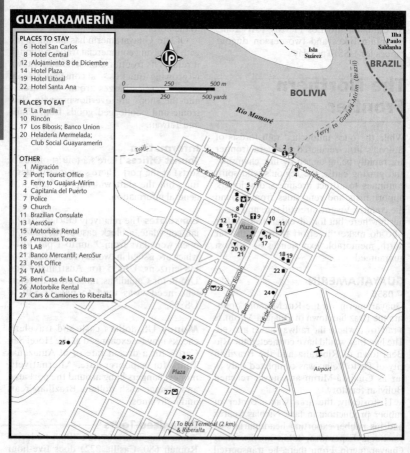

GUAYARAMERÍN

PLACES TO STAY
6 Hotel San Carlos
8 Hotel Central
12 Alojamiento 8 de Diciembre
14 Hotel Plaza
19 Hotel Litoral
22 Hotel Santa Ana

PLACES TO EAT
5 La Parrilla
10 Rincón
17 Los Bibosis; Banco Union
20 Heladería Mermelada;
    Club Social Guayaramerín

OTHER
1 Migración
2 Port; Tourist Office
3 Ferry to Guajará-Mirim
4 Capitanía del Puerto
7 Police
9 Church
11 Brazilian Consulate
13 AeroSur
15 Motorbike Rental
16 Amazonas Tours
18 LAB
21 Banco Mercantil; AeroSur
23 Post Office
24 TAM
25 Beni Casa de la Cultura
26 Motorbike Rental
27 Cars & Camiones to Riberalta

Places to Stay

The most mellow budget place is *Hotel Litoral* (☎ 2016), which charges US$3 per person for clean rooms with baths and refreshingly tepid showers. Rooms with double beds are US$8.25. In the courtyard there's a snack bar and a TV set eternally playing Brazilian *novelas* (soap operas) to a full house. Opposite is the quiet and shady *Hotel Santa Ana* (☎ 2206), with similar amenities for US$5 (US$8.50 with bath).

The low-budget *Hotel Central* (☎ 2042), on Santa Cruz, charges US$4 per person for rooms with shared baths. Even cheaper is *Alojamiento 8 de Diciembre*, which charges US$3 per person. *Hotel Plaza* (☎ 2086), on the plaza, has clean rooms with private baths and a pleasant ambience for US$5 per person.

If you can't cope with the heat, head for *Hotel San Carlos* (☎ 2419; fax 2150), which has a swimming pool as well as a restaurant, sauna (redundant in Guayaramerín), hydromassage, billiard room and 24-hour hot water. Singles/doubles with private baths, TV and air-con cost US$24/34 with breakfast.

Places to Eat

The ***Rincón***, on Federico Román in the plaza, provides home cooking for the many Brazilian expats and visitors. Try an enormous *prato feito* (almuerzo, Brazilian style); *baião de dois com carne de sol*; Brazil's national dish *feijoada carioca*; or pizza, fish, chicken and beef dishes. It charges in reais, making it a bit more expensive than the Bolivian-run restaurants.

Churrasquería Patujú, on 6 de Agosto, serves up tasty, good-value steak-oriented meals. At the similarly beef-oriented ***La Parilla***, almuerzos cost US$1.50 and evening meals go for around US$3.50. At the more quiet out-of-town steak house ***Churrasquería Sujal***, you'll find set almuerzos for US$1 and à la carte dinners for US$3.50. It's most readily accessed by motorbike taxi.

Heladería Mermelada, on the plaza, serves mountainous fruit and ice-cream creations, while ***Los Bibosis*** is popular for drinks and snacks – most of the town's lager louts spend their days here.

Shopping

Currently, Guayaramerín is enjoying a commercial blitz, thanks to its designation as a duty-free zone (authorities couldn't fight the illicit trade, so they decided to sanction it). With the decline of the Brazilian real, it's currently less enthusiastically popular with the crowds of Brazilians who once flocked to this schlock-shoppers' paradise, but market prices are still quoted in reais and are generally lower here than over the river. There's nothing of exceptional interest, but it's a good place to pick up knock-off Adidas bags and Nike shoes, Indian drawstring skirts, and fake brand-name electronic goods.

For local artesanía, visit Caritas, near the airfield, which sells some locally produced wooden carvings for reasonable prices.

Getting There & Away

Air Guayaramerín's airport is right at the edge of town. AeroSur (☎ 3594 or 3271) flies to Trinidad (US$84) daily except Sunday, with same-day connections to Santa Cruz

Memories of Mad María

In 1907, the US company of May, Jeckyll & Randolph began work on a 364km railway to link the village of Santo Antônio on the Rio Madeira to the Bolivian town of Riberalta. The original idea was to compensate Bolivia for the loss of the Acre territory, which was annexed by Brazil in 1903, by providing a transportation outlet to the Atlantic that was otherwise blocked by the Mamoré rapids 25km north of Guayaramerín. German, Jamaican and Cuban workers, and even Panama Canal hands, were brought in to work on the project. When the track was finished in 1912, more than 6000 workers had perished from malaria, yellow fever, gunfights and accidents, and the railway came to be known as *A Via do Diabo* (the Devil's line).

The towns of Guajará-Mirim and Porto Velho owe their existence to the project, but since the railroad never arrived at Riberalta and the world market price of rubber plummeted while it was still under construction, the line became a white elephant before the first train even chugged along it. Today the road between Porto Velho and Guajará-Mirim uses the railway bridges, but the line itself is used only occasionally as a tourist novelty from the Porto Velho end.

Marcio Souza chronicles the whole brutal story in his book *Mad María*, which is mandatory reading for anyone interested in how humanity briefly conquered this small parcel of the Green Hell.

(US$147) and La Paz (US$162). To or from Cobija (US$68), they fly on Monday, Wednesday and Thursday. LAB (☎ 3788 or 3541) flies four times weekly to Cochabamba (US$114) and on Tuesday, Thursday and Sunday to Santa Cruz (US$147), with connections to La Paz (US$162). There are also Tuesday and Saturday flights to Cobija (US$68).

With TAM (☎ 3924), you can fly to Rurrenabaque (US$90) and La Paz (US$100)

on Monday and Friday, to Cochabamba (US$100) on Tuesday and Thursday, and to Trinidad (US$65) and Santa Cruz (US$100) on Wednesday and Sunday.

Bus With the exception of Riberalta, the only bus services to and from Guayaramerín operate during the dry season – roughly between May and October. Most terminals are at the southern end of town, beyond the market. To Riberalta (two hours, US$3.50) several companies each have two to four daily departures. In the dry season, Flota Yungueña runs to Rurrenabaque (19 to 42 hours, US$20) and La Paz (35 to 60 hours, US$32), via Santa Rosa and Reyes, daily except Monday and Saturday at 8 am.

Transportes Guayara leaves for Cobija (14 hours, US$19) on Monday, Wednesday and Friday at 7 am. Trans-Amazonas goes to Trinidad on Thursday at 8:30 am, and Flota Yungueña does the same run on Monday, Thursday and Sunday at 7:30 am.

Beware that if enough tickets aren't sold, any of these runs may be summarily canceled.

Car & Camión Cars and camiones to Riberalta leave from opposite the 8 de Diciembre bus terminal. Camiones charge the same as buses but make the trip in less time. For more comfortable travel, cars charge US$5 and spare you exposure to the choking red dust that gets into everything. To Cobija, YPFB gasoline trucks and a white Volvo freight carrier depart occasionally from the same place as the camiones to Riberalta.

Boat From the port, cargo boats leave more or less daily for Trinidad, a five- to seven-day trip up the Río Mamoré; a notice board outside the port captain's office lists upcoming departures. Expect to pay about US$35 with food. See Trinidad, earlier in this chapter.

Getting Around
Guayaramerín is small enough to walk just about anywhere. There are no automobile taxis, but motorcycle taxis and auto rickshaws (resembling the *tuk-tuks* of Thailand) charge US$0.50 to anywhere around town.

To explore the area, you can hire motorbikes from the plaza for around US$2 per hour, but you can negotiate lower rates on all-day rentals – about US$20 for 24 hours. Don't be tempted to take a swig of the stuff sold in Coke bottles on the street; it's gasoline for the motorbikes!

CACHUELA ESPERANZA
Now all but abandoned, this tiny Río Beni settlement 40km northwest of Guayaramerín was the capital of the economic empire built by Nicolás Suárez. Its location was dictated by the Beni and Mamoré rapids, which halted all Atlantic-bound traffic.

In its heyday, Cachuela Esperanza (Hope Rapids) was a self-contained marvel: Homes and offices were clean and modern and the private hospital and doctors were the finest and best equipped in Bolivia. Suárez imported North American limousines for his personal use on roads he built himself, and a theater was constructed so that an invitation could be extended to the opera star Theda Bara. Everything had to be imported up the Madeira and Mamoré, then disassembled and carried past the rapids; Suárez even brought in a steam locomotive, which today graces the town center.

The town has now been partially restored. You can see the small, white church, which was built high on an outcrop of solid rock overlooking the rapids, and the remains of the home of Nicolás Suárez (he died in 1940). Oddly, the town's main – and mutually incompatible – pursuits are now logging and harvesting Brazil nuts.

The town has a couple of small and basic guesthouses, but there are currently no hotels or other amenities.

Getting There & Away
At least once daily, Transportes Beni connects Guayaramerín with Cachuela Esperanza, but it operates according to no fixed schedule.

Over the River & into Brazil

The happy words on the railway water tower in the Brazilian town of Guajará-Mirim (pronounced 'gwa-zha-**ra** mee-**reeng**'), over the Río Mamoré from Guayaramerín, read *Seja Bem Vindo* – Be Welcome! – and travelers can pop across on a day visit without restrictions.

Between early morning and 6:30 pm, frequent motorboat ferries cross the river between the two ports; they cost US$0.80 from Bolivia and US$1.50 from Brazil. After hours, there are only express motorboats charging US$4 to US$5.50 per boat. Once you're over the river, the Portuguese words *onde fica* (pronounced **awn**-jee fee-ca), meaning 'where is,' will go a long way, and the ubiquitous *gracias* is replaced by *obrigado* (bree-**gah**-doo) if you're a man or *obrigada* (bree-**gah**-dah) if you're a woman.

While you're here, check out the Museu Histórico Municipal de Guajará-Mirim, in the old Madeira-Mamoré railway station, which focuses on regional history and contains the remains of some of Rondônia's fiercely threatened wildlife. Note the tree full of moth-eaten dead animals, the brilliant butterfly collection, the hair-raising assortment of enormous bugs, the huge anaconda that stretches the length of the main salon, the *sucurí* (the snake of your nightmares), an eye-opening history of Brazilian currency inflation, a stamp display in which Hungary is identified as Belgium, and the hideously lovable turtle that inhabits one aquarium. The collection of historical photographs includes an especially intriguing portrayal of an Indian attack taken in the 1960s. Also check out the classic steam locomotives in the square outside – especially the smart-looking *Hidelgardo Nunes*. The museum is open weekdays from 8 am to noon and 2:30 to 6:30 pm, and weekends and holidays from 9 am to noon and 3 to 7 pm. Admission is free.

To travel farther into Brazil or to enter Bolivia here, you'll have to complete border formalities. The Bolivian immigration office is at the port. On the Brazilian side, you pass through customs at the port in Guajará-Mirim and have your passport stamped at the port. They may also ask you to visit the Polícia Federal, on Avenida Presidente Dutra, five blocks from the port. Leaving Brazil, you may also need to pick up a stamp at the Bolivian Consulate in Guajará-Mirim.

Although officials don't always check, technically everyone needs a yellow-fever vaccination certificate to enter Brazil here. If you don't have one, head for the convenient and relatively sanitary clinic at the port on the Brazilian side.

For onward travel, at least eight daily buses connect Guajará-Mirim and Porto Velho (5½ hours, US$11) along an excellent road, commonly known as the Trans-Coca highway. In addition, Brazilian government boats ply the Ríos Mamoré and Guaporé from Guajará-Mirim to the military post at Forte Príncipe da Beira in two to three days. They then continue to nearby Costa Marques, where food and accommodations are available. Inquire about schedules at the not-so-helpful Capitânia dos Portos (☎ 541 2208).

RIBERALTA
☎ 0852

Riberalta sits at an elevation of 175m on the banks of the Río Beni near its confluence with the Madre de Dios, and on the highway linking La Paz to Guayaramerín, making it a hub of sorts. It's the major town in Bolivia's northern frontier region, with a rapidly increasing population that is currently about 60,000.

Riberalta was once a thriving center of rubber production, but with increased competition from Asian countries and the development of synthetics, that industry declined. Since the opening of the road link to La Paz, Riberalta's importance as a river port has also ebbed. The town has fallen back on its current mainstay industry: the cultivation, production and export of Brazil nuts and Brazil nut oil.

AMAZON BASIN

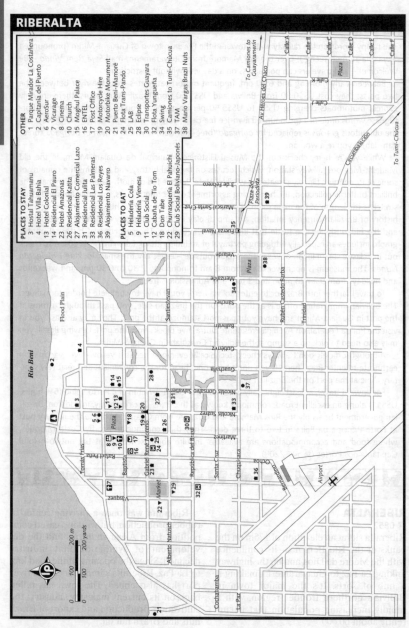

RIBERALTA

PLACES TO STAY
3 Hostal Tahuamanu
4 Hotel Villa Bahía
13 Hotel Colonial
14 Residencial El Pauro
23 Hotel Amazonas
26 Residencial Kattia
27 Alojamiento Comercial Lazo
31 Residencial Julita
33 Residencial Las Palmeras
36 Residencial Los Reyes
39 Alojamiento Navarro

PLACES TO EAT
5 Heladería Cola
9 Heladería Vienesa
11 Club Social
12 Cabaña de Tío Tom
18 Don Tabe
22 Churrasquería El Pahuichi
29 Club Social Boliviano-Japonés

OTHER
1 Parque Mirador La Costañera
2 Capitanía del Puerto
6 AeroSur
7 Vicarage
8 Cinema
10 Church
15 Moghul Palace
16 ENTEL
17 Post Office
19 Motorcycle Hire
20 Motorbike Monument
21 Puerto Beni-Mamoré
24 Flota Trans-Pando
25 LAB
28 Eclipse
30 Transportes Guayara
32 Flota Yungueña
34 Swing
35 Camiones to Tumi-Chúcua
37 TAM
38 Mario Vargas Brazil Nuts

Hero or Bad Guy?

The life of Roberto Suárez Gómez reads like a spy novel in which the hero (or villain, depending on your point of view) always stays one step ahead of the CIA – or, in this case, the US Drug Enforcement Agency (DEA). The great-nephew of Nicolás Suárez, he amassed a fortune from the cocaine trade. Throughout Bolivia, people perpetuate legends of the philanthropic deeds performed by this enigmatic man, who became a folk hero among his compatriots. One story has him landing unannounced in a Piper aircraft at Reyes airport, walking into a particularly poor neighborhood and flinging large quantities of cash into the air for the local people. From there, he reportedly proceeded to the local drinking establishment and declared an open bar for the evening. Other tales speak of his donations to rural schools, development projects and health clinics. And, of course, now and again he's been known to make significant contributions to the federal government.

Information

As a service to travelers, Brother Casimiri at the vicarage changes US dollars cash, traveler's checks and verifiable personal checks. Although there are lots of 'compro dólares' signs in shops around town, they change only cash, and at a relatively poor rate.

Riberalta's post office and ENTEL office are near the main plaza. Keep in mind that the town's municipal water supply is contaminated; the heat and open sewers create a rather pungent atmosphere. Drink only bottled or well-purified water.

Things to See & Do

Riberalta is a pleasant enough town, but it doesn't have a lot for visitors. In the paralyzing heat of the day, strenuous activity is suspended and locals search out the nearest hammock. If you're feeling motivated, don't miss the novel **monument** to Riberalta's favorite invention – the motorbike – on Avenida Nicolás Suárez. Riders, which include a shoeshine kid, are fashioned from machine parts.

For some minor amusement, stroll past the bizarre **Moghul palace**; although the prevailing theme is clearly Rajasthani, the architecture schizophrenically integrates Roman columns and arches, a couple of lounging lions and some raised-relief palm trees, as well as an odd grassy knoll that sprouts from the roof.

The **Parque Mirador La Costañera**, on Riberalta's river bluff, overlooks a broad, sweeping curve of the Río Beni and affords the standard Amazonian view over water and rain forest. Planted in cement 20m above the river here sits the steamer *Tahuamanu*, which could readily pass for the *African Queen*. Inaugurated in 1899, it served in the Acre War (1900-04) and the Chaco War (1932-35), and was in fact the first and last steamer used in the Bolivian Amazon.

Alternatively, you can rent a motorbike and explore the surrounding jungle tracks or take a swim in the river; locals will know where it's safe. At **Puerto Beni-Mamoré**, within walking distance of the center, you can watch the hand-carving and construction of small boats and dugouts by skilled artisans. Two kilometers east of the plaza along Ejército Nacional, you can visit an old rubber plantation, watch coffee beans being roasted and visit a carpentry workshop. Riberalta carpenters specialize in high-quality rocking chairs and other furniture made from tropical hardwoods.

The **Mario Vargas Brazil nut factory**, one of many in Riberalta, is happy to conduct tours. Here over 6000 Riberalta women enjoy a smashing career cracking Brazil nuts. Once extracted, the nuts are dried for 24 hours prior to shipment to prevent their going rancid, and the shells are hauled off to massive dumps to be turned into road-building and patching material. In 1994 the region exported eight million kilograms of the nuts. Perhaps even more significant is the fact that this renewable resource protects rain forests that might otherwise fall to logging operations. So go out and buy more Brazil nuts!

Tumi-Chúcua once served as the Summer Institute of Linguistics of the Wycliffe Bible Society and as the headquarters for translation of the Bible into local indigenous languages. When the work was finished, most of the Indians left and the site and school were turned over to the Bolivian government. With a pleasant lake, gardens and a picnic site, it's now Riberalta's get-away-from-it-all spot. It lies 25km from town on the road toward Santa Rosa. Lifts are easiest to come by on weekends, particularly with the camionetas that leave from the Plaza del Periodista, southeast of the center.

Places to Stay

The cheapest place to stay is *Alojamiento Navarro*, which is popular with itinerant workers. Dormitory accommodations cost US$2 (don't leave things in your room) and doubles are US$3. Note that this neighborhood, which isn't on the municipal water system, has the only good tap water in Riberalta! Another more central cheapie is the friendly but dingy *Residencial El Pauro* (☎ 8452), where you'll pay US$3 for basic digs. *Residencial Julita* may be a bit dingy, but the friendly owner charges just US$2.50 per person.

The best value is the spotless *Residencial Los Reyes* (☎ 8018), near the airport, where US$3 per person gets you a room without bath and US$5/9 pays for a single/double with bath. The shady courtyard provides a respite from the afternoon heat, and iced water and hot coffee are always available.

The friendly *Alojamiento Comercial Lazo* (☎ 8326), with a talkative parrot who's especially chatty in the early morning, has basic rooms for US$3/4 with shared baths and US$ 5/7 with private ones. Rooms with very ratty (and rather ineffective) air-conditioning cost US$14/21.

Residencial Katita (☎ 8386), a friendly and welcoming new place with a public restaurant, charges just US$3 per person. The atmosphere is tropical at *Hotel Amazonas* (☎ 8339), a favorite with local business travelers that has rooms with private baths for US$7/12. A carpeted three-bed suite with TV is US$25. The scene is enhanced by the presence of two friendly little jochis (see Places to Eat).

The quirky *Hotel Colonial* (☎ 8212) isn't the best, but it's well meaning and charges only US$5 per person with cold showers (US$7.50 for hot ones) and breakfast (which includes toast, eggs and coffee). The breakfast is also available to nonguests for US$1.50.

The quiet B&B-style – and very pink – *Residencial Las Palmeras* (☎ 8353), 15 minutes' walk from the center, offers clean accommodations for US$14/20 with private baths and breakfast.

The most upmarket choice is *Hostal Tahuamanu* (☎ 8006), just a block off the plaza toward the river. Rooms with shared bath and breakfast cost US$10/15; with a private bath, they go for US$17/21; and with air-conditioning, the price is US$21/25. Not quite as classy but still nice and similarly priced is the laid-back *Hotel Villa Bahía*, overlooking the river. Here you'll pay US$20/23 for a room with breakfast, bath and air-conditioning.

Places to Eat

For an unforgettable Riberalta specialty, sample its famous Brazil nuts – locally called *almendras* – which are roasted in sugar and cinnamon and sold by children around the bus terminals and the airport for US$0.20 per packet. Another local specialty, which can't be recommended (for sentimental and ecological reasons), is *carne de jochi*. The jochi, or agouti, is a lively long-legged rodent that scurries around these rain forests and is, in fact, the only wild creature with jaws strong enough to penetrate the shell of the Brazil nut.

The reliable *Cabaña de Tío Tom*, on the plaza, serves good coffee, ice cream, juices, shakes, flan and sandwiches, as well as Beni beef. What's more, the sidewalk seating provides a front-row view of the nightly Kawasaki derby on the plaza. It also serves breakfast, but doesn't open until at least 8:30 am. An alternative, also on the plaza, is

Don Tabe, which serves breakfast from 8:30 am. If you're up earlier, go to either the *market* or Hotel Colonial, which serve early birds from 7 am. The plaza also has two heladerías, *Vienesa* and *Cola*.

Club Social, on the plaza, serves inexpensive set lunches, superb filtered coffee, and drinks and fine desserts, but be sure to determine the prices in advance. This isn't to be confused with *Club Social Boliviano-Japonés*, near the market, which doesn't serve anything Japanese, but does dish up Bolivian and Amazonian standbys. *Chu rrasquería El Pahuichi* is big on Beni beef, and the outdoor seating makes it ideal on a warm, clear night.

Entertainment

The two main discos are *Swing*, on Manuel Oliva at Rubén Castedo, and *Eclipse*, on Gabriel René Moreno at Gutiérrez; the latter is the better of the two. Neither is anything special, but they're popular with Riberalta youth who migrate to them when they've tired of video games and buzzing around the plaza on motorbikes.

Getting There & Away

Air The airport is a 15-minute walk from the plaza. LAB (☎ 2239) and AeroSur (☎ 2798) fly several times weekly to Trinidad (US$84), with connections to La Paz (US$162), Santa Cruz (US$147) and Cochabamba (US$114). LAB also flies three times weekly to and from Cobija (US$68) and Guayaramerín (US$30). With TAM (☎ 2646), you can fly to Guayaramerín (US$15), Rurrenabaque (US$90) and La Paz (US$100) on Monday and Friday, and to Trinidad (US$65) and Santa Cruz (US$100) on Wednesday and Sunday. In the rainy season, however, flights are often canceled and you may be stuck awhile. Airport clocks will tell you how late you are in both local and UTC time.

Flights from Riberalta are subject to an AASANA tax of US$1.20 and US$0.60 municipal tax.

Bus During the very muddy and soggy rainy season from November to March, the Guayaramerín road opens sporadically, but at such times, the La Paz road is closed.

The bus terminal lies about 3km from the center, along the Riberalta road. In the dry season, several flotas do daily runs between Riberalta and Guayaramerín (two hours, US$3.50). Alternatively, wait for a car or camión along Avenida Héroes del Chaco. This pleasant but typically dusty trip passes through diminishing rain forest. At the balsa crossing en route, local children hawk the unusual *pacay* pods as snacks; just peel them and chew on the sweet, pulpy beans.

All flotas between Guayaramerín and Cobija (12 hours, US$15), Rurrenabaque (17 to 40 hours, US$18) and La Paz (35 to 60 hours, US$30) also stop at Riberalta en route. Several agencies also go to Trinidad (17 hours, US$21) daily. Trans-Pando Turismo leaves for Cobija from the Hotel Amazonas at least three times weekly.

Boat The Beni passes through countless twisting kilometers of virgin rain forest and provides Bolivia's longest single-river trip. Unfortunately, boats upriver to Rurrenabaque are now rare and, in any case, they normally only run when the road becomes impassable (October to May). For information on availability of transportation to Rurrenabaque, check the notice board at the Capitanía del Puerto at the northern end of Calle Guachalla. Plan on at least US$35 for the five- to eight-day trip, including meals and hammock space. Peru-bound travelers may also find cargo boats to Puerto Heath, where they can look for onward boats to Puerto Maldonado in Peru.

Getting Around

Motorbike taxis will take you anywhere for US$0.50. Colectivos, which are rare, charge the same per person. You can also rent motorbikes from unmotivated taxistas at the corner of Nicolás Suárez and Gabriel René Moreno. The going rate is about US$20 per 24-hour day. You'll need a driver's license from home.

El Chaqueo: The Big Smoke, Fire & Rain

Every year in September, the skies over Bolivia fill with a thick pall of smoke, obscuring the air, canceling flights, aggravating allergies and causing respiratory strife and conjunctivitis all around the country. Illimani is obliterated from the La Paz skyline and deprives visitors to Lake Titicaca of the normally spectacular view of the Cordillera Real. It also causes problems for aviation, which will be apparent when you fly into Trinidad or Guayaramerín and don't see the ground until you bump down on it!

This is all the result of *chaqueo*, the slashing and burning of the rain forest for agricultural and grazing land, which has been going on for hundreds of years. A prevailing notion is that the rising smoke forms rain clouds and ensures good rains for the coming season. In reality, the hydrological cycle, which depends on transpiration from the forest canopy, is interrupted by the deforestation, resulting in diminished rainfall. In extreme cases, deforested zones may be baked by the sun into wastelands. The World Bank estimates that each year Bolivia loses 115,000 to 200,000 hectares of forest in this manner.

Beni ranchers have long set fire to the savannas annually to encourage the sprouting of new grass. Now, however, the most dramatic defoliation occurs along the highways of the northern frontier, around Cobija, Riberalta and Guayaramerín. In the mid-1980s, this was largely virgin wilderness accessible only by air and river, but the new roads connecting the region to La Paz have turned it into a free-for-all. Forest is consumed by expanding cattle ranches, and only charred tree stumps remain. Although the burned vegetable matter initially provides rich nutrients for crops, those nutrients aren't replenished. After two or three years, the land is exhausted and takes 15 years to again become productive. That's too long for most farmers to wait, and most just pull up stakes and search for more virgin forest to burn.

Ironically, all this burning is prohibited by Bolivian forestry statutes, but such laws are impossible to enforce in an area as vast as the Bolivian lowlands. When relatively few people were farming the lowlands, the effects of chaqueo were minimal, but given Bolivia's current annual population growth rate of 2.4%, the country must feed an additional 170,000 people each year. Because much of this population growth is in the rural sector, more farmers' children are looking for lands of their own.

Although the long-term implications aren't yet known (but you'll get a good idea by looking at the devastated Brazilian states of Acre and Rondônia), the Bolivian government has implemented a program aimed at teaching forest-fire control and encouraging lowland farmers to minimize the chaqueo in favor of alternatives – presumably mulching and composting – that don't drain the soil of nutrients. Despite those efforts, it seems that the chaqueo will be a fact of life in Bolivia for many years to come.

RIBERALTA TO COBIJA

Just a few years ago, the route between Riberalta and Cobija was a penetration-standard track negotiated only by hardy 4WD vehicles and large, high-clearance camiones. Nowadays, it's a good high-speed gravel track that connects the once-isolated Pando department with the rest of the country. In the few years it has been open, the road has attracted unprecedented development. Virgin rain forest is being cleared at a rate of knots and scarcely a scrap remains untouched.

At Peña Amarilla, two hours from Riberalta, the route crosses the Río Beni by balsa raft. On the western bank, to the south of the road, is a friendly woman who sells empanadas and other snacks at fair prices. The most interesting crossing on the trip, however, traverses the great Madre de Dios, a river of truly Amazonian proportions. From the eastern port, the 45-minute crossing begins with a 500m cruise along a backwater tributary onto the great river itself. Along the way, listen for the wonderful and intriguing jungle chorus that characterizes this part of the country.

The last major balsa crossing is over the Río Orthon, at Puerto Rico. Here the balsas cross slightly downstream, dodging swimmers as they go. From Puerto Rico to Cobija, development is rampant, and little has escaped being cleared, burned, logged, settled and converted to cattle pasture. The scene is of charred giants, a forest of stumps and smoking bush; and at some times of the year the sun appears like an egg yolk through all the thick smoke.

COBIJA
☎ 0842

Tropical Cobija, with 15,000 very hot and sticky people, sits on a sharp bend of the Río Acre and serves as the capital of the Pando, Bolivia's youngest department. The name of the town means 'blanket,' and not surprisingly, the climate creates the sensation of being smothered beneath a whopping \ duvet. With 1770mm of precipitation annually, it's Bolivia's rainiest and most humid spot.

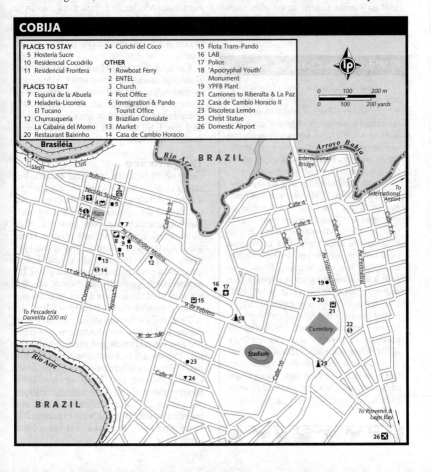

COBIJA

PLACES TO STAY
5 Hostería Sucre
10 Residencial Cocodrilo
11 Residencial Frontera

PLACES TO EAT
7 Esquina de la Abuela
9 Heladería-Licorería
    El Tucano
12 Churrasquería
    La Cabaína del Momo
20 Restaurant Baixinho

24 Curichi del Coco

OTHER
1 Rowboat Ferry
2 ENTEL
3 Church
4 Post Office
6 Immigration & Pando
   Tourist Office
8 Brazilian Consulate
13 Market
14 Casa de Cambio Horacio

15 Flota Trans-Pando
16 LAB
17 Police
18 'Apocryphal Youth'
    Monument
19 YPFB Plant
21 Camiones to Riberalta & La Paz
22 Casa de Cambio Horacio II
23 Discoteca Lemón
25 Christ Statue
26 Domestic Airport

Cobija was founded in 1906 under the name 'Bahía,' and in the 1940s it experienced a boom as a rubber-producing center. When that industry declined, so did Cobija's fortunes, and the town was reduced to little more than a forgotten village, tucked away in the farthest corner of the republic. The original intent was to include Vaca Diez province, with Riberalta as the Pando capital (and Cobija left out in the cold, so to speak). However, when Riberalta opted to stay with Beni department, Cobija didn't protest and happily took over the role of departmental capital.

Cobija's most recent town plan shows lots of streets that have now been overgrown by jungle. In fact, it once appeared that the town might someday be entirely swallowed up, but thanks to the road from Riberalta, a Japanese-funded hospital, a high-tech Brazil nut processing plant, and a pork-barrel international airport, its fortunes may be turning around. The big question is, why?

Information

The Pando tourist office on the plaza operates sporadically, but it wasn't staffed at the time of writing. For information on Brazil, head for the Brazilian consulate (☎ 2110), on the corner of Calle Beni and Avenida Fernández Molina. It's open weekdays from 8:30 am to 12:30 pm. Bolivian immigration is in the Prefectural building on the main plaza; it's open weekdays from 9 am to 5 pm.

Casas de Cambio Horacio and Horacio II change reais, bolivianos and US dollars at official rates, and will occasionally change traveler's checks for an inordinate 10% commission. The post office is on the plaza and the ENTEL office is a block away, toward the river.

Things to See

Cobija isn't laid out in a grid pattern but rather rambles over a series of hills, giving it a certain desultory charm. Of interest in the center are the remaining tropical wooden buildings, which are now giving way to modern brick, concrete and plaster. There are still a few nice old structures around the plaza and on the outskirts, and lovely avenues of royal palms around the plaza. It's also worth dropping by the church, which is open most of the day, for a look at the series of naive paintings from the life of Christ.

In Cobija's hinterlands, you can visit rubber and Brazil nut plantations, and there are also several lakes and places to observe rain forest wildlife, but transportation is difficult. The very adventurous can hire a motorized dugout and head upriver from nearby Porvenir to visit remote villages around the Peruvian border, but it's recommended to take a guide with experience in navigating the overgrown and convoluted waterways.

A Wild Sloth Chase

In his book *In Patagonia*, Bruce Chatwin describes visiting the Patagonian cave, west of Puerto Natales (Chile), in which he finds the remains of a human-sized ground sloth that was clearly not a fossil. For as long as anyone can remember, forest Indians of Brazil, Bolivia and Peru have reported seeing such a creature, which they call *mapinguari*.

Scientists call this enigmatic creature *Mylodontid*, and in 1994 American ornithologist Dr David Oren conducted scores of interviews with forest dwellers regarding the creature. All the interviewees came up with basically the same story: that mapinguari lived only in the deepest forest and had shaggy red hair, club feet, long claws, powerful jaws, a booming cry, an apelike face and a particular fondness for palm hearts (yes, fortunately, it's a vegetarian). It's reported to have a bad habit of spraying a defensive chemical deterrent, which allegedly paralyzes its enemies, and also has bony armor plating embedded in the skin, much as its presumed predecessor, the *Megatherium*. Dr Oren concluded there were enough signs of its existence to warrant a scientific investigation, but we're still waiting for further evidence.

If you're really bored, check out the monument in front of the old hospital. It commemorates an apocryphal local youth who, during the Brazilian takeover of the Acre, shot a flaming arrow and lit the fire that sent invading Brazilians packing back across the river.

Special Events
Cobija holds a Feria de Muestras, featuring local artisans, from August 18 to 27. It takes place at the extreme western end of town, near the Río Acre.

Places to Stay
The *Residencial Frontera* (☎ 2740) is clean but a bit overpriced, with rooms at US$5 per person with shared baths and US$8/10 for singles/doubles with private baths. It's pleasant if you can get a room with a window onto the patio. *Residencial Cocodrilo* (☎ 2215), on Avenida Fernández Molina, charges US$3/8 for clean but far from opulent quarters. The pleasant *Hostería Sucre* (☎ 2797), just off the plaza, charges US$11/15 for rooms with bath and breakfast.

Places to Eat
In the early morning, the market sells chicken empanadas, fresh fruit and vegetables, and lots of canned Brazilian products. Unfortunately, nothing stays fresh very long in this sticky climate, and most people wouldn't touch the meat sold in the market. For a tropical treat, head for the juice bar on the plaza.

Cobija's nicest eatery is *Esquina de la Abuela*, on Avenida Fernández Molina, which sports outdoor tables. Fresh, well-cooked chicken and meat dishes cost US$3 to US$4. If you really want to pig out, finish off with an ice-cream sundae at *Heladería-Licorería El Tucano*, across the road.

On the same street, about five minutes' walk from the center, is *Churrasquería La Cabaína del Momo* (long names seem to be in vogue in Cobija). Here you can eat churrasco for US$2 on an elevated balcony. *Curichi del Coco*, which is better known as a disco, also serves beef and other traditional meals.

For lunch and dinner, you may enjoy *Pescadería Danielita* (☎ 2658), which specializes in freshwater fish dishes. Sadly, a profusion of obnoxious drunks may create some discomfort. Another good choice is *Restaurant Baixinho* (the name is Portuguese for 'shorty'), which is run by an affable chap who's at least 2m tall.

Entertainment
Cobija isn't exactly a hopping place. Most local youths hang out at *Discoteca Lemón* or across the street at the Curichi del Coco karaoke bar (see Places to Eat).

Getting There & Away
Air For some bizarre reason, Cobija has two airports. Despite the fact that the white elephant Aeropuerto Internacional Anibal Arab can accommodate 747s, most flights use the domestic airport just outside the town. Unfortunately, air services are sporadic at best, and although both LAB and AeroSur advertise services, it's largely a matter of luck to connect with something. You'll generally have the best luck flying with TAM or heading for Riberalta and looking for an onward flight from there.

The LAB office (☎ 2170) is on Avenida Fernández Molina, near the Policía Nacional. TAM (☎ 2267) flies directly to and from La Paz (US$92) on Wednesday and Friday; on Tuesday, it flies from La Paz to Cobija, Riberalta (US$44), Guayaramerín (US$49) and Cochabamba (US$65).

Bus In the dry season, buses to Riberalta (12 hours, US$15) and Guayaramerín (14 hours, US$19) leave at 6 am daily. There you can connect with services from Riberalta to Rurrenabaque, Trinidad and La Paz. Three times daily, Flota Cobija connects Cobija with the village of Porvenir (one hour, US$1) 30km to the south.

Camión In the dry season, you can travel directly between La Paz and Cobija by camión for a well-bargained US$30 to US$40. In the wet season, camiones may still get through, but plan on at least three hot, wet days to reach the highlands.

To/From Brazil Travelers to or from Brazil need entry/exit stamps from immigration in Cobija and from the Polícia Federal, just outside Brasiléia. A yellow-fever vaccination certificate is required to enter Brazil from Cobija, but there's no vaccination clinic in Brasiléia, so if your health records aren't in order, you'll have to track down a private physician.

It's a long, hot slog from Cobija across the bridge to Brasiléia, but with some negotiation, taxis will take you from Cobija to the Polícia Federal in Brasiléia, wait while you complete immigration formalities, then take you to the center or to the rodoviária (bus terminal). Alternatively, take the rowboat ferry across the Río Acre (US$0.50). At the Brazilian landing, you're greeted by a topiary turkey, from where it's a 1km hike to the rodoviária and another 1.5km to the Polícia Federal. Dress neatly (no shorts!) or they may refuse to stamp your passport. It's open daily from 8 am to noon and 2 to 5 pm. To change money in Brasiléia, be sure to check the official rates before handing money over to a shopkeeper. Note that none of the banks in Brasiléia accepts traveler's checks.

From Brasiléia's rodoviária, several daily buses leave for Rio Branco (six hours, US$15), where you'll find flights and bus connections to points all over Brazil.

Getting Around

Motorbike and automobile taxis around Cobija charge a set US$0.50 to anywhere in town, including the domestic airport. Taxis to the international airport cost US$3; over the international bridge to Brasiléia, they're US$1.

AROUND COBIJA

On the Chivé road, 150km south of Cobija, is Lago Bay, a freshwater lake for picnicking and fishing near the Río Manuripi. *Complejo Turístico* rents basic cabañas here. To get there, hitch in a private vehicle or camión (US$3), or take a taxi (US$15) as far as San Silvestre, 60km from Cobija. There you'll find small boats for the 1½-hour trip downstream to Lago Bay.

Language

Spanish

Most travelers in South America either arrive with at least a basic knowledge of Spanish or very quickly acquire a working vocabulary of 300 to 500 words. English in Bolivia won't get you very far, but fortunately it's not difficult to learn the basics of Spanish. After a short course or self-teaching program, you won't be able to carry on philosophical or political discussions but will have a basis for communication on which you can improve your skills.

For those who haven't studied Spanish, the following is a brief rundown of basic grammar and pronunciation, and common words and phrases. For a more comprehensive reference, track down Lonely Planet's *Latin American Spanish phrasebook*.

Pronunciation

Vowel pronunciation in Bolivian Spanish is easy and consistent:

- **a** similar to 'father'
- **e** similar to 'grey'
- **i** similar to 'marine'
- **o** similar to 'old'
- **u** usually similar to 'pool'; see **gu** below
- **y** same as **i** above

Spanish consonants are more or less the same as their English counterparts, but with a few variations:

b   resembles the English 'b,' but is a softer sound produced by holding the lips nearly together. When beginning a word or when preceded by 'm' or 'n,' it's pronounced like the 'b' in 'book' (bomba, embajada). The Spanish 'v' is pronounced almost identically; for clarification, Spanish speakers refer to 'b' as 'b larga' and to 'v' as 'b corta.'

c   soft (as 's') before *i* or *e* ; hard (as 'k') before *a, u, o* or a consonant

d   a cross between English 'd' and 'th'

g   soft before *i* or *e* (like German 'ch,' something like an English 'h' but with more friction); otherwise, it's like the 'g' in 'go.'

gu   a hard 'g' sound (like the 'g' in 'get') when followed by *e* or *i*, in which case the **u** is silent unless accompanied by a dieresis: *ü*. When **gu** appears in front of an *a* or *o*, or the **u** appears as ü, the **gu** is pronounced more or less like in the English 'guano.'

h   never pronounced

j   pronounced as English 'h,' only with more friction

ll   often pronounced as 'll y' in 'will you'; in Bolivia, it often sounds more like the simple English 'y'

ñ   the equivalent of the 'ny' in 'canyon'

qu   a hard 'k' sound, with the *u* silent

rr   a rolled or trilled Spanish *r*

r   a slap of the tongue against the palate; sounds like a very quickly spoken 'd' in 'ladder.' At the beginning of a word or following 'l,' 'n' or 's,' it is rolled strongly, though some Bolivians pronounce it as 'zh' (like the 's' in the English 'pleasure').

v   is pronounced like the Spanish 'b.'

x   as in 'taxi'

z   pronounced as 's'

Stress

For words ending in a vowel or the letters 'n' or 's,' stress is placed on the next-to-last syllable. For words ending in a consonant other than 'n' or 's,' the stress is placed on the final syllable. Any deviation from these rules is indicated by an acute accent placed over the stressed vowel. For example: *camión* (truck), *sótano* (basement) or *almacén* (shop). Accents are often omitted from single-syllable words that would technically require one, such as *más* (more), *trés* (three) or *grán* (great). The word *él* only takes an accent when used as 'he' or 'him,' and *qué* takes one when it's used as the interrogative 'what?' Accents may also be used to break up the vowel sounds in a diphthong (vowel combination), as in *increíble* (incredible) or *artesanía* (arts and crafts).

Gender & Plurals

Nouns ending in *a* are generally feminine, and the corresponding definite articles are *la* (singular) and *las* (plural). Those ending in *o* are usually masculine and require the definite articles *el* (singular) and *los* (plural). There are, however, hundreds of exceptions that can only be memorized or deduced by the referent of the word.

Plurals are formed by adding *s* to words ending in a vowel and *es* to those ending in a consonant. Articles, adjectives and demonstrative pronouns must agree with the noun in both gender and number.

Basics

Yes.	*Sí.*
No.	*No.*
Please.	*Por favor.*
Thank you.	*Gracias.*
It's a pleasure.	*Con mucho gusto.*
Sorry.	*Disculpa.* (familiar)
	Disculpe. (formal)
When?	*¿Cuándo?*
How?	*¿Cómo?*
How's that again?/	*¿Cómo?/*
Pardon?	*¿Perdón?*
What?	*¿Qué?*
Where?	*¿Dónde?*

Greetings

Good morning.
Buen día/Buenos días.
Good afternoon/Good evening.
Buenas tardes.
Hello.
Hola.
See you later.
Hasta luego.

Small Talk

What is your name?
¿Cómo se llama (usted)?
My name is…
Me llamo…
How are you?
¿Qué tal?/¿Cómo estás? (familiar)

¿Cómo está? (formal)
Where do you come from?
¿De dónde es (usted)?
I'm from…
Soy de…
Where are you staying?
¿Dónde estás alojado? (familiar)
What is your profession/work?
¿Cuál es su profesión/trabajo?
son/daughter
hijo/hija
husband/wife
marido/esposa
Indian/subsistence farmer
campesina/o
(if in the city)
chola/o (never *indio*)
mother/father
madre/padre

Language Difficulties

Do you speak Spanish?
¿Habla usted español?
Do you speak English?
¿Habla inglés?
Do you understand me?
¿Me entiende?
I (don't) understand.
(No) entiendo.
Please write that down.
Escríbalo, por favor.

Getting Around

I want to go to…
Quiero ir a…
Where is…?
¿Dónde está…?
What time does the next plane/bus/train leave for…?
¿A qué hora sale el próximo avión/bus/ tren para…?
Where from?
¿De dónde?
Where can I buy a ticket?
¿Dónde puedo comprar un boleto?
I'd like a (one-way/roundtrip) ticket.
Quisiera un boleto (de ida nomás/de ida y vuelta).

bus	*bus*
bus terminal	*terminal terrestre/*
	terminal de buses

train	*tren*
railway station	*estación de ferrocarril*
plane	*avión*
flight	*vuelo*
truck	*camión*
backpack/rucksack	*mochila*
tent	*carpa*
mountain	*montaña/cerro/ nevado*
mountain pass	*paso/pasaje/abra/ portachuelo*

Directions

to the right	*a la derecha*
to the left	*a la izquierda*
Go straight ahead.	*Siga derecho.*
around there	*por allá*
around here	*por aquí*
downhill	*para abajo*
uphill	*para arriba*
here	*aquí*
there	*allí/allá*
north	*norte*
south	*sur*
east	*este/oriente*
west	*oeste/occidente*

Accommodations

Do you have any rooms available?
    ¿Hay habitaciones?
I'd like a single/double room.
    Quisiera una habitación simple/doble.
How much is it per night/per person?
    ¿Cuánto cuesta por noche/por persona?
Does it include breakfast?
    ¿Incluye el desayuno?
Can I see it?
    ¿Puedo verlo?

hotel	*hotel*
lodging	*alojamiento*
guesthouse	*pensión/residencial/ casa de huéspedes*
hostel	*hostal*
youth hostel	*albergue juvenil*

Around Town

Where can I change money/traveler's checks?
    ¿Dónde se cambia moneda/ Dónde se cambian cheques de viajero?

Where is the toilet?
    ¿Dónde están los servicios?
    ¿Dónde está el baño?
    (*servicios* may be identified by the initials *SS.HH*)
Where is the…?
    ¿Dónde está el/la…?
    ¿Dónde se queda el/la…?
What time does it open/close?
    ¿A qué hora se abre/se cierra?

bank	*banco*
block	*cuadra*
church/temple/ cathedral	*iglesia/templo/ catedral*
city	*ciudad*
embassy	*embajada*
exchange house	*casa de cambio*
market	*mercado*
police	*policía*
post office	*correo*
town square	*plaza*
tourist office	*oficina de turismo/ el turismo*

Shopping

I would like (a)…
    Quisiera (un/a)…
How much is this?
    ¿Por cuánto sale esto/Cuánto cuesta esto/ Cuánto vale esto?
It's very/too expensive.
    Es muy/demasiado caro.
Do you have anything cheaper?
    Hay algo más barato?
I'll take it.
    Lo llevo.
Buy from me!
    ¡Cómprame!
Don't you have smaller change?
    ¿No tiene sencillo?

shop	*tienda/almacén*
more	*más*
less	*menos*
bigger	*más grande*
smaller	*más pequeño*

Weather

How's the weather?
    ¿Qué tiempo hace?
It's hot/cold.
    Hace calor/frío.

It's raining/snowing	*llueve/nieva*
rain	*lluvia*
snow	*nieve*
wind	*viento*
spring	*primavera*
summer	*verano*
autumn	*otoño*
winter	*invierno*

Health/Emergencies

Help!
    ¡Socorro/Auxilio!
Call the police!
    ¡Llame a la policía!
I've been robbed!
    ¡Me han robado!
I'm lost.
    Estoy perdido/a.
I need a doctor.
    Necesito un médico.
Where's the nearest hospital/pharmacy?
    ¿Dónde está el hospital/la farmacia
        más cercano/a?
I'm pregnant.
    Estoy embarazada/encinta.

I'm…	*Soy…*
diabetic	*diabético/a*
epileptic	*epiléptico/a*
asthmatic	*asmático/a*

Time

What time is it?
    Qué hora es/Qué horas son?
It's one o'clock.
    Es la una.
It's two o'clock.
    Son las dos.
half past two
    las dos y media
quarter past two
    las dos y cuarto
two twenty-five
    las dos con veinticinco minutos
twenty to two
    veinte para las dos
in the afternoon
    de la tarde
in the morning
    de la mañana

midnight	*medianoche*
noon	*mediodía*

at night	*de la noche*
today	*hoy*
tomorrow	*mañana*
yesterday	*ayer*
day before yesterday	*anteayer*
day after tomorrow	*pasado mañana*

Days of the Week

Monday	*lunes*
Tuesday	*martes*
Wednesday	*miércoles*
Thursday	*jueves*
Friday	*viernes*
Saturday	*sábado*
Sunday	*domingo*

Numbers

1	*uno*
2	*dos*
3	*tres*
4	*cuatro*
5	*cinco*
6	*seis*
7	*siete*
8	*ocho*
9	*nueve*
10	*diez*
11	*once*
12	*doce*
13	*trece*
14	*catorce*
15	*quince*
16	*dieciseis*
17	*diecisiete*
18	*dieciocho*
19	*diecinueve*
20	*veinte*
21	*veintiuno*
30	*treinta*
31	*treinta y uno*
40	*cuarenta*
41	*cuarenta y uno*
50	*cincuenta*
60	*sesenta*
70	*setenta*
80	*ochenta*
90	*noventa*
100	*cién(to)*
101	*ciento uno*
200	*doscientos*
201	*doscientos uno*

300	trescientos	800	ochocientos
400	quatrocientos	900	novecientos
500	quinientos	1000	mil
600	seiscientos	100,000	cien mil
700	setecientos	one million	un millón

Aymará & Quechua

Here's a brief list of Quechua and Aymará words and phrases. The grammar and pronunciation of these languages are quite difficult for native English speakers, but those who are interested in learning them will find language courses in La Paz, Cochabamba and Sucre.

Dictionaries and phrasebooks are available through Los Amigos del Libro and larger bookstores in La Paz, but to use them you'll first need a sound knowledge of Spanish. Lonely Planet's *Quechua phrasebook* provides useful phrases and vocabulary in the Cuzco (Peru) dialect, but it will also be of use in the Bolivian highlands.

Pronunciation of the following words and phrases is similar to the way they would be pronounced in Spanish. An apostrophe indicates a glottal stop (the 'sound' in the middle of 'Oh-oh!').

Basics

English	Aymará	Quechua
Where is…?	Kaukasa…?	Maypi…?
to the left	chchekaru	lokeman
to the right	cupiru	pañaman
How do you say…?	Cun sañasa uca'ha…?	Imainata nincha chaita…?
It is called…	Ucan sutipa'h…	Chaipa'g sutin'ha…
Please repeat.	Uastata sita.	Ua'manta niway.
It's a pleasure.	Take chuima'hampi.	Tucuy sokoywan.
What does that mean?	Cuna sañasa muniucha'ha?	Imata'nita munanchai'ja?
I don't know.	Janiwa yatkti.	Mana yachanichu.
I'm hungry.	Mankatawa hiu'ta.	Yarkaimanta wañusianiña.
How much?	K'gauka?	Maik'ata'g?

Some Useful Words

English	Aymará	Quechua
cheap	pisitaqui	pisillapa'g
distant	haya	caru
downhill	aynacha	uray
father	auqui	tata
food	manka	mikíuy
friend	kgochu	kgochu
grandfather	achachila	awicho-machu
grandmother	hacha-mama	paya
Hello!	Laphi!	Raphi!
I	Haya	Ñoka
lodging	korpa	pascana
mother	taica	mama
near	maka	kailla
no	janiwa	mana

English	Aymará	Quechua
river	*jawira*	*mayu*
ruins	*champir*	*champir*
thirst	*phara*	*chchaqui*
to work	*irnakaña*	*lank'ana*
trail	*tapu*	*chakiñan*
very near	*hakítaqui*	*kaillitalla*
water	*uma*	*yacu*
when	*cunapacha*	*haiká'g*
yes	*jisa*	*ari*
you	*huma*	*khan*

Numbers	Aymará	Quechua
1	*maya*	*u'*
2	*paya*	*iskai*
3	*quimsa*	*quinsa*
4	*pusi*	*tahua*
5	*pesca*	*phiska*
6	*zo'hta*	*so'gta*
7	*pakalko*	*khanchis*
8	*quimsakalko*	*pusa'g*
9	*yatunca*	*iskon*
10	*tunca*	*chunca*
100	*pataca*	*pacha'g*
1000	*waranka*	*huaranca*
one million	*mapacha'*	*hun*

Glossary

abra – opening; refers to a mountain pass, usually flanked by steep high walls

abuna – see *buna*

achachilas – Aymará mountain spirits, believed to be ancestors who look after their *ayllus* and provide bounty from the earth

alcaldía – municipal/town hall

almuerzo – lunch; in a restaurant, generally refers to an economical set lunch, which usually consists of three or more courses

Altiplano – High Plain; the largest expanse of level (and, in places, arable) land in the Andes. It extends from Bolivia into southern Peru, northwestern Argentina and northern Chile.

Alto Perú – the Spanish colonial name for the area now called Bolivia

anillos – literally 'rings'; the name used for main orbital roads around some Bolivian cities

anticuchos – beef-heart shish-kebabs

apacheta – mound of stones on a mountain peak or pass. Travelers carry a stone from the valley to place on top of the heap as an offering to the *apus*. The word may also be used locally to refer to the pass itself.

api – syrupy form of *chicha morada* made from maize, lemon, cinnamon and sugar

apu – mountain spirit who provides protection for travelers and water for crops, often associated with a particular *nevado*

arenales – sand dunes

artesanía – locally handcrafted items, or a shop selling them

ayllus – loosely translates as 'tribe'; native groups inhabiting a particular area

Aymará or **Kolla** – indigenous Indian people of Bolivia. 'Aymará' also refers to the language of these people. Also appears as 'Aymara.'

azulejos – decorative tiles, so-named because most early Iberian azulejos were blue and white

bajones – immense flutes introduced by the Jesuits to the lowland Indian communities. They are still featured in festivities at San Ignacio de Moxos.

balsa – raft. In the Bolivian Amazon, balsas are used to ferry cars across rivers that lack bridges.

barranca – cliff; often refers to a canyon wall

barranquilleros – wildcat gold miners of the Yungas and Alto Beni regions

barrio – district or neighborhood

bodega – boxcar, carried on some trains, in which 2nd-class passengers can travel; or a wine cellar

bofedales – swampy alluvial grasslands in the *puna* and Altiplano regions, where Aymará people pasture their llamas and alpacas

boletería – ticket window

bolivianos – Bolivian people; also, the Bolivian unit of currency

bombas de gasolina – gasoline pumps

brazuelo – shoulder (of meat)

buna – giant biting rain-forest ant, over 1cm long (also called *abuna*)

buñuelo – sticky type of doughnut dipped in sugar syrup

bus cama – literally 'bed bus'; a bus service with fully reclining seats that is used on some international services, as well as a few longer domestic runs. It's often substantially more expensive than normal services.

cabaña – cabin

cama matrimonial – double bed

camarín – niche in which a religious image is displayed

camba – a Bolivian from the Eastern Lowlands; some highlanders use this term for anyone from the Beni, Pando or Santa Cruz departments (oddly enough, the same term applies to lowlanders in eastern Tibet!)

cambista – street moneychanger

camino – road, path, way

camión – flatbed truck; a popular form of local transportation

camioneta – pickup truck (ute), used as local transportation in the Amazon Basin

camote – Amazonian sweet potato

campesinos – peasants or common folk, normally of indigenous heritage

cancha – open space in an urban area, often used for market activities; soccer field

carpa – heavy canvas tarpaulin

casilla – post-office box

cédula de identidad – Bolivian national identity card

cena – dinner; in restaurants, a set dinner menu, usually a very economical option

cerrado – sparsely forested scrub savanna, an endangered habitat that may be seen in Parque Nacional Noel Kempff Mercado

cerro – hill; this term is often used to refer to mountains, which is a laughably classic case of understatement given their altitudes!

chairo – mutton or beef soup with *chuños*, potatoes and *mote*

chacra – cornfield

cha'lla – offering or toast to an indigenous deity

chancao – chicken with yellow pepper and tomato-and-onion sauce; a Tarija specialty

chapacos – residents of Tarija; used proudly by *tarijeños* and in misguided jest by other Bolivians

chaqueo – annual burning of Amazonian rain forest to clear agricultural and grazing land; there's a mistaken belief that the smoke from chaqueo forms clouds and ensures good rains.

charango – a traditional Bolivian ukelele-type instrument

charque kan – meat jerky (often llama meat) served with mashed *choclo*. *Charque* is the source of the English word 'jerky.'

chicha – popular beverage that is often alcoholic and made from fermented maize; it may also be made from such ingredients as *yuca*, *camote* or *mani*.

chicharrón de cerdo – fried pork

chirimoya – custard apple, a green scaly fruit with creamy white flesh

choclo – large-grain Andean maize

cholo/a – Quechua or Aymará person who lives in the city but continues to wear traditional dress

chompa – sweater, jumper

chullo – traditional pointed woolen hat, usually with earflaps

chullpa – funerary tower, normally from the Aymará culture

chuños – freeze-dried potatoes

churrasco – steak

clase especial – 2nd class

colectivo – minibus or collective taxi

Colla – alternative spelling for *Kolla*

comedor – dining hall

comercio de hormigas – literally 'ant trade'; smuggling of goods from Argentina into Bolivia on the backs of peasants

COMIBOL – Corporación Minera Boliviana (Bolivian Mining Corporation), now defunct

confitería – snack bar

contrabandista – smuggler

cordillera – mountain range

cuñapes – cassava and cheese rolls

DEA – Drug Enforcement Agency, the US drug-offensive body sent to Bolivia to enforce coca-crop substitution programs and to apprehend drug magnates

denuncia – affidavit

derecho – a right; a privilege provided in exchange for a levy or tax

dueño/a – proprietor

edificio – building

EFA – Empresa Ferroviaria Andina; the new private railway company, also known as FVA, or 'Ferroviarias Andinas'

ejecutivo – executive

Ekeko – household god of abundance; the name means 'dwarf' in Aymará

empanada – meat or cheese pasty

ENFE – Empresa Nacional de Ferroviarios (the old Bolivian national railway authority, now defunct)

ENTEL – Empresa Nacional de Telecomunicaciones (Bolivian national communications commission)

Entelito – 'Little ENTEL,' a small outlet providing ENTEL services

esquina – street corner, often abbreviated *esq*

estancia – extensive ranch, often a grazing establishment

falso conejo – literally 'false rabbit'; greasy, animal-based concoction

FAN – Fundación Amigos de la Naturaleza; the conservation group in charge of Parque Nacional Noel Kempff Mercado

feria – fair, market
ferretería – hardware shop
ferrobus – bus on rail treads
flota – long-distance bus company
fricasé – pork soup, a La Paz specialty
FVA – see EFA

garapatillas – tiny ticks that are the bane of the northern plateaus and savanna grasslands
gaseosa – soft drink
guardaparque – national park ranger

hechicería – traditional Aymará witchcraft
hoja de ruta – circulation card
hornecinos – niches commonly found in Andean ruins, presumably used for the placement of idols and/or offerings
huemul – Andean deer

iglesia – church
Inca – dominant indigenous civilization of the Central Andes at the time of the Spanish conquest; refers both to the people and to their leader
ingenio – mill; in Potosí, it refers to silver smelting plants along the Ribera, where metal was extracted from low-grade ore by crushing it with a mill wheel in a solution of salt and mercury.

jardín – garden
javeli – peccary
jefe de la estación – stationmaster
jipijapa – the fronds of the cyclanthaceae fan palm (*Carludovica palmata*).
jochi – agouti, an agile, long-legged rodent of the Amazon basin. It's the only native animal that can eat the Brazil nut.

Kallahuayas – itinerant traditional healers and fortunetellers of the remote Cordillera Apolobamba. Also spelled 'Kallawayas.'
koa – sweet-smelling incense bush (*Senecio mathewsii*), which grows on Isla del Sol and other parts of the Altiplano and is used as an incense in Aymará ritual; also refers to a similar-smelling domestic plant *Mentha pulegium*, which was introduced by the Spanish
Kolla – the name used by the Aymará to refer to themselves

Kollasuyo – Inca name for Bolivia, the 'land of the Kolla,' or Aymará people. The Spanish knew the area as Alto Perú, 'upper Peru.'

LAB – Lloyd Aéreo Boliviano, the Bolivian national airline
La Diablada – Dance of the Devils, a renowned Bolivian carnival held in Oruro
lago – lake
laguna – lagoon; shallow lake
legía – alkaloid usually made of potato and *quinoa* ash that is used to draw the drug from coca leaves when chewed
licuado – fruit shake
liquichiris – harmful spirits who suck out a person's vitality, causing death for no apparent reason
llajhua – hot tomato sauce
llanos – plains
llapa – bargaining practice in which a customer agrees to a final price provided that the vendor augments or supplements the item being sold
llareta – combustible salt-tolerant moss (*Azorella compacta*) growing on the salares of the southern Altiplano that oozes a turpentine-like jelly used by locals as stove fuel; also spelled *yareta*
locoto – small, hot pepper pods
loma – mound or hillock, sometimes artificial
lomo – loin (of meat)

Manco Capac – the first Inca emperor
mani – peanuts
maracuya – passion fruit
mariguí – a small and very irritating biting fly of the Amazon lowlands. The bite initially creates a small blood blister and then itches for the next two weeks, sometimes leaving scars.
masaco – *charque* served with mashed plantain, yuca and/or maize, a Bolivian Amazonian staple
mate – tea
menonos – Mennonites of the Eastern Lowlands, Paraguay, northern Argentina and southwestern Brazil
mercado – market
mestizo – person of Spanish-American and indigenous parentage or descent; architec-

tural style incorporating natural-theme designs

micro – small bus or minibus

milanesa – a fairly greasy type of beef or chicken schnitzel

minifundio – a small plot of land

mirador – lookout

mobilidad – any sort of motor vehicle

mote – freeze-dried maize

moto-taxi – motorbike taxi, a standard means of public transportation in the Eastern Lowlands and Amazon Basin

mudéjar – Spanish name for architecture displaying Moorish influences

ñandu – rhea, a large, flightless bird also known as the South American ostrich

nevado – snowcapped mountain peak

oca – tough edible tuber similar to a potato

Pachamama – the Aymará and Quechua goddess or 'earth mother'

pacumutu – enormous chunks of beef grilled on a skewer, marinated in salt and lime juice, with cassava, onions and other trimmings. This dish originated in Beni department.

pahuichi – straw-thatched home with reed walls, a common dwelling in Beni department

paja brava – spiky grass of the high Altiplano

panqueques – pancakes

parrillada – meat grill or barbecue

pastel – a deep-fried *empanada*; may be filled with chicken, beef or cheese

peajes – tolls sometimes charged at a tranca or toll station

pejerrey – the most common fish served in Bolivia. It's tasty, and is found everywhere from the Altiplano to the Amazon.

peña – folk-music program

piso – floor

pomelo – large, pulpy-skinned grapefruit

pongaje – nonfeudal system of peonage inflicted on the Bolivian peasantry; abolished after the April Revolution of 1952

prato feito – Portuguese for 'full plate'; a veritable feast of Brazilian carbohydrates, including *maccarão* (pasta), *arroz e feijão* (beans and rice) and *farofa* (manioc flour); available in places with strong Brazilian influences

pukacapa – circular *empanada* filled with cheese, olives etc

pullman – 'reclining' 1st-class rail or bus seat; it may or may not actually recline

puna – high open grasslands of the Altiplano

quebrada – ravine or wash, usually dry

Quechua – highland (Altiplano) indigenous language of Ecuador, Peru and Bolivia; language of the former Inca empire

quena – simple reed flute

queñua – dwarf shaggy-barked tree *(Polylepis tarapana)* that grows at higher altitudes than any other tree in the world; it can survive at elevations of over 5000m.

quinoa – highly nutritious grain similar to sorghum, used to make flour and thicken stews; grown at high elevations

quirquincho – armadillo carapace used in the making of *charangos*; nickname for residents of Oruro

radiales – 'radials,' the streets forming the 'spokes' of a city laid out in *anillos*, or rings. The best Bolivian example is Santa Cruz.

ranga – tripe with yellow pepper, potato and tomato-and-onion sauce; a Tarija specialty

real – Brazilian unit of currency, pronounced 'hey-**ow**'; the plural is *reais*, pronounced 'hey-**ice**'.

refugio – mountain hut

río – river

roca – rock

saíce – hot meat and rice stew

salar – salt pan or salt desert

salteña – delicious meat and vegetable pasty, originally created in Salta, Argentina, but now a staple in the Bolivian diet; it's a popular mid-morning snack.

saya – Afro-Bolivian dance that recalls the days of slavery in Potosí. It's featured at festivities.

SENATUR – Secretaria Nacional de Turismo (Bolivian national tourism authority)

seringueros – rubber tappers in the Amazon region

silpancho – similar to *milanesa*, only pounded even thinner and allowed to absorb even more grease. It is said that you can view a solar eclipse through a properly prepared silpancho.

singani – distilled grape spirit

soroche – altitude sickness, invariably suffered by newly arrived visitors to highland Bolivia

surazo – cold wind blowing into lowland Bolivia from Patagonia and Argentine pampa

surtidores de gasolina – gas dispensers/ stations

Tahuatinsuyo – the Inca name for their entire empire

tallerines – long, thin noodles

tambo – wayside inn, market and meeting place selling staple domestic items; the New World counterpart of the caravanserai

taxista – taxi driver

termas – hot springs

terminal terrestre – long-distance bus terminal

thimpu – spicy lamb and vegetable stew

thola – small desert bush

tienda – small shop, usually family-run

tinku – traditional festival that features ritual fighting, taking place mainly in northern Potosí department. Any blood shed during these fights is considered an offering to Pachamama.

totora – type of reed, used as a building material around Lake Titicaca

tranca – highway police post, usually found at city limits

tranquilo – 'tranquil,' the word most often used by locals to describe Bolivia's relatively safe and gentle demeanor. It's also used as an encouragement to slow down to the local pace of life.

tren expreso – reasonably fast train that has 1st- and 2nd-class carriages and a dining car

tren mixto – very slow goods train. Any passengers normally travel in *bodegas*.

tren Wara Wara – slow train on the Red Occidental that stops at most stations

trufi – collective taxi or minibus that follows a set route

tucumana – empanada-like pastry stuffed with meat, olives, eggs, raisins and other goodies, which originated in Tucuman, Argentina. It's served as a morning snack in parts of Bolivia.

vicuña – a small camelid of the high puna or Altiplano, a wild relative of the llama and alpaca

viscacha – small long-tailed rabbitlike rodent *(Lagidium viscaccia)* related to the chinchilla; inhabits rocky outcrops on the high Altiplano

wiskería – classy bar

yagé – a hallucinogenic drug used by certain tribes of the upper Amazon

yareta – see *llareta*

yatiri – traditional Aymará healer/priest or witch doctor

yuca – cassava (manioc) tuber

zampoña – pan flute made of hollow reeds of varying lengths, lashed together side by side. It's featured in most traditional music performances.

Acknowledgments

THANKS

Thanks to the following intrepid readers whose letters provided useful information, insight and amusing anecdotes:

Jadwiga Adamczuk, Clair & George Alkire, Spencer Allman, Robert Anderegg, Matt Anderson, Corthout Andre, Matt Andrews, Marleen Andries, David Appleton, Danilio Barreto de Araujo, Charles Arnade, Johan Aronsson, Marcelo Arze G, Maike Aselmeier, Valeria Audivert, Per Sigvald Austrheim, Marco Ayllon, Eric Baehler, John Bains, David Baker, Jared Baker, Corina Bakker, Mauricio Balcazar, Daphna Bardin, Sheldon Barnes, Dom Barry, Christiane Batt, Patrick Bauer, Andrew Beattie, Bernd Becker, Robert Bednarik, Alistair Beel, Jochen Beisser, Annelies Van Den Berg, Itamar Berger, Dymphie Van Den Bergh, Lucas Bergmans, Mauricio Bergstein, Thomas Best, Ruth Bitterlin, Brett Blosser, Eyal Blum, Inge Bollen, Martinette Boonekamp, Phillip Boorman, RJ Boule, Anthony Boult, Myrt Bradley, Gareth Brahams, Stuart D. Bresnick, H. Brook Randal, Matthew Brown, Dorte Bruin Christensen, Carola Burman, G Buscher, Jeanine Buschor, Jasper F Buxton, R Calla, Eileen Cameron, Margaret Cantrell, Charles Carey, Anna Carin Gustafson, Ernest Carour Aramayo, Michael Chapman, Mikkel Clausen, Rachel Clemons, Catrina Clowes, Catriona Clowes, A Coffee, Kevin & Dale Coghlan, Geoffry & Phyllis Cohl, Richard Colfer, Roman Colmar, Glenn Costello, Zod Crawshaw, Steve Creamer, Anna & Jacek Czarnoccy, An & Michel Dalleur, Michelle Damm, Rene David, Mary Davis, Peter de Noord, Chris de Smidt, Gaston Delgadillo, Fiona Denholm, Joris Depoortere, Filippo Dibari, Louise Van de Kop, Debbie Dolar, Eva Dolne, Khamer Done, Laurent Duquesne, Suzanne DuRard, Erica Dyllan, Peter Eberle, Hanne Eilhardt Pederson, Camilla Einarsson, Linton Elliot, C Engelhart, Peter Eshelby, Karin & Jan Evertsen, Craig Faanes, Barrie Fairley, Thomas Farrell, Tom Farrell, Joel Fentin, Cecilia Ferreira, Tracy Ferrell, Rosie Field, Sue Flentge, Heinz Flnck, Gustaaf Franck, Jan Fredrik Oisund, Philip Fryer, Maria Gallup, Tim Gatto, Kees van der Geest, Rita George, Stecv Gerv, Stacy Gery, Beatrice Ghiragossian, Sheryl Gibbs, James Gibson, Bernadette Gillivan, Charlie & Ruth Gilmore, Vincent Ginabat, Neil Gollins, Antonio Gonzalez, Nicolas Gonzalez, Jerry Graham, Kate Warren, Chad & Sara Green, Marko Grgin, Nienke Groen, Linda Gruneisen, Salvador Guerra, Mark Guttenplan, Greg & Joanne Hampson, Frank Harmsen, Fred Harris, Claudio Hartmann, Colin Harvey, Hillary Haskins, Mathew & Kate Heal, Michelle Hecht, Martina Heidbnchel, Maaike Heikoop, Peter Hertrampf, Richard Hill, Andreas Hitzcar, Sarah Holman, Ken Holmes, Miranda Hoogendoorn, Andy Hoover, R Horber, Matthew Houlson, Haldo Hulk, Peter Irvine, Claude A Jakob, James Jamison, Jan Janousek, Marcel Jares, Cintia Jasminoy, Amanda Jayne, Myles Jelf, Marcelo Jenny, Schona Jolly, Laura Barcley, Iain Bartlett, Helen Butler, Jo Jon, Martin Jones, Alfonso F. del Granado Jr, Jakob K, Kjetil Karlson, Ben Katz, Rebekah Keates, Lucas Kellet, Keith Kelly, J Kent Willis, Fritz & Ursula Kersting, Diana Kirk, Bill Kisliuk, Christa Kleine, Kay Knightley Day, Piotr Kobus, D Koch, Elizabeth Koffel, Heidi Konecny, Jenifer Kooiman, Maaike van der Kooy, Esteban Krixchcautzky, Pieter Kroese, William Kroll, Mike Krosin, Steffi & Rainer Kubenka, Nina C Kulas, Hans J Kurtzhals, Nina Kyelby, Amababel La Paz, Andrew Land, Christine Lang, Sam Latz, Roger Lawrence, Ron Leach, Marcel Leijzer, Albrecht Lenz, Kathy Leonard, Colin Lewis, R Lightbulb Winders, Michiel van Lint, Elliott Linton, Coraleigh Listen, Ellen & Jos Lommerse, Wilfred Lopez, Dr Gaston Delgadillo Lora, Dikrfln P Lutufyan, Ende MacDonnell, Brad Mackay, Thomas Maier, Suzanna Mak, Richard Manasseh, Arturo Martinez, Claire Martin, Jane Martin, Andres Marlinez Crespo, Kathryn Martys, Chuck R Mason, Malcolm Massey, Tim Maxwell, Elizabeth McInerney, Elizabeth McLaughlin, James McNamee, Debbie Melendez, Richard Melgarejo, Karin Melick-Barthelmess, Les Melrose, Alex Messinger, Linda Miemeyer, Danielle Morris, Michelle Mundy, Peter Murray, StellaElise Nair,

BJ Narkoben, Gil & Arnon Nashilevich, Albi Ness, Laura Neville, Nina Newhouser, Jon Newman, Karin Nichelsen, Katie Nicholls, Bernhard Niederle, Morten Nielsen, Aernout Nieuwkerk, W Nijssen, Michael Ny, Stacia Nyllan, Matt O'Brien, Jeremy O'Connell, Diane O'Connor, Karin Offer, Louise Olle, Jenny O'Sher, Stefan Ott, Birke Otto, Spiras & Julie Pappas, Kerry Parker, Paolo Paron, William Pate, Lynn H & Michele G Patterson, Svenja Pelzel, Justin Perkins, Nathalie Perrena, Samantha Peters, Eric Peterson, Anna-Maria Petricelli, Tanner Philip, Kurt Pluckinger, Lidy van der Ploeg, Andreas Poethen, Ronald Poppe, Annabel Quiroga, Kumi Rattenbury, Diederik Ravesloot, Diederille Ravesloot, Bruno Raymann, Wisi Reding, Nicolien Reith, Tim Renders, Scott Ringgold, Vanessa Rodd, Monica Rodriguez, Stefan Roemer-Blum, Henrik Ronning, Miga Rossetti, Cristin L Ruggles, Eleanor Ryan, Ofer Sadan, Hugh Saffery, Bill Safranek, Ian Samways, Emily Sayce, Emile Schenk, Andreas Schilling, Caroline Andrews & Paul Schmutz, Alicia Schnell, Dominic Schnider, Marion Schwinghammer, Jonathan Sear, Dr Agustin Segui, Peter & Florence Shaw, Susannah Shellnut, Albert Shwiening, Ondrej Simetka, Judith Slot, Andrea Smith, Brian Smith, Duncan Smith, Rachel Smith, Joris Smits, Pascal Sommacal, Ross Spencer Cohen, Bettina & Urs Springer, Greg Stace, Nick Stamatiadis, Ilona Statius Muller, J Stavenuiter, Paul Steng, John Straube, Louise Sullivan, Kathie & Mark Sund, Heini Surola, Melanie Surry, Paul Svedersky, Tracey Swallow, Shona Taner, Caroline Tanguay, Marlene Taussig, Paul Tetrault, Steffi Theuerkorn, Mari Tomine Lunden, Jacques Trudeau, Martin Ulman, Christian Ulrich, Niels Ulrich, FHD van Batenburg, Peter van Dijck, C van Hilten, A Van Hoorn, Floris van Overveld, Alma van Steenbergen, Bart Van Overmeire, Ron Vermaas, Lysette & Martin Visser, Karen Von Muehldorfer, Clive Walker, Julius Walker, Jeff Wallace, Josh Wallenstein, Thomas A Weber, Julie Wedding Bulstad, Barbara Wegelin, Goeran Werner, Peter & Monika Wernli, Ceinwen West, Dalma Whang, Douwe Wijmenga, L Williams, Deborah Willott, Joanne Winston, Edward Witaszek, Liz Wood, Faeze T Woodville, Saskia Wortelboer, John Zazzara, Petra Zellmer, Sabine Zimmermann.

LONELY PLANET

You already know that Lonely Planet produces more than this one guidebook, but you might not be aware of the other products we have on this region. Here is a selection of titles which you may want to check out as well:

South America on a shoestring
ISBN 0 86442 656 9
US$29.95 • UK£17.99

Brazil
ISBN 0 86442 561 9
US$19.95 • UK£12.99

Peru
ISBN 0 86442 710 7
US$17.95 • UK£11.99

Read This First: Central & South America
ISBN 1 86450 067 0
US$14.99 • UK£8.99

Latin American Spanish phrasebook
ISBN 0 86442 558 9
US$6.95 • UK£4.50

Healthy Travel Central & South America
ISBN 1 86450 053 0
US$5.95 • UK£3.99

Available wherever books are sold.

Index

Abbreviations

A – Argentina
B – Brazil

C – Chile
Pa – Paraguay

Pe – Peru

Text

Bold indicates maps.

Bold indicates maps.

Boxed Text

MAP LEGEND

ROUTES

City	Regional	
	..........Freeway	..........Pedestrian Mall
	......Primary Road	..........Steps
	......Primary Dirt	..........Tunnel
	......Secondary Road	..........Trail
	......Tertiary Road	..........Walking Tour
	......Tertiary Dirt	..........Path

TRANSPORTATION

..........Train		..........Bus Route
..........Metro		..........Ferry

HYDROGRAPHY

......River; Creek		..........Spring; Rapids
..........Canal		..........Waterfalls
..........Lake		..........Dry; Salt Lake

ROUTE SHIELDS

(1) Bolivia Red Fundamental
(BR 364) Brazil National Highway
(1) Peru Carreteras Sistema Nacional
(701) Bolivia Red Complementaria
(11) Chile Ruta Nacional
(113) Peru Carreteras Sistema Departamental

BOUNDARIES

..........International		..........County
..........Provincial		..........Disputed

AREAS

..........Beach	..........Cemetery	..........Golf Course	..........Reservation
..........Building	..........Forest; Reserve	..........Park	..........Sports Field
..........Campus	..........Garden; Zoo	..........Plaza	..........Swamp; Mangrove

POPULATION SYMBOLS

✪ NATIONAL CAPITAL ...National Capital	● Large City ....Large City	● Small City ....Small City
◉ Provincial Capital .....Provincial Capital	● Medium City ....Medium City	● Town; Village ....Town; Village

MAP SYMBOLS

▪ ....Place to Stay	▼ ....Place to Eat	● ....Point of Interest

..........Airfield	..........Church	..........Museum	..........Skiing - Downhill
..........Airport	..........Cinema	..........Observatory	..........Stately Home
..........Archeological Site; Ruin	..........Dive Site	..........Park	..........Surfing
..........Bank	..........Embassy; Consulate	..........Parking Area	..........Synagogue
..........Baseball Diamond	..........Footbridge	..........Pass	..........Tao Temple
..........Battlefield	..........Gas Station	..........Picnic Area	..........Taxi
..........Bike Trail	..........Hospital	..........Police Station	..........Telephone
..........Border Crossing	..........Information	..........Pool	..........Theater
..........Buddhist Temple	..........Internet Café	..........Post Office	..........Toilet - Public
..........Bus Station; Terminal	..........Lighthouse	..........Pub; Bar	..........Tomb
..........Cable Car; Chairlift	..........Lookout	..........RV Park	..........Trailhead
..........Campground	..........Mine	..........Shelter	..........Tram Stop
..........Castle	..........Mission	..........Shipwreck	..........Transportation
..........Cathedral	..........Monument	..........Shopping Mall	..........Volcano
..........Cave	..........Mountain	..........Skiing - Cross Country	..........Winery

Note: not all symbols displayed above appear in this book

LONELY PLANET OFFICES

Australia
Locked Bag 1, Footscray, Victoria 3011
☎ 03 8379 8000 fax 03 8379 8111
email talk2us@lonelyplanet.com.au

USA
150 Linden Street, Oakland, California 94607
☎ 510 893 8555, TOLL FREE 800 275 8555
fax 510 893 8572
email info@lonelyplanet.com

UK
10a Spring Place, London NW5 3BH
☎ 020 7428 4800 fax 020 7428 4828
email go@lonelyplanet.co.uk

France
1 rue du Dahomey, 75011 Paris
☎ 01 55 25 33 00 fax 01 55 25 33 01
email: bip@lonelyplanet.fr
www.lonelyplanet.fr

World Wide Web: www.lonelyplanet.com *or* AOL keyword: lp
Lonely Planet Images: lpi@lonelyplanet.com.au